ADAMS

RESUME ALMANAC

ADAMS MEDIA CORPORATION
Holbrook, Massachusetts

Credits
Robert L. Adams, *Senior Editor*
Laura Morin, *Managing Editor*
Richard Staron, *Managing Editor*
Christine Bannen, *Editorial Assistant*
Marcie DiPietro, *Editorial Assistant*

Special thanks to the following contributors:
Christine Roane, *The Bakos Group,* Springfield, Massachusetts
Dorothy Malcolm, *Career Pro,* Copley Square, Boston, Massachusetts
Cheryl Comstock and Jaquelyn Larson, *The Focus Group,* Chapel Hill, North Carolina
Deborah Shapiro, *Parnell Personnel Consultants, Inc.,* Newton, Massachusetts

Published by Adams Media Corporation
260 Center Street, Holbrook, MA 02343

ISBN: 1-55850-358-7

Printed in Canada

J I H G F E D

Library of Congress Cataloging-in-Publication Data
The editors of Bob Adams, Inc.
The Adams resume almanac / the editors of Bob Adams, Inc.
p. cm.
Includes bibliographical references and index.
ISBN 1-55850-358-7
1. Resumes (Employment). 2. Cover Letters. I. Bob Adams, Inc.
HF5383.A27   1994
808'.06665—dc20   4-8685
                                     CIP

This publication is designed to provide accurate and authoritative information with regard to the subject matter covered. It is sold with the understanding that the publisher is not engaged in rendering legal, accounting, or other professional advice. If legal advice or other expert assistance is required, the services of a competent professional person should be sought.
— From a *Declaration of Principles* jointly adopted by a Committee of the American Bar Association and a Committee of Publishers and Associations

Product or brand names used in this book may be trademarks or registered trademarks. For readability, they may appear in initial capitalization or have been capitalized in the style used by the name claimant. Any use of these names is editorial and does not convey endorsement of or other affiliation with the name claimant. The publisher does not intend to express any judgment as to the validity or legal status of any such proprietary claims.

This book is available at quantity discounts for bulk purchases.
For information, call 1-800-872-5627 (in Massachusetts, call 617-767-8100).

Visit our home page at http://www.careercity.com

Table of Contents

Chapter 10

Chapter 11

Chapter 13

Health and Medical

Chapter 18

Chapter 19

Chapter 20
Students 639

Special Situations

The Majors

How to Use This Book

The *Adams Resume Almanac* is a comprehensive guide to crafting a job-winning resume. To get the most from this book, we suggest you begin by looking over Part I: All About Resumes and Part II: All About Cover Letters. In these pages you will find general guidelines for writing more effective cover letters and resumes, examples of different resume formats, four resume make-overs, fifty sample cover letters, and more.

From there, you can focus on your own special situation (your occupation, your status as a student or career changer, etc.) by turning to Part III: Sample Resumes. Look to the chapter(s) that are applicable and try to find a resume format that best suits your experience and job objective.

It should be emphasized that you need not strictly adhere to one resume. The advantage of having so many different styles and formats is that you can pick and choose elements from numerous resumes and custom design your resume to fit your needs.

PART I
All About Resumes

1
Writing Your Resume

When filling a position in today's competitive job market, a recruiter will often have one hundred or more applicants, but time to interview only the five or ten most promising ones. So the recruiter will have to reject most applicants after a brief skimming of their resumes. You could say that the resume is more the recruiter's tool for eliminating candidates than the candidate's tool for gaining consideration.

Unless you have phoned and talked to the recruiter—which you should do whenever you can—you will be chosen or rejected for an interview entirely on the basis of your resume and cover letter. Needless to say, each must be outstanding. Visit our web site for late-breaking information: http://www.careercity.com/edge/getinter/getinter.htm#Resume

Resume Length
Unless you are applying for a top-level position, your resume should ideally fit onto a single page. If your resume is too long, you should consider trimming the content. Keep in mind that your resume is not meant to be a comprehensive, detailed history of your career, but a summary of your experience, qualifications, and skills.

Paper Size
Use standard 8 1/2" x 11" paper. Recruiters handle hundreds of resumes; if yours is on a smaller sheet, it is likely to be lost in the pile, and if it is oversized, it may get crumpled and have trouble fitting in a company's files.

Paper Color
White and ivory are the only paper colors considered acceptable for resumes and cover letters.

Paper Quality
Standard, inexpensive office paper (20 pound bond) is generally acceptable for most positions. Executive and top-level positions may require more expensive stationery papers with a heavier weight or special grain.

Typesetting
Modern photo-composition typesetting gives you the clearest, sharpest image, a wide variety of type styles and effects such as italics, boldfacing, and book-like justified margins. Although typesetting is considered by some to be the best resume preparation proc-

ess, it is the most expensive and least flexible. A typeset resume needs to be reset with every change.

Computers, Word Processing and Desktop Publishing

The most flexible way to type your resume is on a computer or word processor. This allows you to make changes almost instantly, and to store different drafts on disk. Word processing and desktop publishing systems also give you many different options that a typewriter does not, such as boldfacing for emphasis, different "fonts" or typefaces, and justified margins.

The end result, however, will be largely determined by the quality of the printer you use. A dot matrix printer is inappropriate for a resume because the type is much rougher than that of a typewriter. You need at least "letter quality" type. (Do not use a "near letter quality" printer.) Laser printers provide the best quality lettering from a computer.

Typing

Household typewriters and office typewriters with nylon or other cloth ribbons are not acceptable for typing the resume you will have printed. If for some reason you decide against word processing or typesetting, hire a professional with a high quality office typewriter with a plastic ribbon (usually called a "film ribbon").

Printing

Find the best quality offset printing process available. Do not make your copies on an office photocopier. Only the personnel office may see the resume you mail; everyone else may see only a copy of it. Copies of copies quickly become illegible. Some professionally maintained, very high quality photocopiers are of adequate quality, if you are in a rush, but top quality offset printing is best.

Proofreading Is Essential

Whether you typed it yourself or paid to have it produced professionally, mistakes on resumes can be embarrassing, particularly when something critical (such as your name) is misspelled. No matter how much money you paid to have your resume written or typeset, you are the only one who will lose if there is a mistake. So proofread it as carefully as possible. Get a friend to help you read your draft aloud as your friend checks the proof copy. Then have your friend read aloud while you check. Next, read it word by word to check spelling and punctuation.

If you are having your resume typed or typeset by a resume service or a printer, and you can't bring a friend or take the time during the day to proof it, pay for it and take it home. Proof it there and bring it back later to have it corrected and printed.

If you wrote your resume on a word processing program, use that program's built-in spelling checker to double-check for spelling errors. Most quality word processors include this convenient feature; however, a spelling checker is not a substitute for proofreading your resume. It must still be proofread to ensure that there are no errors. (Bear in mind that a spelling checker cannot flag errors such as "to" for "two," or "bills" for "skills.")

Types of Resumes

There are three basic types of resumes. The chronological and functional resume formats are probably best known; the chrono-functional resume is a more recent innovation that combines the two basic resume formats.

The Chronological Resume

The chronological resume is actually a reverse chronological resume—items are listed in reverse chronological order, with your most recent schooling or job first. Names, dates, and places of employment are listed, and education and work experience are grouped separately.

This is the most common and readily accepted resume format. You should use a chronological resume if you have no large gaps in your work history and if your previous jobs relate to your current job objective. This format is a good choice for professionals moving up the career ladder.

The Functional Resume

Far less common is the functional resume. The functional resume focuses on the skills and talents you have developed and de-emphasizes job titles, employer names, and dates. The main purpose of a functional resume is to better the chances of candidates whose qualifications might look weak on a chronological resume or who are in the midst of a career change and wish to deflect attention from recent employment experience. For example, an army officer, a teacher or a homemaker seeking a position at a large corporation might choose a functional resume.

The Chrono-functional Resume

The chrono-functional resume can be a powerful and flexible tool for the job seeker with a solid employment background and special skills he/she wants to emphasize. Like the chronological resume, it chronologically lists job history and education, while allowing the job seeker to highlight what makes his/her qualifications especially marketable.

This type of resume is a good choice for recent graduates with some job experience, career changers, and at-home parents returning to the job market.

What Comes First?

If you are a recent college grad, your education should appear first and should be outlined in considerable detail. Experience should only be listed first when you have at least two years of full-time career experience. Job experience should be listed in reverse chronological order, with your most recent job emphasized most.

Show Dates and Locations

Unless you are using the functional resume format, your resume should clearly show the dates and locations of your employment. List the dates of your employment and education on the left of the page; put the names of the companies you worked for and the schools you attended a few spaces to the right of the dates. Lastly, align the city and state where you studied or worked with the right margin.

Avoid Sentences and Large Blocks of Type

Your resume will be scanned, not read. Short, concise phrases are much more effective than long-winded sentences. Consider the difference between these two examples:

Long-winded

Over the course of the months of December 1993 and January 1994, I completely redid the inventory system at my place of employment, which ended up resulting in a final savings of a great deal of money, perhaps $10,000. It was also considerably easier to perform office tasks efficiently under the new arrangement, not only for myself, but also for others who worked with me at the store.

Clear and concise

Winter, 1993:

Designed and implemented new inventory system, resulting in a cost savings of approximately $10,000 and increased employee efficiency.

Make sure that everything is easy to find. Avoid paragraphs longer than six lines and never go ten or more lines in a paragraph. If you have more than six lines of information about one job or school, rewrite the material into two or more paragraphs.

Highlight Relevant Skills and Responsibilities

Slant your past accomplishments toward the type of position that you hope to obtain. Do you hope to supervise people? If so, state how many people, performing what function, you have supervised.

Bear in mind that your resume is an advertisement for yourself, not an affidavit. Do not feel compelled to list every job you've ever had. Instead, focus on the positions you've had that relate to your current objective or that speak most positively of your experience.

Education

If you have many years of professional experience related to your current job objective, listing your education is optional. For instance, the Chief Executive Officer of a major corporation with over twenty years experience need not include his/her education on a resume.

However, if you are a recent college grad, your educational credentials should be the focal point of your resume. Be sure to mention degrees received and any honors or special awards. Note individual courses or research projects that might be relevant for employers. For instance, if you are a liberal arts major, be sure to mention any courses you may have taken in such areas as accounting, statistics, computer programming, or mathematics, even if these do not reflect your main interests at school.

Should You Include a Job Objective?

If written well, a job objective can give a resume focus and direction. If written poorly, it can immediately eliminate you from consideration. If you choose to use a job objective, the best advice is to keep it very general so as not to limit your opportunities. It should express a general interest in a particular field or industry ("an entry-level position in advertising"), but should not designate a particular job title ("a position as Senior Agency Recruitment Specialist").

Also, avoid writing an objective that focuses on your needs rather than the needs of the employer. Employers want to know what you can do for them, not what they can do for you. For example, a poor job objective might read, "A position where I can travel and use my foreign language skills that offers ample growth opportunities" whereas a strong job objective might read, "To contribute relevant experience and educational background to a challenging position in Human Services."

Personal Data

It is not imperative that you include personal data, but if you do, keep it very brief—two lines maximum. A concise reference to commonly practiced activities such as golf, skiing, sailing, chess, bridge, tennis, etc., can prove to be an interesting conversation piece during an interview. Do not include your age, weight, height, marital status, or any similar item.

References

Stating that "References are available upon request" is optional. On the up side, doing so enables you to change your references and to know when they are going to be contacted. However, you should not feel obligated to sacrifice other, more important information to fit this on your resume.

Resume Content

Be factual.

In many companies, inaccurate information on a resume or other application will be grounds for dismissal as soon as the inaccuracy is discovered. Protect yourself.

Be positive.

You are selling your skills and accomplishments in your resume. If you achieved something, say so, and put it in the best possible light. Don't hold back or be modest— no one else will. At the same time, however, don't exaggerate to the point of misrepresentation.

Be brief.

Include the relevant and important accomplishments in as few words as possible. A vigorous, concise resume will be examined more carefully than a long-winded one.

Emphasize relevant experience.

Highlight continued experience in a particular type of function or continued interest in a particular industry. De-emphasize any irrelevant positions.

Stress your results.

Elaborate on how you contributed to your past employers. Did you increase sales, reduce costs, improve a product, implement a new program? Were you promoted?

Use action verbs.

Action verbs make a resume come alive. Which are right for your resume?

accelerated	chaired
accomplished	collaborated
achieved	compiled
administered	composed
advised	computed
analyzed	conducted
appointed	constructed
arranged	consulted
assisted	created
attained	delegated
balanced	demonstrated
budgeted	designed
built	developed
calculated	devised
cataloged	directed

edited
educated
encouraged
established
evaluated
examined
executed
expanded
expedited
extracted
facilitated
formulated
founded
generated
headed
helped
identified
illustrated
implemented
improved
increased
initiated
innovated
instructed
integrated
interpreted
launched
maintained
managed
marketed
mediated
monitored
negotiated
operated
organized
performed

persuaded
planned
prepared
presented
prioritized
processed
produced
programmed
promoted
proposed
provided
published
recruited
regulated
reorganized
represented
researched
resolved
restored
restructured
retrieved
reviewed
revised
scheduled
shaped
sold
solved
streamlined
summarized
supervised
taught
trained
upgraded
utilized
worked
wrote

Sample Chronological Resume

Chris Smith
178 Green Street
Washington, DC 20057
(202) 555-5555

EXPERIENCE
1985-present UNIVERSITY OF VERMONT   BURLINGTON, VT

Associate Professor of Graphic Arts. Foster an atmosphere that encourages talented students to balance high-level creativity with emphasis on production. Instruct apprentices and students in both artistry and technical operations, including plate making, separations, color matching, background definition, printing, mechanicals, and color corrections. Instruction in black and white, and color.

1987-present DESIGN GRAPHICS   BARRE, VT

Assistant Manager (part-time). Create silk screen overlays for a multitude of processes. Velo bind, GBC bind, perfect bind. Prepare posters, flyers, and personal stationery. Control quality, resolve printing problems, and meet or beat production deadlines. Work with customers to assure specifications are met and customers are satisfied.

EDUCATION
1982-1985 NEW ENGLAND SCHOOL OF ART AND DESIGN   BOSTON, MA
Ph.D. in Graphic Design

1978-1982 UNIVERSITY OF MASSACHUSETTS   BOSTON, MA
B.A. in Art History, minor in Computer Science

AFFILIATIONS
Treasurer of Bookbuilders of Washington Society. Member of the National Association of Graphic Designers.

INTERESTS
Canoeing, volleyball, outdoor sports, photography.

REFERENCES
Available upon request.

Sample Functional Resume

Chris Smith
178 Green Street
Washington, DC 20057
(202) 555-5555

Summary

Solid background in plate making, separations, color matching, background definition, printing, mechanicals, color corrections, and supervision of personnel. A highly motivated manager and effective communicator. Proven ability to:

- Create commercial graphics
- Control quality
- Resolve printing problems

- Produce embossing drawings
- Color separate
- Analyze consumer acceptance

Qualifications

Printing: Black and white, and color. Can judge acceptability of color reproduction by comparing it with original. Can make four or five color corrections on all media. Have long developed ability to restyle already reproduced four-color art work. Can create perfect tone for black-and-white match fill-ins for resume cover letters.

Customer Relations: Work with customers to assure specifications are met and customers are satisfied. Can guide work through entire production process and strike a balance between technical printing capabilities and need for customer approval.

Management: Schedule work to meet deadlines. Direct staff in production procedures. Maintain quality control from inception of project through final approval for printing.

Specialties: Make silk screen overlays for a multitude of processes. Velo bind, GBC bind, perfect bind. Ability to prepare posters, flyers, and personal stationery.

Personnel Supervision: Foster an atmosphere that encourages highly talented artists to balance high-level creativity with a maximum of production. Meet or beat production deadlines. Instruct new employees, apprentices and students in both artistry and technical operations.

Experience

Associate Professor of Graphic Arts, University of Vermont, Burlington, VT (1985-present).
Assistant Manager (part-time), Design Graphics, Barre, VT (1987-present).

Education

New England School of Art and Design, Ph.D. 1985
University of Massachusetts, B.A. 1982

Sample Chrono-functional Resume

Chris Smith
178 Green Street
Washington, DC 20057
(202) 555-5555

QUALIFICATIONS

Solid background in plate making, separations, color matching, background definition, printing, mechanicals, color corrections, and supervision of personnel. A highly motivated manager and effective communicator. Proven ability to:

- Create commercial graphics
- Control quality
- Resolve printing problems

- Produce embossing drawings
- Color separate
- Analyze consumer acceptance

EXPERIENCE

UNIVERSITY OF VERMONT   BURLINGTON, VT
Associate Professor of Graphic Arts   **1985-present**
- Foster an atmosphere that encourages talented students to balance high-level creativity with emphasis on production.
- Instruct in both artistry and technical operations, including plate making, separations, color matching, background definition, printing, mechanicals, and color corrections.
- Instruct in black and white, and color.

DESIGN GRAPHICS   BARRE, VT
Assistant Manager (part-time)   **1987-present**
- Create silk screen overlays for a multitude of processes.
- Velo bind, GBC bind, perfect bind.
- Prepare posters, flyers, and personal stationery.
- Control quality, resolve printing problems, and meet or beat production deadlines.
- Work with customers to assure specifications are met and customers are satisfied.

EDUCATION

NEW ENGLAND SCHOOL OF ART AND DESIGN   BOSTON, MA
Ph.D., Graphic Design   **1985**

UNIVERSITY OF MASSACHUSETTS   BOSTON, MA
B.A., Art History   **1982**

AFFILIATIONS

Treasurer of Bookbuilders of Washington Society.
Member of the National Association of Graphic Designers.

2
Resume Make-overs

While a good resume can open doors for you, a bad resume can close them just as easily.

In this chapter, we include four poorly written resumes and point out some of their most glaring flaws. After some re-writing and rearranging, we've transformed them into interview-winning resumes. You can see the difference for yourself . . .

You can view additional examples on our web site at: http://www.careercity.com/edge/experts/artrose/Rosenfaq.htm

PROFESSIONAL (Before)

Chris Smith
178 Green Street
Albany, NY 12208
(518) 555-5555

OBJECTIVE
I am looking for a position as an administrative assistant in a large company.

EDUCATION
Hofstra University, Hempstead, NY
Bachelor of Arts, English, 1985

Albany High School, Albany, NY
Diploma, 1980

PROFESSIONAL EXPERIENCE
LOYALTY INVESTMENTS, Albany, NY
Administrative Assistant, 1990-present
Responsibilities include: computer work, typing, filing, and answering phones. Answer to the CFO. Interface with sales consultants, vendors, and clients. I am very organized and hard-working and have strong people-skills.

THE GYMNASTIC SCHOOL, Albany, NY
Instructor, 1988-1990
Worked as recreational program coordinator and coach.

GROVER FINANCE, Buffalo, NY
Telemarketing Sales Representative, 1985-1988
Handled customer inquiries in a timely fashion. Responsible for keeping logs of daily calls and monthly sales.

THELMA'S SUPERMART, Albany, NY
Stockperson (part-time), 1983-1985
In charge of checking in stock and taking inventory. Started out as a bagger and was promoted to stockperson.

STUDENT-PRO PAINTING, Albany, NY
Painter, Summers 1981-1984
Member of a high school house-painting team. Painted local houses, fences, and businesses.

REFERENCES
Furnished upon request.

■ Objective is too specific.

■ Education is listed first, without detail and job descriptions are bland and brief.

PROFESSIONAL (After)

CHRIS SMITH
178 Green Street
Albany, NY 12208
(518) 555-5555

OBJECTIVE
To contribute acquired skills to an administrative position.

SUMMARY OF QUALIFICATIONS
- More than four years of professional experience in administration, sales, and coaching/instructing.
- Computer experience includes spreadsheets, work processing and graphics software programs.
- Proven communication abilities, both oral and written.
- Developed interpersonal skills.
- Ability to achieve immediate and long-term goals and meet operational deadlines.

PROFESSIONAL EXPERIENCE

1990-Present **LOYALTY INVESTMENTS, Albany, NY**
Administrative Assistant
Provide administrative support for new business development group; assist C.F.O. with special projects. Ensure smooth work flow; facilitate effectiveness of 14 sales consultants. Direct incoming calls; initiate new client application process, maintain applicant record data base. Oversee office equipment maintenance. Assisted in design and implementation of computer automation system. Aided in streamlining application process.

1988-90 **THE GYMNASTIC SCHOOL, Albany, NY**
Instructor
Planned/designed/implemented recreational program for 70 gymnasts at various skill levels. Evaluated/monitored new students' progress; maintained records. Coached/choreographed competitive performances; motivated gymnastics team of 20. Set team goals/incentives to maximize performance levels.

1985-88 **GROVER FINANCE, Buffalo, NY**
Telemarketing Sales Representative
Secured new business utilizing customer inquiries and mass mailing responses; provided product line information to prospective clients. Initiated loan application/qualifying processes. Maintained daily call records and monthly sales breakdown. Acquired comprehensive product line knowledge and ability to quickly assess customer needs and assemble appropriate financial packages.

EDUCATION
Hofstra University, Hempstead, NY
Bachelor of Arts, English, 1985
Concentration: Business Dean's List, G.P.A. 3.3

REFERENCES
Furnished upon request.

- ■ Jobs held during college are omitted, while more recent and relevant work experience is emphasized.

- ■ Resume emphasizes contributions, achievements, and problems candidate has solved throughout his/her career.

LITTLE JOB EXPERIENCE (Before)

Chris Smith
178 Green Street
Decatur, GA 30032
(404) 555-5555

OBECTIVE:
To find work as a women's clothing designer, preferably evening-wear.

PERSONAL
I am extremely creative and have always been very interested in clothing design, since the first time I played dress-up in my mother's closet. Even though I have had no specific work experience with fashion design, I am sure I have the creativity and talent necessary to become a great women's clothing designer. My idols are Jacqueline Smith and Anne Klein; my favorite fashion magazine is Sassy Fare.

EDUCATION:
Deverling School of Fashion Design, Decatur, GA
A. A. Fashion Design, 1994

WORK EXPERIENCE
THE TUDOR CASTLE, Athens, GA, 1994-Present
  • Reported to head buyer about window displays.
  • Perused fashion magazines on off-time
  • Compiled lists of up-and-coming styles for the next clothing season, provided head buyer with information.
  • Went to fashion shows in New York, Milan, and Paris; assisted in the buying process.

TANGLEWOOD'S Decatur, GA, 1993-1994
  • In charge of designing and putting together in-store and window displays.
  • Required to work with manager planning budgets for displays.

FOLLEN'S VIDEO EMPORIUM, Decatur, GA, 1993
  • Maintained daily bookkeeping.
  • Customer service and some sales.
  • Rented video and electronic equipment.

REFERENCES
Available upon request.

■ Personal background reads like a self-aggrandizing essay.

■ Spelling errors, inconsistencies in punctuation, and drab language weaken resume.

LITTLE JOB EXPERIENCE (After)

Chris Smith
178 Green Street
Decatur, GA 30032
(404) 555-5555

OBJECTIVE
To apply my seven years of experience with women's apparel, as well as my educational background, to a career in fashion design.

SUMMARY
- Area of expertise is creativity—from conception and design to marketing and sales.
- Self-starter with involved style of productivity and workmanship.
- Excellent communicator; adept at sizing up situations and developing new ideas or alternative courses of action in order to design, sell, or increase production.

QUALIFICATIONS
Design:
Conceptualized, coordinated, and designed in-store and window displays, including massive front window of major fashion center. Operated within a streamlined material budget appropriated by the manager, yet consistently generated award-winning window themes for $2.1 million department store.

Buying:
Attended fashion shows in New York, Milan, and Paris; assisted in the buying process. Perused fashion magazines on off-time; provided head buyer with information about upcoming styles.

EMPLOYMENT
DISPLAY COORDINATOR/ASSOCIATE BUYER, The Tudor Castle, Athens, GA 1989-1994

WINDOW DRESSER, Tanglewood's, Decatur, GA, 1987-1990

EDUCATION
Deverling School of Fashion Design, Decatur, GA
A.A. Fashion Design, 1994

REFERENCES Available upon request.

- Format enables candidate to highlight valuable skills and de-emphasize his/her short work history.

- Candidate includes only information pertaining to his/her field of interest.

CAREER CHANGER (Before)

CHRIS SMITH
178 Green Street
New Brunswick, NJ 07102
(201) 555-5555

OBJECTIVE
A job in the field of international corporate relations in which I will have the opportunity to travel and use my travel expertise.

PERSONAL
I am well-traveled, having visited France, Italy, and Germany on many occasions. I also can speak and write fluently in French and have read up on the history of that country while taking college courses in Paris. My world experience alone makes me an ideal candidate for an international position.

EXPERIENCE
Rutgers University, New Brunswick, NJ
Assistant to the Director, Foreign Language Department   June 1993-Present
Oversee marketing, publications, and advertising for Travel Abroad Programs. Write and design camera-ready ads, brochures, and flyers using desktop publishing system. Wrote, edited, and supervised production of departmental newsletter. Develop travel itineraries and budgets.

Executive Secretary to the Dean   July 1992-May 1993
Prepared departmental revenue and budget. Monitored registration progress. Processed faculty appointments and tenure reviews. Wrote minutes for administrative meetings. Compiled and edited faculty brochure. Worked on development proposals and college fundraising campaign. Organized special events.

Faculty Secretary   September 1991-June 1992
Office support for faculty members. Responsible for letters of appointment. Prepared exams and course/instructor evaluations. Assisted with registration and student inquiries.

EDUCATION
RUTGERS UNIVERSITY, New Brunswick, NJ
BA in French Language and Culture Studies, 1991

REFERENCES
Furnished Upon Request.

■ Chronological format is a poor choice for career changers, because it emphasizes candidate's work experience in a different field, rather than stressing transferable skills.

■ Job objective addresses the desires of the candidate rather than the needs of the employer.

CAREER CHANGER (After)

CHRIS SMITH
178 Green Street
New Brunswick, NJ
(201) 555-5555

OBJECTIVE:
Position in INTERNATIONAL CORPORATE RELATIONS which utilizes and challenges my business experience and knowledge of French Customs, Business Practices, and Language.

SUMMARY OF QUALIFICATIONS:

Communication:
Fluent in French, written and verbal. Knowledge of French culture and customs. Extensive travel in France, Italy, and Germany.

Marketing:
Oversaw marketing, publications, and advertising for Travel Abroad Programs. Wrote and designed camera-ready ads, brochures, and flyers using desktop publishing system. Wrote, edited, and supervised production of departmental newsletter. Developed travel itineraries and budgets. Compiled and edited faculty brochure.

Administration:
Prepared departmental revenue and budget. Monitored registration progress. Processed faculty appointments and tenure reviews. Wrote minutes for administrative meetings. Office support for faculty members. Responsible for letters of appointment. Prepared exams and course/instructor evaluations. Assisted with registration and student inquiries.

Fundraising:
Worked on development proposals and college fundraising campaign. Organized special events.

EXPERIENCE:
RUTGERS UNIVERSITY, New Brunswick, NJ
Assistant to the Director, Foreign Language Department, June 1993-Present
Executive Secretary to the Dean, July 1992-May 1993
Faculty Secretary, September 1991-June 1992

EDUCATION:
RUTGERS UNIVERSITY, New Brunswick, NJ
BA in French Language and Culture Studies, 1991
Study Abroad Program, Paris, September 1989-August 1990

REFERENCES:
Furnished upon request.

■ Functional skills are highlighted while unrelated work experience is de-emphasized.

■ Relevant personal information is effectively assimilated into candidate's summary of qualifications.

STUDENT (Before)

CHRIS SMITH
178 Green Street
Burlington, VT 0540
Phone: 802/555-5555

education
1988-1992   **UNIVERSITY OF VERMONT**   **BURLINGTON, VERMONT**
Bachelor of Arts degree, May 1992. Major: Women's Studies. Minor: Art.
3.5 grade point average.

experience
summer   **OFFICE OF THE PUBLIC DEFENDER**   **BURLINGTON, VERMONT**
1991   Summer Intern. Performed research, attended court sessions, posted bail for
defendants. Liaison with District Attorney's Office.

summers   **SWEETWATER'S RESTAURANT**   **BURLINGTON, VERMONT**
1989-1990   Began work as hostess, promoted to wait staff. Also relief bartender.

part-time   **ACADEMIC COMPUTING SERVICES**   **UNIVERSITY OF VERMONT**
1989-1992   Computer counselor for campus computer lab. Hardware maintenance and
software troubleshooting.

part-time   **UNIVERSITY BOOKSTORE**   **UNIVERSITY OF VERMONT**
1988-1989   Cashier/Clerk. Acted as cashier, stocked shelves, and miscellaneous other duties.

interests   Painting, sculpture, and aerobics.

references   Personal references available upon request.

■ Resume looks stark and unappealing.

■ Education, usually a student's strongest credential, is listed only briefly.

STUDENT (After)

CHRIS SMITH

School Address:
178 Green Street
Burlington, VT 05401
Phone: (802) 555-5555

Permanent Address:
23 Blue Street
Manchester, NH 03104
Phone: (603) 444-4444

Education
1988-1992 **UNIVERSITY OF VERMONT**   **BURLINGTON, VERMONT**

Awarded Bachelor of Arts degree in May 1992, majoring in Women's Studies, minoring in Art. Courses include Economics, Statistics, Political Science, and Public Speaking. Thesis topic: The Political Economy of Our Domestic Health Care System. 3.5 grade point average. Awarded the Bailey-Howe Scholarship in 1990.

Contributing editor for campus newspaper, The Cynic. Member of the Outing Club. Member of Varsity Crew Team. Designed and painted university-sponsored mural with the theme of cultural diversity.

Experience
Summer **OFFICE OF THE PUBLIC DEFENDER**   **BURLINGTON, VERMONT**
1991

Summer Intern working with five attorneys. Performed extensive research to support court cases, attended court sessions, posted bail for defendants. Handled confidential documents and paperwork. Liaison with District Attorney's Office.

Summers **SWEETWATER'S RESTAURANT**   **BURLINGTON, VERMONT**
1989-1990

Began work as hostess, promoted to wait staff. Also relief bartender.

Part-time **ACADEMIC COMPUTING SERVICES**   **UNIVERSITY OF VERMONT**
1989-1992

Computer counselor for campus computer lab. Maintained hardware and worked on network and mainframe. Troubleshot software, hardware, and printing problems. Instituted "Freshman Orientation Session" for new lab users.

Part-time **UNIVERSITY BOOKSTORE**   **UNIVERSITY OF VERMONT**
1988-1989

Cashier/Clerk. Acted as cashier, stocked shelves, and performed other duties.

Personal Enjoy painting, sculpture, aerobics, and camping. Member of the National
Background Organization of Women.

References Personal references available upon request.

■ Education is detailed, including impressive scholarships, activities, and other accomplishments.

■ Instead of listing job responsibilities, candidate's specific on-the-job achievements are cited, no matter how small.

PART II
All About Cover Letters

3
Writing Your Cover Letter

Rule Number 1

Always mail a cover letter with your resume. You'd be foolish not to. In a letter, you can show an interest in the company that you can't show in a resume. You can also show more about yourself, while highlighting one or two of your skills or accomplishments the company can put to good use. This chapter spells out what you need to know to make your cover letters the powerful tools they can be.

First off, your letter should be addressed to either the hiring authority for the position you're interested in, or the human resources director. Be sure to include the contact's full name and title, preceded by "Mr." or "Ms." If you're not sure who you should send your letter to, call the company and find out. Above all, be sure to spell your contact's name correctly!

In the cover letter, you need to mention: 1) the job or type of job for which you're applying, and 2) any other information that's important to your situation—for example, dates when you will be available for an interview; the best time of day or night you can be reached; and salary information, if it has been requested; 3) a brief statement highlighting your skills and experience in your resume that you think qualify you for the job.

Remember that you want to highlight skills and experience mentioned on your resume, not just parrot back your resume in letter form. If you're applying for a job that doesn't fit directly into your experience, make sure you explain how your background and qualifications match the requirements of the position. Be specific but concise.

Look at it this way. Your cover letter is more important than your resume itself, since if it doesn't impress the reader, he or she may not even look at your resume. And the easiest way to impress the reader is by doing your homework and finding out as much as you possibly can about each firm you're applying to. For example, we, the publishers of this book, have a relatively small staff. Even so, we too receive many resumes, both when we have job openings and when we don't. And speaking from experience, it is all too common for us to receive a resume from someone who is clearly qualified, but has no idea at all what type of company we are or even what type of books we publish. One candidate, whose resume outlined solid experience, wrote as an aside that working for our company was especially attractive to him because he'd always wanted to work in

Connecticut. (We're located in Massachusetts.) So please, do your homework. It will certainly pay off in the end.

Keep in mind, too, that the appearance of your cover letter is just as important as that of the resume. Each letter should be individually typed. You are sending a "business letter," so be professional. There are typing services available in most cities which can produce individually typed letters at a reasonable cost.

Another important rule: As important as your cover letter is, keep it to one page, if possible. Remember, the key is to state the facts and be quick about it.

For more detailed information about writing cover letters, visit our web site at: http://www.careercity.com/edge/getinter/getinter.htm#Cover Letters

General Model for a Cover Letter

Your Address
Your Phone

Date

Contact Person Name
Title
Company
Address

Dear Mr./Ms._____:

Immediately explain why your background makes you the best candidate for the position that you are applying for. Keep the first paragraph short and hard-hitting. Detail what you could contribute to this company. Show how your qualifications will benefit this firm. Remember to keep this letter short; few recruiters will read a cover letter longer than half a page.

Describe your interest in the corporation. Subtly emphasize your knowledge about this firm (the result of your research effort) and your familiarity with the industry. It is common courtesy to act extremely eager to work for any company that you interview with.

In the closing paragraph you should specifically request an interview. Include your phone number and the hours when you can be reached. Alternatively, you might prefer to mention that you will follow up with a phone call (to arrange an interview at a mutually convenient time within the next several days).

Sincerely,

Signature

Your full name
(typed)

Enc. resume

General Model for a Follow-up Letter

Your Address
Your Phone

Date

Contact Person Name
Title
Company
Address

Dear Mr./Ms._____:

Remind the interviewer of the position for which you were interviewed, as well as the date. Thank him/her for the interview.

Confirm your interest in the opening and the organization. Use specifics to emphasize both that you have researched the firm in detail and considered how you would fit into the company and the position.

Like in your cover letter, emphasize one or two of your strongest qualifications and slant them toward the various points that the interviewer considered the most important for the position. Keep the letter brief; a half-page is plenty.

If appropriate, close with a suggestion for further action, such as a desire to have additional interviews. Mention your phone number and the hours that you can best be reached. Alternatively, you may prefer to mention that you will follow up with a phone call in several days.

Sincerely,

Signature

Your full name
(typed)

Enc. resume

4
Cover Letter Samples

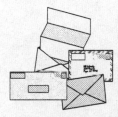

On the following pages are fifty sample cover letters that can be used to help you develop your own. When writing yours, think of it as a one-page summary of who you are, why you're interested in the employer, and how your skills will benefit that particular organization.

The cover letter samples include:

- Responses to Classified Advertisements
- "Cold" Cover Letters to Potential Employers
- "Cold" Cover Letters to Employment Agencies
- "Cold" Cover Letters to Executive Recruiters
- Networking Letters
- Follow-up Letters (After Telephone Conversation)
- Follow-up Letters (After Informational Interview)
- Follow-up Letters (After Job Interview)
- Rejection of Offer Letters
- Acceptance Letters
- Thank You Letters (After Hire)

RESPONSE TO A CLASSIFIED ADVERTISEMENT

178 Green Street
Birmingham, AL 35294
(205) 555-5555

October 2, 1995

Pat Cummings
Vice-President, Editorial
Any Corporation
1146 Main Street
Chicago, IL 60605

RE: Publisher's Assistant Position

Dear Ms. Cummings:

Your recent advertisement in the Chicago Times interests me, as my experience matches your requirements.

You Require:	I Offer:
IBM Word Processing	MS Word, WordPerfect
Publishing experience	Two years experience as a freelance proofreader
Bachelor's degree	B.S. in Business Administration

I would appreciate the opportunity to discuss how I might contribute to your organization. I will call your office the week of October 10th to schedule an interview at your convenience. In the meantime, I may be reached at the above-listed phone number.

Thank you for your consideration.

Sincerely,

Chris Smith

Chris Smith

Enc. resume

RESPONSE TO A CLASSIFIED ADVERTISEMENT

178 Green Street
Waterbury, CT 06708
(205) 555-5555

December 5, 1995

Pat Cummings
General Manager
Any Corporation
1140 Main Street
Chicago, IL 60605

Dear Mr. Cummings:

My interest in the position of Masonry Supply Manager (New York Post, November 30) has prompted me to forward my resume for your review and consideration.

During the past ten years, my experience has been concentrated in the masonry and plastering products supply industry with a building materials firm. During my six years as General Manager, I took an old line business, which had undergone several years of poor management, and reversed the trend. I upgraded the firm's image, and customer and vendor relations, which subsequently increased the dollar volume and bottom line profits by 300%.

I am presently looking for a position where my experience will make a positive contribution to the start-up or continuing profitable operation of a business in which I am so well experienced.

I will contact you in a few days to arrange a meeting for further discussion. In the interim, should you require additional information, I may be reached at (203) 555-5555 between 9 A.M. and 5 P.M.

Sincerely,

Chris Smith

Chris Smith

Enc. resume

RESPONSE TO A CLASSIFIED ADVERTISEMENT

178 Green Street
Tiverton, RI 02878
(401) 555-5555

August 21, 1995

Pat Cummings
Vice-President of Public Relations
Any Corporation
1140 Main Street
Chicago, IL 60605

Dear Ms. Cummings:

Please accept this letter as an application for the Events Planner position advertised in the Providence Journal on August 20. My confidential resume is enclosed for your review.

The position described is exactly the opportunity I am looking for. I am confident my six years experience in public relations, coupled with my drive and enthusiasm, would enable me to make a significant contribution to your organization.

I believe the most important qualification of an Events Planner is the ability to plan well and soundly, and then to imbue a staff with the spirit of teamwork—in other words, to provide leadership and effective administration. I would describe myself as a well organized, results-oriented, and effective problem-solver.

I welcome the opportunity to meet with you to further discuss my qualifications and your needs. Thank you for your time and consideration.

Sincerely,

Chris Smith

Chris Smith

Enc. resume

RESPONSE TO A CLASSIFIED ADVERTISEMENT

178 Green Street
Washington, DC 20057
(202) 555-5555

October 31, 1995

Pat Cummings
Human Resources Director
Any Corporation
1140 Main Street
Chicago, IL 60605

Dear Mr. Cummings:

I'm writing in response to the Writer/Researcher position advertised in the Washington Post on October 30. Please allow me to outline my skills as they apply to your stated requirements:

Writing Experience: I have authored or co-authored five books on sports and communications. In addition, I have been a reporter for both magazines and newspapers for many years. I have written over 3,500 articles for publication, on topics ranging from crime to sports to medicine to humor. I know how to conceive of and research topics, and I am comfortable writing on almost any subject and in a range of styles. I am confident I would have no trouble matching the established style of your book series.

Editing Experience: I have copyedited a number of books on business topics and worked as an editor for several newspapers. I am capable of doing either minor polishing or major rewriting and, more importantly, of being able to tell which is needed. In addition, I taught English Composition and Writing for the Print Media on the high school level for five years.

I have enclosed a resume as well as a brief sample of my writing for your review. I look forward to meeting with you to discuss further how I could contribute to your organization.

Sincerely,

Chris Smith

Chris Smith

Enc. resume

RESPONSE TO A CLASSIFIED ADVERTISEMENT

178 Green Street
Girdletree, MD 21829
(301) 555-5555

October 13, 1995

Box 212-A
Chicago Tribune
Chicago, IL 60605

RE: Sales Manager position

The Sales Manager position advertised in the Chicago Tribune on October 12 intrigues me. I believe you will find me well-qualified.

I am an innovative achiever. I feel that in a growth industry like cable television, there is a need for a representative who can meet and beat the competition. I feel that I have all the necessary ingredients to contribute to the success of Any Corporation, and if necessary, I am willing to take a step backwards as long as there is potential for forward momentum. All I need is a starting point.

The enclosed resume summarizes my proven track record as the Vice-President of Sales for a two million dollar operation. I have strong communications skills and the ability to prepare and make presentations to decision makers on all levels.

I feel that a personal meeting would give us the opportunity to discuss your short- and long-term objectives and my ability to direct your organization towards successfully achieving those goals.

Thank you for your attention to this matter. I look forward to speaking with you.

Sincerely yours,

Chris Smith

Chris Smith

Enc. resume

RESPONSE TO A CLASSIFIED ADVERTISEMENT

178 Green Street
Fox, OR 97831
(503) 555-5555

May 23, 1995

Mr. Pat Cummings
Chairperson
Chicago Municipal Court
1140 Main Street
Chicago, IL 60605

Dear Chairperson Cummings:

Your advertisement in the May 30th issue of Lawyers Monthly is of great interest to me. I feel that I have the qualifications necessary to effectively handle the responsibilities of Administrative Judge.

During the past four years as Assistant Attorney General, I gained broad experience in the litigation of personal injury actions and workers' compensation claims. In this position, I made extensive use of my legal knowledge as well as of my research, analytical, writing, and judgmental skills. I am confident of my ability to provide the expertise necessary for the professional representation of an Administrative Judge.

The enclosed resume describes my qualifications for the position advertised. I would welcome the opportunity to personally discuss my qualifications with you at your convenience.

Sincerely,

Chris Smith

Chris Smith

Enc. resume

RESPONSE TO A CLASSIFIED ADVERTISEMENT

178 Green Street
Stoughton, MA 02072
(617) 555-5555

July 27, 1995

Pat Cummings
Administrator
Any Corporation
1140 Main Street
Chicago, IL 60605

RE: Assistant Hospital Administrator position

Dear Ms. Cummings:

I am writing in response to your advertisement in this past week's *Boston Phoenix*.

I recently took a sabbatical and finished my Bachelors Degree in May at Emerson College. I am currently seeking full-time employment.

My employment background consists of twelve years at the Deaconess Hospital, where I provided a wide range of administrative, financial, and research support to the Chief Executive Officer. I have a strong aptitude for working with numbers and extensive experience with computer software applications.

I would be interested in speaking with you further regarding this position. I am confident that my background in administrative support, as well as my word processing, database, and spreadsheet skills, which will be an asset to Any Corporation.

Thank you in advance for your consideration.

Sincerely,

Chris Smith

Chris Smith

Enc. resume

RESPONSE TO A CLASSIFIED ADVERTISEMENT

178 Green Street
Ecru, MS 38842
(601) 555-5555

November 1, 1995

Pat Cummings
Office Manager
Any Corporation
1140 Main Street
Chicago, IL 60605

Dear Mr. Cummings:

Your October 30 advertisement in The Jackson Review calls for an Administrative Assistant with a background rich in a variety of administrative skills, such as mine.

As an extraordinarily organized and detail-oriented individual with five years experience in administration, I believe my qualifications match your requirements. My strengths also include independent working habits and superb computer skills. As an Administrative Assistant at Lambert Hospital, I was in charge of all computer support, word processing, data base, spreadsheet, and administrative functions, including all purchasing, equipment maintenance, daily office operations, supervising of staff and volunteers, and coordinating various projects with staff and outside vendors.

I would appreciate the opportunity to discuss this position with you at your convenience, as it sounds like an exciting opportunity. If you have any questions, do not hesitate to contact me at the above listed phone number or at (601) 444-4444.

Sincerely,

Chris Smith

Chris Smith

Enc. resume

RESPONSE TO A CLASSIFIED ADVERTISEMENT

178 Green Street
Knoke, IA 50553
(515) 555-5555

February 3, 1995

Pat Cummings
Senior Marketing Manager
Any Corporation
1140 Main Street
Chicago, IL 60605

Dear Ms. Cummings:

In response to your advertisement in the February 1 edition of the New York Times for an International Purchasing Agent, I would like to submit my application for your consideration.

As you can see, my qualifications match those you seek:

YOU REQUIRE:	I OFFER:
A college degree	A Bachelors degree in English from Long Island University
Fluency in Italian and French	Fluency in Italian, German, and French
Office experience	Experience as a receptionist at a busy accounting firm
Typing skills	Accurate typing at 60 WPM
Willingness to travel	Willingness to travel

I feel that I am well qualified for this position and can make a significant contribution to Any Corporation. My salary requirement is negotiable.

I would welcome the opportunity for a personal interview with you at your convenience.

Sincerely,

Chris Smith

Chris Smith

Enc. resume

RESPONSE TO A CLASSIFIED ADVERTISEMENT

178 Green Street
Shoshoni, WY 82649
(307) 555-5555

September 18, 1995

Pat Cummings
Partner
Any Corporation
1140 Main Street
Chicago, IL 60605

Dear Mr. Cummings:

I am writing in response to your advertisement in the September 17th edition of the New York Times. I have recently graduated from New England School of Law and it is my intention to relocate to Chicago. I have enclosed my resume for your consideration.

My work experience and my scholastic endeavors have thoroughly prepared me for employment in a firm that specializes in various segments of law. This fall and past summer, I have been working for a small general practice firm where I am entrusted with a great deal of responsibility. I write appellate briefs, memoranda in corporate, contract, and criminal law, and I draft complaints and answers. I also actively participate in attorney-client conferences by questioning clients and by describing how the law affects the clients' suits.

I would appreciate the opportunity to meet with you and discuss how my qualifications could be guided to meet your needs.

Thank you for your time and consideration. I look forward meeting with you at your convenience.

With best regards,

Chris Smith, Esq.

Chris Smith, Esq.

Enc. resume

"COLD" COVER LETTER TO A POTENTIAL EMPLOYER

178 Green Street
Miami, FL 33054

November 11, 1995

Pat Cummings
Personnel Manager
Any Corporation
1140 Main Street
Chicago, IL 60605

Dear Ms. Cummings:

After fifteen years as a District Sales Manager, I am seeking new opportunities and am forwarding my resume for your consideration.

Equally important as my experience in new business development for multimedia products is my interest in becoming an integral part of a young, aggressively expanding organization such as Any Corporation. Energetic and enthusiastic, I am confident of my ability to stimulate company growth and profits through successful follow-through on corporate sales and marketing programs.

I can be reached at the above address or by phone at (305) 555-5555. Thank you for your consideration.

Sincerely,

Chris Smith

Chris Smith

Enc. resume

"COLD" COVER LETTER TO A POTENTIAL EMPLOYER

178 Green Street
Little Rock, AR 72204
(501) 555-5555

July 7, 1995

Pat Cummings
Personnel Manager
Any Corporation
1140 Main Street
Chicago, IL 60605

Dear Mr. Cummings:

My desire to locate a responsible position in plant management has prompted me to forward the attached resume for your consideration.

Please note that, in addition to more than five years of vocational training and hands-on experience with automated, semi-automated, and mechanical plant equipment and systems, I have also been involved in purchasing and negotiations. Although presently employed in a responsible position, I feel that an association with your firm may offer better growth potential than I can foresee with my present employer.

Thank you for your consideration. I look forward to hearing from you.

Sincerely,

Chris Smith

Chris Smith

Enc. resume

"COLD" COVER LETTER TO A POTENTIAL EMPLOYER

178 Green Street
Bunkie, LA 71322
(318) 555-5555

December 5, 1995

Pat Cummings
Human Resources Manager
Any Corporation
1140 Main Street
Chicago, IL 60605

Dear Ms. Cummings:

I am writing to inquire about opportunities for computer programmers in your organization.

I offer extensive knowledge of five computer languages and strong management, sales, and sales support experience. As a Computer Specialist, I was responsible for the management of a center handling the complete line of Honeywell computers and peripherals for home and commercial use. In addition to a B.S. degree in Business Administration, I will receive a certificate in Programming this May.

I feel confident that given the opportunity, I can make an immediate contribution to Any Corporation. I would appreciate the opportunity to meet with you to discuss your requirements. I will call your office on Tuesday, December 12, to schedule an appointment. Thank you for your consideration.

Sincerely,

Chris Smith

Chris Smith

Enc. resume

"COLD" COVER LETTER TO A POTENTIAL EMPLOYER

178 Green Street
Gardenia, ND 58739

April 15, 1995

Pat Cummings
Personnel Manager
Any Corporation
1140 Main Street
Chicago, IL 60605

Dear Mr. Cummings:

Having had the opportunity to meet with Deborah Sturgis and the rest of the staff at the Fargo office, I am very much interested in career opportunities at Any Corporation.

I am planning a permanent relocation to the Chicago area in late summer. I am submitting my resume for consideration in areas where I can apply my experience and education in accounting towards reaching mutually beneficial goals.

Please note that I am currently completing my senior year at North Dakota University and will receive my B.S. degree with a major in accounting and a concentration in computer programming in May. Throughout school, and during full-time and part-time employment, I have continued to strengthen my focus in these areas. In addition, I have excellent problem-solving skills and feel that, if given the opportunity, I would be an immediate as well as a long-term asset to your firm.

My resume is a good summary but I strongly feel that it is during a personal interview that my potential to be of service to your organization would be more fully demonstrated. I plan to be in the Chicago area the week of May 1 and would welcome the opportunity to meet with you. I will follow up with a phone call on April 25 to arrange such a meeting. In the interim I can be reached at the above address or by telephone at (701) 555-5555.

Thank you for your time and consideration.

Sincerely,

Chris Smith

Chris Smith

Enc. resume

"COLD" COVER LETTER TO A POTENTIAL EMPLOYER

178 Green Street
New York, NY 10020
(212) 555-5555

March 13, 1995

Pat Cummings
Personnel Director
Any Corporation
1140 Main Street
Chicago, IL 60605

Dear Ms. Cummings:

I am writing to inquire about upcoming entry-level editorial openings with Any Corporation.

I am presently a senior in good standing at New York University, due to graduate in May. I am pursuing a Bachelor of Arts degree with a major in Journalism and a minor in both Economics and English Literature. I am proficient in both WordPerfect and Microsoft Word for Windows, and am familiar with both IBM and Apple operating systems. I am presently working as a Research Intern for the Economics Division of Tradewinds Publishing in Newark.

Enclosed you will find a copy of my resume. Letters of recommendation from employers and professors, as well as writing samples, will gladly be provided upon request. I will contact you next week about the possibility of arranging a meeting at your convenience.

I look forward to speaking with you.

Sincerely,

Chris Smith

Chris Smith

Enc. resume

"COLD" COVER LETTER TO A POTENTIAL EMPLOYER

178 Green Street
Ranier, OR 97048
(503) 555-5555

May 31, 1995

Pat Cummings
Personnel Manager
Any Corporation
1140 Main Street
Chicago, IL 60605

Dear Mr. Cummings:

Are you currently seeking a security specialist to maintain or upgrade the security of your organization? If so, I would like to apply for the position.

During the past twenty years, I have gained experience and education encompassing all aspects of law enforcement, and security procedures and implementation.

I feel confident that I can make an immediate contribution to Any Corporation, and I believe that a personal conversation would be to our mutual advantage. I will call your office on Tuesday, June 8, to schedule an appointment at your convenience.

Thank you for your attention. I look forward to speaking with you.

Sincerely,

Chris Smith

Chris Smith

Enc. resume

"COLD" COVER LETTER TO A POTENTIAL EMPLOYER

178 Green Street
Shawnee Hills, OH 43965
(216) 555-5555

October 4, 1995

Pat Cummings
Personnel Manager
Any Corporation
1140 Main Street
Chicago, IL 60605

Dear Ms. Cummings:

My interest in joining Any Corporation as a licensed electrician has prompted me to forward my resume for your review.

I have six years of experience, two as an apprentice and four as a licensed electrician, handling all kinds of electrical installations, working with electrical contractors, and as a subcontractor. Presently I am investigating new opportunities in which to apply my education and experience with a well established company. I am capable of working independently or as a member of a team, and feel confident of my ability to provide quality performance in any assignment that I undertake.

The resume is merely a brief review of my experience; during a personal interview we could further discuss my qualifications. I am very much interested in joining Any Corporation and look forward to your reply.

Sincerely,

Chris Smith

Chris Smith

Enc. resume

"COLD" COVER LETTER TO A POTENTIAL EMPLOYER

178 Green Street
Cinnaminson, NJ 08077
(609) 555-5555

November 1, 1995

Pat Cummings
President
Any Corporation
1140 Main Street
Chicago, IL 60605

Dear Mr. Cummings:

My interest in Any Corporation's growth and innovation in the field of multimedia technology has prompted me to forward my resume as an initial application for a position within your management structure.

During the past fourteen years, my experience has ranged from senior auditor with Keane & Co. Peripherals to my current position as Vice-President/Controller of a $90 million, multi-plant CD-ROM manufacturing operation. I believe that my expertise and entrepreneurial insight can be utilized to the advantage of a growing enterprise with a need for effective and efficient financial management and cost control.

If your company can use a profit-oriented and financially astute executive, I would like to discuss my qualifications with you during a personal interview. Thank you for your time and consideration.

Sincerely,

Chris Smith

Chris Smith

Enc. resume

"COLD" COVER LETTER TO A POTENTIAL EMPLOYER

178 Green Street
Proctorsville, VT 05153
(802) 555-5555

July 7, 1995

Pat Cummings
Personnel Manager
Any Corporation
1140 Main Street
Chicago, IL 60605

Dear Ms. Cummings:

In the interest of investigating career opportunities with your company, I am enclosing my resume for your consideration and review.

As you will note, I have fifteen years of educational and media experience. I am proficient in the operation of a wide variety of photographic, video, and audio equipment. I am regularly responsible for processing, duplicating, and setting up slide presentations, as well as synchronized slide and audio presentations.

I believe that my qualifications would make me an outstanding asset to your organization. I would very much appreciate the opportunity of a personal interview, at your convenience, to further discuss my abilities and the needs of Any Corporation.

I look forward to hearing from you.

Sincerely,

Chris Smith

Chris Smith

Enc. resume

"COLD" COVER LETTER TO A POTENTIAL EMPLOYER

178 Green Street
Manchester, NH 03104
(603) 555-5555

July 31, 1995

Pat Cummings
Human Resources Director
Any Bank
1140 Main Street
Chicago, IL 60605

Dear Mr. Cummings:

Having majored in mathematics at Rice University, where I also worked as a Research Assistant, I am confident that I would make a successful addition to your Economics Research Department.

In addition to my strong background in mathematics, I offer significant business experience, having worked in a data processing firm, a bookstore, and a restaurant. I am sure that my courses in statistics and computer programming would prove particularly useful in an entry-level position.

I am attracted to Any Bank by your recent rapid growth and the superior reputation of your Economic Research Department. After studying different commercial banks, I have concluded that Any Bank will be in a strong competitive position to benefit from upcoming changes in the industry, such as the phasing out of Regulation X.

I would like to interview with you at your earliest convenience.

Sincerely,

Chris Smith

Chris Smith

Enc. resume

"COLD" COVER LETTER TO A POTENTIAL EMPLOYER

178 Green Street
Little Compton, RI 02837
(401) 555-5555

August 27, 1995

Pat Cummings
Personnel Manager
Any Corporation
1140 Main Street
Chicago, IL 60605

Dear Ms. Cummings:

During the past fourteen years, my experience has been in all phases of custom casework and millwork manufacturing. Currently, I am investigating new opportunities in the Chicago area where my family and I are planning permanent relocation.

The enclosed resume summarizes my background and experience in the above areas. I am highly motivated, profit-oriented, and recognized for my ability to direct a manufacturing function and produce quality goods within cost budget and time schedules.

I am very much interested in joining your organization, and I am currently available for interviews. I will call you on Thursday, September 4, to confirm that you received my resume and answer any questions you might have.

Sincerely,

Chris Smith

Chris Smith

Enc. resume

"COLD" COVER LETTER TO A POTENTIAL EMPLOYER

178 Green Street
Emmans, PA 18049

July 18, 1995

Pat Cummings
Chief Executive Officer
Any Corporation
1140 Main Street
Chicago, IL 60605

Dear Mr. Cummings:

My interest in continuing my professional career in the health care field has prompted me to submit my resume for your review.

For fifteen years, I have dedicated myself to providing quality health care in medical staff support in diverse areas including patient care, orientation and training of volunteer staffs, inventory control, facilities reorganization, and service coordination.

The enclosed resume summarizes my background and experience in these and other areas. I will be glad to furnish you with any additional information during a personal interview or by phone at (215) 555-5555.

Thank you for your time. I look forward to your response.

Sincerely,

Chris Smith

Chris Smith

Enc. resume

"COLD" COVER LETTER TO AN EMPLOYMENT AGENCY

178 Green Street
Falndreau, SD 57028

March 4, 1995

Pat Cummings
Director
Any Corporation
1140 Main Street
Chicago, IL 60605

Dear Ms. Cummings:

During the past ten years, my experience has been in the liability insurance field in positions ranging from Transcriber to Senior Field Claims Representative. Currently, I am seeking a new association with an underwriter or a corporate liability insurance department where there is a need for expertise in claims settlement from fact-finding analysis to negotiation.

I am hoping that among your many clients, there may be one or two who are looking for someone who is knowledgeable in the area of corporate liability insurance. If so, I would like to explore the opportunity. I may be reached at (605) 555-5555 during regular business hours or at (605) 444-4444 evenings.

I look forward to hearing from you.

Sincerely,

Chris Smith

Chris Smith

Enc. resume

"COLD" COVER LETTER TO AN EMPLOYMENT AGENCY

178 Green Street
Salamanca, NY 14779
(716) 555-5555

May 13, 1995

Pat Cummings
Director
Any Corporation
1140 Main Street
Chicago, IL 60605

Dear Mr. Cummings:

In July of this year, I will be permanently relocating to the Chicago area. I am forwarding the attached resume for your evaluation because of my desire to contribute my comprehensive experience in real estate/property management to a locally-based company.

I have two years of direct experience involving all aspects in the management of 275 apartments and four commercial units in three buildings. My diverse responsibilities include a range of activities from advertising and promotion of apartments to competitive analysis of rate structures.

My experience also includes contractor negotiations, liaison with government and service agencies, personnel relations, financial management, and other functions basic to effective management of complex properties.

If you know of any company with a current need for a bright, outgoing property manager with an orientation to sales, please do not hesitate to contact me.

Thank you for your consideration.

Sincerely,

Chris Smith

Chris Smith

Enc. resume

"COLD" COVER LETTER TO AN EXECUTIVE RECRUITER

178 Green Street
Mustang, OK 73064
(405) 555-5555

February 17, 1995

Pat Cummings
Executive Recruiter
Any Corporation
1140 Main Street
Chicago, IL 60605

Dear Ms. Cummings:

During the past twelve years, I have played a key role as Materials and Plant Manager in the profitable operation of a $5 million paper conversion and printing plant.

I am currently exploring opportunities at medium to large scale manufacturing/ distribution operations where there is a need for an experienced executive capable of making decisions to improve operations, reduce costs, and increase profits.

With my present employer, I have:

- held converting costs to a 2% annual increase during the last five years—well under the rate of inflation and the increase in energy costs,
- reduced annual energy costs by almost 30%,
- reduced warehousing costs by $75,000 annually without affecting service, and
- reduced essential material costs by 60%.

The enclosed resume summarizes my background, experience, and other achievements.

Please contact me if my qualifications may be of interest to any of your client companies or if you would like to further discuss my background. I would, of course, be happy to meet with you to further discuss the details of my experience.

Sincerely,

Chris Smith

Chris Smith

Enc. resume

"COLD" COVER LETTER TO AN EXECUTIVE RECRUITER

178 Green Street
Erwin, TN 37650
(615) 555-5555

October 30, 1995

Pat Cummings
Executive Recruiter
Any Corporation
1140 Main Street
Chicago, IL 60605

Dear Mr. Cummings:

During the past fifteen years, I have held senior-level positions ranging from Senior Consultant with a CPA firm, where I specialized in Corporate Financial Planning, to my current job as Chief Financial Officer.

Although I am presently involved in interesting and challenging projects, I am considering a change, preferably to a firm that seeks a high-energy, self-starter for its management team. I have established a fine track record in financial and strategic planning which has produced high-profit results and encompassed:

- Multimillion dollar improvement in cash flow
- Reduction in operating costs and increased profitability of a rapid growth service organization ($15 million to $25 million within two years)
- Profit and business planning, financial evaluation, and long-range financial forecasting for a $150 million group of operating companies
- Negotiation for public and private funding totaling $25 million

My salary requirement is in the $100,000–$120,000 range with appropriate benefits. I would be willing to relocate for the right opportunity.

If it appears that my qualifications meet the needs of one of your clients, I would be happy to further discuss my background with either you or the client. I will be contacting your office in the near future to determine the status of my application.

Sincerely,

Chris Smith

Chris Smith

Enc. business profile

"COLD" COVER LETTER TO AN EXECUTIVE RECRUITER

178 Green Street
Kalamazoo, MI 49006

June 15, 1995

Pat Cummings
Executive Recruiter
Any Corporation
1140 Main Street
Chicago, IL 60605

Dear Ms. Cummings:

My experience encompasses over ten years of decision-making responsibility for human resource development, manpower planning, and labor law and relations affecting hundreds of employees in the public and private sectors. In addition to training and supervision of sizable staffs, I have been involved in collective bargaining for management, wage and salary administration, employee benefits, safety and training, and making and enforcing labor law considerations.

I am currently interested in a firm that offers stability, growth, and profits. I am willing to relocate if offered a challenging assignment. My salary requirement is $45,000–$55,000.

I have enclosed my resume for your review. If I may provide you with additional information, please call me at (616) 555-5555. I look forward to discussing my qualifications with you in more detail.

Sincerely,

Chris Smith

Chris Smith

Enc. resume

"COLD" COVER LETTER TO AN EXECUTIVE RECRUITER

178 Green Street
Irmo, SC 29063

October 25, 1995

Pat Cummings
Executive Recruiter
Any Corporation
1140 Main Street
Chicago, IL 60605

Dear Mr. Cummings:

During the past twenty years, I have gained experience ranging from National Sales Manager/Director of Marketing to CEO of a $25 million athletic shoe manufacturer. I have earned the reputation for being a highly skilled senior-level manager in the areas of manufacturing, new business startup and management, company reorganization and expansion, and design and development, at both regional and national levels.

Although my positions have been challenging and fast-paced, at this point in my career, I am seeking new opportunities in an advisory capacity, which may ultimately lead to an equity position. I am looking for an environment where my expertise, creativity, and motivation can be fully utilized towards upgrading and/or expanding new or existing businesses. My salary requirement is $80,000–$100,000.

If you would like any additional information, please do not hesitate to call me at (803) 555-5555. I am best reached weekdays between 8:00 A.M. and 1:00 P.M.

I look forward to your response.

Sincerely,

Chris Smith

Chris Smith

Enc. resume

"COLD" COVER LETTER TO AN EXECUTIVE RECRUITER

178 Green Street
Gusher, VT 84030
(802) 555-5555

April 1, 1995

Pat Cummings
Executive Recruiter
Any Corporation
1140 Main Street
Chicago, IL 60605

Dear Ms. Cummings:

I have played a key role in designing, implementing, reorganizing and managing operations, manufacturing, materials, engineering, and quality assurance functions for nationally and internationally recognized corporations.

Currently, I am seeking a position with a company that can benefit from my twenty years of progressively responsible management experience in the above areas. My expertise is diverse and includes:

- five years as Director of Operations for a $60,000,000 manufacturer;
- more than six years as Materials Manager with a multi-plant, multi-warehouse, $10 million manufacturer of industrial rubber products;
- over nine years as Manufacturing Coordinator with a toy manufacturer;
- physical set-up of new or expansion of existing manufacturing and support facilities;
- manpower planning;
- industrial union relations;
- capital equipment investment and materials purchases.

My product knowledge includes thorough familiarity with metal, wood, plastic, ceramic, and rubber products.

I have enclosed my resume for your review. Should you be conducting a search for someone with my background, at the present time or in the near future, I would greatly appreciate your consideration. I would be happy to discuss my background in greater detail with you, on the phone or in person. Thank you for your time.

Best wishes,

Chris Smith

Chris Smith

Enc. resume

NETWORKING LETTER

178 Green Street
Burbank, CA 91501

January 18, 1995

Pat Cummings
Director
Any Corporation
1140 Main Street
Chicago, IL 60605

Dear Mr. Cummings:

   At the suggestion of Walter Durrane, I am enclosing my resume for your consideration pertaining to consulting or related assignments with Any Corporation.

   I have recently retired from a long and successful general medical practice. However, as an active professional, I am interested in contributing my expertise as a representative for a public agency such as the Fraud Control Unit at Any Corporation. I have been actively involved as an evaluator and consultant for insurance companies, attorneys, industrial, and other insured claims, and I would like to transfer these skills in the continuation of my profession.

   I look forward to meeting you to further discuss my ability to fulfill your requirements. In the interim, I may be reached at the above address or by phone at (818) 555-5555.

Sincerely,

Chris Smith

Chris Smith

Enc. resume

NETWORKING LETTER

178 Green Street
Moses Lake, WA 98837
(509) 555-5555

June 30, 1995

Pat Cummings
Producer
Any Corporation
1140 Main Street
Chicago, IL 60605

Dear Ms. Cummings:

Peggy Sullivan recently indicated to me that you may have an opening for a set designer and suggested that I contact you. I seek a creative position involving stage design in television.

I was graduated in December from Purdue University with a Bachelor's degree in Theater Arts and a concentration in Studio Art. In addition to modern drama and music and sound in theater, I studied set creation and design, intermediate painting, and wood cutting. As a member of the drama club, I designed and helped create props for numerous campus productions, including A Midsummer Nights Dream and Vinegar Tom.

As for work experience, I co-designed and co-created the props and decorations for a new miniature golf course with a tropical island theme, which was immensely popular. I also gained valuable skills working as an apprentice to a busy carpenter and painting houses for a large company.

Enclosed is my resume as well as some photographs of my work. I have some interesting ideas for the sets of "Wheel of Trivia" and "Late Night Videos" which I would like to discuss with you in a personal interview. I may be reached at the above listed number after 1:00 P.M. on weekdays.

Thank you for your consideration of my application.

Sincerely,

Chris Smith

Chris Smith

Enc. resume

NETWORKING LETTER

178 Green Street
Zephyr Cove, NV 89448
(702) 555-5555

March 30, 1995

Pat Cummings
Senior Loan Administrator
Any Corporation
1140 Main Street
Chicago, IL 60605

Dear Mr. Cummings:

I truly enjoyed our conversation last week at the Racquet Ball Club. I hope you enjoyed the remainder of your Las Vegas stay.

As you may recall, I will be graduating from the University of Las Vegas in May with a degree in Finance. For the past three months, I have been interning at Marshall Howe and Company. I have learned the auditing and payment coordination aspects of the business in depth, gaining praise for my motivation, professionalism, and willingness to take on new tasks.

Currently, I am looking for an entry-level Finance position within a dynamic company. I would greatly appreciate any assistance you could provide. Enclosed is my resume and a letter of recommendation for your review.

Thank you in advance for your help. It is greatly appreciated!

Sincerely,

Chris Smith

Chris Smith

Enc. resume
    letter of recommendation

NETWORKING LETTER

178 Green Street
Wolfeboro, NH 03894
(603) 555-5555

June 27, 1995

Pat Cummings
Principal
Any School
140 Main Street
Chicago, IL 60605

Dear Ms. Cummings:

It was a pleasure to speak with you a few months ago at the "National Women in Education Convention" in Boston.

As you may recall, I was then working as an English teacher at Amos Academy in Manchester, New Hampshire. However, due to extensive cuts in the faculty budget and my own lack of seniority, my position has been eliminated.

During our conversation, I remember you mentioned your search for an English teacher for grades 7 and 8. I realize that much time has passed, and this position has more than likely been filled. However, I was hoping that you may know of a similar opening within your district or that you may have some suggestions as to others with whom it might be beneficial for me to speak.

I can be reached at the telephone number listed above. I would appreciate any leads you could give me.

Again, I very much enjoyed our conversation.

Sincerely,

Chris Smith

Chris Smith

Enc. resume

NETWORKING LETTER

178 Green Street
Dazey, ND 58428
(701) 555-5555

June 2, 1995

Pat Cummings
Director of Marketing
Any Corporation
1140 Main Street
Chicago, IL 60605

Dear Mr. Cummings:

It was a pleasure talking with you during our flight to Rome last April. I hope you enjoyed your trip!

As you may recall, at the time I was a senior at Harvard University studying marketing and sales. You were kind enough to give me your business card with instructions to contact you once I was "liberated from the Fetters of Academia." Finally, that day has arrived!

Although I am a recent graduate, I have held several internships at major Boston corporations. Mine is not the hesitant approach of the neophyte; I know how to buy and sell in an aggressive, no-holds-barred manner while retaining the diplomacy necessary to garner respect.

I've enclosed my resume for your reference and file. If you know of anyone seeking a fresh new addition to their marketing team, please let me know.

Thank you in advance for your assistance.

Best wishes,

Chris Smith

Chris Smith

Enc. resume

NETWORKING LETTER

178 Green Street
Savage, MT 59262
(406) 555-5555

September 28, 1995

Pat Cummings
Telecommunications Consultant
Any Corporation
1140 Main Street
Chicago, IL 60605

Dear Ms. Cummings:

Several years ago I was a classmate of your son Dustin at the University of Miami. When I bumped into him last week in Billings, Montana, of all places, he informed me that you deal closely with several leading specialists in the telecommunications field and suggested I contact you immediately.

I am interested in joining a company where I can contribute strong skills and education in communications. I offer:

- Bachelor of Arts degree in Communication Science
- Familiarity with all areas of marketing, public relations, and advertising
- One year experience as a Promotions Intern at a radio station
- Fluency in German

I would greatly appreciate any advice and/or referrals you might be able to give me. I will call you in a few days to follow up.

Thank you for your time.

Sincerely,

Chris Smith

Chris Smith

Enc. resume

FOLLOW-UP LETTER (After Telephone Conversation)

178 Green Street
Weymouth, MA 02190
(617) 555-5555

September 12, 1995

Pat Cummings
Human Resources Director
Any Corporation
1140 Main Street
Chicago, IL 60605

Dear Mr. Cummings:

It was good talking with you again today. As promised, I am enclosing my resume for your information.

In addition to a B.S. in Biology, I have five years of experience in a laboratory setting. This includes preparation and performance of experiments, as well as analysis, writing, and presentation of results.

Currently, I am investigating new opportunities where I can continue to develop my skills and apply my knowledge toward broader responsibilities and advancement. Any assistance you might give me towards this endeavor will be sincerely appreciated.

Again, thank you for taking time out of your busy schedule to aid me in my job search. Your confidence in my abilities is greatly appreciated.

Sincerely,

Chris Smith

Chris Smith

Enc. resume

FOLLOW-UP LETTER (After Telephone Conversation)

178 Green Street
Boise, ID 83725
(208) 555-5555

August 3, 1995

Pat Cummings
Vice-President
Any Corporation
1140 Main Street
Chicago, IL 60605

Dear Ms. Cummings:

I am forwarding my resume in regards to the opening we discussed in your Marketing Department.

Although I am currently employed in a management position, I am interested in a career change, especially one where I can combine a thorough knowledge of boating with my sales, marketing, and communication skills. I am an imaginative, well organized self-starter with strong interest in boating. As a semi-professional sailboat racer, I twice won national honors and participated in the races at Cape Cod. In addition, I have made lasting contacts with owners and officials.

After you have had the chance to review my resume, please contact me so that we can further discuss the possibility of my joining your staff. I am confident that my business background and knowledge of boats will enable me to have a favorable impact on both your sales and image.

Thank you for your attention, and I look forward to speaking with you again to learn more about this opportunity.

Sincerely yours,

Chris Smith

Chris Smith

Enc. resume

FOLLOW-UP LETTER (After Telephone Conversation)

178 Green Street
New York, NY 10027
(212) 555-5555

July 1, 1995

Pat Cummings
Controller
Any Corporation
1140 Main Street
Chicago, IL 60605

Dear Mr. Cummings:

Thank you for taking time out of your busy schedule to speak with me yesterday regarding the Export Manager position. My interest in this position and in Any Corporation is stronger than ever, particularly because it would afford the opportunity to become less desk-bound—an occupational hazard in my most recent employment.

Pursuant to our conversation, I have compiled a supplement to my resume, detailing my experience relevant to the position of Export Manager. As I explained to you, my family has been involved in the fashion industry for most of my life. While not formally employed by them, I have actively assisted/advised both my mother and my uncle on their European outlets, acquiring considerable expertise and knowledge of the fashion accessory and perfume industry.

In regard to salary requirements, I did a brief cost survey of the Chicago area and happily discovered a favorable difference between that area and where I reside in New York. I would, therefore, be able to consider a salary somewhat lower than we discussed—perhaps in the low fifties—since my living expenses would be so significantly decreased.

I am very enthusiastic about the prospect of re-entering a field where my interpersonal skills and familiarity with European culture and fashion will be more fully utilized.

I look forward to hearing from you again in the near future.

Sincerely,

Chris Smith

Chris Smith

Enc. resume

FOLLOW-UP LETTER (After Informational Interview)

178 Green Street
Toast, NC 27049
(919) 555-5555

July 26, 1995

Pat Cummings
Associate Professor of Psychology
Any Corporation
1140 Main Street
Chicago, IL 60605

Dear Ms. Cummings:

It was a pleasure seeing you again today. I appreciate the time you found in your busy schedule to meet with me.

It was interesting to learn about the use of interactive toys and models in child psychology. I have already been to the library to borrow the book by Leonard Finn that you recommended so highly. I am looking forward to reading about his ideas on child's play before the latency period.

I will be contacting Mr. Finn within the next few days to set up an appointment. I will let you know how everything is progressing after I have met him.

Again, thank you for your assistance. You will hear from me soon.

Sincerely,

Chris Smith

Chris Smith

FOLLOW UP LETTER (After Job Interview)

178 Green Street
Chicago, IL 60605
(312) 555-5555

August 5, 1995

Pat Cummings
Vice-President of Operations
Any Corporation
1140 Main Street
Chicago, IL 60605

Dear Mr. Cummings:

I greatly enjoyed our meeting yesterday. I would like to reiterate my interest in Any Corporation's opening for a Materials Manager.

As I explained during our conversation, I feel confident that my qualifications match the requirements of the position. I offer twelve years experience working as Manager of Warehousing and Distribution and as Senior Buyer for a large metropolitan hospital. Briefly, my accomplishments include:

Reducing expenditures of all in-house medical and non-medical supplies by 20% through cost-effective negotiations, purchasing, and control.

Automating inventories which increased efficiency and decreased costly errors, thus saving over $10,000 annually.

Designing a functional warehouse layout which effectively reduced the selection and distribution process for warehoused materials and provided more stringent controls.

Reducing shrinkage, damage, and obsolescence of inventory by 33%.

Thank you for the time and courtesy you and your associates extended to me. I will look forward to hearing from you.

Sincerely,

Chris Smith

Chris Smith

FOLLOW-UP LETTER (After Job Interview)

178 Green Street
Luna, NM 87824
(505) 555-5555

December 2, 1995

Pat Cummings, MD
Director, Pediatric Medicine Fellowship Program
Any Hospital
1140 Main Street
Chicago, IL 60605

Dear Dr. Cummings:

Thank you for allowing me to interview for the fellowship position in your department at Any Hospital. I appreciated the opportunity to meet with the faculty and the staff; everyone was most hospitable.

I was impressed with the program and in particular the thought which has gone into the fellowship curriculum development and research guidance. I came away very enthusiastic about the position.

Please extend my thanks to Dr. Lee, Dr. Murphy, and Dr. Sloat for a thoughtful discussion relative to the Emergency Medicine Fellowship Program. Being part of such a team is, indeed, an enticing prospect.

If you have any further questions please do not hesitate to contact me. I look forward to hearing from you.

Sincerely,

Chris Smith

Chris Smith

cc. Joan Lee, MD
Brian Murphy, MD
Susan Sloat, MD

FOLLOW-UP LETTER (After Job Interview)

178 Green Street
Wicomico, VA 23184
(804) 555-5555

July 4, 1985

Pat Cummings
Human Resources Director
Any Corporation
1140 Main Street
Chicago, IL 60605

Dear Mr. Cummings:

I enjoyed meeting with you yesterday. Thank you for taking the time out of your busy schedule to talk with me about the current sales position available with Any Corporation.

I would like to stress my interest in this position. The prospect of having the freedom to run my own sales territory like my own business is exciting and appealing to me.

My background includes extensive team selling, and I would like to emphasize that all decisions regarding structure of presentations, targets, and general selling strategy within the downtown Lynchburg territory were principally my responsibility. I had the freedom to set pricing structure and tailor product packages as I saw fit to best make the sale. I thrived on that freedom and was successful.

As a follow up to our meeting, I will write a rough business plan, as we discussed, and I will contact Jordan Banks for further insight into the position.

Thank you again for your time. I look forward to meeting with you again in August at the Chicago office.

Sincerely,

Chris Smith

Chris Smith

cc. J. Banks

FOLLOW-UP LETTER (After Job Interview)

178 Green Street
Flat, AK 99584

November 19, 1995

Pat Cummings
President
Any Corporation
1140 Main Street
Chicago, IL 60605

Dear Ms. Cummings:

It was a pleasure meeting you today. I appreciate you taking the time from your hectic schedule to speak with me about your opening for an Executive Assistant.

The position is exciting and seems to encompass a diversity of responsibilities. I believe that with my experience and skills, I would be able to contribute significantly to your business.

I look forward to hearing from you in the near future. If you need further information, please feel free to call me.

Sincerely,

Chris Smith

Chris Smith
(907) 555-5555

FOLLOW-UP LETTER (After Job Interview)

178 Green Street
Fort Wayne, IN 46803
(219) 555-5555

January 23, 1995

Pat Cummings
Executive Director
Any Hotel Chain
1140 Main Street
Chicago, IL 60605

Dear Mr. Cummings:

I would like to thank you for meeting with me on Friday regarding the position of Hotel Manager. I enjoyed learning more about this opportunity and Any Hotel Chain.

I would like, also, to reiterate my interest in the position. I feel that it would be an exciting opportunity and feel my track record shows I would be a successful candidate.

I am looking forward to hearing your final decision. Thank you again.

Sincerely,

Chris Smith

Chris Smith

REJECTION OF OFFER LETTER

178 Green Street
Rupert, ID 83350
(208) 555-5555

May 15, 1995

Pat Cummings
Art Director
Any Corporation
1140 Main Street
Chicago, IL 60605

Dear Ms. Cummings:

I would like to use this opportunity to thank you for taking the time to meet with me last week.

However, after careful thought and consideration, I must decline your tempting offer for the position of Assistant Art Director. I've decided that my interests and career goals lie elsewhere at this point in my life. Perhaps our needs will coincide at a later date.

Thank you again. Best wishes for your continued success.

Sincerely,

Chris Smith

Chris Smith

REJECTION OF OFFER LETTER

178 Green Street
Winterthur, DE 19735
(302) 555-5555

February 14, 1995

Pat Cummings
Vice-President, Research and Development
Any Corporation
1140 Main Street
Chicago, IL 60605

Dear Mr. Cummings:

Thank you for taking the time to meet with me on Friday to discuss the opportunities for employment within your Research and Development Department.

While I appreciate your generous offer, I have decided to withdraw from consideration for the position. I have accepted a position elsewhere which I feel is better suited to my long-term needs.

Again, many thanks for your time. I wish you the best of luck in your future endeavors at Any Corporation.

Sincerely,

Chris Smith

Chris Smith

ACCEPTANCE LETTER

178 Green Street
Weeping Water, NE 68463
(402) 555-5555

May 21, 1995

Pat Cummings
Human Resources Director
Any Corporation
1140 Main Street
Chicago, IL 60605

Dear Ms. Cummings:

I would like to express my thanks for selecting me as the new Benefits Administrator for Any Corporation. This is an exciting opportunity, and I am eager to join your ranks.

I have turned in my resignation to my present employer, and I will begin working for you three weeks from today. During the interim, I will remain in contact with both you and Rick Starchon in order to ensure that my initiation is a smooth one.

Again, thank you for your confidence and support. I look forward to fulfilling your expectations.

Sincerely,

Chris Smith

Chris Smith

ACCEPTANCE LETTER

178 Green Street
Green Bay, WI 54301

March 17, 1995

Pat Cummings

Any Corporation
President
1140 Main Street
Chicago, IL 60605

Dear Mr. Cummings:

I have received your letter of March 10, and am thrilled to accept Any Corporation's offer to become your new Labor Relations Specialist.

I have formally resigned from the Blackwell Company, and will be relocating to the Chicago area within the next four weeks. I will be able to better pinpoint an exact starting date within the next few days.

You will be hearing from me again soon to finalize the remaining details of our agreement.

Thank you again for giving me this opportunity to become a part of the Any Corporation team. If you have any questions or require additional information, please do not hesitate to call me at (414) 555-5555.

Sincerely,

Chris Smith

Chris Smith

THANK YOU LETTER (After Hire)

178 Green Street
Twodot, MT 59085
(406) 555-5555

October 14, 1995

Pat Cummings
Managing Editor
Any Corporation
1140 Main Street
Chicago, IL 60605

Dear Ms. Cummings:

I am happy to inform you that I have just accepted an offer for employment as an Acquisitions Editor at Dandelion Publishing Group. I should begin work there the first week of November.

I would like to thank you for all of your help during my job search, specifically for putting me in touch with Ninona Punder at Dandelion's Billings Office.

If there is ever anything that I can do for you, please do not hesitate to contact me. Yours was a favor I shall not soon forget.

Again, many thanks and best wishes.

Sincerely,

Chris Smith

Chris Smith

THANK YOU LETTER (After Hire)

178 Green Street
El Segundo, CA 90245
(310) 555-5555

December 22, 1995

Pat Cummings
Software Engineer
Any Corporation
1140 Main Street
Chicago, IL 60605

Dear Mr. Cummings:

I am pleased to inform you that my job search has come to a successful conclusion. Yesterday, I was offered a position with L. GWA PO Inc., a Japanese software conglomerate that has recently opened a branch office in Los Angeles. I am delighted to be able to participate once again in the fast-paced world of computer technology.

I would like to extend my warmest thanks to you for your kindness and encouragement during my job search. The next time you visit LA, please be sure to let me know.

Happy holidays and best wishes for the new year!

Sincerely,

Chris Smith

Chris Smith

PART III
Sample Resumes

5
Resumes for Special Situations

 Writing a resume can seem like an even more formidable task when you find yourself in what we call "special situations." Perhaps you lack paid job experience, have been out of the workplace to raise children, are concerned about possible discrimination because of age or disability, or are trying to enter a field in which you have no practical experience. Not to worry! The key to improving your resume in these special situations is to emphasize your strengths. Focus on your marketable skills (whether they were acquired in the workplace or elsewhere), and highlight impressive achievements, relevant education and training, and/or related interests. And of course, you should take care to downplay or eliminate any information that may be construed as a weakness.

For example, if you are a "displaced homemaker" (a homemaker entering the job market for the first time), you can use a functional resume to highlight the special skills you've acquired over the years while downplaying your lack of paid job experience. If you are an older job candidate, use your age as a selling point. Emphasize the depth of your experience, your maturity, your sense of responsibility, and your positive outlook. Changing careers? No problem! Instead of focusing on your job history you should emphasize the marketable skills you've acquired that are considered valuable in the position you're seeking. For example, let's say your career has been in real estate and, in your spare time, you like to run in marathons. Recently, you heard about an opening in the sales and marketing department at an athletic shoe manufacturer. What you need to do is emphasize the skills you have that the employer is looking for. Not only do you have strong sales experience, you're familiar with the needs of the company's market, and that's a powerful combination!

Throughout this chapter, you'll find creative resume solutions for even the most daunting career obstacles. Use them as a guideline for creating your own job-winning resumes.

You can find more examples of creative resume solutions on our web site at: http://www.careercity.com/edge/experts/bnadler/nadler.htm

50-PLUS JOB CANDIDATE (Management)

CHRIS SMITH
178 Green Street
Huntington, WV 25702
(304) 555-5555

OBJECTIVE:
A position in small plant management. Willing to relocate and/or travel.

SUMMARY OF QUALIFICATIONS:
More than thirty years of experience encompassing plant management to include sales, production, plant maintenance, systems, personnel, and related functions. Hired, trained, and supervised personnel. Additional experience as Sales Counselor in the educational field. Good background in customer relations and human resources.

CAREER HIGHLIGHTS:
The Westview Schools, Huntington, WV
Career Counselor   1981-Present
Contact and interview teenagers, young adults, and adults with reference to pursuing courses of higher education leading towards careers in a variety of business professions (secretarial, accounting, court reporting, business management, public relations, fashions and merchandising, computer and machine operating and programming, machine accounting, etc.). Administer aptitude tests to applicants and advise prospective students as to their aptitudes and best courses to pursue.

Greenbriar Corporation, Huntington, WV
General Manager   1972-1981
Assumed responsibility for management of this firm which originally employed twelve. Selected, set up, equipped, and staffed new facilities; hired, trained, and supervised skilled production personnel; set up incentive plans; quality production and cost controls; systems; plant maintenance; handled payroll, billing, credit and collection, purchasing, and finance.

Rosemont Inc., Charleston, WV
Assistant Plant Manager, Laundry Company   1962-1972
Supervised all personnel in this plant which employed 250 people. Handled customer relations, complaints, quality control, and related functions.

EDUCATION:
Northeastern University, Boston, MA
BSBA degree
Industrial Relations and Accounting.

- Resume stresses candidate's extensive experience and significant accomplishments.

- Background summary accentuates candidate's acquired professional skills and impressive track record.

ALL EMPLOYMENT AT ONE COMPANY (Administrator)

Chris Smith
178 Green Street
St. Louis, MO 63130
(314) 555-5555

PROFESSIONAL EXPERIENCE:
MARCA INFRARED DEVICES, St. Louis, MO
Manufacturers of infrared sensing and detecting devices.

1991-Present **Administrator**
Control, track and maintain engineering personnel status, capital expenditures, and perform budget support for engineering departments.
- Automate weekly labor reports to calculate effectiveness and utilization and report against plan.
- Automate calculation of vacation dollars used in engineering budget planning.
- Automate capital equipment planning cycle.
- Act as capital expenditure liaison for all of engineering.
- Maintain engineering personnel status and monitor performance to plan.
- Perform year-end close-out on all engineering purchase orders.
- Control, track and maintain all contractor and consultant requisitions.
- Cross-train in library functions involving documentation ordering and CD ROM usage.

1990-91 **Documentation Control Clerk**
Controlled, tracked and maintained all changes to engineering documentation.
- Trained personnel in status accounting function and audit performance.
- Downloaded engineering and manufacturing tracking files from mainframe to MacIntosh.

1987-90 **Documentation Specialist**
Controlled, tracked and maintained all changes to manufacturing and engineering documentation.
- Generated parts lists and was initial user of computerized Bills of Material.
- Directed changes in material requirements to material and production control departments.

1985-87 **Configuration Management Analyst**
Controlled, tracked and maintained all changes to engineering documentation.
- Chaired Configuration Review Board.
- Presented configuration status reports at customer reviews.

1984-85 **Inside Sales Coordinator**
- Served as first customer contact.
- Directed customer calls and customer service.
- Maintained literature files and processed incoming orders.

EDUCATION:
B.S. - Biology, Washington University 1984

- Brief description of current employer adds weight to already strong qualifications.

- Dynamic action verbs give resume impact.

ALL EMPLOYMENT AT ONE COMPANY (Financial Analyst)

Chris Smith
178 Green Street
Newberg, OR 97132
(503) 555-5555

PROFESSIONAL EXPERIENCE
Portland Memorial Hospital, Portland, OR

1992-Present **Administrative/Financial Analyst, Department of Medicine**
Responsible for monitoring the financial and performance indicators of the managed care Health Program. Calculate and substantiate annual financial settlements. Supervise claims authorization process. Serve as liaison between the contracting parties for financial issues. Develop computer database systems. Assisted the Project Director with the development and implementation of a hospital based PPO for Portland Memorial employees.

1990-1992 **Research Funding Coordinator, Division of Hematology and Oncology**
Managed active, pending, and planned sponsored research programs. Instrumental in obtaining funding sources via a network research funding database. Prepared grants and monitored grant expenditures. Analyzed monthly financial reports and prepared budget projections. Managed and coordinated international research fellowship programs and blood donor programs. Developed and monitored an encumbrance database.

1988-1990 **Accounts Payable Supervisor, Research Administration**
Managed the administrative process of goods acquisitions and services for all research departments within the Hospital. Created and maintained an encumbrance database and distributed financial reports to investigators. Supervised the Accounts Payable Coordinator.

1986-1988 **Research Data Coordinator/Unit Assistant, Oncology Department**
Coordinated an outpatient hematology and oncology research study with the Chief of Hematology. Researched medical history, coordinated with Blood Bank Outpatient Laboratories and data entry. Scheduled outpatient testing for oncology patients. Instrumental in the development of a Breast Clinic and Chief Residents Clinic.

1985-1986 **Administrative Assistant, Materials Management**
Assistant to Both the Director of Materials Management and the Purchasing Manager.

EDUCATION
1988 George Tex College, Newberg, OR
Political Science and Sociology, B.A.
Presidential Honors.

1983 Linfield College, McMinnville, OR
College course work consisting of accounting and history concentrations.

1982 University of Oregon, Eugene, OR
Medical Assisting, A.S.

COMPUTER SKILLS
Lotus, dBase, Paradox, WordPerfect.

■ Chronological format emphasizes a clear career path.

■ Candidate's highest educational achievement is shown before other, less significant degrees.

ALL EMPLOYMENT AT ONE COMPANY (Vice-President)

Chris Smith
178 Green Street
Pocatello, ID 83204
(208) 555-5555

SUMMARY OF QUALIFICATIONS:
- Over 12 years experience in inventory control management.
- Strong background in customer service.
- Excellent interpersonal skills.

EXPERIENCE:

J.C. RIVINGTON & CO, Pocatello, ID
(An Employee-Owned company since 1978)
Manufacturer/Distributor of premier quality Photo Frames.

1991-Present VICE-PRESIDENT Inventory Management/Administrative Services
Monitored the Production/Distribution/Inventory Control Systems, and the Import Purchasing, Product Costing Department. Managed the Distribution, Electronic Data Processing, and Communications Departments.

1987-1991 DIRECTOR Inventory Control/Materials
Managed/controlled the Production/Inventory Control System including Finished Goods, Work-In-Process, and Raw Materials, translating Sales Forecasts into production/inventory budgets and plan. Directed and monitored the Purchasing Dept., both domestic and foreign purchases including goods purchased for resale. Chaired weekly Production Meetings to set/communicate priorities to Plant, Warehouse, Purchasing, and Customer Service managers. Designed/computerized a Product Costing System initially utilized as a marketing tool.

1983-1987 MANAGER Inventory Control/Materials
Performed Production/Inventory Control managerial functions of Finished Goods, Work-In-Process, and Raw Materials to meet company inventory investment objectives, to provide even production budgets on factory floor, and to meet agreed upon targeted levels of customer service.

1980-1983 OFFICE MANAGER
Supervised, directed and coordinated Customer Service/Order Dept., Communications including Word Processing, Switchboard, and Mail Room, Data Processing, Credit & Collection, Accounts. Payable and Accounts. Receivable Departments. Established company newsletter.

EDUCATION:

Northwestern College, Orange City, IA
Master of Business Administration, 1980.

Iowa State University, Ames, IA
Bachelor of Science in Management, 1978.

- Format de-emphasizes the fact that all candidate's work experience is at one company.

- Resume illustrates continual career progression.

AT-HOME DAD REENTERING THE WORK FORCE (Sales)

CHRIS SMITH
178 Green Street
Holland, MI 49423
(616) 555-5555

SUMMARY OF QUALIFICATIONS
- Excellent interpersonal and communication skills; cooperative, patient, supportive and loyal team player.
- Highly adaptable and comfortable with unconventional/alternative settings and situations; familiar with academic, domestic and creative routines and structures.
- Ability to ensure a project or task is completed accurately and in a timely fashion; strong on follow-up.
- Energetic and vital; remain active member of community organizations, while raising a large family.

EXPERIENCE

MICHIGAN HISTORICAL SOCIETY, Holland, MI   1992-Present
Researcher/Projects and Editorial Assistant - Part-time Volunteer
Research and work includes fact finding for the Michigan Tree Research Project; and a four-year study on In-depth Biographical History of Viking Presence in Early Michigan.

MICHIGAN MENTAL HEALTH CENTER, Detroit, MI   1991-Present
Co-Leader, Substance Abuse Program - Part-time Volunteer
Assist the Day Hospital staff with transition patients; assist on a team therapy program as well as in "modules" such as health awareness, gardening and literature groups.

HOLLAND PUBLIC WORKS DEPT.,   Summers 1979 - Present
Activities Coordinator
Supervise local children in a variety of activities at the town playground; crafts, sports, games, etc. Requires knowledge of CPR and First Aid.

SHARONA REALTORS, Ypsilanti, MI   1978-79
Sales Representative

MICHIGAN STATE, East Lansing, MI   1976-78
Instructor, Art History
Developed curriculum; taught rudimentary aesthetics, method, and appreciation of modern American Art; monitored student progress, intervened where necessary.

EDUCATION

DETROIT SCHOOL OF PHOTOGRAPHY, Detroit, MI.   1982
Graduate, Applied Photography.

DREXEL, Philadelphia, PA. Bachelor and Master of Arts: History.   1976

■ Resume focuses on candidate's past job experience while incorporating functional qualifications.

■ Use of boldface and underlining provides a clean and crisp presentation.

AT-HOME MOM REENTERING THE WORK FORCE (Interior Design)

CHRIS SMITH
178 Green Street
Mesa, AZ 85203
(602) 555-5555

Summary of Qualifications
- Strong management background; owned and operated a successful interior design store for nine years.
- Experience in delegating authority; managed retail staff of six, and later performed volunteer work with countless children and adolescents.
- Superior training/teaching skills; patient and supportive, having years instructional background in crafts, swimming, sports, CPR, cooking, etc.
- Communicate well with children.
- Strong team player; enthusiastic attitude motivates increased productivity in others.

Experience   **Girl Scouts of America**, Mesa, AZ   1989-Present (Part-time)
Brownie Troop Leader, ages 10-11
Lead weekly troop meetings; work with girls towards achievement of merit badges in camping, cooking, sewing, and crafts. Organize monthly overnight trips to local campgrounds. Teach practical first aid techniques and CPR. Facilitate discussions on personal safety when unaccompanied by an adult; teach girls methods of dealing with unsolicited attention from strangers, peer pressure, drug and alcohol abuse, and eating disorders. Organize annual cookie drive; profits garnered support Girl Scouts across America in both their performance of community service and their journey towards personal growth.

Weight Watchers, Mesa, AZ   1990-Present (Part-time)
Meeting Leader
Educate and motivate members toward healthy lifestyle changes. The topics change weekly and range from healthful eating habits and exercise to behavior modification techniques. Manage cash and bookkeeping for each meeting.

Baroque Backdrops and Designs, Mesa AZ   1980-1989
Business Owner/Manager (Interior design company)
Performed all aspects of retail and office management, sales, purchasing, closet and space design, estimates, planning, installations, inventory control, brochure designs, and text publishing. Maintained office and inventory control on a MacIntosh.

Community Involvement
Parks and recreational department, Mesa, AZ   Spring 1987-Present
Coach Girls' Softball Team, ages 12-14
Saint Martha's Church Choir, Mesa AZ   1992-Present
Play organ for three services every Sunday morning
CCD Instructor, Mesa, AZ   1989-1990
Taught Catholic doctrine to elementary school children in preparation for Sacrament of First Communion.

Education
Stonehill College, Easton, MA
B.A. Early Childhood Education, 1975

- Job descriptions are brief and punchy, without being choppy.

- Volunteer work and community service lend strength to this resume.

AT-HOME MOM REENTERING THE WORK FORCE (Nursing)

Chris Smith
178 Green Street
Upper Montclair, NJ 07043
(201) 555-5555

CAREER OBJECTIVE
To utilize my extensive experience in nursing in a challenging position within the health care industry.

PROFESSIONAL EXPERIENCE
1988-92   MONTCLAIR MEMORIAL HOSPITAL, Montclair, NJ
R.N. Staff Nurse
Addictions Treatment Program
Patient care on 40-bed Mental Health Unit, assessing patients in crisis, interviewing and counseling, administering medication, Emergency Room consulting, collaborating with health care providers.
- Assess and evaluate patients with substance abuse problems.
- Responsible for the verification and pre-certification of insurance providers.
- Assess medical complications.
- Lead and co-lead educational groups for patients and their families.
- Collaborate with Treatment Team to implement in-patient and after care plans.

1985-88   **Staff Nurse/Psychiatric Addiction Emergency Service**
- Assessed of addicted and psychiatric patients to determine severity of illness and level of care needed.
- Collaborated with health care providers and medical team.

1983-85   MONMOUTH COLLEGE/NURSING PROGRAM, West Long Branch, NJ
Instructor/Medical Assisting Techniques
- Instructed students in the arts and skills of office medical procedures.
- Organized and planned curriculum, tested and graded students in written and practical methods.

1981-83   CITY OF NEWARK SCHOOL DEPARTMENT, Newark, NJ
Substitute School Nurse
- Administered first aid for students in K-12.
- Eye and ear testing, counseling and health teaching.

EDUCATION
JERSEY CITY HOSPITAL SCHOOL OF NURSING, Jersey City, NJ
Registered Nurse: Registration Number 10468, 1981.

ACTIVITIES
Volunteer, Cedar Grove Nursing Home, 1993-present.
Forward, Women's Soccer League, 1993-present.

■ Job objective gives resume focus without limiting candidate's opportunities.

■ Personal interests and activities are relevant to candidate's field of interest.

CAREER CHANGER (Advertising)

Chris Smith
178 Green Street
Austin, TX 78746
(512) 555-5555

OBJECTIVE:
To contribute over eight years experience in administration, promotion, and communication to an entry-level position in **advertising**.

SUMMARY OF QUALIFICATIONS:
- Performed advertising duties for small business.
- General knowledge of office management.
- Ability to work well with others, in both supervisory and support staff roles.
- Experience in business writing and communication skills.
- Type 55 words per minute.

SELECTED ACHIEVEMENTS AND RESULTS:
Administration:
Record keeping and file maintenance. Data processing and computer operations, accounts receivable, accounts payable, accounting research and reports. Order fulfillment, inventory control, and customer relations. Scheduling, office management, and telephone reception.

Promotion:
Composing, editing, and proofreading correspondence and PR materials for own house cleaning service. Large scale mailings.

Communication:
Instruction, curriculum and lesson planning; student evaluation; parent-teacher conferences; development of educational materials. Training and supervising clerks.

Computer Skills:
Proficient in MS Word, Lotus 1-2-3, Excel, Filemaker Pro, and ADDS Accounting System.

WORK HISTORY:
Teacher; Self-Employed (owner of housecleaning service); Floor Manager; Administrative Assistant; Accounting Clerk.

EDUCATION:
Southwestern, Georgetown, Texas, BS Education, Summa Cum Laude, 1986
Georgetown Center for Adult Education, Bookkeeping & Accounting, Intermediate Microsoft Word, Introduction to Excel, FileMaker Pro

AFFILIATIONS:
National Association of Advertising Executives.

■ Job objective focuses on the needs of the employer, not the job candidate.

■ Job-related affiliations demonstrate candidate's active participation in field.

CAREER CHANGER (Computer Programming)

Chris Smith
178 Green Street
Hollywood, CA 90210
(213) 555-5555

OBJECTIVE
A position in computer programming.

SKILLS SUMMARY

More than eleven years of progressive experience in professional office setting. Accurate, precise, dedicated, self-motivated; able to set effective priorities to achieve immediate and long-term goals and meet operational deadlines. Excellent communication skills.

HARDWARE

IBM 386, 486, 3090; HP 9000; Apple Plus II, Compaq

SOFTWARE

C++, Cobol, Cobol II, Fortran, Pascal, Basic, Powerbuilder

EDUCATION

LOYOLA MARYMOUNT UNIVERSITY, Los Angeles, CA, 1990-present
Courses in MIS, Computer Science. Computer Programming
LOMA LINDA UNIVERSITY, Riverside, CA, 1986
Courses in Accounting Principles
CALIFORNIA STATE COLLEGE, Sacramento, CA
Bachelor of Science, Elementary Education, 1984

EXPERIENCE HIGHLIGHTS

ERICKSON CORPORATION, Hollywood, CA   6/90-Present
Accounting Clerk
Processed Accounts Payable. Acted as vendor and upper-level project personnel liaison. Developed monthly cost accruals. Maintained daily field order log utilizing Lotus 1-2-3. Assisted with payroll data input and craft layoffs.

TRIDENT BANK, Anaheim, CA   2/88-6/90
Proof Operator
Micro-encoded deposited checks using NCR proof machine.

THE SOUP MASTER, International Headquarters, Burbank, CA   6/86-10/87
Assistant Bookkeeper
Coordinated Accounts Receivable/Payable. Compiled nationwide franchise financial/payment reports. Dispatched Area Director Royalty Reports; recorded payments. Developed General Ledger summaries. Promoted to International Accounts from Regional Accounts.

LOS ANGELES PUBLIC SCHOOL SYSTEM, Los Angeles, CA   6/84-6/86
Teacher
Taught Elementary, High School, and Adult students in Mathematics and General Studies.

■ Qualifications pertaining to candidate's field of interest are positioned in top half of resume.

■ Valuable computer skills are highlighted in a separate section.

CAREER CHANGER (Daycare)

Chris Smith
178 Green Street
Sioux Falls, SD 57105
(605) 555-5555

OBJECTIVE
A position as a daycare worker utilizing experience caring for people of all ages.

SUMMARY OF QUALIFICATIONS
- Strong nurturing capabilities, as well as ability to comfort those in times of crisis.
- Excellent communication skills.
- Extremely patient and calm at all times, including high pressure situations.
- Able to diagnose needs of others.

EXPERIENCE

CHARGE NURSE/STAFF NURSE - ONCOLOGY, DIALYSIS UNIT
Sioux Falls Hospital, Sioux Falls, SD   **January 1989-Present**
- Provide clinical services to 40 patients on the Oncology/Dialysis Unit.
- Delegate work assignments and supervise performance of licensed staff, evaluate nursing activities to ensure patient care, staff relations, and efficiency of service.
- Visit patients to verify that nursing care is carried out as directed and treatment administered in accordance with physicians.
- Participate in orientation and instruction of personnel and interact with all hospital departments in order to provide patient care.
- Responsible for direct ordering of drugs, solutions and equipment; maintain records on narcotics.
- Administer prescribed medications and treatments, prepare equipment and assist physicians during treatments and examinations.
- Provide patient education, assess and provide patients' needs, and serve as a resource person for patients and families.
- Hands-on experience with the administration of chemotherapy, narcotic pain control, and other protocols.

REGISTERED NURSE - MEDICAL/SURGICAL FLOOR
Brookings Medical Center, Brookings, SD   **June 1980 - December 1988**
- Assumed responsibility as Staff Nurse as well as Charge Nurse; supervised a professional nursing staff on a 35-bed floor.
- Covered all areas of surgical/medical clinical treatment and care with other responsibilities similar to above.
- Trained new nurses.

EDUCATION
South Dakota State University   **May 1980**
Brookings, South Dakota
Nursing Certificate/Registered Nurse

■ Stating that "references are available upon request" is not essential; most employers will assume that references are available.

■ Clean layout makes resume easy to read.

CAREER CHANGER (Education)

CHRIS SMITH
178 Green Street
Aberdeen, SD 57401
(605) 555-5555

OBJECTIVE:

To contribute acquired teaching skills at the Secondary Level.

EDUCATION:

SIOUX FALLS COLLEGE, Sioux Falls, SD
Master of Science in Education (January, 1994)
Bachelor of Science in Biology (May, 1987)

CERTIFICATION:

South Dakota, 9-12 Secondary

RELATED EXPERIENCE:

8/94 - DOWNEY HIGH SCHOOL, Aberdeen, SD
Present **Student Teacher**
Assist in the teaching of ninth grade Earth Science. Plan curricula for laboratory experiments and lead post-lab discussions. Administer weekly quizzes. Confer with parents and teaching staff.

9/92-2/94 HAVEN HILLS HIGH SCHOOL, Sioux Falls, SD
Student Teacher
Assist in the preparation of instructional materials for tenth grade Social Studies class. Help teach and evaluate students. Advise students regarding academic and vocational interests.

OTHER EXPERIENCE:

7/89 - NORTHERN LIGHTS PUBLISHING COMPANY, Sioux Falls, SD
Present Freelance Editor

5/87-7/89 Administrative Assistant

MEMBERSHIPS:

Big Sister Program
Volunteer Tutors of Sioux Falls

■ Boldfacing calls attention to relevant experience and qualifications.

■ Volunteer work and community service lend strength to this resume.

CAREER CHANGER (Fashion Design)

Chris Smith
178 Green Street
Decatur, GA 30032
(404) 555-5555

OBJECTIVE
To apply my seven years of experience with women's apparel, as well as my educational background, to a career in fashion design.

SUMMARY
- Area of expertise is creativity - from conception and design to marketing and sales.
- Self-starter with involved style of productivity and workmanship.
- Excellent communicator; adept at sizing up situations and developing new ideas or alternative courses of action in order to design, sell, or increase production.

QUALIFICATIONS
Design:
Conceptualized, coordinated, and designed in-store and window displays, including massive front window of major fashion center. Operated within a streamlined material budget appropriated by the manager, yet consistently generated award-winning window themes for $2.1 million department store.

Buying:
Attended fashion shows in New York, Milan, and Paris; assisted in the buying process. Perused fashion magazines on off-time; provided head buyer with information about upcoming styles.

EMPLOYMENT
DISPLAY COORDINATOR/ASSOCIATE BUYER, The Tudor Castle, Athens, GA 1989-1994

WINDOW DRESSER, Tanglewood's, Decatur, GA, 1987-1990

EDUCATION
Deverling School of Fashion Design, Decatur, GA
A.A. Fashion Design, 1994

REFERENCES Available upon request.

■ Functional format is ideal choice for career changers.

■ Candidate includes only information pertaining to his/her field of interest.

CAREER CHANGER (International Business)

CHRIS SMITH
178 Green Street
New Brunswick, NJ
(201) 555-5555

OBJECTIVE:
Position in INTERNATIONAL CORPORATE RELATIONS which utilizes and challenges my business experience and knowledge of French Customs, Business Practices, and Language.

SUMMARY OF QUALIFICATIONS:

Communication:
Fluent in French, written and verbal. Knowledge of French culture and customs. Extensive Travel in France, Italy, and Germany.

Marketing:
Oversaw marketing, publications, and advertising for Travel Abroad Programs. Wrote and designed camera-ready ads, brochures, and flyers using desktop publishing system. Wrote, edited, and supervised production of departmental newsletter. Developed travel itineraries and budgets. Compiled and edited faculty brochure.

Administration:
Prepared departmental revenue and budget. Monitored registration progress. Processed faculty appointments and tenure reviews. Wrote minutes for administrative meetings. Office support for faculty members. Responsible for letters of appointment. Prepared exams and course/instructor evaluations. Assisted with registration and student inquiries.

Fundraising:
Worked on development proposals and College fundraising campaign. Organized special events.

EXPERIENCE:
RUTGERS UNIVERSITY, New Brunswick, NJ
Assistant to the Director, Foreign Language Department, June 1993-Present
Executive Secretary to the Dean, July 1992-May 1993
Faculty Secretary, September 1991-June 1992

EDUCATION:
RUTGERS UNIVERSITY, New Brunswick, NJ
BA In French Language and Culture Studies, 1991
Study Abroad Program, Paris, September 1989-August 1990

REFERENCES:
Furnished upon request.

■ Resume is geared towards candidate's field of interest.

■ Functional skills are highlighted while unrelated work experience is de-emphasized.

CAREER CHANGER (Nursing)

Chris Smith
178 Green Street
Hartford, CT 06120
(203) 555-5555

OBJECTIVE
A nursing position in a metropolitan hospital.

SUPPORTIVE QUALIFICATIONS
- Over five years experience in the Medical/Health Care arenas.
- Broad-based knowledge of all aspects of Nursing.
- Calm under pressure; cooperative, flexible team player.
- Bilingual: fluent in English and Portuguese

EDUCATION

St. Joseph's Nursing School, Hartford, CT
B.S., Nursing   May 1994

STUDENT TRAINING AND EXPERIENCE

Lafayette Hospital, Hamden, CT
Nursing Aide   1994
Responsible for tasks on the Cardiac and Psychiatric Units.
Assisted in patient care; counseled patients and families on a
variety of health and diet issues.

Primrose Hospital, Fairfield, CT
Cardiac Nursing Aide   1993
Led group sessions, focusing on risk factors including smoking,
cholesterol, exercise, blood pressure, and diet.

Meadowcroft Hospital, Greenwich, CT
Maternity-Rotation Assistant   1992
Administered to patients' needs for physical and émotional
support. Taught caretaking classes for new parents.

Ferncliff Hospital, Danbury, CT
Nursing Intern, Intensive Care Unit   1990-91
Worked closely with staff at major trauma certified facility.
Continuous measurement of intracranial pressure, blood pressure,
and cardiac indexes.

Berrylane Nutrition Center, Bridgeport, CT
Clinical Practice Assistant   1989-90
Assist in preparation of nutritional care plans.

PREVIOUS WORK HISTORY

Naugatuck Bottle Co., Hartford, CT
Golem Manufacturing, Hartford, CT

■ Extensive training and educational background supplement resume's impact.

■ Foreign language skills further strengthen candidate's qualifications.

CAREER CHANGER (Public Relations)

CHRIS SMITH
178 Green Street
Juneau, AK 99801
(907) 555-5555

PROFESSIONAL OBJECTIVE
A position in public relations in which to apply interpersonal, organizational, and conceptual skills

SUMMARY
- Over three years experience in public relations
- Proven ability to plan and supervise major special events
- Knowledge of all aspects of media relations
- Skilled educator and pubic speaker

RELATED EXPERIENCE
1994 to present ALASKANS FOR A CLEANER WORLD, Juneau, AK
Public Relations Coordinator
- Contribute time and creative services to non-profit organization
- Plan and supervise special events
- Organized first annual "A Breath of Life" Walk-a-thon, raising over $15,000
- Handle all aspects of media relations
- Educate public about enviromental issues
- Speak at local schools to encourage environmental awareness

1993 to present MT. JUNEAU MEDICAL CENTER, Juneau, AK
Coordinator, Department of Neurosurgery
- Promote department; oversee public relations
- Coordinate all communications for medical and non-medical activities within department
- Serve as liaison between administrations of two hospitals, physicians, and nurses
- Educate in-house staff, patients, and families on techniques, equipment, and related subjects

UNRELATED EXPERIENCE
UNIVERSITY HOSPITAL, Anchorage, AK
Staff Nurse, Surgical Intensive Care Unit, 1991 to 1993
Senior Staff Nurse, Neurological/Neurosurgical Floor, 1989 to 1991

PRESENTATIONS & LECTURES
Have given over 25 presentations and lectures to various schools, hospitals, in-house staff, and professional associations

COMPUTER SKILLS
IBM: WordPerfect, Lotus 1-2-3, Paintbrush
Macintosh: MacWrite, Excel

EDUCATION
UNIVERSITY OF ALASKA, Anchorage, Alaska
Bachelor of Science degree in Nursing, 1989

- Related work experience is accentuated while unrelated experience is de-emphasized.

- Summary grabs the reader's attention with powerful skills and qualifications.

CAREER CHANGER (Publishing)

Chris Smith
178 Green Street
Savannah, GA 31401
(912) 555-5555

OBJECTIVE:
To obtain an entry-level position in the publishing industry.

QUALIFICATIONS:

Editorial:
- Working knowledge of all aspects of the English language.
- Demonstrated copyediting and proofreading skills.
- Author of self-published book titled <u>Birding in the South</u>.
- First-hand knowledge of the book publishing industry.

Prepress:
- Supervise all aspects of book production.
- Assist with layout and formatting process.
- Prepare and organize art work for reproduction.
- Review and approve proofs.

Operations:
- Manage inventory control.
- Filled orders.
- Coordinate shipping and billing.

Promotion:
- Coordinate preparation and distribution of flier to bookstores.
- Design and place advertisement in <u>Publisher's Weekly</u>.
- Promote book at local book signing.

Computers:
- Thorough knowledge of Microsoft Word, Corel Ventura, Lotus 1-2-3, Excel, and Windows.

WORK EXPERIENCE:
1984-Present SAVANNAH SCHOOL DISTRICT, Savannah, GA
<u>Reading Specialist</u> (1991-Present), Implement the Publishing Center for Students.
<u>Coordinator/Teacher of the Gifted</u> (1988-1990), Advisor for school newspaper.
<u>Teacher, Fourth Grade</u> (1984-1987), Coordinated procedures for Writing Center.

EDUCATION:
College of Charleston, Charleston, SC
Bachelor of Arts in Elementary Education, May 1984.

■ Job objective is brief and to the point.

■ Resume emphasizes qualifications pertaining to candidate's job objective.

CAREER CHANGER (Travel)

Chris Smith
178 Green Street
Puyallup, WA 98374
(206) 555-5555

OBJECTIVE
A career in the travel industry that draws upon my administrative and communication skills.

SUMMARY OF QUALIFICATIONS
- Over ten years administrative experience.
- Experience booking flight and hotel accommodations for corporate officers and their families.
- Excellent language/communication skills; speak fluent Italian, French, and Spanish.
- Extensive experience in phone inquiries; able to remain calm and diplomatic under stressful conditions.
- Organized and efficient; able to plan ahead with an eye for potential problems; skilled at implementing solutions to ensure maximum effectiveness of plans.

RELATED EXPERIENCE
NOONAN GRAPHICS, Vancouver, WA   1989-94
Public Relations Assistant
Coordinated the creative and production phases of monthly informative catalog. Answered customer mail; filled out of state orders; created a computer filing system on various customer inquiries. Acted as a liaison between international clients and top management; utilized extensive language skills.

BUCHELL AND GORMAN, INC., Puyallup, WA   1985-89
Administrative Assistant
Provided administrative support and general office assistance. Composed monthly marketing forecast reports; communicated via fax with foreign clients about shareholder status and marketing procedure. Maintained liaisons between client and production staff. Prepared contract bids.

OTHER EXPERIENCE
Insurance Agent, Daycare Worker, Retail Sales Associate, and Front Desk Clerk.

EDUCATION
University of Washington, Seattle, WA
A.S. Business Administration 1982

East Seattle High School, Seattle, WA
High School Diploma, 1979

REFERENCES
Available upon request.

■ Unrelated work experience and limited education are de-emphasized.

■ Format is organized and visually appealing.

CURRICULUM VITAE (College Administrator)

CHRIS SMITH, Ph.D.

178 Green Street
Pittsburgh, PA 15213
(412) 555-5555

OBJECTIVE:
To secure a challenging college administration position which will assist the young adult in maximizing his/her potential.

SUMMARY OF QUALIFICATIONS:
- Designing, implementing and evaluating programs to facilitate the adjustment, achievement, retention and career planning of female college students in their first and ensuing years of study.
- Counseling the college woman with varied personal and academic problems.
- Proposal writing, budget planning and analysis.
- Managing personnel, staff development and evaluation.
- Creating strategies and managing admissions and recruitment programs.
- Teaching experience in university and public school environments.
- Planning, organizing and implementing activities for cultural and personal enrichment.
- Active participation in university-wide and community activities.

EMPLOYMENT EXPERIENCE:
1979 - **BROWN UNIVERSITY**, Providence, RI
Present **Director of Women's Studies** (1991-Present)
Plan, administrate and evaluate a comprehensive freshman academic support program. Coordinate activities including academic advising, academic placement and academic, personal and career counseling; administrate placement tests, new student orientation, parent/student workshops cultural activities, academic tracking and early warning system for "at risk" freshman, provide group counseling services and student workshops.
- Initiated a Newsletter and a Recognition dinner for women's achievements in academics, activities and sports.
- Established parent workshops on college adjustment and financing education and women's workshops on sexual harassment, date rape, relationships and eating disorders.
- Cultural awareness activities instituted included a guest lecture series, field trips to the Boston Art Museum and the Ryder Early American Collection, and a study tour to retrace the stops in the Flight of Paul Revere.
- Established phone interviews with parents with permission of the student to discuss various problems, such as anorexia nervosa, academic probation, and substance abuse.

(continued)

- A curriculum vitae, often called a CV for short, is usually more extensive than a typical resume.

- Curricula vitae are standard for medical, legal, and academic professions.

EXPERIENCE: (continued)

Admissions Director (1988-1991)

Managed the admissions and recruitment program, creating and designing strategies to enhance the total program, concept and mission.

- Developed a marketing plan for recruitment; wrote recruitment brochures for the Office of Admissions and academic departments of the university.
- Supervised professional and clerical staff; provided and encouraged in-service training and professional growth.
- Compiled data for statistical reporting to various state and federal agencies.
- Served as representative to the Academic Council.
- Acted as liaison between the Office of Admissions, faculty, the administration and the alumni.
- Maintained a positive working relationship between high school and community college counselors and the Office of Admissions.

Assistant to the Admissions Director (1979-1988)

- Developed high school recruitment programs.
- Visited high school and local two year college for the purpose of recruitment.
- Evaluated transcripts of transfer students for transferable credits.
- Served as foreign student advisor.
- Substituted for Director in her absence.

TEACHING EXPERIENCE:

1987 -
Present **BROWN UNIVERSITY**, Providence, RI

- Teach Women's Orientation, a two-hour required course for all students. Units include Eating Disorders, Value Clarification, Relationships, Substance Abuse, Domestic Violence.
- Also taught Emotion Exploration Course, 1991 and 1992.

EDUCATION:

BROWN UNIVERSITY, Providence, RI
Ph.D. in Sociology, 1974

CARNEGIE MELLON UNIVERSITY, Pittsburgh, PA
Master of Education - Counseling Major, 1972

MIDDLEBURY COLLEGE, Middlebury, VT
Bachelor of Arts in Elementary Education - Art Minor, 1968

CURRICULUM VITAE (Doctor)

Chris Smith

Curriculum Vitae

178 Green Street
New York, NY
(212) 555-5555

Date of Birth: 8/16/65
Place of Birth: Manhattan, NY
Marital Status: Single

EDUCATION:

1993-1994 NEW YORK UNIVERSITY HOSPITAL, New York, NY
Residency in Gynecology
1992-1993 BROOKLYN HEALTH CLINIC, Brooklyn, NY
Internship in Internal Medicine
1988-1992 JOHNS HOPKINS UNIVERSITY, Baltimore, MD
M.D.
1984-1988 LOYOLA UNIVERSITY, New Orleans, LA
B.A., History

CERTIFICATION:

National Board of Medical Examiners - Part I, May 1990; Score 425
National Board of Medical Examiners - Part II, October 1992; Score 400
National Board of Medical Examiners - Part III, July 1993; Score 430

RESEARCH EXPERIENCE:

Investigated the study of a particular protein which is known to dephosphorylate cell fat from 7/9/87 to 10/04/87 in the laboratory of Dr. G. Bartlett, Chairman, Department of Physiology at Johns Hopkins Health Science Center at Baltimore. Experiments were concerned with structural analysis of fats and fat-binding protein isolated from animal blood cells. The project provided experience in techniques for isolation of actin and for characterization of proteins by sodium acetyl iodine-phenalamine powder electrostasis.

EXTRACURRICULAR ACTIVITIES:

1986-1988 Senior Baseball Team, New Orleans, LA
1987-1988 Loyola Baseball Team
1984-1988 Pi Kappa Alpha Fraternity
1988-1992 John Hopkins University Hockey Team
1990-1992 John Hopkins University Rugby Team

PROFESSIONAL AFFILIATIONS:

1988-1992 Member, American Medical Association
1991-1992 Member, Medical Society of the State of New York
1993-1994 Member, Massachusetts Society of Gynecologists/Obstetricians
1993-1994 Member, American Society of Gynecologists/Obstetricians

- Candidate lists education, certification, activities, and affiliations without further description.

- Valuable research experience is provided in detail.

DISPLACED HOMEMAKER (Administration)

CHRIS SMITH
178 Green Street
Grenvil, NE 68941
(402) 555-5555

Objective:
An entry-level administrative position.

Summary of Qualifications:

ADMINISTRATION:
Accurate typing at 60 words per minute. Thoroughly experienced in all aspects of office administration, including record keeping, filing, and scheduling/planning.

ACCOUNTING:
Coordinate finances for a middle income family of five on a personal computer. Process accounts payable in a timely manner without compromising facets of the expenditure budget. Monitor checking account closely.

COMPUTERS:
Lotus 1-2-3, Microsoft Word, WordPerfect, IBM Compatible.

ORGANIZATION:
Organize a rotating carpool with five other mothers. Make several copies and distribute at least one month in advance.

Organize a monthly women's writing group concerned with reclaiming the feminine voice. Develop writing exercises that address the hidden spiritual elements in modern women's lives. Motivate members to channel stress, uncertainty, and fear into the gift of creativity. Act as mentor and friend.

LEADERSHIP:
President of Grenvil Historical Society, an organization of fifteen members concerned with educating public about Grenvil town history and preserving historic landmarks. Develop calendar of events; invite guest speakers, organize fundraising events. Provide meeting place, as well as materials and refreshments.

Coach a girls' soccer team, ages 7-11, in the Grenvil Youth Outreach Program (GYOR) from September to November. Provide players with the instruction, motivation, support, and outlook that will enable them to come away from each game with satisfaction and pride, no matter what the score.

Notable Accomplishments:
Organized fundraiser to renovate the Henry Wallace House; raised over $5,000.
Several short stories published in regional literary magazines, including *The Loft*.

Education:
Grenvil Community College, Grenvil, NE
Courses in Creative Writing, Word Processing, and Accounting.

■ Functional format is ideal for homemakers entering the job market for the first time.

■ Resume emphasizes skills that can be transferred to the workplace.

DISPLACED HOMEMAKER (Caretaking)

CHRIS SMITH
178 Green Street
Baton Rouge, LA 70807
(504) 555-5555

Objective:
To provide care in an adult home or child daycare environment.

Skills:
Care-Providing

- Provided care for a paraplegic in a private home setting for five years.
- Maintained a daily log of all medication administered.
- Coordinated a biweekly story hour at two local nursing homes.
- Delivered groceries to homebound seniors twice a week for two years.
- Administered medication.
- Acted as an assistant to seniors in wheelchairs through private and public transportation.

Communication

- Organized the care of an elderly relative within a nursing home for three years.
- Bargained with contractors about the adaptation of private homes for special needs adults.
- Provided counseling to the elderly, clarifying their wants and needs.
- Improved communication with support services for an elderly couple in order to improve their quality of life.
- Organized a pet visiting hour by acting as a liaison between two nursing homes and the local animal shelter.

Planning

- Organized day trips to local museums, parks, and shopping centers.
- Developed calendar of monthly in house events for two nursing homes.
- Planned biweekly shopping lists for several elderly individuals according to their physicians' specifications.
- Organized successful "Friend in Deed" program in which mobile seniors visited the homes of their house-bound peers.

Education:
Lexington High School, Lexington, KY

■ Resume is tailored specifically to candidate's job objective.

■ Candidate's many achievements are emphasized.

DISPLACED HOMEMAKER (Food Service)

CHRIS SMITH

178 Green Street
Cheyenne, WY 82009
(307) 555-5555

Objective:
A position in Food Service in the public school system.

Related Experience:

Jameson Homeless Shelter   Cheyenne, WY
Weekday server. Act as a liaison between homeless and a national food distributor, securing special requests and unanimously favored items.

St. Bernadette's Parish   Cheyenne, WY
Coordinate annual bake sale; provide approximately ten percent of the bakery items sold.

Brady Family   Cheyenne, WY
Act as live-in nanny for eight-year old twin boys; duties include the preparation of their meals and snacks on a regular basis.

Lion's Club Carnival   Cheyenne, WY
Work the concession booths at annual carnival each June; prepare and serve such items as fried dough, sweet sausage, pizza, and caramel apples; maintain a receipt record of profits for event administrators.
Conduct informal cooking classes out of the Payne Community Center kitchen on a weekly basis.

Awards:
Award-winning country style cook.
Placed first in national fruit-based pie competition.
Won cash prize for best pot roast recipe, *Reader's Digest*.

Education:
Cheyenne Community College, Cheyenne, WY
Associates Degree, Home Economics

Interests:
Gourmet cook, Little League softball coach, avid gardener

References:
Available upon request

■ Awards heading draws attention to candidate's significant accomplishments.

■ Personal interests can provide a great topic for conversation during a job interview.

DISPLACED HOMEMAKER (Management)

CHRIS SMITH
178 Green Street
Stoneham, MA 02180
(617) 555-5555

Objective:
To secure a position as a management trainee

Summary of Skills:
Administration
- Led meetings of fifteen participants
- Created tentative plans for the quarterly meetings
- Supervised team of seven volunteer firefighters
- Scheduled musicians for the Bang's community center during the summer music festival
- Coordinated weekly films for "Culture on the Common" program during one summer
- Kept receipt records for yearly Exotic Foods Fest with revenue in excess of $50,000

Communication
- Developed grant requests for team of volunteer firefighters
- Led Christian youth group weekend retreats each month
- Tutored teenagers with math anxiety
- Spoke before groups of concerned teachers, parents, and citizens regarding adolescent violence
- Conducted telephone surveys assessing the overall happiness of teenagers with the local school system

Planning
- Coordinated youth group travel plans
- Planned calendar of events for recently opened teen center
- Developed new feedback oriented lesson plans for high school classrooms

Education:
Massasoit Junior College, Canton, MA
A.S. Management, 1978
Honor society

Computer Skills:
Lotus 1-2-3, Microsoft Word

Interests:
Hiking, camping, and antique collecting

References:
Available upon request

■ Functional format focuses attention on candidate's major skills and accomplishments.

■ Strong action verbs bring resume to life.

FORMER SMALL BUSINESS OWNER (Desktop Publishing)

Chris Smith
178 Green Street
Clarksville, TN 37044
(615) 555-5555

OBJECTIVE
A challenging position in the field of sales and electronic publishing.

SUMMARY OF QUALIFICATIONS
- More than fifteen years of Art Director/Buyer and graphics/design production experience in the publishing field; extensive knowledge of type and mechanical preparation, budgeting and scheduling.
- Excellent interpersonal, communication, and managerial skills; adept at coordinating and motivating creative artists to peak efficiency.
- Aware of cost management and quality control importance on all levels.
- Self-motivated; able to set effective priorities and meet impossible deadlines.
- Productive in fast-paced, high-pressure atmosphere.

PROFESSIONAL EXPERIENCE
1978-1994   NO CONTEST GRAPHICS, Nashville, TN
Owner/President, Art Director/Buyer
Coordinate operations, 12-member production staff, freelance desktop publishers and illustrators. Maintain overview of works-in-progress to produce at optimum efficiency. Provide/advice to personnel in designing materials to appropriately meet client needs; conceptualize product; delegate staff to make decisions. Commission freelance agents by utilizing nationwide illustrator four-color manuscripts using watercolor illustrations, photography, or graphics. Act as liaison between executive personnel and staff. Budget each project; motivate artistic staff and typesetters to meet projected deadlines and remain within cost-efficient parameters. Projects include: greeting cards, care package kits, magazine fragrance inserts, cereal boxes, toy packages, coloring books (cover and contents), holographic bumper stickers, and retail store signs and logos.

1976-1978   NEW JERSEY LITHOGRAPH, Newark, NJ
Head of Typesetting & Design Department
Supervised staff in design and execution of print materials for commercial printer.

EDUCATION
CENTENARY COLLEGE, Hackettstown, NJ
A.S. in Technical Illustration, 1977

ART INSTITUTE OF NEWARK, Newark, NJ
Certified in Graphic Design, 1975

■ Resume format is neat and professional.

■ Resume emphasizes contributions, achievements, and problems candidate has solved throughout his/her career.

FORMER SMALL BUSINESS OWNER (Environmental Services)

CHRIS SMITH
178 Green Street
La Jolla, CA 92093
(619) 555-5555

OBJECTIVE
A position utilizing my experience in recycling and developing environmentally-conscious programs.

SUMMARY OF QUALIFICATIONS
- Acquired the first recycling permit in the City of San Diego for ferrous and non-ferrous metal, aluminum, high-grade paper and plastic.
- Developed profitable pilot program for community and industrial recycling.
- Recovered non-ferrous and precious metals from waste solutions, photo and electrical scrap.
- Conducted research and formulated chemical process to liquefy Styrofoam into reusable plastic.

EXPERIENCE
1988 to   CALIFORNIA RECYCLE RENEGADES, INC., San Diego, CA
1994   **Owner/President**
Established First Aluminum Recycling in San Diego. Developed programs for expansion from ferrous and non-ferrous metals to high grade paper, aluminum, and plastic. Conducted pilot program; formulated a network in Sable Park and Briody Hills for voluntary recycling. Provided containers biweekly for aluminum, glass, and newspaper. Picked up and processed material, sending check for proceeds to community associations.

EDUCATION
University of California, Riverside—Bookkeeping
M.A. Business Administration 1986

University of California, Berkley
B.A. Environmental Science 1984

AFFILIATIONS
Member of Pacific Community Association.

REFERENCES
Available upon request.

■ Job-related affiliations demonstrate candidate's active participation in field.

■ Summary of qualifications highlights candidate's achievements.

FREELANCER (Broadcasting)

CHRIS SMITH
178 Green Street
Lawrence, KS 66049
(913) 555-5555

FREELANCE PRODUCTION

Writer/Producer/Director/Editor: Training videotape for Child Services of Squaw Valley, Incorporated; tape is designed to instruct current and prospective members of the Council on Children in the most effective and efficient conductance of Board functions (1994).

Writer: series of short videotapes on recreational drinking use for Social Science Research and Evaluation, Incorporated. Program depicts strategies teens may use to avoid problems associated with drinking; to be shown in high schools throughout Kansas. Worked as Camera Operator during production (1994).

Internship: Special Projects Department of WNP-TV; assisted in preliminary research/writing and in the scheduling and logistical planning of location shooting for documentary, "Milk Carton Kids; An American Crisis," aired January, 1994; acted as Production Assistant. Screened potential interview candidates. Production Assistant for "Madness to my Method," a 8-part documentary series on obsessive compulsive disorders (1993).

Producer/Writer/Editor: Two PSA's for the Kansas Commission for the Deaf, to be aired throughout the state of Kansas (1993).

Camera Operator/Editor: "Missing Buttonholes", 4th program to be used by Kansas State University's Broadcast Journalism Department (1993).

Producer/Writer/Assistant Editor: Volunteer Recruitment PSA for Specialized Ambulatory Care Clinic, Wichita, KS (1991).

EDUCATIONAL BACKGROUND

KANSAS STATE UNIVERSITY, Manhattan, KS
Master of Science Degree in Broadcasting.
- Concentration, Television Production and Writing.
- Assistant Director: "Dinnertime Mind Dance" for Cablevision of Lawrence (1993).
- Grade point average: 3.4/4.0
- Awarded $2,000 scholarship from School of Public Communication (1992).

REFERENCES

Excellent references available upon request.

- Functional resume format is perfect for candidate's needs.

- Strong educational credentials strengthen resume.

FREELANCER (Publishing)

Chris Smith
178 Green Street
Richmond, VA 23294
(804) 555-5555

SUMMARY
Freelance writer and editor specializing in children's textbooks.

EXPERIENCE

Freelance Writer   1991-Present
Ben Curtis and Company: Gifted Child Program, grades 7-12
Tallvia Kincaide, Inc.: Writing Handbooks, grades 7-9
Jean K. Simmons Company: Ancient Civilizations Textbook, grade 12
Jean K. Simmons Press: Literature Program, grades 9-12
Create original manuscripts for student textbooks, annotated teacher's editions, and numerous ancillaries. Materials include the following: teaching apparatus; questions for responding, analyzing, and interpreting; thinking, writing, language, and vocabulary exercises and worksheets; multi-page writing workshops; end-of-unit features for writing and language skills; and collaborative learning activities. Design prototypes for textbook and ancillary features. Conduct multicultural literature searches.

Senior Editor, Secondary English, Jean K. Simmons Press   1986-1991
Project supervisor for Teacher's Editions of a composition and grammar program, levels 6-9. Edited author manuscript for "Writing is Fun," level 7 & 8. Wrote manuscript for "Writing is Fun," levels 9, 10, 11, and 12, including instruction, model paragraphs, and assignments. Developed content and approach for units on critical thinking and word processor use.

Editor, Secondary English, Educational Press   1984-1986
Project supervisor for Teacher's Editions and Teacher's Resource Masters of vocabulary program, levels 9-12. Edited author manuscript for four levels of pupil books for vocabulary program. Wrote exercises, reading comprehension passages, and activities to support instruction. Conducted writing workshops for teachers as follow-up to sales.

Associate Editor, Secondary English, Educational Press   1982-1984
Developed explanatory material and features for teacher's editions for grammar and composition program, levels 9-12. Contributed to the development of vocabulary program, including writing, editing, and selecting appropriate art.

EDUCATION

Clark University, Worcester, MA. Master of Arts, Education   1982
Boston College, Chestnut Hill, MA. Bachelor of Arts, English   1980

REFERENCES
Available upon request.

■ Resume lists candidate's clients in italics with a general overview of duties below.

■ Resume emphasizes candidate's strong work history.

FREQUENT JOB CHANGER (Copywriter)

Chris Smith
178 Green Street
Fort Worth, TX 76114
(817) 555-5555

SPECIAL SKILLS
Experienced and competent with MacIntosh, IBM and Lotus systems. Solid communication skills, in person and by phone. Possess strong work ethic and enthusiasm. Strong organizational skills.

EMPLOYMENT

Copywriter/Service Director
WDDE Radio Station, Fortworth, TX   1993-present
- Compose copy for advertisements and promotions.
- Edit client copy, client newsletter and executive correspondence.
- Communicate with clients and listeners by phone.
- Produce commercials.
- Organize and oversee copy and taped spots.
- Delegate on-air personalities for recording.
- Coordinate technical aspects of on-air programming.

Claims Coder
Texas Mutual Inc., Dallas, TX   1992-1993
- Process claims reports and encode data to computer system.
- Review and revise reinsurance files.
- Conduct inventory.
- Balance daily accounts for each computer system.

Mathematics Tutor
University of Dallas, Irvine, TX   1991-1992
- Tutor individual college students.

OTHER EMPLOYMENT
Receptionist, Research Assistant, Lifeguard.

EDUCATION
Graduated Dave Erickson "Public Speaking" course, 1993
University of Dallas, Irvine, TX, 1992, Graduated Summa Cum Laude
Bachelor of Science Degree in Education, Minor in English
- Member of Kappa Krappa Gamma Honor Society
- Dean's List four years

SPECIAL INTERESTS
Volunteer at MiCasa, A Dallas Battered Women's Shelter
Surfing, Window Shopping, and Canoeing

REFERENCES AVAILABLE UPON REQUEST

- Dynamic action verbs give resume impact.

- Chrono-functional resume format is a good choice for frequent job changers, particularly if there is no clear career path.

GAPS IN EMPLOYMENT HISTORY (Editor)

CHRIS SMITH
178 Green Street
Sumter, SC 29150
(803) 555-5555

Objective:
An editing position within a major publishing house.

Summary of Qualifications:
- More than seven years of writing/editing experience.
- Adept at managing multiple responsibilities simultaneously.
- Experienced at delegating authority and motivating others to ensure efficiency and productivity.
- Computer knowledge includes Lotus 1-2-3, Microsoft Word, WordPerfect, Pagemaker, and DOS.

Work Experience:

Editor-in-Chief, Renegade Magazine
Sumter, SC
Selected submissions, edited and wrote headlines for submissions and columns, laid out page, recruited columnists, trained associates from 1990-1993. Frequent copy editing and research.

Associate Editor, Modern Daze Magazine
New York, NY
Wrote articles for both the magazine and its associated newsletter, *Disembodied Voices*. Edited features and department articles from 1984-1988. Read and critiqued assigned articles from contributing editors.

Copy Editor, Heathcliff's Garden Magazine
Boston, MA
Edited news stories, wrote headlines, assisted with layout of page, occasionally solicited advertising and helped with distribution from 1980-1982.

Other Experience:
Writer, professional musician, world traveler.
(Details available upon request.)

Military:
Army Corporal (honorable discharge).

Education:
University of Richmond, Richmond, VA
Bachelor of Arts, English, 1978
Le Student Roma, Rome, Italy
Intensive study of Italian language and culture, 1991

- Gaps in employment history are obscured by placing dates of employ in job descriptions.

- Functional format is another good option for candidates with gaps in employment history.

IMMIGRANT (Senior Accountant)

CHRIS SMITH
178 Green Street
Kankakee, IL 60901
(815) 555-5555

EXPERIENCE

K.T. BIRCHWOOD AND SONS, Chicago, IL
Senior Accountant, December 1994-Present
Responsible for G.L. processing reporting, initially for six companies, also bank reconciliation, etc. Involved in preparation for Chapter 11 filing (1994), subsequent reporting requirements, also handling account receivables and internal audits.

ESSEX COMPUTER, LTD., Glasgow, Scotland
Assistant Financial Accountant, 1988-1994.
Maintained the general ledger system; oversaw the preparation of the month end and year end financial reports, audit reports, budgets, and variance analysis of the monthly financial package for submission to U.S. Headquarters. Maintained capital assets, depreciations schedules and reconciliation of Bank Accounts. Maintained the operation of the accounts payable system with vendors, also involved in the set-up and modification of a new computer system. Experience using micros, primarily Multi-plan and Lotus. Member of steering committee selected a new general ledger package, which is currently used at this facility.

S.G.R., LTD., Glasgow, Scotland
Temporary Accountant, 1987-1988
Maintained and reconciled all bank and investment accounts. Performed inventory control. Involved in inter-company accounting with foreign subsidiaries.

UPSCALE ENTERPRISES, Glasgow, Scotland
Accounts Assistant, 1984-1987
Performed all bookkeeping functions of company; creditors (including foreign currency), contract payments, debtors, payroll, management accounts, profit and loss by flight reports, budget and costing.

EDUCATION

COLLEGE OF COMMERCE, Glasgow, Scotland
Certificate in Business Studies, 1984-1988
Major: Accounting

NORTHERN ENTERPRISE OF CERTIFIED ACCOUNTANTS, Glasgow, Scotland
Exempt—Level I, have passed subjects in Level II.

PERSONAL

Work permit

■ Work permit information is optional on a resume. If desired, it could alternatively be expressed in a cover letter.

■ Specific contributions display candidate's achievements and problem-solving abilities.

LAID OFF (Recruiter)

CHRIS SMITH

178 Green Street
Boone, NC 28607
(704) 555-5555

SUMMARY
Over five years of experience recruiting high technology, support staff and marketing personnel. Expertise in recruiting and marketing engineers, programmers and other professionals in the Management Information Systems, Software Development environments and related support positions for a wide range of client firms in the electronics and software industries.

EXPERIENCE
1991-1994   **Professional Recruiter** - Elworth Associates, Boone, NC
Hired and placed hourly skilled, unskilled, technical and non-technical personnel. Initiated recruiting program in search for critically needed electronic technicians. Established sources for non-professional people and participated in extensive field trips to technical, business and secretarial schools.

Promoted to Professional Employment Recruiter and established and maintained agency contacts with reference to professional personnel, administrative and technical. Traveled 15-20% of the time. Extensive field recruiting trips to universities, career centers, conferences; and major United States cities. Recruited degreed engineers for all types, physicists, administrators, controllers, accountants, EDP, sales and marketing personnel.

1990-1991   **Independent Consultant/Contract Recruiter**
Clients: Amy Corporation, Kerrigan Inc., MPB
Recruited top MBAs for major corporations.

1989-1990   **Technical Recruiter** - The Scorpio Group, Durham, NC
Recruited engineers, programmer/analysts and technicians for satellite and telecommunications, signal processing, C3, electronic warfare, artificial intelligence and data base development.

EDUCATION
Bachelor of Arts, Duke University, 1989
Major in Psychology
Minor in Business Administration

REFERENCES
Excellent references available upon request

- A resume should never indicate a candidate's reason for leaving his/her past jobs.

- Job descriptions indicate impressive promotions and achievements.

MILITARY BACKGROUND (Intelligence Specialist)

Chris Smith
178 Green Street
Appleton, WI 54912
(414) 555-5555

Professional Experience

UNITED STATES NAVY   1990-1994
Intelligence Specialist
- Served as intelligence analyst in photographic interpretation for FIRST at NAS Boston and Fleet Intelligence Center Pacific
- Participated in intelligence operations on month long active duty assignments.
- Edited and compiled contingency briefs for fleet surface ships at Commander Naval Surface Force, Miami.

UNITED STATES NAVY   1986-1990
Intelligence Specialist
- Served as Intelligence Assistant at Commander Naval Surface Force, U.S. Pacific Fleet, Miami, 1987-1990
- Edited and compiled point papers on foreign navies
- Briefed shipboard intelligence officers on intelligence collection effort
- Performed various other functions including standing watch, serving as classified control custodian, and clerical and editorial duties
- Performed administrative duties in Special Security Office at Fleet Intelligence Center Pacific, Los Angeles, CA

Education

Marquette University, College of Liberal Arts, Milwaukee, WI
Bachelor of Arts in Soviet Politics
GPA in major: 3.5/4.0
Study Abroad: Hamburg, St. Petersburg, Moscow, Paris, 1993
Five-week study of Soviet languages

Military Training:
Basic Training, Maui, Hawaii, 1986
Intelligence Specialists "A" School, Bangor, Maine, 1986
Shipboard Intelligence School, Miami, Florida, 1987
National Imagery Interpretation Rating Scale School, Miami, 1987

Additional Information

- Fluent in German, French, Russian
- Received two Naval Certificates of Achievement, 1987, 1992
- Clearance-Top Secret

■ Resume includes candidate's relevant additional information.

■ Layout is clean and well-organized.

MILITARY BACKGROUND (Supervisor)

Chris Smith
178 Green Street
Vancouver, WA 98665
(206) 555-5555

CAREER OBJECTIVE
To secure an **Administrative/Supervisory** position in the Human Services field.

SYNOPSIS
Self-starter with involved style of leadership. Excellent communicator with the ability to elicit interest, enthusiasm, drive and energy using a common sense approach. Adept at sizing up situations, analyzing facts and developing alternative courses of action in order to achieve, even exceed desired results.

QUALIFICATIONS
- Extensive supervisory experience.
- 6 years counseling up to 120 soldiers with subsequent referrals when necessary.
- Exceptional training and instructional skills.
- Strong administrative and organizational abilities.
- Relevant course work in college and U.S. Army professional training.
- Bilingual: English and Spanish.

EXPERIENCE
1984-1994   U.S. ARMY   **Squad Leader/Training NCO**
From initial tour of duty to honorable discharge, details have included military driver, senior gunner, squad leader, acting platoon sergeant, and training NCO.
- Command inspections and training 120-man Air Defense Artillery Battery with an 18-hour world wide mission in the 7th ID (L).
- Trained and targeted career progression for soldiers on staff.
- Directly responsible for the discipline, training, morale and quality of life of one particular soldier.
- Accountable for training records, personnel performance, strength reporting, and weight control.
- Liable for personnel processing, NCO Evaluation Reports, evaluations, awards, in/out processing, legal actions and orders.

AWARDS
- Army Service Medal
- U.S. Defense Medal
- Four Army Good Conduct Medals
- Four Officer Development Ribbons

EDUCATION
Farmville High School, Farmville, VA
Graduate Diploma, 1984

■ Impressive awards indicate candidate's potential to excel.

■ Qualifications call attention to candidate's relevant supervisory and administrative experience.

NO CLEAR CAREER PATH (Accounting)

Chris Smith
178 Green Street
Rockford, IL 61108
(815) 555-5555

OBJECTIVE:
An entry-level accounting position.

SUMMARY OF QUALIFICATIONS:
- Excellent interpersonal skills.
- Possess strong leadership qualities.
- Computers: Lotus 1-2-3, Microsoft Word and MASS-11.
- Four years of collections experience. Successfully collected 90% of company's overdue accounts.
- Experience in accounts payable and accounts receivable.
- Knowledge of spreadsheets and accounting software.

PROFESSIONAL EXPERIENCE:
1990-Present   ALBRIGHT SERVICES CORPORATION, Rockford, IL
               <u>Shareholder Services Representative</u>
- Maintain telephone contact with clients, shareholders, and dealers.
- Handle account adjustments; respond to inquiries; research account balances and stop payments.

Summers   <u>Special Police Officer</u>
1988 - 1990
- Possessed full police authority.
- Responsible for night beat on Main Street.
- Performed arrests and bookings as necessary.

1989-1990   BILL MITCHELL GUBERNATORIAL CAMPAIGN, Chicago, IL
            <u>Legislative Intern</u>
- Provided office assistance including data entry, research, memo writing, document delivery, and various organizational duties.
- Instituted new filing system which increased departed by 15%.

OTHER EMPLOYMENT:
Bartender, Carpentry Assistant, Lifeguard.

EDUCATION:
NORTHWESTERN UNIVERSITY, Evanston, IL
B.A. in American Studies, 1990
Graduated Cum Laude

INTERESTS:
Enjoy SCUBA Diving and Jogging.

REFERENCES:
Available Upon Request.

■ Statistics and dollar figures quantify candidate's accomplishments.

■ Summary of qualifications draws attention to skills related to candidate's job objective.

NO CLEAR CAREER PATH (Human Resources)

Chris Smith
178 Green Street
Wise, VA 24293
(703) 555-5555

OBJECTIVE   An entry-level position in Human Resources.

SUMMARY OF QUALIFICATIONS
- Trained in basic computer skills.
- Developed interpersonal skills; excellent mediation abilities.
- Proven supervisory abilities; deal equitably with all levels.
- Function well both independently and as team member.
- Adapt easily to new concepts; adept at handling multiple responsibilities.
- Extensive experience in training; able to explain procedure and garner significant results within a brief time span.
- Charismatic, assertive personality; skilled at commanding the attention of others.

WORK HISTORY

1984 - Present   ARMY NATIONAL GUARD, Richmond, VA
Assistant Section Coordinator, Sergeant/ E-5
Coordinate training of soldiers, creating schedules, overseeing adherence to rules, assisting in directing operations, and attending weekly meetings.

1991 - Present   BENNIE WARD'S STYLE SHINDIG, Winchester, VA
Sales Associate
Provided customer assistance. Acknowledged as one of top salespeople; consistently met/exceeded sales goals.

1988-91   MARTELL BLUE SECURITY SERVICES, Salem, MA
Security Shift Supervisor
Handled employee ID checks; secured building; ensured other site call ins. Worked independently on on-site assignments.

1985-88   VIRGINIA SAMARITAN ASSOCIATION, Charlottesville, VA
Fundraiser
Utilized telephone techniques to raise funds for organizations.

1982-85   FIRST NATIONAL BANK OF LEXINGTON, Lexington, VA
Teller
Processed withdrawals and deposits; tallied vault moneys.

EDUCATION   RICHMOND JUNIOR COLLEGE, Richmond VA
Associates Degree in Management Science
Major: Business Administration

REFERENCES   Furnished upon request.

■ Job objective is brief and to the point.

■ Functional resume format is another good choice for candidates with no clear career path.

OVERSEAS EMPLOYMENT HISTORY (Field Administrator)

Chris Smith
178 Green Street
Seal Cove, ME 04674
(207) 555-5555

OBJECTIVE A challenging international career where I can contribute extensive experience in administration and management.

CAREER EXPERIENCE

WELBRUN STATE UNIVERSITY, European Region, Berlin, Germany   1992-Present
Field Administrator/Manager
Administer all office activities. Serve as liaison on military based college, resolving military-civilian, faculty-student clashes. Requires ability to maneuver politically, observing military priorities. Coordinate with Education Service Officer, Education Center staff, and faculty in planning educational programs for community. Assist students in course registration and planning individual academic/vocational needs. Process registration forms and financial reports. Maintain/update classroom files and rosters. Initiate/distribute publicity.

UNIVERSITY OF MASSACHUSETTS, European Sect, Paris, France   1990-1992
Field Registrar
Managed office in planning/implementing educational program for military community. Initiated innovative marketing policy and personal outreach program; increased student enrollments from 250 to 700 per year. Assisted students as needed; prepared/processed registration forms and financial packets. Reviewed lecturer applications; assisted in transition into area. Planned/organized student tours and field trips.

ILSESFORD, Paris, France   1988-1990
Retail Manager
Supervised retail store complex operations including: Retail Store, Barber shop, Pick-up Point, Theater, and temporary concessions. Tripled sales. Monitored Retail Store renovation, inventory, fixed assets, custodial funds, and cash/receipts. Implemented data compilation to support inventory budget requirements, projected sales, and annual forecast. Interviewed, hired/terminated, trained and cross-trained personnel. Acted as liaison between military commander and the community.

THE GUIMBLEY SCHOOL, Lancaster, England   1986-1988
Administrative Assistant
Supervised/implemented clearance updating for 2,000 personnel files to improve faculty academic qualifications. Assisted Associate Dean: transcribed edited reports and correspondence, clarified new Academic Affairs procedures/policies, processed/revised/completed reports, catalogs.

EDUCATION **WELBRUN STATE UNIVERSITY**, European Region, Berlin, Germany
M.P.A., Public Administration, Cognate: Counseling, 1992

UNIVERSITY OF MASSACHUSETTS, European Division, Paris, France
B.A., Business Management, cum laude, 1990

■ Job objective focuses on the needs of the employer, not the job candidate.

■ Specific contributions display candidate's achievements and problem-solving abilities.

PART-TIME EMPLOYMENT HISTORY (Retail Manager)

CHRIS SMITH
178 Green Street
Johnson, VT 05656
(802) 555-5555

OBJECTIVE
To join a dynamic sales staff with a firm that has a need for a highly motivated representative skilled in retail markets.

SUMMARY OF PROFESSIONAL EXPERIENCE
- Four years of substantial experience in positions as Sales Representative, Retail Sales Manager, and Warehouse Manager with retail and a major wholesale organization.
- Assumed responsibility for divisional sales from $1.4 million to $2.1 million within one year.
- Hands-on experience in sales, inventory control and promotion of chemicals, furniture, clothing and seasonal products.
- Skilled in developing special merchandising effects to increase product visibility and sales.

WORK HISTORY
Raintree, Inc.
Seasonal Specialty Stores, Raintree Industries, Johnson, VT
Retail Manager (Part-time)   (1993-Present)
- Hire, train, schedule and supervise a highly productive staff of 11 selling and promoting a diverse product mix.
- Develop, implement, and expand seasonal merchandise and presentations for year-round sales. Greatly expanded product knowledge and sales through use of in store video and other image equipment.
- Select and purchase all billiard equipment and accessories.
- Prepare inventory projections, work on sales promotions (in-store and chain-wide). Excellent consumer base resulting in strong repeat business.
- Maintain financial control of all debits/credits.

Wholesale Warehouse Manager, (Part-time)   (1992-1993)
- Supervised a staff of 6 and controlled all aspects of shipping and receiving. Directed fleet scheduling maintenance as well as building maintenance control and security for this facility.

Sales Representative (Part-time)   (1991-1992)
- Increased all aspects of wholesale pool and supply and accessory business. Control of expanding sales and sales force. Established new sales and accounts within the New England area.

EDUCATION
Cornell University, Ithaca, NY
B.A. Business Administration, 1991.

■ Part-time experience may be treated like full-time experience on a resume.

■ Statistics and dollar figures quantify candidate's accomplishments.

PHYSICALLY CHALLENGED (Broadcasting)

CHRIS SMITH

178 Green Street
New York, NY 10023
(212) 555-5555

Objective:
A challenging mid-level position in broadcasting.

Summary of Qualifications:
Over ten years experience in recording engineering, background vocals, producing, mixing/editing.

Experience:

1991 -
Present

Vogue Recording Studio, New York, NY
Recording Engineer
- Clarify session requirements.
- Mix and edit demo tapes and albums.
- Maintain and repair audio equipment.
- Support video production department.

1985-1990

WMLC AM, Radio 15, New York, NY
Radio Personality
- Associate Producer and Programmer for live talk shows.
- Audio and Sound Engineer for commercials.
- Run syndicated talk board operations.
- Produce comedy bits for weekly comedy show.
- Interview call-ins on the air.

Education:

New York University, New York, NY
Studies include broadcasting, public speaking and audio engineering. School Radio Station General Manager. Braille Tutor. 1982-1985.

License: Third Class Broadcasting

Interests: Standup comedy, playing guitar, traveling

References: Available upon request

Personal: Willing to travel

■ Unless it is immediately relevant to candidate's job objective, there is no reason to indicate a physical impairment on a resume.

■ Personal interests give a candid snapshot of candidate as a person.

PHYSICALLY CHALLENGED (Engineering)

CHRIS SMITH
178 Green Street
Casper, WY 82604
(307) 555-5555

OBJECTIVE
An Engineering position in the field of Electro-Optics.

WORK EXPERIENCE

1993-Present   JT Technology   Casper, WY
ASSISTANT ENGINEER
- Provide engineering support to various sensor and electro-mechanical areas.
- Solve engineering-related problems for production department; assist through direct observation, positive communication and dynamic interaction between production floor and test engineering management.
- Perform equipment and component testing; troubleshoot malfunctions; assist engineers with special projects and with department support tasks as required.
- Monitor current developments in the engineering fields for possible practical applications.

1990-1993   Charles Technology Corporation   Casper, WY
ASSISTANT ENGINEER
- Supervised various test engineering projects which required operating specialized equipment, documenting test results and making reports of findings to engineering management.
- Implemented software/hardware modifications and engineering changes requested by company clients.
- Assisted senior engineers with projects and performed support duties as needed.

1988-1990   Dishwashers, Etc.   Green Bay, WI
APPLIANCE TECHNICIAN
- Made household and commercial service calls to troubleshoot malfunctions, repair and/or replace various appliances.
- Installed new equipment; interacted with customers and coworkers in a pleasant and efficient manner.

EDUCATION

Associates of Science Degree in Electronic Technology, 1990
Green Bay Community College, Green Bay, WI
GPA 3.5/4.0

ACTIVITIES

New York Marathon
Placed 5th, Wheelchair Division - 1993

■ Education is listed towards bottom of resume because candidate's practical experience outweighs his/her degree.

■ Resume emphasizes contributions, achievements, and problems candidate has solved throughout his/her career.

PHYSICALLY CHALLENGED (Medical Research)

CHRIS SMITH
178 Green Street
Arlington, VA 22207
(703) 555-5555

PROFESSIONAL EXPERIENCE
1991 to Present   **Research Assistant**
CITY HOSPITAL   Washington, D.C.
Pathology Unit
- Establish protocols and procedures on cell culture and freezing methods.
- Maintain and establish Transgenic, Oscular Meloma Cell Lines, and In Vitro Studies.
- Perform chemotherapy toxicity studies, Cytospins, Dot Blots, DNA Extractions.
- Maintain and breed transgenic SV40, CDI Nude, NIH III, Bg-NU-Xid and blood sampling.
- Maintain mouse colonies; supervise dissections, autopsy reports, In Vitro injections and record keeping.
- Perform various other laboratory and maintenance processes.

November 1988 to June 1991   **Skin Bank Technician**
ARLINGTON HOSPITAL BURN INSTITUTE   Arlington, VA
- Harvested and processed post-mortem (Cadaver) allo-graphs, under sterile technique.
- Processed human/artificial tissue for freezing (auto-grafts, pig skin biobrane).
- Researched In Vitro culture cells, auto and all-graft cells in mice.
- Vax and digital computer, word II processing.
- Maintained all laboratory equipment.

1984 to November 1987   **Research Clinical Technician**
FARRELL & OKELUND RESEARCH ASSOCIATES   Alexandria, VA
- Performed F.D.A. and I.R.B. pharmacokinetic research studies, including statistical analyses of safety and human tolerance studies in bioavailability, bioequivalence, cardiology, alpha and beta blockers, hypertension, neurology, and endoscopy ulcer studies.
- Administered protocols and case report forms.
- Performed various clinical nursing and laboratory duties.

1982 to 1983   **Laboratory Technical Assistant**
ENGELMAN LABORATORIES   Bethesda, MD
- Performed various clinical laboratory functions.

EDUCATION
Bachelor of Science Degree in Biology
Gallaudet College for the Deaf
Washington, D.C., 1982

■ Candidate's most relevant work experience is prioritized throughout resume.

■ Bullets make resume easy to read.

RETIREE REENTERING THE WORK FORCE (Principal)

CHRIS SMITH
178 Green Street
Arkadelphia, AK 71923
(501) 555-5555

OBJECTIVE
To contribute extensive experience and administrative skills to a part-time teaching position.

EXPERIENCE
ARKANSAS PUBLIC SCHOOL SYSTEM

1982 to 1991   **Principal - Retired**
RODHAM ELEMENTARY SCHOOL   Arkadelphia, AR
- Oversaw all operations for entire school.
- Supervised and evaluated teachers and teaching assistants.
- Developed curriculum for mainstream and special needs children.
- Developed curriculum for mainstream and special needs children.
- Directed staff meeting, oriented new administrative and teaching staff.

1976 to 1982   **Principal**
HOPE CLINTON JUNIOR HIGH SCHOOL   Arkadelphia, AR
- Directed and facilitated all operational procedures.
- Developed curriculum and supervised staff.
- Created and implemented educational program enhancements.
- Directed staff meetings, informed staff of district ordered changes.

1973 to 1976   **Teaching Assistant Principal**
NOAH JUNIOR HIGH SCHOOL   Arkadelphia, AR
- Served as acting principal and directed operational processes.
- Assisted and supervised teaching staff.
- Interfaced with parents/teachers for educational program development.

1965 to 1973   **Teaching Assistant Principal**
DAMON ELEMENTARY SCHOOL   Conway, AR
- Assisted principal in the coordination of educational programs.
- Purchased books and various educational aids.

1954 to 1965   **Teacher**
CONWAY JUNIOR HIGH SCHOOL   Conway, AR
- Instructed students in math and science.

EDUCATION
JOHN BROWN UNIVERSITY, Siloam Springs, AK
Masters Degree: Education, 1949
Bachelor of Arts Degree: History, 1945

CERTIFICATION
State Teacher Certification

■ Job objective focuses on the needs of the employer, not the job candidate.

■ Including professional licensure and accreditations can be essential for certain fields of work.

CHRIS SMITH

178 Green Street
Fairfax, VA 22030
(703) 555-5555

SKILLS

Research	WordPerfect
General office skills	Microsoft Word
Writing	Lotus 1-2-3

WORK EXPERIENCE

Legal Assistant
Parnell & Swaggert
Fairfax, VA   1993-Present
Responsible for corresponding via courier, telephone, letter, and facsimile with clients, attorneys, Secretaries of State, U.S. Dept. of State, and foreign associates in matters of intellectual property law, primarily trademarks. Meet with clients regarding applications/registrations of trademarks and direct either U.S. Commissioner or foreign agent how to proceed. Other duties include: compiling information from other Ladas & Parry branches, paying our debit notes and billing clients.

Legislative Intern
Office of Senator Fisher
Washington, D.C.   Summer 1993
Responsible for legislative correspondence, involving case work. Assisted and Labor and Human Resources Committee Judiciary Sub-Committee, and Fund for a Democratic Majority. Projects included research, writing, covered hearings and wrote memos.

Legislative Aide
Office of Senator Florio
Washington, D.C.   Summer 1992
Responsible for overseeing communications between Senator Florio and the general public.

EDUCATION
George Mason University, Fairfax, VA
BA, Law and Society, 1992

HONORS & AWARDS
Oxford Honor Scholar
Who's Who Among Students, 1990
Student Government Award

■ Impressive awards further enhance candidate's credentials.

■ Resume emphasizes valuable
skills.

SHORT EMPLOYMENT HISTORY (Operations Clerk)

CHRIS SMITH
178 Green Street
Kenosha, WI 53141
(414) 555-5555

Objective
A position within the operations department of a reputed brokerage firm.

Summary of Qualifications
- Detail-oriented; establish effective priorities.
- Able to implement decisions and expedite work flow to meet deadlines.
- Comfortable providing unlimited support during times of high pressure and stress.

Experience

KASS AND SON, INC., Kenosha, WI
Operations and Process Clerk (1994-Present)
- Open, log, reconcile, and verify new accounts.
- Reconcile daily customer service/new accounts input against computer printouts. Research/correct problems.
- Maintain/update files.
- Handle high-volume mailings to welcome new clients and initial mailing of Electronic Funds Transfer forms/letters.
- Recommend procedural changes to facilitate work flow.
- Interact with branch representatives.
- Assist with special projects as required including bookkeeping, handling President's incoming calls, and responding directly to customer inquiries.
- Converted manual check processing to electronic function.
- Eliminated major filing backlog.

Other Experience

Camp Teutonahwa, Butte, MT
Administrative Assistant (Part-time)
Billings Middle School, Billings, MT
Administrative Assistant (Part-time)

Volunteer Work

Jewish Education Association, Kenosha, WI
Resource Coordinator
Barbara Walsh Soup Kitchens, Bozeman, MT
Kitchen Worker/Shelter Coordinator

Education

Widener University, Chester, PA
B.A. Management, 1988
President of Class, 1986-88
Formed Widener Chapter of Y.B.P.A. (Young Business People of America).
Membership began at 15 students; by 1993, it had swelled to 174.

- Impressive qualifications and volunteer and educational experience help to compensate for candidate's short employment history.

- Resume accentuates relevant experience; unrelated jobs are listed under "Other Experience."

CHRIS SMITH
178 Green Street
Raleigh, NC 27611
(919) 555-5555

OBJECTIVE:
A long-term position in administration.

SKILLS & QUALIFICATIONS:
- Five years Accounting, Financial & Administrative experience.
- Computer knowledge includes IBM, APPLE, and HONEYWELL.
- Outstanding communications and organizational skills.

EXPERIENCE:

11/94-Present   CARMICHAEL ENTERPRISES, Raleigh, NC
Accounting Clerk/Data Entry
Temporary Position
Prepare and maintain all general ledger accounts, records, and files. Input data on various computer systems, including IBM, Apple, and Honeywell.

6/94-10/94   CHAVEZ INVESTMENTS, Winston-Salem, NC
Customer Service Representative
Temporary Position
Responded to questions and assisted shareholders in regards to their stocks, bonds, equity and money market accounts, as well as tax questions. Approved check disbursements and utilized IBM computer system.

11/93-6-94   JOHN HANCOCK LIFE INSURANCE CO., Boston, MA
Purchasing Clerk
Temporary Position
Maintained general supply inventory levels and purchased general supplies and specially requested items and materials. Negotiated price and coordinated delivery with various vendors. Prepared purchase orders. Assisted in other administrative activities.

4/88-12/92   SCANLON CORPORATION, Chapel Hill, NC
Residential Counselor
Assisted and counseled mentally retarded and emotionally disabled adults in reading, math, personal hygiene and motor skills.

OTHER EXPERIENCE:
Other temporary assignments have included: Receptionist, Order Entry Clerk, Switchboard Operator, Proofreader.

EDUCATION:
Clydeston Business School Certification, 1992
Kennedy High School Graduate, 1988

■ Long-term temporary assignments may be treated like full-time permanent positions on a resume.

■ Short-term assignments are listed under "Other Experience."

WEAK EDUCATIONAL BACKGROUND (Assistant Manager)

Chris Smith
178 Green Street
Myrtle Beach, SC 29577
(803) 555-5555

OBJECTIVE

To apply skills attained through experience in supervision of Parking Facilities to the position of Assistant Manager of Parking Facilities.

SUMMARY

- Proven abilities have resulted in rapid advancement to a supervisory position.
- Self-motivated, people-oriented, consistently responsible.
- Familiar with all prerequisite functions of maintaining a smooth-running Parking Facility.
- Sworn Deputy Sheriff, Birchwood County.

EXPERIENCE

1984-
Present **SPORT AUTHORITY ROLLINS AIRPORT**, Lexington, SC

1989- **SUPERVISOR OF PARKING FACILITY**
Present Oversee collection of all moneys. Maintain public relations and customer service. Resolve all problems. Administer work schedules, payroll, assignment of duties, and various other functions. Attend to snow removal. Represent Port Authority at scheduled court appearances.

1989 - **PRESIDENT OF LOCAL CHAPTER OF NAGE**
Present Represent all cashiers and attendants. Settle all problems pertaining to Parking Facilities. Negotiate contracts.

1987-89 **ASSISTANT SUPERVISOR/CASHIER**
Assisted supervisor. Collected all parking fees. Achieved high standard of customer relations.

1984-87 **ATTENDANT**
Patrolled and maintained cleanliness standards of Parking Facility. Assisted customers.

OTHER EXPERIENCE

Skilled carpenter's helper; advanced to highest skilled fish cutter within one year and then elected shop steward. (Total experience, 4 years.)
Truck driver, class 2 license to Lead Bartender/Beverage Manager/Assistant Manager. (Total experience 6 years.)

REFERENCES

Furnished upon request.

- Listing educational background is optional if candidate has lots of work experience.

- Relevant work experience is emphasized while other positions are de-emphasized.

WEAK EDUCATIONAL BACKGROUND (Money Market Accountant)

Chris Smith
178 Green Street
Troy, MI 48098
(313) 555-5555

OBJECTIVE:
To fully utilize over ten years of experience in investment accounting within an allied field.

SUMMARY:
Experience in monitoring money flow in money market funds and mutual funds, as well as calculating the yield for various money market accounts, and pricing mutual funds.

EXPERIENCE:

GERGEW SERVICE COMPANY   Troy, MI
Senior Money Market Accountant   1989-Present
Determined daily available cash, calculated daily yields and dividends. Posted general ledger. RECONCILED trial balance accounts. Acted as liaison between fund traders and custodian banks. Prepared audit schedules. Assisted in training new personnel. Used both P.C. and CRT.

Mutual Fund Accountant   1986-89
Functions included daily pricing of common stock and bond funds, accruing and reconciling interest and dividend accounts, reconciling trial balance accounts and daily contact with brokers to obtain stock and bond quotes.

TIMBERCREST COMPANY,   Boston, MA
Assistant Supervisor   1985-86
Prepared schedules for fund audits. Prepared reports for fund managers. Assisted fund accountants with month-end trial balance reconciliation. Trained new personnel.

Fund Accountant   1983-85
Manually priced funds and posted journals and ledgers through trial balance. Heavy daily contact with brokers.

OTHER QUALIFICATIONS:
LICENSED MICHIGAN REAL ESTATE BROKER, 1982

EDUCATION:
Waterford High School, Waterford, MI
Graduated 1981

■ Summary is concise and adds punch to resume.

■ Work experience is emphasized, while limited education is de-emphasized.

6
Accounting and Finance

Nature of Work

Those professionals who work in accounting and finance prepare, analyze, and verify financial reports that furnish valuable, up-to-date information to managers in all business, industrial, and governmental organizations. Others in the finance field, those grouped into the category of financial managers, prepare the reports required by a firm to conduct its operations and to satisfy tax and regulatory requirements. These professionals are the hidden support structure of a company, for they develop information to assess the present and future financial status of the firm.

Budget analysts serve as a financial plan for controlling future operations and as a means of analyzing the organization's spending behavior. Cost estimators develop information about the cost of future projects for owners to use in making bids for contracts or to determine if the organization is getting good value for its money. Actuaries assemble and analyze statistics to calculate the probabilities of death, sickness, injury, disability, unemployment, and property loss.

Employment

Most professionals in the accounting and finance field work in urban areas where accounting firms and the central or regional offices of businesses are concentrated. Schools, hospitals, retail stores, trucking companies, chemical plants and nearly every major industrial, commercial, and governmental operation has a need for skilled professionals to monitor their finances.

Training

Though entry requirements vary by specific job, most firms require their applicants to hold at least a bachelor's degree in accounting, business administration, or a related field. Most also prefer applicants who possess a strong knowledge of computers and their applications in accounting and internal auditing.

Previous experience in accounting, billing, or finance can help an applicant get a job. Many colleges offer students the opportunity to gain experience through summer or part-time internship programs conducted by business firms. Such training is invaluable in gaining permanent employment in the field. Solid math and communications skills are very important as well.

Job Outlook

The job prospects for accountants and other finance professionals will be better than average for the next decade, mainly because more and more new businesses will be coming into existence. Each of these businesses will need their share of employees to set up books, prepare taxes, and give management advice.

Earnings

Those employed in accounting and finance can usually expect to earn a starting salary of $22,000 to $25,000. The middle salaries range from $25,000 to $34,000, while senior professionals earn anywhere from $40,000 to $60,000+. A beginning public accountant employed by a public accounting firm can expect to earn about $25,300, while a top level financial manager might earn over $68,000.

ACCOUNTANT (General)

CHRIS SMITH
178 Green Street
Loretto, PA 15940
(814) 555-5555

OBJECTIVE

An accounting position offering the opportunity to utilize my professional financial expertise, extensive business experience, and ability to interact with senior management and with the business community on a worldwide basis.

SUMMARY OF QUALIFICATIONS

- **Accountant** and **Administrative Manager** of medium-sized motor components manufacturing and distribution company serving national and international markets
- Hands-on experience with firm of Certified Public Accountants and Auditors
- **Certified Public Accountant** and **Auditor**

PROFESSIONAL EXPERIENCE

1988-
Present
LISMORE SHIPPING CO., LTD., Loretta, PA
Accountant
- Managed, developed, and maintained all aspects of finance, accounting, foreign exchange dealings, marketing, and data processing of company and its overseas offices in London and New York
- Controlled budget, cash flow, and capital expenditure
- Reviewed, analyzed, and evaluated finances and securities pertaining to advances and shipping for client base of about 200
- Established and maintained close relationships with bank executives, auditors, and attorneys, ensuring compliance with all regulatory bodies

1983-1988
RABINO PRODUCTS, Meadville, PA
Accountant
- Developed and implemented corporate and project-oriented financial strategies
- Provided financial overview and leadership for all major operating considerations and activities, including development of business and profit plans
- Controlled line management for all accounting, production costing, EDP, and financial functions

1981-1983
MANNINGS, DAWE, AND BOND, Pittsburgh, PA
Auditor
- Audited private companies, listed companies, partnerships, and individual businesses
- Prepared financial statements and schedules

EDUCATION

UNIVERSITY OF PENNSYLVANIA, Philadelphia, PA
Bachelor's Degree, with major in Accountancy, Marketing, and Business Finance, 1981

■ Summary of qualifications highlight candidate's strengths.

■ Bullets make resume easy to read.

ACCOUNTANT (Senior)

CHRIS SMITH
178 Green Street
Billings, MT 59105
(406) 555-5555

EMPLOYMENT HISTORY

July 1989 to **ROSS PECOE, INC., Billings, MT**
Present (A $20 million publicly held company that develops, manufactures and markets proprietary x-ray systems)

Senior Financial Analyst/Accountant (July, 1990 to Present)
- Assist controller in preparation of financial statements and all SEC reporting.
- Assist in the consolidation of three European subsidiaries.
- Review work of staff accountant and approve journal transactions for data entry.
- Assist with the corporate budget in preparation and maintenance of budgets and projections using both Excel and Lotus for Windows.
- Prepare monthly budget to actual reports and distribute to managers.
- Manage accounting duties of a venture capital funded start-up organization, Beta Technologies, Inc. (sister company to Ross Pecoe Inc.), including financial reporting and coordinating annual audit with external auditors.
- Implemented the ASK MANMAN computer information system.

Senior Accountant (July, 1989 to July, 1990)
- Assisted with monthly closings and financial reporting.
- Worked directly with controller in preparation for Primary and Secondary Public Stock Offerings.
- Implemented Solomon III General Ledger Accounting Package, including the installation and set-up of all modules required by accounting, the development of procedures to be used by this new system, the training of staff on the system, and the formatting of several financial reports.
- Installed and maintained a seven-user Novel Network.

March 1987 **STEADFAST CORP., Cherry Creek, MT**
to July 1989 (A venture capital funded software development firm)
Staff Accountant
- Administered single-user Solomon III Accounting System.
- Assisted in general ledger close including foreign currency translation of foreign subsidiaries.
- Monitored cash and accounts receivable.
- Trained new employees to administer the accounts payable and order entry functions.

EDUCATION

Bronte College, New Castle, ME
Master of Science in Accountancy, expected completion August, 1993
Carroll College, Helena, MT
Bachelor of Arts in Business Management, December, 1986

COMPUTER SKILLS

Excel, Lotus 1-2-3 (Windows), ASK ManMan General Ledger, Solomon General Ledger, Novell Network

---

■ Computer skills are highlighted.

■ Brief descriptions of employers add weight to already strong qualifications.

ACCOUNTING ASSISTANT

CHRIS SMITH
178 Green Street
Chicago, IL 60604
(312) 555-5555

OBJECTIVE
A career in the financial field where budgeting experience will be advanced.

SUMMARY OF QUALIFICATIONS
- More than sixteen years of progressive experience in budget control, public relations, and sales.
- Excellent interpersonal and negotiating skills; adept at defusing potential problems.
- Proven oral and written communication abilities.
- Adaptable to new concepts and responsibilities.
- Proficient in handling diverse tasks simultaneously.

PROFESSIONAL EXPERIENCE

STATE TREASURY, Chicago, IL   1985-Present
Accounting Assistant
Administer budget, payroll, and personnel for a 322-person staff and $7 million budget. Attend state house meetings. Act as liaison with Budget Bureau. Pay Treasury bills; ensure payroll coverage. Determine emergency allotment needs. Utilize IBM and Hewlett Packard Computer Systems. Assist with public relations, opening/closing monthly and yearly budgets, and payroll. Negotiate contract work. Interface with clients from presentations and determining needs through completion of services. Act as liaison with accountants.

CRAVEN TRANSPORT, Midway Airport, Chicago, IL   1980-1985
Budget Director
Set up/implemented $7 million budget and payroll for main branch and subsidiaries. Negotiated contracts with air freight agencies working directly with owner.

NANETTE CONSTRUCTION, Elsah, IL   1974-1980
Budget Director
Actuated original budget for new company; ensured appropriation of moneys for payroll. Administered all office functions utilizing IBM Computer System.

EDUCATION

Western Illinois University, Macomb, IL   1972-1974
Major: Business Management

REFERENCES

Furnished upon request.

- Strong action verbs bring resume to life.

- Candidate's most relevant work experience is prioritized throughout resume.

ACCOUNTING CLERK

CHRIS SMITH
178 Green Street
Brimfield, MA 01010
(413) 555-5555

OBJECTIVE
An assistant accounting position in a progressive organization that offers opportunities for advancement.

SUMMARY OF QUALIFICATIONS
- More than three years accounting experience.
- Extensive computer experience.
- Developed interpersonal skills, having dealt with a diversity of professionals, clients, and staff members.
- Self-motivated; able to implement decisions and set effective priorities to achieve both immediate and long-term goals.

EXPERIENCE
4/94-pres. APPLEDYNE CORP., Brimfield, MA
Accounting Assistant
Prepare, monitor, and maintain computerized accounts payables and receivables. Verify accuracy of purchase orders and invoices. Resolve problem areas. Monitor IBM accounting system for internal software companies. Implemented a billing system to maintain cordial relations with clients, resulting in a 10% increase in new client acquisition. Delegate as troubleshooter. Design an employee check-cashing center within company. Received written commendation from Appledyne president, John Pacs.

4/93-4/94 TERRIO LYCRA CORP., Amherst, MA
Accounts Receivable/Payable Clerk
Maintained computerized Accounts Receivable/Payable; handled outgoing communications on IBM word processing system. Generated/mailed A/P checks.

7/91-4/93 MAYFLOWER DATING SERVICE, Manomet, MA
Accounting Clerk/Assistant to Vice-President of Finance
Generated income statements, balance sheets, general ledger, checks and reports; entered payable vouchers; received/deposited monthly rent checks.

EDUCATION
JASPER COLLEGE, Nashua, NH
B.S., Mathematics, 1991
G.P.A. 3.0/4.0

COMPUTERS
Proficient in Lotus 1-2-3 and Microsoft Word.

- Specific dates of employment (month and year) are ideal for candidates with no gaps in work history.

- Separate heading of "Computers" emphasizes candidate's technical knowledge.

ACCOUNTING MANAGER (Funds)

CHRIS SMITH
178 Green Street
Bakerton, KY 42711
(606) 555-5555

EMPLOYMENT HISTORY

1990 to **CHET HORN INC., Bakerton, KY**
Present **Accounting Manager**
- Directed a staff of five. Responsible for the Custody Operations work necessary to maintain client's asset base. (International Bond Funds, Equity Funds, Single Country Funds and Pension Funds.)
- Anticipated client needs and responded to their requests. Maintained an excellent service record during a growth period that increased our team's asset responsibility from $6 billion to $7.1 billion in one year.
- Expanded market awareness by attending focus sessions and seminars on the constantly changing foreign markets.
- Improved GCAS productivity by designing the Brown Brothers Monthly Custody Operations Package. Collaborated with the client to test and convert to an automated transmission process. Trained account staff and management peers to utilize bank's on-line security system.

Account Manager
- Monitored and executed currency and security settlements in global markets (including Emerging Markets).
- Supported internal and external audit requests by successfully reconciling all currency and security discrepancies with clients and sub-custodians.
- Accomplished team goals by cross-training with other Account Managers and taking on additional responsibilities, including a weekly review of overdrafts for all funds in the team.

1989 to **SUNNYVALE AND SON, Lexington, KY**
1990 **Fund Accountant**
- Settled bond and equity transactions in the United States markets. Prepared weekly and monthly financial statements for mutual funds.
- Assumed sole responsibility for researching past due interest, dividend receivables, claiming brokers. Reduced the volume by 60% in one year.

EDUCATION

Moorehead State University, Moorehead, KY
Master of Science, 1992
Concentration: Finance

Cumberland College, Williamsburg, KY
Bachelor of Science, 1989
Concentration: Finance and Economics

COMPUTERS

Software knowledge: Microsoft Word, Lotus 1-2-3, Pascal, FORTRAN

■ Consistent verb tense makes for easy reading.

■ Use of dollar figures and percentages lend weight to the resume by emphasizing accomplishments.

ACCOUNTING MANAGER (General)

CHRIS SMITH
178 Green Street
Bangor, ME 04401
(207) 555-5555

EXPERIENCE

Parnotti, Inc.., Bangor, ME   1990-Present
General Accounting Manager for $80 million medical diagnostics manufacturer. Supervise five accountants, manage accounts payable, cash, fixed assets, and payroll functions. Prepare monthly and quarterly accounting and employee benefits reports. Monitor license agreements, computing and paying royalties. Analyze and report monthly and annual capital budgets.

Cost Accounting Manager, 1986-90.
Prepared monthly manufacturing accounting report. Patented product royalties computation and payment. Supervised two cost accountants. Maintained extensive written and verbal communication with operations and finance upper management and staff.

The Raisty Group, Deepwater, NJ   1984-86
Senior Financial Analyst. Monitored annual budget preparation and consolidation of departmental budgets. Prepared financial information for use by internal management and parent company management. Wrote the first "Raisty Budget Manual" used by all department heads during annual budget preparation.

Koravetsos, Inc., Atlantic City, NJ   1982-84
Staff Accountant. Audited and prepared tax returns for real estate developers and limited partnerships.

EDUCATION

Colby College, Waterville, ME 1982
Master of Business Administration degree: concentration in Finance.

University of Maine, Waterville, ME 1980
Bachelor of Arts degree: major in Accounting, minor in Business Administration.
Sarno Corporation scholarship recipient.

CERTIFICATION

Passed all four parts of the *Certified Public Accountant* exam, May 1981.

MEMBERSHIPS

National Society of Certified Public Accountants, October 1981-Present.
New Members Committee Chairperson, 1984-85, Vice Chair 83-84.
American Institute of Certified Public Accountants, 1985-89.

■ Boldfacing, underlining, and clean type make for a clear and crisp presentation.

■ Resume illustrates continual career progression.

ACCOUNTS PAYABLE CLERK (General)

CHRIS SMITH
178 Green Street
Newark, NJ 07102
(201) 555-5555

OBJECTIVE

Seeking a position in administrative support where acquired accounting skills will be advanced.

WORK EXPERIENCE

5/89 to Present **BETTY LOU'S LINGERIE, Newark, NJ**
Accounts Payable/Payroll Department
Light typing, filing and other general office duties. Key in bills on a Wang computer and print all checks for 6 different offices. Assist in payroll preparation by calculating all time sheets and related duties.

1986 to 5/89 **DYNAMO DANCE SUPPLIES, Teaneck, NJ**
Accounts Payable
Set up all invoices to match purchase orders for input into computers. Added up all invoices to match check amounts. Responsible for filing, sorting mail and general office duties.

1984 to 1986 **LEDA AND THE SWAN PETSITTERS, New Brunswick, NJ**
General Office Worker
Acted as cashier, light typist, bank depositor, and key punch operator. Handled filing, and accounts payable/receivable. Heavy customer contact.

COMPUTERS

Lotus 1-2-3, PC-Calc, Multimate, JERSEYPRO.

EDUCATION

1985-1986 DIRK JUNIOR COLLEGE, Camden, NJ
Completed courses in Accounting, Typing and Data Processing.

SPECIAL INTERESTS

Camping, fishing, and jogging.

REFERENCES

Furnished upon request.

■ "Special Interests" provides personal touch.

■ Work experience is emphasized, while limited education is de-emphasized.

ACCOUNTS PAYABLE CLERK (Senior)

CHRIS SMITH
178 Green Street
Burbank, CA 91501
(818) 555-5555

EMPLOYMENT HISTORY

1988 to **SIENNA SIGH HERBALISTS**, Burbank, CA
Present **Senior Accounts Payable Administrator** (1988 to Present)
- Manage entire accounts payable function at Corporate Headquarters.
- Coordinate efforts for accounts payable personnel at three branch locations;
- Complete weekly check disbursements for all Sienna locations. Payments averaging in excess of $500,000.
- Inform Corporate Treasurer of weekly cash requirements, give input of required vendor payments and credit terms for extremely sensitive cash management function.
- Issue weekly and monthly accounts payable distribution reports, work with Corporate Accountants as to accounts payable interface with the general ledger.
- Maintain total outstanding payable balance, including collection of outstanding credits.
- Manage Japanese accounts payable on Lotus System.
- Cross-train as replacement for Senior Payroll Administrator on APD system.
- Cross-train for filing of Federal, State and Unemployment Taxes.

Factory Accountant/Accounts Payable (1986-1988)
- Recorded and analyzed direct labor and standard costs.
- Posted all invoices to general ledger.
- Maintained and collected all receivables from Reece's foreign affiliates and outside vendors.
- Assisted in general ledger monthly closings.

1984 to **THE HOLISTIC HEALING CENTER**, San Francisco, CA
1986 **Bookkeeper**
- Managed weekly payroll for 37 employees.
- Filed state and federal taxes.
- Maintained human resources duties.
- Oversaw full accounts payable duties.
- Posted of cash receipts.
- Composed and posted JE to GL through trial balance.

TECHNICAL SUMMARY

Lotus 1-2-3, WordPerfect, IBM PC, ADS PC, Real World Accounting software, IBM System 36 and 38, Harris Data and Computer Associates Software

EDUCATION

University of Nevada at Las Vegas: Bachelor of Science, Accounting, 1983

■ Resume emphasizes candidate's strong work history.

■ Strong action verbs bring resume to life.

ACCOUNTS RECEIVABLE CLERK

CHRIS SMITH

---

178 Green Street   Newark, NJ 07107   (201) 555-5555

CAREER HISTORY

THE FULLER COMPANY, Newark, NJ   1990-Present
Assistant Manager—Accounts Receivable
- Maintained $10,000 petty cash fund and $15,000 American Express Travelers' Checks account.
- Documented "proofed" checks and moneys for deposit and coordinated with other departments to resolve problems with checks that failed to clear.
- Posted receivables to electronic spreadsheet (Lotus 1-2-3) and month-end journal entries on MILLENNIUM system-a highly technical software application.
- Researched interdepartmental queries and provided results to requester.
- Performed traditional accounting functions.

Financial Associate-Accounts Payable
- Audited documents to include expense reports, invoices, and check requests for payment.
- Generated disbursement instructions for accounts.
- Assigned and maintained vendor identification files through an on-line computer system.
- Developed and maintained 1099 tax information on vendor.
- Assisted in establishing and validating travel reimbursement programs.

B. PARR AND ASSOCIATES, West Orange, NJ   1988-1990
Bookkeeper
- Performed all accounting functions to include journal entries, accounts payables, receivables, petty cash, deposits, bank reconciliations and trial balance.
- Calculated payroll deductions and processed payroll.
- Responsible for monthly, quarterly and year end payroll and sales tax forms.
- Effective in phone collection of overdue accounts, generating invoices and statements.

HACKENSACK HOME FURNISHINGS, Hackensack, NJ   1985-1988
Manager/Bookkeeper
- Brought company to full operational status.
- Responsible for inventory, orders, sales, rent-to-own contracts and supervisor of part-time employees.
- Performed all bookkeeping, banking, sales, payroll taxes and bank reconciliations.

EDUCATION

Kean College of New Jersey, Union, N.J.
AS in Accounting, December 1984.

■ Use of concrete examples accen-   ■ Resume emphasizes candidate's
tuates candidate's achievements.   strong career history.

ACTUARIAL ANALYST

CHRIS SMITH
178 Green Street
Boston, MA 02115
(617) 555-5555

PROFESSIONAL OBJECTIVE
A challenging position which effectively utilizes professional experience, analytical skills, and commitment to success.

PROFESSIONAL BACKGROUND
1988 to   BLUE CROSS/BLUE SHIELD, Boston, Massachusetts
Present   Actuarial Analyst
...Set rates, determine liabilities, and prepare forecasts for largest health insurance company in Massachusetts.
...Calculate and document HMO rates and rates for new benefits.
...Analyze underwriting results, payment experience, and enrollment statistics for upper management.
...Compile accurate statistical information and reports.
...Compute monthly unpaid claim liabilities and retrospective refund liabilities for corporations.
...Liaison between State Division of Insurance and Actuarial Department for State audit. Report directly to principal auditor.
...Project Leader for setup of automated completion factor programs.
...Utilize computerized system to access necessary information.

1985 to   JAYSON ASSOCIATES, Stoneham, Massachusetts
1988   Computer Operator
...Operated IBM 360 Computer to run variety of jobs for wholesale medical supply distributor.

EDUCATION BACKGROUND
QUINCY JUNIOR COLLEGE, Quincy, Massachusetts
...Associates Degree in Business Administration (1988)

COMPUTERS
Knowledge of IBM-based systems.
Software includes: Lotus 1-2-3, Multimate, dBase III Plus, FORTRAN, Pascal.

INTERESTS
Boating, skiing, backgammon.

- Format is clear and visually appealing.

- Use of ellipses differentiates this resume from others using bullets.

ASSISTANT PORTFOLIO MANAGER

CHRIS SMITH
178 Green Street
Arlington, VA 22201
(703) 555-5555

PROFESSIONAL OBJECTIVE
Seeking new challenges in **Finance,** where relevant education, experience and analytical, customer service, follow-up and problem-solving skills will be utilized and advanced.

CAREER HISTORY
1990-Present CANNON, SLOAT, ERICKSON, AND BANKS, INC., Arlington, VA
Assistant Portfolio Manager
- Set up all systems and files for Reconciliation Department; assumed responsibility for procedures and documentation relevant to this new unit (300 accounts).
- Ensure that all account monies are fully invested and that transaction requests are fulfilled in a timely and accurate manner.
- Personally responsible for portfolio of 18 accounts.
- Prepare cash flow analyses and verify/submit client quarterly reports.
- Maintain research files of stocks and bonds; assess and select municipal bonds presented by Brokers.
- Interact with bank and in-house Trading Department.

1989-1990 O'CONNOR PRINTING, Alexandria, VA
Promotional Sales Representative
- Generated new business and established new accounts through cold-calling, follow-up and the provision of detailed service and pricing information.

1988-1990 VIRGINIA STATE REPRESENTATIVE ELECTION COMMITTEE, Charlottesville, VA
Assistant Campaign Manager
- Assisted in the development and implementation of promotional programs; set up and coordinated fundraisers.

EDUCATION
SWEET BRIAR COLLEGE, Sweet Briar, VA
Bachelor of Science Degree in **Management/Finance,** January, 1988.

Course work included:

Management Information Systems	Managerial Accounting
Financial Accounting	Stock Market Investments
Data Processing Statistics	International Economics
Money and Banking	Monetary Management

Internship: Served VTA Advisory Board as Assistant Budget Analyst.
- Reviewed budget proposals from various departments; broke down and analyzed previous budgets, verified figures and made recommendations to Budget Director based on results.

- Resume includes course work that corresponds to the position desired.

- Work history is stated in reverse chronological order, with most recent employment listed first.

AUDIT MANAGER

CHRIS SMITH
178 Green Street
Pawtucket, RI 02860
(401) 555-5555

OBJECTIVE
An Audit Management position with the possibility of cross-functional responsibilities in Project Development.

SUMMARY OF QUALIFICATIONS
Versatile, respected management professional with high standards of integrity. Adept at sizing up situations, analyzing facts, and developing alternative courses of action in order to increase productivity. Form quality liaisons and relationships easily, and instill a high level of confidence at all levels.

PROFESSIONAL EXPERIENCE

Auditing Manager   1989-Present
MINISTRY OF NATIONAL EDUCATION   Hamburg, Germany
- Controlled contract management of an education improvement project.
- Assisted Execution Bureau in establishing Accounting System.
- Controlled all project financial operations; verified financial statements, justification of expenses, requests, and disbursements.
- Established internal control systems for various investment categories.

Financial Advisor   1986-1989
NATIONAL PORT AUTHORITY   Port au Prince, Haiti
- Established control mechanism for financial plans and budgets; monitored the management of all financial resources and established a treasury service.
- Restructured Control and Budget Service; updated accounting procedures.
- Implemented an evaluation system for budget execution; took corrective actions as necessary; updated and restructured the Procurement Service.
- Monitored accuracy and timely transmittal of monthly financial statements; assisted in the establishment of a computerized accounting system.
- Member, Supervisory Board of Management Information Systems; controlled all financial resources.

Chief Financial Analysis/Evaluation and Control Department   1982-1986
MINISTRY OF PLANNING   Port au Prince, Haiti
- Analyzed development projects' annual operations plans, internal and external, physical and financial project executions.
- Participated in social housing project financed by the United Nations.
- Represented the Ministry at the Management Board of Canadian Government Retrocession Funds.

EDUCATION
BOSTON UNIVERSITY, Boston, MA, B.A. Economics, 1980.

- Job descriptions detail candidate's responsibilities and accomplishments.

- Education is listed at bottom of resume because candidate's practical experience outweighs his/her degree.

AUDITOR (Internal)

CHRIS SMITH
178 Green Street
Kent, Ohio 44242
(216) 555-5555

PROFESSIONAL EXPERIENCE

5/90 to   VORHEES MEDICAL INSTRUMENTS, Kent, Ohio
present   **Senior Internal Auditor**
- Supervise financial and operational audits of construction projects, subsidiaries, special projects and employee benefit packages.

1/89 to   SUGAR AND SPICE APPAREL, Gambier, Ohio
5/90   **Staff Accountant**
- Participated in the auditing of client companies' financial statements.

6/83 to   JAMESTOWN OIL CORPORATION
1/89   Houston, Texas, 10/86 to 1/89
Operations Auditor
- Performed operational audits and wrote audit programs for various company affiliates.

Micah, Saudi Arabia, 11/83 to 10/86
Project Auditor
- Audited and coordinated payments of 54 pipeline construction contractors. Project successfully complete within $2 billion budget.
- Supervised staff of two in the preparation of a $12 million quarterly invoice.

Houston, Texas, 6/83 to 11/83
Operations Auditor Trainee
- Performed service station audits and region functional audits.

EDUCATION

OHIO STATE UNIVERSITY, Columbus, Ohio
Currently enrolled in part-time MBA program
BOWLING GREEN STATE UNIVERSITY, Bowling Green, Ohio
Bachelor of Arts Degree in Business Administration, 1983
Dale Carnegie Course in Effective Speaking and Human Relations

CERTIFICATION

Certified Public Accountant Examination
Passed, November, 1990 Pennsylvania
Certified Internal Auditor Examination
Passed, May, 1989

- "Certification" heading draws attention to candidate's specific professional qualifications.

- Specific dates of employment reflect candidate's rapid career advancement.

AUImGr (IRS)

AUDITOR (IRS)

CHRIS SMITH
178 Green Street
Birmingham, AL 35294
(205) 555-5555

OBJECTIVE
A challenging position within the fields of Tax Accounting or Investment.

SUMMARY OF QUALIFICATIONS
- Thorough knowledge of individual income, employment and excise tax laws and regulations, IRS Service policies, selected tax forms. Experienced in preparation of individual and employment tax returns. Proficient accounting, bookkeeping, and problem-solving skills.

EMPLOYMENT HISTORY

10/89 to Present   **Taxpayer Service Representative**
INTERNAL REVENUE SERVICE   Birmingham, AL
- Respond to customer inquiries, regarding tax filing procedures and policies for individual income and businesses.
- Explain various IRS bills and notices to taxpayers and set up installment agreements.
- Maintain knowledge of current IRS tax documents, enforcement policies, forms, laws, notices, regulations, Service organization and policies.
- Develop understanding of "tiered" interview techniques, to determine taxpayers ability to pay outstanding tax obligations.

1/89 to 5/89   **Intern**
PRICE, PATTON, AND TATE   Atlanta, GA
- Operated QUOTRON machinery, posted trades and performed general office and receptionist duties.

Summer 1988   **Sales Intern - China Department**
JAKES DEPARTMENT STORE   Selma, AL
- Provided customer service and resolved consumer and departmental complaints.
- Created displays and initiated sale of merchandise.
- Controlled inventory and trained employees.

Summer 1987   **Ticket Salesperson**
BUDGIE BUS TOURS   Montgomery, AL
- Maintained bookkeeping records, deposited currency and resolved customer complaints.
- Commended for achievement of second highest ticket seller in twelve years.

EDUCATION
ARMSTRONG STATE COLLEGE   Savannah, GA
Bachelor of Arts Degree: Management, May 1989

COMPUTERS
IBM Mainframe, DOS, WordStar, Lotus 1-2-3

- Job objective is supported by the facts and accomplishments stated in resume.

- Summary of qualifications emphasizes candidate's skills in concise terms.

BANK ADMINISTRATOR

CHRIS SMITH
178 Green Street
Boulder, CO 80309
(303) 555-55555

OBJECTIVE
A challenging career where administrative experience, motivation and a commitment to excellence will be utilized and advanced.

SUMMARY OF QUALIFICATIONS
- Five years of progressive, professional experience; extensive mutual funds background.
- Computer experience includes: Wang word processor, Data General, and IBM.
- Developed interpersonal and communication skills, having dealt with a diversity of professionals, clients, and staff members.
- Self-motivated; able to set effective priorities to achieve immediate and long-term goals and meet operational deadlines.
- Adapt easily to new concepts and responsibilities.
- Function well independently and as team member; respond best in fast-paced, high-pressure environment.

PROFESSIONAL EXPERIENCE
BOULDER BANK & TRUST CO., Boulder, CO   8/89-7/94
Senior Specialist, 7/93-7/94
Controlled correspondence flow. Input/output data utilizing Data General System. Completed back log and time sheets. Supervised support staff. Generated reports. Well-versed in Securities and Exchange Commission rules and regulations.

Priority Response Administrator, 12/92-7/93
Administered/resolved shareholder inquiries; enhanced time frame. Researched complex and lengthy data maintaining rigid deadlines. Handled general clerical responsibilities; generated reports.

Priority Response Specialist, 8/92-12/92
Dealt with share owners; provided information on work itemization, research, and adjustments. Handled special projects and clerical functions.

Shareholders Communications Specialist, 2/91-12/92
Communicated directly with shareholders by telephone and letter; provided information on mutual funds, net asset values, policies, and procedures. Analyzed, calculated, and adjusted daily shareholder account activities.

Customer Service Representative, 8/89-1/91
Researched/corrected billing errors; utilized C.R.T. system. Provided account information.

RELEVANT EDUCATION
Certified in ABCD Bank Training Program, 1989

- Layout is clean and well-organized.

- Resume de-emphasizes the fact that candidate's experience is at one company.

BANK TREASURER

CHRIS SMITH
178 Green Street
Rome, GA 30161
(706) 555-5555

PROFESSIONAL OBJECTIVE
A treasurer position in banking.

SUMMARY OF QUALIFICATIONS
- Extensive experience in Business Development, Commercial Loan Operations, Credit Analysis, Loan Review, Asset/Liability Review, Financial Analysis, and Planning
- Refinement and implementation of management systems, administrative policies and operational procedures.
- Experience hiring/terminating, training, scheduling, motivating, and supervising staffs.
- Forecasting, preparing, and monitoring expenditures of operational budgets.
- Exceptional interpersonal, client service, liaison, and follow-through skills.

PROFESSIONAL BACKGROUND
WYNDCREST BANK, Rome, GA
Treasurer (1989 to Present)
- Manage day-to-day operations and develop new business at branch with staff of 16 to 20 and deposit base of $16 million.
- Work with ATM and acquired maintenance skills.
- Hire/terminate, schedule, evaluate, and supervise administrative and support staff.
- Conduct long range and day-to-day planning for branch.
- Provide customer service through resolution of problems, explanation of bank services and policies, and knowledge of financial planning.

Branch Manager (1984 to 1989)
- Supervised total operation of branch with $7 million deposit base in Rome Center.
- Within three-month period, added 220 deposit accounts and increased deposits to bring branch's deposit base by 244%.
- Trained personnel in Creative Merchandising, Marketing, and Sales Development.
- Implemented turn-around for Winter Square Branch with 36 employees and $22 million in assets.
- Streamlined and reorganized Customer Service Operations.

EDUCATIONAL BACKGROUND
PAINE COLLEGE, School of Banking, Augusta, GA
Certificate of Completion, 1984
ATLANTA INSTITUTE OF BANKING, Atlanta, GA
Maintained A Average through completion of eight courses, 1984
OGLETHORPE UNIVERSITY, Atlanta, GA
Bachelor of Science in Business Administration, 1983

PROFESSIONAL AFFILIATIONS
Rome Business Association Member

- Dynamic action verbs give resume impact.

- Statistics and dollar figures quantify candidate's accomplishments.

BILLING CLERK

CHRIS SMITH
178 Green Street
Derry, NH 03038
(603) 555-5555

SUMMARY OF QUALIFICATIONS:
Professional experience includes the following areas:
- Office supervision, prioritizing and coordination office work flow.
- Porcessing billing and collecting delinquent accounts.
- Resolving customer problems and complaints.
- Familiar with utility, insurance and credit environments.

SKILLS:

IBM and Wang PC's, Lotus 1-2-3, Tesseract, TELEX terminals, typing, calculator.

EXPERIENCE:

REGIONAL WATER QUALITY CONTROL AUTHORITY, Derry, NH
Senior Customer Service/Billing Clerk (1992-Present)
- Process semi-annual sewer bills, calculating interest and penalty charges.
- Answer customer inquiries, problems and complaints, composing correspondence.
- Process all procedures and collect delinquent accounts.
- Compile and prepare monthly cash flow reports.
- Act as Supervisor when needed, prioritizing and coordinating office work flow.

THE PRAGMATIC INSURANCE COMPANY, Manchester, MA
Administrative Technician - Service Bureau, Group Administration (1988-1992)
- Processed and billed clients choosing C.O.B.R.A. (benefits continuation).
- Provided customer service, researched accounts and informed clients of their monthly rate and payment.
- Processed and deposited monthly payments.
- Created and maintained monthly rosters.

COMMERCIAL REPORTS & TITLE AGENCY, Nashua, NH
Office Manager (1984-1988)
- Interviewed, hire, train and supervise office employees.
- Traveled throughout the state of New Hampshire, completing title searches and credit reports and supervising field staff.
- Assisted clients with any mortgage or title insurance questions.

EDUCATION:

Pennsbury High School, Levittown, PA - Diploma (1976)

■ Valuable computer and administrative skills are highlighted.

■ Work experience is emphasized, while limited education is de-emphasized.

BILLING SUPERVISOR

CHRIS SMITH
178 Green Street
Miami, FL 33054
(305) 555-5555

EXPERIENCE

The Pearl Co.   Miami, FL
Limited Partnerships Accounting and Administration
BILLING SUPERVISOR   9/88 to Present
Created/implemented billing system for reimbursing departmental salaries,
rent and out-of-pocket expenses. Initiated Accounts Receivable system using
Data General and Lotus. Researched and projected yearly management fees and
cash distributions. Supervised daily preparation of invoices and reconciling
monthly bank statements.

CONTROL ACCOUNTANT   6/86 to 9/88
Monitored daily reconciliation of transfer agent and share-holder records
for Mutual Fund Division. Supervised daily posting and reconciliation of
demand deposit accounts and settlement with client's share and dollar
positions. Reconciled and reported net changes in Fund daily share
positions.

Bank of Miami   Miami, FL
CASH CONTROLLER   11/85 to 6/86
Monitored incoming shipments of coin and currency, handling large cash
orders from banks and companies. Filled out currency transaction reports.
Distributed and collected moneys from tellers.

FOREIGN TELLER   3/85 to 10/85
Bought and sold foreign currency and travelers checks. Performed wire
transfers. Typed bank drafts. Maintained exchange rates.

COMMERCIAL TELLER   7/84 to 4/85
Cashed and deposited customer checks. Verified signature of business and
individual customers. Typed cashier and certified checks. Trained new
tellers. Assisted supervisor with automatic teller machines.

EDUCATION

Rollins College   Winter Park, FL
B.S., BUSINESS ADMINISTRATION candidate   1985 to Present

Boca Raton Jr. College   Boca Raton, FL
A.S., ACCOUNTING   1985
Major: Accounting

TECHNICAL SKILLS

Experience in certification stamp, protechtograph machine, regiscope, CRT
and data entry. Proficient in Lotus and Multi-Mate.

- ■ Promotions within both companies demonstrate candidate's strong work performance.

- ■ No descriptive copy on education allows candidate to emphasize work history.

BOOKKEEPER (Agency)

CHRIS SMITH
178 Green Street
Albuquerque, NM 87140
(505) 555-5555

OBJECTIVE
A challenging career opportunity in Accounting/Bookkeeping.

SUMMARY OF QUALIFICATIONS
- More than 18 years experience in Accounting/Bookkeeping.
- Able negotiator/liaison, dealing with professionals, clients and staff.
- Accurate, organized, aware of importance of meeting deadlines and maintaining smooth work-flow.
- Computer literate.

EXPERIENCE
CHUTES AND LADDERS DAYCARE CENTER, Albuquerque, NM
Agency Bookkeeper   5/91-Present
Handle cash disbursement, verify vendor invoices, generate weekly checks. Administer General Ledger, fund coding and checkbook maintenance for agency accounts. Record transactions; maintain up-to-date bank balances. Prepare/post disbursements and monthly invoices to state and municipal contractors.

Voucher Bookkeeper   6/90-5/91
Processed current/outstanding requests for reimbursement for over 300 providers (3,000 payments). Dealt with underpayment/overpayment and rate changes; verified adjustment requests against payment history; issued/recorded advance payment checks. Ensured immediate update of computerized fiscal files and accounts payable to meet rigid deadline schedule. Assisted providers; verified payments for auditors. Oversaw part-time staff.

Assistant Bookkeeper   4/88-6/90
Supervised current/outstanding invoice payment approval, computerized data input, invoice verification, posting to Ledger and dispatching checks.

SAWYER REALTY TRUST, Las Cruces, NM   9/84-4/88
Part-time Bookkeeper
Recorded rent payments, paid banks/vendors, reconciled bank statements.

EDUCATION
NEWBURY JUNIOR COLLEGE, Boston, MA
Associate Degree in Accounting, 1984

MONTREAL UNIVERSITY, DIVISION OF CONTINUING EDUCATION,
Montreal, Canada
Bachelor of Arts Degree, Teaching/Education (equivalent)

■ Specifically listing quantity of work produced indicates candidate's ability to handle heavy work loads.

■ Summary of qualifications highlights candidate's achievements.

BOOKKEEPER (General)

CHRIS SMITH
178 Green Street
Dickinson, ND 58601
(701) 555-5555

OBJECTIVE
To contribute acquired bookkeeping/office management skills to an organization offering opportunities for advancement.

SUMMARY OF QUALIFICATIONS
- Over three years of bookkeeping and managerial experience.
- Adept at motivating/delegating staff to increase efficiency and profit margin.
- Developed interpersonal and communication skills, having dealt with a diversity of professionals, clients, and staff members.
- Self-motivated; able to set effective priorities to achieve immediate and long-term goals and meet operational deadlines.
- Adapt easily to new concepts and responsibilities.

PROFESSIONAL EXPERIENCE

BITTERROOT NATURAL FOODS, Bismarck, ND   1991-Present
Manager/Bookkeeper
Supervised staff. Provided customer service. Administered bookkeeping, cash intake/reconciliation, and order placement.

DIVA HAIR SCHOOL, Grand Forks, ND   1988-1991
Office Manager, Administrative Office
Supervised operations and retail counter. Tracked student hours; prepared job postings. Maintained inventory. Utilized IBM compatible word processing system.

ADDER AND SONS, Dickinson, ND   1986-1988
Verification/Payables Clerk
Verify/Balance invoices, folders and check books. Assist in processing Accounts Receivable.

THE DARNELL BANK, Tar Creek, ND   1984-1986
Teller
Handled cash transactions and customer service.

EDUCATION

MINOT STATE COLLEGE, Minot, ND   1984-1985
Courses in Accounting and Management

COMPUTERS

Proficient in MacIntosh and IBM compatible

- Job-related course work is included.

- Chrono-fuctional format provides both a summary of qualifications and dates of employment.

BOOKKEEPING CLERK

CHRIS SMITH
178 Green Street
Eden Prairie, MN 55347
(902) 555-5555

<u>**OBJECTIVE**</u>

A challenging position in bookkeeping.

<u>**PROFESSIONAL EXPERIENCE**</u>

ASSOCIATES, INC., Eden Prairie, MN
Bookkeeping Clerk, 1992-Present
• Monitor general ledger and investors' monthly reports.
• Oversee A/R and A/P staff to ensure accuracy of accounts.
• Monitor payroll taxes for accuracy and on-time payments.
• Manage multiple accounts for real estate developer with commercial and residential properties in several states.

MORNINGSIDE CO., Hopkins, MN
Bookkeeping Clerk, 1990-1992
• Supervised general ledger through trial balance, as well as A/P, payroll, and payroll tax returns.
• Converted bookkeeping procedures from one write system to in-house computer system.
• Coordinated department's work flow.

Accounts Receivable Clerk, 1989-1990

HAWTHORNE MEDICAL CENTER, Howard Lake, MN
Secretary, Cardiac Care Unit, 1987-1989
• Scheduled patients for appointments and tests.
• Answered phones, troubleshoot problems.
• Transcribed doctors' orders, order supplies.
• Maintained patient records, set up charts.

EXCELSIOR CORP., Mankato, MN
Secretary to Vice-President, 1985-1987
• Performed office duties such as monitoring personnel files, scheduling, and paying operating expenses.

Receptionist, 1984-1985
• Answered phones, scheduled travel, acted as liaison between management and staff.

<u>**EDUCATION**</u>

SOUTHWEST STATE UNIVERSITY, Marshall, MN
Accounting Courses, 1988-1989

■ Boldface and underlining attracts attention to key information.

■ Resume illustrates continual career progression.

BUDGET ANALYST

CHRIS SMITH
178 Green Street
Los Angeles, CA 90031
(310) 555-5555

EXPERIENCE

2/91-   **Golden Life Insurance Company**   Los Angeles, CA
Present BUDGET ANALYST
- Balance $1.3 billion budget maintained on IBM mainframe
- Reconcile accounts on ISA/ABC system to other financial systems
- Assist management in budget preparation
- Conduct training classes on the financial system for upper-level management
- Prepare comparison of expense to budget reports for executives
- Submit accounts and I.R.S. filing for the Political Action Committee.
- Generate financial analysis projects using Focus Report Writing and Lotus 1-2-3, including macro programming

6/87-   **The Pacific**   Los Angeles, CA
2/91   FUNDING ANALYST
- Prepared contract proposals and illustrative cost calculations
- Constructed Actuarial Valuation Report for individual clients
- Determined the minimum and maximum contribution allowable by law for the I.R.S.
- Assured accuracy of the data base
- Developed plan costs and analyzed actuarial gains/losses

ACCOUNTING TECHNICIAN
- Managed money market mutual fund for 60 corporate clients
- Balanced Trial Balance and generated journal entries
- Maintained, compared and reconciled the fund on three computer systems
- Communicated with other departments, field personnel, and clients
- Prepared financial statements
- Assisted system analysts in preparation and implementation of new computer system

EDUCATION

UNIVERSITY OF WASHINGTON   Seattle, WA
Bachelor of Science Degree in Finance

ACTIVITIES

Swimming, reading, crafts, travel

■ Bullets make resume easy to read.   ■ Job descriptions are thorough.

CERTIFIED PUBLIC ACCOUNTANT (CPA)

CHRIS SMITH, CPA
178 Green Street
Houston, TX 77029
(713) 555-5555

EXPERIENCE

1/88 to present   **Mastermind Engineering**   Houston, TX
Accounting Manager
- Complete SEC Reporting and Disclosure forms.
- Manage general ledger closing and maintenance.
- Supervise and review all areas of accounting and finance.
- Administrate 401K pension plan.
- Implement accounting/payroll/manufacturing software.

3/82 to 12/87   **Dunphy & Reilly, Inc.**   Houston, TX
Senior Internal Auditor
- Conducted operational and financial audits of manufacturing subsidiaries.
- Designed and implemented audit programs to test the efficiency of all aspects of accounting controls.
- Recommended changes and improvements to corporate and divisional management.
- Trained and supervised staff auditors in all aspects of the audit engagement.
- Involved with corporate management in areas of acquisition and corporate development.

5/80 to 3/82   **Churchill North**   Houston, TX
Supervising Senior Accountant
- Supervised, planned, and budgeted audit engagements.
- Prepared financial statements and tax filings.
- Reported directly to management regarding internal control, making recommendations for improvement.
- Recruited, trained, supervised and evaluated staff accountants.
- Gained experience from a variety of client assignments, including those in manufacturing, real estate and nonprofit industries.
- Proficient in the use of spreadsheet packages.

CERTIFICATION   CPA, State of Texas

EDUCATION   **UNIVERSITY OF TEXAS**   Houston, TX
Bachelor of Science, Accountancy, May 1980
Associate in Science, Management, May 1978
- Overall GPA 3.4/4.0
- Accountancy GPA 3.6/4.0
- Participated in Accounting Honors Program

REFERENCES   Available upon request

■ Including professional licensure and accreditations can be essential for certain fields of work.

■ Specific dates of employment (month and year) are ideal for candidates with no gaps in work history.

CHIEF FINANCIAL OFFICER (CFO)

CHRIS SMITH
178 Green Street
Marylhurst, OR 97036
(503) 555-5555

EMPLOYMENT HISTORY

1986 to Present **KALEIDOSCOPE HOTELS, INC.**, Marylhurst, OR
Vice-President of Finance & Administration, (1990 to Present)
Directed and oversaw the accounting function for thirteen hotels located throughout Northwest with annual sales in excess of $120M. Supervised Home Office staff of twenty with extended authority over 100 field employees.
- Directed the annual budget process from original business plan to final approval.
- Administered self-insurance programs for Workers' Compensation by directing attorney selection, investigations and claim settlements.
- Designed system to track capital spending.

Company (Corporate) Controller, (1988 to 1990)
Reported all consolidated financial performance for the divisions of Kaleidoscope, which consisted of hotels, residential apartments, telecommunications stations and a construction division. Supervised a staff of fifteen.
- Directed selection and implementation of new accounting software for real estate divisions of the company, and new payroll system for entire company which processed payroll for 6,000 employees in seven states.
- Integral member of team that implemented change from a premium-based Workers' Compensation insurance policy to a self-insured one.

Assistant Controller, (1986 to 1988)
- Supervised an office staff of ten in the daily accounting function.
- Set-up accounting offices in all thirteen hotels in the division.
- Chaired committee that selected automated time and attendance payroll system for entire company which ultimately achieved annual savings of over $500K.

1983 to 1986 **HUBERT FINE FRANCHISE SYSTEMS, INC.**, Holyoke, MA
Accounting Manager, (1985 to 1986)
Responsible for accounting functions and preparation of annual budget for this "spin off" corporation of Marriott Corporation's purchase of the Howard Johnson Company. Supervised a staff of six.
- Worked with Marriott Corporation on pre- and post-acquisition adjustments.

Staff Accountant, (1983 to 1985)
Prepared corporate financial statements for senior management and annual audit.

EDUCATION

Oregon State University, Corvallis, OR
Bachelor of Science, Accounting, 1983

COMPUTER PROGRAMS

Microsoft Word, DOS, Lotus 1-2-3, Pascal

■ Employment history provides brief job summaries while highlighting specific accomplishments.

■ Chronological format illustrates a clear career path.

COLLECTIONS OFFICER

CHRIS SMITH
178 Green Street
Scituate, MA 02066
(617) 555-5555

EXPERIENCE:

11/90-6/94   NANTASCOT BANK, Scituate, MA
International Loan/Collection Specialist
Provided and/or coordinated full loan service functions to International Corporate, Commercial, and Correspondent Financial concerns. Researched and resolved customer problems and inquiries. Processed ingoing and outgoing documentary collections. Maintained and updated all loan and loan-related documentation, including foreign tax credit system. Utilized IBM PC, on-line system.

10/89-6/94   JEREMY PEARL FURNITURE, Weymouth, MA
Credit Collector (part-time)
Telephone collections of past due accounts. Informed customers in regard to their account status and payment options. Credit bureau and fraud account functions. Related typing and data entry. Successfully collected 75% of assigned accounts.

12/88-7/89   HOUSES-R-US REALTORS, Weymouth, MA
Receptionist
Answered phones and provided customer support. Responsible for typing and researching.

7/85-11/88   MASSBANK, Boston, MA
Trade Service Assistant
Assisted and informed customers regarding debits and credits to their accounts. Accurately compiled and updated customer files using IBM PC. Maintained word processing seminar reservation list.

EDUCATION:

1986-1988   UNIVERSITY OF MASSACHUSETTS, Boston, MA
Courses in Personnel Management, English, Communications

1984-1986   QUINCY COLLEGE, Quincy, MA
Courses in Communications, Typing, English

References Available Upon Request

■ Limited education is strengthened by listing applicable course work.

■ Resume emphasizes candidate's strong work history.

CREDIT ANALYST

CHRIS SMITH
178 Green Street
Grace City, OH 58445
(216) 555-5555

SUMMARY:
- Five years experience in retail banking and commercial lending.
- Adept at credit/financial analysis.
- Proficient in analysis of financial statements.
- Fluent in Dutch; knowledgeable in conversational and written German.
- Naturalized U.S. Citizen.

EDUCATION: OHIO STATE UNIVERSITY - Graduate School of Management, Columbus, OH
M.B.A., Concentration: Finance, May 1994
Courses included: International Finance, Money and Capital Markets, Investments, Corporate Finance, Corporate Financial Reporting, and Global Macroeconomics.
- GPA in Major: 3.8/4.0

Bachelor of Science, Business Administration, 1989
Concentration: Accounting and Finance

EXPERIENCE: WISTERIA BANK, Grace City, OH
Commercial Loan Credit Analyst, 1992-Present
Provide analytical services as part of lending team. Analyze/evaluate financial statements. Develop pro-forma statements and cash flow projections. Document findings; prepare independent recommendations on advisability of granting credits for corporate lenders.

Senior Personal Banker, 1991-1992
Assisted in branch administration. Oversaw branch overdraft reports. Reviewed/executed consumer loans. Supervised the vault area; audited tellers; provided customer service.

Personal Banker, 1989-1991
Established/serviced professional clientele accounts. Expedited investments in treasury bills, repurchase agreements, CD's, retirement accounts, and discount brokerage for bank clients. Assisted branch corporate lender weekly on a revolving commercial loan.
- Sold 16 retirement accounts in one day; resulted in an IRA sales award for branch.
- Achieved several awards for bank product sales.

COMPUTERS: Lotus 1-2-3, IBM, MS-DOS, word processing software

---

■ Statistics and dollar figures quantify candidate's accomplishments.

■ Professional memberships show commitment to field.

CREDIT MANAGER

CHRIS SMITH
178 Green Street
Billings, MT 59102
(406) 555-5555

OBJECTIVE:

A responsible position in credit management.

WORK HISTORY:

WARD COLLECTIONS AGENCY, Billings, MT   7/87 to Present

5/93 to Present   **District Manager**

- Handled collections for major, local and national clients with a staff of 55 employees. Hired and trained sales and collections personnel; performed evaluations and salary reviews.
- Evaluated attorney performance and audit results.
- Implemented Human Resource policies at branch level for all sales, clerical and collection personnel.
- Produced over $10 million in revenue and $3 million in profit.
- Increased revenues and profits by 18%.

6/90-5/93   **Assistant Branch Manager**

- Reported to the Executive Vice-President of MONEY Assistance Agency. Servicing for the $75 million corporation.
- Set up office and hired personnel.
- Established a training program and supervised production. Set goals at 15% profit margins. Collected $2 million in 4 years.
- Achieved a 200% growth in collection of moneys leading to department expansion from three to eleven employees.

7/86-6/90   **Division Supervisor**

- Reported to the Executive Vice-President of MONEY Assistance Agency.
- Provided client servicing for the $75 million corporation.
- Set up office and hired personnel.
- Established a training program and supervised production.
- Set goals at 15% profit margins.
- Collected $2 million in 4 years.
- Achieved a 200% growth in collection of monies leading to department expansion from three to eleven employees.

EDUCATION:

B.S. Degree in Management, (1987)
Rocky Mountain College, Billings, MT

Associate Degree in Management and Marketing, (1984)
Alverno College, Milwaukee, WI 53215

PROFESSIONAL MEMBERSHIPS:

Credit Managers of America
Creditors Council on Fraud

■ Specific dates of employment (month and year) are ideal for candidates with no gaps in work history.

■ Percentages and dollar amounts quantify candidate's accomplishments.

FINANCIAL ANALYST

CHRIS SMITH
178 Green Street
Omaha, NE 68182
(402) 555-5555

OBJECTIVE
To contribute financial skills to an organization offering managerial opportunities.

SUMMARY OF QUALIFICATIONS
- More than three years of progressive experience in the financial field.
- Developed interpersonal and communication skills, having dealt with a diversity of clients, staff members.
- Self-motivated; able to set effective priorities and implement decisions to meet operational deadlines.
- Adapt easily to new concepts and responsibilities.

PROFESSIONAL EXPERIENCE

8/88-
Present

BRIDELL BANK AND TRUST CO., Omaha, NE
Corporate Accounting Analyst, Comptrollers Division
Prepared/analyzed income-related statements, balance sheet and earnings schedules for $9 billion corporation and subsidiaries. Compiled 10k, annual, federal reserve, management, and analyst reports. Utilized trend reports to analyze balance sheet and income statement key ratios. Prepared Gap report; established General Ledger accounts.

2/88-6/88

Summers 1985, 1986
CARTEL, BANK, Wayne, NE
Intern, Presidential Suite CSR
Serviced depositors with accounts in excess of $100,000; reconciled accounts. Handled bookkeeping, customer relations, and check verification.

8/87-12/87

THE BANK OF ROME, Rome, Italy
Relationship Analyst - AIESEC Intern
Researched financial reports to support quantitative analysis of bank's relationship with foreign correspondents.

EDUCATION

UNIVERSITY OF NEBRASKA AT OMAHA, Omaha, NE
Bachelor of Science, Finance, May 1987

COMPUTER SKILLS

Lotus/Symphony, DOS, IBM mainframe, WordStar, Lotus macros. Knowledge of basic programming.

- ■ Separate category for computer experience calls attention to candidate's technical knowledge.

- ■ Highly specific job descriptions illustrate depth of candidate's knowledge and experience.

FINANCIAL CONSULTANT (Consumer Markets)

CHRIS SMITH
178 Green Street
Princeton, NJ 08540
(609) 555-55555

EXPERIENCE: **XYZ FINANCIAL CONSULTANTS,** Princeton, NJ
July 1990- Present
Financial Consultant, Consumer Markets
- Developed $11 million client base through aggressive prospecting campaign.
- Successfully built portfolios that include stocks, bonds, options, and insurance products for more than 450 clients.
- Implemented financial plans and operations through account development and growth.

October 1988-July 1990
Sales Associate
- Worked directly with the firm's top producer, profiling high net worth individuals for future business.
- Generated $20,000 in commissions for top producer through new account openings.
- Analyzed existing portfolios, assisting in development of accounts.

September 1986-October 1988
Customer Account Representative
- Supervised more than 35,000 accounts in the areas of trade settlement, NASD regulations, and customer inquiries.
- Reported recommendations to upper management.
- Acted as liaison between sales force and New York operations.

RELATED TRAINING: Successfully completed XYZ Financial Consultant Sales Training and Advanced Training programs at Princeton, NJ, headquarters.
Licensed in Series 6,7,63 and health and life insurance.

EDUCATION: IONA COLLEGE, Iona, NY
Bachelor of Arts degree in Economics, 1988
Concentration: Business Management

COMPUTER SKILLS: Lotus 1-2-3, JERSEYPRO, IBM compatible.

- Related training accentuates specific professional qualifications.

- Job descriptions include candidate's on-the-job accomplishments.

FINANCIAL CONSULTANT (General)

CHRIS SMITH
178 Green Street
Cookeville, TN 38502
(615) 555-5555

Objective A challenging position in the field of FINANCIAL COUNSELING, dealing directly with clients developing comprehensive financial plans.

Education Central Michigan University, Mount Pleasant, MI, 1991
Certificate in Investment Planning.

Northwestern University, Evanston, IL
Bachelor of Science Degree in Business Administration. (G.P.A. 3.7). 1988
Honors Graduate, Concentration in Marketing.

Experience Hillside Estates, Kalamazoo, MI, 1989-Present
Managing and monitoring all phases of the organization. Applied knowledge of market conditions and sales methods. Interfacing with clients and buyers in the sale and resale of manufactured homes. Interviewed and hired potential employees.

Springhouse Restaurant, Springfield, ND, 1985-1988
Assistant Manager. Coordinated restaurant operations; Trained and motivated employees in customer relations and the methods of maintaining good employer-employee relationships.

Foreign Friends, Inc., Chicago, IL, 1987
Participant in an intensive summer program culminating in four weeks of travel in South Africa; organized and executed programs to provide immunization shots. Became extremely aware of the need of flexibility in adjusting to changing conditions.

Affiliation Member of International Association of Financial Planners.

Strengths Self-motivating, excellent communication skills, able to deal effectively and productively with management, co-workers and the public, goal oriented, capable of the sustained effort necessary to take a project from conception to completion.

Interests Sailing, skiing, scuba diving, hiking, piano.

References Available upon request.

- Format draws attention to clearly stated objective.

- Impressive GPA lends weight to educational background.

FINANCIAL MANAGER (General)

CHRIS SMITH
178 Green Street
Seattle, WA 98122
(206) 555-5555

EMPLOYMENT HISTORY

January, **THE ATHENA GROUP, Seattle, WA**
1989 to **Manager of Finance**
Present Manage a group of three associates responsible for producing financial reports, all aspects of budgeting a $52M office, A/R, A/P, petty cash, expense reports, revenue collection and monthly closing for office of 284 associates. Responsibility to produce systems that generate the necessary financial information to determine our profitability. Systems track accrual revenue, accrual profit, cash revenue, cash profit, expenses by sub-groups and a new cost accounting system.

- Upon hiring into this position in July of 1992, had written off $3M of unbillable or uncollectable business. The office posted a 0% profit. Currently, looking to make a 5% accrual profit for this fiscal year.
- Designed a billing tracking system to allow team managers to determine where they stood on a monthly basis for revenue collection. The system projects where the team is in accordance with where they need to be in order to meet the goal of 5%.

Systems Analyst, Finance & Administration
Systems analyst for WANG minicomputer with 10 users. Administered COBRA software application, Health Care/Dependent Care Reimbursement System.

- Assisted in implementing new health care system. Installed remote connection for off-site claims processing.
- User liaison for billing system in place in 40 offices throughout US and Canada. Designed training materials, performed on-site training, troubleshooting via telecommunications.

Sept. 1987 to **FANFARE INTERNATIONAL, Tacoma, WA**
January, 1989 **Programmer/Analyst/Consultant**
- Provided large utility client with database software to track political campaign contributions. System provided feedback on how campaign contributions were distributed versus the way "supported" legislators voted on key issues.

EDUCATION

Longfellow University, Wordsworth, WA
Master's degree in MIS, anticipated December 1994

Barley College, Sioux City, Iowa
Bachelor of Arts in Economics, 1987
Minor in Computer Science

COMPUTERS

Languages: dBase, Clipper, RBase, BASIC, Pascal, DYNAMO
Applications: Lotus 1-2-3, WordPerfect, Windows, Excel, Symphony, OnLan, Carbon Copy
Operating Systems: DOS, Novell, IBM MVS
Hardware Platforms: PC's, WANG minicomputer, DEC PDP 1170, IBM 9370

- Computer section provides detail about candidate's technical knowledge.

- Candidate's work experience reads like a series of accomplishments, not just a list of job duties.

FINANCIAL PLANNER (Health)

CHRIS SMITH
178 Green Street
Tallahassee, FL 32307
(904) 555-5555

EMPLOYMENT HISTORY

1990 to Present **HEALTH PROVIDERS, Tallahassee, FL**
Director, Financial Planning and Reporting
Oversee all aspects of internal and external reporting including preparation of the annual report as well as quarterly and monthly reports to the Board of Directors and Senior Management. Coordinate development of the financial plan and track financial performance against plan. Supervise a department of twelve professionals.

- Successfully guided the financial planning and reporting function through significant transition as management restructured the Corporation to meet customer expectations. Results include Board and Management level reporting structured along business unit and product lines, significantly enhancing effectiveness.
- Selected and implemented Windows based LAN using advanced database, spreadsheet and desktop publishing software to create an integrated financial modeling, planning and reporting process. Reduced analysis and production time by 30%.
- Leader of successful integration project which merged financial operations/staff with corporation. Served as project leader reporting to CFO on all aspects of this six-month integration project. Completed project on time and within budget.
- Directly involved with senior management on an ongoing basis.

1987 to 1990 **THIBERGE TECHNOLOGIES, Miami, FL**
Manager, Accounting/Consolidations
Managed the Corporate Accounting function including foreign and domestic Consolidations for 15 Subsidiaries. Supervised three professionals and one clerical.

- Successfully managed the transition of the accounting function through decentralization of the entire company within timetable set by senior management.
- Selected, installed and implemented Micro Control (IMRS) consolidations software at corporate headquarters. Streamlined consolidation process, enhancing accuracy and reducing closing time by 25%.

1985 to 1987 **INTERNATIONAL CONSULTANTS, Boca Raton, FL**
Assistant Controller
Compiled financial, bank and tax reports. Served as principal liaison with bankers and outside auditors. Managed G/L, F/A, Consolidations and foreign exchange.

- Directed accounting function in a high growth environment. Managed function during expansion, growing from 8 to 30 professional and clerical staff.

EDUCATION

Florida University
Bachelor of Science, 1984
Major in Accounting and minor in Computer Science

COMPUTERS

PASCAL, FORTRAN, Lotus 1-2-3, IBM, Word

■ Job descriptions are straightforward and understandable.

■ Bullets call attention to candidate's achievements.

INSURANCE UNDERWRITER (General)

CHRIS SMITH
178 Green Street
Tempe, AZ 85287
(602) 555-5555

CAREER HISTORY

1979 to   SCRIMSHAW INSURANCE CO., Tempe, AZ
Present   **Underwriter, Personal Lines Insurance**, 1988 to Present
- Analyzed all personal lines of business to determine acceptability and to control, restrict or decline according to company guidelines.
- Handled computer- and manually-issued policies.
- Assisted in training Administrative and technical personnel either by direct training or set up of training schedules.
- Facilitated implementation of new programs by training new personnel.
- Kept abreast of changing policies, rates and procedures, explaining coverage, rules, forms and decisions to Agents, staff and insured.
- Briefed Agents on new services to stimulate sales.
- Responsible for all personal lines of business for the states of Arizona and New Mexico.
- Assisted in ensuring achievement of company productivity and profitability objectives.
- Resolved client grievances and misunderstandings.

Assistant Supervisor, Manual Rating and Policy Writing, 1984 to 1986
- Implemented Supervisory Controls; Delegated responsibilities, set objectives and monitored work.
- Evaluated staff performances based on results expected and achieved.
- Conducted audits.
- Implemented new programs through staff briefing, ongoing training and updating materials.

Senior Rater, 1984
- Rated and coded all lines of business for personal lines.
- Trained other Raters and introduced the Merit Rating Surcharge Program for Arizona Automobile (Commonwealth of Arizona).

Unmatched Mail Clerk, Record Department, 1979 to 1984
- Responsible for incoming mail for personal and commercial lines of business.

EDUCATION

- Underwriter Trainee, 1986 to 1987
- Completed program at Jones Underwriting School in Phoenix, Arizona and trained for 1 year to become an Underwriter.
- Ongoing Education has included the following classes: Effective Letter Writing, How to Conduct an Interview, Career Workshop, Speed Reading, Xerox Sales Course, Underwriting School (6-week program), Senior Underwriting Seminar, Listening Seminar, Supervisory Seminar.

■ Education section focuses on valuable job-related training.

■ Resume illustrates continual career progression.

INSURANCE UNDERWRITER (Senior)

CHRIS SMITH
178 Green Street
Gallant, AL 35972
(205) 555-5555

PROFESSIONAL BACKGROUND

1985 to **CONFEDERATE INSURANCE COMPANIES, Altoona, AL**
Present Senior Underwriter Analyst
- Responsible for underwriting complex commercial property referral accounts up to $200 million covering one-half of United States for property and casualty carrier for all lines.
- Advise and provide support for field staff and agents.
- Assist in development of training programs and manuals.
- Interpret state insurance regulations and legislation.
- Review corporate financial data and participate in audits.
- Write underwriting manuals for company personnel explaining underwriting philosophy and complicated insurance concepts.

Senior Property Underwriter
- Evaluated risks and contributed to departmental marketing through personal calls on agents to provide assistance, generate new business, and educate.
- Trained Underwriter Trainees and Underwriters.
- Authorized work from line Underwriters within Branch Letter of Authority.

1981 to **DALFINO & CONNELLY INSURANCE COMPANIES, Attalla, AL**
1984 Senior Commercial Property Underwriter
- Responsible for underwriting commercial packages for metropolitan and rural agencies in Wyoming and Colorado.
- Promoted from Assistant Commercial Underwriter to Underwriter and to Senior Underwriter.

1979 to **WALTON INSURANCE COMPANY, Gadsden, AL**
1980 Rate and Code Supervisor
- Managed Rate and Code operations including the issuance of policies and calculation of rates.
- Hired/terminated, trained, scheduled, and supervised staff of 15 Commercial and Personal Lines Raters.

1976 to **ALLSURE INSURANCE COMPANY, Birmingham, AL**
1978 Assistant Commercial Package Underwriter
- Underwrote commercial packages.
- Promoted from Commercial Package Rater to Assistant Commercial Package Underwriter in 1977.

EDUCATIONAL BACKGROUND

BIRMINGHAM-SOUTHERN COLLEGE, Birmingham, AL
Bachelor of Science Degree, 1976
Major: Management, Minors: Psychology, Economics

■ Layout is clean and well-organized.

■ Resume emphasizes candidate's strong career history.

INVESTMENT BROKER

CHRIS SMITH
178 Green Street
Dover, NH 03820
(603) 555-5555

OBJECTIVE   A challenging position in Investment Banking.

SUMMARY OF QUALIFICATIONS

- Performed various prospecting duties, including: acquiring of clientele for brokers, qualifying investors, conducting stock research and implementing procedures to organize client holdings.
- Obtained Series 7 and 63 Stock Broker Licensure.
- Experienced in coordinating sports activity programs for young people.

EXPERIENCE   **Prospector**   6/93 to Present
DOWNTOWN DOVER ASSOCIATES   Dover, NH
- Conducted stock research and updated various transactions.
- Contacted potential clients and assisted in establishing a clientele base.
- Implemented procedures for the organization of client holdings.

Prospector   8/92 to 5/93
BURKE & LAWLOR   Dover, NH
- Assisted in establishing and maintaining a client base for brokers.
- Contacted clients, researched stock and updated transactions.

Prospector   9/91 to 8/92
LAWRENCE, INC.   Dover, NH
- Solicited potential clients for brokers.
- Qualified investors and conducted stock research.

On-Site Coordinator   Summers - 89 to 91
DOVER PLAYGROUNDS   Dover, NH
- Supervised over 200 program participants.
- Calculated payroll for ten staff members.
- Coordinated scheduling for over eighty basketball games.
- Assigned referees and performed officiating duties.

EDUCATION   UNIVERSITY OF NEW HAMPSHIRE, 8/90 to Present   Dover, NH
Major: Economics
- Accumulated 117 credit hours and financed 100% of education expenses.
- Activities: Economics Society

INTERESTS   Basketball, Rugby Football Club, Golf, Reading

REFERENCES   Furnished upon request.

■ Achievements and activities are highlighted under education.

■ Personal interests can provide a great topic for conversation during a job interview.

JUNIOR ACCOUNTANT

CHRIS SMITH
178 Green Street
Boise, ID 83725
(208) 555-5555

EMPLOYMENT HISTORY
SPUD TRUST, Boise, ID

Junior Accountant (April 1993 to Present)
Supervise the Accounts Payable unit. Prepare monthly journal entries, oversee cash disbursements, expense recording and petty cash reconciliation. These responsibilities are in addition to the Accounting Technician position.

Accounting Technician (September 1989 to April 1993)
Process Accounts Payable, Agency Commissions and Policyholder Refunds for five companies. Prepare Travel and Entertainment reconciliations for all Vice-President expenses as well as reconciliation spreadsheets for all company telephone charges. Responsible for printing all vendor, claims, refund and agency commission checks, coding invoices, month end closing, filing, 1099 processing and vendor calls. Handle all telephone inquiries with verbal and written correspondence. Support the secretary for the Vice-President of Accounting.

Secretary to Vice-President of Finance (December 1987 to September 1989)
Type all correspondence and memos. Type, proofread and distribute all financial statements. Handle incoming calls to Accounting and Data Processing department and schedule all appointments. Assist in the processing of policyholder refunds, claims, agency commission checks. File accounts payable back-up.

EDUCATION
The Computer Network, Boise, ID
Completed Word Processing Certificate program, November, 1986
Fluent in Spanish

TECHNICAL SUMMARY
Lotus 1-2-3, Allways and Microsoft Word on IBM PC and MacIntosh, Wang Word processor, J.D. Edwards, Mapics, Symphony, IBM Text Management system, Wang, AS400, PC, Network.

REFERENCES
Available upon request.

■ Technical summary accentuates candidate's computer knowledge.

■ Resume format illustrates continual career progression.

LOAN ADMINISTRATOR

CHRIS SMITH
178 Green Street
Collister, ID 83706
(208) 555-5555

OBJECTIVE
To obtain a position within a multi-branch bank as a loan administrator.

WORK EXPERIENCE
1991- Bank of Boise, Collister, ID
Present **Loan Administrator,** Commercial Real Estate Division.
Duties include disbursement and tracking of loans, maintenance of the same and close contacts with customers and legal firms. Administer accounts and maintain contacts within bank and in the Pocatello office.

1988-1990 Garden City National Bank, Garden City, ID
Bank Reconciliation Clerk
Edited journal entries prior to posting. Processed invoices for payment. Determined proper budget account for coding of receipts. Reconciled bank accounts in U.S. currencies. Communicated with banks to clarify and resolve outstanding items as required.

1985-1987 The Tyler Corporation, Narupa, ID
Accounting Assistant, Finance Department
Verified accuracy and proper authorization of bills prior to payment, then processed bills. Reconciled accounts and wrote journal vouchers.

EDUCATION
College of Idaho, Caldwell, ID
Associates Degree, Accounting, 1985

COMPUTERS
Lotus 1-2-3, Wang word processor, Microsoft Word, WordPerfect, and IBM-compatible.

References available upon request.

■ Job objective is clearly defined.

■ Resume is easy and quick to read; only relevant details are included.

LOAN SERVICER

CHRIS SMITH
178 Green Street
Salt Lake City, UT 84117
(801) 555-5555

OBJECTIVE
A challenging position in the Business/Financial area.

SUMMARY
- Developed interpersonal skills.
- Self-motivated and able to function well in high-stress atmosphere.

EXPERIENCE

7/87-Present **THE MORMON BANK,** Salt Lake City, UT
Loan Servicer, Commercial and Real Estate Loans
Prepare customer billing and weekly/monthly reports; resolve customer problems. Set up/maintain customer legal and credit files. Record and adjust income in General Ledger. Process loan payments onto computerized system. Maintain tax and Insurance Escrow accounts; remit payments to respective institutions. Review loan documents. Responsible for general Portfolio management.

2/86-12/86 **ISLAND OF JAMAICA,** Negril, Jamaica
Cooperative Officer
Responsible for promotion and supervision of co-operative Societies, mainly Commercial Credit Unions.

11/83-12/86 **RICHARD'S RESTAURANT,** Montego Bay, Jamaica
Manager
Managed daily retail store functions. Supervised staff and inventory control. Maintained Accounting System; ensured viability and profitability of business.

9/78-9/83 **ISLAND OF JAMAICA,** Education Dept., Negril, Jamaica
School Teacher
Instructed children ages 10-13 in Mathematics, English Language, Reading, Social Studies, History.

VOLUNTEER POSITIONS
Appointed by government to local government administration; Member of Village Council, 5/83 to 12/86.
Elected member and subsequently Chairman of Board of Directors, Credit Union, 7/83-12/86.

EDUCATION
UNIVERSITY OF LIMBURG, The Netherlands
General Certificate in Education
Courses in Cooperative Principles, General Accounting and Financial Management

REFERENCES FURNISHED UPON REQUEST.

■ Volunteer positions highlight candidate's leadership qualities.

■ Education focuses on related course work.

MANAGEMENT ACCOUNTANT (Airline)

CHRIS SMITH, CMA, CPA
178 Green Street
Houston, TX 77251
(713) 555-5555

EXPERIENCE:

BLUE MOON AIRLINES - 1025 Blue Moon Boulevard, Houston, TX
Positions:
Senior Financial Analyst, Flight Operations (3/93-Present)
Manager, Cargo Accounting Automation (11/90-3/93)
Manager, Cargo Payables and Processing (12/88-11/90)
Supervisor, Freight & Mail Audit (9/86-12/88)
Responsibilities and Accomplishments:
- Prepared annual budgets, monthly forecasts, and strategic plans for operating department. Department budget was over $3 billion - 25% of total company budget. Increased sophistication and accuracy of budgeting and forecasting.
- Conducted detailed studies to identify cost savings. Contributed to productivity improvements saving $20 million annually. Recommended internal control procedures that saved $250,000 per year.
- Compared actual expenses to budget and investigated variances. Created various computer models and analytical tools to facilitate variance analysis.
- Summarized monthly financial results and reported to upper management.
- Monitored financial performance of 60 cost centers. Provided administrative support for personnel requisitions, capital requests, and budget preparation.
- Calculated monthly revenue. Prepared journal entries and audit schedules.
- Monitored accounts receivables of $35 million and initiated collection efforts.
- Supervised as many as 20 management employees and 60 clerks. Conducted system training for employees. Encouraged participation and empowered employees to take initiative. Developed a positive work environment.
- Integrated Blue Moon and In Flight airlines accounting functions following merger.

CERTIFICATION:

CERTIFIED PUBLIC ACCOUNTANT
State of Texas (1992)
CERTIFIED MANAGEMENT ACCOUNTANT
Institute of Management Accountants (1987)

EDUCATION:

RICE UNIVERSITY - Houston, TX
Graduated May 1984 - Bachelor of Accounting Science
Student Senate Vice-President and Chairman of the Senate Finance Committee

COMPUTER SKILLS:

PERSONAL COMPUTER
Proficiency with Lotus 123, WordPerfect, Harvard Graphics and LAN environment.
MAINFRAME
Planned, developed, and implemented two computer systems. Familiar with IBM and Unisys platforms - including MSA Ledger, TSO, DB2, QMF/SQL, and MAPPER. Demonstrated ability to query mainframe database and extract relevant information.

- Candidate avoids repetition by listing job titles and focusing on on-the-job responsibilities and accomplishments.

- Statistics and dollar figures quantify candidate's accomplishments.

MANAGEMENT ACCOUNTANT (Restaurant)

CHRIS SMITH
178 Green Street
Killington, VT 05751
(601) 555-5555

OBJECTIVE

A position in management accounting.

EDUCATION

University of Vermont, Burlington, VT
Bachelor of Science in Accounting, May 1993
Dean's List Student-GPA: 3.1-Honors Internship Program
Executive Vice-President/Fundraising Chairman - Zeta Beta Tau Fraternity: Organized special events that raised over $15,000. Lead meetings and coordinated activities. Acted as liaison between faculty and campus community. Served as a Big Brother, Burlington Boy's Club.

TECHNICAL SUMMARY

Lotus 1-2-3, WordPerfect 5.1, dBase+, Realworld Accounting Package

EMPLOYMENT HISTORY

1992 to **THE SIZZLER STEAK HOUSE,** Killington, VT
Present Management Accountant
Managed accounting operations and accounts payable department. Ensured use of correct accounts payable control factors. Reconciled bank and credit card accounts. Reviewed the general ledger and made adjustments for inter-company transactions. Prepared road tax documents for trucks throughout New England states. Monitored inventory transfers among branch locations.

1988 to 1991 **DIAL TONES,** Burlington, CT
Manager/Pay Phone Technician
Performed business and technical activities. Provided supervision, performance evaluation and training to technical staff of 7, delegating authority to collect revenues while maintaining equipment. Reconciled bank accounts and handled administrative record keeping.

1989 to 1992 **MAPLE TREE ARENA,** Burlington, VT
Manager
Directed concession activities for consecutive seasons, including financial record keeping, bank account reconciliation and food preparation. Directly supervised staff of 20 employees.

VOLUNTEER WORK

THE BURLINGTON SOUP KITCHEN, Burlington, Vermont
VERMONT VOLUNTEER INCOME TAX ASSISTANCE, Burlington, VT

ACTIVITIES

Achieved Brown Belt Karate Status
Uechi Karate Academy - Middlebury, Vermont
Tennis, Hockey

■ Volunteer work section accentuates community service.

■ Education section stresses relevant achievements.

MORTGAGE UNDERWRITER

CHRIS SMITH
178 Green Street
Conyers, GA 30207
(404) 555-5555

OBJECTIVE

To utilize analytical, communications, training and language skills in a financial institution or funding foundation.

SUMMARY OF QUALIFICATIONS

- More than three years of experience ranging from Compliance Administrator to Underwriter with a major, multi-branch mortgage company.
- Bachelor of Arts Degree in Political Science with minor in Spanish (Honors).
- Strong organizational skills and the ability to prepare and make presentations to individuals or groups.
- A team player with good management, coaching, teaching and communication skills necessary to promote services or concepts.
- Capable of rapid orientation and open to company-sponsored training in new areas which pose good career potential.

EXPERIENCE

UNDERWRITER
Finn Mortgages, Conyers, GA   1990-1994

- Evaluated the subject property and financial strength and credit worthiness of the borrowers.
- Authorized to approve loans of up to $300,000 based on documentation requirements of secondary market.
- Examined, evaluated and recommended approval of customer applications for jumbo loans and prepared jumbo loan packages (to $700,000) for review by major private investors.
- Served as advisor and answered general underwriting questions for loan processors and originators.

As Assistant Underwriter:
- Processed residential loan applications from initial application to closing.
- Assisted busy marketing representative in the origination process.
- Reviewed borrowers' loan applications to insure completeness of data; verified information listed on applications and obtained additional documents required for sale of loans to secondary market.
- Dealt with borrowers, attorneys, brokers and underwriters.
- Walked borrowers through the application process and trained assistant underwriters in new branches.

EDUCATION

Emory University, Atlanta, GA
Bachelor of Arts Degree, 1989
Major: Political Science - Minor: Spanish
Manager of Women's Varsity Softball Team 1986-1988
Member of IASEC (International Association of Students in Business and Economics)

- Summary of qualifications highlights candidate's achievements.

- Listing candidate's authorization level indicated high level of seniority.

PAYROLL MANAGER

CHRIS SMITH
178 Green Street
St. Paul, MN 55105
(612) 555-5555

CAREER
OBJECTIVE To secure a Senior Level position as Payroll Manager.

EXPERIENCE
1992 to   JASMINE HEART, INC., St. Paul, MN
Present   **PAYROLL MANAGER**
Management of multi-state payroll for 150 shops in North American and 10 shops in Canada for well-known apparel and home decor company.
- Act as systems administrator for combined Human Resources and Payroll System (produce 5,500 W-2s and 200 T-4s).
- Act as liaison between Finance, Human Resources, corporation executives and outside vendors.
- Monitor all payroll tax liabilities, filings, journal entries, accounts payable, wire transfers for direct deposits.

Accomplishments
- Continued operation of payroll Department in Newark, New Jersey while simultaneously re-establishing department in new St. Paul headquarters.
- Coordinated entire department move to new headquarters and oversaw all human resources payroll-related issues.
- Identified programming errors in Human Resources Payroll System; directed and oversaw corrections.

1988 to   ADAGIO LEASING, INC., Mankato, MN
1992   **PAYROLL MANAGER**
Supervised department team of 7. Coordinated a $40 million payroll for 3,000 employees.
- Managed and controlled 18 separate multi-state payrolls with 8 weekly union and non-union payrolls and 9 biweekly payrolls.
- Acted as interface liaison for all payroll coordination and assimilation for executive level financial departments and Internal Human Resources.

Accomplishments
- Allocated 6 months to correct, organize and implement 18 separate payrolls.
- Converted existing manual-worksheet system to full on-line computerized system.
- Revised procedures for customer audits of Adagio records, thus increasing revenue.

EDUCATION STATE UNIVERSITY OF NEW YORK AT CORTLAND - B.S., EDUCATION 1988

COMPUTERS Managistics/ADP on line payroll system, Comchea, Lotus 1-2-3, LAN, Windows, IBM PC

- Specific professional accomplishments are listed for each position held.

- Education is listed towards bottom of resume because candidate's practical experience outweighs his/her degree.

STAFF AUDITOR

CHRIS SMITH
178 Green Street
Loretto, PA 15940
(814) 555-5555

PROFESSIONAL EXPERIENCE

DEVONSHIRE EQUIPMENT, INC., Loretto, PA   1990-Present
Staff Auditor
- Plan, identify, and test controls; present findings and recommend actions to management.
- Assist in the audits of New England, Northwest, New Jersey, Washington, D.C., Southeast, and Great Lakes Districts and U.S. Areas General Ledger Group.

BILL CHESTNUT & COMPANY, Greensburg, PA   1988-1990
Staff Auditor
- Participated in audits of $4 billion bank, major manufacturing company, mutual fund, software distribution company and large urban transportation company.

GROVE CITY COLLEGE, Grove City, PA   1987
Tutor/Instructor, Introduction to Financial Accounting
- Formulated, administered, and graded exams
- Tutored individuals in a self-paced course

LONDON COMMERCIAL BANK, London, UK   1986
Intern
- Conducted over 50 on-site investigations of firms with assets up to $2M; assessed "fair" valuation of assets
- Assisted evaluation of $80M brewery
- Identified potential bank investments by analyzing financial statements and determining relevant accounting ratios.
- Submitted written reports to financial officer.

EDUCATION

Mercyhurst College, Erie, PA
M.B.A., 1990

Grove City College, Grove City, PA
B.A., Economics, 1988

REFERENCES

Available on request.

- Bullets make resume easy to read.

- Specific dates of employment (month and year) are ideal for candidates with no gaps in work history.

STOCK BROKER

CHRIS SMITH
178 Green Street
Nashville, TN 37203
(615) 555-5555

OBJECTIVE
A challenging career in trading.

SUMMARY OF QUALIFICATIONS
- Brokerage License, series 7 & 63.
- Two years of progressive, financial experience.
- Developed interpersonal abilities.
- Self-motivated; able to achieve immediate and long-term goals and meet operation deadlines.
- Respond well in high-stress atmosphere.

EXPERIENCE

COPPERDASH ASSOCIATES, Nashville, TN   2/88-Present
Fund Accountant
- Report directly to Portfolio Manager and Traders on investment cash availability.
- Buy commercial paper for private accounts.
- Track stocks and bonds; record dividend/interest payments.
- Monitor/report portfolio security changes.
- Interface with Brokers and Banks regarding trade settlements.
- Analyze/prepare performance reports for Board of Directors and Shareholders, utilizing market invoices.
- Run industry comparisons.
- Assist Public Accountants, prepare audit papers, price out daily net worth for NASD, book accounting transactions (shares, securities, expenses, receipts, disbursements and dividends).
- Analyze current market condition; forecast dividend/interest payments and fund expenses.

EDUCATION

CAMPBELL COLLEGE, Bules Creek, NC
B.A., Accounting Finance, 1987
OXFORD UNIVERSITY, Oxford, England
One year abroad, 1984

COMPUTERS

Lotus 1-2-3 and Shaw Data

REFERENCES

Furnished upon request

- Lines, boldface, and choice of print make for a clean, crisp, visually appealing resume.

- Resume focuses employer's attention on candidate's latest, most relevant experience in detail.

TAX ACCOUNTANT

CHRIS SMITH
178 Green Street
Selden, NY 11784
(516) 555-5555

SUMMARY

Accomplished, versatile and well-credentialed executive with extensive experience in all aspects of the financial function for leading manufacturing and financial companies. Demonstrated record of success in building smooth-running, cost-effective operations.

EMPLOYMENT HISTORY

1987 to Present **BANCE FINANCE, Selden, NY**
Tax Accountant
Served as an AVP of Tax specializing in acquisitions, divestiture and corporate reorganizations.

- Conceived a special tax structure resulting in $7.25 million of savings in Federal tax in sale of subsidiary.
- Planned and implemented "tax-shelter" of consolidated Life/P&C income. Projected annual savings of $20 million.
- Automated compliance through purchase/implementation of new software.

Assistant Treasurer (1987 to 1992)
Controlled and improved all financial aspects of this $4 billion insurance company, including cash flows, accounts receivable, accounts payable, investments, taxation, financial trend analysis and budgeting.

- Conceived, recommended and implemented new holding company structure to shelter state taxes. $1 million in annual savings.
- Implemented controls to insure the utilization of "terms" on accounts payable. $2 million in annual savings.

1985 to 1987 **BANKERS UNION, Saugerties, NY**
Federal Tax Manager
Handled all aspects of taxation for over 100 subsidiary companies including tax planning, tax compliance, capital gains strategy and audit resolution.

1979 to 1985 **TI-KI SURF EQUIPMENT, Honolulu, Hawaii**
Tax Analyst
Hired initially as an Internal Accountant, was quickly promoted to Financial Analyst and subsequently to Tax Analyst. Was responsible for designing and supporting financial reporting for seven foreign operations.

EDUCATION

University of Hawaii
Bachelor of Science in Accounting, May 1979

University of New York
Master of Science of Taxation, May 1983
Master of Business Administration in Finance, May, 1987

- Resume emphasizes contributions, achievements, and problems candidate has solved throughout his/her career.

- Strong educational credentials strengthen resume.

TAX INSPECTOR

Chris Smith
178 Green Street
Butte, MT 59404
(406) 555-5555

PROFESSIONAL OBJECTIVE
A challenging, growth-oriented position in which professional experience, academic background, technical skill, and a commitment to excellence will have valuable application.

PROFESSIONAL EXPERIENCE
1984-Present **INTERNAL REVENUE COMMISSION,** Sydney, Australia
Tax Inspector/Higher Tax Office
- Review both individual and corporate tax files for completeness and accuracy.
- Consult with tax claims in resolving conflicts and/or resolve inequities resulting from misinformation, lack of information at time of initial filing.
- Respond to inquiries on tax matters as to policies and procedures.
- Determine penalties as directed by statute and process claims for collection procedure.
- Strong interpersonal, public relations, and communication skills required.
- Examined corporate payroll records for accuracy.
- Executed collections through direct subscription to the Office of the Collector General.
- Supervised, trained, scheduled, and monitored 11 employees.
- Compiled monthly statistic base for permanent records and data for regional/national reports.
- Monitored job performance and bid selections of traders and vendors.

1977-1984 **THE REVENUE COMMISSION SOCIAL CLUB,** Canberra, Australia
Director
- Managed overall operation of the Club, which represented employees of the revenue commissioners.
- Maintained facility consisting of two bars, function rooms, gymnasium, saunas, indoor football arena, and ancillary space areas.
- Hired/terminated, supervised, trained, and motivated staff.
- Oversaw office management, bookkeeping/accounting and member accounts.
- Arranged for equipment replacement, control, ordering, bid-purchases.

REFERENCES
Available upon request.

- Resume format is neat and professional.

- Education is omitted due to candidate's extensive work experience.

VICE-PRESIDENT OF ADMINISTRATION AND FINANCE

CHRIS SMITH
178 Green Street
Dodge City, KS 67801
(316) 555-55555

SUMMARY OF QUALIFICATIONS
- Extensive experience in providing administrative, managerial and operational guidance for the financial services industry.
- Thorough knowledge in managing administrative sales and secured loan programs, preparing budgets and developing product pricing policies.
- Supervised, trained and developed staffs of numerous sizes.
- Proficient in monitoring numerous custody accounts in a timely and accurate fashion.
- Participation with affiliates in the capacities of president, executive committee member, speaker/panel member and general member.

EXPERIENCE

1/86 to Present   **Vice-President Administration-OIC-Custody Services**
THIRD BANK OF KANSAS   Dodge City, Kansas
Manager of the administrative department. Provide handling and record keeping services for corporate, fiduciary and personal custody accounts with assets totaling $20 billion.
- Prepare budgets and develop product pricing policies.
- Manage administrative sales and secured loan programs.
- Direct administrative processes for a sizable potion of the department's largest and most complex accounts.
- Extensive involvement in the analysis of new accounting systems, to determine customer needs.
- Develop and maintain strong securities operational knowledge.

9/75 to 1/86   **Client Manager - Custody Services**
- Administered over 200 custody accounts, which included direct contact with customers, attorneys, investment advisors, mutual funds, brokers and accountants.
- Acted as liaison between the operations support areas and the customer contact department. Reported problems and operational errors.
- Participated in the trust systems conversion team, which was responsible for the successful conversion to the on-line accounting system.

SEMINARS

Harbridge House, Inc., - Senior Management Program
Thomas Blodgett Associates - Consultative Selling Skills Program

PROFESSIONAL AFFILIATIONS
- Member - Executive Committee - Past President - Securities Operations Association of The Heartland
- Speaker/Panel Member - Kansas Bankers Association; speaking at various Trust Operations Seminars.
- Past President - Bank of Heartland Supervisors' Association

---

■ Seminars and professional affiliations demonstrate candidate's dedication to the field.

■ Chrono-functional format is more flexible than a chronological resume, but stronger than a functional resume.

VICE-PRESIDENT OF FINANCE

CHRIS SMITH
178 Green Street
Buffalo, NY 14212
(716) 555-5555

EXPERIENCE

NIB, Inc.   *Buffalo, NY*
V.P.-Finance   *1989-1993*
Provide administrative leadership to the corporation. Led team in the development of a mission statement, strategic plans, and related business plans to grow company 100% in a three-year time period. Researched, planned, and established a satellite manufacturing plan in less than six weeks. Established full-system integration with the corporate office. Coordinate all legal, tax and insurance contracts. Developed the company profit sharing, section 125, 401(k) and other benefit plans.

Ryder Group, Inc.   *Poughkeepsie, NY*
Finance Manager   *1982-1988*
Increased levels of management responsibility for financial accounting, analysis, budgeting, credit and collection for a four billion dollar international manufacturing company. Coordinated financial consolidations, analysis, budgeting, acquisition and divestiture support. Prepared consolidated statements in GAAP and SSAP formats. Supervised four exempt and four non-exempt employees with dotted-line authority over eight Plant Controllers.

Jameil Jones Systems
Cost Accounting Manager   *1980-1982*
Developed cost systems for eight construction branches and two manufacturing divisions. Key member of negotiation team and audit coordinator for the divestiture program involving these divisions. Reviewed and approved standard costs, transfer prices, budgets, physical inventory valuation and cost estimates. Sales were 62 million. Supervised staff of four nonexempt employees.

Crichton Co., CPA's
Staff Accountant   *1978-1980*
Prepared financial statements, footnotes, and other tax and financial information. Performed compliance testing and the study of internal control. Supervised and reviewed junior accountants.

ACHIEVEMENTS

Management and Treasury
- Founded and operate a successful contract manufacturing corporation
- Developed investment guidelines, banking relationships, and cash planning programs. These programs reduced corporate borrowing, improved cash flow and increased other income
- Led employee meetings in incentive bonus, profit sharing, 401(k), safety and corporate philosophy
- Successfully established a new operating division in six weeks
- Developed a comprehensive risk management program that improved coverage and reduced cost
- Provided significant shareholder assistance in tax and financial planning

EDUCATION

New York University, New York
B.A. Accounting, May 1978

■ Achievements section attracts employer's attention to the candidate's most impressive professional accomplishments.

■ Use of paragraphs rather than bullets is preferable for more senior positions.

7
Administration

Nature of Work
Those who are employed in administration work throughout the private industry and government. Among their various duties, they coordinate and direct supportive services such as secretarial and correspondence, prepare travel plans, process information, and schedule and distribute materials. Bank tellers handle a wide range of banking transactions, such as cashing checks, accepting deposits and loan payments, and processing withdrawals. Administrative assistants perform and coordinate office activities to ensure that information is disseminated in a timely fashion to staff and clients. Those in material recording and dispatching occupations keep track of orders for personnel, equipment, and materials.

Employment
The majority of administrative professionals work in travel, management, business, social, and health service organizations. Others are found in manufacturing, wholesale and retail trade, and in government.

Training
Within the realm of administrative services, most employees require a high school diploma. Courses in speech, office practices, and business math provide a helpful background. Strong typing, computer, and communications skills are a definite advantage.

Job Outlook
Employment of administrative workers is expected to experience average growth through the year 2005, as most professions within this field are versatile and can be placed in virtually every kind of industry. Employment is not dependent on any single sector of the economy.

However, two professions within administration services will suffer a marked decline in employment: bank tellers and telephone operators. Both jobs will fall prey to the rapid technological advances taking place in automation. The new generation of automated teller machines has taken the place of human bank tellers in the processing of transactions, such as deposits to multiple accounts. Telephone operators will find their jobs being phased out by automated switchboards and technologically advanced voice mail systems. Certain banks and telephone companies have already decided not to replace tellers or operators who leave, a sign that the transformation is already well underway.

Earnings

Many administrative workers are part-time, and although this is convenient for mothers or students, there are not typically any benefits for non-full-time employees. The higher wages in administrative services can be found in the larger, more metropolitan corporations as opposed to smaller, suburban operations. Salaries vary a great deal for administrative assistants, reflecting differences in skill, experience, and level of responsibility, ranging from $20,5000 to $32,900. Bank tellers generally earn an annual salary of $10,000 to $25,000. Clerical supervisors and managers have a median annual salary of $15,000 to $44,700+. On the average, general office clerks garner a yearly wage of $16,000.

ADMINISTRATIVE ASSISTANT (Department of Health)

CHRIS SMITH
178 Green Street
Milwaukee, WI 53202
(414) 555-5555

OBJECTIVE
To obtain a challenging position as Administrative Assistant.

SUMMARY
- Highly developed interpersonal skills.
- Self-motivated to ably coordinate daily office functions.
- Knowledgeable regarding technical and medical terminology.
- Familiar with computer operation.
- Responsible for training of new personnel.

EXPERIENCE

5/86-Present **DEPARTMENT OF HEALTH**
Standards and Quality, Milwaukee, WI
Administration Assistant
Handle incoming calls and mail. Greet visitors. Resolve inquiries. Prepare and type office reports. Maintain supervisor and staff member appointments and travel calendars. Verify, revise, and arrange appointments, conferences, and meetings. Act as liaison to supervisor regarding meetings and conferences. Maintain control records and follow-ups on work in progress. Establish file-coding system. Train incoming staff. Maintain time and attendance records as well as instructional and reference manuals.

7/81-5/86 **VETERAN'S HOSPITAL**, Lacrosse, WI
Claims Development Clerk
Managed clerical functions including: incoming calls; maintenance and update of files, logging, and special determinations reports in all Administrative Law Judge cases; typing contracts, reports, and general correspondence. Dealt with receipt of checks and attendant recording duties. Computed and interpreted claims processing. Directed inquiries and maintained cordial relations with the public. Trained new clerks.

EDUCATION
1978 ST. JOHN'S CATHOLIC COLLEGE, Madison, WI
Major: Business Management/Human Services, Bachelor's degree

COMPUTERS
DOS, IBM Mainframe, Microsoft Word, PASCAL

REFERENCES
Available upon request.

■ Computer knowledge, usually a requirement in the administrative field, is highlighted on this resume.

■ Job objective is clearly defined.

ADMINISTRATIVE ASSISTANT (Education)

CHRIS SMITH
178 Green Street
Grand Rapids, MI 49428
(616) 555-5555

OBJECTIVE
An Administrative Assistant position in a progressive organization.

PROFILE
- Ability to execute a number of projects simultaneously
- Skilled in administrative and office procedures
- Competent with IBM computer and numerous software applications
- Excellent organization and communication skills

EXPERIENCE
ANASTASIA INSTITUTE, Grand Rapids, MI 1990-Present
Administrative Assistant
Office management, word processing, spreadsheet, and billing. Coordinate assignment of 1500 students to applicable academic counselors, monitor progress of problem students under disciplinary action. Handle student complaints about racism, sexual harassment, etc.

DIABETES CENTER, Holland, MI 1987-90
Administrative Secretary
Planned and executed bimonthly weekend patient conferences. Coordinated finances, material, registration. Coordinated catering for special events. Budgeted and facilitated four-day professional seminar.

AIDS ASSOCIATION, Kalamazoo, MI 1984-87
Meeting Coordinator
Organized and supervised all meeting planning activities, coordinated direct mail campaigns for fundraising and special events, wrote and placed press releases in local media.

EDUCATION
BACHELOR OF ARTS/COMMUNICATION STUDIES
Kramer College, Kalamazoo, MI 1983
G.P.A. 3.25; Graduated Cum Laude

CERTIFICATE IN MEETING MANAGEMENT
Landsend College, Holland, MI 1989

SOFTWARE SKILLS
Proficient in WordPerfect 5.1; Multimate; Lotus 1-2-3; Q&A; Professional Write; Wang Working Knowledge - dBase III+; CRT IMS System, Microsoft Word 4; Microsoft Excel; Pro-Cite 2.0; Display Write; Raiser's Edge

---

- Job objective is brief and to the point.

- Valuable computer skills are highlighted in a separate section.

ADMINISTRATIVE ASSISTANT (Investments)

CHRIS SMITH
178 Green Street
Albany, NY 12208
(518) 555-5555

OBJECTIVE
To contribute acquired skills to an administrative position.

SUMMARY OF QUALIFICATIONS
- More than four years of professional experience in administration, sales, and coaching/instructing.
- Computer experience includes spreadsheets, work processing and graphics software programs.
- Proven communication abilities, both oral and written.
- Developed interpersonal skills.
- Ability to achieve immediate and long-term goals and meet operational deadlines.

PROFESSIONAL EXPERIENCE
1990-Present LOYALTY INVESTMENTS, Albany, NY
Administrative Assistant
Provide administrative support for new business development group; assist C.F.O. with special projects. Ensure smooth work flow; facilitate effectiveness of 14 sales consultants. Direct incoming calls; initiate new client application process, maintain applicant record data base. Oversee office equipment maintenance. Assisted in design and implementation of computer automation system. Aided in streamlining application process.

1988-90 THE GYMNASTIC SCHOOL, Albany, NY
Instructor
Planned/designed/implemented recreational program for 70 gymnasts at various skill levels. Evaluated/monitored new students' progress; maintained records. Coached/choreographed competitive performances; motivated gymnastics team of 20. Set team goals/incentives to maximize performance levels.

1985-88 GROVER FINANCE, Buffalo, NY
Telemarketing Sales Representative
Secured new business utilizing customer inquiries and mass mailing responses; provided product line information to prospective clients. Initiated loan application/qualifying processes. Maintained daily call records and monthly sales breakdown. Acquired comprehensive product line knowledge and ability to quickly assess customer needs and assemble appropriate financial packages.

EDUCATION
Hofstra University, Hempstead, NY
Bachelor of Arts, English, 1985
Concentration: Business; Dean's List, G.P.A. 3.3

REFERENCES
Furnished upon request.

■ Summary grabs the reader's attention with powerful skills and qualifications.

■ Resume emphasizes contributions, achievements, and problems candidate has solved throughout his/her career.

ADMINISTRATIVE ASSISTANT (Personnel)

```
                        CHRIS SMITH
                       178 Green St.
                    Pinesville, LA 71359
                      (318) 555-5555
```

<u>WORK EXPERIENCE</u>

THE LAPIS CORPORATION, Pinesville, LA   9/88-Present
<u>Personnel Administrative Assistant</u>
- Maintained files.
- Prepared records for off-site storage.
- Designed forms for archives.
- Developed effective space management plan for on-site records.
- Improved tracking system resulting in few lost files.
- Handled employment verifications and designed forms to expedite process.

GLADE GROVE COLLEGE, Baton Rouge, LA   12/84-8/88
<u>Records Coordinator for Development</u>
- Recorded gifts made to the college.
- Maintained files.

<u>Coder</u>   12/81-12/84
- Translated data from surveys into numerical code for data entry.
- Edited computer printouts.
- Performed quality control.

PAISLEY TELECOMMUNICATIONS, New Orleans, LA   6/72-12/81
<u>"Advantage" Coordinator</u> [The "Advantage" is an auto dialer.]
- Tested and programmed each unit.
- Schedule site visits and installations.
- Kept inventory.
- Assisted customers with questions and problems.

<u>Interviewer</u>   4/71-5/72
- Conducted public opinion surveys.

<u>EDUCATION</u>

Biltmore College, Dallas, Texas   1972
Associates degree in Marketing.

References are available upon request.

■ Work experience is emphasized, while limited education is de-emphasized.

■ Clean layout makes resume easy to read.

ADMINISTRATIVE ASSISTANT (Recent Grad)

Chris Smith
178 Green Street
Stanford, CA 94305
(415) 555-5555

Experience: **Stanford Law School**
9/92- **Administrative/Research Assistant**
Present Provide support for legal, doctoral candidate. Coordinate manuscript production phases. Research changes in case law pertaining to "Mechanisms of the Supreme Court and Human Rights."

11/92- **Administrative Assistant**
Present Edit Stanford Law School journal. Provide administrative support to Editor-in-Chief.

3/93- **Administrative/Research Assistant**
Present Utilize data-base, periodical governmental reports for country-specific research on legal, economic, and political issues. Manage manuscripts from production through publication.

Fall 1992 **Special Events Coordinator**
Organized Annual Stanford Law School Alumni Conference.

Education:
1992 **Michigan State University**
BA: International Politics & History
Studied in Madrid, Spain, Fall 1991.

1991 **Bucknell University**
International Law, East European/Russian Economics, Graduate English

Skills: Computers-Microsoft Word
Databases-Westlaw, Internet
Languages-Fluent in Spanish; working knowledge of French

Interests: Travel, swimming, in-line skating, surfing.

References: Available upon request.

■ Listing foreign language skills and international travel enhances candidate's credentials.

■ Personal interests can provide a great topic for conversation during a job interview.

ADMINISTRATIVE ASSISTANT (Wholesale Distributor)

CHRIS SMITH
178 Green Street
Dallas, TX 75275
(214) 555-5555

OBJECTIVE
To secure a challenging position as an Administrative Assistant.

SUPPORTIVE QUALIFICATIONS
- 3 years as an administrative assistant.
- 4 years experience working in the medical/health care arena.
- 2 years education and training in Secretarial Sciences.

STRENGTHS

Detail-oriented	Organized
Patient	Prioritize Accurately
Positive Attitude	Work Well Under Pressure

PROFESSIONAL EXPERIENCE

MUSTANG DISTRIBUTORS, Dallas, TX **Administrative Assistant**
1993-Present Performed general secretarial tasks, typing reports and correspondence on MacIntosh equipment; arranged meetings, expense reports, and travel vouchers. Designed computer automation system; assisted in its implementation.

TEXAS MEDICAL CENTER, Austin, TX **Unit Secretary**
1990-Present Transcribed doctors' orders for patients' records on computer; answered telephones in busy office.

GRANITE INVESTMENT RESOURCE CENTER, Dallas, TX **Data Entry**
1988-1990 Input account transactions and transfers into computer.

SEUSS HEALTH, Houston, TX **Data Entry**
1986-1988 Input medical information, maintained computer files; managed nightly upkeep and documentation of triage information, medication and treatments.

BROWNWOOD HOSPITAL, El Paso, TX **File Clerk, Medical Records Department**
1984-1986 Filed, answered phones, researched patient information for various departments.

EDUCATION

DALLAS COMMUNITY COLLEGE; course work in Secretarial Sciences and Business, 1984-1986.

REFERENCES

Furnished upon request

- Layout is clean and well-organized.

- Resume includes course work that corresponds to the position desired.

ADMINISTRATIVE DIRECTOR

CHRIS SMITH
178 Green Street
Washington, D.C. 19180
(202) 555-5555

EMPLOYMENT HISTORY

ADMINISTRATIVE DIRECTOR 1991-Present
Georgetown Medical School, Dept. Psychiatry, Washington, D.C.
Coordinate the administrative/logistics aspects of a multi-study research program on the genetic transmission of mental illnesses. Design, implement, and manage a relational database for each of the studies; write and maintain appropriate documentation; produce reports and statistics as required. Identify, assist in the recruiting of, and follow through the protocol study subjects; screen normal controls and family members for medical exclusions; coordinate the chart review process. Develop, organize, and implement administrative procedures and policies; draft the administrative procedures sections of the Study Procedures Manuals. Coordinate medications and hospitalizations history review process for psychiatric patients after neuropsychological testing is completed.

COMPUTER EDUCATION COORDINATE 1988-1991
Washington D.C. Bar Association
Coordinated and administered the Computer College Program to educate attorneys in the uses and advantages of computers in the law office. Developed curriculum, promoted and implemented educational seminar series; assisted in teaching and presentations; selected sites. Established state-wide lawyers' computer-user group; edited and contributed to newsletter; planned meetings and agendas; developed membership; promoted student user groups with law schools.

LEGAL SECRETARY 1987-1988
Randell & Jenks, Boston, MA
Developed and implemented systems to streamline office procedures. Monitored attorneys' daily activities for time records; allocated monthly charges to appropriate cases and matters; drafted bills. Assisted paralegals with assignments. Reorganized attorneys' files.

ADMINISTRATIVE ASSISTANT - EXEMPT STAFF 1985-1987
Catholic University, Washington, D.C.
Coordinated and administered the Professional Summer Program developed for the Navy community. Assisted with catalog preparation and program marketing; prepared and monitored budgets; oversaw lecturer negotiations, site selection, social amenities, and travel management.

EDUCATION

American University, Washington, D.C.
B.A. Economics, 1984

■ Dynamic action verbs give resume impact.

■ Education is listed towards bottom of resume because candidate's practical experience outweighs his/her degree.

BANK TELLER

CHRIS SMITH
178 Green Street
Baltimore, MD 21202
(301) 555-5555

OBJECTIVE
To utilize banking and sales experience, in the Hospitality or Business arena.

SUMMARY OF QUALIFICATIONS
- Skilled in the production and dissemination of correspondence, materials management, maintenance of filing systems, mail processing and data entry.
- Proficient in the execution of banking processes, daily transaction reconciliation, sale of bank products, customer service, consistent input of recommendations for procedural enhancement and personnel management.

PROFESSIONAL EXPERIENCE
1989 - BANK OF BALTIMORE, Teller   Baltimore, MD
Present
- Process various account transactions, reconcile and deposit daily funds.
- Inform customers of bank products, refer public to designated personnel, provide account status data, and handle busy phone.
- Execute signature functions and provide input for system enhancement.
- Orient, train, supervise, and delegate tasks for new hires.
- Serve as Team Leader for Christmas Clothing Campaign for Homeless.

1987-98 MEYER, GREEN AND FAZIO, Office Assistant   Princess Anne, MD
- Collected, sorted and distributed incoming mail. Processed outgoing mail.

1986-87 TANNENBAUM SOCIETY, Sales Associate   Washington, DC
- Serviced customers, reconciled cash drawer.
- Created effective product displays.

1984-86 KENT AND LANE ASSOCIATES, Office Assistant   Richmond, VA
- Produced correspondence, responded to public inquiries, monitored and maintained confidential records.

EDUCATION
GENEVA COLLEGE, Annapolis, MD
Associate degree in Business/Travel, 1984

COMPUTERS
Lotus 1-2-3, WordPerfect 5.1, IBM Compatible, Sabre

- For office support positions, typewritten resumes are generally acceptable.

- Company names and dates are listed on the left margin while locations are listed on the right margin.

DATA ENTRY SUPERVISOR

CHRIS SMITH
178 Green Street
River Forest, IL 60305
(312) 555-5555

CAREER OBJECTIVE
To secure a Supervisory position in data analysis/data entry.

SUMMARY OF QUALIFICATIONS
- Over 13 years of data entry and administrative experience.
- Well-developed managerial abilities.
- Proven communications and written capabilities; report writing based on findings in database.
- Strong interpersonal skills, having dealt with a diversity of professionals, clients, and staff.
- Cooperative and flexible team player; equally effective working independently.

PROFESSIONAL EXPERIENCE

MORTEK ANALYSTS, River Forest, IL   1988-Present
1990-Present **Data Analyst III**
Collect data and analyze documents with on-line database. Retrieve records from the Registry of Deeds, vital statistics. Compile and generate reports of finds. CAST entry and maintenance, CAPS statistical reports production (M204 system). Log and analyze specific calls (TOLLS). Act as liaison to U.S. Attorneys Office. Gather and analyze case materials; conduct physical case reviews. Act as Interim Supervisor; train, assist and supervise staff of six.

1988-1990 **Data Entry Supervisor**
Supervised staff of four. Processed data entry inputs and Seizure/Motor Vehicles reports; updated Personnel files and DEAS-Accounting system. Prepared biweekly Progress Reports; maintained relevant records.

BLUE ANGEL ASSOCIATES, Chicago, IL
1986-1988 **Data Entry Operator**
Cooperated with Chief Operator transcribing prescription drug data for reimbursement. Required speed, accuracy and attention to critical money fields.

AWARDS
- 1988 Merit Award for excellence as a supervisor.
- Presidential Award 1989 for outstanding performance.

EDUCATION AND TRAINING
High School Diploma, 1984

COMPUTER SKILLS
Lotus 1.2.3, dBase III, dBase IV, WordPerfect 5.1

■ Awards heading draws attention to candidate's significant accomplishments.

■ Work experience is emphasized, while limited education is de-emphasized.

DISPATCHER (Medical)

CHRIS SMITH
178 Green Street
Hickory, NC 28601
(704) 555-5555

Professional Objective
A dispatching/management position within the medical field.

Summary of Qualifications
- Four years experience in supervising service technicians, handling public's questions and complaints, and servicing patients' medical equipment.
- Effective in developing rapport with depressed patients.
- Willing to travel or relocate.

Professional Experience
1990 to GALLIMORE HOME HEALTH CARE; Hickory, NC
Present **Medical Technician/Dispatch Supervisor**
- Schedule and supervise twelve drivers.
- Handle patients' inquiries and complaints.
- Monitor equipment and supply inventories.
- Service patients' equipment/develop rapport with them.
- Accomplishments: Improved efficiency of method of routing drivers and of method of briefing them on their assignments.

1988-1990 CARE PROVISIONS; High Point, NC
- Set up medical equipment for patients.

Education
1988 JOHNSON STATE COLLEGE, Johnson, VT
Bachelor of Science, Business Management

Computers
Lotus 1-2-3, Microsoft Word 4.0, WordPerfect 5.1, dBase III.

■ Indicating a willingness to relocate on a resume can be advantageous.

■ Valuable computer skills are highlighted in a separate section.

DISPATCHER (Terminal/Freight)

CHRIS SMITH
178 Green Street
Erie, PA 16563
(814) 555-5555

OBJECTIVE:
A Dispatching position with a growth-oriented organization. Willing to relocate and/or travel.

SUMMARY OF QUALIFICATIONS:
- *Terminal, customer service, human resource, financial management skills.*
- *Daily reporting, record keeping, dispatching.*
- *Excellent organizational and communication skills.*
- *Relate well with personnel, management and clientele at all levels.*
- *Present a positive and productive image of the company.*
- *Ability to promote team work for efficient operation of company.*
- *Formulate cost saving procedures to assure effective use of manpower.*

PROFESSIONAL EXPERIENCE:
DISPATCHER - Duffield Freight Inc., Erie, PA (1991-Present)
- Act as dispatcher, set up pick-up and deliveries, update computer, route drivers, customer service, troubleshoot.
- Check logs for accuracy and DOT regulations.
- Explain procedures to and review work of new drivers to assure accuracy of paperwork.
- Interact with other terminals regarding problem solving.

**ACCOUNT EXECUTIVE - Bedelia Transportation Company,
Gwynedd Valley, PA** (1989-1991)
- Solicited outbound and inbound freight.
- Handled special tariffs and claims, dispatching and setting up freight programs.
- Provided customer profile and customer relations.

LINE DISPATCHER - Sycamore Freight, Haverford, PA (1987-1989)
- Set up manpower and yard schedules of inbound and outbound schedules; determined dispersal of dispatch drivers. Kept computer updated; handled maintenance problems and customer relations.

EDUCATION:
Eastern College, St. David's, Pennsylvania
Bachelor of Science Degree, 1987
Major: Business Administration

■ Use of boldface and italics provides a clean and crisp presentation.

■ Summary grabs the reader's attention with powerful skills and qualifications.

EXECUTIVE ASSISTANT

Chris Smith
178 Green Street
Erie, PA 16541
(814) 555-5555

Objective:
To provide efficient and effective administrative support.

Experience:

1989-
Present

Redmond Computer, Inc., Erie, PA
Administrative Assistant to the Chief Executive Officer
Coordinated and prioritized the daily activities of the Chairman of the Board. Performed the administrative functions in support of the CEO. Required an in-depth knowledge of the Company, the industry, the financial community, the investors, the customers, the educational community, etc. Interacted and assisted in the preparation for the Board of Directors meetings. Recorded and distributed the minutes of management meetings.

1986-89

Steppenwolf Associates, Pittsburgh, PA
Administrative Assistant to the President and Chief Executive Officer
Prioritized the daily activities of the CEO. Set up and maintained a "tickler system." Composed, and edited correspondence on behalf of the President.

1982-86

Jasmine, Rain, Inc., Beaver Falls, PA
Administrative Assistant to the Chief Operating Officer
Interacted on behalf of the COO in sensitive customer and employee relationships. Recorded and distributed minutes of the Management Committee. Maintained and distributed monthly department reports.

Education:

1985-
Present

University of Pennsylvania Continuing Education Program: Management, Business, Computer Skills and Marketing, French and Italian. Cutter College: Computer Literacy, Shorthand Refresher and Medical Language.

Computers:

PC Computers (IBM and clone), Wang Word Processing, DEC word processing. Literate in most PC software, WordPerfect (5.1), Word, Multimate, Professional Write, ChiWriter, Sidekick, Org Plus, Spotlight, Symphony, and All-in-One. Proficient in shorthand, typing, adding machines, and calculators.

- Job objective focuses on the needs of the employer, not the job candidate.

- Separate category for computer experience calls attention to candidate's technical knowledge.

EXECUTIVE SECRETARY (Banking)

CHRIS SMITH
178 Green Street
Brattleboro, VT 05301
(802) 555-5555

OBJECTIVE
To secure a position with a strong company as Executive Secretary

SUMMARY OF QUALIFICATIONS
- Gained extensive knowledge of bank administrative policies and procedures through six years of bank experience
- Able to supervise employees and work with all levels of management in a professional, diplomatic and tactful manner
- Rapidly analyze/recognize department problems and solutions
- Work on multiple projects under pressure and meet strict deadlines and budget requirements

EMPLOYMENT EXPERIENCE
BRATTLEBORO SAVINGS BANK, Brattleboro, VT
Executive Secretary (1990-Present)
- Act as Executive Secretary to Senior Vice Present Commercial Division
- Set up Commercial Loans on System
- Prepare monthly reports for Board of Directors
- Update commercial loan files with regard to financial statements, financial information, etc.
- Maintain appraisal files
- Coordinate loan renewals with Loan Officer

SPARTAN TRUST COMPANY, Montpelier, VT
Executive Secretary (1987-90)
- Acted as Secretary to the Executive Vice-President and Senior Loan Officer
- Manage secretarial staff supporting the Commercial Loan Officers
- Coordinate staff meetings and presentations to Board of Directors
- Prepare monthly departmental and divisional reports for distribution
- Update and maintain Policy and Procedure Manual on a timely basis

Commercial Finance Assistant (1985-87)
- Prepare daily client loan advances and loan payment activity
- Maintain monthly client loan/collateral statements
- Maintain collateral availability controls by formula
- Perform analysis of client files
- Assist in preparation of departmental reports and loan agreements

COMPUTER SKILLS
IBM PC, Q & A, WordPerfect 5.2, Lotus 123

■ Job descriptions are straightforward and understandable.

■ Stating that "references are available upon request" is not essential; most employers will assume that references are available.

EXECUTIVE SECRETARY (Sales)

CHRIS SMITH
178 Green Street
Manchester, NH 03104
(603) 555-5555

Experience

1991-Present **Shrike Oil Co., Manchester, NH**
Executive Secretary - Sales
- Support the Director of Sales
- Support Field Sales Representatives and Regional Managers
- Generate sales reports
- Sales promotions/contests
- Statistic and data gathering
- Assist Marketing department when needed
- Manage travel arrangements
- Plan meetings
- Attend trade shows

1987-91 **Romeo Associates, Bedford, NH**
Administrative Assistant - International Sales
- Supported the Director of Sales and Contracts Administrator
- Managed all correspondence
- Supervised export control
- Managed customer service and repair parts administration

1980-87 **Jenks Systems, Nashua, NH**
Secretary - Marketing
- Maintained personnel records
- Managed travel arrangements
- Supervised typing correspondence
- Directed contact with customer base

Education

1980 • Quinipeac College, Derry, NH
Bachelor of Arts; Business Administration
1988 • Seminars; Assertiveness training; public speaking

Computers

Microsoft Word, Excel, WordPerfect, Lotus 1-2-3, IBM Compatible

Skills

Typing 80 WPM, Dictaphone, E-Mail

Affiliations

Professional Secretaries International

■ Job-related affiliations and seminars indicate candidate's commitment to his/her field.

■ Resume includes course work that corresponds to the position desired.

FILE CLERK

CHRIS SMITH
178 Green Street
Cohasset, MA 02025
(617) 555-5555

OBJECTIVE

A position as a File Clerk in a progressive organization.

SKILLS

Typing 70 wpm accurate   Word Processing
Calculator   CRT
Adding machine

EMPLOYMENT

January 1994-Present
Brigham & Women's Hospital, Boston, MA
File Clerk. Type; maintain patient filing system.

September 1993-January 1994
ProTemps Employment, Quincy, MA
Clerk/Typist. Responsible for typing; filing; and CRT.

May 1992-September 1993
Cohasset Cleaners, Cohasset, MA
File Clerk. Performed clerical duties; processed mail, daily reports and
correspondence; retrieved/updated/corrected files.

EDUCATION

1992-1993
The Burdett School, Boston, MA
Courses in Typing, Filing, Word-processing, Computers (IBM:
WordPerfect, Lotus 1-2-3, Spreadsheets)

References Available Upon Request

■ Job objective is supported by the facts and accomplishments stated in resume.

■ Listing typing speed is appropriate for most office support positions.

GENERAL OFFICE CLERK

Chris Smith
178 Green Street
Boston, MA 02215
(617) 555-5555

SKILLS:
- *Typing 65+ wpm.*
- *Strong knowledge of general accounting procedures.*
- *Ability to work under pressure in a fast-paced environment and manage multiple tasks.*
- *Ability to work independently with good organizational and communication skills.*
- *Experience working for a large corporation.*
- *Professional appearance and attitude.*

EXPERIENCE:

1989-
Present

CARTER TRUST
Office Clerk

Boston, MA

Transcribe statements from insureds, typed letters to attorneys, insureds, and other insurance companies. Manage timely payment of worker's compensation checks and the timely filing of workers' compensation forms; type confidential material such as employee appraisals for the Claims Manager. Extensive workload on IBM 3090 processing insurance claims, payments, and recovery checks. Print checks to insureds and vendors. Answer telephone inquiries from insureds, claimants, and agents.

1985-1989

FEDERAL UNION INSURANCE CO.
Clerical Supervisor

Boston, MA

Supervised the clerical staff consisting of three clerical employees. Acted in the capacity of Administrative Assistant to the Claims Manager, typed letters to attorneys, insureds, etc., and handled special projects and reports from the Boston office.

1981-1985

MAPLEROOT HIGH SCHOOL
Payroll Clerk

Belchertown, MA

Handled a monthly payroll for 500 hourly employees. Prepared quarterly federal withholding tax returns and labor statistics report.

EDUCATION:

H.S. Diploma
Certificate in WordPerfect 5.1
Certificate in Lotus 1-2-3

COMPUTERS:

WordPerfect 5.1, Lotus 1-2-3, E-Mail, IBM System

REFERENCES:

Furnished upon request.

■ Skills section focuses employer's attention on candidate's relevant qualifications.

■ Work experience is emphasized, while limited education is de-emphasized.

INVENTORY CONTROL ANALYST

CHRIS SMITH
178 Green Street
Providence, RI 02903
(401) 555-5555

CAREER OBJECTIVE
A technical/administrative support position in inventory analysis.

BACKGROUND SUMMARY
A dedicated, conscientious individual with a solid background in inventory control. Demonstrated ability to identify, analyze and solve problems. Knowledgeable in all facets of inventory control. Experienced in data entry. Proven ability to work independently or with others. Work well in a fast-paced environment. Organized. Excellent attendance record.

CAREER HISTORY
SULLIVAN DATA SYSTEMS, Providence, RI
Inventory Control Analyst   (1986-Present)
Inventory Control Clerk II   (1982-86)
- Analyzed, investigated and resolved inventory discrepancies identified through section inputs and daily cycle count procedures.
- Served as a principal consulted on plant inventory systems.
- Assisted in reviewing and revising physical inventory procedures.
- Coordinated and assisted in conducting physical inventories.
- Created and maintained filing systems on a personal computer. Generated reports from files created.
- Assisted in liquidation of excess and used computer equipment.
- Trained new departmental personnel on data entry procedures using a CRT.
- Demonstrated knowledge of Lotus 123 and Excel software applications.
- Created and maintained daily, monthly and yearly reports for upper management.
- Conferred with management on a daily basis.
- Coordinated projects with co-workers at multiple plant sites.

EDUCATION
Roger Williams College, Bristol, RI, 1968-72

CONTINUING EDUCATION
Sullivan Data Systems
ISO 9000 Awareness Training (International Standardization Organization)
QWG (Quality Work Group)

■ Continuing education indicates candidate's ongoing commitment to his/her career.

■ Background summary includes strong well words like "dedicated" and "conscientious."

MAIL ROOM SUPERVISOR

CHRIS SMITH
178 Green Street
Biddeford, ME 04005
(207) 555-5555

OBJECTIVE
To secure a full-time mailroom management position.

EXPERIENCE

11/87-   LANCELOT, INC., Biddeford, ME
Present **Supervisor, Mailroom Services**
         Coordinate incoming mail, disperse inter-building correspondence. Manage
         courier   services   and   shipping/receiving.   Administer   employee
         evaluations/appraisals, schedule hours. Research and account for certified,
         registered, and express mail. Responsible for office supply procurement.
         Obtain/maintain lease agreements for electronic machinery and equipment.

1986-87 BIRCH, INC., Saco, ME
         Supervisor, Mailroom Services
         Shipped weekly overseas pouches and biweekly payroll to 35 domestic offices.
         Sorted/distributed in-house payroll for 600 employees. Coordinated in-house
         and U.S. office stock distribution. Acted as building management contact and
         Chief Fire Warden for 100,000 square feet of office space. Assisted in
         office relocations throughout U.S.

1984-86 DATEL EXPRESS, Saco, ME
         Courier
         Delivered time sensitive packages throughout Boston area. Sorted
         incoming/outgoing express packages.

1981-84 PORTLAND FINANCE, Portland, ME
         Supervisor, Incoming Mail/Messengers and Stock Distribution
         Managed computer facility forms and negotiable forms stored in in-house
         vault.

EDUCATION

1982-85 NORTHWESTERN UNIVERSITY, Chicago, IL
         Major: Business Administration

1980-81 UNIVERSITY OF MASSACHUSETTS, Amherst, MA
         Major: Business Administration

■ Boldfaced job titles accentuate candidate's career progression.

■ Including a telephone number is essential on a resume.

OFFICE MANAGER (Computers)

CHRIS GREEN
178 Green Street
Berkeley, CA 94720
(415) 555-5555

OBJECTIVE
An OFFICE MANAGEMENT position in the Computer field.

SKILLS PROFILE
- Demonstrated planning, controlling, organizing and leadership skills. Offer 10+ years of management experience encompassing personnel functions, client relations and facilities management.
- Human resource skills include determining staffing needs, selecting, hiring, assigning and supervising.
- Articulate and expressive speaker. Presented numerous well-received client seminars on product features. Conducted intensive on-site training sessions for PMS clients and installation staff.

EXPERIENCE
TOUCHSTONE SYSTEMS, INC. - Berkeley, CA
OFFICE MANAGER   1990-present
Direct and coordinate all aspects of installation, troubleshooting, training and general customer service operations for the Norwalk branch of TS, INC. Provide all maintenance functions and management of security systems. Administer property management budget with sensitivity to cost control. Respond immediately to building emergencies and implement appropriate course of action. Determine office staffing needs, write and place employment ads, interview and select qualified personnel. Provide orientation and training in company policy and practices, operations and customer service techniques.

QUARTERMAIN CONTRIBUTORS, INC. - San Diego, CA
BRANCH MANAGER   1988-90
Provided leadership and direction for TS systems installers/trainers outside of the San Diego metropolitan area. Selected, trained, directed and evaluated the performance of technical support staff, ensuring compliance with the highest possible quality performance standards.

PERCELL ASSOCIATES - Los Angeles, CA
OFFICE MANAGER   1986-88
Managed and oversaw all office functions encompassing the control of annual operating budgets. Sources and negotiated purchasing of cost effective, quality equipment and supplies.

EDUCATION
BACHELOR OF SCIENCE IN MANAGEMENT, 1986
Pepperdine University, Malibu, CA
Additional courses, workshops and seminars include:
PERSONNEL * WORK TEAMS * BUSINESS WRITING * ORGANIZATION SKILLS

COMPUTER SKILLS
Hardware: IBM * DEC
Communications: PCANYWHERE * QMODEM * PROCOMM
Software: MULTIMATE * PROFESSIONAL WRITE * ONE-WRITE PLUS * WINDOWS * LOTUS 1-2-3

■ Job objective is brief and to the point.

■ Applicable course work, workshops, and seminars are highlighted.

OFFICE MANAGER (Construction)

CHRIS SMITH
178 Green Street
Rhododendron, OR 97049
(503) 555-5555

OBJECTIVE A management or administrative position that will utilize and challenge proven skills and varied experience.

EDUCATION Willamette University, Salem, OR
B.S., Management, 1986
Spanish minor

EXPERIENCE

1989- **Office Manager**
Present RITTER CONSTRUCTION, Rhododendron, OR
Provide payroll, bookkeeping, personnel, inventory, and job scheduling management for this medium-size construction company. Assist in estimating process. Prepare accounts receivable and payable. Maintain good customer and vendor relations.

1896-1989 **Senior Service Representative**
LEHMAN BANK, Monmouth, OR
Opened new accounts and cross selling of bank services. Conducted branch audits. Performed daily balancing and troubleshooting of ATM system. Extensive customer service and public relations.

1983-1986 **Nurse's Aide**
CUTTER MEMORIAL HOSPITAL, Salem, OR
Directed patient care and nursing support.

1982-1983 **Sales Associate**
BERKOWITZ DRUGS, Salem, OR
Retail sales responsibility included customer service, cash register operation, merchandising, and inventory control.

PERSONAL Real Estate Salesperson's License (Oregon)
Notary Public
Experience with IBM PC-based computer systems
Fluent in French, Conversational Spanish

■ Candidate's most relevant work experience is prioritized throughout resume.

■ Clean layout makes resume easy to read.

OFFICE MANAGER (General)

CHRIS SMITH
178 Green Street
Wayne, NE 68787
(402) 555-5555

OBJECTIVE

To contribute developed skills to a challenging Office Manager/Secretarial position with a progressive organization offering opportunities for growth and advancement.

SUMMARY OF QUALIFICATIONS

- More than twenty years office experience including knowledge of typing and word processing (several systems).
- Self-motivated; able to implement decisions and set effective priorities to achieve both immediate and long-term goals.
- Bilingual - Spanish and English.
- Excellent communication skills, both oral and written.
- Proven interpersonal skills, having dealt with a variety of professionals and clients.

PROFESSIONAL EXPERIENCE

1991-Present EMERSON ASSOCIATES, Wayne, NE
Office Manager
Arrange logistics for office expansion and relocation. Establish office procedures and systems. Actuate/implement filing system, client billing system and bookkeeping. Order supplies; maintain inventory. Handle word processing and receptionist responsibilities.

1982-1991 RUNNING FAWN HOUSING COMMISSION, Primrose, NE
Administrative Assistant
Functioned as principal support staff person to Executive Director, providing comprehensive administrative and clerical support services. Organized/managed work schedule. Coordinated communications flow with commissioners, staff, Mayor's Office, public and private officials and general public. Prepared Director's scheduled events; organized/presented information in a useful format. Administered work-flow.

1977-1982 COMMISSION ON JEWISH AFFAIRS, Table Rock, NE
Administrative Assistant
Management of office included: typing, recording minutes at commission meetings, handling incoming calls, assisting general public, and maintaining office supplies. Coordinated information release to press, legislators and interested individuals.

1974-1977 PAUA SHELL HOSPITAL, Broken Bow, NE
Personnel Assistant
Provided administrative support to Personnel Recruiter and Personnel Representative. Screened applicants; checked references; scheduled interviews. Prepared candidates for typing tests. Answered incoming calls. Typed all office materials and correspondence.

Receptionist
Utilized Wang Word Processor. Greeted/screened applicants.

■ Job objective is supported by the facts and accomplishments stated in resume.

■ Education is omitted due to candidate's extensive work experience.

OFFICE MANAGER (International Business)

Chris Smith
178 Green Street
Sheboygan, WI 53081
(414) 555-5555

SUMMARY OF QUALIFICATIONS

- Supervisory/management experience.
- Fluent in Japanese and French languages; lived, worked, and studied in both Japan and France.
- Broad computer experience includes: Lotus, WordPerfect, IBM and MacIntosh.
- Self-motivated and detail-oriented.
- Able to motivate staff to facilitate work flow and meet operational deadlines.

EDUCATION

Ithaca College, Ithaca, NY
B.A., International Relations, December 1987

Universite de Paris, Paris, France
Courses in French Business and Japanese Language

PROFESSIONAL EXPERIENCE

Leary Company, Sheboygan, WI   1989-Present
Office Manager, Project Development Department
- Supervise staff in a diversity of projects. Office communications in Japanese.
- Write/control monthly $200,000 budget.
- Oversee public relations, advertising, association memberships, and donations.
- Coordinate opening of Sheboygan office, interacting with designers, architects, lawyers, and landlord; arranged Opening Party for 300 guests.
- Develop nationwide relocation policy/orientation program for new employees.
- Maintain employee benefits.
- Determine program content, budget, advertising, and student selection for Leary's summer internships in Tokyo for American students.
- Supervise creation of new magazine in Japanese; conducted market research, article research and writing, layout and design.
- Conceptualize/develop Japanese Business Library containing 2000 books for public use.
- Actuate/implement accounting system/program on Lotus 1-2-3.

The Rivers Edge Products, Oshkosh, WI   1988-1989
Software Development, Advertising Department
- Assisted in development and marketing of on-line computer magazine.
- Miscellaneous duties.

■ Relevant work experience is emphasized while other positions are de-emphasized.

■ Summary of qualifications illustrates candidate's key credentials.

OFFICE MANAGER (Legal)

Chris Smith
178 Green Street
Montpelier, VT 05602
(802) 555-5555

PROFILE   Office management professional totally involved and dedicated to the services and quality of an organization, while maintaining strong work ethics and standards.

SUPPORTIVE QUALIFICATIONS/ACHIEVEMENTS
- Over eight years experience in office management and operations.
- Over fifteen years in all areas of legal secretarial work; four years involvement in bookkeeping and payroll.
- Computer Skills: 32 Meg Central Processing/Unix; Lotus 1-2-3; IBM PC compatible stand-alone configuration; WordPerfect Version 5.1; OfficePower, and Quicken Version 4.0 software.
- Demonstrated training skills; instructed each secretary in policies and procedures of organization, kept them updated on changes in the law, including maintenance of the law library.
- Proven communications and interpersonal skills: writing, speaking, listening; responsible for even planning, all advertising, and designing letterhead for firms' business stationary.

PROFESSIONAL EXPERIENCE

Duvell and Aldrich, P.C.   Montpelier, VT
Legal Office Manager/Bookkeeper   1986-Present
- Purchase and coordinate installation of all office equipment and its maintenance.
- Hire, supervise and coordinate schedules of support staff; responsible for needs of newly hired staff.
- Open, close and create case files and lists; manage personal injury protection files.
- Maintain account records on computer and hard copy; accounts payable and receivable; financial reports; client funds; distribute settlement funds.
- Assist operators with word processing, software/hardware programs; maintain computer reference library and system logbook.
- Provide auxiliary and continued support to attorneys specifically in personal injury law.

Cattail Associates   Johnson, VT
Legal Secretary - Admiralty/Federal/State Workers' Compensation   1985-1986

Artesia, Klebnick, and Rowe   Plainfield, VT
Legal Secretary - Small Claims and Collections   1983-1985

Cascade and Jergen   Poultney, VT
Legal Secretary - Business Law   1981-1983

Bird, Spoon and Mann   Castleton, VT
Legal Secretary - Corporate Litigation   1979-1981

EDUCATION

Johnson State College, Johnson, VT
Candidate for B.S. in Business Administration, 1996

■ Profile is concise and adds punch to resume.

■ Resume emphasizes qualifications pertaining to candidate's job objective.

ORDER ENTRY CLERK

CHRIS SMITH
178 Green Street
Lincoln, NE 68522
(402) 555-5555

CAREER OBJECTIVE
A position in general clerical or customer services.

CAREER HISTORY

THE BULLFROG COMPANY, Lincoln, NE   1990-Present
Order Entry - Parts Department
- Processed and shipped orders within 12 hours of receipt from Bull Group Field Engineers in the U.S. and abroad.
- Met or exceeded daily deadlines.
- Used computer application to track orders and determine status and availability of parts.
- Generated daily reports on status of orders.
- Prepared and used reports to identify and resolve order processing problems.
- Worked independently.
- Kept supervisors informed on daily basis.
- Established and maintained functional files.
- Invested and resolved complaints from Field Engineers.
- Coordinated with multiple departments and shippers to ensure timely deliveries.

K.T. INC., Norfolk, NE   1987-1989
General Office Administrator
Customer Services
Secretary/Receptionist
- Typed letters and reports.
- Maintained files.
- Answered inquiries about customers accounts.
- Received payments and balanced statements.
- Posted accounts receivable and payable.

EDUCATION

Marcelle Junior College, Omaha, NE
B.A., Computer Science, Expected 1995.

- Job descriptions are brief and punchy, without being choppy.

- Clean layout makes resume easy to read.

RECEPTIONIST (General)

CHRIS SMITH
178 Green Street
Laramie, WY 82071
(307) 555-5555

QUALIFICATIONS:
- Over 25 Years Secretarial/Administrative Experience
- Skills: Typing (65 wpm), Dictaphone, Multi-line Phones/Switchboard, Ten Key (110 kspm) Digital DECmate computer, bookkeeping, credit checks, statistical typing.
- Extensive business experience including accounting firms, legal firms, financial firms, insurance companies, transportation companies, medical environments, government agencies and non-profit groups.
- Offer common sense, ability to take initiative, quality orientation and the ability to see a job through.
- Outstanding communications skills . . . Extremely hardworking and dedicated.

EMPLOYMENT: MARSTON CONVENT, Laramie, WY, 1988-Present
Receptionist
Answer phone, greet visitors and provide information, tours, and literature. Record and monitor thank-you notes for all received donations. Perform light typing, filing, and word processing.

WYOMING PUBLIC TELEVISION, Laramie, WY, 1987-88
Telemarketer
Solicit donations. Monitored the ordering of informative pamphlets, placards, buttons, tee-shirts, etc.

RINALDO RANCH, Laramie, WY, 1983-88
Secretary
Provided word processing, customer relations, some accounts payable processing. Implemented new system for check processing; increased prompt payment of client bills.

WOMANPOWER INC., Laramie, WY, 1975-83
Secretary
Acted as liaison between public and CEO.

STATE HEALTH COALITION, Laramie, WY, 1965-75
Statistical Typist
Prepared health record documentation of infectious disease patients at State hospital. Managed training of new hires.

EDUCATION: TRAINING, INC., Boston, MA, 1965
An office careers training program in bookkeeping, typing, reception, word processing, and office procedures.
ST. JOSEPH'S ACADEMY, Portland, Maine
High School Diploma

- Job objective is unnecessary because resume illustrates a clear career path.

- Work history is stated in reverse chronological order, with most recent employment listed first.

RECEPTIONIST (Imports)

CHRIS SMITH
178 Green Street
Omaha, NE 68182
(402) 555-5555

OBJECTIVE
To contribute acquired clerical/administrative skills to a challenging position.

SUMMARY OF QUALIFICATIONS
- Clerical skills include typing (55 wpm), data entry, word processing, knowledge of Digital and Startel Computer Systems.
- Developed interpersonal skills, having dealt with a diversity of professionals, clients, and staff members.
- Adapt easily to new concepts and responsibilities.
- Proven ability to coordinate and organize priorities to meet scheduled/unscheduled deadlines.
- Developed supervisory abilities; able to designate responsibilities.
- Work well independently and as a team member.

PROFESSIONAL EXPERIENCE

C.C. CROW'S IMPORTS, Omaha, NE   1988-Present
Receptionist/Office Assistant
Requires extensive typing. Handle incoming calls including warehouse lines. Maintain word-processing, data entry, accounts receivable/payable and incoming/outgoing mail. Manage office equipment including Startel Computerized System and fax machine.

SWEETCHEEKS BEAUTY SUPPLIES, Anchorage, AK   1987-88
Receptionist
Referred incoming phone calls to respective parties. Coordinated the travel plans of the president. Performed dictation, data entry, filing, etc.

CHESAPEAK FURNITURE, Fairbanks, AK   1984-88
Customer Service Supervisor
Ssupervised employees to ensure observation of rules/regulations. Provided customer service; resolved customer complaints.

EDUCATION

GAMON JUNIOR COLLEGE, Lincoln, NE
Associate Degree, Business Administration, May 1987

REFERENCES

Furnished upon request.

- Strong action verbs bring resume to life.

- Resume emphasizes qualifications pertaining to candidate's job objective.

RECEPTIONIST (Salon)

CHRIS SMITH
178 Green Street
St. Louis, MO 63130
(314) 555-5555

OBJECTIVE
A challenging position offering opportunities for growth and advancement.

SUMMARY OF QUALIFICATIONS
- Typing (40 wpm), word processing, and accounting; adept with figures.
- Experience dealing with a diversity of professionals, clients, and staff members.
- Proven communication abilities, both oral and written.
- Adapt easily to new concepts and responsibilities.
- Self-motivated; able to set effective priorities to achieve immediate and long-term goals and meet operational deadlines.

PROFESSIONAL EXPERIENCE

DIETER'S SALON, St. Louis, MO   1990-93
Receptionist/General Clerk
Handled incoming calls; scheduled appointments.
Responsible for cash-flow and weekly payroll.
General clerical duties included some accounting, inventory maintenance, and filing.

CHANTILLY LACE APPAREL, Winslow, MO   1988-90
Receptionist
Provided customer services.
Assisted in editing sales circulars.
Greeted business associates.

BALZAC'S, St. Charles, MO   1986-88
Sales Associate/Cashier
Provided customer assistance; registered sales; responded to telephone inquiries. Security related functions included pre-opening employee and fitting room checks.

REFERENCES
Furnished upon request.

■ Education is omitted while practical skills and experience are emphasized.

■ Resume format is neat and professional.

CHRIS SMITH
178 Green Street
Dover, DE 19901
(302) 555-5555

SUMMARY OF QUALIFICATIONS
Administrative professional with high quality skills and experience in the strategic areas of Computer Operations, Customer Service and Administrative Operations
- Seasoned administrator and trainer
- Developed and taught various training sessions on computer hardware/software
- Reorganized numerous departments to increase efficiency, reduce expenses and inventory needs

EMPLOYMENT ABSTRACT
PRATT AUTOMATED SYSTEMS, Dover, DE   1986-Present
Secretary/Receptionist
- Process Account Payable invoices
- Direct incoming correspondence and phone requests to proper personnel
- Verify accuracy of and submit all employee time sheets and expense accounts
- Place and follow-up on all equipment orders
- Demonstrate and train customers on new software programs
- Create a database with information on customers
- Maintaine computers, scanners, printers and plotters
- Operate Source Data Systems Computer for input on service records pertaining to awards, advancements, special pay, emergency data
- Maintain over 1,000 personnel records

SOCIAL SECURITY ADMINISTRATION, Newark, DE   1982-86
Secretary
- Assisted claimants to ensure all SSI claims were processed in a timely manner
- Maintained files on claimants
- Performed receptionist duties

EDUCATION
CURRY COLLEGE, Milton, MA   1987
Course work: English 101, Computer Basics, DOS, Assembly

COMPUTERS
WordPerfect, Lotus 1-2-3, dBase III, DOS, DisplayWrite, Desktop Publishing, experience with spreadsheets inventory management

---

■ Background summary accentuates candidate's acquired professional skills and impressive track record.

■ Job descriptions are brief and punchy, without being choppy.

SECRETARY (Hospital)

CHRIS SMITH
178 Green Street
Washington, DC 20057
(202) 555-5555

OBJECTIVE:
An administrative position within a business setting.

QUALIFICATIONS:
- Over Eight Years Administrative Experience
- Exceptional Organizational Skills
- Outstanding Public Relations and Communications Skills

EXPERIENCE:

JENNINGS HOSPITAL, Washington, D.C.
Secretary-Radiation Therapy Department (1990-present)
Responsible for the administrative organization of the Radiation Therapy Department. This includes the preparation of charts, scheduling, typing and preparing invoices, requisitions, correspondence, answering phones, greeting patients and visitors, filing, inventory control, and general office organization. Serve as liaison between physicians, staff, and patients.

Senior Birth Registrar (1986-90)
Recorded live births and prepared and processed birth certificates, infant data, and associated documentation. Served as liaison between physicians, staff, and patients in regards to legal documentation. Inaugurated a pilot program which facilitated networking between Hospital and Registry of Vital Statistics.

Purchasing Assistant (1984-86)
Assisted in the purchasing of chemical and equipment requisitions. Controlled inventories and distribution. Implemented procedure enhancements.

Patient Observer (1988-89).
Provided emotional support and observation for at-risk patients. Program was administered through the Nursing Office.

EDUCATION:

TRIBORO JUNIOR COLLEGE, Denver, CO
A.S., Business, Major in Executive Secretarial Sciences (1988)

COMPUTERS:

Microsoft Word, Excel, WordPerfect, Lotus 1-2-3, IBM Compatible

---

- Job objective gives resume focus without limiting candidate's opportunities.

- Resume illustrates continual career progression.

SECRETARY (Production)

CHRIS SMITH
178 Green Street
Mitchell, SD 57301
(605) 555-5555

SUMMARY OF QUALIFICATIONS

- Skilled in book production and composition including design composition, production scheduling, desk-top periodical production, and photo-typesetting proofreading.
- Developed interpersonal, communication, and supervisory skills, having dealt with a diversity of professionals.
- Self-motivated. Adapt easily to new concepts and responsibilities.
- Function well independently and as team member; adept at creative problem-solving.

EDUCATION

BLACK HILLS STATE COLLEGE, Spearfish, SD
Bachelor of Arts, December 1989
Major: English   Minor: Psychology

EXPERIENCE

9/88-Present   HARTNICK GRAPHICS, Mitchell, SD
Assistant to Production Manager
Maintained liaisons between clients and production staff. Coordinated production schedules for in-house and freelance personnel. Prepared contract bids. Administered production status records; expedited completed works. Provided secretarial support and general office assistance. Composed monthly marketing forecast reports; corresponded via telex with -international clients regarding foreign government bids and export procedures.

4/84-9/88   ELDERBERRY INC., Huron, SD
Secretary to Director, Sales & Marketing
Performed all typing, tracked field engineers, and ensured smooth work flow. Handled special projects; completed inventory of engineering supplies.

11/83-4/84   TANGIBLES CORP., Sioux Falls, SD
Public Relations Secretary/Editorial Staff Assistant
Responsible for creative and production phases of quarterly publication. Handled public relations and press releases.

COMPUTERS

Familiar with Wang, IBM, NCR, and software programs: Lotus 1-2-3, WordPerfect, Microsoft Word, and Composer II Typesetting.

■ Layout is clean and well-organized.

■ Stating that "references are available upon request" is not essential; most employers will assume that references are available.

SECRETARY (Senior)

CHRIS SMITH
178 Green Street
Providence, RI 02908
(401) 555-5555

OBJECTIVE
To contribute acquired administrative skills to a Senior Secretary/Word Processor position.

SUMMARY OF QUALIFICATIONS
- More than 13 years administrative/clerical experience; type 90 wpm.
- Self-motivated; able to set effective priorities and implement decisions to achieve immediate and long-term goals and meet operational deadlines.
- Proven communication abilities, both oral and written.

PROFESSIONAL EXPERIENCE

CALDYNE ASSOCIATES, Providence, RI   1988-Present
Secretary
Process technical reports, engineering specs, and traffic studies utilizing Multi-mate WP. Type all requisite documents for staff of 30 professionals. Arrange meetings, handle incoming calls. Expedite UPS mailings, Federal Express, faxing and courier services. Type statistical charts, manuscripts, correspondence, and minutes. Order supplies, coordinate daily meetings, arrange luncheons, and administer labor cards.

BRISTOL BANK, Bristol, CT   1984-88
Secretary/Receptionist
Utilized call director, typed reports, letters, and expense sheets. Reserved conference rooms, order supplies. Responsible for calligraphy assignments.

SARGENT AGENCY, Hamden, CT   1981-84
Secretary
Assigned to School of Public Health. Managed typing of medical charts used in textbooks for Government Funded Medical Program in Iran.

EDUCATION
POLLACK SECRETARIAL SCHOOL, Jackson, TN   1979

COMPUTER SKILLS
DOS, Microsoft Word, IBM Compatible, Lotus 1-2-3

REFERENCES FURNISHED UPON REQUEST.

■ Separate category for computer experience calls attention to candidate's technical knowledge.

■ Education is applicable to candidate's job objective and adds weight to resume.

SHIPPING/RECEIVING EXPEDITER

CHRIS SMITH
178 Green Street
Henderson, NV 89014
(702) 555-5555

CAREER HISTORY
THE ALPHA CORPORATION, Henderson, NV
Shipping/Receiving Expediter (1987-Present)
- Entered packing slips, invoices, and other material control information into computer through a CRT.
- Compared and identified contents to packing slips.
- Coordinated with buyers and vendors on problem identification and resolution.
- Scheduled daily deliveries of incoming traffic.
- Transcribed bills of lading.
- Created and implemented an inventory system.
- Conducted physical inventory and updated locations of parts.
- Generated inventory and location reports using Lotus files (self-taught).

Assembler/Material Handler (1985-1987)
- Opened and delivered parts to line.
- Inspected and rejected defective parts.
- Achieved or exceeded production goals.
- Coordinated with co-workers to improve quality of parts.

ROBERT SMITH, INC., Sparks, NV
Clerk (1984-1985)
- Entered purchase orders using a CRT.
- Backed-up computer systems.
- Assisted in maintaining accounts receivable.

Mail Room Clerk (1978-1984)
- Updated/maintained customer files.
- Coordinated and conducted bulk mailings.

EDUCATION
Benton Junior College, Benton Harbor, MI
Associates Degree, Management (1978)

- Resume indicates a series of promotions.

- Education is listed towards bottom of resume because candidate's practical experience outweighs his/her degree.

STAFF ASSISTANT

CHRIS SMITH
178 Green Street
Clinton, MS 39058
(601) 555-5555

OBJECTIVE
To contribute extensive administrative and clerical experience to a challenging position.

SUMMARY OF QUALIFICATIONS
- Adapt easily to new concepts and responsibilities.
- Developed interpersonal, communication, and supervisory skills.
- Self-motivated; able to set effective priorities and implement decisions to achieve immediate and long-term goals and meet operational deadlines.

PROFESSIONAL EXPERIENCE

1990-Present   AUGUSTUS TELEPHONE COMPANY, Clinton, MS
Staff Assistant, Management Job Evaluation, Management Compensation, Human Resources Department
Administer personnel functions and support activities relating to management job evaluation and compensation support. Develop and maintain internal procedures. Control Management Salary Guide. Research and analyze significant data. Coordinate, direct, and mechanize reports and procedures. Requires thorough knowledge of all office equipment and systems.

1988-90   BRAINCHILD, INC., Jackson, MS
Staff Assistant
Reviewed, prepared, processed job/employee change reports for all general departments. Interpreted salary policy. Interfaced with Human Resources Department and upper level management including company officers.

1983-88   TECHNIQUES, INC., Lorman, MS
Staff Assistant
Operations Assistant, Human Resources Department, 1983-85

RELEVANT EDUCATION
Attended in-house seminars and training including Supervisory Relationship Training and Job Evaluation.

COMPUTERS
IBM PC, Mainframe, Focus, Wang Word Processing, dBase, and Multimate

■ Boldface, all-capital headings give resume punch.

■ Relevant education emphasizes training of interest to employers.

STENOGRAPHER

CHRIS SMITH
178 GREEN STREET
REDFORD, MI 48239
(313) 555-5555

OBJECTIVE:
A challenging position as a stenographer in a progressive company.

ACHIEVEMENTS AND QUALIFICATIONS:
- Strong shorthand and speed writing skills at 130 WPM.
- Excel at Gregg Simplified and Diamond Jubilee
- methods; proficient with the Pitman method.
- Area of expertise is the transcription, editing and interpreting of stenographic characters into clear, concise, and precise English.
- Typing skills include word processing at 80 WPM and typewriter production at 65 WPM.
- Recipient of the *Shorthand Award* and *Stenographer of the Year Award* from the Pittman method archives.
- Consistent recognition from the Gregg simplified method archives for excellence in Gregg-style character performance.

EDUCATION:
Salem State College, Salem, MA
A.A Secretarial Sciences, 1987
Katherine Gibbs Secretarial School, Boston, MA
Executive Secretarial program, 1987

PUBLICATIONS:
Stenographer's Notes, co-author D.D. Sweeny;
Whole Word Publishing, Boston, MA 1991

Gregg Shorthand Made Simple, co-author D.D. Sweeny;
Whole Word Publishing, Boston, MA, 1991

EMPLOYMENT:
1992- *Harvard University Admissions,* Cambridge, MA Head Stenographer
Present

1988-1992 *John Ervine Mutual Life Insurance,* Boston, MA Stenographer

- Publications, whether book or magazine, are impressive on a resume.

- Achievements and qualifications give resume impact.

TELEPHONE OPERATOR

CHRIS SMITH
178 Green Street
Pompano Beach, FL 33063
(305) 555-5555

PROFESSIONAL OBJECTIVE A challenging position within the Southern Bell Corporation in Directory Assistance where progressive experience and excellence will be utilized and advanced.

EXPERIENCE Southern Bell Telephone/SBT
Pompano Beach, FL

1982-Present **Operator**
Responsible for customer calls that can't be direct dialed. Knowledge and skill on the OSDI equipment. Ensure repair orders are called into main office. Assist all callers in a timely, courteous fashion.

1977-1982 **411 Directory Assistance Operator**
Provide telephone numbers for callers.
Ensure numerical accuracy and speed.

EDUCATION AND TRAINING Winter Park High School, Winter Park, FL
Graduated 1979

Southern Bell Telephone Company Directory Assistance Operator Seminar 1977

Performed training and work routines under the direction of an SBT company mentor 1977

SKILLS
- OSDI Telecommunications Equipment
- Data Entry
- Type 45 WPM
- Accurate
- Willing to travel or relocate

REFERENCES AVAILABLE UPON REQUEST

■ Objective indicates candidate's desire to advance within current organization.

■ Specialized job training strengthens candidate's qualifications.

TICKET AGENT

CHRIS SMITH
178 Green Street
Melrose, CT 06049
(203) 555-5555

OBJECTIVE
To apply skills attained through experience and education to an entry-position in the field of travel.

STRENGTHS
- Self-motivated and goal-oriented.
- Proven abilities in organization and communication.
- Perform well in high-stress atmosphere.
- Highly developed interpersonal skills, having worked cooperatively with a variety of professionals.
- Experienced traveler.

EDUCATION

Assertiveness Training Courses, The Burke Program, 1991
Computer Programming Workshop
Certified, 1992
University of Bridgeport, Bridgeport, CT
B.A., Public Relations, 1990

WORK EXPERIENCE

TICKET AGENT, Davis Harwin Tours, Ivortyon, CT   1993-Present
Resolved all customer needs. Arranged travel schedules. Handled incoming cash.

MACHINE OPERATOR, Carlisle Sand Inc., Melrose, CT   1991-1993
Duties include sorting and metering mail.

CASUAL DISTRIBUTION CLERK, U.S. Post Office, Hartford, CT   1989-1991
Set up mail room and appropriate forwarding of packages and mail.

MENTAL HEALTH COUNSELOR, Mystic, CT   1986-1989
Counseled, supervised and evaluated clients. Arranged special events for youths.

RECEPTIONIST, Warbell Realty, Hartford, CT   1985-1986
Serviced clients. Arranged appointments. Handled incoming calls. Dealt with general office functions.

REFERENCES

Available on request.

■ Strengths section puts positive twist on candidate's professional skills and qualifications.

■ Job objective helps give resume focus.

TYPIST

CHRIS SMITH
178 Green Street
Tampa, FL 32714
(813) 555-5555

CAREER OBJECTIVE
A clerical/typist position requiring strong skills in computer literacy.

BACKGROUND SUMMARY
Dedicated, trustworthy enthusiastic employee. Loves a challenge and enjoys working with people. Strong background in computer applications. Good humored, friendly and has a positive outlook. Proven ability to take initiative and adapt to changing priorities.

CAREER HISTORY
Contemporary Data Systems, Tampa, FL, 1987-Present
Secretary and Clerk Typist I-III
- Compiled daily reports and prepared documents using Microsoft Word for Windows, WordStar, Windows, and RBase.
- Logged, filed, and retrieved Component Engineering Reports
- Transcribed reports
- Served as department receptionist: Answered and directed incoming phone calls/messages.
- Ordered office supplies for the entire department
- Typed purchase orders, expense reports, recorded and distributed petty cash
- Sent and distributed fax messages
- Made travel arrangements and reservations
- Worked with Telex machine
- Performed duties of company operator as required
- Compiled, printed and distributed various reports
- Coordinated and distributed part numbers for all engineering departments

Tampa Sporting Goods, Tampa, FL, 1987-1988
Sales Clerk (part-time)
- Met and serviced customers
- Responded to customer demands for products of information
- Maintained inventory levels
- Participated in showroom reorganization and presentations
- Conducted physical inventories

EDUCATION AND WORK-RELATED TRAINING
Attending University of Tampa
B.A., Expected 1995
Contemporary Data System, Lotus 1-2-3, WordStar, Quality Work Group, ISO 9000
Type 70 wpm.

■ Background summary gives a snapshot of the candidate's working habits and personality.

■ Education and work-related training direct attention to candidate's valuable computer knowledge and typing skills.

VICE-PRESIDENT OF ADMINISTRATION

CHRIS SMITH
178 Green Street
Elicott City, MD 21042
(410) 555-5555

EXPERIENCE

VICE-PRESIDENT OF ADMINISTRATION
Moon Glass Systems Corporation (manufacturers of electronic components)
Elicott City, MD   1990-Present

- Initially oversaw the construction of two facilities, a 25,000 square-foot. facility in Baltimore and a 47,000 square-foot facility in Columbia.
- Planned and scheduled total move including plant layout, space planning, communications systems planning and purchase, and coordinated total move for 400 employees without any loss in production.
- Promoted to Vice-President of Administration with total responsibility for personnel, safety, security, buildings and grounds, data processing, and outside services in a company which grew from $15 million to $30 million in volume.
- Direct activities pertaining to facilities maintenance including janitorial tasks, preventive maintenance programs, buildings and grounds maintenance, security systems.
- Implement budget and variance policies; establish inventory levels; develop strong receivables program; and prepare and review computerized financial reports for management.

CORPORATE MANAGER, Standards & Controls
Kingsmeade Company
Baltimore, MD   1985-1990

- Developed standards and controls pertaining to several thousand employees. This included indirect support and direct labor at 20 locations.
- Reported to the Vice-President of Materials and Manpower Planning and handled the personnel function for the Standards & Controls Department. Budget responsibility: $4 million in a company with $200 million sales volume.
- Interfaced with all departments on staffing requirements and controls.
- Developed incentive programs; determined staff and requirements; established workplace layouts and material flow.

PLANT MANAGER
Sycamore Co.
Columbia, MD   1982-1987

- Started as a Computer Operator and advanced to Assistant Plant Manager on rotation to 20 plants throughout Columbia. Promoted to Plant Manager; assigned to an unprofitable operation and successfully brought the plant into a profit making operation for the first time within three years. Company employed 50 and produced $6 million in sales.

EDUCATION

Salisbury State College, Salisbury, MD
Bachelor of Science Degree, Business Administration, 1982
Graduated with High Honors

■ Resume illustrates continual career progression.

■ Education is listed towards bottom of resume because candidate's practical experience outweighs his/her degree.

8
Communications

Nature of Work

Those in the communications field range from behind the scenes workers to on-air personalities. Positions involve a great deal of writing, research, and editing. They may also involve work-related travel, odd hours, and extreme pressure to meet deadlines. Communications professionals have to interact with people extensively every day. They are the people who gather and disseminate information about current events, act as advocates for businesses and other agencies, or present television and newsbroadcasts.

Employment

For the most part, communication professionals work in the metropolitan areas where the central media markets and publishing firms are concentrated. Increasingly though, jobs are opening up in suburban media outlets, service, and biotech industries for such positions as public relations workers and technical writers.

Training

With fierce competition to break into the communications field, most employers require a bachelor's degree in public relations, journalism, communications, English, or some related field. Some type of related experience, such as an internship, is a definite advantage. Strong written and oral communication skills are a must, while technical skills such as desk top publishing and broadcast knowledge are clearly an asset.

Job Outlook

The employment of those in communications is expected to experience average growth for all occupations through the year 2005. More jobs will be opening up as more and more businesses come into existence, but the competition for these positions will be great. The toughest obstacles will be for those individuals without the appropriate educational background or work experience. It is expected that the vast majority of jobs will result from the need to replace those professionals who leave their jobs to retire, take another job, or for other reasons.

Earnings

The annual salary range for communications professionals is wide, due to the fact that some individuals working television or radio earn a salary commensurate with their celebrity status, while the starting writer or editor may begin at $15,000 a year. Typically, a broadcast announcer can expect to earn anywhere from $13,000 to $54,000 in radio, and $30,000 to $129,000 in television. Newspaper reporters average $22,000 to $42,000 a week, while writers and editors in the publishing field earn $20,000 to 30,000 a year.

ASSISTANT EDITOR

CHRIS SMITH
178 Green Street
Philadelphia, PA 19103
(215) 555-5555

EXPERIENCE
1989-Present PUBLICATIONS DEPARTMENT, MUNSON MUSEUM, Philadelphia, PA
Assistant Editor
- Proofread and copyedit scholarly archaeological monographs and museum catalogues.
- Assist editor with all aspects of book production; prepare and organize art work for reproduction, supervise paste-up, and review/approve proofs.
- Identify titles to be reprinted, making necessary editorial changes, obtaining estimates, contracting typesetting, printing, and binding services.
- Recommend and supervise freelance artists. Manage a staff assistant.
- Work directly with authors in regard to editing and artwork.
- Promote materials at various conferences. Select appropriate titles and contract with a combined exhibit group.
- Served as Rights and Permissions Editor.
- Managed inventory control of entire publications stock.
- Supervised order filling; coordinated shipping, billing and maintenance of circulation records.

1984-89 VILLANOVA UNIVERSITY, OFFICE OF INTERNATIONAL PROGRAMS FOR AGRICULTURE, Villanova, PA
Assistant to the Director
- Edited and typed grant proposals, research papers and reports.
- Coordinated preparation and distribution of an international newsletter.
- Served as contact between federal agencies and university departments for sponsored foreign students.
- Coordinated arrangements for visitors, seminars, conferences, and overseas and domestic travel.

1982-84 **Project Administrator**
- Controlled export trade of endangered floral species within Pennsylvania for U.S. Fish and Wildlife Scientific Authority.

1979-82 U.S. DEPARTMENT OF LABOR, Scranton, PA
Clerk-Stenographer
- Performed secretarial duties for large technical and professional staffs of the Architecture and Engineering Section and the Community Development Division.
- Served on the Education Committee.

EDUCATION

SWARTHMORE COLLEGE, Swarthmore, PA
Bachelor of Arts Degree in English, 1978; GPA 3.8
Academic Honors: Phi Beta Kappa, Phi Eta Sigma, Dean's List

SKILLS

Lotus 1-2-3, Microsoft Word, WordPerfect, Pascal, FORTRAN, Proficient in Spanish and French

■ Job descriptions are straightforward and understandable.

■ Academic honors and a high GPA make educational background appear more impressive.

ASSOCIATE EDITOR

Chris Smith
178 Green Street
Little Rock, AR 72204
(501) 555-5555

WORK EXPERIENCE

Senior Editor   May 1994-Present
THE SOUTHWEST TRAVEL REPORT   Littlerock, AR
Develop and manage editorial direction and content of start-up monthly regional trade journal covering travel industry. Instrumental in content development and design. Assign and manage contributing writers, report and wrote stories for publication prototype, coordinate art and production elements.

Associate Editor   April 1992-May 1994
THE JENSEN COMPANY   Little Rock, AR
Reported and wrote features for five departments for three trade magazines covering the meeting, convention and incentive travel industries. Assisted in the development of story and art ideas as well as copy editing and proofing.

Assistant Editor   Dec. 1991-March 1992
DEYLAH PUBLISHING   Little Rock, AR
Researched and wrote items for annual fact books and their weekly supplemental updates covering communications industry.

Contributing Editor   Sept. 1988-Nov. 1991
WHERE TO EAT   Little Rock, AR
Wrote articles for monthly restaurant trade newspaper.

Administrative Assistant   April-June 1988
CONWAY ARTS JOURNAL   Conway, AR
Assisted business and marketing directors in direct mail projects, classified advertising, and fulfillment of book and subscription orders.

Editorial Intern   Sept.-Dec. 1987
CONWAY ARTS JOURNAL   Conway, AR
Reported and wrote articles and columns for twice monthly newspaper for the arts and entertainment industry. Position also involved research, fact checking, and production support.

EDUCATION

Hendrix College, Conway, AR
B.A. degree, English/Political Science, 1988
Member-The Society of Professional Journalists

■ Resume indicates a series of promotions.

■ Education is listed towards bottom of resume because candidate's practical experience outweighs his/her degree.

AUTHOR

CHRIS SMITH
178 Green Street
Riverdale, NY 10471
(212) 555-5555

<u>EXPERIENCE</u>

Writer specializing in women's issues, theater and the arts.

Books: <u>Best Plays of 1993; A Collection of Theater Reviews</u> (Farber Publishing, forthcoming)
<u>Best Plays of 1992; A Collection of Theater Reviews</u> (Farber Publishing, 1993)
<u>The Evolution of Feminism in the Theater</u> (Farber Publishing, 1991)
<u>The French Woman: Breaking the Stereotype</u>, by Mimi St. Pierre (Birnblass Press, 1988)
<u>A Tale of Caracas</u>, by Esteban Bolivera (Carolina Publishers, 1985)
Plays with corresponding reviews (multiple authors) published by Carolina Publishers in International Theater, 1982.

Articles: Currently theater columnist for *The New York Review* and editorial writer for *Woman Magazine*. Credits include:

Equality	*Guide to Broadway*	*Our World*
Eve	*Men's World*	*Parent And Child*
Family	*Mother Earth*	*The Renaissance Reader*
The Feminist	*New York Theater Guide*	*Teenage America*
The Great Debate	*NOW*	*Today's Woman*

**Corporate
Clients:** United Feminists, New York Theater Association

Editor: 1977-81: Contributing Editor, *The Feminist*
1973-76: Copy Editor/Proofreader for various clients
1970-72: Manuscript Submissions Coordinate, Non-Fiction Division, Carolina Publishers
1964-69: Senior Editor, *The Renaissance Reader*
1962-1963: Editor, *Mother Earth*
1960-1961: Assistant Editor, *Our World*

<u>EDUCATION</u>

Adelphi University
Garden City, NY
Bachelor of Arts in English Literature
Minor: Journalism

L'Ecole d'Avignon
Avignon, France
Semester Abroad

Universidad de Cordoba
Corboda, Spain
Semester Abroad

■ Candidate's writing experience is emphasized at top of resume.

■ Past job experience is listed and not elaborated on.

BROADCAST PRODUCER

CHRIS SMITH
178 Green Street
Waukesha, WI 53186
(414) 555-5555

<u>EDUCATION</u>

University of Massachusetts, Amherst, MA
Bachelor of Arts in English, 1990

School of the Museum of Fine Arts, Boston, Massachusetts, 1985-1986

<u>TELEVISION PRODUCTION</u>

1989 to   WTOR EDUCATIONAL FOUNDATION, Worcester, MA
1993

Producer
Produced:
Three contract series (20 half-hour programs for each) for U.S. Marines and Stanford University Commission on Extension Services: "Ideologies in World Affairs," "Computer Science I," and "Computer Science II"

"Fighting Mad" — series of two-hour-long group therapy sessions conducted by Dr. Paula Hershey, Hamline University

One-hour special on gay men and AIDS epidemic

"The 21 Inch Classroom" — History, Geology Pilot

"Bob Bersen Reviews"

Wrote/produced:
Half-hour promotional videotape selling ETV for the University of Massachusetts, Amherst.

Half-hour promotional videotape selling ITV for the 21-Inch Classroom

<u>REFERENCES</u>

Available upon request.

■ Format is organized and visually appealing.

■ Resume emphasizes qualifications pertaining to candidate's job objective.

COLUMNIST

CHRIS SMITH
178 Green Street
Elmhurst, IL 60126
(312) 555-5555

EDUCATION

Knox College, Galesburg, IL
BA in Communications
1986-1990

PROFESSIONAL EXPERIENCE

The Windy City
Current columnist, photographer and freelance writer for monthly tourist magazine in Chicago. Write 1000-word column each month entitled "Around the Town." 1993-Present.

The Great Outdoors
Wrote copy for 75-page mail-order camping equipment catalog. Wrote and revised hundreds of 25-word sales descriptions. Met tight deadlines in eight-week freelance project. 1993.

The Index
Full-time staff writer for Knox College alumni magazine. Wrote short news briefs and in-depth features, including several cover stories. As the only staff writer, researched and investigated all major articles and initiated several new story ideas. Current freelance writer. 1992.

Along the Shore
Freelance writer for monthly newsletter for cities surrounding Lake Michigan. 1991.

Trailways
Created, edited and published a newsletter while participating in a hike along the Appalachian Trail. Solicited submissions, edited all copy and desktop published the newsletter on a MacIntosh computer. 1991.

The Knox Collegian
Full-time editor of campus newspaper. Assigned and edited all articles for weekly publication. Involved in all aspects of publication process, including writing, copyediting, proofreading, desktop publishing and layout. Managed staff of 15. 1990.

Tempo
Intern at newsweekly in Chicago. Responsibilities included proofreading, fact-checking and writing 250-word news briefs for "Around the World" section. Wrote an in-depth feature on battered women's shelters in the Chicago area. 1990.

References and all works available upon request

■ Job descriptions are concise and easy to follow.

■ Work history is stated in reverse chronological order, with most recent employment listed first.

COPY EDITOR

CHRIS SMITH
178 Green Street
Columbia, MO 65201
(314) 555-5555

Objective:

A full-time Editing or Researching position

Related Experience:

1993-1994 **Managing Editor,** *The Circle,* **University of Missouri**
Copy Edit and supervise the writing, formatting, and layout process of producing a biweekly college newspaper. Monitor and order supplies. Facilitate monthly payroll.

1993 **Assistant Editor, Book Editing Internship, University of Missouri**
Copy Edit multi-cultural college English teaching text to be published Spring 1995. Conduct correspondence. Confirm references. Suggest editorial changes.

1992 **Teaching Assistant & Writing Center Tutor, English Department, University of Missouri**
Assist instructor in leading class discussion for freshman composition course. Advise class groups on papers. Grade freshman composition papers. Tutor individual students in any curriculum.

1991-1992 **Writer,** *Science World Newsletter,* **University of Missouri**
Interview/Research and write feature articles for biannual college newsletter spotlighting UM faculty/student activities and accomplishments.

1991 **Assistant Editor, Internship,** *The Art Journal*
Aid in submission selection. Manage correspondence. Copy Edit. Collaborate editorial changes with Editor. Confirm references. Write and organize contributor section.

Computer Skills:

QuarkXpress, MacIntosh, Pagemaker, AmiPro, MS Word, WordPerfect (DOS and Windows), Quattro Pro Windows.

Education:

University of Missouri, Columbia, MO
B.A. English Literature, Candidate, 1994
Cumulative G.P.A.: 3.1/4.0 Major: 3.4/4.0

■ Internship experience is valuable for candidates with little job experience, particularly if it corresponds to the position sought.

■ Unrelated work experience is omitted.

CORRESPONDENT

CHRIS SMITH
178 Green Street
Swannanoa, NC 28778
(704) 555-5555

EDUCATION

WAKE FOREST UNIVERSITY, Winston, NC
Master of Arts, Print Journalism, May 1984

SHEFFIELD UNIVERSITY, Sheffield, U.K.
History Degree, June 1983
Literature Degree, June 1982

PRINCETON UNIVERSITY, Princeton, NJ
Summer Program in Anthropology, 1981

EXPERIENCE

1991-   *LE RECORD DU JOUR*
Present   French Daily Newspaper

Responsible for writing stories and features on local affairs for the Cultural and the National Sections. Assignments completed on deadline. Travel extensively throughout France and topical point of interest stories. Have been awarded six GLOBE journalism awards for international reporting. Broke story on Sorbonne smuggling; resulted in the recovery of six pieces of priceless art stolen from the Louvre in 1988.

1984-1990   *TOKYO RECORD*
Japanese Daily Newspaper - English Edition (2nd largest in country)

Responsible for writing stories and features on social and political issues throughout the country.

SKILLS

Lotus, WordPerfect, IBM
35 mm Photography
1/2 inch Videotape
Super 8 Movies
Fluent in French, English and Spanish

PERSONAL DATA

Writing fiction and poetry (novel is pending publication). Traveled extensively throughout the world.

Letters of reference and writing samples will be furnished upon request.

■ Strong educational credentials strengthen resume.

■ Personal interests and activities are relevant to candidate's field of interest.

EDITOR

CHRIS SMITH
178 Green Street
Birmingham, AL 35244
(205) 555-5555

EXPERIENCE

BANKS AND SON INC., Birmingham, AL
Senior Editor, Reference (10/92-Present)
Responsible for the evaluation and acquisition of general trade reference titles.
Assessed the profitability of projects and negotiated contracts.
Involved in all aspects of the publishing process from development and editing to production, publicity, and marketing.
In-house editor for institutional authors such as the American Library Association and the Vintage Motorcycles newsletter.

ROMANCE NOVEL-OF-THE-MONTH CLUB, INC., Kinsey, AL
Associate Director (5/89-10/92)
Evaluated fiction and nonfiction manuscripts.
Managed all club titles in terms of pricing and inventory, and initial, backlist, and premium uses.
Responsible for Club sales budgeting and estimating.
Supervised ten employees.

Managing Editor (1984-5/89)
Deputy Editorial Director of the British division.
Evaluated manuscripts.
Scheduled new and backlist titles in the RNOMC News and in Club advertising.
Supervised two employees.

ILL FATED KISSES, Selma, AL
Editorial Director, (1980-1984)
Supervised the design and production of titles for two continuity programs.
Responsible for identifying, developing, and/or acquiring successful poetry and artwork.

EDUCATION

New York University, New York, New York, 1984
Completed 12 credits in the Masters in Publishing Program
Courses included Publishing Law, Finance, and Subsidiary Rights

Pace University, New York, New York, 1983
B.S. Degree, Magazine Journalism
B.A. Degree, English Literature

- Job descriptions reflect candidate's extensive experience in the publishing business.

- Courses listed under education are related to candidate's field of interest.

EDITORIAL DIRECTOR

CHRIS SMITH
178 Green Street
Longmeadow, MA 01106
(413) 555-5555

PROFESSIONAL OBJECTIVE
A challenging editorial position.

PROFESSIONAL BACKGROUND
1985 to   SONG OF THE MUSE PUBLICATIONS
Present   Longmeadow, Massachusetts
Director of Publications (1988 to Present)
- Responsible for managing operations of poetry, book and periodical publishing.
- Report to Director of Headquarters Operations.
- Book publishing includes 26 titles booklist with nine to ten new titles annually.
- Periodical publishing includes 60-page monthly membership magazine with $25,000 advertising revenue, and 300-page semiannual subscription journal with $48,000 subscription and advertising income.
- Hire/terminate, schedule, train, and supervise staff of five.
- Forecast, prepare, and monitor expenditures of operational budget.
- Coordinate editing, design, composition, mechanical production, and book fulfillment.

Editor, Song of the Muse (1985 to 1989)
- Responsible for editorial content, planning, and graphics for 60-page monthly.
- Directed and approved mechanical preparation and cover design.
- Managed editorial development, editing/rewrite, copy editing, type specs, proofreading, photo/illustration research and selection, and layout.

1978 to 1979   JOURNAL OF ALCOHOLISM
Stoughton, MA
Associate Publisher and Marketing Director
- Responsible for profit and loss of 60 page monthly with circulation of 17,000.
- Realized 25% profit on gross annual revenue of $800,000.
- Coordinated income from subscriptions, conferences and workshops, advertising, and list rentals.

EDUCATIONAL BACKGROUND
TOLEDO STATE UNIVERSITY, Toledo, Ohio
Bachelor of Arts in French, English Minor, 1985

AFFILIATION
Book Builders of Boston

COMPUTERS
Microsoft Word, Pagemaker, DOS, Lotus 1-2-3

■ Statistics and dollar figures quantify candidate's accomplishments.

■ Job-related affiliations demonstrate candidate's active participation in his/her field.

EVENTS PLANNER

CHRIS SMITH
178 Green Street
Miami, FL 33054
(305) 555-5555

OBJECTIVE:

A challenging and responsible Events Planning position offering opportunities for direct client contact, where my experience, education and capabilities can be fully utilized.

EXPERIENCE:

9/88-Present **SEA THE WORLD (INTERNATIONAL CRUISE LINE),** Miami, FL
Passengers: 500 to 2000
Crew Members: 300-800 from over 40 nations
First Purser (8/91-Present)
Responsible for directing activities of four offices and supervising front office personnel. Act as on-board personnel and accounting departments. Supervise staff of up to 10 on embarkation days. On call 24 hours.

- Prepare manifest, port papers for all ports of call, clearance, crew visas and act as liaison between ship and country for all customers and immigration procedures for both passengers and crew.
- Resolve passenger problems and collect accounts. Responsible for $250,00 safe for foreign exchange. Prepare payroll.
- Make all travel arrangements for on-board entertainers, changing twice on each cruise, i.e., booking flights, hotel reservations, etc.
- Plan, schedule, organize and supervise operations for crew benefit events for various organizations at ports of call.
- Oversee all printing/typesetting, i.e., daily programs, literature, menus, maps for shore travel, health programs, invitations, newsletters.
- Order equipment and supplies for hotel department.

Second Purser - Foreign Exchange (2/91-7/91)
Second Purser - Crew (3/90-1/91)
Senior Assistant Purser (5/89-3/90)
Assistant Purser (9/88-4/89)

6/87-8/88 **THE AMBER HOTEL,** Providence, RI
Front Office Sales Agent
Responsible for taking reservations, solving problems and checking guests in and out. Handled conventions of up to 250 as well as transient guests.

EDUCATION:

JOHNSON AND WALES UNIVERSITY, Providence, RI
SCHOOL OF HOTEL RESTAURANT MANAGEMENT
Bachelor of Science (May 1987)

■ Brief description of current employer enhances the weight of candidate's accomplishments.

■ Job descriptions highlight candidate's leadership skills and problem-solving abilities.

INFORMATION SUPPORT SPECIALIST

CHRIS SMITH
178 Green Street
Evansville, WY 82636
(307) 555-5555

OBJECTIVE
A position where I can contribute excellent word processing and administrative skills.

EXPERIENCE
Kimball Equipment Corp., Casper, WY
1990-present
Information Support Specialist
Offer formal and informal training and assistance in the use of end-user computing hardware, software and applications, most specifically Lotus 1-2-3, WordPerfect 5.1, various versions of MS-DOS and graphics packages. Work with user department personnel to ensure adherence to office automation/end-user computing guidelines, standards and procedures. Coordinated with other Information Services staff to provide appropriate education, hardware, software and data required to effectively assist users. Perform problem analysis and resolution activities via company help line.

1985-1989
Supervisor, Word Processing, Word Processing Center
Planned, organized, directed and controlled provision of stenographic, clerical, word/information processing services and company telephone operators. Supervised 13 full-time employees. Duties included determining material, personnel and budgeting needs. Designed work flow systems, defined operating standards and evaluated overall effectiveness. Established cost and quality controls, and monitored performance to insure that proper levels were maintained.

1983-1984
Word Processing Specialist, Word Processing Center
Operated all information processing equipment in Center. Developed thorough knowledge of center procedures and maintenance of records with ability of meeting high priority turnaround time. Functions performed included formatting and producing complex documents, records processing, retrieval of data from electronic files, analyzing requirements for and handling special projects, training center and system personnel in use of information processing equipment. Acted as administrative support specialist and supervisor in their absence.

EDUCATION
Associates Degree, Business Management, 1983
University of Wyoming, Laramie, WY

REFERENCES
Available upon request.

- Education is listed towards bottom of resume because candidate's practical experience outweighs his/her degree.

- Job objective focuses on the needs of the employer, not the job candidate.

JOURNALIST

CHRIS SMITH
178 Green Street
College Park, MD 20742
(301) 555-5555

PROFESSIONAL EMPLOYMENT

May 1985-Present **FREELANCE JOURNALIST & PHOTOGRAPHER.** Cover a variety of current events and general interest topics, including student uprisings in Washington D.C. and town meetings around Virginia and Maryland.

September 1993-present **LECTURER, UNIVERSITY OF MARYLAND, COLLEGE PARK.** Currently teaching English Composition and Ethics and the Media 18 hours a week to first-, second- and third-year students of Journalism.

1991-1993 **LIBRARIAN, SMITH COLLEGE, NORTHAMPTON, MA.** Coordinated undergraduate library assistance. Organized fundraising and library activities.

August 1988-September 1990 **CONTRIBUTING EDITOR & COLUMNIST, READER'S PARADISE MAGAZINE, BOSTON, MA.** Published articles on international politics. Authored a fortnightly column "Washington Update" which tracked legislation proposed in Congress.

August 1986-September 1988 **CONTRIBUTING EDITOR, PALE MOON PUBLISHING CO., BOSTON, MA.** Wrote postscripts and flaps for books, corresponded with authors. Researched and co-authored almanac of resume for publication in trade market.

EDUCATION

1991-1993 Wardell College, Boston, MA - **MASTERS OF FINE ARTS JOURNALISM**

1981-1985 Georgetown University, Washington, D.C. - **BACHELORS OF ARTS PHOTOGRAPHY**

AWARDS

1993 **SPRINGFIELD SOCIETY;** received scholarship for being "most likely to contribute to the field of publishing."

■ Strong educational credentials strengthen resume.

■ Awards heading draws attention to candidate's significant accomplishments.

MANAGING EDITOR

CHRIS SMITH
178 GREEN STREET
ALBANY, NY 12222
(518) 555-5555

PROFESSIONAL EDITORIAL EXPERIENCE

1990-Present   **Managing Editor.** World History Publications, Albany, NY
- Assisting in acquisition of articles for publication in international journals.
- Copy and content editing; close editorial collaboration with authors.
- Establishing publications' style criteria; design and layout.
- Writing and/or editing articles for quarterly newsletter.
- Overseeing work of freelance personnel for graphics, music transcriptions, proofreading, etc.
- Full preparation of camera-ready copy using Page Maker.
- Liaison with publications services for final production of journal, newsletter, monographs, etc.
- Teaching new staff to use computer hardware and programs.

1988-1990   **Editorial Assistant.** Social History Journal, New York, NY
- Copy and content editing.
- Writing or editing short articles.
- Assisting in acquisition of articles for publication.
- Computerization of subscription, circulation, and ledger.
- Teaching new staff to use computer hardware and programs.

FREELANCE WORK

1989-Present   **Series Editor,** John Abbott Publishing, New York, NY
- General editor of monographs in European Studies.
- Working with scholars in various disciplines to review manuscripts.
- Final responsibility for acquiring manuscripts for publication.

EDUCATION

1994   Ph.D., World History, State University of New York at Albany.
1988   MA, Western Civilization, New York University.
1987   BA, Linguistics, New York University.

PUBLICATIONS

ACQUIRED AND EDITED:

Children of Tomorrow. Bannen, Connor J. New York: John Abbott Publishing, 1994.
Issues in Western Civilization. Journal of World History, Vol. V. World History Publications. May 1993.
Issues in the European Community. Europe Today, Vol. X. World History Publications. August 1992.

- Impressive educational background strengthens resume.

- Experience is effectively divided into professional and freelance sections.

PRODUCTION EDITOR

CHRIS SMITH
178 Green Street
Bothell, WA 98012
(206) 555-5555

PROFESSIONAL OBJECTIVE
A position in **Production Editing.**

PROFESSIONAL EXPERIENCE
GRAVES EQUIPMENT CORPORATION, Bothell, WA   1992 to Present
Production Editor
- Write and edit weekly newsletter focusing on news and trends at Graves Equipment Corporation and in the GEC-compatible market; major sections devoted to reporting new GEC-compatible hardware and software products and services as well as general news of companies who sell to GEC-based markets

ZURICH MARKETING GROUP, INC., Seattle, WA   1991-1992
Research Associate
- Assisted development, implementation and analysis of various surveys pertaining to higher education
- Developed script, conducted interviews, analyzed results, and wrote reports summarizing research findings

UNIVERSITY OF WASHINGTON PRESS, Seattle, WA   1988-1991
Manuscript Editor, *Reviews of Genetic Diseases*
- Produced six issues of medical journal; completed work ahead of all scheduling deadlines
- Organized efforts of editorial committee, scheduled, and edited; coordinated layout with printers

THE OAKDALE EXPERIENCE, Seattle, WA   1984-1988
Assistant to the Editor
- Wrote weekly column covering science news; researched and interpreted topics of current interest for Editor and contributing editors
- Edited articles for content and usage; assisted advertisement design; handled layout and typesetting
- Acted as liaison for Marketing Director, Editor, and advertisers

PACIFIC LUTHERAN UNIVERSITY SCHOOL OF MEDICINE, Tacoma, WA   1980-1984
Research Assistant
- Edited three medical textbooks under publisher deadline; coordinated author contributions; assisted writing

EDUCATION
Seattle Pacific University, Seattle, WA
Bachelor of Arts in Neuropsychology, 1980

■ Resume illustrates continual career progression.

■ Use of boldface and underlining provides a clean and crisp presentation.

PROOFREADER

CHRIS SMITH
178 Green Street
Hope, AR 71801
(501) 555-5555

OBJECTIVE
To serve as proofreader for a book publisher.

EXPERIENCE
1989-   Vigilant Widow Publishers, Hope, AR
Present   Proofreader
           Monitor all outgoing business forms, pamphlets, and booklets, for
           mistakes. Train new hires. Manage darkroom. Coordinate efficient
           darkroom procedures.

1985-1989 Saphire Runway Photo, Walnut Ridge, AR
           Photo Lab Assistant
           Proofed outgoing photographs for surface flaws, skin blemishes, etc.
           Operated printer and EP-2 processor.

1983-1985 John's Photo, Birmingham, AL
           Photo Lab Assistant

EDUCATION
Krakotoa State Community College, Eureka, IL
Associates Degree, 1985.

COMPUTERS
WordPerfect, Microsoft Word, Pagemaker.

INTERESTS
Reading, Archery, Photography.

REFERENCES
Available upon request.

■ Job objective is brief and to the point.

■ Personal interests can provide a great topic for conversation during a job interview.

PUBLIC RELATIONS (Fundraising)

CHRIS SMITH
178 Green Street
Tallmadge, OH 44278
(216) 555-5555

SUMMARY:

- Recognized for ability to plan, organize, coordinate and direct successful fundraising programs, volunteer committees, public relations programs, and educational programs.
- Broad knowledge of legislative procedure.
- Extensive volunteer recruiting and training.

EXPERIENCE:

Ohio Association for Multiple Sclerosis, Akron, OH
Public Relations Manager
Fundraising Director (1991-present)
- Served as Consultant to seven chapters in Ohio on campaign problems and activities.
- Organized state-wide and regional campaign meetings and developed fundraising programs.
- Chairperson for Committee for a Healthier Ohio.
- Special assignments included reviewing all state legislation concerning Association for MS and its programs; staffing Legislative Advisory Committee and following through on specific bills; acting as Training Coordinator for five three-day orientation courses held for new employees.

Campaign Director (1989-1991)
- Administered $1 million campaign, including every aspect of fundraising.
- Recruited 40,000 volunteers.
- Wrote campaign letters; ordered all campaign material; staffed Campaign Advisory Committee; coordinated and directed chapter-wide meetings; conducted staff meetings.
- Maintained campaign records; tested new materials and ideas; assisted chapter department heads and the executive director.

National Lung Association,, Sandusky, OH
Campaign Director (1986-1989)
- Directed complete direct mail fund raising campaign ($250,000); formulated policy in the areas of scheduling, list building, coding and testing; cooperated with public relations director in developing campaign materials; trained and supervised up to fifty office volunteers.

EDUCATION:

MS degree in Public Relations, 1985 - University of Dayton, Dayton, OH
BA degree in Government, 1981 - Macalester College, St. Paul, MN

■ Statistics and dollar figures quantify candidate's accomplishments.

■ Job descriptions emphasize candidate's ability to successfully manage and complete projects.

PUBLIC RELATIONS (Special Events)

CHRIS SMITH
178 Green Street
Syracuse, NY 13213
(315) 555-5555

SUMMARY OF QUALIFICATIONS
- Computer literate: Microsoft Word, WordPerfect, Page Maker, File Maker.
- Adept at operating within proposed budget restrictions and time restraints.
- Developed interpersonal skills, having dealt with a diversity of professionals, clients, and staff members.

EXPERIENCE

BIG APPLE, Syracuse, NY
Special Events Coordinator   5/92-Present
- Create/coordinate special events and promotions.
- Manage $425,000 marketing budget.
- Develop/evaluate event and marketing proposals.
- Handle charity fund raising, corporate image positioning, and community outreach activities.
- Act as liaison between company and city and state organizations, media, and vendors; negotiate contracts; coordinate interdepartmental logistics.
- Select/write event advertising, promotional materials, and publicity.

Assistant to the Director of Public Relations   9/91-5/92
- Assisted in promotion and publicity of special events.
- Drafted press releases and speeches.
- Developed press kits; maintained media relations.
- Researched prospective consumer markets; created direct mail lists; updated media lists; compiled publicity files.

SYRACUSE UNIVERSITY, Syracuse, NY   9/90-5/91
Teacher's Assistant
- Aided professor in editing *Working With The Media.*
- Developed lesson plans.
- Graded mid-term and final exams for class of 18 students.

ABC KID CARE, Syracuse, NY   Summers, 1989 & 1990
Coordinator, Day Care Center
- Organized daily activities program for 45 children.
- Supervised three counselors.
- Developed promotional and advertising strategies for potential markets.

EDUCATION
SYRACUSE UNIVERSITY, Syracuse, NY
Bachelor of Arts in Public Relations, May 1992, Magna Cum Laude

■ Summary of qualifications highlights candidate's acquired professional skills.

■ Academic honors, such as graduating magna cum laude, strengthen resume.

PUBLIC RELATIONS ASSISTANT

CHRIS SMITH
178 Green Street
Omaha, NE 68114
(402) 555-5555

SUMMARY OF QUALIFICATIONS

Successful administrative experience with major voluntary health agency ... recognized for ability to plan, organize, coordinate and direct successful fund raising programs, volunteer committees, public relations programs, educational programs ... legislative experience and knowledge ... extensive volunteer recruitment experience ... supervisory experience with both professional and non-professional staffs ... qualified to work with agencies and institutions as well as civic and industrial leaders in the best interest of the organization ... active in community affairs.

EMPLOYMENT EXPERIENCE

Nebraska Heart Society, Inc., Omaha, NB
PR Managerial Assistant , 1990-Present
Serve as consultant to the seven chapters in the state regarding campaign problems and activities; organize statewide and regional campaign meetings; develop fund-raising programs (bequests); conduct the 1991 and 1992 campaigns for the newly merged Central Chapter (Antelope County); 1992 Chairman for the Nebraska Independent Health Agency Committee (solicitation of State employees); 1992 Secretary for the Combined Federal Campaign (Federal employee campaign); Special Assignments: Responsible for reviewing all State legislation regarding any relationship to the Heart Society and its programs, and bringing specific bills to the attention of the proper committee or individual. Staff the Legislative Advisory Committee and follow through regarding specific bills. Act as Assistant Training Coordinator for four two-and-one-half day orientation courses held for new employees. Assist in developing the course. Speaker at several campaign conferences.

Directorial Assistant (Greater Omaha Chapter), 1988-1990
Supervised all chapter campaign duties as well as assisted the Executive Director with administrative responsibilities such as personnel and budget.

EDUCATION

Dillard University, New Orleans, LA
M.S. degree, Public Relations, 1988

University of Michigan at Flint
B.A. degree, Government, 1986

PERSONAL

Willing to relocate and travel.

- Summary of qualifications gives a picture of candidate's as an employee and a person.

- Unrelated work experience is omitted.

PUBLICIST

CHRIS SMITH
178 Green Street
Pullman, WA 99164
(509) 555-5555

OBJECTIVE:

Publicist position at ABC Corporation.

EXPERIENCE:

CNBS TELEVISION, "Confrontations," Pullman, WA   1991-Present
Production Assistant
Book main guests and panelists. Generate and research story ideas. Conduct video research. Edit teases for show. Organize all production details for studio tapings. Troubleshoot equipment malfunctions. Monitor lighting and TelePrompter. Coordinate publicity ads in local newspapers.

BARSTOW COMPANY, Seattle, WA   1989-1991
Publicity Assistant
Publicized new books and authors. Assisted in booking media tours (TV, radio and print). Wrote and designed press releases. Fulfilled review copy requests. Conducted galley mailings and general office work.

WNBN-TV, Tacoma, WA   1988-1989
Production Intern
Assisted producers of a live, daily talk show. Researched and generated story ideas. Pre-interviewed possible guests. Logged tapes. Went out on shoots and wrote promotional announcements. Produced five of my own segments for the show.

THE BENEDICT COUNCIL, UNIVERSITY OF WASHINGTON, Seattle, WA   1987-1988
Promotional Assistant
Implemented promotional campaigns for concerts on campus. Wrote and designed promotional advertisements. Initiated student involvement with program.

THE CHERRY HAIKU, INC., Seattle, WA   1986-1987
Art Assistant
Responsible for paste-ups/mechanicals. Operated Photostat camera; coordinated logistics for photo shoots. Participated in "brainstorming" sessions with creative team.

EDUCATION:

UNIVERSITY OF WASHINGTON, Seattle, WA
B.A., Cum Laude May, 1988
Major: Communication
Minor: English

- Resume emphasizes contributions, achievements, and problems candidate has solved throughout his/her career.

- Job objective refers to a specific job opening advertised in a classified advertisement.

RADIO ANNOUNCER

CHRIS SMITH
178 Green Street
Baltimore, MD 21217
(301) 555-5555

PROFESSIONAL OBJECTIVE
A rewarding and challenging position as an ANNOUNCER.

EDUCATION BACKGROUND
NORDSTROM BROADCASTING SCHOOL, Baltimore, MD
Received Certificate for 11-month Broadcasting Program, 1982
Courses included: Announcing, Speech, Technical Lab, News, Sales and Copy Writing.

PROFESSIONAL EXPERIENCE
1989 to   THE DIVINING ROD, Baltimore, MD
Present   Announcer
- Responsible for providing adult contemporary music and announcing for private club.
- Set up equipment, select music, and engineer show.
- Operate own equipment which includes lighting and broadcasting system.
- Conduct various promotions, and accept requests from audience.

1985-89   WXTS FM 95, Baltimore, MD
Producer
- Responsible for coordinating adult contemporary music programming, commercials, giveaways, long-distance requests, production and engineering for Jolene Sunny's Night Show from 6 to 9 p.m.
- Conduct listener music surveys.

1982-85   TRAVELIN' TUNES, Baltimore, MD
Disc Jockey
- Responsible for playing music at weddings, christenings, banquets, etc., all across Maryland.
- Played all varieties of music including: Big Band, Irish, Top 40 and adult contemporary.

PERSONAL
Willing to travel and relocate.

AUDITION TAPE ENCLOSED.

- Indicating a willingness to relocate on a resume can be advantageous.

- Nontraditional typeface is acceptable for certain creative industries.

RADIO PROGRAM DIRECTOR

CHRIS SMITH
178 Green Street
Darlington, SC 29532
(803) 555-5555 (Day)
(803) 444-4444 (Evening)

OBJECTIVE

A responsible programmer's position with an established radio station with a Soft or Mainstream Adult Contemporary format.

SUMMARY

- Bachelor of Science Degree, Mass Communication/Psychology (May 1988): Almost 10 years of accumulated part- and full-time experience in diverse areas of AM announcing, newscasting, and audio production, as well as associated areas of writing, reporting and promotion.
- Experience includes working regular on-air shift for well-positioned stations in a good-sized markets — Experience also includes production of commercials, promotional & public service announcements and program hosting; as well as working with/troubleshooting & problem-solving on equipment including Control Boards, Cart Machines, Reel-to-Reel Machines, Mixers & STL's.
- Relate well to wide range of adult audience interests. Knowledge of music from 1930's to present. Knowledge also includes understanding of Mutual, ABC, CBS, NBC, CNN, NPR, APR and a wide variety of Sports Networks. Developed excellent following or highly commended by superiors & fellow workers in every position held.

BROADCAST EXPERIENCE

1992-Present **WKSU AM 1320**
Radio Program Director **Florence, SC**
Background Information: WKSU is a locally programmed, 5,000 WATT station:
Developed and organized own format for a variety of music programs; served as liaison between audience, sponsors, and station manager.

1989-1990 **WGON AM 560**
Announcer **Conway, SC**
Background Information: WGON is a locally programmed, 5,000 WATT station, offering an Adult Contemporary, full-service format: WGON is the #2 station in the Conway market, and is rated as a format leader in Radio & Records Directory, successfully competing against 40 stations whose broadcasts are in the same market area.

- Full-time announcer — Five-hour shift — Nostalgia format — coordinated production of commercials, promotional and public service announcements; handled certain technical and/or administrative functions, as required.

1988-1989 **WLMB AM 980**
Announcer (Evenings) **Myrtle Beach, SC**
Background Information: Myrtle Beach is the nation's 100th largest radio market — 5th-rated (Arbitron) WLMB is a 1,000 WATT full-service, locally programmed AM station in a 10-station "medium size" market (Arbitron) — Also one of Radio & Records format leaders — Responsibilities included:

- Full-time announcer in the 6-11 P.M. time slot. Produced commercials, promotional and public service announcements, as well as handled certain technical and/or administrative functions when short handed, as required.

■ Specific background information about radio stations add depth to candidate's job descriptions.

■ Job objective is clearly defined.

REPORTER

CHRIS SMITH
178 Green Street
Greenville, SC 29613
(803) 555-5555

OBJECTIVE:

To contribute researching and writing skills to a position as **Reporter** or **Editorial Assistant.**

WRITING DISTINCTIONS:

- Superior Scholar Award for "Jack-O-Lantern Dreams," a creative-writing Senior Project, comprised of seven poems and four prose pieces about growing up in a Jehovah's Witness family. Spring, 1994
- Amazon Expedition Article, accepted by *Charleston Record* "Travel" section. Fall, 1993
- Researched and wrote historical articles for "The Insider's Guide to Greenville."
- Published short stories in "Gnashings," the Furman student literary magazine. Spring, 1994

EDUCATION:

FURMAN UNIVERSITY, Greenville, SC
Bachelor of Arts, May 1994
Major: English

SYRACUSE UNIVERSITY, Sydney, Australia   Fall 1992
Concentration: Language and History, Fall 1992

WORK EXPERIENCE:

EYE ON GREENVILLE, Greenville, SC   Summer 1993
Reporter/Editor
- Researched and wrote articles; assisted in determining editorial content.

English Peer Tutor   Fall 1991, Spring 1993
- Provided one-on-one interaction in basic writing with a Freshman student; emphasized grammar and writing skills.

POINT MAGAZINE, Charleston, SC   Summer 1992
Intern
- Assisted writers in research; prepared media kits for potential advertisers.

REACH, Furman journal of student scholarship   Spring 1991
Member, Editorial Committee
- Evaluated and selected articles.

COMPUTERS:

Lotus 1-2-3, Microsoft Word, Pagemaker, IBM Compatible

- ■ Writing distinctions enhance candidate's credentials.

- ■ Experience studying and traveling abroad strengthens candidate's educational background.

SYMPOSIUM COORDINATOR

CHRIS SMITH
178 Green Street
Sacramento, CA 95823
(916) 555-5555

EXPERIENCE

Fairgate Corporation, Burbank, CA   1993-Present
Symposium Coordinator. Serving as the planner and coordinator of the company's annual supplier symposium. Responsible for setting up and maintaining a supplier database of over 500 records. Responsible to company purchasing teams for the coordination and update of information. Acting as liaison for Fairgate to the Symposium guests. Deadline-oriented position with a strict schedule. Learned the value of attention to details and fine-tuned my ability to handle multiple tasks simultaneously.

Earlcort Enterprises, San Rafael, CA   1991-1993
Creative Consultant. Serving in a variety of positions including marketing, advertising and public relations and the drafting of business plans for a growing list of clients. Extensive communication skills and people skills added to the responsibility of the position.

Jen Brooks and Associates, San Jose, CA   1988-1991
Part-time freelance work for Public Relations Firm. Assignments have included several articles and photographs. Maintain an on-going relationship.

Sterling Sparrow Salon, Hollywood, CA   1987-1988
Receptionist. Answered phones, greet customers, handle inquiries, take messages, book and confirm appointments. Kept books, compiled daily and weekly sales reports. Handle banking functions, close out registers. Controlled inventory. Trouble-shot office-related problems.

Sandalwood Fragrances, Ventura, CA   1986-1987
Receptionist. Processed Accounts Payable and Accounts Receivable. Performed computer input and light typing. Answered phones, filed, and performed miscellaneous office tasks.

EDUCATION

Boston College, Chestnut Hill, MA
B.A. English, 1986

OTHER SKILLS

Extensive experience with MacIntosh and IBM compatible systems. Proficiency in WordPerfect, Lotus 1-2-3, Microsoft Word, Excel, DOS, D-Base III, Paradox, Freelance Graphics and Harvard Graphics, QuarkExpress.

■ Relevant freelance and part-time positions are incorporated into the resume alongside full-time positions.

■ Valuable hardware and software skills are highlighted in a separate section.

TELEVISION DIRECTOR

CHRIS SMITH
178 Green Street
New York, NY 10036
(212) 555-5555

PROFESSIONAL EXPERIENCE

1992 to Present **CBS NEWS, New York, NY**
Director
- Direct live taping of 30-minute newscasts.
- Direct all studio personnel, equipment, and scheduling.
- Rotated through several positions in 1992, including Assistant Director, Technical Director, Audio Engineer, and Floor Manager.

1989 to 1992 OWL EYES PRODUCTIONS, Albany, NY
Associate Producer/Production Coordinator
- Coordinated freelance production of television commercials for local and national affiliates.
- Booked talent, handled casting contracts.
- Coordinated travel and wardrobe arrangements.
- Administered budgets for wardrobe, props, and food & beverage.
- Supervised all operations on shooting days.

1989 FREELANCE
Production Coordinator
- Coordinated production of award-winning music video by The Starstruck Souls.
- Coordinated production of commercial for Paragon Park at Lost Haven Beach, Massachusetts.

1987 to 1989 **Production Assistant**, Foster Productions, Kingston, NY
- Assisted in the production of industrial and medical films, business presentations, videotaping of plays, fashion show, etc.

EDUCATION

Syracuse University
Syracuse, NY
BFA in Broadcasting & Film, 1987
Minor: Psychology

INTERESTS

Travel, playing guitar, photography

■ Resume tracks candidate's long list of impressive accomplishments and promotions.

■ Personal interests give a candid snapshot of candidate as a person.

TELEVISION PRODUCER

Chris Smith
178 Green Street
Washington, DC 20005
(202) 555-5555

PROFESSIONAL EXPERIENCE

1989 to   THE TRELLIS FUND NETWORK RADIOTHON, Washington, DC
Present   **Executive Producer**, 1991 and 1992 Radiothons
- Coordinate all activities for and produce Trellis Fund Radiothon. Administer $95,000 budget.
- Hire and supervise production and engineering staff. Coordinate network stations. Write instructional booklets.
- Format program and compile log. Book guests, interview patients, and set up features.
- Develop and implement marketing plans.

Producer, Trellis Fund Council Annual Tribute to Washington Congressman Bob Tibbing, 1991.
- Produced and directed banquet show/video presentation.
- Oversaw lighting and stage design. Formatted, booked guests, hired and supervised production staff.

1988   WRK-TV, Immokalee, FL
Freelance Associate Producer, "Neighbor to Neighbor"
- Produced segments of live talk show.
- Booked guests, researched guests and topics.
- Scripted promos and opens; coordinated graphics.

1982-1987 WRK-AM, Immokalee, FL
Producer, Music and Talk Shows
- Produced, booked guests, screened phone calls, took transmitter readings.

1976-1982 WMOT-AM, Pensacola, FL
Sports Producer, Pensacola Pirates Radio Network
- Produced Pirates Pre-Game Show. Oversaw production of broadcasts
- Wrote and produced features. Gathered scores and booked guests.
- Developed new programs. Assisted network coordinator.

News/Sports Intern, Summer 1975
- Edited network feeds, wrote copy. Assisted reporters and field reports.

AWARDS

Stateside Press, Best Sports Coverage, Pensacola, FL, 1981
For work as WMOT-AM Co-Producer of "Coverage of the 14th Annual Pensacola Road Race"

EDUCATION

Florida Atlantic University, Boca Raton, FL
Bachelor of Arts in Political Science, 1976

- Impressive credentials and awards further enhance candidate's qualifications.

- Resume illustrates continual career progression.

TELEVISION PRODUCTION ENGINEER

CHRIS SMITH
178 Green Street
Sweet Briar, VA 24595
(804) 555-5555

CAREER OBJECTIVE
A position as TELEVISION PRODUCTION ENGINEER.

PROFESSIONAL EXPERIENCE

ENGINEERING DEPARTMENT/PRODUCTION ENGINEER   1987-Present
WNPQ - Bristol, VA
Responsible for all technical/engineering aspects of production including lighting, camera operation, and TelePrompter functioning for studio and location shoots. Supervise tape recording in 1", 3/4" VHS and 1/2" Beta cam modes. Troubleshoot equipment malfunctions. Analyze problems and implement effective solutions including technical adjustments and minor repair work. Perform grip work and miscellaneous support tasks as required. Meet all management established production deadlines.

VIDEO POST PRODUCTION/AUTOMATION TECHNICIAN   1984-1987
Rochelle Technical Systems - Lexington, VA
Specialized in programming computer applications to perform multiple tasks carried throughout a network to televisions, VCR's and control equipment. Edited commercial spots onto two-hour working tapes. Gained a strong background in computer automation and graphics.

PRODUCTION ASSISTANT/INTERN   Summer 1984
Blacksburg Medical Center - Blacksburg, VA
Served as Production Assistant on six Medical Digest shoots, produced exclusively for broadcast on WWLP 22. Handled lighting, TelePrompter, camera operation and 3/4" broadcast quality tape recording. Maintained highest possible production standards. Resolved malfunctions and technical problems in a timely and cost-effective manner.

INTERN   Spring 1984
Emerald Valley Unit Production - Sweet Briar, VA
Worked on three camera sets in positions from Grip up to Camera Director. Handled both technical and creative aspects while working in a highly active environment.

EDUCATION & TRAINING
ASSOCIATES DEGREE TELECOMMUNICATIONS TECHNOLOGY, 1984
Sweet Briar College - Sweet Briar, VA

COMPUTERS
Microsoft Word and WordPerfect

■ Internships demonstrate candidate's determination to break into a competitive field.

■ Work experience is emphasized, while limited education is de-emphasized.

TRANSLATOR

CHRIS SMITH
178 Green Street
New Haven, CT 06511
(203) 555-5555

STRENGTHS AND QUALIFICATIONS

- High levels of enthusiasm and commitment to a successful sales, marketing or communications career.
- Strong leadership qualities; able to schedule priorities and perform/delegate accordingly to effectively accomplish tasks at hand.
- Working knowledge of both written and verbal Japanese and French.
- Broad perspective of Japanese people, culture, and customs, as well as Japanese-American diplomatic relations.
- Computer literate in most popular software, including WordPerfect 5.0 and 5.1 (including Japanese WordPerfect), Lotus 1-2-3, DrawPerfect and Computer Aided Design (CAD).

JAPANESE-AMERICAN RELATIONS

Served as liaison between Japanese diplomats and the Japanese-American Relations Group and with the Japanese press during the Prime Minister's stay.

Translated correspondence and filed inquiries from the Japanese population in the Boston business community.

Organized travel itineraries for Japanese officials visiting the New England area.

SALES/MARKETING/ENTREPRENEURIAL SKILLS

Founded International Resumes, a company designed for the creation of English and Japanese resumes, and ran it from 1989-1991.

Designed and circulated posters, banners and invitations in order to introduce the Japanese community to New England.

EDUCATION

Yale University, New Haven, CT
M.A., East Asian Studies, expected to be received June 1995

Harvard University, Cambridge, MA
B.A. Psychology and Japanese Studies, May 1989

EMPLOYMENT HISTORY

1991-Present	**Technical Writer/Junior Programmer**	Universal Programs, Inc., New Haven, CT
1989-1990	**Assistant to the Japanese Ambassador**	Japanese Embassy, Washington, D.C.
Summers 1989-90	**Sales Representative**	Carlisle's Inc., West Hartford, CT
1987-1988	**Marketing Representative**	A.M. Keegan & Company, Easton, MA

■ Functional portion of the resume focuses on candidate's unique qualifications, skills, and accomplishments.

■ Chronological portion of the resume briefly summarizes candidate's employment history.

TYPESETTER

CHRIS SMITH
178 Green Street
Knoxville, TN 37801
(615) 555-5555

EXPERIENCE Oakridge Industries, Knoxville, TN   1991-Present
Typesetter
Typeset manuscripts for various magazines, advertisements, financial reports, catalogs, graphs, newsletters, etc., on an MCS 6400 Compugraphic System. Fit layouts supplied by customers and coded all manuscript geared to the system.

Butterfield Corporation, Grand Prairie, TX   1987-1991
Typesetter
Typeset manuscript of legal cases for courts and law books on a Compugraphic 7500, 7700 and 2750.

Alder, Inc., Granbury, TX   1984-1987
Marketing Editor
Oversaw status of work output and interviewed potential employees. Other duties consisted of typesetting manuscripts for various magazines, text books, sports directories, and advertisements, using Pro-count, AKI Autocomp PCI-100 systems. Also marked up manuscript in accordance with customer specifications, using computer coding geared to interact with various equipment corporations. Experienced in usage of Video Display Terminal editing system, as well as Typositor.

Camacho and Briar, Inc., Dallas, TX   Summer 1983
Typesetter and Proofreader
Served as a Typesetter and Proofreader for marketing materials, including fliers, advertisements, and posters. Experienced with Digital PDP11 computer.

OTHER
Asher and Lynn, Dallas, TX   Summer 1982
Served as a Secretary to the College Editorial Department.

Sunchise and Wright, Dallas, TX   Summer 1981
Served as an Assistant Bookkeeper in the Accounting Department.

EDUCATION
St. Edward's University, Austin, TX
B.A. in English, 1984

■ Relevant work experience is emphasized while other positions are de-emphasized.

■ Job objective is unnecessary because resume illustrates a clear career path.

WRITER

CHRIS SMITH
178 Green Street
Indianapolis, IN 46205
(317) 555-5555

SUMMARY OF QUALIFICATIONS

- Experienced in the general planning and detailed execution of projects.
- Have written numerous in-house company documents including program proposals, five-year plans, research reports and executive correspondence.
- Participated in marketing teams which conceived, wrote and produced direct mail campaigns and support materials for a sales force.
- Flexible in assuming a leadership role, collaborating with colleagues, or supporting a department head or executive.
- Have written and edited over 200 audio-visual scripts and 100 related booklets for science, mathematics and social studies education.

PROFESSIONAL EXPERIENCE

Writing/ Writer/Editor/Consultant
Editing FREELANCE EMPLOYMENT, 1990-Present, Indiana State
For Business: Wrote numerous planning, policy, and procedural documents; produced in-depth reports which required extensive research and analysis; wrote letters and memos for executive signature.

For Science Education: Wrote clear, accurate audio-visual programs for students; developed useful, informative support materials for educators.

Management The Ruby Shoes Press, Terra Haute, IN
/Publishing **Editorial and Development Manager**   1979-1990
- Began as freelance writer and progressed to the management of company's AV editorial and production.
- Refined and administered annual budget of $300,000 for development of new programs.
- Recruited and supervised ten in-house editors and an average of thirty freelance writers, artists, and producers.
- Conceived, scheduled, and produced over 120 AV programs and an equal number of teaching guides.
- Collaborated on marketing plans for all AV products. Delivered presentations of new products to sales force.
- Developed award-winning programs that ranked among the company's best sellers.

EDUCATION

NEW YORK UNIVERSITY, New York, New York;
Masters Degree in English, 1978
- Teaching Fellowship, 1977-1978

COLUMBIA UNIVERSITY, New York, New York;
Bachelor of Arts Degree in English, 1974
- Minors in Biology and Chemistry.

COMPUTERS

IBM Windows, Lotus, WordPerfect, Aldus Pagemaker

■ Chrono-functional format is more flexible than a chronological resume, but stronger than a functional resume.

■ Summary of qualifications highlights candidate's achievements.

9
Computers and Mathematics

Nature of Work
Computer and math professionals define, analyze, and resolve business problems. Computer systems analysts utilize their knowledge of computer systems to examine problems and design solutions. This process may include planning new computer systems or devising ways to apply existing systems to operations still done manually. Computer programmers write, update, and maintain the detailed instructions that list in a logical order the steps the computer must follow.

Mathematicians are engaged in a wide variety of activities, ranging from the creation of new theories and techniques to the translation of economic, scientific, engineering, and managerial problems into mathematical terms.

Operations research analysts help organizations coordinate and operate in the most efficient manner by applying scientific methods and mathematical principles to organizational problems.

Employment
Most computer professionals work in urban areas for data processing firms, government agencies, insurance companies, banks, and firms that manufacture durable goods. Mathematicians most commonly hold faculty positions at colleges and universities, as well as in the government and in service and manufacturing industries.

Training
Logical thinking, and superior analytical and reasoning abilities are essential for computer and math professionals. The ability to concentrate and pay close attention to detail is also important. A college degree is almost always required, and in many cases a graduate degree is preferred. Prior work experience is an advantage.

Job Outlook
The prospective job growth outlook for computer-oriented professions is expected to be much better than average far into the future, due to the constant advances in computer technology. *The best bets:* managers, systems analysts, computer scientists, and operations research analysts. Employment of data processing equipment repairers will also grow faster than the industry average because of the need to maintain all that hardware. Programming and administrative support jobs like data entry keyers, secretaries, and computer operators will grow more slowly since the improvements in automation have

helped increase productivity. Other occupations, including technical writers, teachers, accountants, and engineers, will grow about as fast as the industry average.

In contrast, employment of mathematicians and statisticians is expected to increase more slowly through the same time period. However, an increasing number of workers have job titles which reflect the end product of their work rather than the discipline of mathematics used in that work. Therefore, although employment of mathematicians will not increase much, those with degrees in mathematics should have good job opportunities.

Earnings
In 1990, systems and research analysts averaged between $30,000 to $50,000 per year. Median earnings of programmers were about $34,000 per year. Mathematicians with a bachelor's degree earned an annual salary of approximately $27,000, while a master's degree earned $31,000 and a Ph.D. earned $42,800.

APPLICATIONS PROGRAMMER (General)

CHRIS SMITH
178 Green Street
Los Altos, CA 91335
(415) 555-5555

Objective

Innovative applications programmer seeks a challenging position where creative ideas can be fully developed into computer software and hardware products.

Background Summary

Strong programming and problem analysis skills proven under high-pressure environments. Developed effective design and organizational skills from large engineering projects that shaped production testing and data collection processes. Well developed interpersonal and communication skills.

Career History

Harley Morrison Associates   1987-Present
Los Altos, CA
Systems Engineer
- Designed and implemented real-time "Build-to-Order" manufacturing test systems to meet new marketing strategies and reduce overhead costs.
- Designed network based applications for manufacturing process control and test data collection improving product quality and manufacturing efficiency.
- Knowledgeable with Arcnet and Ethernet Network topologies in large-scale networking environments.
- Developed custom software and computer hardware for testing, process control and data collection enhancing product reliability.
- Supplied technical support to foreign and domestic facilities in California, Virginia, and Beijing.
- Trained and supervised ten foreign and domestic test engineers and technicians.
- Isolated computer system failures to component level.
- Evaluated test procedures and documentation.
- Adapted manufacturing test process to new computer technologies and customer specifications.

Richard Rondoni Business Machines   1980-87
Reseda, CA
Co-Op Engineer
- Designed and maintained computer based electronic test hardware.
- Developed hardware control software and computer interface circuitry.
- Correlated production data using dBase.
- Published failure and analysis reports.

Education

The University of California at Santa Barbara   1979
Bachelor of Science in Electrical Engineering

Computers

COBOL, Natural, Turbo Pascal, Pascal, C, IBM 3090, IBM 3083, IBM

- Background summary accentuates candidate's acquired professional skills and impressive track record.

- Bulleted statements are powerful and concise.

APPLICATIONS PROGRAMMER (Senior)

CHRIS SMITH
178 Green Street
Huntington, WV 25701
(304) 555-5555

OBJECTIVE

To contribute relevant experience and education background to the position of **Computer Programmer/Software Engineer.**

SUMMARY OF QUALIFICATIONS

- Proficient in the design and implementation of program enhancements, including an on-line message system, database repair/trouble-shooting utilities and a release system to update clients on the current version of software.
- Demonstrated ability in the provision of client support services.

EXPERIENCE

6/1989 to Present   **Senior Programmer - Patient Scheduling System**
TESSERACT CORPORATION   Huntington, WV
A privately owned software company specializing in the needs of the health care industry.
- Design and implementation of new system enhancements.
- Sole development of new generator product. Designed file structure and conducted actual coding based on functional specification requirements.

3/1988 to 6/1989   **Programmer/Analyst**
- Installed software for new clients and provided on-site support.
- Developed on-line message system for members of the programming group.
- Instituted utilities which aided in the detection and evaluation of client bugs and made repairs to the client database.
- Supported existing clients and resolved critical issues/problems in a timely fashion.

EDUCATION

MARSHALL UNIVERSITY, 1993-Present   Huntington, WV
Enrolled in Graduate Mathematics program (Part-time)

WEST VIRGINIA UNIVERSITY, 1985-1989   Morgantown, WV
Bachelor of Science Degree: Computer Science Engineering

COMPUTERS

Programming Languages: C++, C, Jam, Pascal, LISP, IBM, PL/1, Prolog, AION
Databases: SQL/DS, Oracle
Hardware: HP 9000, IBM 3090

REFERENCES FURNISHED UPON REQUEST

- Job objective is supported by the facts and accomplishments stated in resume.

- Continuing education indicates candidate's ongoing commitment to his/her career.

APPLICATIONS PROGRAMMER (Senior)

CHRIS SMITH
178 Green Street
New York, NY 10003
(718) 555-5555

EMPLOYMENT
HISTORY

BENTLEY LIFE INSURANCE, New York, NY   1988-Present
Programmer Analyst/Senior Programmer
- Supervised and guided junior programmers in the team on various PC Illustration System Projects.
- Developed, maintained, and supported Sales Illustration Systems in "C."
- Developed a Front End System for the Bentley Sales Illustration Systems in OS/2 Presentation Manager.
- Wrote the "Illustration Software Installation" routine in INSTALIT software.
- Designed a file transfer process to and from the Mainframe to PC using NDM (Network Data Mover) software.
- Hands-on experience with PC hardware, DOS, MS Windows, IBM OS/2, Novell Software, Emulation Software (Rumba, Extra, etc.), Dial-In Software (SimPC, XTalk, etc.) and have understanding of Token Ring LAN.
- Wrote DOS Batch files for Illustration Software Installation routine.
- Developed an Executive Information System on the mainframe using COBOL 2. Became very familiar with mainframe production environment.
- Maintained and supported the existing COBOL mainframe on-line and batch systems.

SHADOW ASSOCIATES, Hartford, CT   1986-1988
Computer Programmer
- Designed product and sales tracking programs for company computer system.
- Monitored product availability and inventory for branch sites, display new product releases and access daily proceed information.
- Maintained/expanded client base.

EDUCATION

New York University, New York, NY
Master of Science in Electrical Engineering, 1986
Program emphasis: Software Engineering and Computer Networks

Oxford University, Oxford, England
Bachelor of Science in Engineering (Electronics Option), 1984
Program emphasis: Digital Communications and Engineering Management

TECHNICAL
SUMMARY

Hardware:	IBM PC, IBM Mainframe
Software:	MS Windows, Rumba, Novell
Op Systems:	MS-DOS, OS-2, MVS
Languages:	C, COBOL, COBOL II, Pascal, FORTRAN, Visual Basic, Assembly

■ Resume emphasizes contributions, achievements, and problems candidate has solved throughout his/her career.

■ Bullets make resume easy to read.

COMPUTER OPERATIONS SUPERVISOR

CHRIS SMITH
178 Green Street
Portland, OR 97504
(503) 555-5555

PROFILE

- Proficient using variety of computer systems and PC software.
- Ability to prioritize and meet operational deadlines in a demanding, fast-paced environment.
- Conscientious and detail-oriented.
- Strong communication, organizational, and problem-solving skills.

EMPLOYMENT

1973-1993 **First National Bank of Oregon,** Portland, OR
Computer Operations Supervisor
Over twenty years experience in operations area of data processing. Responsible for the running and monitoring of all systems, running of all back-ups as well as daily applications and handling various use requests. Knowledge of tape library functions, output operation, and maintenance of output devices.

COMPUTER SKILLS

IBM/PC:	WordPerfect, Lotus 1-2-3, MS Windows, MS Word for Windows, MS Excel for Windows
MacIntosh:	MS Excel, MS Word, Aldus Pagemaker
Systems:	Vax 8530, 8650, 11/785, 11/780
	BM System 38, System 88, pick/series 1 (4964), System 3
	IBM OS 3090 mainframe, 370 DOS mainframe
	Data General MV10000, Wang vs100, PDP 11/70

OFFICE SKILLS

Accounting, Keyboarding, Multi-Line Telephones, 10-Key Pad, Photocopy and Fax Machines, Microfiche, Filing, Record Keeping

EDUCATION

Portland School, Inc., Portland, OR
Certificate: January, 1974
Intensive 18-Week Micro-Computer Specialist Training Program

References Furnished Upon Request

- With 20 years professional experience, candidate opts for chronological format to accentuate relevant qualifications.

- Clean layout makes resume easy to read.

COMPUTER OPERATOR

Chris Smith
178 Green Street
Belleville, IL 62221
(618) 555-5555

OBJECTIVE: A position in computer operations offering opportunities for advancement.

WORK EXPERIENCE: **Computer Operator**, summers, 1991-1993
Mayfair Products, Inc., Kent, OH

- Sole individual in charge of operating computer systems, entering data and compiling records in 1991. Assisted with operations in 1993.
- In charge of accounts receivable, billing and invoices.
- Processed back-up at the end of the day.
- Provided general office assistance.

Computer Operator, summer, 1990
Agamemnon Electroplating, Kent, OH
- Assisted in the operation of the computer systems.
- Served as assistant to the Office Manager.

EDUCATION: Kent State University, Kent, OH
Bachelor of Arts, Economics, May 1993

Economic courses include Human Resources, Law and Economics, Statistics, and Monetary Theory

Other areas of study include Financial and Administrative, Accounting, Corporation Finance, and extensive Computer Programming.

ACTIVITES AND HONORS: Third Place in the Kent Financial and Administrative Accounting Achievement Awards. Dean's List. Yearbook Editor. Big Sister to incoming Freshmen. Spanish Club, Intramural Sports.

LANGUAGES: Fluent in Spanish and German.

References available upon request

■ For recent grads, extracurricular activities demonstrate potential for productivity.

■ Foreign language skills can be beneficial on a resume.

COMPUTER TECHNICIAN

CHRIS SMITH
178 Green Street
Olympia, WA 98505
(206) 555-5555

Employment Experience:
Pisces Data Systems, Inc. - July 1985 to Present.
Olympia, WA

Pre-Sales Technical Support:
Support the Eastern Area sales staff, which averages about five reps. Work closely with the sales reps to formulate and implement sales strategies. Working with prospects to understand business problems and propose appropriate technical solutions. Write and deliver technical product presentations. Develop and deliver customer product demos. Design proposed system configurations and write proposals.

Key Achievements:
Managed large data migration effort. Designed and implemented an open-systems migration plan that replaced a large Control Data mainframe with a Silicon Graphics compute server and a network of thirteen SGI workstations. This effort included: system installation and configuration, development of file migration utilities, conversion of in-house FORTRAN code, conversion of over 50,000 files and developing and delivering system-administrator and end-user training.

Education:
Washington State University, Pullman, WA
B.S. in Graphic Communications, 1985

Programming Languages:
FORTRAN   C   VAX Assembler

Operating Systems:
UNIX   MS-DOS   NOS   NOS/VE   AOS/VS

Hardware Experience:
Control Data mainframes
Silicon Graphics servers and workstations
Sun workstations
DEC workstations
Hewlett-Packard workstations
PCs
MacIntosh

Professional Awards:
Control Data Professional Excellence Award, 1988
Control Data Sales Analyst of the Month, 1990

■ Key achievements are emphasized in a separate section.

■ Impressive credentials and awards further enhance candidate's qualifications.

DEVELOPMENTAL ENGINEER

CHRIS SMITH
178 Green Street
Schenectady, NY 12305
(518) 555-5555

PROFESSIONAL SKILLS

Summary: Nine years experience with all aspects of system architecture, algorithm, and software design, development, and implementation. Nearly all of these designs included parallel or massively parallel architectures.

Design, development, and implementation of complex real-time simulation/stimulation systems. This includes architecture and algorithm development for closed- and open-loop simulation/stimulation, and data acquisition and analysis development.

Signal processing algorithm design and implementation.

Military Specification (2167A) software design methodologies.

Hardware: UNIX workstations, VAX, Intel Hypercube (386 and i860 based), Intel Touchstone Delta, Cray, various DSP chips and array processors.

Languages/ C, FORTRAN, Pascal, assembler and machine language for assorted processors. UNIX,
OS: VMS, DOS, managed a small VMS installation.

PROFESSIONAL EXPERIENCE

1984 to Future Systems, Schenectady, NY
Present

1990 to Principal Developmental Engineer, Advanced Technology Center
Present

- Researched and identified a modern replacement hardware architecture for existing real-time simulation/stimulation laboratory
- Led the design and implementation of advanced fault-tolerant signal generation software on massively parallel DSP based computer
- Researched, identified, and developed a high speed, data communication system connecting an Intel Hypercube and a Sun Sparc workstation
- Developed and implemented algorithms for rapid low rank updating and downdating of Choleski matrix factors. These algorithms are based on hyperbolic Householder transforms and are optimized for use with parallel processors. This is a new technology development for wide-band signal synthesis.

1988 to 1990 Senior Developmental Engineer, Precision Weapons Operation
- Lead engineer in field of stability analysis for systems of spinning rigid and deformable bodies
- Managed scheduling and work assignments for team of researchers
- Awarded Keller Technical Achievement award for major contributions in the field of nonlinear dynamical system analysis
- Led the development efforts for various real-time and non real-time simulations.

(continued)

■ Summary of professional skills highlights candidate's key credentials.

■ Candidate's breadth of professional experience is sufficient to use a two-page resume.

PROFESSIONAL EXPERIENCE (continued)

1984 to 1988   Senior Developmental Engineer, Underseas Systems Division
- Lead Engineer Feller Real Time Simulation Laboratory. This hardware-in-the-loop simulation consisted of a large number of parallel processors communicating through a shared memory interface. It encompassed many diverse engineering disciplines including kinematic and dynamical systems analysis, real-time embedded software design, data acquisition and analysis.
- Responsible for overall system design and implementation for a major real-time simulation/stimulation effort
- Managed scheduling and work assignments for simulation group
- Designed and analyzed massively parallel, DSP based, real-time computer systems and the associated algorithms for various new business ventures
- Became expert in distributed, real-time algorithm and software design and implementation
- Developed and implemented control system for an unstable vehicle
- Performed environmental modeling

EDUCATION

May 1990   M.S. Aerospace Engineering and Mechanics, Rensselaer Polytechnic Institute

March 1982   B.S. Aerospace Engineering and Mechanics, Rensselaer Polytechnic Institute

DIRECTOR OF INFORMATION SERVICES

CHRIS SMITH
178 Green Street
Ithaca, NY 14850
(607) 555-5555

SUMMARY OF QUALIFICATIONS
- Extensive experience in COBOL Programming.
- Proven managerial abilities.
- Self-motivated; able to set effective priorities to achieve immediate and long-term goals and meet operational deadlines.
- Developed interpersonal skills, having dealt with a diversity of professionals, clients, and staff members.
- Function well in fast-paced, high-pressure atmosphere.

EXPERIENCE

NEW YORK INSTITUTE OF CERTIFIED PUBLIC ACCOUNTANTS,
New York, NY   1986-Present
Director of Information Services
Controlled Programming & Systems, Computer Operations, Data Entry, Membership Records, and Membership Promotion and Retention Departments. Implemented complete financial reporting systems, magazine subscription fulfillment, order entry, inventory, invoicing, accounts receivable, CPE course scheduling and evaluations, membership records and dues accounting, computerized production of publications, committee appointments and sundry applications. Utilized Burroughs B-2900 Computer Systems, with various peripheral equipment and 35 on-line CRT terminals (COBOL computer language). Retired to open Real Estate Agency.

BROMIDE, INC., Albany, NY   1980-1985
Systems Representative
Assisted salesmen in technical presentations for prospective clients; advised and implemented client conversion and installation of new computer systems.

BROWN UNIVERSITY, Providence, RI   1978-1979
Analytical Chemist, Division of Sponsored Research

LIVERPOOL GRAMMAR SCHOOL, Liverpool, England   1977-1978
General Science and Math Teacher

EDUCATION
UNIVERSITY OF DUBLIN, Dublin, Ireland
Bachelor of Science, 1976

- Summary of qualifications accentuates candidate's acquired professional skills and impressive track record.

- Relevant work experience is emphasized while other positions are de-emphasized.

HARDWARE ENGINEER

CHRIS SMITH
178 Green Street
Rochester, NY 14624
(716) 555-5555

Summary of Over four years experience in the computer engineering field, with responsibilities including
Qualifications: architectural, ASIC, and board level design on products ranging from low-cost desktop
workstations to high performance graphics workstations.

Experience: **Starr Computer, Inc.** **Rochester, NY**
1990 to Senior Hardware Engineer
Present Designed an intelligent, cache-coherent, Futurebus+, single board computer running
VxWorks Real-Time OS on an Intel 80960CA with Ethernet, SCSI, and serial ports.
- Defined the architecture for the I/O board.
- Performed schematic capture, PLD design, and board layout.
- Simulated the design with RTL and Verilog.
- Debugged the board and system.

1987-1990 **Browning Corporation** **Buffalo, NY**
Senior Hardware Engineer (1989-1990)
Lead a design group for a 30K gate LSI 100K gate array for I/O.
- Created a gate array design environment using Synopsys and Verilog.
- Designed the Ethernet interface and part of the I/O Gate Array.
- Defined the I/O for a low-cost Magnus 88110 system with EISA.

Hardware Engineer II (1987-1989)
Designed part of the first Magnus 88000 based workstation.
- Defined the I/O architecture.
- Designed the Ethernet interface.
- Developed the PROM I/O drivers for graphics and keyboard.
- Assisted test engineering with the ramp up for workstation product.

1986-1987 **Purdue University** **West Lafayette, IN**
Graduate Research Assistant
Programmed part of a single user PLATO operating system.
- Wrote I/O device drivers, graphics device drivers, kernel routines, and portions of the
compiler.

Education: **Purdue University** **West Lafayette, IN**
- Master of Science in Electrical Engineering, May 1987.
- Bachelor of Science in Computer Engineering, January 1986.

Skills: Design Tools: LSI Logic, Synopsys, Verilog, Ikos, Mentor, ABEL, RTL.
Programming Languages: Assembler (PDP11, 8086, 68000, 88100), Basic, C, C++,
FORTRAN, FP, Lisp, Pascal, Path Pascal, PL/1, TUTOR.
Operating Systems and software environments: UNIX, AOS/VS, Domain, NOS, PLATO,
X-windows, OSF/Motif.

■ Technical knowledge is high-lighted in skills section.

■ Summary of qualifications gives an overview of candidate's career.

INFORMATION ANALYST

CHRIS SMITH
178 Green Street
Philadelphia, PA 19104
(215) 555-5555

TECHNICAL SUMMARY
Software: WordPerfect, Lotus 1-2-3, Freelance, Paradox, cc:Mail, Direct Access, Fastback Plus, DOS, Windows.

Hardware: IBM, DEC, Compaq, Toshiba 386 and 486 PC's and laptops; LANpress print servers, HP laser and Epson FX printers, Cabletron MMACs, various Ethernet networking devices, CD-ROMs.

EMPLOYMENT HISTORY
1986 to Present
PENNSYLVANIA POWER COMPANY, Philadelphia, PA

Information Analyst
- Perform Novell system administration tasks on a 33-file server, 3,000-user network.
- Participate as a team member in implementing new ways of serving VAX and IBM-host users.
- Proven skills include problem solving in a Novell network and IBM microcomputer system environment.
- Set up remote workstations accessed via Novell Access Servers, terminal servers, and ISNs.
- Update existing systems with Novell Netware by installing network interface cards, appropriate IPX/NETX drivers, memory upgrades and additional fixed storage space.
- Implement IBM 3270 SAA gateway software and upgrades.
- Administer print queues and print servers (LANpress and Netport).
- Maintain UPS, tape backup units, IBM PS2 95XP 486 file servers, Cabletron MMAC hubs, including IRMs and TPMIMs, CD-ROMS, and additional storage devices.
- Develop system configurations with an emphasis on memory optimization for various PCs on the network including Compaq, DEC, Microsmart, IBM and Toshiba.
- Provide user training in office applications including WordPerfect, Lotus 1-2-3, Paradox, Freelance, and cc:Mail.
- Provide DOS and Windows operating systems support.
- Support PC tools such as Norton Utilities, Direct Access, Fastback, and QEMM.

EDUCATION
Drexel University, Philadelphia, PA
Master of Business Administration, May, 1993

Temple University, Philadelphia, PA
Bachelor of Science in Information Systems, June, 1986

■ Valuable software and hardware skills are highlighted in a separate section.

■ Bullets make resume easy to read.

LAN ADMINISTRATOR

CHRIS SMITH
178 Green Street
Albuquerque, NM 87104
(505) 555-5555

CAREER SUMMARY

An experienced professional with expertise in the design and development of multi-user database management systems running on a Local Area Network. Skilled in LAN management and USER training.

BUSINESS EXPERIENCE

JEFFERSON MANUFACTURING CORP., Albuquerque, NM   1988 to Present
Documentation Development Coordinator
Analyze, develop, and maintain application software for engineering LAN. Provide training and user support for all applications to LAN users. Maintain departmental PC workstations including software installation and upgrades.

- Reduced data entry errors and process time by developing an on-line program which allowed program managers to submit model number information.
- Replaced time-consuming daily review board meetings by developing a program which allowed engineers to review and approve model and component changes on-line.
- Developed an on-line program which reduced process time, standardized part usage, and which allowed engineers to build part lists for new products and components.

Computer Systems Analyst   1984-1988
Responsibilities included database management systems analysis and design, workstation maintenance and repair, and LAN management.

- Reduced process time and purchasing errors by developing an on-line program which allowed the purchasing department to track the status of all purchasing invoices.
- Developed a purchase order entry program for the purchasing department which improved data entry speed and reduced the number of data entry errors.

LAFAYETTE, INC., Albuquerque, NM   1979-1984
Engineering Technician III
Prototyped and tested new PC products, drawing schematics and expediting parts for these new PC products. Designed and coded multi-user database management software for engineering use.

- Expedited the parts for 25 or more telecommunications terminal prototypes. Built, troubleshot, and transferred those prototypes to various departments for testing.

EDUCATION

Associates Electronics Engineering Technology, University of Notre Dame 1979
Continuing education training courses includes Advanced Digital Electronics, C Language Hands-On Workshop, Visual BASIC Programming, and Structured Analysis and Design Methods.

COMPUTER EXPERIENCE

IBM PC Compatibles, Tape Backup Systems, Local Area Networks, MS-DOS, Lotus 1-2-3, dBase III, DBXL\Quicksilver, Clipper, C Language, Netware 3.11, MS Windows, Visual BASIC, and SQL Language.

■ Bullets draw attention to professional achievements.

■ Continuing education indicates candidate's ongoing commitment to his/her career.

MANAGER OF NETWORK ADMINISTRATION

<u>CHRIS SMITH</u>
178 Green Street
Cranston, RI 02920
(401) 555-5555

Experience

Travis Computer, Inc.   **Cranston, RI**
Manager of Network Administration - 6/92 to present
- Manage staff of three Network Administrators and network of 100+ UNIX machines and 250+ users. Network consists of 10 server machines (8 Travis, 2 IBM), 30+ UNIX workstations, 4 GatorBoxes, dialin and dialout lines, uucp, T1 connection to a West Coast company, many X terminals and exabyte backup.
- Work consists mainly of future planning for growth of a diverse and distributed network and hands-on work with network tools and problem solving.
- Enhance and maintain extensive network tools that allow a network that spans 3 backbones to appear as one entity. Highly automated and user friendly network.
- Member of team to transition Travis into several spin-off companies. Entails network design, execution and subsequent move to new locations.

Network Administrator - 4/91 to 6/92
Daily administration of UNIX network including tool enhancement and modification, problem solving, YP maintenance, account creation, mail, news, uucp, installing and upgrading systems.
- Planned and executed a company move at the home office and assisted in planning of company move of the Gulf Coast office. Included space planning, network design and implementation.
- Wrote proposals for gaining Datel access, security and a general plan to move the network into the future.

Lafayette Donlin Laboratory   **Easton, PA**
Member Assistant Staff - 7/88 to 2/91
- Software Engineer for real-time integrated, airborne radar system. Code design and generation in 'C.'
- Wrote code that operated hardware over a DVL bus.

Pollack and O'Keefe   **Bethlehem, PA**
Computer systems Coordinator - 1/86-6/88
Responsible for computer systems used by CAD, Accounting, Word Processing and Engineering departments.

Computer Experience

Hardware: Travis, IBM, TITAN, Cayman GatorBox, MacIntosh.
Software: UNIX SV.3, SV.4
Language: Gould, VAX 11/780
Familiar with Ultrix, MS-DOS.

Education

Pennsylvania State University   **University Park, PA**
BS in Applied Mathematics, 1986.

■ Candidate focuses on his/her strongest point: lots of related job experience.

■ No job objective is needed since resume emphasizes a clear career path.

MIS MANAGER

CHRIS SMITH
178 Green Street
Cambridge, MA 02139
(617) 555-5555

TECHNICAL SUMMARY

Hardware Platforms:	PC's, Workstations, Mainframes, Servers
Operating Systems:	VMS, MVS, DOS, ULTRIX/UNIX, CP/M
Networks:	DECNET, TCP/IP
Approaches:	OODB, Client Servers, Remote Data Access, RDB, DBMS, CAD/CAM, EDI, CASE, 4GL's

EMPLOYMENT HISTORY

NILES CORPORATION (1982 to Present)

Ultrix Systems and Software, MIS Manager (1991 to Present)
Developed and implemented an overall information architecture for the manufacturing and engineering operational units of the low end business. Directed the efforts focused on utilizing client/server technology for manufacturing plants in the United States and Canada. Managed 24 professionals and an annual budget of $2.7 million, as well as a computer resource group that serviced 1,200 customers. Managed downsizing which resulted in budget reductions.

Consultant & Information Systems Marketing (1988 to 1991)
Major responsibility was to be the MIS subject matter expert for the development of courses designed to educate senior sales and software service people on MIS functions, its problems, and Digital's solutions. Designed and implemented various seminars and symposiums for the purpose of educating customers. All these activities resulted in increased sales and the establishment of new accounts.

Field Service Logistics (FLS) IS Manager (1986 to 1988)
Directed the design, development and implementation of the New Business Process. Directed and managed a staff of senior MIS professionals which implemented the MRPII application in multiple locations. The result was a 25% savings in inventory and expense reductions of $10 million.

MIS Manager, Low-End Business Center (1985 to 1986)
Directed MIS activities in support of order processing business unit with high-volume activity. In order to stabilize the operations, analyzed the operation, hired staff, proposed investments, and drove solutions. The result was smoother operations, quicker response to customers' orders, and reduced indirect labor costs.

Manager, Personal Data Systems (1982 to 1985)
Managed and directed the PDS Department in the pursuit of its long-range plan, the main focus of which was to deliver a distributed data base system. Resulted in reduced labor costs at headquarters and quicker response to employees.

EDUCATION

Massachusetts Institute of Technology (1986). Master of Science in Computer Science
Boston University (1972). Bachelor of Business Administration (Accounting)
Currently enrolled in the Certified Financial Planning program

---

- Technical summary clearly spells out candidate's computer skills.

- Use of boldface and underlining provides a clean and crisp presentation.

OPERATIONS ANALYST

CHRIS SMITH
178 Green Street
Sunset, SC 29685
(803) 555-5555

OBJECTIVE

A position as a computer operations analyst.

SUMMARY OF QUALIFICATIONS

- More than 18 years computer experience.
- Dedicated professional; set effective priorities to achieve immediate and long-term goals.
- Self-motivated; able to implement decisions to ensure smooth work flow.

EXPERIENCE

LARCHMONT MUTUAL, Sunset, SC
Operations Analyst, 1991 to Present
Translate information requirements into logical, economical, and practical system designs for large systems; cooperate with users and Senior Operations Analyst. Evaluate corporate requirements; investigate alternatives to identify/recommend best design. Prepare flowcharts; synthesize gathered information and present in logical/manageable components. Write detailed specifications; coordinate system testing; develop practical solutions to problems. Prepare associated documentation, user manuals, and instructions for complete operation of system. Assist junior personnel.

Console Operator, 1985 to 1991
Maintained/monitored Financial Information Services Equipment: IBM 4214 VM/SP system, IBM 4381 and 3090 MVS/XA and DOS/.VSE Mainframes, IBM 4248 and 4245 printers, IBM 3380 Disk Packs, IBM 4320 tape drives and IBM 3480 cartridge drives. Ran daily productions schedule; routed/printed productions jobs; maintained system controller and lines.

Senior Quality Reviewer, 1978 to 1985
Scrutinized percentage of claims processed to ensure correct coding of claims; reported statistical errors.

Data Entry Clerk, 1976 to 1978
Processed Data Entry; required knowledge of Medicare operational guidelines and Medical Terminology.

- Resume indicates a series of promotions.

- Education is omitted due to candidate's extensive work experience.

PRODUCT SUPPORT MANAGER

CHRIS SMITH
178 Green Street
Raritan, IL 61471
(309) 555-5555

TECHNICAL SUMMARY

Evaluated both hardware and software workstation configurations. Migrated entire organization to Microsoft Windows, Novell Netware network, and Microsoft SQL Server. Certified Lotus Notes Engineer.

EMPLOYMENT HISTORY
L. MULLINS SOFTWARE INC., Raritan, IL
Manager, Product Support (1989-Present)
- Manage the staff and operation of 40 technical product support specialists.
- Ensure superior levels of customer satisfaction with Product Support by hiring and retaining talented staff and providing technical and service skills training along with measurable standards of service performance.
- Determine which products and technologies are supported by Product Support Group.
- Responsible for acquiring training for product support specialists on new products and technologies.
- Contribute to various technical publications such as monthly newsletter, biannual software guide, technical notes, and white papers.
- Evaluated and developed in several front-end applications such as Powerbuilder, Forest & Tress and back-end database solutions such as Microsoft SQL Server.
- Responsible for creating summary, functional specifications and design specification.
- Developed summary project plans, cost-benefit analyses, and business rational for completion of each project.
- Monitored project progress. Documented and reported project status to Vice-President of Information Services as well as the user community.
- Identified and controlled all project schedule variances with gnatt charts and project management software tools.

FOLSOM AND RUSSO COMPONENTS, Sweetwater, IL
Manager, End User Computing (1984-1989)
- Managed and implemented local area and all associated applications.
- Developed, implemented, and maintained standards and guidelines for personal computer hardware (IBM-compatible and MacIntosh) and software.
- Managed hardware and software acquisition.

EDUCATION
Butler University, Indianapolis, IN
Master of Business Administration, 1984
Concentration in Information Systems

University of Illinois at Chicago
Bachelor of Science in Business Management, 1982

- Technical summary stresses candidate's achievements.

- Candidate's highest educational achievement is shown before other, less significant degrees.

PROJECT MANAGER

Chris Smith
178 Green Street
Rocky Mount, NC 27804
(919) 555-5555

PROFESSIONAL OBJECTIVE

Seeking further challenges as a **Project Manager** or related position where a diverse background and proven technical expertise will be utilized and advanced.

PROFESSIONAL EXPERIENCE

Quonto Information Systems, Rocky Mount, NC
Senior Systems Analyst, 1991-Present
- Member of a team selected to establish Quonto in the U.S.; report directly to the Chief Executive.
- In charge of specification, development, and installation of a sales/marketing and accounting software used in conjunction with the company developed Property Management System.
- Evaluate and develop applications development tools.
- Hire, train, monitor and supervise programming staff.
- Write software utilizing BASIC, ASSEMBLER, and COBOL.
- Client contact involves coordination and delivery of sales presentations and maintaining a positive and professional relationship through cooperative interaction.

Milton Data Processing, Reading PA
Systems Analyst, 1988-1991
- Designed, programmed and acted as project leader for the development of patient administration system.
- Evaluated and marketed patient administration and laboratory systems including composition of technical proposals and cost-benefit analyses.

Programmer, 1981-1988
- Functioned as part of a team responsible for the development of accounting software for microcomputers.

COMPUTER EXPERIENCE

Software: COBOL, BASIC, ASSEMBLER PC/DOS, RPG2, CDE/BTL, IMAGE 3000
Hardware: ICL 1900, ICL 1500, HP 3000, IBM PC, SORD M23

■ Resume stresses valuable management skills in addition to technical knowledge.

■ Resume illustrates continual career progression.

STATISTICIAN

CHRIS SMITH
178 Green Street
Cleveland, OH 44125
(216) 555-5555

CAREER OBJECTIVE

To secure an entry-level position in a large organization, preferably within the Accounting-Finance arenas, where I can contribute specialized statistical knowledge.

SUMMARY OF QUALIFICATIONS

- Broad knowledge of SAS Programming.
- Six years experience in the field of bookkeeping.
- Two years productive work experience in a statistics capacity.
- Computer Skills: SAS Programming; Statistics on Minitab; C-Language; DOS; Microsoft; WordPerfect.
- Relevant course work conducive to field.

Strengths

ANALYTICAL * PRECISE * ACCURATE * CONFIDENT * ORGANIZED * METICULOUS * DILIGENT * FAST LEARNER * GOAL-DIRECTED * EXCELLENT INTERPERSONAL SKILLS * MEET DEADLINES * CALM UNDER PRESSURE

EXPERIENCE

1993-Present   CLEVELAND MEDICAL CENTER, Cleveland, OH   **Data Entry**
- Part-time Health Service research for a three-year diabetes study involving questionnaires, processing data with resulting statistics.

1987-1993   JONES SURVEY & ENGINEERING, Cleveland, OH   **Bookkeeping**
- Summer employment and part time balancing accounts payable and receivable, processing time sheets, payroll, data entry, word processing. Mortgage survey field work including measurements, distance, assuring their conformation with zoning regulations.

PROFESSIONAL AFFILIATIONS

SCIENCE CLUB AT OBERLIN COLLEGE * GAMMA PHI BETA SORORITY

EDUCATION

OBERLIN COLLEGE, Oberlin, Ohio
B.A. Mathematics/Statistics; Minor in Business Administration, Graduated 1993.

REFERENCES

Available upon request.

- Resume emphasizes qualifications pertaining to candidate's job objective.

- Job objective gives resume focus without limiting candidate's opportunities.

SUBCONTRACTOR (Programming)

CHRIS SMITH
178 Green Street
New York, NY 11215
(212) 555-5555

**WORK
EXPERIENCE:**

New York Department of Public Welfare - 1989-Present
Subcontractor
Designed and developed programs for new reporting system plus maintenance
programming on existing reporting system.
Software used: OS/JCL, COBOL, TSO/SPF, VSAM, EASYREV

Rowe Street Bank and Trust - New York, NY, 1988-1989
Subcontractor
Maintenance Programming on the Trust Accounting System to add tax withholding on
interest and dividend income.
Software used: OS/JCL, PLI, ROSCOE, CMS, DATACOM

New York Hospital - Hempstead, NY, 1986-1988
Subcontractor
Program design and development for the existing Medicaid billing system.
Software used: OS/JCL, COBOL, TSO/SPF

New England Life Insurance Co. - Elmira, NY, 1984-1986
Subcontractor
Maintenance Programming to handle year-end changes to the agent commission system.
Software used: OS/JCL, COBOL, TSO/SPF

Atwood Corporation - Amherst, NY, 1982-1984
Programmer/Analyst
Programming and design on a portfolio management system.
Software used: COBOL, OS/JCL, ES

E. Walker and Associates, Inc. - Houghton, NY, 1981-1982
Programmer/Analyst Intern
Application programming and program design involving four projects at three separate
client locations. Experience in project leadership and user interface.
Software used: COBOL, PL/I, TSO/SPF, IMS, OS/JCL, CMS

EDUCATION:

Houghton College, Houghton, NY
B.S. in Computer Science
Graduated - January, 1982

- Resume emphasizes candidate's strong work history.

- Job objective is unnecessary because resume illustrates a clear career path.

SYSTEMS ANALYST (Custom Products)

CHRIS SMITH
178 Green Street
Chapel Hill, NC 27514
(919) 555-5555

CAREER OBJECTIVE:
Detailed and quality-oriented systems analyst seeking a position in developing custom products.

SUMMARY OF QUALIFICATIONS:
Extensive experience in customizing computer systems to meet customer contract requirements. Twenty years of diversified experience in testing subassemblies and electronic components to ensure a quality product.

CAREER HISTORY:
GORDON AND BYRON ASSOCIATES, Chapel Hill, NC
Custom Products Engineer (Level II) 1989-Present
- Research the customer requirements document to resolve non-compliant issues.
- Develop and control bills of material and put into effect a customer change control procedure.
- Write a specification document for the customer product.
- Develop and coordinate a test plan to test the product to ensure reliability.
- Organize the development of custom parts. Coordinate the design effort to ensure the product is launched on schedule and within budget.
- Travel to manufacturing site to resolve problems during pilot run. Meet with customer for product acceptance and sign off.
- Respond and resolve all field problems with customer products.

Test Engineer (Level I and II) 1986-1989
Developed test software and hardware used to test computer subassemblies on functional and in-circuit test systems.

EDUCATION:
Degree of Associate in Applied Business, 1984
Major: Computer Information Systems
Northeastern University, Boston, MA
Member of the Phi Theta Kappa Society

Certificate as an Electronic Technician, 1980
ITT Technical Institute

COMPUTERS:
- FORTRAN, Pascal, XII Windows
- CBDS, CADAM, CATIA, Oracle
- UNIX, VM/CMS
- IBM 3090

- Format is organized and visually appealing.

- Job objective focuses on the needs of the employer, not the job candidate.

SYSTEMS ANALYST (Industrial)

CHRIS SMITH
178 Green Street
Appleton, WI 54912
(414) 555-5555

SUMMARY OF ACCOMPLISHMENTS

- Set up the interfacing of mini computer to PC in order to archive daily receipts onto optical disks.
- Created a device driver for a new disk system, and developed a new operating system to handle the new driver.
- Qualified all of Devlin software onto a new computer system.
- Built a new method of handling orders into the system.
- Rewrote accents receivable program system to handle long-term notes.
- Suggested an improvement in board revectoring at Price Computer which was later implemented.

EMPLOYMENT HIGHLIGHTS

1989-Present **Systems Analyst** DEVLIN INDUSTRIES, Appleton, WI
Create or change programs; generate new reports; new ways of retrieving information in and out of computer; responsible for making system more efficient.

1988 **Typesetting Operator** OSHKOSH NEWS, Oshkosh, WI
Interim position with tasks that covered production of all type for several area newspapers.

1985-1988 **Production Assistant** PRICE COMPUTER, Madison, WI
Worked in Production Department on board repair, board revectoring, equipment assembly, basic production on electronic manufacturing.

PROFESSIONAL AFFILIATIONS

MADISON COMPUTER SOCIETY * ASSOCIATION OF COMPUTING MACHINERY

EDUCATION

MILWAUKEE SCHOOL OF ENGINEERING, Milwaukee, WI. Two Bachelor of Science Degrees: Computer Science/Systems and Applied Physics/Astronomy. Graduated, January 1985.

COMPUTER LITERACY

Hardware: PDP 11 Series * IBM PC, 286, 386, 486 * CDC 170 Series Mainframe
Languages: PDP 11 Assembly * 386 Assembly * C * Turbo Pascal * FORTRAN 77 * FORTH * Z80 Assembly * LISP
Systems: CDC-NOS * MS-DOS * Concurrent DOS * RT-11 RSTS * UNIX
Software: Paradox 3.5 * Search Express 2.51 * Word Star 5.0 * Monarch * ProComm 2.6

■ Summary points to candidate's specific contributions and problem-solving abilities.

■ Job-related affiliations demonstrate candidate's active participation in his/her field.

SYSTEMS ENGINEER

CHRIS SMITH
178 Green Street
Charlotte, NC 28214
(704) 555-5555

BACKGROUND

Extensive and diversified computer hardware and software knowledge in personal computers. Expertise in prototype computer testing. Excellent investigative and research skills. Self-taught in many programming languages, word processors, operating systems, database and spreadsheet software applications.

TECHNICAL QUALIFICATIONS

Programming Languages - Borland C, QBasic, FORTRAN, WordBasic
Operating Systems - MS-DOS, Windows, Novell Netware
Database - FoxPro, askSam
Spreadsheets - Lotus, Excel
Word Processors - WordStar, WordPerfect, Word for Windows, Word for DOS

SUMMARY OF ACCOMPLISHMENTS

- Organized preproduction testing of computer prototype
- Researched, wrote and edited test procedures that were used for testing of computer prototypes
- Correlated and verified technical information and communicative style in test procedures written by engineers/technical writers
- Co-authored Maxmillian (MDS) Microsoft DOS 5.0 software test plan and was presented with plaque for acknowledging outstanding efforts on development of DOS 5.0
- Wrote database application to track problems found during developmental stages of product, and to generate reports on outstanding issues found during product development
- Designed storage/retrieval and tracking system and cost analysis for manufactured products
- Developed computer engineering test tools
- Analyzed, developed and implemented new work-related quality processes to improve product testing
- Created software applications that automated work-related processes such as generating status and engineering change request reports

CAREER HISTORY

Maxmillian Data Systems, **Systems Engineer,** Charlotte, NC
Gilford College, **Instructor,** Greensboro, NC

EDUCATION

BGS, Duke University, Durham, NC
Majors: Industrial and Systems Engineering, Computer Computational Mathematics, Mathematics

■ Functional format focuses attention on candidate's major skills and accomplishments.

■ Dynamic action verbs give resume impact.

SYSTEMS PROGRAMMER

CHRIS SMITH
178 Green Street
Little Rock, AR 72209
(501) 555-5555

SUMMARY OF QUALIFICATIONS
- Thorough knowledge in the development and implementation of computer programs, including formulation of preventive maintenance programs, institution of assembler modules, provision of technical support and customization of existing formats.
- Skilled in the transformation of system font to alternative alphabets.

PROFESSIONAL EXPERIENCE
1990-Present   **Systems Programmer**   Little Rock, AR
PUBLIC AUTHORITY FOR CIVIL INFORMATION
- Maintained over 300 and developed 75 assembler modules.
- Formulated screen manager program, utilizing Assembler and Natural languages, to trace input and output to the VTAM buffer.
- Installed and customized Omegamon 695 and 700 on IBM mainframes.
- Developed program to monitor complete security control blocks, using Assembler and Natural.
- Produced a stand alone IPL and created a backrest on IBM 3380 DASD.

1981-90   **Partner/Technical Manager**   Fayetville, AR
- Initiated start-up activities and implemented operational procedures.
- Designed and managed the implementation of a network providing legal community with a direct line to supreme court cases, using Clipper on IBM 386's.
- Developed a system which catalogued entire library inventory, using Turbo Pascal on IBM AT.
- Utilized C to create a registration system for university registrar on IBM AT.

EDUCATION
ARKANSAS TECH UNIVERSITY   Russellville City, AR
Completed course work in Advanced IBM 370 Assembler, SNA Fundamentals, MVS/ESA Architecture, Natural 2 Programming Language, MVS/XA Concepts and Facilities, MVS/XA Job Control Language, MVS/XA System Problem Determination, ACF/VTAM Concepts, MVS/XA Using Utility Programs, MVS/XA Using and Creating Procedures.

UNIVERSITY OF ARKANSAS AT PINE BLUFF
Bachelor of Science Degree: Mathematics and Computer Science, 1981

COMPUTER SKILLS
- Programming Languages: Assembler, C, COBOL, Natural, Turbo Pascal, dBASE III+, and Clipper.
- Software: VTAM, Complete, TSO, JES 2, ACF 2, Omegamon 695 and 700, and Adabas.
- Operating Systems: MVS/XA, MVS/SP, MS-DOS and VMS.
- Hardware: IBM 3090 Model 2, IBM 3083 mainframe, IBM 3880 Storage Controller, IBM 3380 DASD, IBM 3725 Communication Controller, IBM 3800 Laser Printer, VAX 11, IBM AT and IBM 386

■ Impressive educational background strengthens resume.

■ Separate category for computer experience calls attention to candidate's technical knowledge.

TECHNICAL ENGINEER

CHRIS SMITH
178 Green Street
Albany, NY 12207
(518) 555-5555

PROFESSIONAL EXPERIENCE

TECHNICAL ENGINEER   1988-Present
MERCER INC., Albany, NY
Plan, coordinate, and execute hardware, software and network installation, configuration, maintenance, troubleshooting and repair operations for service contract clients. Specialize in maintaining IBM and Mac PCs, and peripherals with emphasis on networking environments.

- *Develop and implement service schedules, systems and procedures to assure delivery of quality, cost-efficient technical services.*
- *Quickly diagnose causes of systems failures and malfunctions to ensure highest operating efficiencies, reliability, and quality performance standards.*
- *Respond immediately to emergency situations with sensitivity to deadlines and customer needs.*
- *Assist network engineers with installation and troubleshooting of Appleshare and Novell systems.*
- *Analyze client equipment and operations to determine servicing and supply needs.*
- *Monitor and maintain cost-effective inventories of supplies, tools and materials.*
- *Investigate, test, and implement improvements to existing procedures.*
- *Consistently manage time and multiple tasks to meet deadline, established objectives, and quality performance standards.*
- *Foster clear communications and maintain excellent staff and client working relations.*

MANAGER OF INFORMATION SYSTEMS   1982-1988
KRITEL ASSOCIATES, INC., Schnectady, NY
Directed and supervised all MIS, related activities for a financial services firm supplying critical, timely information to corporate client base. Administered DISTON's 2 Novell 2X networks, maintaining peak operating efficiencies and providing user training for all hardware and software applications. Controlled budget costs for purchasing and operations.

LICENSES AND CERTIFICATIONS
CANDIDATE FOR CERTIFIED NETWARE ENGINEER/C.N.E. * CERTIFICATION IN MACINTOSH CPU, PRINTER, AND POWERBOOK REPAIR * CERTIFIED IN OKIDATA & EPSON LASER AND IMPACT PRINTERS * CERTIFICATION IN HEWLETT PACKARD LASER JET PRINTERS

TECHNICAL EXPERTISE
- **Hardware proficiencies:** IBM: AT, XT, PS2 * MACINTOSH * HP: II-IIISI LASER PRINTERS, COLOR PLOTTERS * OKIDATA * EPSON * DEST OCR SCANNERS * STORAGE DIMENSIONS E/O SCSI DRIVE
- **Networks:** APPLETALK * ETHERTALK * NOVELL NETWARE 2X, 3X * CABLING, NODES, PERIPHERALS
- **Software applications:** DOS, MACINTOSH OPERATING SYSTEMS * MS WINDOWS 3.0, 3.1 * WINDOWS APPLICATIONS * CWP 5.1 * WORD * EXCEL * LOTUS * WORDPERFECT 5.1 * DISPLAYWRITE 4 * QUICKEN 3.0 * PAGEMAKER 4.0 * HARVARD GRAPHICS 2.3 * PUBLISH/TEXT PAC OCR * NUTSHELL PLUS II * PARADOX 3.0

- Professional licensure and certifications add weight to resume.

- Use of boldface and italics provides a clean and crisp presentation.

10
Education and Library Science

Nature of Work

Educators play a vital role in the development of children. Kindergarten and elementary school teachers introduce young people to numbers, language, science, and social studies. Secondary school teachers delve more deeply into these subjects while also helping students learn more about themselves and the world around them.

Librarians make information available to people. They manage staff, oversee the collection and cataloging of library materials and direct information programs for the public.

Employment

Kindergarten, elementary, and secondary school teachers held 2.8 million jobs in 1990. Nine out of ten were in public schools. Employment is distributed geographically, much the same as the population. Librarians held about 149,000 jobs in 1990. Most were in school and academic libraries; others were in public or special libraries. A small number worked for hospitals, religious organizations, and governments.

Training

All fifty states and the District of Columbia require that public elementary and secondary school teachers be certified. Usually certification is granted by the state board of education or a certification advisory committee.

Requirements vary by state. However, all states require a bachelor's degree and a completion of an approved teacher training program with a prescribed number of subject and education credits and supervised practice teaching.

Job Outlook

Employment for kindergarten and elementary teachers is expected to grow at an average pace for all occupations through the year 2005. Employment for special education and secondary school teachers is expected to increase much faster than average.

Graduates of library science should have favorable job prospects largely due to the decline in the number of such qualified people during the 1980s.

Earnings

According to the National Education Association, public elementary and secondary school teachers averaged $33,000 for the school year. Earning in private schools were generally lower. In some public schools, teachers earn extra income for coaching sports or extracurricular activities.

Salaries of librarians vary by the individual qualifications and by the type, size, and location of the library. Starting salaries of graduates of accredited library school master's degree programs averaged $25,300 in 1990, and ranged from $23,400 in public libraries to $26,200 in school libraries. In college and universities, the average beginning salary was $24,000, while librarians in the federal government averaged $41,200.

ARCHIVIST

Chris Smith
178 Green Street
Chapel Hill, NC 27514
(919) 555-5555

EXPERIENCE:
6/93-Present UNIVERSITY OF NORTH CAROLINA, Chapel Hill, NC
Archivist
- Handle daily operations of College Archives, including: cataloging, photo indexing, and reference service.
- Manage school records.
- Work with alumni and local community to expand collection.
- Organize annual Alumni weekend events and displays.

9/91-5/93 **Technical Services Librarian**
- Maintained and updated catalog.
- Oversaw retrospective conversion of bibliographic data in preparation for implementation of on-line catalog.

9/89-8/91 MUSEUM OF SOUTHERN HISTORY, Chapel Hill, NC
Library Assistant
- Transferred newspaper clippings to microfilm.
- Cataloged Civil War era monograph collection.

EDUCATION:
University of North Carolina, Chapel Hill, NC
Master of Science in Library Science, 1991

Wingate College, Wingate, NC
Bachelor of Arts in English, 1987

MEMBERSHIPS:
Southern Personal Computer Users Group
- Program Committee, 1990-1992
- Board of Directors, 1992-Present

The Society of American Archivists
- Secretary of the Southern Chapter, 1993-Present

ACCOMPLISHMENTS:
Received "Alumni Appreciation Award" for organizing 1993 reunion.

■ Job descriptions are brief and punchy, without being choppy.

■ Accomplishments heading draws attention to impressive award.

ART INSTRUCTOR

CHRIS SMITH
178 Green Street
Gary, IN 46408
(219) 555-5555

AREAS OF EXPERTISE:

Art	Crafts Instruction
Education	Program Coordination
Teaching/Training	Curriculum Development

PROFESSIONAL HIGHLIGHTS:

Art Instructor 1976 to present
GARY REGIONAL SCHOOL DISTRICT Gary, IN
Responsible for curriculum development; teach aesthetics, art history, and appreciation. Oversee studio work; manage supply inventory and control budget.
* Implemented curriculum with classes for gifted art students, 1983

Arts & Crafts Program Director/Instructor 1984-1988
GARY PARKS AND RECREATIONAL ASSOCIATION Gary, IN
Created and facilitated arts & crafts activity programs including sewing, weaving, knitting, 3-dimensional work, sculpting, clay, paris craft, jewelry, enameling, painting, and drawing. Successfully controlled department budget; selected, purchased and managed supplies; supervised and directed arts aides in various duties. Produced annual arts show with competition winners traveling to compete in national show in Washington, DC.
* Commended for exceptional Arts & Crafts display, 1986
* Arranged school tours with Parks and Rec members demonstrating break-dancing styles & graffiti art, 1984

Basic Skills Teacher 1980-1984
INDIANA EDUCATIONAL PROGRAM Gary, IN
Tutored individuals in reading, math, and oral language skills; assessed students' accomplishments and prepared educational plans based on life and career skills. Responsible for directing and supervising teaching aides.

LICENSES/CERTIFICATES:
State of Indiana Elementary Education Certificate
Elementary & Secondary Education Certificate in Art

EDUCATION:

Bachelor of Fine Arts in Art Education 1976
INDIANA UNIVERSITY Bloomington, IN
(Cum Laude)

Graduate Studies include: Problem Solving Computer Using Pascal/Graduate Teaching of Reading/Child Behavior and Development/Independent Study: Painting/Special Problems, Communications Studies/Ceramic Chemistry/Special Problems, Painting/Psychological Statistics/Physiology/Ceramics/Intern Teaching

---

■ Candidate's areas of expertise are listed first to attract employer's attention.

■ Continuing education indicates candidate's ongoing commitment to his/her career.

ASSISTANT DEAN OF STUDENTS

CHRIS SMITH
178 Green Street
Pittsburgh, PA 19213
(412) 555-5555

OBJECTIVE
A position requiring proven organizational, administrative and
interpersonal skills in an academic environment.

EXPERIENCE
ASSISTANT DEAN OF STUDENTS - Carnegie Mellon University, Pittsburgh, PA   1991-Present
- Supervise housing in four Residence Halls, as well as the Residence Life staff of four professional Resident Directors and fourteen student Resident Assistants.
- Recruit, select, train and supervise Resident Staff.
- Plan and arrange social, cultural, and recreational activities of various student groups; meet with student and faculty groups to plan activities.
- Conduct orientation programs for new students with other members of faculty and staff; counsel students on methods for improving their organizations and promote student participation in social, cultural and recreational activities. Coordinate the preparation and publishing of student affairs calendar and advertising/press releases.
- Initiate and advise Student Advisory Committee on the campus food service to assure that food service management include student preferences in daily menus.
- Supervise major campus events: New Student Orientation; Parents' Weekend.
- Interact with Campus Police on various campus-based problems & issues; as well as with Health Services Clinic and Counseling Center, the college food service, housekeeping, and physical plant.
- Serve on and actively contribute to committees; Student Life and Student Wholeness Committees; the Alcohol Alert Team; and the Drug Task Force.

COORDINATOR OF STUDENT ACTIVITIES - Carnegie Mellon University, Pittsburgh, PA   1986-1991
- Developed a comprehensive student activities program focusing on development of student's leadership skills. Prepared and conducted workshops on Public Speaking, Assertiveness Training, Time Management, and Conflict Confrontation.
- Instrumental in involving International students in campus activities: International Week, International Buffet Dinner (Round table discussion between American and International Students), instituted an International theme on the campus center concourse.

EDUCATION
Master of Education, Program Evaluation and Research, May 1985
University of Pennsylvania, Philadelphia, PA

Bachelor of Arts degree in Psychology, May 1983
Allegheny College, Allegheny, PA

- Job descriptions highlight candidate's leadership skills and problem-solving abilities.

- Resume format is neat and professional.

COACH

CHRIS SMITH
178 Green Street
Orono, ME 04473
(207) 555-5555

PROFESSIONAL OBJECTIVE
A challenging position as Hockey Coach at the college level.

PROFESSIONAL EXPERIENCE
1989-Present UNIVERSITY OF MAINE, Orono, Maine
Assistant Varsity Hockey Coach
- Goaltender Coach
- Scouted opposing teams in preparation for games
- Responsible for recruitment of potential student athletes

1988-1989 SAINT JOSEPH'S COLLEGE, North Windham, Maine
Assistant Varsity Hockey Coach
- Participated in all phases of coaching, training and preparation of hockey team
- Assisted in recruiting efforts for the 1979-1980 season

ADDITIONAL EXPERIENCE
1984-1987 STATE HOCKEY SCHOOL OF MAINE, Augusta, Maine
Hockey Instructor, Summer program
- Program Director, 1981-1984
- Head Goaltending Director, 1977-1984

1983 MAXFIELD ALL-AMERICAN HOCKEY SCHOOL, Orono, Maine
Hockey Instructor

1982 NATIONAL SPORTS CAMP OF AMERICA at UNIVERSITY OF MAINE, Orono, Maine
Hockey Counselor and Instructor

EDUCATION UNIVERSITY OF MAINE, Orono, Maine
Masters of Science degree in Human Movement, Health and Leisure, 1987
- Starting Varsity Hockey Goal Tender, 1978-1981
- All-Star Goal Tender, Bangor Tournament, 1978
- Outstanding Goal Tender, Portland Tournament, 1978
- All-East, 1978
- Captain, NCAA Division I Champions, 1981

Bachelor of Science degree in Human Movement, Health and Leisure, 1981

■ Resume emphasizes qualifications pertaining to candidate's job objective.

■ Unrelated work experience is omitted.

COLLEGE PROFESSOR

CHRIS SMITH
178 Green Street
Malvern, PA 19355
(215) 555-5555

SUMMARY OF QUALIFICATIONS

- Ten years teaching experience at college level.
- Academic counselor to students attending Drexel University.
- Six years as a Professor, Drexel University, teaching Criminal Law, Legal Aspects of Criminal Procedures, Crime in America, The Courts & Criminal Procedures, Juvenile Procedures, and Business and Administrative Management.
- Strong communications skills as author, lecturer, teacher, debater, and negotiator dealing with individuals and groups in the disciplines of law and business administration.
- Excellent relationship builder with students, faculty, and administration.

EXPERIENCE

Professor, Drexel University, Philadelphia, PA (1989-Present)
Conduct college-level courses in Business and Legal Studies to university students and serve as academic advisor for students. Prepare and present lectures to students on law and business practices; research and compile bibliographies of specialized materials for outside reading assignments; stimulate class discussions. Plan, coordinate and participate in special events involving university and community officials. Member of Student Affairs faculty committee.

Assistant Professor, Dickinson College, Carlisle, PA (1984-1988)
Taught seven core courses in Business Administration and Law Enforcement. The latter included Criminal Law, Legal Aspects of Criminal Procedures; Crime in America; The Courts & Criminal Law, Legal Aspects of Criminal Procedures; Crime in America; The Courts & Criminal Procedures; and Juvenile Procedures. Planned lectures, administered examinations, and assisted students outside of classroom.

EDUCATION

John Carroll University, University Heights, OH
Juris Doctor Degree, 1993

Case Western Reserve University, Cleveland, OH
Master of Arts in Business Administration, 1983

North Carolina State University, Raleigh, NC
Bachelor of Science in Criminal Justice, 1980

■ Summary highlights candidate's experience and expertise in his/her field.

■ Strong educational credentials strengthen resume.

COMPUTER TEACHER

CHRIS SMITH
178 Green Street
Libertyville, IL 60048
(708) 555-5555

SKILLS:

- Computers: MacIntosh, IBM, Apple
- Software: MacIntosh - Microsoft Word 5.0, Microsoft Works 3.0, Pagemaker 4.0/5.0, Claris Works, Excel, FileMaker Pro, FoxPro; IBM - Microsoft Word for Windows, WordPerfect 5.0

EDUCATION AND TRAINING:

DePaul University	Bachelor of Arts Degree, Education
Chicago, IL	Illinois Teacher Certificates (Nursery-8th)

EXPERIENCE:

Computer Teacher 1986-Present
Libertyville Middle School, Libertyville, IL

- Taught Basic Programming and computer applications to seventh graders, and LOGO and applications to Special Education seventh graders;
- As a replacement teacher, provided students with a smooth transition from their original teacher;
- Developed a catalog of available software for staff members;
- Modified public domain software/programs for implementation of curriculum;
- Provided staff with support via in-service workshops and one-on-one instruction to facilitate their use of computers for classroom management and for implementation of curriculum by increasing computer use by staff from 3 to 25 teachers, and Computer Lab use by staff from 30 hours to 236 hours a year.

Bookstore Manager 1984-1985
Concordia Preparatory School, River Forest, IL

- Purchased and sold all required textbooks for this independent private school (Pre-K through 12);
- Designed, purchased and sold all school logo products;
- Within first six months of employment, turned operation around from a net loss to a net gain situation;
- Computerized and reorganized entire bookstore operation and procedures enabling students to purchase their books more efficiently.

Chapter 1 Basic Skills Teacher, Community Education Computer Instructor, Home Instructor
Aurora Board of Education, Aurora, IL 1980-1983

- Taught remedial reading and math to Chapter 1 students (K-8);
- Created and implemented computer curriculum for adults (Basic programming and applications).

■ Computer skills, essential for this position, are prominently listed.

■ Job descriptions are straightforward and understandable.

DAYCARE WORKER

CHRIS SMITH
178 Green Street
Delaware City, DE 19706
(302) 555-5555

EDUCATION:
University of Delaware, Newark, DE
Bachelor of Arts, 1993
Major: Early Childhood Education; GPA in Major: 3.5/4.0

CERTIFICATION:
Delaware State K-5

TEACHING EXPERIENCE:
Head Teacher: City Child Care Corporation, Delaware City, DE
September 1994-Present
Taught educational and recreational activities for twenty children, ages five to ten years, in a preschool/playcare setting. Planned and executed age-appropriate activities to promote social, cognitive and physical skills. Developed daily lesson plans. Observed and assessed each child's development. Conducted parent/teacher orientations and meetings. Organized and administered various school projects.

Teacher: Little People Preschool and Daycare, New Castle, DE
June 1993-August 1994
Taught educational and recreational activities for children, ages three to seven years, in a preschool/daycare setting. Planned, prepared and executed two week units based upon a theme to develop social, cognitive and physical skills. Lessons and activities were prepared in Mathematics, Language Arts, Science and Social Studies. Observed and assessed each child's development and followed up with parent/teacher discussions.

Student Teacher: Rolling Elementary School, Newark, DE
January-May 1993
Taught and assisted a kindergarten teacher in a self-contained classroom of twenty-eight students. Planned and instructed lessons and activities in Mathematics, Science and Social Studies.

Teacher's Aide: Y.M.C.A. Daycare Center, Wilmington, DE
June-August, 1992

Teaching Intern: Freud Laboratory School, Newark, DE
January-May 1991

Teaching Intern: Green Meadow Elementary School, Newark, DE
January-May 1990

Teaching Intern: Delaware State College Daycare Centers, Dover, DE
October-December 1989

■ "Certification" heading draws attention to candidate's specific professional qualifications.

■ Internships and student teaching positions strengthen resume, since candidate has short employment history.

DEVELOPMENTAL EDUCATOR

CHRIS SMITH
178 Green Street
Jamaica, NY 11413
(212) 555-5555

OBJECTIVE
A senior-level position in development and/or alumni relations with a non-profit organization or institution.

SUMMARY OF QUALIFICATIONS
- Ten years of experience in development with non-profit service organizations, universities, and educational institutions catering to the arts.
- Experience ranges from Secretary to Director of Development, to current position of Director of Development.
- Expertise in mass media communications, special events organization, budget planning and multi-office coordination for national development program.
- Well qualified to assume full responsibility for directing and supporting a well organized development or alumni relations program.

EXPERIENCE
DIRECTOR OF DEVELOPMENT - Paisley Star School for the Arts Development Office, Jamaica, NY
Director of Development   1988-Present
- Coordinate all fund-raising, public relations, alumni relations and publications for this private Boarding and Day secondary school for students in the arts, while actively developing Trustee, Alumni and Parents Association Boards.
- Supervise a support of eight as well as volunteers in the planning, organization, and running of reunions, special events and innovative functions with great success.
- Wrote, designed, and coordinated the production of publications; composed mass media communications and instituted a new newsletter; increased annual fund by 100%.
- Key participant in $8-million capital campaign structuring, set-up of special committees, etc.; laid groundwork for entire Campaign for the enhancement of educational programs.

Assistant to the Director of Development   1984-1988
- Assumed full responsibility for the set of systems, procedures and direction of the Alumni Annual Fund. Administered direct mail, processed responses and returns, acknowledged donor gifts and maintained current records of approximately 10,000 alumni.
- Served as Ad Book Coordinator for the Annual Paisley Star Gala Dance Performance. Sold and wrote ads and program copy, designed layout, and coordinated printing production. Ad book garnered several thousands of dollars in additional revenue.
- Extensively involved in public, community, and alumni relations as well as media releases and relations.

EDUCATION
- Bates College, Lewiston, ME
  B.A., Communications 1982

■ Job objective is clearly defined.

■ Resume emphasizes contributions, achievements, and problems candidate has solved throughout his/her career.

ESL TEACHER

CHRIS SMITH
178 Green Street
San Francisco, CA 94111
(415) 555-5555

OBJECTIVE

To contribute relevant experience, educational background and linguistic skills to a full-time Teaching of English as a Second Language position.

SUMMARY OF QUALIFICATIONS

- Instructed various populations in English and Sign Language, tutor in Chinese and coordinate communication and cognitive development activities for special needs individuals.
- Proficient in the provision of counseling services and initializing patients' existing motor capabilities to develop basic skills.
- Experienced in working with adults/children from diverse cultural backgrounds.
- Fluent in Chinese and English; extensive language training in French and Latin.
- Exceptional communication/interpersonal and organization skills.

EXPERIENCE

ERVINE PRISON   San Francisco, CA
1991-Present   **Interpreter, Chinese/Vietnamese**
Act as interpreter/translator for prisoners and prison officials. Sit in on trials, and probate/appellate hearings. Act as liaison between lawyers and their other incarcerated clients.

CHINESE-AMERICAN CIVIC ASSOCIATION   San Francisco, CA
1988-1991   **Teacher**
Instruct Chinese and Vietnamese adults in English as a second language.

RYDELL CORPORATION   San Francisco, CA
1984-1988   **Counselor/Interpretor**
Conduct individual and group counseling for the elimination of inappropriate behaviors in young adults suffering from autism and cerebral palsy. Consultation with psychiatrists, psychologists and health professionals for the coordination of treatment plans. Monitor clients to assess effectiveness of treatment plans. Instruct clients in various basic skills, including communication, reading, writing and math. Initiated cognitive development activities.

EDUCATION

SCHOOL FOR INTERNATIONAL TRAINING   Orange, CA
Master of Arts in Teaching
Concentration in Teaching of English to Speakers of Other Languages (ESOL)

UNIVERSITY OF MIAMI
Bachelor of Arts Degree: Human Services   Miami, FL

REFERENCES FURNISHED UPON REQUEST

- Chrono-functional format is more flexible than a chronological resume, but stronger than a functional resume.

- Unrelated work experience is omitted.

FOREIGN LANGUAGE TEACHER

CHRIS SMITH
178 Green Street
Echo, Oregon 97826
(503) 555-5555

OBJECTIVE

A teaching position with an established university seeking the services of a highly commended educator, with total capability in the teaching and translation of French.

TEACHING EXPERIENCE

Teacher of French Literature & Language: 1992-Present
Smith College, Northampton, MA

Professor of French Language: 1990-1992
Faculty of Literature and Human Science, University of Vermont, Burlington, VT
- Continually active in all aspects of the education process and administration

Head of French Language Department: 1985-1990
College of Translation, Pratt University, Brooklyn, NY
- Teaching, Translation, French & Persian Literature, Art, History
- Full curriculum - all aspects of administration - public service

Professor for French & Persian Language & Literature: 1980-1985
College of Translation, New York University, NY, NY
- Teaching, Translation, French & Persian Literature, Art, History
- Full academic schedule - research, writing, public service

Educational Advisor: 1978-1980
Technical Committee, Office of Foreign Language, Boston College, Chestnut Hill, MA
- System-wide curriculum development, French & Persian Literature & Language

Teacher of French Language & Literature: 1975-1977
Stoughton High School, Stoughton, MA
- Full academic schedule - active in school affairs

EDUCATION

Ph.D., Harvard University, Cambridge, MA: 1975
- French Literature

M.A. *(Highest Honors)*, Hood College, Frederick, Maryland: 1973
- French Literature

B.A. *(Highest Honors)*, University of Illinois at Chicago: 1971
- French Literature

- Job objective focuses on the needs of the employer, not the job candidate.

- Resume emphasizes candidate's strong work history.

GUIDANCE COUNSELOR

CHRIS SMITH
178 Green Street
Irvine, CA 92717
(714) 555-5555

OBJECTIVE

To secure a position as a guidance counselor in grades K-8.

EDUCATION

UNIVERSITY OF CALIFORNIA   Irvine, CA
M.Ed., Counselor Training/Psychology
Concentration on *School Guidance in Primary Grades*
• Certification upon graduation; May 1995

PEPPERDINE UNIVERSITY   Malibu, CA
B.A., Psychology; Minor, Sociology   May 1993

QUALIFICATIONS
• Experience with children with behavioral problems and handicaps including deafness, mental retardation, cerebral palsy, and eating disorders.
• Proven adaptability and expertise working with multi-cultural populations, particularly Hispanic students.
• Fluent in American Sign Language; Conversant in Spanish.
• Excellent communication and interpersonal skills, verbal and written.
• Organized; meet deadlines.

EXPERIENCE

ADAIR SCHOOL   Irvine, CA
Intern/Guidance Counseling, K-8   1994-Present

UCAL/IRVINE   Irvine, CA
Research Assistant   1993-Present
• Conducted extensive research at this Institute for People with Disabilities.

PEPPERDINE UNIVERSITY HOSPITAL SCHOOL   Malibu, CA
Volunteer/Recreational Therapist, Ages 2-21   1993

PROFESSIONAL AFFILIATIONS
• Counseling Association of California
• PTA, California chapter

Excellent References Available On Request

■ Chrono-functional format emphasizes candidate's education, qualifications, and relevant internship, while de-emphasizing lack of professional work experience.

■ Professional memberships show candidate's commitment to his/her field.

HEAD TEACHER

CHRIS SMITH
178 Green Street
Deltona, FL 32738
(207) 555-5555

EDUCATION

ECKERD COLLEGE, St. Petersburg, FL
Bachelor of Science Degree
Major: Elementary Education
Specialization: Moderate Special Needs

FLAGLER COLLEGE, St. Augustine, FL
Major: Speech Pathology and Audiology

PROFESSIONAL EXPERIENCE

MEADOW BROOK ELEMENTARY SCHOOL, Deltona, FL   1990-Present
Head Teacher, Resource Room, grades 4-6.
Major emphasis on successfully mainstreaming learning disabled students into regular education,
Social Studies, Science, and Mathematics classes. Established close working relationships and
regular education staff to modify curriculum to meet the needs of special education students.
Coordinated, designed and implemented individual IEP goals in Reading and Language Arts.
Supervised instructional aides.

JAMIE FENTON SCHOOL, Pine Castle, FL   1988-1990
Head Teacher, self-contained language/learning disabilities program, grades K-5.
Designed and implemented individual IEP's, responsibly arranged and chaired CORE's for each
student. Coordinated efforts of each specialist involved on TEAM. Developed curricula in all
content areas. Effectively established excellent rapport with regular education staff which earned
recognition of the special education class. Screened potential candidates for program, reporting
directly to the SPED administrator. Supervised student teachers and instructional aides.

BORDEN HOME AND SCHOOL FOR BOYS, Winter Park, FL   1987-1988
Head Teacher, self-contained emotionally disturbed and learning disabilities class, ages 8-12.
Developed positive behavior modification techniques to coincide with success-oriented group and
individual lesson plans. Integral member of TEAM, coordinating IEP's, case-conferences, parent
contact, and psychological support. Supervised student teachers.

THE SOUTHERN HOME FOR RUNAWAYS, Orlando, FL   1985-1987
Head Teacher, self-contained emotionally disturbed and learning disabilities class, ages 10-15.
Developed and successfully implemented IEP's. Planned and presented curriculum. Supervised and
trained student interns.

■ Layout is clean and well-organized.

■ Unrelated work experience is omitted.

LIBRARIAN

CHRIS SMITH
178 Green Street
Burlington, VT 05401
(802) 555-5555

PROFESSIONAL EXPERIENCE

1978 to present   KATHRYN F. BELL LIBRARY
Burlington, VT
Librarian, 1986-present
- Cover the circulation desk.
- Give instructional guidance to patrons, including use of index tools and card catalog; answer reference questions.
- Shelf books, journals, and audiovisuals.
- Give instruction on use of AV equipment.
- Check new book orders to prevent duplication.
- Record incoming periodicals and microfilm and identify and strip same for security.
- Maintain Reference Search File.
- Photocopy from journals and microfilm upon request.
- Compile statistics on door count, circulation, photocopies, and reference questions
- Knowledgeable in library services, policies and procedures, copyright and photocopy policies and procedures, circulation, basic filing, and the NLM Classification System, ALA filing rules, mesh headings, and various indexes.

Library Assistant, 1978-1986
- Supervised the library, maintaining quiet and order.
- Supervised the evening clerk.
- Performed many general library tasks as described in current position.
- Compiled and circulated LIL (Lates in Literature) reference packet for physicians.

1970 to 1977   EAST CATHOLIC HIGH SCHOOL, Rutland, VT
Librarian/Audio Visual Coordinator
- Supervised library and aided staff.
- Responsible for all library duties.
- Ordered software, and maintained all audio visual equipment; instructed teachers on equipment use; scheduled equipment usage.
- Supervised student assigned study periods.
- Maintained positive working relationship with teachers and students.

EDUCATION

SIMMONS COLLEGE, Boston, MA
Masters of Library Science, 1970

BURLINGTON COMMUNITY COLLEGE, Burlington, VT
Bachelor of Arts in English, 1968

- Extensive professional experience is presented in an orderly, bulleted format.

- Candidate's highest educational achievement is shown before other, less significant degrees.

LIBRARY TECHNICIAN

Chris Smith
178 Green Street
Norwood, MA 02062
(617) 555-5555

EDUCATION:
Simmons College, Boston, MA
M.S., Library Science, Graduated Cum Laude 1989

Northeastern University, Boston, MA
B.S., Computer Science, Graduated 1983

AREAS OF EFFECTIVENESS
- Analysis
- Research
- Numerical Ability
- Troubleshooting Skills

EXPERIENCE:
BOSTON PUBLIC LIBRARY, Boston, MA   1988-Present
Systems Coordinator
- Coordinate the automation of all PCs, VMS-base, UNIX and Dumb terminals.
- Ensure all PCs are up and running on a 24-hour basis.
- Troubleshoot, run codes, keep systems operating smoothly.
- Train librarians and library staff on use of systems, particularly VMS-base and UNIX.
- Provide instant access to newsprint publications on microfiche; maintain terminals.
- Assist librarians to develop materials to aid the public.

THOMAS CRANE LIBRARY, Quincy, MA   1985-1988
Computer Assistant
- Assisted Systems coordinator in maintaining all PCs and Dumb terminals.
- Ensured smooth running of all UNIX systems on a daily basis.
- Assisted librarians and public in the use of PCs.

PROFESSIONAL AFFILIATIONS
- Library Technicians of Boston

■ Clean layout makes resume easy to read.

■ Impressive educational background strengthens resume.

MUSIC TEACHER

CHRIS SMITH
178 Green Street
Boston, MA 02114
(617) 555-5555

PROFESSIONAL OBJECTIVE
Seeking a position as a college-level music teacher.

PROFESSIONAL EXPERIENCE

Teaching
- Juilliard School, New York, NY   1992-1993
  Taught private guitar lessons. Co-led workshops in jazz improvisation and ensemble techniques in New York City High Schools
- University of Pennsylvania and Temple University, Philadelphia, PA   1991
  Co-led two day workshops in jazz performance
- Des Moines House of Music, Studio East Music, West Music, New York and Rock Hard Music, NY   1990

Performance
- Guitarist in concert with the Bugles, Don Wrensly, Mel Fanfare, the Joe Bob Brown Band, and Prudence Jackson and the Waifs.
- Guitarist, *Dirt and Wine* and *Enrique Smith's Dream,* University of Pennsylvania and the inaugural ball for the governor of Pennsylvania.
- Recordings include: guitar work on themes for the Boston Bruins; a documentary film "Whimsy of the Co-Dependent Heart," and more than a dozen demos and jingles for independent producers.

Musical Direction/Writing
- Music Director, *On the Trellis,* Boston, MA, 1993, Pelican Productions
- Co-Writer and Music Director, *Cry, Sapphire Girl, Cry,* University of Michigan, 1988, as part of the artist-in-residence program.
- Co-Writer and Music Director, *Warm Rain: One Woman's Battle with Body Acceptance,* Devlin Theater, San Francisco, CA; Mechely Theater, New York.
- Music Director and Composer, *Buttercup Hates Acorn, A Love Story,* San Francisco Theater.
- Co-Writer and Arranger of 50 songs in the pop and jazz fields.

EDUCATION
- Juillard School, New York, NY. Professional Music Diploma, May 1990
- Berklee College, Boston, MA. Jazz arranging, harmony and improvisation, 1988
- University of Pennsylvania, Philadelphia, PA. Bachelor in Musical Theory and Composition, 1987

CERTIFICATION/RECOGNITION
- Certified Teacher in New York Private Secondary Schools, 1990
- Juillard Scholarship Recipient, 1989
- Outstanding Soloist Award, Montreal Jazz Festival, 1988

■ Functional format focuses attention on candidate's major skills and accomplishments.

■ Including dates is ideal for any resume format, but are not mandatory for a functional resume.

NANNY

Chris Smith
178 Green Street
Livermore, CO 80536
(303) 555-5555

RELATED EXPERIENCE:

1993- Private residence, Livermore, CO
Present **NANNY**
Care for twin boys from the age of two months through two years. Assist in selecting toys and equipment, provide environmental stimulation, personal care and play.

1991-1993 Baby Bear Preschool, Keystone, CO
TEACHER
Taught infant, preschool and after school programs. Planned curriculum, organized activities, and communicated with parents and staff regarding children's growth and development. Suggested equipment to enrich children's experiences and helped create a stimulating environment.

1989-1991 This Little Piggy Daycare Center, Dove Creek, CO
TEACHER
Planned and implemented curriculum for infants. Communicated with parents and other staff regarding daily progress of children.

1987-1989 The Kid Corral, Wild Horse, CO
TEACHER
Planned and implemented curriculum for toddler program. Enriched children's experiences through play, music, and art.

1985-1987 Ivywild Coalition for Retarded Citizens, Ivywild, CO
CARE GIVER
Provided care in clients' homes, administering physical therapy when necessary. Planned activities to stimulate and improve children's skills and environment.

EDUCATION:
Metropolitan State College, Denver, CO
Completed 30 credits in Education with an emphasis on the Daycare setting. Minor: English.

INTERESTS:
Reading, music, arts and crafts.

REFERENCES:
Excellent references available upon request.

- Since candidate did not earn advanced degree, resume simply cites areas studied and credits earned.

- Activities give candidate's resume a personal touch.

PHYSICAL EDUCATION TEACHER

Chris Smith
178 Green Street
Toledo, OH 43606
(419) 555-5555

SUMMARY OF QUALIFICATIONS

Enthusiastic and positive attitude, experienced in making group presentations and teaching a wide range of students of all ages. Strong analytical and problem-solving abilities, welcoming new challenges. Goal- and results-oriented, able to motivate others to perform at their highest levels. Combine mathematical background with writing, planning and organizational abilities. Eager to learn new skills and procedures.

COACHING EXPERIENCE

BRENNEN HILL SCHOOL DISTRICT, Toledo, OH   1982 to Present
Emphasize building self-esteem and character through developing realistic expectations and high standards. Serve as mentor and role model in assisting students to reach their goals.

Head Winter Track Coach-Junior High   1984-Present
- Team finished 4 seasons undefeated.
- 5 teams recorded first place finishes in Brennen Hill District Competitions.

Head Boy's Basketball Coach-Junior High   1986-Present
- Teams recorded 2 undefeated seasons.
- Achieved 3 additional first place finishes in B.H.S. League.

Head Football Coach-Junior High   1986-Present
- Team achieved 3 undefeated seasons with 1 additional first place finish in their league.

EDUCATION
Baldwin College, Berea, OH
Master's degree in Education, 1981

CERTIFICATION
Ohio, Secondary Mathematics Education

■ Summary of qualifications illustrates candidate's key credentials.

■ Resume emphasizes achievements; doesn't simply list job responsibilities.

PRINCIPAL

CHRIS SMITH
178 Green Street
Williamsburg, VA 23185
(804) 555-5555

OBJECTIVE
A challenging HIGH SCHOOL ADMINISTRATIVE position.

PROFILE
- Offer masters degrees in School Administration and Biology/Immunology enhanced by 15 years of teaching and student guidance experience combined with a 10-year corporate Marketing and Management background.
- Facilitator of the Discipline Committee. Initiated, organized and orchestrated numerous class trips and education expeditions with durations of up to 2 weeks.
- Self-starter with strong planning, controlling, organizing and leadership skills. Consistently meets deadlines and objectives; works well under pressure.
- Articulate and effective communicator with proven ability to work with diverse populations of students at a variety of academic levels. Consistently maintain excellent relations with students, parents, faculty and administrators. Works well as part of a team or independently.
- Track record for identifying complex administrative problems; resourceful in developing and implementing creative solutions resulting in increased productivity with enhanced sensitivity to costs and efficiency.

EDUCATION
MASTER OF SCIENCE IN SCHOOL ADMINISTRATION, 1993
College of William and Mary - Williamsburg, VA

MASTER OF SCIENCE IN BIOLOGY/IMMUNOLOGY, 1985
James Madison University - Harrisonburg, VA

MASTER OF SCIENCE IN SCIENCE EDUCATION/ENVIRONMENTAL SCIENCES, 1981

BACHELOR OF SCIENCE IN BIOLOGY, 1975
Drew University - Madison, New Jersey

(continued)

- The first page of resume outlines candidate's key skills and educational qualifications.

- The second page focuses attention on specific professional experience and licensure.

HEAD TEACHER   1983-Present
The Adams School   Williamsburg, VA
Responsible for planning, developing, preparing and implementing an effective science curriculum, management and student assessment. Devise and prepare daily lesson plans, materials, teaching aids and demonstrations to effectively convey critical concepts and factual knowledge in Biology, Physical Science, Physics, Earth Science and Oceanography. Develop engaging daily classroom presentations; assign work projects; review and discuss lesson objectives and class performance. Stimulate and motivate students by generating excitement and enthusiasm; encourage exploration of new concepts, joy in learning and pride in performance. Provide clear explanations, creative approaches and extra tutoring as required. Compose and administer exams and grade student performance. Advise and counsel individual students in academic areas and on aspects of student life. Communicate with parents on their child's progress, fostering excellent professional relations. Interact positively with faculty members and administrators. Provide educational leadership through serving on committees and executing special projects to further high educational standards.

HIGH SCHOOL TEACHER   1982-1983
West Harris High School   Harrisburg, VA
  • Presented Biology and Physical Science classes at the high school level.

MIDDLE SCHOOL TEACHER   1981-1982
Reede Middle School   Harrisburg, VA
  • Taught an Earth Science curriculum to eighth grade students.

TEACHER   1976-1978
Melbourne Academy   Madison, NJ
  • Instructed students in Biology, Marine Biology/Ecology.

LICENSES & CERTIFICATIONS
VIRGINIA • NEW JERSEY PERMANENT CERTIFICATION IN BIOLOGY, CHEMISTRY, EARTH SCIENCE AND PHYSICAL SCIENCE

SCHOOL PSYCHOLOGIST

CHRIS SMITH
178 Green Street
Dubuque, Iowa 52001
(319) 555-5555

CAREER HISTORY

1986-Present   DUBUQUE SCHOOL DEPARTMENT, Dubuque, Iowa
School Psychologist/Guidance Counselor
- Provide individual and group counseling to children aged 5-15 as well as to adults and parents.
- Serve as Consultant to teachers, principals, administrators and other personnel.
- Develop behavioral strategies to assist with controlling problem pupils in the classroom; observe and assess classroom behavior and performance.
- Conduct educational and psychological testing; interpret results and design/implement individualized plans for students which include short- and long- term goals.
- Serve as liaison with outside agencies (D.S.S., D.Y.S., O.F.C.) and the courts and escort children/adolescents to court when necessary.
- Provide expert testimony and support for children and parents.
- Prepare, compile and present materials such as evaluations, test results and the testimony of other parties.
- Develop and conduct lectures/seminars for teacher in-service training.
- Chair meetings for the staff and other school department personnel.
- Determine educational requirements for special needs children and ensure the implementation of individualized treatment/educational plans; assess needs and progress on an ongoing basis.
- Participate in team assistance for chronically or terminally ill children.
- Assist in the development of appropriate educational materials.

1982-Present   PRIVATE PRACTICE, Dubuque, Iowa
Psychologist
- Provide assessment, counseling and therapeutic group services to parents without partners and the children of divorced parents.
- Develop and conduct presentations for community, church and special interest groups either seeking understanding of the problems or striving to set up their outreach/support services to deal with these situations.
- Also work with individuals, families and groups in adjusting to the death of a parent or loved one and in dealing with alcoholism, success and stress.

EDUCATION

1982   UNIVERSITY OF IOWA, Iowa City, IA; C.A.E.S. Counseling/Clinical Psychology

1975   UNIVERSITY OF IOWA, Iowa City, IA; M.E.D. School Psychology

1971   SIMPSON COLLEGE, Indianola, IA; Certification in Special Needs

1966   TAYLOR UNIVERSITY, Upland, IN; B.A., Sociology/Psychology.

■ Candidate's private practice is listed in employment section of resume.

■ Impressive educational background strengthens resume.

SPECIAL NEEDS EDUCATOR

CHRIS SMITH
178 Green Street
Salt Lake City, UT 84112
(801) 555-5555

EDUCATION:

University of Wisconsin, Milwaukee, WI
B.S., Education, 1977

Montclair State College, Upper Montclair, NJ
General Curriculum, two years

CREDENTIALS:

Life Language Learning Disabilities, Utah
Learning Disabilities and Emotional Disturbance, K-12, Wisconsin
Teaching Emotionally Handicapped Certificate, New Jersey
Multiple Subject Teaching Credential, K-12, Oregon

EXPERIENCE:

Salt Lake Independent School District, 1988-Present
Valley Middle School, Salt Lake City, UT
Teacher - Self-contained, Severe Emotional Disabilities Classroom

Streaming Meadows Psychiatric Hospital, Summer 1989
Salt Lake City, UT
Ninth Grade Summer School Teacher - Multiple Subjects

Cedar City Independent School District, 1986-1988
Cedar Middle School, Cedar City, UT
Special Education Teacher
Behavior Adjustment Classes for Severely Emotionally Disabled Children
• Participated in Curriculum and Staff Development
• Revised Grade Six Special Education Mathematics Curriculum Guide

Social Vocational Services, 1984-1985
Group Home, Medford, OR
Home Manager
• Supervision, IPP implementation for six autistic children.

Madison Schools, 1982-1984
Madison Grammar School, Madison, WI
Primary Behavior Disorder Teacher, grades 1-3

Milwaukee Public Schools, 1978-1982
Marquette Elementary School, Milwaukee, WI
Continuing Substitute (2nd grade)

■ Impressive credentials are accentuated under a separate heading.

■ Work history is stated in reverse chronological order, with most recent employment listed first.

TEACHER (Preschool)

CHRIS SMITH
178 Green Street
Summerfield, OK 74966
(918) 555-5555

OBJECTIVE   To join the teaching or management staff of a quality preschool.

EXPERIENCE   MISS NICOLE'S DAYCARE, Summerfield, OK   1990-Present
Head Teacher - Toddlers, ages 3 and 4
- Design a developmentally sound curriculum to enhance the social, physical, intellectual well-being of the children in this day care program.
- Plan and implement activities to achieve curriculum goals in a comfortable and secure atmosphere.
- With assistance from Child Care Coordinator, design and arrange space allowing for a variety of activities to promote children's independence in using the classroom.
- Supervise Teacher, Assistant Teacher and other support staff; conduct weekly meetings for planning and supervision.
- Maintain safety of classroom environment and inform Child Care Coordinator when repairs are needed.
- Hire and train new staff when necessary; conduct on-site orientation for new staff while program is on-going.
- Plan and coordinate arrangements for field trips; coordinate the meeting or pick-up of children from bus stops and classrooms.
- Prepare menus and documentation for the nutrition program, according to the Bureau of Nutritional guidelines, order food, and plan and serve nutritious snacks daily.

SUMMERFIELD SCHOOL SYSTEM, Summerfield, OK   1989-1990
Substitute Teacher
- While attending college, taught classes in various school systems at elementary and secondary levels. January 1990 - June 1990, worked as a permanent substitute with the Summerfield School System.
- Prepared teaching outline for course of study, lectured, demonstrated and used teaching aids to present subject matter to class, and prepared, administered and corrected exams.

EDUCATION
University of Massachusetts, Boston, MA
Bachelor of Science in Elementary Education/Sociology, 1988

CERTIFICATION
Elementary Education Grades K - 6

References available upon request

■ Including professional licensure and accreditations can be essential for certain fields of work.

■ Specific achievements and dynamic action verbs give resume impact.

TEACHER (Kindergarten)

CHRIS SMITH
178 Green Street
Winesburg, OH 44690
(614) 555-5555

OBJECTIVE

To contribute developed skills to a challenging teaching position.

SUMMARY OF QUALIFICATIONS
- More than 9 years teaching experience - ages 3 months to 6 years. Relate well with children.
- Able to present materials interestingly, making the introduction to learning fun. Utilize music.
- Practical knowledge of Spanish.
- Proven interpersonal skills, having worked with and supervised a diversity of professionals, clients and staff.
- O.F.C. and Infant Toddler qualified.

EDUCATION

KENT STATE UNIVERSITY, Kent, OH
B.S., Education, 1980
Major: Early Childhood Education

State-certified to teach Kindergarten through grade 8.

PROFESSIONAL EXPERIENCE

1/81-Present O'DONNELL CENTER PRESCHOOL, Winesboro, OH
Head Teacher, Kindergarten, 1983-Present
Supervised teachers, Youth Corp. Workers and Student Volunteers. Planned and conducted daily curriculum. Cooperated in over-all planning of preschool program. Observed/recorded behavior and progress of children; planned individual education follow-up to prepare students for first grade.

Perceptual Motor Instructor, Infant/toddler to Age 5, 1981-1983
Planned/implemented special training periods, recorded progress, evaluated needs, submitted weekly reports. Cooperated with Special Education Coordinator on program goals and scheduling needs of individual children. Motivated staff in this specialized area.

Assistant Teacher, ages 3-5, 1/81-6/81

9/80-12/80 RETTMAN SCHOOL, Cincinnati, OH
Student Teacher, Pre-Kindergarten & Grade 3

RELATED ACTIVITIES

9/81-3/82 DUVAL CENTER, Dayton, OH
Preschool Teacher, Family Religious Education Program
Interpreted Spanish Language. Tutored English as a Second Language.

- Personal interests and activities are relevant to candidate's field of interest.

- Foreign language skills further strengthen candidate's qualifications.

TEACHER (Elementary School)

CHRIS SMITH
178 Green Street
Charleston, SC 29424
(803) 555-5555

EMPLOYMENT

1978 to present — IMMACULATE CONCEPTION SCHOOL, Charleston, SC
Fifth Grade Teacher, 1983 to present
- Assisted in setting up the new curriculum; selected materials, designed learning area and advised on physical set-up of classroom.
- Develop and implement curricula, lesson plans, special projects and exercises to increase dexterity, alertness and coordination.
- Committee Chairperson for School Accreditation Ceremony.
- Member, Handbook Committee; compile, write and analyze school policies and regulations.
- Director of School Bowling League (1984 to present); recruit chaperones, set and collect dues, organize outings and coordinate total program for 125 to 190 4th through 8th graders. (Previously acted as League Treasurer and Chaperone, 1978 to 1984).
- Organize and coordinate annual Sports Banquet.

Fourth Grade Teacher, 1978 to 1983
- Developed curricula and lesson plans and instructed in Reading, Mathematics, Science, Spelling, Language, Art and Religion.
- Participated in and conducted parent-teacher conferences, advising parents on child's progress and how best to reinforce education.

1974 to present — RANE'S DRUG STORE, Charleston, SC
Sales Clerk/Cashier, full-time summers and part-time through the year
- Responsible for cashing out and verification of receipts.
- Prepare sales reports and break downs per department by analyzing and tabulating merchandise-coded receipts.
- Train and supervise part-time employees and new hires.
- Conduct vendor inventories on a regular basis to facilitate timely and efficient ordering and purchasing.
- Set up displays and implement in-store promotions.
- Assist in opening and closing operations.

EDUCATION

CLEMSON UNIVERSITY, Clemson, SC
Bachelor of Science Degree in Education, Early Childhood Education, 1978.
- Minored in Mathematics/Educational Mathematics.
- South Carolina Teaching Certificate.

REFERENCES — Furnished upon request.

- Job descriptions highlight candidate's individual accomplishments, organizational skills, and willingness to take on added responsibilities.

- Although the summer/part-time job listed is not directly related to candidate's field of interest, it serves to accentuate candidate's hardworking nature.

TEACHER (Elementary School)

CHRIS SMITH
178 Green Street
Harrisonburg, VA 22807
(703) 555-5555

OBJECTIVE

Seeking a career continuation as an **Elementary Education Teacher** where education, experience, and developed skills will be of value.

EDUCATION

GEORGE MASON UNIVERSITY, Fairfax, VA
Bachelor of Arts, <u>cum laude</u>, in Elementary Education, 1984
- Dean's List (2 semesters)
- Academic Scholarship
- Education Society, member 1980-1984

EXPERIENCE

1984 to present   JAMES MADISON ELEMENTARY SCHOOL, Harrisonburg, VA
Faculty Member
- Experience in teaching kindergarten and 1st grade in the areas of reading, math, social studies, arts, and music.
- Aid in the selection of textbooks and learning aids.
- Plan and supervise class field trips. Arrange for class speakers and demonstrations.

1982 to 1984   FAIRFAX YMCA, YOUTH DIVISION, Fairfax, VA
Program Assistant/Special Event Coordinator
- Oversaw summer program for low-income youth.
- Budgeted and planned special events and field trips, working with Program Director to coordinate and plan variations in the program.
- Served as Youth Advocate in cooperation with Social Worker to address the social needs and problems of participants.

Fall 1983   GEORGIA MASON ELEMENTARY SCHOOL, Fairfax, VA
Student Teacher
- Taught third grade in all elementary subjects.
- Designed and implemented a two-week unit on Native Americans.

Spring 1983   FAIRFAX KINDERGARTEN, Fairfax, VA
Student Teacher
- Generated a unit on Ezra Jack Keats' storybooks.

Fall 1982   ALLEN SCHOOL, Fairfax, VA
Student Teacher
- Concentrated on instructing lower level reading and math groups, and conducted whole class math lessons.

- Educational awards, like Dean's List standing and academic scholarships, add strength to resume.

- Stating that "references are available upon request" is not essential; most employers will assume that references are available.

TEACHER (Middle School)

CHRIS SMITH
178 Green Street
Jersey City, NJ 07302
(201) 555-5555

OBJECTIVE

To contribute acquired teaching skills at the Junior High or Secondary level.

SUMMARY OF QUALIFICATIONS

- More than thirteen years of teaching experience, particular expertise in Business Education, History, French, and E.S.L.
- Fluent in French and Jamaican.
- Developed interpersonal skills, having dealt with a diversity of professionals, students, and staff members.
- Self-motivated; able to set effective priorities to achieve immediate and long-term goals and meet operation deadlines.
- Adapt easily to new concepts and responsibilities.

EDUCATION

GLASSBORO STATE COLLEGE, Glassboro, NJ
Master of Education, Foundations of Education, 1984
Bachelor of Science, Foundations of Education - Business Education, 1982

RIDGEWOOD COMMUNITY COLLEGE, Ridgewood, NJ
Associate Degree of Arts, Human Services - Office Education, 1980

EXPERIENCE

JERSEY CITY PUBLIC SCHOOLS, Jersey City, New Jersey   1986-Present
Grade 7 Teacher
Prepare instruction materials, supervise classrooms, teach/evaluate students. Confer with parents and teaching staff. Advise students regarding academic and vocational interests.

SCHOOL FOR GIRLS, Jamaica   1984-86
Middle School Teacher
Taught English language to class of 30-40 girls, prepared progress reports.

MAYOR'S OFFICE COORDINATING COUNCIL, Trenton, NJ   1982-84
Intake Counselor
Interviewed training program applicants; determined appropriate candidates for admission.

PROFESSIONAL AFFILIATIONS

Member, Association for Supervision and Curriculum Development.

■ Job objective is clearly defined.

■ Job-related affiliations demonstrate candidate's active participation in his/her field.

TEACHER (High School)

CHRIS SMITH
178 Green Street
Tacoma, WA 98416
(206) 555-5555

PROFESSIONAL OBJECTIVE
Seeking new challenges in the instruction of Mathematics and related courses at high school level.

EDUCATION UNIVERSITY OF WASHINGTON, Seattle, WA; Masters Degree in Secondary Education, 1982.

EVERGREEN STATE COLLEGE, Olympia, WA; Bachelor of Arts Degree in Mathematics, 1979. Graduated Cum Laude.

Teaching Certification, Washington.

PROFESSIONAL EXPERIENCE

1979 to   TACOMA HIGH SCHOOL, Tacoma, WA
present   Chairperson, Mathematics Department, 1984 to present
- In addition to responsibilities as Math Instructor, direct the Math Evaluation Committee for accreditation by the National Association of Schools and Colleges.
- Develop evaluative report for submission to accreditation board; report details and assesses present and future goals, programs, plans and professional performance/development.
- Select and approve all departmental texts; write course descriptions and upgrade as indicated.
- Approve all purchases, justify expenditures and develop/monitor budget.
- Provide input to the hiring/renewal process; evaluate staff teachers.

Mathematics Instructor, 1979 to present
- Instruct the 9-12th grade levels in Trigonometry, Algebra I & II, Geometry, Pre-Calculus and Business Math.
- Teach Honors Algebra I, Geometry and Pre-Calculus; initiate, develop and conduct special Remedial Math Program and after-school tutorial sessions for problems math students.
- Conduct summer school sessions in Remedial Math and SAT preparation (8 weeks each).
- Develop curricula and lesson plans, select texts and design tests.
- Serve as Junior Varsity Baseball and Basketball Coach and Varsity Assistant Coach for Baseball and Basketball teams; Athletic Trainer for sports teams (Football, Baseball and Basketball).

■ Impressive educational background strengthens resume.

■ Professional experience is divided to highlight candidate's impressive promotion to department chairperson.

TEACHER (High School)

CHRIS SMITH
178 Green Street
Baltimore, MD 21218
(301) 555-5555

PROFESSIONAL EXPERIENCE

1970-Present ST. JUDE HIGH SCHOOL, Baltimore, MD
Teacher - Dean of Discipline

Teach primarily Social Studies to students in grades 9-12. Responsible for organizing activities for 9th grade cluster; field trips to museums and to Africa for African-American studies. Serve on numerous committees and boards for multi-cultural activities. Increased Parent Involvement Committee from 10 to 80 parents. Act as Career Cooperating Teacher for student teachers from Harvard School of Education, orienting and training in teaching practicum.

Summers, HIGH SCHOOL STEP PROGRAM AT JOHNS HOPKINS, Baltimore, MD
1972-Present **Counselor**

Supervised 75 high school students. Responsible for helping to bridge gaps, orientation, acclamation and placement of inner city students to the possibility of a college education, in-college and post-college experiences.

1980-1987 MORTIMER PUBLIC HIGH SCHOOL, Baltimore, MD
Teacher-Adult Education

Taught Geography and World History to adults pursing their G.E.D.s.

EDUCATION

LOYOLA COLLEGE, Baltimore, MD
Master of Arts Degree in History
Other relevant courses and training included: Secondary School Principal, Legal Aspects of Education Administration, and Testing and Evaluation.

WAYNE STATE COLLEGE, Detroit, MI
B.A. in French; minor in Chemistry

CERTIFICATION

Maryland Teaching Certificate

■ Candidate's most relevant work experience is prioritized throughout resume.

■ International travel and foreign language skills demonstrate candidate's global and cultural experience.

TEACHER AIDE

CHRIS SMITH
178 Green Street
Kerryville, TX 78028
(512) 555-5555

PROFESSIONAL OBJECTIVE

To obtain a challenging and responsible position in Education or Social Services, providing hands-on experience with adolescents.

EDUCATION

UNIVERSITY OF MASSACHUSETTS, Amherst, MA
Bachelor of Arts, History to be awarded 1996
Academic Scholarship, Honor Society

WORK EXPERIENCE

1994 to RIP VAN WINKLE DAY CARE, Kerryville, TX
Present **Teacher Aide**
Planned curricula for after-school programs, kindergarten through third grade. Organize field trips and also manage a day camp. Responsible for supervising activities and office management.

Summer GRAVEL ROAD RECREATION CENTER, Kerryville, TX
1994 **Assistant Recreation Leader**
Responsible for planning and leading group recreational activities for 20 to 35 children, ages 7 to 14 at neighborhood youth center.

Summer STRAWBERRY HILL DAY CAMP, Prairie View, TX
1993 **Group Leader**
Supervised teenage boys in recreational activities.

Summer PEBBLE BEACH DAY CAMP, Prairie View, TX
1992 **Physical Education Instructor**
Taught dance and self-defense classes for teenagers.

REFERENCES

Available upon request.

■ Education is listed at top of resume while limited work experience is briefly listed.

■ Job objective gives resume focus without limiting candidate's opportunities.

TUTOR

CHRIS SMITH
178 Green Street
Bel Air, MD 21015
(301) 555-5555

EDUCATION

Loyola College, Baltimore, MD   12/93
Bachelor of Arts Degree in English: Professional Writing
Honors: Cum Laude (3.21), Dean's List six of eight semesters

EXPERIENCE

Goden Academy, Baltimore, MD   1/94 to Present
Tutor
Teach English to a senior Japanese student concentrating on special grammar and
compositional needs 6 hours a week.

Ridge Heights Elementary, Baltimore, MD   11/93 to Present
Teaching Assistant
Instruct group of 5 second and third grade students in writing and creative expression.

WPIT, Boston, MA   9/93-7/94
News Journalist Intern
Spent a week in the news room, field reporting, and attending music and promotion
meetings at Boston's #1 radio station. Communicated with traffic center and sourced
news stories.

Loyola College, Baltimore, MD   Summer 1993
Writing Skills Tutor
Assisted the students with their writing and managed the writing skills center during
daily hours.

Camp Lalcota: Bethesda, MD   Summer 1992
Special Needs Counselor
Planned/Supervised daily events. During summer camp aided in the care and feeding
of children from age 6-15.

Loyola College, Baltimore, MD   9/91-5/92
Peer Counselor
Assisted students in social and personal development regarding their adjustment to
college life. Led group and individual counseling sessions.

COMPUTERS

Lotus 1-2-3, Microsoft Word, IBM Compatible

- Educational honors indicates candidate's potential for superior job performance.

- Relevant summer and part-time positions add weight to resume.

VOCATIONAL COUNSELOR

CHRIS SMITH
178 Green Street
Las Vegas, NV 89134
(702) 555-5555

EXPERIENCE

VOCATION HOUSE, Las Vegas, NV (1991-Present)
Interviewer/Vocational Counselor
- Provided on-going vocational counseling to eligible clients and acted as liaison with program administrators.
- Clients represented ex-offenders and unemployed.
- Administered and interpreted basic academic tests to potential employees and reviewed work samples.
- Responsible for documentaries, reports, and records on progress of programs.

LAS VEGAS HALFWAY HOUSES, INC., Las Vegas, NV (1991-1993)
Vocational Counselor
- Primarily responsible for vocational counseling to participants from the offender and ox-offender program
- Administered tests and referred applicants to various training programs.

CITY OF LAS VEGAS, Las Vegas, NV (1989-1991)
Contract Administrator
- Monitored assigned programs by conducting quarterly on-site visitations and reviews.
- Monitored and reviewed monthly invoices and executed quarter and final analysis of performance standards.
- Reviewed budget requirements and advised on budget revision requests.
- Participated in annual program planning and proposal review process.

BEAUCHAMP HOUSE OF CORRECTION, Las Vegas, NV (1989)
Job Counselor
- Provided counseling and testing to work-trainee releases for C.E.T.A. work assignments.

POTTER HALFWAY HOUSES, INC., Las Vegas, NV (1987-1988)
Facility House Manager
- Coordinated daily upkeep of the facility by assigning weekly house details on maintenance and repair.
- Supervised and assigned office spaces and monthly collection of rents.
- Maintained inventory control of supplies, equipment, key control, first aid and hygiene kits.
- Responsible for front desk coverage, sign-in and sign-out logs by occupants, and verified incoming calls.

EDUCATION

University of Nevada, Las Vegas
B.A., Psychology, 1987

■ Resume indicates candidate's extensive background in counseling services.

■ Job descriptions are brief and punchy, without being choppy.

11
Engineering

Nature of Work
Engineers apply the theories and principles of science and mathematics to the economical solution of practical technical problems. Often their work is a link between a scientific discovery and its application. Engineers design machinery, products, systems, and processes for efficient and economical performance. They design industrial machinery and equipment for manufacturing goods, and defense and weapons systems for the armed forces.

Engineers plan and supervise the construction of buildings, highways, and rapid transit systems. They also design and develop consumer products and systems for control and automation of manufacturing, business, and management processes.

Employment
In 1990, engineers held over 1.5 million jobs. Over half of these were in manufacturing industries, mostly in electrical and electronic equipment, aircraft parts, machinery, scientific instruments, chemicals, motor vehicles, fabricated metal products, and primary metal industries. Engineers also worked in the communications, utilities, and construction industries.

Training
A bachelor's degree in engineering from an accredited engineering program is usually required for beginning engineering jobs. Most degrees are granted in branches such as electrical, mechanical or civil engineering.

Graduate training is essential for faculty positions but is not required for the majority of entry-level engineering jobs. Many engineers obtain a master's degree to learn new technology, to broaden their education, and to enhance promotion opportunities.

Job Outlook
Employment opportunities in engineering are expected to continue to be good through the year 2005. This is due to the fact that the number of degrees granted in engineering is not likely to increase much beyond present levels, and the need for engineers will be greater as companies increase investments in plant and equipment to further increase productivity. Furthermore, more engineers will be needed to improve deteriorating roads, bridges, water and pollution control systems, and other public facilities.

Earnings

Starting salaries for engineering graduates with a bachelor's degree averaged $31,900 a year in private industry in 1990; those with a master's degree and no experience earned $36,200; and those with a doctorate degree earned $50,400.

AEROSPACE ENGINEER

CHRIS SMITH
178 Green Street
Pittsburgh, PA 15201
(412) 555-5555

**CAREER
OBJECTIVE** Research, design and development of mechanical and control systems.

EDUCATION
1993-1994 UNIVERSITY OF PENNSYLVANIA, Philadelphia, PA
M.S. in Mechanical Engineering, May 1994
Areas studied: Advanced System Dynamics and Control, Dynamics, Advance Calculus
and Decision Analysis.

Research Assistantship under Dr. James Kirk in the Aeronautics Department working on
design and oxperimentation of a new space vehicle.

Received Air and Space Fellowship for academic year 1993-94.

1989-1993 UNIVERSITY OF PENNSYLVANIA, Philadelphia, PA
B.S. in Mechanical Engineering, May 1991. Areas studied include Thermodynamics,
Mechanical Behavior of Materials, System Dynamics and Control, Fluid Mechanics,
Design, Aerodynamics, Engineering Management, Technical Writing, and Computer
Programming. GPA 3.8/4.0.

Bachelor's Thesis: "Investigation of the Challenger Explosion: What Went Wrong?"

WORK EXPERIENCE
Summer   ROCKETEER AEROSPACE CORPORATION, Pittsburgh, PA
1993 Worked with flight test engineers on the Board of Safety Standards. Prepared
governmental report based on statistical analysis of several possible control systems.

Summer   FLY AWAY AEROSPACE CORPORATION, Pittsburgh, PA
1992 Worked on development of new engine mathematical model. Implemented new F-15
Simulator program.

January-May UNIVERSITY OF PENNSYLVANIA: DEPARTMENT OF MECHANICAL ENGINEERING,
1992 Philadelphia, PA
Assisted visiting professor with research involving system analysis of a thermodynamic
and hydraulic system.

Summer   ROCKETEER AEROSPACE CORPORATION, Pittsburgh, PA
1991 Worked on the assembly of the cockpit section of the B-14 and C-34 aircraft.

■ Education is focus point of resume since candidate is a recent
grad school grad.

■ Only relevant work experience is
included.

CERAMIC ENGINEER

CHRIS SMITH
178 Green Street
Dill, MT 59725
(406) 555-5555

OBJECTIVE: An engineering position in ceramic product and process development.

EDUCATION: **COLLEGE OF CERAMICS AT EASTERN MONTANA COLLEGE,** Billings, MT
Bachelor of Science in Ceramic Engineering, Cum Laude (January 1992)
G.P.A. - 3.6

EXPERIENCE:
1992-Present **THE DILLINGER MINT,** Bozeman, MT
Ceramic Engineer - Product Design and Development
- Troubleshoot entire porcelain process from design concept through forming, firing and decorating.
- Perform kiln programming, scheduling and maintenance.
- Develop and formulate porcelain slips, glazes and colors.
- Direct group members concerning technical matters.
- Evaluate and develop new materials and processes.
- Provide technical support for overseas vendors and maintain vendor contacts.

Summer 1991 **KTP,** Butte, MT
Summer Intern
- Designed circuits and assembled product assurance test equipment for testing of multilayer ceramic modules.

1989-1990 **RAINBOW WORKSHOP**, Great Falls, MT
Research Assistant - Co-Op Program
- Evaluated processes including slip casting, iso-press, dry press and extrusion using glass powders for prototype development of glass and glass ceramic parts.
- Participated in development of a cost effective process to produce ceramic powders utilizing spray drying and other granulation techniques.

Summer Intern (Summer 1989)
- Assisted in developing glass and glass ceramic prototypes through glass powder techniques.

REFERENCES:
Available upon request.

■ Internship experience is valuable for candidates with little job experience, particularly if it corresponds to the position sought.

■ Dynamic action verbs give resume impact.

CHEMICAL ENGINEER

CHRIS SMITH
178 Green Street
Rochester, NY 14623
(716) 555-5555

WORK EXPERIENCE:
SANFORD CORPORATION, Rochester, NY   1983-Present
Chemical Process Modeling Engineer

Carbon Dioxide Process Simulator
- Applied knowledge of thermodynamics; reactor design; phase separation; fluid compression and expansion; process control to complete simulation from preliminary coding.
- Wrote operations manual.

Computer Models for Hydraulic Devices
- Researched, designed, coded, tested detailed models for submersible centrifugal and hydraulic pumps.

Drilling Control Simulators
- Revised and developed computer models for oil well simulation.
- Utilized knowledge of fluid mechanics, mathematics and computer programming.
- Wrote operations manuals.

SKILLS:
- Computer languages: FORTRAN 77; Hardware: IBM-PC, Intel systems.
- Extensive research experience: quantitative and qualitative analysis of dynamic systems, inorganic chemistry.

EDUCATION:
Bachelor of Science in Chemical Engineering, May 1982
Rochester Institute of Technology, Rochester, NY
Honors: Magna cum laude graduate, member of the Engineering Honor Society of America.

MEMBERSHIP:
American Society of Chemical Engineers
Student Chapter Vice-President, 1992-present

PERSONAL:
Willing to relocate.

■ Resume indicates a series of promotions.

■ Job-related affiliations demonstrate candidate's active participation in his/her field.

CIVIL ENGINEER

CHRIS SMITH
178 Green Street
Bryn Mawr, PA 19010
(215) 555-5555

EMPLOYMENT HIGHLIGHTS

1987-Present Kershaw and Kane Inc., Bryn Mawr, PA
Specialist in the Structural Division
Prepare technical guidelines and master specifications, review project specifications, maintain technical files and bidder lists, provide technical expertise in areas relating to fire resistance, combustibility of building materials and systems in general. Act as a liaison between design and manufacturing in introductions of notebook and desktop products. Create initial process methods, documentation, line balancing, tooling, and fixturing for new and existing products.

1984-87 Bradford A. Sullivan Corp., Meadville, PA
Assistant Manager of the Construction Section
Served as backup to and acted in the absence of the manager. Prepared technical guides for property conservation in the areas of wind, fire, gravity loads, and earthquakes. Performed loss investigations and special inspections in areas of interest. As a staff lecturer, conducted training classes and seminars. Reviewed plans and specifications for loss potential.

1981-84 Dixon & Petrie Division, Pittsburgh, PA
Structural Designer.
Provided structural design and engineering estimates, and specifications for industrial, laboratory, commercial, and power facilities.

1977-81 Building Blocks, Inc., Boston, MA
Structural Designer.
Provided structural design and engineering estimates for highway bridges and waterworks.

1974-77 Stephen G. Fox, Inc., Artemis, PA
Engineer
Participated in bid and cost-plus work, structural design, engineering field supervision, engineering estimates, construction (bid) estimates, and construction coordination on industrial and commercial projects.

LICENSURE Professional Engineer - Pennsylvania

EDUCATION New York University, New York, NY
Bachelor of Science, Civil Engineering, 1973

■ Resume illustrates continual career progression.

■ Including professional licensure and accreditations can be essential for certain fields of work.

ELECTRICAL ENGINEER (Managerial)

CHRIS SMITH
178 Green Street
New London, NH 03257
(603) 555-5555

PROFESSIONAL OBJECTIVE
A leadership position supporting product development or engineering utilizing knowledge of electrical, electronic and mechanical design.

BACKGROUND SUMMARY
Progressive engineering management experience from project manager, group leader, section manager, to engineering manager over four sections and 40 people. Responsible for consumer product development from inception to discontinuance covering mechanical, electromechanical and electrical design.

PROFESSIONAL EXPERIENCE
The C. Marlowe Company, New London, NH
Engineering Manager 1986-Present
- Created International Technical Engineering responsible for technical coordination and support to multiple, global manufacturing sites.
- Created Alpha Test Engineering responsible for creating preproduction engineering prototypes for global marketing use. Planned, hired and trained the staff, provided for procurement, logistics, facilities, and capital equipment.
- Managed $0.6M in expense budget + $2-9M in preproduction engineering prototypes per year.
- Provided definition input to all proposed products as well as resource allocation, scheduling planning, control, problem reporting and solving support.
- Developed major portions of the Quality documentation system for Engineering to comply with ISO 8500.
- Participated in Engineering Documentation Control conversion from manufacturing to stock, from assemble to order. The first product under this system had 700,000 planned configurations.

The Kipling Company, Wolfeboro, NH
Product Design Engineer 1981-86
- Oversaw design engineering for over 200 consumer and PC products, both in assembled form and in kit form.
- Prepared and monitored expense and capital budgets.
- Prepared cost and feasibility studies, analysis of design and product financing.
- Monitored product safety and regulatory compliance and product cost and development schedule.
- Responsible for adding $9M of new product revenue out of $90M total business.

EDUCATION
- New Jersey Institute of Technology, Newark, NJ
  Bachelor of Science, Electrical Engineering, 1980

■ Statistics and dollar figures quantify candidate's accomplishments.

■ Strong action verbs bring resume to life.

ELECTRICAL ENGINEER (Product Development)

CHRIS SMITH
178 Green Street
Dallas, TX 75277
(214) 555-5555

SUMMARY

Degreed Electrical Engineer experienced in leading product development programs for commercial, OEM, and government markets. Capable of administering research and development programs, managing vendor and partner technology relationships, and satisfying customer needs expectations through resourceful problem solving and accurate communications.

PROFESSIONAL EXPERIENCE

Borgman Systems, Dallas, TX 1988-Present
Section Manager, OEM Systems Engineering
- Managed development of customized versions of personal computer products to meet requirements of OEM customers, Japanese government and U.S. Federal government agencies. Supplied all of Spain's personal computer products, with customized security and networking functionality
- Provided OEM customers with problem-solving support and systems integration engineering
- Managed the development of a laptop PC in support of the U.S. Navy Lightweight Computer Unit contract
- Managed the development of customized personal computers for several other Government bids

Section Manager, Design Evaluation
- Managed development support engineering group chartered with personal computer competitive analysis and design verification testing
- Developed competitive analysis processes resulting in more compact computer designs
- Initiated test processes including electrostatic discharge, conducted susceptibility and emissions, and related problem solving to meet regulatory requirements
- Developed test plans and processes to verify the functionality of the computer products

Belle Data Systems, Stephenville, TX 1984-88
Senior Principal Design Engineer
- Developed bus architecture enhancements to a Goldstone 10000 based in-store processor to meet customer performance requirements
- Developed a Goldstone 15000 based cluster terminal controller, emulating an IBM 3650, in a project leader capacity. Developed an PCL 2/6 Channel interface in partnership with Expectations, Inc.

(continued)

■ Summary grabs the reader's attention with powerful skills and qualifications.

■ Specific contributions display candidate's achievements and problem-solving abilities.

PROFESSIONAL EXPERIENCE (continued)

Mitasha Corporation, Galvaston, TX 1981-84
Product Engineer, Microcontroller Operations
- Designed wafer-sort production test hardware for the 6235 microcontrollers, incorporated as a plug-in card to a test system
- Developed test process improvements, resulting in a 85 percent gross margin and fewer customer returns
- Coordinated product engineering activities with the Cairo, Egypt facility

Au Courant Corporation, Houston, TX 1978-81
Electrical Designer
- Developed an Interdesign Monochip analog IC to convert an analog bar code reader signal into a digital representation
- Provided design support to the development of data communications boards

EDUCATION
B.S. in Electrical Engineering, Massachusetts Institute of Technology, Cambridge, MA

Seminars:
Crosby Quality System
Deming Statistical Process Control
Data Communications

OTHER ACTIVITIES
Licensed private pilot, instrument rated
Serve as a director of the local flying club

ELECTRONICS ENGINEER (Experienced)

CHRIS SMITH
178 Green Street
Los Angeles, CA 90007
(213) 555-5555

BACKGROUND SUMMARY
Over eleven years of extensive computer/electronics experience. Versed in both digital and analog electronics with specific emphasis on computer hardware/software. Special expertise in system and component evaluation. Network supervisor responsible for installing/maintaining Arcnet LAN system. Proficient in assembly and C programming languages. Excellent communication skills including written, verbal and interpersonal.

PROFESSIONAL WORK EXPERIENCE
Stevenson Data Systems, Los Angeles, CA 1981-1993
Components Evaluation Engineer 1992-1993
Responsible for the characterization and evaluation of, and approved vendors list for: Power supplies, oscillators, crystals, and programmable logic used in desktop and laptop computers. Evaluated and recommended quality components that increased product profitability. Created and developed power supply test plan used for evaluating third party power supplies. Interacted with vendors to resolve problems associated with components qualification. Technical advisor for Purchasing. Promoted to Engineer II.

Design Evaluation Engineer 1990-1992
Evaluated new computer product designs, solving environmental problems on prototype computers. Conducted systems analysis on new computer products to ensure hardware, software and mechanical design integrity. Designed hardware and software for PC, ISA bus programmable load board used for environmental testing. Performed reliability life testing on computer systems. Installed/maintained 20 user, Novell, Arcnet LAN system. Examined system and sub-system susceptibility to electrostatic discharge in order to meet IEC-801-2 industry standards. Analyzed complete power and load of computer system and subsystem to verify power and load estimations.

Assistant Engineer 1981-1990
Performed extensive hardware evaluation on prototype computers, tested prototype units for timing violations using the latest state-of-the-art test equipment, digital oscilloscopes and logic analyzers. Performed environmental, ESD and acoustic testing. Designed and built a product saver used to protect units under test during environmental testing. Designed and built a power-up test used to test prototype computers during cold boot.

EDUCATION
Bachelor of Science in Electrical Engineering University of Southern California 1990
Associate in Engineering Electronics University of Southern California 1981

- Job descriptions emphasize candidate's accomplishments.

- Work history is stated in reverse chronological order, with most recent employment listed first.

ELECTRONICS ENGINEER (Recent Grad)

CHRIS SMITH
178 Green Street
Houston, Texas 77004
(713) 555-5555

PROFESSIONAL OBJECTIVE
A responsible career opportunity in **Electronic Engineering**.

EDUCATIONAL BACKGROUND
UNIVERSITY OF HOUSTON/UNIVERSITY PARK, Houston, Texas
Bachelor of Science Degree in Electronic Engineering, 1993
Associate Degree in Science, 1990
Associate Degree in Electronic Engineering Technology, 1989

WORK EXPERIENCE
1994 to **MLC CORPORATION,** Houston, Texas
Present *Project Engineer* 6/94-Present
Assist engineers in Research and Development laboratory with design, development and modifications to new instruments.
- Train technicians in use of instrument.
- Test instrument features, circuitry.
- Serve as liaison between Manufacturing and R & D departments.

Engineering Trainee 2/94 to 6/94
- Trainee in the testing of instrument precision and quality involving laser alignment, electronic and other adjustments.

Summer **TEXAS ELECTRIC,** Fort Worth, Texas
1993 *Engineering Intern*
- Constructed test units for automobiles in Electronics Laboratory.
- Fabricated interior of unit from engineering plans.
- Designed and constructed control panel.

Summer **LONE STAR INSTRUMENTS,** Fort Worth, Texas
1992 *Engineering Intern*
- Assisted engineers working on Load Monitors which gauge weight and distribution properties on heavy machine presses.
- Assembled equipment and tested product quality.

REFERENCES
Available upon request.

■ Specific dates of employment (month and year) are ideal for candidates with no gaps in work history.

■ Valuable internship experience enhances candidate's credentials.

ENGINEERING CONSULTANT

CHRIS SMITH
178 Green Street
New York, New York 10027
(212) 555-5555

PROFESSIONAL EXPERIENCE

CONSULTING ENGINEER   1992-Present
The Maupin Consulting Group   New York, New York
Provide professional consulting services to large- and medium-sized corporations with accountability for project management including planning and coordinating client conferences, facilities inspections, developing and implementing recommendations focused on improving efficiencies and cost controls in areas encompassing material management, productivity, customer service delivery, maintenance and general operations. Analyze and diagnose clients' operational structure. Assess financial operating parameters and schedule progress. Develop and implement improved internal controls. Recruit and train talented management to drive the company's strategic plan. Evaluate existing design and fabrication methodologies, manufacturing processes, tooling, mechanical assembly, inspection, and statistical process controls. Troubleshoot; identify actual and potential problem areas and implement solutions to ensure maximum effectiveness. Draw on resource networks in related industries, agencies and professional organizations to assist the client in meeting professional needs. Effectively manage time and multiple tasks to consistently meet deadlines. Foster and maintain excellent staff, customer and community relations.

LOGISTIC ENGINEER/MECHANICAL ENGINEER   1988-1991
The Duessa Corp.   Manhattan, NY
Performed broad, multifunctional responsibilities encompassing management of engineering aspects of parts design, development, testing and developing documentation for maintenance of the company's frigates. Directed, monitored and controlled production of engineering documentation, including quality control, efficiency and project cost considerations. Troubleshot logistics or mechanical problems and implemented effective solutions consistent with the all over Maintenance Plan recommendations. Provided on-going technical assistance and advice, engineering leadership and business support.

INDUSTRIAL ENGINEER   1986-1988
Crow, Jones, and Grey, Inc.   Albany, NY
Performed research utilizing large data base containing customer order information. Identified product flow patterns. Incorporated machine utilization, product handling, in-process inventory and customer delivery factors.

PRODUCTIVITY/MANAGEMENT SERVICES ANALYST   1983-1986
City of Buffalo   Buffalo, NY
Analyzed/developed formal reports. Made and implemented recommendations for improvements in cost management and work efficiencies for municipal service delivery. Evaluated vehicle and equipment usage, inventory controls and computer systems needs. Performed numerous related operational/economic studies.

EDUCATION

Master of Industrial Engineering, 1983
Rensselaer Polytechnic Institute, Troy, NY

Bachelor of Mechanical Engineering, 1980
Polytechnic Institute of New York, Brooklyn

- Small typeface and narrow margins are used to keep resume to one page.

- Education is listed towards bottom of resume because candidate's practical experience outweighs his/her degree.

ENVIRONMENTAL ENGINEER

CHRIS SMITH
178 Green Street
Lewisburg, PA 17837
(717) 555-5555

EDUCATIONAL BACKGROUND:

9/93   BUCKNELL UNIVERSITY
Lewisburg, PA
M.S. in Environmental Engineering
Activities: Implemented campus-wide recycling program; established campus chapter of Save the Planet.

5/89   CLARION UNIVERSITY OF PENNSYLVANIA
Clarion, PA
B.A. in Biology

EXPERIENCE:

8/93-   ENVIRONMENTAL CONSULTANTS
Present   Pittsburgh, PA
Environmental Engineer
- Advise corporate clients of environmentally sound practices.
- Monitor environmental regulations, lobbyist group actions, and court rulings.
- Troubleshoot actual and potential environmental problems via standard and safety control tests.
- Awarded "Most Environmentally Aware Employee of the Year," 1994.

9/89-5/92   THE LEWISBURG ZOO
Lewisburg, PA
Assistant to the Fundraising Director
- Compiled and maintained contact lists.
- Assisted at fund-raisers.
- Managed and edited "What's New at the Zoo?" newsletter.

5/89-9/89   DEPARTMENT OF NATURAL RESOURCES
Washington, DC
Intern
- Conducted hydrologic and hydraulic surveys for dams.
- Performed dam inspections, stream gauging, surveys, and flood insurance study reviews.
- Compiled flood plain delineation data from field surveys and topographic maps.

REFERENCES: Available upon request.

■ Chronological format illustrates a clear career path.

■ Resume emphasizes contributions, achievements, and problems candidate has solved throughout his/her career.

FACILITIES ENGINEER

CHRIS SMITH
178 Green Street
Broomfield, CO 80021
(303) 555-5555

OBJECTIVE: A challenging position in facilities engineering, project engineering, or engineering management.

EXPERIENCE: Facilities Engineer - Breckenridge Company, Broomfield, CO
(1986-Present)
Supervise all phases of maintenance and engineering for this specialty steel company which employs 800, and covers a 60-acre facility.

- Direct multi-craft maintenance, utilities, engineering and construction departments.
- Supervise staff of 100 people and ten supervisors in all phases of maintenance and engineering.
- Plan and install maintenance program and directing all improvement and/or new construction projects starting from studies for justification to project start-up.
- Represented the company as general contractor on project and saved approximately $4 million of the original estimates submitted by outside contractors.
- Direct technicians and supervisor on the design, construction and maintenance of equipment and machinery.
- Established standards and policies for testing, inspection and maintenance of equipment in accordance with engineering principals and safety regulations.
- Prepared bid sheets and contracts for construction facilities and position.
- Full responsibilities for a budget of approximately $10 million annually.
- Extensive involvement in labor relations with various trades.

Project Engineer - Gibralta Corporation, Loveland, CO
(1982-1986)
- Planned and implemented modernization program including the installation of bloom, billet, bar, rod and strip mills as well as the required soaking pits and reheating furnaces.
- Directed a multi-craft maintenance force of approximately 250 craftsmen and supervisors.
- Planned and installed a maintenance program which reduced equipment down-time and increased C/P/T savings, substantially.

ASSOCIATIONS: Member of American Iron and Steel Engineers Association

EDUCATION: University of Colorado at Boulder, Boulder, CO
B.S., Mechanical Engineering, 1982

■ Specific achievements and dynamic action verbs give resume impact.

■ Professional memberships show candidate's commitment to his/her field.

FIELD ENGINEER

CHRIS SMITH
178 Green Street
Oaklawn, IL 60453
(708) 555-5555

OBJECTIVE: A position as _Senior Field Engineer_ - Electronics Systems. Willing to travel and/or relocate. Preference: Foreign assignment.

ACHIEVEMENTS AND QUALIFICATIONS:
More than ten years experience with an internationally known field engineering corporation in both the U.S. and abroad.

- Engineering, cost and administrative responsibility for digital systems and support personnel.
- Maintained and operated UNIVAC and special purpose computers.
- Supported various spacecraft launches.
- Initiated and/or implemented various cost reduction programs resulting in over $20,000 savings in reduced labor and material costs.
- Supervised and coordinated all field engineering functions.
- Served as technical advisor and instructor of formal training to engineers and technicians.

EXPERIENCE: Colfax Corporation, Oaklawn, IL
Senior Field Engineer (1985-Present)
Design modifications which will improve operations while reducing costs of systems. Install design changes as required by NASA. Support various spacecraft launches from the eastern and western launch facilities, and perform M&O for Apollo Lunar Seismic Experiment Package (ALSEP) operations. Handle cost reduction program on the station as required by NASA. This requires full responsibility for assuring that Bermuda (MSFN) adheres to its quarterly budget. Serve as Assistant Project Control Centers Supervisor with responsibility for maintenance and operations of fifteen control centers. Supervise the activities of approximately 200 engineers and technicians; review modifications designed by control center engineers. Provide formal classroom training to newly arrived engineers and technicians. Train engineers and technicians in the maintenance and operation of the R&RR system; initiated 24-hour tracking operations.

Broadmoor Corporation, Detroit, MI
Field Engineer (1977-1985)
Supervised maintenance and alignment of test equipment, preventive maintenance, and operations. Installed design modifications in the Digital Data Assembly System, and the Analog-to-Digital Preselector System. Wrote training material; conducted formal training classes on overall system maintenance and operations.

MILITARY SERVICE:
U.S. Army Security Agency
Rank: Sergeant Major (1972-1977)

TRAINING AND EDUCATION:
Lawrence Institute of Technology, Southfield, MI
Bachelor of Science, Electrical Engineering, 1982

Additional course work and training includes:
FORTRAN Programming, Antenna Position Programming, Tracking Data Processor, and Apollo Timing System

■ Resume emphasizes candidate's strong work history.

■ Including a good military record can be advantageous if it relates to candidate's job objective.

INDUSTRIAL ENGINEER

CHRIS SMITH
178 Green Street
Lake Charles, LA 70609
(318) 555-5555

PROFESSIONAL EXPERIENCE

1985- **LEYNER CORPORATION,** Lake Charles, LA
Present Industrial Engineer
- Provide floor support engineering in printed wire assembly (PWA) and subsystem assembly (SSA) areas.
- Purchase capital equipment. Interface with vendors. Justify expenditures.
- Design plant layout, tooling fixtures, and flow charts of material.
- Program automatic equipment.
- Write process sheets and rework procedures.
- Recommend changes to product to allow ease of manufacture.
- Implement design changes. Initiate methods and process improvements.
- Troubleshoot problems. Effect disposition or rejection of material.
- Provide assistance to all other departments.

1984 **PRUDENCE D. McHARRISON LABORATORY,** Ruston, LA
Summer Engineering Assistant
- Conducted variety of tests including Tensile, Compression, and Creep tests on molded parts.
- Responsible for production of plastic test specimens, and mounting, polishing, and microscopic analysis.
- Designed tools and fixtures for Instron machine.

1982/83 **DUCHESS COMPONENTS,** Baton Rouge, LA
Summers Molding Room Attendant, 1983
- Operated and maintained machine producing epoxy preforms.
- Maintained records on inventory, loss of material, and quality control.

Machine Shop Attendant, 1982
- Operated lathes, milling and grinding machines; monitored welding and heat treatments.
- Read blueprints.

EDUCATION

LOYOLA UNIVERSITY AT NEW ORLEANS, College of Engineering, New Orleans, LA
Bachelor of Science Degree in Industrial Technology, 1985
Minor concentration in Computer Science

PROFESSIONAL AFFILIATIONS/CERTIFICATIONS

Member, Society of Manufacturing Engineers, Leyner Management Club
Certified Manufacturing Technologist and Solderer

- Relevant work experience is emphasized while other positions are de-emphasized.

- Chronological format illustrates a clear career path.

MANUFACTURING ENGINEER

CHRIS SMITH
178 Green Street
Seattle, WA 98103
(206) 555-5555

SUMMARY

Manufacturing engineer with extensive experience in a development and new product introduction environment. Areas of expertise include design for Manufacturability (DFM) of high-density surface mount printed circuit/wiring boards (PWB) and managing contract PWB fabrication.

TECHNOLOGY

- Type 1 (SMT both sides), type II (SMT both sides and PTH) and type III (SMT single side and PTH) PWB assemblies.
- High-density, large (22" x 11"), 6 mil lines and spaces, micro via, high-aspect ratio, fine pitch, 0.093" thick, dry film solder mask, impedance controlled PWBs.
- Range of SMT components include PQFPs (fine pitch technology), PLCCs, SOPs, and discrete chips.
- Futurebus+/Metral and HD+/Litton interconnection technologies.

EXPERIENCE

1990-present **Kai Pacific Computer Inc.,** Seattle, WA
Manufacturing Engineer
Review and modify design of assemblies for manufacturability. Specify the fabrication and assembly process and create assembly instructions for PWBs. Manage PWB fabrication and assembly vendors. Design tooling and fixturing required for assembly and repair of new products. Improved PWB design and manufacturability by creating design guidelines. Solved manufacturability problems of PWBs by influencing engineering to make package type, orientation and spacing modifications. Improved in-circuit/ATE testability of PWBs by reducing tooling hole tolerance and increasing test pad diameter. Managed and coordinated prototype PWB fabrication and assembly vendors to bring in eight different surface mount PWB assemblies built to an aggressive schedule. Wrote the specification for and managed the design and build of a test station for boundary scan and functional testing and de-bug of PWB assemblies. Evaluated and prepared Kai Computer's vendors in Japan for volume manufacture of new products, which entailed travel to Japan. Improved PWB assembly quality and turn-around time by influencing the vendor to add new equipment.

1986-90 **Saturn Computer Inc.,** Auburn, WA
Manufacturing Engineer
Purchased tooling and fixturing required for production and repair of existing products. Solved design, production and material availability problems of existing products through initiating engineering change orders (ECOs) and temporary variance authorizations (TVAs). Managed the testing and shipment of a surface mount video upgrade product. Created a surface mount PWB fabrication specification.

EDUCATION

1982-86 **University of Iowa,** Iowa City, Iowa
Bachelor of Science in Mechanical Engineering (BSME)

■ Summary highlights candidate's experience and expertise.

■ Valuable technical knowledge is emphasized at top of resume.

MARINE ENGINEER

CHRIS SMITH
178 Green Street
Newport, RI 02840
(401) 555-5555

SUMMARY

- Marine/Mechanical Engineer: More than 4 years of progressively responsible hands-on and management experience in the maintenance, repair, modification, overhaul and installation of heavy marine equipment and machinery.
- Expertise with electrical, water, fuel, lubrication, hydraulic, power plant, motor control and related systems and major components.
- Experience includes AC/DC light and power systems, generators, controllers, starters and transformers; communications systems, general electronics, consoles and computers.

EXPERIENCE

1st, 2nd, 3rd ASSISTANT ENGINEER   Nordica Inc.
                                                                          Newport, RI

1st Assistant Engineer: (M/V Maine Sunshine): 1993-Present
- Responsibilities aboard this 15,000 h.p. diesel ship with 2 twin V-14 Enterprise engines and 125 p.s.i. Vaporphase waste heat boiler; supervision of up to 8 assistants in the administration of matters affecting physical operation of the ship, from start-up to shut-down of the main propulsion plant.
- Assigned/scheduled/inspected work; set up preventive maintenance programs; handled inventory management/control, stores/parts/consumables ordering; burning of heavy fuel oil required continual troubleshooting/problem-solving in the maintenance of propulsion system. Hands-on management included 80% of all engines.

2nd Assistant Engineer: 1992-1993
- Supervised 4 assistants in the maintenance of boilers and auxiliary equipment; responsible for fueling, storing and purification of fuel, test/maintenance of correct boiler water and/or main jacket water, and maintenance, repair, overhaul or replacement of related systems and components.

3rd Assistant Engineer: 1991-1992
- Supervised 3 assistants, handled small electrical maintenance, start-up/shut-down of fresh water distillery system, transfer and storage of water, and operation, maintenance and repair of the lubrication system, including storing, transfer and purification.

EDUCATION

Bachelor of Science, Rhode Island Maritime Academy, Providence, RI; 1990
- Marine Engineering
- Naval Science Award for Highest Naval GPA by Engineering Student
- Graduated with Honors

- Resume indicates a series of promotions.

- Impressive honors and award enhance candidate's credentials.

MECHANICAL ENGINEER (Costing and Standards)

CHRIS SMITH
178 Green Street
Taylorsville, IN 47280
(812) 555-5555

OBJECTIVE   A position in quality control/assurance or inspection with a manufacturer of quality engineered products.

EDUCATION   Valparaiso University, Valparaiso, IN
Bachelor of Science degree in Mechanical Engineering, 1985

Senior Design Project: Stress analysis and final drawings for hydroelectric waterwheel and for variable speed transmission. Received Hestinger Award for work in heat transfer and thermodynamics

Undergraduate Teaching Assistant. One of three students selected to weekly lectures and grade examinations for junior Thermodynamics (M.E. 345).

EXPERIENCE   **MECHANICAL COSTING AND STANDARDS ENGINEER**
Katsel Corp., Ltd., Terre Haute, IN   **(1990-Present)**
As Costing and Standards Engineer, operated IBM System 34 MAPICS costing and standards application and implementation. Maintained parts list data to first, second, third, other levels of critical product structure file including subassemblies to complete system. Converted new products, newly released by engineering to sales staff, for order entry, and interacted with accounting department on cost roll-up examination and tracking.

As Mechanical/Industrial Engineer, proposed cost reducing changes to manufacturing. Conducted time study of a complicated manufacturing process; drafted floor plans for manufacturing. Planned large scale changes in 15 workstations to increase efficiency. Recommended changes which were incorporated and project was successfully completed.

MECHANICAL DESIGNER
Enginuity, Staunton, IN   **(1985-1989)**
Design support stands for heat control devices. Perform quality control sample testing of synthetic fibers. Monitor effects of extreme temperature on manufacturing equipment.

REFERENCES   Available upon request.

■ Impressive information on senior project strengthens candidate's educational credentials.

■ Job objective gives resume focus without limiting candidate's opportunities.

MECHANICAL ENGINEER (Transportation)

CHRIS SMITH
178 Green Street
Boston, MA 02115
(617) 555-5555

PROFESSIONAL OBJECTIVE
A challenging position in engineering technologies.

PROFESSIONAL BACKGROUND
1988-1994   MASSACHUSETTS TRANSIT AUTHORITY, Boston, Massachusetts
Maintenance Foreman
- Repair and maintenance of generators, electrical motors, and mechanical systems in shop, yard, and aboard rail units for public transport.
- Assess, determine, and repair mechanical defects toward safety maintenance according to statute and standards of rail service.
- Assemble machines from drawing specifications, wire electrical boards, test and trace defects.
- Repair and maintain heavy duty diesel engines.
- Supervise maintenance staff and monitor performances.
- Plan, project, forecast, and monitor expenditures within budgets.
- Record and report machine performance and arrange for routine checks against requirements for safety.
- Adjust and set governor for maximum efficiency and test fuel injectors.
- Troubleshoot sequence schematic designs and installation of new electrical units.
- Repair and maintain compressors, lighting plants, and both oil and coal fired boilers.

1985-88   LARABY SALES, INCORPORATED, Trent, Ireland
Mechanic/Assembler
- Assembled mechanical goods and products of both foreign and domestic manufacturers for retail distribution.
- Verified safety, fittings, and proper tuning according to manufacturer specifications to meet public and consumer demands.
- Specialty items included both domestic and international high-quality bicycles.

EDUCATION BACKGROUND
CORK TECHNICAL COLLEGE
Cork, Ireland
Senior School Certificate, 1982
Diploma, Mechanical Engineering, 1984

SPECIAL TECHNICAL SKILLS
Operator, Boilers   Technician, Boilers and Diesels
Maintenance, Boilers   Maintenance, Diesel and Diesel Machinery

■ Valuable technical skills are high-lighted under a separate heading.

■ Dynamic action verbs give re-sume impact.

NUCLEAR ENGINEER

CHRIS SMITH
178 Green Street
Tuscaloosa, AL 35401
(205) 555-5555

CAREER OBJECTIVE
A challenging quality assurance position in the nuclear power industry.

SKILLS/ACHIEVEMENTS
- Experienced in all aspects of nuclear power plant operation including, chemistry, radiological controls, health and safety issues, quality assurance, training and project management.
- Highly proficient in identifying actual and potential problem areas, and in implementing solutions to ensure maximum safety, operational and cost effectiveness.

PROFESSIONAL EXPERIENCE
RUCKER ISLAND NUCLEAR FACILITY, Tuscaloosa, AL
ENGINEER LABORATORY DIRECTOR   1992-Present
Coordinated all aspects of operations for the Nuclear Power Training Division. Directed and supervised staff of eight additional trainees in daily reactor and systems maintenance activities. Maintained analytical and radiation monitoring equipment; effected adjustments and repairs and necessary; supervised replacement of reactor components. Ensured compliance with strict quality assurance standards.

ENGINEERING LABORATORY TECHNICIAN   1989-1992
Coordinated Laboratory Division operations. Supervised staff in implementation of chemistry procedures and radiological controls including adjustments, and minor repair and major replacement projects. Responded immediately to emergencies; made adjustments, implemented repairs and submitted detailed reports of findings: acted as Quality Assurance Inspector.

OPERATOR   1987-1989
Responsible for smooth operation of nuclear plant facility; duties included monitoring readings; record keeping; troubleshot problems or abnormal test results; made adjustments and repairs as needed. Served schedule watches as Engineering Laboratory Technician and instructed various training exercises; made effective oral presentation of information; answered technical questions; oversaw hands-on drill activities and assisted with grading student performance.

EDUCATION & TRAINING
ASSOCIATE OF SCIENCE DEGREE IN NUCLEAR TECHNOLOGY, 1990
Tuskegee University, Tuskegee Institute, AL

BACHELOR OF SCIENCE DEGREE IN TECHNICAL ENGINEERING, 1986
Auburn University, Montgomery, AL

■ Candidate's key qualifications are highlighted under skills/achievements heading.

■ Chrono-functional format is more flexible than a chronological resume, but stronger than a functional resume.

PETROLEUM ENGINEER

CHRIS SMITH
178 Green Street
Orem, UT 84058
(801) 555-5555

SUMMARY OF QUALIFICATIONS
- Extensive knowledge of geological formations and conditions.
- Educational background in geology and environmental engineering.
- Ability to perform statistical analyses and present data effectively.

EXPERIENCE
AMEREXPLORE CORP., Provo, UT
PETROLEUM ENGINEER   1989 to 1994
Responsible for exploration in Colorado, Wyoming, Nevada, Oregon, Washington, Arizona, and New Mexico. Studied and evaluated geological formations and conditions related to petroleum generation, migration, and accumulation. Developed drillable petroleum prospects by predicting favorable locations of accumulation. Oversaw drilling operations in Washington and Oregon with 20 to 25 person operating staff.

TAMARACK, INC., Salt Lake City, UT
INTERN   1988
Observed and participated in exploration of mines surrounding Great Salt Lake. Tested petroleum samples gathered. Recorded results of exploration and presented paper to upper-level managers of company.

EDUCATION
UTAH STATE UNIVERSITY
Masters Degree in Environmental Engineering, 1987

UNIVERSITY OF UTAH
Bachelors Degree in Geology, 1984

REFERENCES
Available upon request.

- Boldfacing draws attention to key credentials.

- Related internship experience reinforces candidate's professional experience.

PLASTICS ENGINEER

Chris Smith
178 Green St.
Hemlock IN 46937
(219) 555-5555

OBJECTIVE   A position in **Plastics Engineering.**

EXPERIENCE

Raychem Corporation, Hemlock, IN   1985-1994
GROUP LEADER, INDUSTRIAL VENTURE GROUP - HEATER TECHNOLOGY
GROUP
Responsible for developing self-regulating heated utilizing capacites, ferrites and magnetic metals
for chemical, petroleum and electronic industries. Supervised six-person project team. Group
results:

- U.S. Patent #3441178. Self-regulating heaters employing reactive components. Inventors: Bob
  Whitley, Kyle Kryptonite, and Chet Chester.
- Developed product-market package with $60 million/year projected sales.
- Utilized outside contractors to build a solid-state 20 KHZ power supply that cost 1/5th the cost
  of standard commercial units.

ENGINEER, PROCESS DIVISION
Responsible for evaluating ceramic capacitors for high-temperature environments. Evaluated
capacitors from ten manufacturers. Supervised three-person project team. Group results:

- Identification of Z5U and X75 type ceramic capacitors rated at 240 VAC, 200'C and 0 VAC:
  400'C environment for 10 years.
- Development of a capacitor screening and life projection program - One Raychem first.

ENGINEER, PROCESS DIVISION
Involved in bringing heater from concept through Factory Mutual approval. Group results:

- Helped develop 400'C thick film heater - One Raychem first.
- Participated in the introduction of conductive ceramics into Raychem.

ASSOCIATE ENGINEER, PROCESS DIVISION
Worked on the design and development of a forming machine for processing carbon black loaded
polytetrafluoroethylene in coordination with Stanford University Mechanical Engineering
Department. - One Raychem first.

EDUCATION

M.S. in Chemical Engineering, 1985
Massachusetts Institute of Technology, Cambridge, MA

Research Assistantship, 1983-1984
Investigated fluid flow through paper pulp mat for C.H. Dexter Corporation, Windsor Locks, CT,
and studied viscoelasticity on drop size in simulated polymer suspension reactor.

AFFILIATIONS

- American Institute of Plastics Engineers
- International Society for Hybrid Microelectronics
- American Institute of Chemical Engineers

■ Specific achievements and dynamic action verbs give resume impact.

■ Job-related affiliations demonstrate candidate's active participation in his/her field.

PRODUCT ENGINEER

CHRIS SMITH
178 Green Street
Troy, NY 12180
(518) 555-5555

Experience MDK Incorporated, Troy, NY
Product Engineer (12/92-Present)
Engineer for cable products designed for high-speed applications. Responsibilities include product extension, electrical analysis, release of proposals and products, approval of tools and dies, resolving manufacturing problems, quality assurance, and interacting with customers.

Engineering Analyst (2/91-11/92)
Corporate staff member responsible for electrical engineering computer software packages used internationally. Provided consulting, support, and training of electrical analysis software used to design interconnects. Developed software interface between SPICE and MATLAB. Evaluated new software packages. Administered UNIX environment and specified optimal configurations for engineering packages.

Development Engineer (9/88-2/91)
Designed computer board to board connectors specializing in the electrical characterization of the interface. Provided computer modeling to determine capacitance, inductance, impedance, effective dielectric, propagation delay, and crosstalk for multiple conductors. Performed laboratory testing of samples using oscilloscope, TDR, and spectrum analyzer. Used CAD software to represent 3D models of connector proposals and construct mechanical layout.

Engineer Trainee (Summer, 1988)
Worked with development engineering group. Designed and performed procedure to test filtered connector's response to load conditions.

Computer Operating Systems: UNIX, MS-DOS, Amiga DOS, and PrimOS.
Experience Languages: 68000 Assembler, Intel 80X86 Assembler, Basic, C, FORTRAN.
Software: Ansoft's Maxwell, Aries 3D modeling, MATLAB, Prime's Medusa, Greenfield, Phyllis, SPICE, X-windows, Helmholtz.

Education Master of Science in Engineering anticipated August, 1997
Rensselaer Polytechnic Institute, Troy, NY
Currently pursuing an advanced degree in computer and electrical engineering.

Bachelor of Science in Electrical Engineering December, 1987
Hofstra University, Hempstead, NY

Associate of Arts in Engineering May, 1984
Elmira College, Elmira, NY

■ Resume emphasizes candidate's strong work history.

■ Candidate's highest educational achievement is shown before other, less significant degrees.

12
Executive and Managerial

Nature of Work

Executive and managerial positions exist in all types of business. The responsibilities that people in these positions have range from general supervisory duties to running an entire company.

General managers direct their individual departments activities within the framework of the organization's overall plan, which is designed by the chief executive officer of the company. It is the task of the general manager to motivate workers to achieve their department's goals as rapidly and economically as possibly.

Construction managers plan, budget and direct the entire construction project, often using computers to evaluate various construction methods and to determine the most cost effective plan.

Property managers administer income-producing commercial and residential properties and manage the communal property and services of condominium and community associations.

Employment

Managers are found in at levels in all industries, in all sizes of firms. Executives can be found in public or private companies, as well as government agencies.

Training

The educational background of managers and executives vary as widely as the nature of their responsibilities. Most have some type of bachelor's degree, usually focusing on their business concentration. In an effort to determine the physical and intellectual qualifications of applicants, many organizations require health, psychological, and competency exams.

Job Outlook

Employment of executives and managers is expected to increase as fast as the average for all occupation through the year 2005, as businesses grow in number, size, and complexity. However, in opposition to this growth, intense competition is forcing firms to improve operating efficiency and establish a leaner corporate structure with fewer management positions, thus moderating employment growth.

Earnings

Managers and executives are among the highest paid workers in the nation. However, salary levels vary substantially, depending upon the level of managerial responsibility, length of service, and the type, size, and location of the firm.

ASSISTANT STORE MANAGER

CHRIS SMITH
178 Green Street
Mantua, NJ 08051
(609) 555-5555

OBJECTIVE: To utilize skill in administration, management, and personnel toward further responsibilities in professional administration.

SUMMARY OF QUALIFICATIONS:
- Experience with financial administration of retail sales and service operations.
- Management of high-volume retail operations. Includes supervision of merchandising, asset management, customer service and maintenance. Effect creative marketing programs and maintain compliance with corporate procedure.
- Skill in direction and development of individual and team personnel. Responsible for training, schedule and motivation of staff personnel.

EXPERIENCE:

Assistant Store Manager   **1983 to Present**
LORAX SUPERMARKETS   Woodbury, NJ
- Responsible for control and administration of financial transactions in retail environment. Includes control of cash flow and expenses, internal audit and protection of corporate assets, and establishment of seasonal budgets.
- Manage schedule and procedure of over 175 personnel. Directly supervise all customer services, lottery sales, display merchandising, maintenance, sanitation, and employee training.
- Received awards for best cash variance and payroll percentage. Set goals and adjust departmental budgets by sales projection. Perform internal audits, control expenses, and protect assets.
- Worked part-time 1983-87. Promoted to Assistant Manager in 1992.

COMPUTERS:

IBM WordPerfect, Macintosh FileMaker, Spreadsheet, Lotus 1-2-3.

EDUCATION:

Bachelor of Science in Business Management   **1987**
STOCKTON STATE COLLEGE   Pomona, NJ

VOLUNTEER:

Reader Program at Children's Hospital, Red Cross Blood Donor, Youth Tutor Program.

REFERENCES:
Available upon request.

- Summary of qualifications accentuates strong skills.

- Volunteer work indicates candidate's active involvement in his/her community.

ASSISTANT VICE-PRESIDENT (Banking)

Chris Smith
178 Green Street
Dodge City, KS 67801
(316) 555-5555

— SUMMARY OF QUALIFICATIONS —
Extensive experience in multi-branch operations includes the following areas:
- Successfully developing and personally marketing new products for small business.
- Rewriting and implementing branch system policies and procedures.
- Troubleshooting operations and establishing improved financial controls.
- Budget planning and controls, audits.

— EXPERIENCE —
Dodge City Savings Bank, Dodge City, KS
ASSISTANT VICE-PRESIDENT   1988-1994
- Assisted President and Regional Vice-President in charge of branches.
- Security officer, making and implementing camera placement and procedures for three branches. Wrote security manual.
- Installment loan officer, improving collections and commercial loan documentation.
- Troubleshooting assignments to Philadelphia office, establishing efficient operations and financial controls.

Wichita National Bank, North Newton, KS
ASSISTANT VICE-PRESIDENT-North Newton Office   1983-1988
- Created new position with responsibility for commercial balances/profit and loss in a 10-branch area.
- Established program for business with under $1 million in annual sales, developing products and marketing through personal calls.
- Generated $7 million in deposits and $5 to $6 million in lending.

ASSISTANT VICE-PRESIDENT- Salina Office   1978-1983
- Responsible for supervision and administration of 10-branch personnel, commercial development, and attaining or exceeding budgetary goals in deposit and loan totals.
- Increased deposits from $9 million to $35 million, and loans from $2 million to over $7 million.

ASSISTANT VICE-PRESIDENT- McPherson Office   1975-1978
- Managed staff of 15 employees, increasing deposits 85% to $15 million and loan totals to $4 million.

BRANCH MANAGER- Central Avenue   1971-1975
- Managed new office in competitive banking area with retail orientation. Achieved deposits of $10 million with substantial loan balances.

— EDUCATION —
Southwestern College, Winfield, KS
Accounting and Economics Studies

■ Education is de-emphasized because candidate's work history is strong.

■ Job descriptions highlight candidate's leadership skills and problem-solving abilities.

ASSISTANT VICE-PRESIDENT (Commercial Finance)

CHRIS SMITH
178 Green Street
Brooklyn, NY 11210
(718) 555-5555

PROFILE

- *Offer Masters training in Public Communications and a BA in Economics with distinguished academic performance. Top of class in Brooklyn masters program; Valedictorian of baccalaureate class, 1985.*
- *Business accomplishments include P & L responsibility as Assistant Vice-President of LeBrock, Inc. Generated $25 million in revenues through negotiating purchases of commercial paper and effective structuring of real estate loans.*
- *Outstanding Sales Producer for LeBrock - secure 20% of all company annual revenues in an organization of 15 individuals with financial authority.*
- *Characterized as driven and dedicated to an ideal of quality product and performance. Known for combining creativity, resourcefulness and initiative to build a solid record of professional achievement.*

PROFESSIONAL EXPERIENCE

ASSISTANT VICE-PRESIDENT 1991-Present
Brent LeBrock, Inc. Brooklyn, New York

Coordinate and execute all aspects of revenue development, operations, finance and contract management for a commercial financing enterprise specializing in the food industry generating $50 million in yearly transactions. Develop and maintain a viable network of business contacts and prospects. Work closely with client businesses in evaluating asset base, including appraising business and commercial real estate. Provide consultation to clients in matters of law, finance and related documentation. Structure attractive financial packages; effectively negotiate terms for commercial paper transactions, mortgages, leasing and insurance. Monitor and ensure compliance with financial and legal aspects of all client contracts. Troubleshoot and resolve complex situations.

Formulate and establish procedures facilitating peak operating efficiencies, cost effectiveness and high employee morale. Select and develop support staff in all aspects of activities. Maintain MIS systems including computer database, accounting and business software. Participate in corporate planning and development of effective business strategies, facilitating clear communications between Operations, Legal departments and managing partners.

ASSISTANT MANAGER 1981-91
The Bastille Stores, Inc. Washington, D.C.

Drove sales and supervised all aspects of operations for The Bastille's highest volume Washington, D.C. store, generating $1.9 million in annual sales. Significantly increased sales volume and overall customer satisfaction levels.

EDUCATION

MASTER OF ARTS IN PUBLIC COMMUNICATIONS, anticipated 1995
BACHELOR OF ARTS IN ECONOMICS, 1981
Class Valedictorian • Summa Cum Laude • Alpha Sigma Lambda Honor Society
BROOKLYN COLLEGE - Brooklyn, New York

■ Profile sums up candidate's professional qualifications.

■ Statistics and dollar amounts clearly demonstrate candidate's achievements.

BRANCH MANAGER (Restaurant)

CHRIS SMITH
178 Green Street
Arvin, CA 93203
(805) 555-5555

SUMMARY
- Fifteen years of successful experience in management of three franchise restaurants, including financing, contractual agreements, corporate and personnel relations, property management, facilities design and layout, advertising, promotion, and community relations.
- Experience also includes purchasing, inventory control and management, personnel hiring, training, scheduling and evaluation, security, policy and procedure.
- Proven record as top salesperson. Consistently awarded top-sales manager honors.

PROFESSIONAL EXPERIENCE

1979-present   **PIZZA PALACE**
Branch Manager   **(3 LOCATIONS)**

During this period managed three Pizza Palace restaurant franchises, generating annual sales of over $3.5 million. Managed work force of more than 250. Actively involved in all aspects of successful business operations, including: marketing, advertising and public relations; financing; personnel hiring, training, management, scheduling and relations; property maintenance, repair, modification and management; operations and inventory control; financial management, and associated aspects of administrative detail.

1975-1978   **BUSINESS PRODUCTS, INC.**
Sales Manager   **Bakersfield, CA**

Supervised 25 sales associates for growing office supply company. Kept all records of commissions. Acted as liaison between upper-level management and associates.

1972-1974
Sales Associate

Sold office supplies to various small and large businesses in the Southern California area. Highest earned commission, 1973 and 1974.

EDUCATION
California Polytechnic State University, San Luis Obispo, CA
Bachelor of Arts Degree: 1971
- Concentration in English

REFERENCES
Available upon request.

- Statistics and dollar figures quantify candidate's accomplishments.

- Resume emphasizes achievements; doesn't simply list job responsibilities.

BRANCH MANAGER (Temporary Services)

CHRIS SMITH
178 Green Street
Oxnard, CA 93033
(805) 555-5555

OBJECTIVE

A senior level position in sales with a firm which has a need for a professional capable of generating repeat business in service.

EXPERIENCE

BRANCH MANAGER
Bangtail Temps, Oxnard, CA   **June 1993-Present**
Responsibilities:
- Full responsibility for a $5.5 million dollar temporary services branch including the supervision of outside sales and inside support staffs, and the selection and training of new Sales Representatives.
- Within 4 months, established 10 new corporate clients resulting in $150,000 in new revenue to the company.

BRANCH MANAGER
NETA Temporary Services, Inc., San Mateo, CA   **1991-1993**
Responsibilities:
- After branch consolidation and reorganization by NETA, assumed budget planning/administration, and new business development/account retention responsibility for this branch which generated $1 million in annual volume.
- Obtained new accounts to replace lost business and maintained profitability. Utilized sales expertise, account management, proven sales techniques and strategies to develop a 80% new client base and maintain profit margin.

MAJOR ACCOUNT MANAGER
Transon Electronics, Inc., Torrance, CA   **1981-1991**
- Based on cold-calling, lead development, and appointment generation skills, promoted from Account Representative to Major Account Manager within 6 months. Marketed direct mail pieces to major corporations, direct response agencies, and dealers. Utilized application selling process and new and innovative approaches to consistently achieve and exceed sales objectives.

EDUCATION

Rice University, Houston, TX
Bachelor of Fine Arts/Theatre Arts

Transon Electronics Sales Training Program
Sales Excellence Seminar

REFERENCES

Available upon request.

■ Job objective focuses on the needs of the employer, not the job candidate.

■ Job descriptions refer to promotions and impressive professional successes.

CHIEF EXECUTIVE OFFICER (CEO)

Chris Smith
178 Green Street
Helena, MT 59601
(406) 555-5555

OBJECTIVE

A senior administrative position which would take advantage of 20 years of varied, in-depth background.

CAREER SUMMARY

Executive primarily skilled in banking operations and data processing systems. Strong background in retail banking, marketing, planning, budgeting and P&L management. Demonstrated record of developing and implementing solutions to multidimensional complex operational problems.

EMPLOYMENT

Calliope Savings Bank, Helena, MT   **1991-Present**
PRESIDENT/CEO
Originally hired as Executive Vice-President and subsequently elected President/CEO in June of 1992.
Company provides check processing, consulting, and other services to 40 banks. Developed and conducted corporate planning strategy meetings. In addition to having overall responsibility for operations, also responsible for financial management and P&L for the company, which presently employs 65 people and processes 30 million checks per year. Company turned profit within 2 years of start up. Developed data processing delivery system analysis; recommendations were adopted by 10 banks.

The Prudent Savings Institution, Billings, VT
VICE-PRESIDENT—DIVISION HEAD OF BANKING DIVISION   **1989-1991**
Under the direction of Chairman of the Board, responsible for administrating, planning, and directing retail banking activities. Conferred with senior management and recommended programs to achieve bank's objectives.

VICE-PRESIDENT-MARKETING   **1987-1989**
Administered and directed marketing activities of the bank. Organized and planned actions impacting on various publics supporting bank's markets. Worked with the divisions and outside agencies to develop plans which supported division's objectives. Supervised the following; liaison with advertising and public relations firms; the development and sales of bank services to various businesses and development and control of the advertising and public relations budgets.

(continued)

■ Two-page format is appropriate for senior-level positions.

■ Bold, uppercase print draws attention to candidate's impressive job titles.

<u>EMPLOYMENT</u> (continued)

      VICE-PRESIDENT-SAVINGS DIVISION   **1984-1987**

      ASSISTANT VICE-PRESIDENT-SAVINGS DIVISION   **1980-1984**

      PROGRAMMER   **1977-1980**

<u>EDUCATION</u>
      Bowdoin College, Brunswick, ME
      B.A., English, 1973

      Colby College, Waterville, ME
      M.A., Finance, 1977

<u>SPECIAL EDUCATION</u>
      Graduate School of Savings Banking
      NAMSB-Carroll College 1980

      Management Development Progam-NAMSB
      University of Montana-1982

      Marketing School
      Rocky Mountain College-1984

      Various courses in: Economics, Finance, Law, Public Speaking, Speed Reading and
      Banking

<u>PROFESSIONAL ACTIVITIES</u>
      Contributor, <u>Hiking for Stress Relief</u>
      Contributor, <u>Horizons in Corporate Clout</u>
      Rocky Mountain College 1986-1992
      Assistant Professor of Business, University of Montana

<u>HOBBIES</u>
      Hiking, jogging, mountain climbing

CHIEF OPERATIONS OFFICER

CHRIS SMITH
178 Green Street
San Diego, CA 92106
(619) 555-5555

OBJECTIVE: The opportunity to be associated with a dynamic, progressive organization in need of an experienced executive qualified in the fields of training, recreation, and/or education.

SUMMARY OF QUALIFICATIONS:
- Planning and supervising air operations for training activities.
- Manpower, equipment, and facility coordination.
- Personnel training, evaluation, and scheduling.
- Administration and supervision of the maintenance and preparation of records, reports, and correspondence.
- Troubleshooting and resolving operational and training problems.
- Extensive experience as instructor, lecturer, administrator.

EXPERIENCE: U.S. Navy, San Diego, CA   1985-1994
Chief, Operations Plans Division
Responsibilities:
- Coordinate the preparation, production, and revision of combat mission folders.
- Develop alert force procedures.
- Organize a smooth functioning administration and operational division to accomplish the requirements within the severely limited allotted time.
- Maintained detailed knowledge of all aspects of plans to include maintenance, logistics, communications weapons.
- Direct the staff of enlisted and officer personnel.

EDUCATION: University of Notre Dame, Notre Dame, IN
BA Degree
Major: Political Science

MILITARY: United States Navy
Second Lieutenant 1991
Served in Desert Storm, Stationed in Turkey
Honorable Discharge, May 1994

COMPUTERS: Lotus 1-2-3
WordPerfect
Logistics Radar Equipment

PERSONAL: Willing to relocate.

■ Military service accentuates candidate's leadership capabilities and strong work ethic.

■ Separate category for computer experience calls attention to candidate's technical knowledge.

CLAIMS EXAMINER

CHRIS SMITH
178 Green Street
Caldwell, ID 83605
(208) 555-5555

OBJECTIVE: A challenging and responsible position where my experience as a Claims Examiner for Medical Assistance recipients and provider liaison can be utilized in support of company goals.

SUMMARY: Over eight years experience in positions of increasing responsibility with rapidly growing Health Maintenance organization includes the following:
- Organizing and establishing policies for Medical Assistance Organization.
- Extensive customer service and provider communication.
- Staff supervision and coordination.
- Auditing and quality control.
- Utilizing Com Tec and Disc Corp computer system.

EXPERIENCE:

1986-Present **IDAHO HMO**, Boise, ID
Quality Control Coordinator (1991-Present)
Maintain daily, weekly and monthly statistics on 25 claims examiners, reporting claim error through paper tracking and daily audit report. Interact with State Health auditors yearly. Make adjustments to claims and maintain relationships with providers.

Senior Claims Examiner/Unit Leader (1989-90)
Trained and supervised three claims examiners, processing claims for 15,000 Medical Assistance recipients. Responsibilities included coordination of benefits, determination of eligibility, extensive provider relations and customer service communication.

Claims Examiner (1987-88)
Created new position, organizing and establishing policies for a Medical Assistance Organization which grew from 250 members in 1987 to its present 15,000. Processed medical and dental claims, referrals, encounters, eye and prescription claims. Maintained heavy telephone contact with customers. Negotiated rates with providers and Health Partners administration.

1985-1986 **NEW LOOKS**, Caldwell, ID
Assistant Manager
Trained and supervised staff of 20 employees for women's clothing store. Responsible for sales, customer service, inventory, payroll, merchandising, management reporting, and problem solving.

■ Summary grabs the reader's attention with powerful skills and qualifications.

■ Resume indicates a series of promotions.

CONTROLLER (General)

CHRIS SMITH, C.P.A.
178 Green Street
Richmond, VA 23225
(804) 555-5555

SUMMARY OF QUALIFICATIONS
- Over twenty years of progressive, professional accounting and supervisory experience.
- Computer skills include: Lotus 1-2-3, Taxware Systems, IBM PC, and Microsoft Word.
- Proficient in Spanish and some knowledge of French.
- Self-motivated; able to set effective priorities and implement decisions to achieve immediate and long-term goals and meet operational deadlines.

EDUCATION

Passed C.P.A. Examination, January 1989

UNIVERSITY OF VIRGINIA, Charlottesville, VA
Certificate in Accountancy with High Honors, 1988 G.P.A.: 3.6/4.0

UNIVERSITY OF MADRID
Graduate School of Spanish Literature, 1972

UNIVERSITY OF RICHMOND, Richmond, VA
Bachelor of Arts, Modern Languages, 1971 G.P.A.: 3.0/4.0

PROFESSIONAL EXPERIENCE

KENDALL MANAGEMENT GROUP, Richmond, VA   1992-Present
Controller
Initiate and maintain general ledgers for three closely held corporations. Compile financial statements. Process payroll, payables and receivables. Prepare budget and cost reports.

B.T. JOHNSON, C.P.A., Richmond, VA   1989-Present
Staff Accountant
Prepare individual, corporate, and fiduciary income and estate tax returns. Generate compilations and financial statement audits. Research tax issues.

ASHLAND AUTHORITY, Ashland, VA   1973-1989
Assistant Terminal Agent
Supervised ten ticket agents. Implemented Accounting Department policies. Assisted in conversion of sales reporting to Lotus 1-2-3.

■ Strong educational credentials strengthen resume.

■ Foreign language skills further strengthen candidate's qualifications.

CONTROLLER (International)

CHRIS SMITH
178 Green Street
Roanoke, VA 24018
(703) 555-5555

EXPERIENCE:

1988- STARON PROMOTIONAL CORP.   Roanoke, VA
Present *Controller*
Financial responsibilities: Accounts Receivable/Payable, verify and authorize invoices, establish and approve credit lines for clients and suppliers, process payroll, compile and audit monthly, quarterly, and yearly cash disbursement and financial reports.
Import & export responsibilities: comply with customs and importing regulations, coordinate all aspects of import and export shipments.
Other responsibilities: Process daily banking transactions, open and negotiate domestic and international Letters of Credit, calculate salespeople's commissions.

1985-1988 MILITARY OF TURKEY   Istanbul, Turkey
Contract Administrator
Prepared quotations and performed administration of high-dollar contracts for American companies. Position included financial follow-up on the execution of contracts, and administration of technical and contractual modifications.

1983-1985 TURKISH EMBASSY   Washington, D.C.
Buyer - Procurement Mission
Performed high-dollar procurement of aviation systems and spare aircraft parts. Gained experience in all aspects of purchasing process, utilizing computerized purchasing systems. Served as liaison between Turkish Users and U.S. Vendors, handled negotiation of prices and conditions.

1981-1983 UNIVERSITY OF TURKEY   Istanbul, Turkey
Teaching Assistant
Research Assistant and Student Advisor in School of Business Administration, Financial Studies.

EDUCATION: UNIVERSITY OF TURKEY   Istanbul, Turkey
Graduate School of Business Administration
MBA, 1983 - Major: Finance

TURKISH INSTITUTE OF TECHNOLOGY   Istanbul, Turkey
BS in Industrial & Management Engineering, 1976
Graduated with Honors.

REFERENCES: Available upon request.

■ Foreign work experience is invaluable.

■ Use of boldface and italics provides a clean and crisp presentation.

DIRECTOR OF OPERATIONS

CHRIS SMITH
178 Green Street
Tacoma, WA 98447
(206) 555-5555

SUMMARY

- Over 15 years in shopping center management
- 20 years in retail
- Strong background in shopping center operations: Budget development, expense control, negotiating service/systems contracts, communications and administration

EXPERIENCE

1979 to Present HILLSTON MANAGEMENT CO., INC.
Tacoma, WA
Director, Shopping Center Operations (1988-present)
- Oversee operations for 10 high-volume shopping centers.
- Hire, train, and motivate Operations Managers.
- Prepare budgets and control expenses for each center.
- Negotiate and award company-wide security, maintenance, and other service contracts.

General Manager, Whitman Mall (1985-1987)
- 1.5 million sq. ft. center in Tacoma, WA
- Managed leasing, maintenance, security, promotions, advertising, budget development, expense control, and accounts receivable.
- Fostered effective tenant and public relations.

General Manager, Corbain Mall (1983-1984)
- 800,000 sq. ft. center in Seattle, WA.
- Coordinated tenant construction, pre-opening activities, and grand opening.

General Manager, Pacific Mall (1979-1982)
- 600,000 sq. ft. center in Walla Walla, WA.

1970-1975 HEALD SALES CORP.
Tacoma, WA
Credit Operations Manager - Central Office
Store Credit Manager - Tacoma, WA

EDUCATION

Pacific Lutheran University, 1975
B.S. Business Administration

■ Summary is concise and adds punch to resume.

■ Relevant work experience is emphasized while other positions are de-emphasized.

DISTRICT MANAGER

CHRIS SMITH
178 Green Street
Chickasha, OK 73023
(405) 555-5555

OBJECTIVE:

A district management position. Willing to travel and/or relocate.

PROFESSIONAL EXPERIENCE:

JESSAMINE BOOKSTORES INC., Chickasha, OK
District Manager, Oklahoma   1991-Present
- Oversee all operations of ten retail bookstores in Oklahoma.
- Advise store management on personnel functions, merchandising, loss prevention, and customer service; communicate and ensure compliance with company policies, procedures, and programs.
- Open new stores; hire staff; oversee initial set-up.
- Research competition relative to title selection, pricing, merchandising and sales programs.

WHIPPORWHILLBOOKS, New York, NY
District Manager, West Coast   1988-91
- Managed operations as above for total of five districts in Los Angeles, San Francisco, San Diego, San Gabriel, and San Fernando.
- Performed extensive hiring, training, and developing of store managers.
- Set individual store and district sales goals.
- Named District Manager of the Year for Western United States, 1990, 1991.

Store Manager, New York   1986-88
- Oversaw daily store operations; hired, trained, and developed personnel; performed merchandising functions; tracked and reported sales; handled inventory, bookkeeping, cash administration, etc.

Assistant Manager, New York   1985-1986
- Assisted manager in day-to-day operations; managed store in his absence.

EDUCATION:

Southwestern University, Georgetown, TX
Bachelor of Arts in English Literature, May 1984

COMPUTERS:

MacIntosh FileMaker, Microsoft Word, Spreadsheet, ManagePro.

- Indicating a willingness to relocate on a resume can be advantageous.

- Resume indicates a series of promotions.

EXECUTIVE MARKETING DIRECTOR

CHRIS SMITH
178 Green Street
Alexandria, LA 71301
(318) 555-5555

OBJECTIVE
A Senior Management position.

QUALIFICATIONS
- Thoroughly familiar with the design, installation, implementation and/or conversion of data processing systems for major areas of bank operations which require in-depth knowledge of departmental functions.
- Well qualified in areas of planning and setting objectives, sales and customer relations, and training programs dealing with both company and banking personnel.
- Establish and currently maintain excellent contacts with business and industry.
- Proven expertise in personnel management, employee training, marketing, innovative ability in application development, problem definition and solutions, and the ability to manage working teams.

EXPERIENCE
Heidelburg Computer Corporation, Alexandria, LA
Executive Marketing Director   1952-Present
General Information:
Began as a trainee assigned to work with units specifically designed for banks. Continued in this area through punched card accounting and computer-oriented data processing hardware and software. Promoted to Executive Marketing Director with responsibility for:
- Supervise staff of eight (marketing, systems engineers, customer education, field engineers) and direct efforts of productive sales and systems engineering team.
- Work with three major accounts (Commercial banking, teleprocessing network for mutual savings, and a major bank holding company); provide services involving annual revenue of over $4 million.
- Coordinate sales support activities, troubleshoot problem areas, and resolve problems by working in close cooperation with company's divisions (field engineering, systems design division, supply division, administrative staff, local branch management).
- Organize top-level presentations for sales involving million dollar company/customer commitments.
- Maintain top-level contacts within customer organizations, and advise on matters pertaining to long-range overall system planning.
- Direct investigative effort prior to system design, and instruct customer/personnel.
- Serve as a consultant and advisor to other marketing personnel in the organization.
- Serve as a guest lecturer at Heidelburg schools.

EDUCATION
Fort Lewis College, Durango, CO
Bachelor of Science, Business Administration, 1952

■ Qualifications section highlights candidate's areas of expertise.

■ Unrelated work experience is omitted.

FIELD ASSURANCE COORDINATOR

CHRIS SMITH
178 Green Street
Danville, VA 24541
(804) 555-5555

EMPLOYMENT HISTORY

1991 to Present
BRACH HEALTH CORPORATION, Emory, VA
Field Assurance Coordinator
- Assure compliance of all complaint activity with Division, Corporate, and Regulatory requirements.
- Provide technical support troubleshooting customer problems.
- Coordinate recall actions.
- Participate in relocation efforts of product complaints from Emory, VA to the corporate office in Miami, FL.
- Maintain corporate product complaint database.
- Supervise temporary personnel.
- Interface with hospitals, dealers, and sales representatives in regard to product complaints.

1989 to 1991
T.M. LEARY MEDICAL SUPPLIES, Ferrum, VA
Customer Service/Technical Service Representative
- Provided product, price, and technical information to customers, dealers, and sales staff.
- Expedited and coordinated movement of product through repair and upgrade processes.
- Assisted sales force in developing and maintaining lease and rental programs.
- Initiated $30,000 in customer sales through sales incentive program.
- Developed and maintained infusion pump loaner program.

1988 to 1989
GINSBERG DEFENSE, Birdsnest, VA
Inspector Technician
- Audited processed for the MX missile program.
- Performed visual inspection in classified areas on cable and subassemblies used in electronic warfare.
- Instructed productivity program.

1986 to 1988
KERROUAC ASSOCIATES, Lively, VA
Inspector Technician
- Inspected electro-mechanical and circuit-card assemblies to various military specifications.

EDUCATION
Ferrum College, Ferrum, VA
Associates in Business Administration, 1991

TECHNICAL SUMMARY
WordPerfect, Microsoft Word, DOS, Lotus 1-2-3, Windows

■ Font gives resume clean and professional appearance.

■ Reverse chronological format focuses employer's attention on candidate's most current position.

FOOD SERVICE MANAGER

CHRIS SMITH
178 Green Street
Saint Matthews, KY 40272
(502) 555-5555

PROFESSIONAL OBJECTIVE

A position in Administration or Management in which over ten years of outstanding managerial experience will have valuable application.

PROFESSIONAL EXPERIENCE

1984 to present **LLOYD CORPORATION**, Louisville, KY
GRACE COMPANY, Jeffersonville, KY
Food Service Manager, 1987 to present
- Supervise, hire/fire, train, and schedule cafeteria staff of 25
- Act as liaison to executive staff
- Coordinate all kitchen operations; handle merchandising, ordering, and purchasing
- Supervise catering of special events
- Administer executive dining, preparation, and service
- Prepare bookkeeping, inventory control, and other reports

HAMMOND COMPANY, New Albany, KY
Manager, Executive Dining Rooms, 1984 to 1987
- Supervised, hired/fired, trained, and scheduled staff of 15
- Administered all aspects of executive dining
- Coordinated special parties and events

1980 to 1983 JENNINGS CLUB, Buechel, KY
Head Waiter
- Supervised all dining room operations
- Acted as assistant to manager, training and briefing new employees

1976 to 1980 LIGHTHOUSE RESTAURANT, Shively, KY
Waiter
- Worked part-time while attending school to help finance education

EDUCATION

Bellarmine College, Louisville, KY
Bachelor of Arts in Philosophy, 1980

INTERESTS

Fishing, cooking, reading mysteries

REFERENCES

Furnished upon request

■ Education is listed towards bottom of resume because candidate's practical experience outweighs his/her degree.

■ Personal interests can provide a great topic for conversation during a job interview.

GENERAL MANAGER (Nightclub)

CHRIS SMITH
178 Green Street
Hyannis, MA 02601
(508) 555-5555

PROFESSIONAL EXPERIENCE

AMBER REIGN, Hyannis, MA   *1986-Present*
General Manager
- Manage all nightclub/restaurant operations. Volume: $10,000/night.
- Maintain all accounting, cash, bar/food/inventory cost, payroll, and administrative controls.
- Monitor sales at Ticketron outlet and supervise ticketing system.

Achievements
- Conceived, opened, and managed Amber Reign, increasing overall volume by 60%.
- Developed "Hear Them Roar," a Women's Comedy Competition, which became a successful, repeat promotion at Amber Reign and later went on to a national tour in 1992.

CAPE COD CUTIES, Hyannis, MA   *1982-1986*
General Manager
- Managed all aspects of this growing chain of New England Hair Salons.
- Supervised staff of 12 employees, ensuring efficient customer service in this high-volume, tourist-oriented selling space.
- Hired/fired staff. Responsible for payroll/accounts payable utilizing IBM PC.

EDUCATION

University of Massachusetts - Boston
Course work in General Management Practices, Business & Finance, Accounting, 1986-1987.

Aquinas Junior College
A.S. Marketing, 1981

COMPUTER SKILLS

Microsoft Word
Lotus 1-2-3
FileMaker

REFERENCES

Furnished upon request.

■ Resume emphasizes achievements; doesn't simply list job responsibilities.

■ Resume includes course work that corresponds to the position desired.

GENERAL MANAGER (Printing Company)

CHRIS SMITH
178 Green Street
New London, CT 06320
(203) 555-5555

EXPERIENCE

6/93 to Present · **Manager**
DICKENS PRINTING COMPANY · *New London, CT*
- Facilitate the operation of and provide maintenance services for a combined commercial multicolor and thermographic stationary printer.
- Estimate job costs and schedule production.
- Ensure project compliance with customer specifications.
- Delegate responsibilities, train, supervise and evaluate staff.

9/91 to 5/93 · **Manager**
HARDY PRESS · *Hartford, CT*
- Serviced customers, dealt with vendors, and estimated project costs.
- Scheduled projects and monitored production to ensure compliance with customer specifications.
- Delegated responsibilities, scheduled work week, trained, supervised, developed and evaluated staff members.

5/89 to 8/91 · **Project Coordinator**
COPY CAT COPIERS · *Fairfield, CT*
- Provided estimates on projects.
- Sourced vendors and conducted purchasing procedures.
- Standardized procedures for estimating, purchasing and order documentation during a high-growth period.

ACCOMPLISHMENTS
- Elected as member of The Executive Finance Committee; assisted in the evaluation and subsequent adjustment of company procedures; influential in changes which generated an increase in gross sales from $5 to $8.5 million.
- Headed standardization project which promoted a reduction in errors and maximized profits.
- Implemented the Profit Enhancement System for estimating and costing.

EDUCATION

1991 to 1994
CONNECTICUT COLLEGE · *New London, CT*
Certified in numerous management, employee relations and computer seminars

FAIRFIELD UNIVERSITY · *Fairfield, CT*
Bachelor of Arts in Liberal Arts Studies, 1989

- Accomplishments section accentuates candidate's ability to maximize profits.

- Continuing education indicates candidate's ongoing commitment to his/her career.

GENERAL MANAGER (Furniture Company)

CHRIS SMITH
178 Green Street
Baltimore, MD 21239
(301) 555-5555

OBJECTIVE To maximize professional and organizational skills in a general management position.

RELEVANT EXPERIENCE

1/94-Present

GENERAL MANAGER
Sweet Dreams Furniture Company, Baltimore, MD
Manage staff of five. Analyze market and target direct market areas. Perform spreadsheet analysis utilizing Lotus 1-2-3, i.e., budget analysis, projections, payroll and bookkeeping. Created custom forms and tables through Lotus Works Database Services; compatible with dBase III.

7/89-12/93

BUSINESS/OFFICE MANAGER
Rose & Flo Bake Shops, Baltimore, MD
Coordinated the effectiveness of staff members' functions with the implementation of a computerized purchasing and billing system. Supervised a staff of 10-13, including interns. Performed Human Resource management duties, i.e., recruitment, selection, training and development, benefits, policies and procedures. Increased sales by 75%, and reduced cost 30%, utilizing marketing techniques. Negotiated purchases of computer equipment and contracted alternative delivery systems. Maintained public relation contacts with local and regional media, and implemented new marketing promotions. Office procedures also included taxation, bookkeeping, coding, and billing.

SKILLS

Proficient in WordPerfect, Lotus 1-2-3, and Pagemaker, dBaseIII.

EDUCATION

Dickinson College, Carlisle, Pennsylvania
BACHELOR OF ARTS, Human Resources, May 1989
Dean's List
Editor-in-Chief of the Yearbook, 1988-89.

INTERESTS

Baking, Sailing, Reading Poetry.

References Available Upon Request

- Computer proficiency is stressed within the job descriptions as well as in the skills section.

- Personal interests give resume a personal touch.

HMO ADMINISTRATOR

CHRIS SMITH
178 Green Street
Fairbanks, AK 99508
(907) 555-5555

OBJECTIVE

To secure a challenging Management position in a Health Insurance company.

PROFESSIONAL EXPERIENCE

1991-Present VEDDER COMMUNITY HEALTH PLAN, Fairbanks, AK
Multi-Specialty Float
Currently trained in at least 10 departments to ensure smooth operations in medical assisting or administrative work. Some departments include Internal Medicine, Nutrition, Pediatrics, Visual Services, OB-GYN, Radiology, Pharmacy, Main Desk, Building Services.
- Member, *Lark Leadership Committee* for unification and cooperation of interpersonal relations among management and staff.
- Member, *Lark Diversity Committee* to promote awareness of the similarities in values despite diversities among multicultural staff.

1989-1991 **Hospital Admissions Coordinator**
Scheduled examinations/surgeries, including emergencies. Set up operating rooms. Coordinated in-patients' hospital rooms and physicals. interviewed patients for information before surgery/examinations. Informed patients of necessary requirements before surgery.
- Received **Dunstable Award** for highly developed level of responsibility and commitment to member satisfaction. June 1991.
- Awarded **Gold Star Award** 1990 for implementing new practices and procedures which remain a permanent part of hospital admissions.

1987-1989 **Medical Assistant**
Scheduled appointments for gynecology and obstetrics. Booked appointments exclusively for OB-GYN specialist. Answered/screened patient phone calls, channeled them to proper doctor. Maintained records, data input.

1982-1987 THE LEE HUANG RESIDENCE, Fairbanks, AK
Childcare Governess
Provided quality homecare for two children in their parents' absence. Oversaw general supervision of home. Creatively organized activities.

EDUCATION

UNIVERSITY OF ALASKA, Fairbanks, AK. **Candidate for M.Ed.,** 1995.
ALASKA PACIFIC UNIVERSITY, Anchorage, AK. B.A. Liberal Arts, 1991.
Courses: Accounting I; Business Communication; Algebra I.

■ Bullets draw attention to candidate's relevant professional memberships and awards.

■ Each job description is related and contributes to candidate's professional objective.

HOSPITAL ADMINISTRATOR

CHRIS SMITH
178 Green Street
Detroit, MI 48203
(313) 555-5555

PROFESSIONAL OBJECTIVE
A challenging, growth-oriented position in HEALTH CARE MANAGEMENT/ADMINISTRATION.

PROFESSIONAL EXPERIENCE
THE DETROIT MEDICAL CENTER, Detroit, MI
Hospital Director, 9/88–Present
- Supervise/coordinate administrative services for City' public health care program.
- Handle health care and hospitalization for indigents, low-income, and welfare patients, consistent with care afforded insurance and fee-for-service patients.
- Troubleshoot staff/general administration conflicts and issues.
- Resolve policy issues; develop reports and documents for budgeting proposals and expenditure control.

Central Administrator, Emergency Services, 4/82–9/88
- Coordinated all administrative details of Emergency Room health care.
- Assisted medical team in providing prompt support services for the health care delivery system.
- Supervised ward secretaries, interpreters, and ancillary personnel.
- Prepared budget and monitored expenditures.

Unit Manager, 6/80–4/82
- Provided administrative support to Intensive Care Units, Operating Rooms, and Medical/Surgical Floors.
- Handled vendor relations and inventory control.
- Supervised secretarial staff and ancillary personnel.

ADDITIONAL EXPERIENCE
- Additional experience includes Central Administrator, Night Admitting Manager, and Ward Secretary. 1972–1980.

EDUCATIONAL BACKGROUND
UNIVERSITY OF DETROIT MERCY, Detroit, MI
M.S. Degree: Health Service Administration, 1980

MICHIGAN HOSPITAL ASSOCIATION, Detroit, MI
Certificate: Management Development, 1976

MICHIGAN STATE UNIVERSITY, East Lansing, MI
B.A. Degree: English, 1972

BOARD MEMBERSHIPS
Elected to Board of Directors, Department of Public Health, 9/93-Present.

- Specific dates of employment (month and year) are ideal for candidates with no gaps in work history.

- Impressive educational background strengthens resume.

IMPORT/EXPORT MANAGER

CHRIS SMITH
178 Green Street
Pueblo, CO 81004
(719) 555-5555

CAREER HISTORY

1988 to   THE MORIN COMPANY, Pueblo, CO
present   <u>Import/Export Manager</u>, 1992-present
- Handle established accounts and all new calls/sales for European, Japanese and U.S. exports.
- Prepare price quotations and government tenders; advise on delivery and order specifications.
- Write new product proposals and manufacturing documents, determining needs and coordinating assembly of all necessary materials.
- Process orders, credit memos, letters of credit, substitutions, return authorizations and product complaints.
- Maintain extensive written, verbal and fax communications with U.S. and overseas customers and dealers; provide product and delivery information.
- Liaison with all facets of corporate and subsidiary operations including warehouse, manufacturing, advertising, marketing, research and development and the legal department.
- Ensure proper and timely filling and delivery of each order; resolve collections problems and account discrepancies.

<u>Administrative Assistant, International Marketing</u>, 1989-92
- Provided back-up to 8 world-wide International Marketing Assistants and 3 Marketing Managers; cross-trained in all clerical and Marketing functions.
- Handled European business overflow for assistants and managers; processed orders, invoices and requests.

<u>Bilingual Executive Secretary to the General Manager of European Exports</u>, 1988-89
- Provided general secretarial support in all marketing/distribution functions.
- Translated all Spanish and Portuguese documents; made all travel arrangements.

EDUCATION

UNIVERSITY OF COLORADO, Boulder, CO
Bachelor of Arts Degree in Spanish, graduated *Cum Laude*, 1987

SKILLS

IBM CRT, IBM PC, fluent in Spanish, knowledge of Portuguese.

■ Foreign language skills are extremely valuable for candidates in the import/export field.

■ Underlining job titles draws attention to candidate's career progression.

INSURANCE CLAIMS CONTROLLER

CHRIS SMITH
178 Green Street
Birmingham, AL 35229
(205) 555-5555

PROFESSIONAL OBJECTIVE
Seeking greater opportunity for achievement in the field of Accounting Management in the Insurance and Financial areas.

PROFESSIONAL EXPERIENCE

1981 to present
SHELDON INSURANCE AGENCIES, Birmingham, AL
Claim Control Supervisor, 1987-Present
Responsible for maintenance coordination of existing claim support systems, development of financial and operational reports from new claim processing system, and establishment and performance of all draft controls and related analyses.
- Coordinate required IRS reporting for claim payments and abandoned personal property review.
- Monitor balances and collection of sundry ledger receivables.
- Develop accruals for liabilities.

Operations Accountant, 1985-1987
Performed confirmation of processed premium transactions. Instrumental in hard development of expense budget and calendarized plan.
- Reported directly to management; provided analyses of monthly plan variances.
- Developed premium reporting specifications and enhancements on an as-needed basis.
- Monitored aging of all receivables and letter of credit balances.

Senior Operations Analyst, 1982-1985
Generated required premium accruals for unprocessed transactions. Coordinated development of management reports with staff. Performed on-going analyses of financial results.

Financial Analyst, 1981-1982
Provided financial systems reports to field underwriting offices. Prepared short- and long-range plans and expense budgets, as well as the monthly servicing carrier profit and loss statement.

1979 to 1981
CROWEL COMPANY, INC., Auburn, AL
Management Report Analyst
Created standardized and specially requested financial exhibits for senior management.

EDUCATION

1980
AUBURN UNIVERSITY, Auburn, AL
B.S., Accounting

- Specific dates for positions within the same company impress employer with candidate's rate of career advancement.

- Stating that "references are available upon request" is not essential; most employers will assume that references are available.

INSURANCE COORDINATOR

CHRIS SMITH
178 Green Street
Laurel, MS 39440
(601) 555-5555 (Day)
(601) 444-4444 (Evening)

SUMMARY OF QUALIFICATIONS
- More than eight years of progressive, professional administrative, clerical, and supervisory experience. Extensive mortgage banking and basic accounting background.
- Self-motivated; able to set effective priorities to achieve immediate and long-term goals and meet operational deadlines.
- Able to work independently and as team member; adept at motivating staff to ensure smooth work-flow and increased productivity.

RELEVANT EXPERIENCE
REGINALD WARSAW SYSTEMS, Laurel, MS, 1987-Present
Insurance Coordinator, 1990-Present
Coordinate quality assurance: system verification, policy/transaction entry, output verification, and in-house personnel/customer education. Act as a liaison between end users and technical personnel. Analyze documented systems problems; recommend solutions and detailed specification. Establish and execute Test Matrices; execute Batch Test cycles; verify test results; report to upper management. Maintain and document system support files.

Customer Service Clerk, 1987-1990
Provided general customer services operating with tight deadlines.

DARVWEILLER TEMPORARY EMPLOYMENT AGENCY, Jackson, MS
Clerical/Administrative Assistant, 1986-1987
Assignments included Sawyer Bank as Mutual Funds Researcher.

EDUCATION
MISSISSIPPI UNIVERSITY FOR WOMEN, Columbus, MS
B.A. Business Management, 1987

COMPUTER SKILLS
IBM 3090, Ps/Z, XT/2000 and 3050, Workstation, and Harris; software training includes OS/JCL and TSO, Easytrieve, Microsoft Works, WordPerfect, Paradox 3, Lotus 1-2-3, dBase III Plus, DOS, and CA-7.

REFERENCES
Furnished upon request.

■ Summary is concise and adds punch to resume.

■ Separate category for computer experience calls attention to candidate's technical knowledge.

INVENTORY CONTROL MANAGER

CHRIS SMITH
178 Green Street
Fort Bragg, NC 28307
(919) 555-5555

PROFESSIONAL BACKGROUND
1988 to DEPARTMENT OF DEFENSE, Logistics Division, Supply Branch, Ft. Bragg, NC
Present Commodity Manager, Inventory Control
- Supervise staff of 10; Train, schedule, evaluate and delegate responsibilities—monitor work done and give final approval upon completion.
- Coordinate procurement and delivery of military supplies including electronics, modules, boards, guidance systems, tanks, aircraft, weapons, petroleum products, and spare parts.
- Receive bills of lading and resolve discrepancies with original orders.
- Input receipt of materials and monitor inventory via CRT.
- Interpret government rules and regulations regarding ordering and receipt of supplies; Ensure proper application of all other procedures and policies.
- Review damaged Item listings, determine whether to repair, and ship to repair shop.
- Complete financial paperwork ensuring orders are within budgetary requirements.
- Complete paperwork for inventory, shipping, purchasing, accounting, and end-of-month reports.
- Received awards for "Outstanding Performance," 1993, 1994.

1985 to NATIONAL GUARD, Raleigh, NC
1988 Communications Supervisor
- Coordinated all communications and electronic supplies for the North Carolina National Guard.
- Trained, scheduled, evaluated, and motivated as many as 40 workers.
- Developed and implemented innovative system for ordering supplies and tracking inventory control.
- Input data and monitored inventory via computerized system.
- Forecasted, prepared, and monitored expenditures of operational budget.

EDUCATIONAL BACKGROUND
Asheville High School, Asheville, NC, 1985.

TRAINING

Supply Systems; Storage Management; Logistics Organization; Equal Opportunity; Application of Management Improvement Techniques for 1st Line Supervisors; Procurement; Financial Management in Stock Control Systems; Management of Materials Handling Equipment.

■ Job descriptions highlight candidate's leadership skills and problem-solving abilities.

■ Relevant military training and experience takes precedence over limited education.

MANAGEMENT CONSULTANT

CHRIS SMITH
178 Green Street
Westhampton, MA 01027
(413) 555-5555

EDUCATIONAL BACKGROUND
VANDERBILT UNIVERSITY, Nashville, TN;
Master of Arts Degree in Political Science, 1980.

UNIVERSITY OF THE SOUTH, Sewanee, TN;
Bachelor of Arts Degree in Political Science, 1978.

PROFESSIONAL BACKGROUND
(1991-Present) *Management Consultant,* Kimberly Neumann, Inc., Westhampton, MA
- Provide assessment and consultation in the areas of human resources, health care, administration and economic development, with emphasis on full utilization of staffing, capital equipment and all other resources.
- Served as Chief Project Officer for firm with emphasis on marketing, coastal zone planning, and intergovernmental relations services.

(1988-1991) *Staff Consultant/Political Scientist,* National Commission For The Protection Of Animals In Scientific Experiments, Hadley, MA
- Developed and implemented general surveys regarding animal experimentation activities in social and behavioral sciences.
- Project management responsibilities for National Animal Experimentation Conference, securing over 25 scholarly research papers.

(1983-1988) *Executive Director,* Northampton Health Clinic, Northampton, MA
- Directed operations of a federally-funded ambulatory care center offering medical, dental, and mental health services.
- Reduced agency debt by more than $250,000 through reorganization of billing system.

(1981-1983) *Executive Director,* William Stoughton Children's Center, Springfield, MA
- Established collaborative in mental health services with an area program utilizing funding from national and local non-profit organizations.

(1980-1981) *Associate Director for Programs and Planning,* North Prospect Community Development Corporation, Amherst, MA
- Managed daily operations and supervised programs for this community-based social services organization with $1 million budget.

AFFILIATIONS
Volunteer Researcher for the Animal Protection Agency, 1983-1984.
National Management Organization (NMO), 1981-1984.

■ Strong educational credentials strengthen resume.

■ Affiliations listed are related to candidate's professional experience.

MANAGER (Non-Profit and Charities)

Chris Smith
178 Green Street
Fort Wayne, IN 46803
(219) 555-5555

EXPERIENCE

GARY Y.M.C.A.   Gary, IN
ASSOCIATE EXECUTIVE DIRECTOR   1991-Present

Supervision
Supervised seven full-time program directors and non-exempt administrative staff. Recruited, hired, trained and evaluated full- and part-time staff. Organized and conducted staff meetings and training events. Responsible for career development for full-time professional staff.

Management
Financial management of $2 million multi-department annual budget. Developed and projected new annual budget, balanced and allocated funds and ensured branch departments met financial goals. Operations management of program areas: Adult Fitness, Aquatics, Youth Sports and Fitness, Gymnastics, Day Camp, Fitness Center, Membership, Member Services, office administration and facility maintenance. Administered safety and risk management procedures for the branch.

Fundraising
Chaired 1991 Annual Support Campaign and Community Gifts Chair of the 1992 Annual Support Drive. Organized campaign activities, recruited and trained volunteers, managed telephone solicitations, developed prospects and implemented related administrative procedures.

Programs/Services
Managed multi-program areas, scheduling, enrollment and member evaluations. Established program guidelines and criteria. Managed and supervised membership department and front desk area, program registration and member services/relations.

Community Relations
Responsible for administration and allocation of scholarship/financial aid funds. Assisted in volunteer development program. Direct responsibility to branch Board of Directors and program committees. Responsible for Public Service Announcements and public relations via presentations at various community organizations.

Promotions and Marketing
Planned and managed promotion budget, promotional print scheduling, hired graphic contractors and media advertisers. Created, planned and implemented in-house promotions. Collected and analyzed database of demographics and trends related to marketing membership and programs.

SENIOR PROGRAM DIRECTOR AND PHYSICAL DIRECTOR   1986-1991
Direct supervision and management of the following departments: Adult Fitness, Fitness Center, Corporate Fitness, Gymnastics, Youth Physical, Day Camp and Community Services. Supervised approximately fifty part-time employees and one hundred volunteers. Conducted program and membership open-house promotions.

EDUCATION

GARY COMMUNITY COLLEGE   Gary, IN
Continuing education courses in marketing, MIS, and organizational communication.   1986

DEPAUW UNIVERSITY   Greencastle, IN
Bachelor of Science, Physiology and Biology   1985

■ Chrono-functional format is more flexible than a chronological resume, but stronger than a functional resume.

■ Continuing education indicates candidate's ongoing commitment to his/her career.

MANUFACTURING MANAGER (Automotive)

CHRIS SMITH
178 Green Street
Woodstock, VT 05091
(802) 555-5555

OBJECTIVE:

A position in manufacturing with a firm in need of an individual with a broad technical as well as management background in the machining and manufacturing fields.

EXPERIENCE:

Manufacturing Manager
Gladstone Motor Company, Montpelier, VT   1989-Present
- Oversaw modernization and reorganization of this engine plant contracted for remanufacture of Dane Motor Company engines.
- Set up controls for workers in manufacturing departments and machine shop which included: grinding, boring, and honing operations.
- Initiated improved quality control system to meet Dane specifications for full-year warranty. System resulted in reduction of rejects to less than 4% on 500-600 engines completed monthly.
- Established purchasing policies utilizing second and third sources for parts which resulted in Baur-Dane assuming more competitive pricing position.
- Classified purchasing details on 80 different production engines; implemented inventory control; greatly improved ordering efficiencies; and set up effective marketing service policies.

Accomplishment: Through expanded automation effected a labor cost reduction of $12 million annually. This was on $82 million in annual sales and the difference between a loss and substantial profit for management.

Manufacturing Manager
P.I.L. Engineering Company, Inc., Colchester, VT   1986-1989
- Supervised production machine shop which subcontracted to manufacture precision machine parts and assemblies for the electronic industry.
- Developed and implemented manufacturing, cost control and quality control programs; successfully developed business to $8.2 million in annual sales.

General Manager
Ferou Maintenance, Rutland, VT   1983-1986
- Shouldered full responsibility for this tractor-trailer maintenance company servicing the Shaw Line Haul Fleet consisting of 500 trailers and 200 tractors traveling New England and upper New York State.
- Recruited and hired 60 mechanics operating on three shifts.
- Initiated many vehicle design changes which were adopted by the Stanza Motor Company.
- Designed unique field service trucks on which specifications were written for national application.

■ Bold type, underlining, and/or italics draws attention to key information.

■ Job descriptions detail candidate's responsibilities and accomplishments in concise terms.

MANUFACTURING MANAGER (Computer)

CHRIS SMITH
178 Green Street
Beetown, WI 53802
(414) 555-5555

CAREER OBJECTIVE
A results-oriented supervisor seeks a managerial opportunity in which to help to improve production by leading a team effort directed at achieving company goals.

SUMMARY OF QUALIFICATIONS
Over 15 combined years of expertise in supervision including electronic assembly for a major computer manufacturer, and injection molding operations for a prominent plastics company. Because of ability to adjust and learn new skills quickly, have often been called upon to start up new operations. Excel in training employees to do jobs correctly the first time. Computer proficient including Word and Windows.

CAREER HISTORY

Berryman Systems, Beetown, WI   **1985-Present**
General Supervisor
- Performed a full range of supervisory functions that included selecting/training personnel, planning work loads, promoting quality and department efficiency, maintaining discipline and safety
- Improved productivity from 45 parts per hour to over 600 parts per hour by using existing equipment
- Achieved a superior appraisal for personal performance in 1993
- Developed detailed process and orientation packets for new employees
- Awarded three bonuses and two letters of appreciation for superior efforts put forth by team in surpassing daily production targets and producing high quality products (1991-1992)
- Developed soldering workshop for new employees
- Selected to attend training session on workmanship standards, inspection, rework and repair offered by the National Electronics Training Center of Wisconsin
- Promoted to general supervisor on new second shift. Responsible for up to 120 hourly workers and 5 section supervisors
- Promoted to section supervisor for constantly meeting and surpassing production and quality requirements
- Developed a method (template overlay) which resulted in eliminating 75% of inspection costs

(continued)

■ Job objective focuses on the needs of the employer, not the job candidate.

■ Job descriptions accentuate candidate's specific contributions and accomplishments.

CAREER HISTORY (continued)

Bruce & Wayne Components, **Gotham, WI**   **1983-1985**
Production Manager
- Directed up to 50 employees in the operation and maintenance of high-tech machinery
- Placed in charge of operations whenever general manager left the plant
- Selected to assist general manager to phase out operations at Siren location and move operations to Gotham

Plath Music Industries, **Rice Lake, WI**   **1980-1983**
Manager, Electronic Technician
- Directed up to 20 employees in the assembly of home entertainment and audio visual equipment. Areas of supervision included solderwave equipment, repair, personnel, mechanical and electrical sub assembly

EDUCATION
St. Norbert College
B.S., Industrial Technology, 1980

COMPUTER SKILLS
Lotus 1-2-3, WordStar, Microsoft Windows

OPERATIONS MANAGER (Distributor)

CHRIS SMITH
178 Green Street
Upper Arlington, OH 43221
(614) 555-5555

OBJECTIVE A Management position where experience, education, and communication skills will be fully utilized in a growth-oriented environment

SUMMARY OF QUALIFICATIONS
- Comprehensive knowledge of all functional areas of business operations
- Strong initiative in decision-making and assumption of responsibilities
- Self-starter capable of motivating others
- Excellent communication and organization skills
- Effective time management

PROFESSIONAL EXPERIENCE
OHMON EQUIPMENT COMPANY, Columbus, OH
Operations Manager, 1982-Present
- Directed all administrative functions for distributor of machinery
- Hired, fired, motivated, and evaluated staff of up to 15 in office, sales, and warehouse
- Ordered all equipment and supplies
- Managed accounts payable/receivable and financial statements; proved effective in collection of outstanding accounts
- Generated sales to national and midwest area client firms
- Provided information to engineers on appropriate equipment to meet their needs, within budgetary limits
- Worked with purchasing agents; expedited customer service needs
- Coordinated sales reports with available inventory
- Scheduled all shipments, ensuring on-time delivery

HATTRICK EQUIPMENT RENTALS, Grove City, OH
Assistant Supervisor, 1978-1981

EDUCATION CAPITAL UNIVERSITY, Columbus, OH
Bachelor's Degree in Accounting, 1977

REFERENCES Available upon request

- Summary of qualifications highlights candidate's acquired professional skills.

- Most recent work experience is emphasized.

OPERATIONS MANAGER (Financial Services)

CHRIS SMITH
178 Green Street
Chester, PA 19013
(215) 555-5555

SUMMARY OF QUALIFICATIONS

- Self-motivated; able to set effective priorities to achieve immediate and long-term goals, ensure smooth work-flow and meet operational deadlines.
- Developed interpersonal and communications skills, having dealt with a diversity of professionals, clients, and staff members.
- Computer-trained: WordPerfect, Lotus 1-2-3, FileMaker.

PROFESSIONAL EXPERIENCE

CARTER FINANCIAL SERVICES, Chester, PA   8/92-Present
Operations/Staff Manager, Corporate Finance Group, 9/94-Present
Provide short-term assistance to areas with unexpected volumes; assist with procedure writing, work flow analysis, and special projects. Assist in restructuring of work processing; prepare monthly quality analysis reports on team productivity.

Supervisor, Transaction Processing Department, 1/93-9/94
Hired, trained, and supervised staff of 12; maintained employee records, performance evaluations, and recommendations. Ensured timely processing of client/shareholder transactions.

Supervisor, Research Department, 8/92-1/93
Supervised staff of 10. Analyzed research requests; allocated work; microfilm activities and maintenance of film documentation and archive inventory records.

CHESTERTOWN INSURANCE COMPANY, Chester, PA   9/89-8/92
Sales Agent
Developed, implemented, and coordinated life/health insurance programs for clients; counseled clients on program benefits provided by respective employers.

EDUCATION

CARTER FINANCIAL SERVICES, Chester, PA
Operations Management Training Program, 3/94-9/94

WIDENER UNIVERSITY, Chester, PA
B.A. History, 1992

PERSONAL

Willing to travel and/or relocate.

- Specific dates of employment (month and year) are ideal for candidates with no gaps in work history.

- Participation in company-sponsored training programs adds depth to candidate's educational background.

OPERATIONS MANAGER (Human Services)

CHRIS SMITH
178 Green Street
Phoenix, AZ 85023
(602) 555-5555

PROFESSIONAL EXPERIENCE

1987 to Present   LASSITER HUMAN SERVICES, Phoenix, AZ

Operations Manager, 1989 to Present

Manage and coordinate all touring activities including scheduling, travel and accommodations planning, and international support for 150 students traveling to approximately 200 cities annually.

- Integral member of management team involved in goal planning, forecasting, cast evaluation, and problem solving.
- Lead and provide guidance to cast members.
- Manage, train, and support up to 15 public relations representatives in the program's marketing effort.
- Train, supervise, and evaluate operations interns.
- Select and train advance cast personnel in specific city travel and performance guidelines including logistics, scheduling, cultural information, and team communication.
- Direct and facilitate planning meetings; act as liaison between cast members, management and sponsors.
- Logistics Coordinator for city-to-city travel in 20 countries on 5 continents; ensure safety compliance.
- Conduct daily status/informational meetings.
- Maintain Operations Department budget.
- Interview cast applicants, and assess and determine eligibility and qualifications.
- Currently assigned to the training and development of Health Services Coordinators; developed new training program to accommodate shift in coordinator's role and created present training manual; oversee health care of 550 crew, staff, and trainees; train participants to deal with emergency situations, illness, nutrition, and the unique problems encountered in foreign cities.

Health Services Coordinator, 1987 to 1989

- Assumed increasing operations responsibilities.
- Oversaw the health and nutritional needs of the cast and staff during tour, including health maintenance, emergencies, counseling, direct care, and coordination with physicians.
- Directed meal planning, budgeting, and preparation.
- Presented self health care seminars.

1984 to 1987   KEEGAN MEDICAL CENTER, Lake Havasu City, AZ

Staff RN/Rehabilitation and Medical Unit

- Assumed Charge responsibilities when necessary.
- Practiced Modular Nursing; directed and supervised aides and LPNs in direct patient care.
- Selected member, Stroke Education Committee, involved in the implementation of patient/family educational programs.
- Interdisciplinary Team volunteer, Hospice of the Southwest, 1985-1987.

EDUCATION

University of Arizona, Tucson, AZ
B.S. Nursing, 1983

- Most recent job experience is described in detail; previous positions are listed more briefly.

- Education is de-emphasized because candidate's work history is strong.

PRESIDENT (Banking)

CHRIS SMITH
178 Green Street
Helena, MT 59601
(406) 555-5555

OBJECTIVE: A **Senior Management** position which would take advantage of more than twenty years of varied, in-depth background.

CAREER SUMMARY:

Executive skilled in Banking Operations and Data Processing Systems. Strong background in Retail Banking, Marketing, Planning, Budgeting and P & L Management. Demonstrated record of developing and implementing solutions to multidimensional complex operational problems.

CALLIOPE SAVINGS BANK, Helena, MT

1991-Present *President*

Originally hired as Executive Vice-President and subsequently elected President in June of 1992. Company provides check processing, consulting and other services to 40 banks. Developed and conducted corporate planning and strategy meetings. In addition to having overall responsibility for operations, also responsible for financial management and P & L for the company. Company presently employs 65 people and processes 30 million checks per year. Company turned profit within 2 years of start-up. Developed data processing delivery system analysis. . . recommendations were adopted by 10 banks.

1980-1991, THE PRUDENT SAVINGS INSTITUTION, Billings, MT
(Asset size: one billion dollars)

1989-1991 *Vice-President - Division Head of Banking Division*

Under the direction of Chairman of the Board, responsible for administrating, planning and directing the retail banking activities of the Bank. Conferred with Senior Management and recommended programs to achieve Bank's objectives. Responsibility included: Personnel, Salary Administration, Budget Administration, Performance Planning, Sales Management and other duties related to operational areas.

1987-1989 *Vice-President - Marketing*

Administrated and directed marketing activities of the Bank. Organized and planned actions impacting on various publics supporting Bank's markets. Worked with Divisions and outside agencies to develop plans which supported Division's objectives. Supervised the following: Liaison with Advertising and Public Relations firms; the development and sales of Bank services to various businesses; and development and control of the Advertising and Public Relations budgets.

1984-1987 *Vice-President - Savings Division*

(continued)

■ Chronological format illustrates a clear career path.

■ Summary grabs the reader's attention with powerful skills and qualifications.

1980-1984   ***Assistant Vice-President*** - *Savings Division*

1974-1980   ***Programmer***

EDUCATION:

BOWDOIN COLLEGE, Brunswick, ME
Bachelors Degree, English, 1973

COLBY COLLEGE, Waterville, ME
Masters Degree, Finance, 1977

SPECIAL EDUCATION:
Graduate School of Savings Banking

NAMSB - Carroll College - 1980
Management Development Program - NAMSB

University of Montana - 1982
Marketing School

*Rocky Mountain College -*1984
Various courses in: Economics, Finance, Law, Public Speaking, Speed Reading and Banking.

PROFESSIONAL ACTIVITIES:

Contributor, Hiking For Stress Relief	Present
Serve on Horizons in Corporate Clout	Present
Assistant Professor of Business, Rocky Mountain College	1986-1992

HOBBIES:

Hiking, Jogging, Mountain Climbing

REFERENCES:

Furnished upon request.

PRESIDENT (Marketing)

CHRIS SMITH
178 Green Street
Camden, NJ 08034
(609) 555-5555

CAPABILITIES
Advertising/Sales
Product/Market Research
In-House Publications
Marketing/Consumer Products
Mail Order/Catalog Sales
Merchandising
Architectural Design/Residential Construction

OBJECTIVE
To join a firm in need of an individual skilled in advertising, market research, sales and merchandising of consumer-oriented product lines. Will consider flex-time, per diem or project assignments.

SUMMARY OF QUALIFICATIONS
- Experienced in the management of a catalog business from product research and procurement to ultimate sale.
- Strong background in catalog development, media selection and advertising design.
- Expertise in the development and maintenance of complex customer database, inventory control systems, and forms design.
- Additional experience with educational materials cataloging, preparation of instructional inserts, and corporate communications.
- *Bachelor of Science in Business with concentration in Advertising.*
- Strong sales, marketing, organizational, and communication skills directed towards merchandising consumer-oriented products and public relations publications.
- Especially skilled in developing sales techniques designed to increase customer loyalty and sales volume.
- Experience with trade show, auctions, lot bidding, pricing, packaging, and customer service.
- Capable of working effectively in a number of areas requiring creative, innovative thinking and the ability to deal with people using an individual or team approach.

(continued)

■ For upward-bound professionals with a strong track record, the chrono-functional resume is the strongest tool available.

■ Two pages is an acceptable length for top positions.

(continued)

EXPERIENCE

PRESIDENT/GENERAL MANAGER
The Windmere Corp., Camden, NJ   **1989-Present**
Responsibilities and accomplishments:
- Successfully started this mail-order business specializing in American Antiques and related collectibles to an international customer base.
- Manage full range of sales functions from research and procurement of products for resale through selection of and advertising in publications.
- Set up systems, procedures, and techniques for establishing and maintaining an up-to-date customer base and detailed information as to past purchases and types of collectible wants.
- Designed forms, implemented inventory control system and developed quality packaging and mailing methods to assure quality customer service. Maintained direct contact with clients via mail or phone communication.
- Attend auctions and special conferences in Boston, Los Angeles, Houston, Detroit and other metropolitan cities.
- Hire, train, and supervise the activities of personnel in related merchandising and customer service functions.

CORPORATE COMMUNICATIONS ASSISTANT
Bird, Inc., Convent Station, NJ   **1985-89**
Responsibilities and accomplishments:
- Assisted the Director of Public Relations. Controlled all aspects of a bimonthly, in-house publication distributed to employees and their families.
- Traveled to various Bird locations to conduct on-site interviews with employees and management, planned and scheduled photo sessions, wrote articles on employees and company events, and coordinated printing and distribution.

Related areas of experience:
- For two years, was employed by Hayden Education Company. Cataloged and wrote instructional materials for the assembly of educational products for science curricular. Worked closely with the R&D Department during final product development. Assisted Customer Service Manager during major promotional campaigns via direct contact with end-users.

EDUCATION
Fairleigh Dickinson University, Madison, NJ
Bachelor of Science in Business with Minor in Advertising, 1985

ASSOCIATIONS
American Management Association

INTERESTS
Cycling, fishing, woodwork

PRODUCT MANAGER

CHRIS SMITH
178 Green Street
Dunnellon, FL 34433
(813) 555-5555

OBJECTIVE

A position requiring comprehensive product management, product/protocol development and clinical research/nursing skills to obtain FDA product approval.

EXPERIENCE

Estrade, Inc., Dunnellon, FL   **October 1992-Present**
Product Manager

- Provide a comprehensive coordination of all product development activities, from research to market, to fulfill the ultimate objective of a commercially marketable product.
- Devise, implement and evaluate training and educational materials for providers of ALT services.
- Follow-up on the continuous assessment and evaluation of product application needs and ALT provider needs through collaboration with multidisciplinary team (clinical research, process development, research and development, and regulatory affairs).
- Assist in the strategic planning for the development of further applications for ALT and the adaptation of cell processing techniques for other clinical indications.
- Assemble and manage multidisciplinary project teams for product development of each application of ALT.
- Prepare and present the clinical aspects of protocols to physicians' investigative groups.

Manager - Clinical Services   **October 1989-September 1992**

- Developed, managed and provided ongoing evaluation of clinical training and staff development plans for use in fifteen company-operated outpatient treatment centers and participating clinical research facilities throughout the country.
- Participated in the hiring, orientation and technical training of clinical personnel. Provided ongoing assessment of clinical performance including annual performance evaluations.
- Designed and implemented Clinical Quality Assurance/Quality Improvement Plans for use in company-operated outpatient treatment centers.

St. Theresa's Hospital   **1983-1989**
Staff RN

- Provided primary nursing care of critically ill pediatric patients in a tertiary care facility. Responsible for patient and family education for discharge planning and home care placement.

EDUCATION

Boston College, Chestnut Hill, MA
Bachelor of Science Degree - Nursing, 1983

COMPUTER LITERACY

Windows, Microsoft Word, E-Mail, Patient Data Systems. Work with systems consultants on the design and implementation of data management systems including remote access.

■ Job objective is clearly defined.

■ Note candidate's successful career transition.

PRODUCTION MANAGER

CHRIS SMITH
178 Green Street
St. Paul, MN 55105
(612) 555-5555

CAREER OBJECTIVE

Efficient supervisor seeks a team leader position to help increase productivity and meet or exceed company goals.

BACKGROUND SUMMARY

Extensive and diversified supervisory experience in computer, office furniture, and boat manufacturing operations. Particularly effective in increasing productivity and capacity. Demonstrated ability to learn new skills quickly. Able to supervise new departments without prior experience and meet production goals. Successfully motivate employees. Excellent interpersonal skills. Gained reputation for honesty and placed in a position of trust.

SUMMARY OF ACCOMPLISHMENTS

- Supervised the start-up of second shift shipping department. Trained new employees, reached full capacity while maintaining quality and production goals.
- Instructed Quality Development courses.
- Participated in upgrading assembly systems at Lennon and Epstein Systems.
- Consistently met and/or surpassed production goals. Supervised same day shipping of orders.
- Participated with Lennon management team in the move of logistics, service operations from St. Paul to Winona facility. Received cash achievement award for this project.
- Operated computerized warehouse management, inventory control and order processing systems.
- Researched requirements and supervised the development of a high-tech paint laboratory including procurement and staffing.
- Planned, arranged and supervised rework groups which traveled to on-site locations to perform engineering repairs and other problem-solving activities.
- Supervised development of new preassembled components of cabin cruisers at Howell Boat Company.
- Consistently built and maintained strong relationships with vendors and customers through close and effective communication.
- Supervised, scheduled and coordinated production of four departments in a metal fabrication operation.

(continued)

- Since candidate has held six jobs as production supervisor, he/she chooses not to repeat same job description six times.

- Instead, candidate summarizes work history under "Summary of Accomplishments."

(continued)

CAREER HISTORY
Epstein Systems, St. Paul, MN

Production Supervisor   1991-Present
Shipping
Production Supervisor   1987-1991
Publications Assembly
Production Supervisor   1985-1987
Maintenance

Lennon Metal, Winona, MN

Production Supervisor   1982-1985
Welding/Assembly
Production Supervisor   1980-1982
Shipping

Howell Boat Company, Duluth, MN

Production Supervisor   1976-1980
Wood Assembly/Finishing
Gelcoat Gun Operator   1972-1976

EDUCATION
University of Minnesota, Duluth, MN
B.A. Business Administration, 1982

Mankato State University, Mankato, MN
A.S. Electronic Technology, 1972

TRAINING
Word for Windows, dBase III, Lotus 1-2-3
Orienting New Employee Seminar, Advanced Quality Circle Leader Training, QED
Paint Defects, Paint Systems, Blueprint Reading, Arc Welding
Engineering Drawing, Time and Motion Study

PROGRAM MANAGER

CHRIS SMITH
178 Green Street
Shawnee, OK 74801
(405) 555-5555

BACKGROUND SUMMARY
Extensive experience in customer relations with a major manufacturer of electronic kit products. Special program management skills utilizing the team concept for product development. Program manager for successful federal contracts and the development of four commercial micro computer systems.

CAREER HISTORY
RICOCHET DATA, Shawnee, OK   1990-Present
Program Manager
Develop and coordinate short- and long-range plans for the design and introduction of new microcomputer products.
- Create work breakdown structure. Identify required resources.
- Develop master charts to track major milestones and critical path activities.
- Served on a management task force assigned to develop a set of work instructions for the introduction of outsourced products.
- Reduced product time to market by 25%.

LORENZ COMPANY, Oklahoma City, OK   1976-1990
Computer Sales Coordinator   1985-1990
Provided customer assistance in selecting the computer components best suiting their requirements.
- Evaluated customer needs and recommended the best hardware and software solution.

Retail Store Manager   1981-1985
Managed the Lorenz factory retail store providing sales and service for over 200 products.
- Generated gross annual sales in excess of $2 million for four consecutive years.
- Managed a sales and service staff of eight people.
- Provided superior customer service and support.

Product Technical Consultant   1976-1981
Provided technical consultation to customers via telephone and letter on any problem they might experience during the assembly and operation of their kit.
- Maintained sixty to eighty customer contacts per day.
- Developed an in-depth technical knowledge of the product line.
- Improved customer relations.

EDUCATION
Oral Roberts University, Tulsa, OK
B.A. Management, 1984

Phillips University, Enid, OK
Certification: Broadcaster Transmitter Service
Certification: Radio and Television Service

■ Bullets call attention to candidate's major successes.

■ Including professional licensure and accreditations can be essential for certain fields of work.

PROJECT MANAGER

CHRIS SMITH
178 Green Street
Bozeman, MT 59715
(406) 555-5555

PROFESSIONAL EXPERIENCE

1991-1994 FERRIS CONSTRUCTION CORPORATION   Bozeman, MT
<u>Project Manager/Superintendent</u>
Oversaw daily field and office operations of a construction corporation handling commercial and residential projects.
- Provided on-site management and quality control to ensure projects met time and budget requirements, and were built in accordance with contract documents.
- Coordinated and scheduled subcontractors and suppliers.
- Worked closely with architects and engineers in reviewing drawings and specifications.
- Scheduled, conducted and participated in project meetings.
- Oversaw cost control/coding and payroll.
- Prepared budgets, estimates, bids, proposals, schedules, contracts, subcontracts, and work scopes.
- Negotiated subcontract agreements, purchase orders and general contracts with clients.

1988-1990 SONORA ASSOCIATES   Anceney, MT
<u>Superintendent</u>
Managed all aspects of commercial construction projects.
- Coordinated subcontractors and suppliers.
- Provided quality control on various projects.
- Worked closely with designers, engineers and architects to ensure projects were built in accordance with contract documents.
- Supervised carpenters/laborers and subcontractors.
- Generated daily/weekly progress reports.
- Reviewed subcontracts and implemented operations.

1983-1988 M. CARDILLO & SONS CONSTRUCTION COMPANY   Belgrade, MT
<u>Carpenter Foreman</u>
Oversaw all daily carpentry-related operations.
- Provided quality control.
- Hired, trained and supervised up to 10 carpenters/helpers.
- Logged time for payroll.

1977-1982 Various Contractors throughout Montana
- Gained experience in union/nonunion, rough/finish, and residential/commercial construction. Later developed specialty in finish work.

LICENSURE   Montana Supervisor's License #325925

EDUCATIONAL BACKGROUND

MONTANA STATE UNIVERSITY, Bozeman, MT
Construction Management, 1977

- ■ Education is de-emphasized because candidate's work history is strong.

- ■ Layout is clean and well-organized.

PROPERTY MANAGER

CHRIS SMITH
178 Green Street
Golden, CO 80401
(303) 555-5555

PROFESSIONAL OBJECTIVE

Seeking new challenges in Property Development and Management. Offering experience and skill in negotiations, management, purchasing, leasing, staff supervision and construction/renovation.

EXPERIENCE

1978 to present PETERSON PROPERTIES, Golden, CO
Property Manager, 1981 to present
- Negotiate lease and rental agreements; oversee capital improvements, maintenance and modifications for 175 residential units and 150,000 square feet of commercial space in 7 different buildings.
- Hire, supervise and train staff of 50, including maintenance, construction, security and clerical personnel; coordinate with in-house legal staff.
- Prepare yearly cash budgets for each property; assist legal staff in the preparation and presentation of materials and pleadings for tax proceedings, rent control hearings and building permit applications.
- Design and consult on building renovations; solicit and assess bids; hire and oversee subcontractors.
- Serve as Investment Appraiser, traveling to various property sites and preparing financial analyses and feasibility studies of possible property acquisitions.
- Supervised 4-condominium, $500,000 construction project; assessed property and negotiated purchase; obtained permits and appropriate designs; consulted and assisted General Contractor; hired and supervised subcontractors.
- Participated in the negotiation of a $3.5 million lease for Peterson-owned commercial property.

Construction Manager, 1978 to 1980
- Functioned as Project Manager for the conversion of 75 apartment units to condominiums.
- Designed and implemented renovation plans, obtained permits and ordered all materials.
- Hired, supervised and scheduled crews; ensured compliance with work schedule and design plans.

EDUCATION COLORADO COLLEGE, Colorado Springs, CO
Bachelor of Science Degree in Finance, May, 1977.

LICENSES Real Estate Salesman's License, State of Colorado, 1980
Notary Public, State of Colorado, 1977

■ Statistics and dollar figures quantify candidate's accomplishments.

■ Candidate's work experience reads like a series of accomplishments, not just a list of job duties.

REGIONAL MANAGER

CHRIS SMITH
178 Green Street
Wheatland, ND 58079
(701) 555-5555

SUMMARY OF QUALIFICATIONS

- A high-energy, self-motivated, self-starter with the ability to develop and establish an efficient, highly productive work force.
- Expertise in staffing, training, motivation and evaluation of personnel to assure adherence to quality service, product specifications, and customer satisfaction.
- Active participation in development of Manager Training Program and Employee Certification Program.
- Sound knowledge of sales projections, budgets, cost-control systems and standardized procedures designed for stable operations and bottom-line profits.

EXPERIENCE

REGIONAL MANAGER
The Supreme Eatery, Hunter, ND   **1993-Present**

- Responsible for management of 10 stores. Oversee performance of approximately 150 employees including managers and assistant managers. Report to Director of Store Operations.
- Work with store managers on budgets, and management tracking. Open new stores, and negotiate and set up contracts for purchasing of foods, beverages and maintenance with local vendors and service companies.
- Worked with Training Manager on a Manager Training Program and Employee Certification for all employees designed to teach product specifications and procedures for customer service and quality product preparation.
- Conduct coaching, counseling, and motivational sessions, and work with store managers on budget responsibility and projections.
- Developed check list for opening, closing, safety, sanitation, security, and daily operations for use by managers in each unit.

ASSISTANT GENERAL MANAGER
The Roadside Restaurant, Gardner, ND   **1989-1993**

- Started as an Assistant Manager and was promoted to Assistant General Manager.
- Directed all personnel operations including the recruitment, training, evaluation and pay administration for 75 employees.
- Assisted in Employee Certification Process for 50 employees. Achieved total certification within two months. This resulted in increased efficiency and improved employee morale.
- Maintained inventory levels and supervised ordering. Increased sales by instituting daily specials and a Sunday Brunch. Significantly streamlined operations and lowered costs while maintaining high quality standards.

EDUCATION

North Dakota State University, Fargo, ND
Bachelor of Arts in English Literature, 1988

■ Summary of qualifications highlights candidate's acquired professional skills.

■ Resume tracks candidate's long list of impressive accomplishments and promotions.

RETAIL STORE MANAGER

CHRIS SMITH
178 Green Street
Los Angeles, CA 90035
(310) 555-5555

OBJECTIVE: A **Retail Management** position.

EXPERIENCE:
6/92-Present   SPINNER RECORDS CORPORATION, Los Angeles, CA
Manager   5/94-Present
- Operated Spinner's largest volume store (approximately $50,000/week).
- Hire, train, and coordinate a staff of 26.
- Direct sales floor activities.
- Handle all merchandising, inventory control, ordering, cash control, and maintenance functions.
- Coordinate special promotions and events.
- Prepare daily sales reports.
- Interact with corporate personnel at all levels.
- Assist in developing local marketing and advertising strategies.

Assistant Manager   6/92-4/94
- Oversaw full range of retail management responsibilities.
- Assisted in merchandising.
- Opened/closed store; handled customer service complaints and cash control.
- Supervised and motivated employees.

4/90 -5/92   SANTA ANA SHOPS, Santa Ana, CA
Assistant Manager
- Handled hiring, merchandising, and cash control for this small convenience store.
- Supervised 15 employees.
- Opened and closed market.
- Prepared bank deposits and daily sales reports.

ACHIEVEMENTS:
- Won two merchandising display contests.
- Received the "Super Spinner" Sales Award for exceeding sales goals, 1994.

REFERENCES:
Furnished upon request.

■ Specific dates of employment (month and year) are ideal for candidates with no gaps in work history.

■ Impressive achievements further enhance candidate's qualifications.

SERVICE MANAGER

CHRIS SMITH
178 Green Street
Mill Valley, CA 94941
(415) 555-5555

SUMMARY OF QUALIFICATIONS

- Expertise encompasses all phases of Field Service support and reports including: Labor distribution, contract, billable and warranty service report processing, expense, accounts payable, parts orders, warranties, repairs, maintenance orders and related documentation.
- Effectively provide administrative support to District Service, Zone Manager and Service Technicians.
- Extensive customer contact in troubleshooting, and resolving problems pertaining to service disputes or service contract renewals.

EXPERIENCE

SERVICE COORDINATOR
Western Services Group, Oakland, CA   1988-Present

- Provide administrative support to District Service Manager and 6 Service Technicians servicing approximately 200 hospitals. Train and supervise assisting personnel.
- Monitor open incidents, report calls and maintain and monitor Field Service Engineers tracking logs.
- Involved in daily contact with customers to troubleshoot and resolve problems pertaining to billing, unpaid tax balances, excessive charges or short payments, warranties, service contract renewals, and other service-related matters while maintaining good customer relations.
- Generate and maintain service-related and quotation correspondence. Process contract proposals, agings, contract agencies, and contract terminations. Prepare warranty certificates to assure issuance of commissions to correct salesmen.
- Maintain Return Authority log encompassing credit, inventory and repair exchange inventory, and issue or monitor credits to service customers.
- Audit travel and expense reports, process general vouchers, hours for payroll and purchase orders for vendors.

ACCOUNTS RECEIVABLE/CREDIT & COLLECTION AGENT
Sampson and Company, San Francisco, CA   1979-1986

- Advanced from Accounts Receivable Clerk to progressively responsible positions involving finance, credit/collection, and record keeping for domestic and foreign markets.
- Responsibilities included: Cash receipts, disbursements, adjustments, closings, preparation of worksheets, computer input, and projection of cash flow.
- Handled collection for one parent company and three subsidiaries. Decreased outstanding accounts receivable balances substantially and retained excellent customer relations.
- Directed credit investigations. Successfully resolved all disputes.

EDUCATION

Santa Clara University, Santa Clara, CA
Bachelor of Arts Degree, Human Services, 1978
Minor: Business

■ Specific numeric and dollar figures quantify candidate's achievements.

■ Job descriptions are very specific.

TELECOMMUNICATIONS MANAGER

CHRIS SMITH
178 Green Street
Bremerton, WA 98310
(206) 555-5555

OBJECTIVE   Management position requiring strong communications, sales, supervisory and customer relations skills in the field of Financial Services.

EXPERIENCE   THE SHERWOOD CORPORATION, Bremerton, WA

Telecommunications Director
1991-Present
Successfully manage 80 Problem/Resolution Telephone Representatives. Develop and implement customer service procedures. Responsible for year-end positive variance of $5.2 million budget.

Manager, Problem Resolution Center
1989-1991
Effectively developed rotational instruction for inbound telephone managers and supervisors. Areas included Account Analysis, Trading Support, Management Support and Payments.

Manager, Telephone Operations
1988-1989
Planned and scheduled 24-hour operations and ongoing training for 600 telephone representatives at new operations center in Bremerton. Relocated from native Vermont as part of start-up team.

Supervisor, Retail Sales, Woodstock, VT
1987-1988
Promoted to supervisor of 15-30 representatives. Responsible for individual and group performance and productivity.

Telephone Representative
1986-1987
One of the first Sherwood telephone representatives to be fully cross-trained in sales, customer service, and mutual fund trading.

EDUCATION   **Heritage College,** Toppenish, WA
Bachelor of Science Candidate.
History/Political Science Major
Estimated completion, December, 1996

- Specific numeric and dollar figures quantify candidate's achievements.

- Resume indicates a series of promotions.

TRANSPORTATION MANAGER

CHRIS SMITH
178 Green Street
Flushing, NY 11385
(718) 555-5555

PROFESSIONAL OBJECTIVE
A challenging, growth-oriented position in **TRANSPORTATION INDUSTRIES.**

PROFESSIONAL EXPERIENCE
1990-1995 **MARCONI SYSTEMS**, Flushing, NY
Shift Supervisor/Chief Operator
- Supervised shift of 10 employees in monitoring, repairing, and installing electronic protective systems for both domestic and corporate clients.
- Maintained control console for incoming calls on a guard-express with on-call duty, 24 hours daily, in emergency situations.
- Reviewed client needs and made recommendations as to what services best met customer requirements.
- Expedited emergency services to a 75,000 individualized program.
- Strong interpersonal and communication skills required.

1985-1990 **NEW YORK STATE LABORATORIES**, Elmira, NY
Maintenance
- Maintained general laboratory with regard to safety and sanitation within a strict health environment.
- Maintained inventory control of supplies and equipment orders and re-order storage units.
- Responded to departmental work-orders on special needs and maintenance repair.

MILITARY
UNITED STATES ARMY
Mogadishu, Somalia
Rank: E-4, Honorable Discharge
Shipboard Duty: USS Jagger, USS Richards, and USS Wyman

EDUCATION
DUNCAN INSTITUTE OF TECHNOLOGY, New York, NY
Studies: Engineering & Drafting, 1984

NEW YORK SCHOOL OF STEAM ENGINEERING, New York, NY
Certificate: Steam Engineering, 1983

NEW YORK TECHNICAL HIGH SCHOOL, New York, NY
Diploma, Engineering/Drafting, 1982

LICENSURE Auxiliary Police Officer

■ Job objective gives resume focus without limiting candidate's opportunities.

■ Use of boldface and italics provides a clean and crisp presentation.

VENDING MANAGER

Chris Smith
178 Green Street
Yuma, AZ 85365
(602) 555-5555

PROFESSIONAL OBJECTIVE
Seeking a challenging position which will utilize and advance Supervisory/Managerial skills and a commitment to excellence.

PROFESSIONAL EXPERIENCE
PLUMMER FOOD SERVICES, Yuma, AZ
Vending Manager, 1/91-present
- Interview, hire, train, schedule and supervise 45 service representatives including 3 territorial supervisors.
- Purchase merchandise from wholesale operations.
- Responsible for overall inventory control for $4.5 million department.
- Perform payroll functions including maintenance of records and payroll adjustments.
- Fill in for service representatives when necessary.
- Maintain close contact with president of company regarding determination of staffing and equipment requirements.
- Responsible for implementing maintenance programs for a fleet of 42 vehicles.
- Directly responsible for cost reduction and improved efficiency; assisted in pulling company out of bankruptcy.

THE LOTHROP CORPORATION, Chandler, AZ
Operations Consultant, 4/90-10/90
- Assigned to Regional Headquarters to troubleshoot and work on special projects.
- Surveyed accounts for new bid proposals.
- Consulted with management regarding improvements, cost reduction and quality control throughout western United States.

Director of Operations, Vending/Food Services, 7/89-4/90
- Supervised 4 managers, 2 mechanics, and 30 general staff of vending operations with gross sales of over $1 million annually; responsible for technical support of 600 pieces of equipment.
- Purchased all products from wholesale operations; handled accounts payable, payroll, and preventive maintenance programs for all equipment.
- Adhered to Federal, State, and Local laws governing food service operations and fair labor practices.

Operations Supervisor, 10/87-7/89
- Assumed overall responsibility for vending operations.
- Hired, trained, and supervised staff.
- Doubled account sales.

General Supervisor, 6/87-10/87
- Supervised staff of 30.
- Determined and monitored all vending routes of Southeastern branch; conducted daily field inspections.
- Communicated and followed up with various account executives.

- Candidate's work experience reads like a series of accomplishments, not just a list of job duties.

- Percentages and dollar amounts quantify candidate's accomplishments.

VICE-PRESIDENT (Construction)

CHRIS SMITH
178 Green Street
Laconia, NH 03102
(603) 555-5555

OBJECTIVE
An Executive Management position in REAL ESTATE OPERATIONS/DEVELOPMENT/MARKETING.

SELECTED CAREER HIGHLIGHTS
- *Multidisciplined Professional:* Real Estate background encompassing Business Development, Strategic Planning, Marketing, and Construction Project Management.
- *Marketing Edge:* Developed a vital network of business and industry contacts instrumental in Raze's acquisition of key contracts with the China Society, Jen Bright, and Weld Corporations.
- *Technical Expertise:* Offer BSME with proven abilities to estimate costs, design and install electrical, telecommunications, fire and life safety and related technological systems.
- *Project Executive:* Full profit and loss accountability for key client projects involving scheduling, cost accounting, cash flow analysis, purchasing and professional relations.
- *Human Resource Management:* Recruit, assign, motivate and evaluate management and support staff. Develop and implement progressive policy for 500 employees.
- *Cost Conscious:* Developed innovative cost-saving programs including cellular telephone service and Raze' T-Bar Systems.
- *Sales Achiever:* Reputation for excellent sales presentations. Closed the largest single sale within Meyer for an infrared lighting control system.
- *Skilled Negotiator:* Deal successfully with U.S. and Asian corporate representatives. Handled prime contractor negotiations, secured an equity position with RSSO for Raze' 1500 room Manhattan Ritz Hotel.

PROFESSIONAL EXPERIENCE
RAZE REALTY & CONSTRUCTION COMPANY, INC. - 1986-Present
SENIOR VICE-PRESIDENT/
EXECUTIVE VICE-PRESIDENT & PROJECT EXECUTIVE:
RAZE CONSTRUCTION CORPORATION   Laconia, NH
Coordinate and execute a variety of construction management projects for a leading real estate development firm specializing in hotel, office and commercial facilities construction and renovation. Home office responsibilities include driving marketing and sales efforts, developing and presenting proposals with cost estimates; negotiate terms of customer contracts with domestic and international corporations. Provide quality preconstruction consulting, design and project management services. Provide critical strategic planning; execute project staging and logistics.

Field services include all aspects of design, planning and execution of assigned construction and tenant installation projects for commercial clients. Analyze existing and proposed designs with a specialty in electrical and telecommunications systems; suggest improvements to plans, methods, and materials. Schedule projects, select and procure materials; assign personnel and engage qualified subcontractors. Oversee all phases of project execution; approve engineering/design changes; troubleshoot and resolve complex technical problems, consistently meeting project deadlines and highest possible quality standards. Maintain clear communications and positive relations with clients, subcontractors and the community.

(continued)

- Two pages is an acceptable length for top positions.

- For upward-bound professionals with a strong track record, the chrono-functional resume is the strongest tool available.

- Head of Raze Technologies Group, handle all technology-related installations on trading floors, security, life safety and high-tech wiring systems.
- Serve on Raze's Personnel and Marketing committees.
- Highly skilled in use of computer systems; utilize numerous software programs for effective project scheduling and cost accounting applications.
- Expert troubleshooter; identify complex problems; resourceful and inventive in implementing creative solutions with enhanced sensitivity to cost, efficiency, and deadlines.

Projects include:

- *FOUR CROWS: Managed construction of the 350-room, 4-star luxury hotel, tallest in the world.*
- *THE CHINA SOCIETY: Executed this below-sidewalk expansion with extreme sensitivity to ongoing operations.*
- *DURITZ HOUSE HOTEL: Executed room renovations, new ballroom and lobby in original Art Deco style.*
- *THE HORATIO HOTEL: Undertook gut renovation including new room construction, public spaces, ballroom.*
- *SCHULTZ HOTEL: Developed architectural and systems design alternatives and cost estimates for extensive renovation.*
- *PENELOPE INN: Local Law 16 upgrade.*
- *GUSTAV KLIMT CENTER: Completed an infrastructure upgrade; installed security and building automation.*
- *HOTEL MONROE in Boston*
- *MYOKO AMERICA: Handled bidding and purchasing of cabling and installation for trading floors of U.S. branch of Asian trading company.*

PROJECT MANAGER   1976-1985
LINDSEY, KEENE, INC.   North Conway, NH

Estimated project costs, sourced and negotiated purchasing, scheduled, directed and coordinated a variety of quality office building projects. Responsible for managing construction projects and ensuring compliance with regulatory requirements and highest quality standards. Controlled and managed overhead and project budget costs; approved selection of subcontractors, systems and materials decisions. Performed cost accounting and administrative tasks ensuring peak profit performance.

Projects include:

- BIDLAW INSURANCE: Managed construction projects in 2 company buildings.
- SPECIFIC OIL: Oversaw construction for corporate guest facilities.

ADDITIONAL EXPERIENCE

ADJUNCT ASSISTANT PROFESSOR   1990-Present
Boston University Real Estate Program   Boston, MA

EDUCATION
BACHELOR OF SCIENCE IN MECHANICAL ENGINEERING, 1976
Massachusetts Institute of Technology, Cambridge, MA

Additional courses, workshops and seminars include:
Several REAL ESTATE topics and MANAGEMENT seminars

VICE-PRESIDENT (Sales and Marketing)

CHRIS SMITH
178 Green Street
Minneapolis, MN 55404
(612) 555-5555

OBJECTIVE:
The opportunity to utilize background and experience in National/International Marketing, Sales & Purchasing in a Marketing & Sales or Off-Shore Sourcing position.

PROFESSIONAL EXPERIENCE:
Littleton and Keats, Minneapolis, MN
VICE-PRESIDENT   1990-Present
Background Information: For this $10 million, industry-leading producer of toys and related items manufactured & sold Nationally/Internationally through Toy Stores, Supermarket Chains, as well as Catalogs. Started as Purchasing Manager, assuming additional responsibilities for outside sales, and on basis of outstanding success in the development and handling of key accounts & general operations, advanced to current position of Vice-President in charge of Sales & Product Development.

ACCOMPLISHMENTS INCLUDE:
- Personal Sales over $4 million/year, while managing/working with network of over 46 sales organizations employing 150 sales representatives.
- Managed Development, Sourcing, Manufacturing and Importation of total Doll and Doll Accessory product lines from Far East & Europe. *Reduced cost of manufacture by 15%.*
- Added $350,000 at significant margin to Gross Sales through establishment of new division marketing line of Doll accessories. Developed new fashions projected at $600,000 first year sales.
- Developed new Sales Accounts, through establishment of national rep./distributor organization, from annual sales of $250,000 *to current volume of $850,000.*

Cattail Inc., Buffalo, NY
GENERAL MANAGER   1984-1990
- Supervised 30, including 8 inside & 9 outside sales personnel in the marketing & sales of all product lines, while setting up telemarketing program, developing special promotions, organizing/managing trade show participation, sourcing, and handling new product evaluations.
- Worked closely with 90 major manufacturers' representative organizations or individuals.
- Turned inventory up to 6 times/year.
- Negotiated several exclusive lines with companies responsible for production of over 50% of gross volume.
- Increased sales during this period from $2 million to $4.5 million.

■ Background information on present employers adds weight to already strong qualifications.

■ Statistics and dollar figures quantify candidate's accomplishments.

WAREHOUSE MANAGER

Confidential Resume of
CHRIS SMITH
178 Green Street
Hoboken, NJ 07030
(201) 555-5555

SUMMARY OF QUALIFICATIONS
- Large volume warehouse experience
- Special handling requirement experience
- Inventory, quality control and sanitation abilities
- Experience in truck fleet operations

EXPERIENCE

9/91 to Present AMERICAN CRYSTAL COMPANY, Hoboken, NJ

5/92 to Present Warehouse Manager
- Supervise staff of 17
- Manage a 25,000-square-foot warehouse with 7 bays and 3 fork lifts
- Schedule all employees
- Handle all special handling freight requirements
- Oversee rate negotiations, breakage and inventory control
- Service company-owned retail locations as well as a variety of distributors
- Direct rerouting and management of a 12-truck delivery fleet

9/91 to 5/92 Warehouse Supervisor
- Supervised four warehouse manager who were required to supply weekly reports regarding productivity numbers, expenses, overtime and overall operations
- Operated and directed activities in four warehouse operations representing supervision of 32 people and 35,000 square feet of warehouse space

6/89 to 9/91 CORNUCOPIA SHOPS, Hoboken, NJ
Assistant Warehouse Superintendent
- Supervise 175 warehouse employees in a 50,000 square foot warehouse
- Worked with both inbound and outbound dry groceries and non-foods; shipments totaled over 50 trailers a day moving 275,000 cases per week
- Prepared employee schedule
- Oversaw shipping, receiving, and inventory control

EDUCATION
Hoboken Community College, Hoboken, NJ
A.S. Business Administration, 1991

■ Header indicates candidate's desire for confidentiality.

■ Work experience is emphasized, while limited education is de-emphasized.

13

Health and Medical

Nature of Work

Health and medical workers help people prevent and deal with illness, work toward achieving and maintaining healthy lifestyles, and help to address and resolve related issues, such as insurance and medical claim forms. Medical and nurse practitioners work directly with patients and their families in dealing with health problems. Pharmacists and health care support workers assist patients by providing medical advice regarding prescriptions, insurance claim forms, and related issues. Researchers work to find and improve medical treatments and techniques.

Employment

Health care workers and managers are employed by hospitals and subsidiary service providers such as alcohol and drug abuse rehabilitation clinics, hospice facilities, home health care providers, and nursing homes. Doctors and dentists have the option of going into private or group practice. Research and teaching opportunities are available at university medical centers, teaching hospitals, and in the upstart biotechnical field.

Training

Nursing certification or medical licensure, combined with clinical or residence experience, are required to practice medicine. On the administrative side of the health care field, employers look for a business and/or health services administration background and a bachelor's or master's degree depending on the level of the position sought. A Ph.D. is usually required in teaching, consulting or research.

Job Outlook

Employment of medical and health care professionals is expected to grow faster than the average for all occupations through the year 2005, due to continued expansion of the health industry. The population is growing and aging, and health care needs increase sharply with age. In addition, new technologies permit health care workers to do more tests, perform more procedures, and treat conditions previously regarded as untreatable. Despite efforts to control costs, the payment of most services through private insurance, Medicare, and Medicaid will continue to encourage growth.

Earnings

In 1990, the average annual salary for dieticians, occupational therapists, recreational therapists, and speech pathologists was between $25,000 and $30,000. Pharmacists, physical therapists, physicians' assistants, and registered nurses earn between $35,000 and $40,000. At the other end of the spectrum, doctors have a yearly income of between $96,000 and $220,000.

CARDIOLOGIST

CHRIS SMITH, M.D.
178 Green Street
Payne Gap, KY 41537
(606) 555-5555

OBJECTIVE
A professional career opportunity in which to practice clinical cardiology in a group practice or hospital setting.

SUMMARY OF QUALIFICATIONS
- Two years as Cardiology Fellow with extensive experience covering full spectrum of clinical cardiology.
- Experience encompasses: Cardiac Catheterization and Angioplasty, Cardiac Pacing and Electrophysiology, Echocardiography, Exercise testing and nuclear imaging, In-patient and out-patient hospital care of cardiac patients.
- Two years of experience as a Clinical Instructor in Medicine at St. Martha's Hospital teaching interns, residents and medical students.
- Board Certified - Internal Medicine; Board Eligible in Cardiology.

EXPERIENCE
CARDIOLOGY FELLOW   **1993-Present**
St. Martha's Hospital, Payne Gap, KY
Responsibilities:
- As a Cardiology Fellow, utilize sophisticated, state-of-the-art systems, procedures and techniques, covering the full spectrum of clinical cardiology.
- Currently involved in research encompassing clinical evaluation of the Bundeen Cross Coronary Stent.
- Researching and preparing a review article dealing with Ventricular Arrhythmias.

INTERNSHIP AND RESIDENCY IN INTERNAL MEDICINE   **1990-1993**
St. Martha's Hospital, Payne Gap, KY
- With this 600-bed hospital, handled rotating assignments involving Intensive Care (Medical ICU, CCU); Emergency; In-patient/out-patient practice of general adult medicine.

EDUCATION
Boston College School of Medicine, Chestnut Hill, MA
MD Degree

University of Pennsylvania, Philadelphia, PA
Bachelor of Science Degree in Pre-Professional Studies

PROFESSIONAL QUALIFICATIONS
Diplomate, American Board of Internal Medicine
Board Eligible in Cardiology

■ Job objective clarifies candidate's career goal.

■ Summary of qualifications illustrate candidate's key credentials.

CHIROPRACTOR

DR. CHRIS SMITH
CHIROPRACTOR

178 Green Street
Dedham, MA 02026
(617) 555-1212

PROFESSIONAL HISTORY
Greater Boston Chiropractic Center, Boston, MA
Chiropractic Therapy, 1985 - Present

- Provide spinal manipulation and handle necessary muscular-skeletal needs of sports-injured patients.
- Alleviate pain in elderly and work-related injured patients.
- Assist the industrial accident injured in regaining strength and stamina.
- Provide information for insurance companies, workman's compensation, and third party billing procedures.

EDUCATION
Palmer College of Chiropractics, Davenport, IA
M.D., Degree
Graduated, 1985

University of Massachusetts, Boston, MA
B.S., Pre-Med
Graduated, 1983

CERTIFICATION / PROFESSIONAL AFFILIATIONS
Certified by the Commonwealth of Massachusetts

American Chiropractic Association
Massachusetts Chiropractic Society
Greater Boston Chiropractic Society
Sports Injury Council of the American Chiropractic Association

PUBLICATIONS
Spine, October 12, 1991, Volume 9.
"Correlations of Spinal Biomechanics and Childhood Asthma."

Journal of the ACA, May 3, 1989, Volume 19, Issue 5.
"Further Effects of Calcium on Geriatric Osteoporosis Patients."

■ Certification/professional affiliations section demonstrates candidate's active participation in field of medicine.

■ Publications indicate candidate's contributions to medical research literature.

CLINICAL DIRECTOR

CHRIS SMITH
178 Green Street
Cincinnati, OH 45221
(513) 555-5555

<u>EXPERIENCE</u>

KEITAL HOSPITAL, Cincinnati, OH
10/91-Present
Director, Clinical Services (5/91-Present)
- Services include emergency services, day services, outpatient services (adults and children) family therapy training program and psychology internship program.
- Provide direction and administration for large ambulatory services department in an urban mental health center. $3 million operating budget. 2000 active patients. 50,000 annual visits.
- Supervise 75 clinical, administrative, and staff employees.
- Coordinate program analysis, planning, and development.

Director, Emergency Psychiatric Services and Day Programs (8/88-5/91)
- Clinical and administrative responsibility for emergency service and psychiatric day programs.
- Managed thirty professional staff members.
- Maintained fiscal accountability, including the implementation, monitoring, and modification of operating budget.
- Responsible for management of psychiatric on-call physicians.

Director of Adult Day Treatment Programs (6/86-8/88)
- Oversee treatment activities for 50 patients involved in the acute day hospital and the long-term day treatment program.
- Coordinated treatment and discharge planning.

Psychologist (6/82-6/86)
- Provided group, family and individual treatment counseling for adults and adolescents in the day hospital setting.
- Provided assessment, contracting, treatment planning, and crisis intervention.

<u>EDUCATION</u>

Oberlin College, Oberlin, OH
Master's Degree in Counseling Psychology, 1982

Ohio State University, Lima, OH
Bachelor's Degree in Psychology, 1980
Honors Graduate

<u>LICENSE</u>

L.C.S.W., Level II Social Worker
State of Ohio

- Specific dates of employment (month and year) are ideal for candidates with no gaps in work history.

- Resume illustrates continual career progression.

DENTAL ASSISTANT

CHRIS SMITH
178 Green Street
Poughkeepsie, NY 12601
(601) 555-5555

OBJECTIVE

A position as a Medical Assistant or related position of responsibility where there is a need for clinical as well as administrative experience.

SUMMARY OF QUALIFICATIONS

- Over five years of experience as a Dental Assistant, and Medical Receptionist assisting in direct patient care and patient relations.
- Honor Graduate as Medical Assistant from National Education Center.
- Sound knowledge of medical terminology and clinical procedures.
- Certified in: First Aid; Cardiopulmonary Resuscitation; Electrocardiography.
- Additional experience as Receptionist/Secretary with an executive search/management consulting firm, financial management company, and realty firms.

HEALTH CARE EXPERIENCE

Dr. Herbert Dickey, M.D., Brooklyn, NY   **1993-Present**
- Perform accounts payable/receivable.
- Schedule patients for appointments.
- Prepare patients for surgical procedures; record temperature and blood pressure, insert intravenous units, and administer sedatives.
- Provide post-operative care; record vital signs every ten minutes until consciousness; establish patient comfort; provide necessary information to patients regarding new medications/possible side-effects.

Drs. William and Joseph Janell, New York, NY   **1992-93**
- Began as Dental Trainee, advanced to Dental Assistant.
- Sterilized instruments, processed X-rays, scheduled appointments, maintained patient relations.

Externship   **1990**
Internal Medicine Associates, Brooklyn, NY
- Multi-disciplined practice, including gastroenterology, rheumatology, endocrinology and cardiology.
- Took vital signs, performed urinalysis, EKGs, and blood chemistries. Maintained patient charts.

EDUCATION

State University of New York, Biminghamton, NY
A.S. Biology

COMPUTERS

Microsoft Word, Lotus 1-2-3

■ Summary of qualifications highlights candidate's achievements.

■ Education is listed towards bottom of resume because candidate's practical experience outweighs his/her degree.

DENTAL HYGIENIST (A)

CHRIS SMITH
178 Green Street
Upper Montclair, NJ
(201) 555-5555

OBJECTIVE

A full-time position as a Dental Hygienist in a private practice.

EMPLOYMENT

Dr. Rettman, D.M.D., Upper Montclair, NJ
Dental Hygienist   (1988 to present)
- Provide prophylaxis treatment to patients in a variety of situations; teeth cleaning, gum massage, oral hygiene education, and periodontal scaling.
- Monitor radiographs. Administer novocaine prior to painful procedures.
- Provide secretarial assistance: telephones, paperwork, scheduling, etc.

Dr. Grohowski, D.M.D., Princeton, NJ
Dental Assistant   (1985 to 1988)
- Assisted dentist in prophylactic procedures: provided necessary tools, sterilized equipment, comforted patients.

EDUCATION

Kelly School of Dental Hygiene, New York, NY
A.S. in Dental Hygiene, 1985
Course work included: Chemistry, Radiology, Nutrition, Periodontology, Pathology, Anatomy, Dental Equipment, Oral Embiology, Psychology, and Pharmacology.

LICENSURE

New Jersey Dental Hygiene License
National Board Dental Hygiene Exam (written - 90)
N.E.R.B. Dental Hygiene Exam (Clinical - 93, written -90)

REFERENCES

Available upon request.

■ Job objective is brief and to the point.

■ Use of boldface and italics provides a clean and crisp presentation.

DENTAL HYGIENIST (B)

Chris Smith
178 Green Street
Simi Valley, CA 93063
(805) 555-5555

OBJECTIVE

Seeking a full-time position as a Dental Hygienist in a private practice with a strong emphasis on prevention.

EDUCATION

Cooper School of Dental Hygiene, University of California
A.S. in Dental Hygiene, 1988
Course work included:

Chemistry/Biochemistry	Anatomy/Physiology
Radiology	Oral Embridogy
Nutrition	Dental Materials/lab
Periodontology	Psychology/Sociology
Pathology	Pharmacology

Dental Hygiene Lecture and Clinical Rotations:
Watersville School, Veteran's Administration Hospital

LICENSURE

California Dental Hygiene License
National Board Dental Examination (written-90)
N.E.R.B. Dental Hygiene Examination (clinical-95, written-84)

EMPLOYMENT

1989-Present   Dr. Race Banner, D.M.D., Eastham, MA
Dental Hygienist
- Perform prophylaxis, periodontal scaling, oral hygiene education, sealants, and radiographs. Occasional assisting and reception; related paperwork and scheduling.

1983-1989   Dr. John E. Quest, D.M.D., Bourne, MA
Assistant/Receptionist
- Provided general clinical and office support on a temporary basis.

PERSONAL

- Member, American Dental Hygiene Association.
- National Student Dental Hygiene Association, Past Member, Class Historian.

REFERENCES

Available upon request.

■ Relevant course work adds depth to candidate's educational background.

■ Including professional licensure and accreditations can be essential for certain fields of work.

DENTAL TECHNICIAN

CHRIS SMITH
178 Green Street
Kerryville,TX 78028
(512) 555-5555

OBJECTIVE
A full-time position in the field of Dental Technology.

PROFESSIONAL EXPERIENCE
LIBERTY SOLDIERS HOME, Kerryville, TX   1987–Present
Dental Technician
- Construct and repair full or partial dentures, metal or porcelain crowns, inlays, and bridges according to dental impressions and dentist's prescription.
- Utilize hand tools and dental laboratory equipment including curing tanks, grinders, polishers, lathes, drills, high heat furnaces, and dental surveyors to replace missing teeth and to restore teeth.
- Advise dental students on various phases of laboratory technology.
- Maintain and document related information and records.
- Monitor inventory and replenish stock when necessary.

EDUCATION
TEXAS TECH UNIVERSITY, Lubbock, TX   1986-1987
Certificate in Dental Technology
Lab work included:
- All aspects of Dental Laboratory
- Crown and bridge
- Porcelain fused to metal
- Dentures
- Partial dentures
- Mouth guards, retainers

PROFESSIONAL AFFILIATIONS
Dental Technicians of America (DTA)
Dental Hygiene Lecturer: Lubbock Elementary Schools, Veteran's Hospital, Southern Baptist Community Health Center and various local nursing homes

INTERESTS
Folk music, animation festivals, herbal gardens.

■ Job-related affiliations demonstrate candidate's active participation in his/her field.

■ Personal interests can provide a great topic for conversation during a job interview.

DENTIST

CHRIS SMITH D.M.D.
178 Green Street
Bellingham, WA 98225
(206) 555-5555

EXPERIENCE

1992-Present   **Owner-General Practice**
ZILAH DENTAL ASSOCIATES   **Bellingham, WA**
- Purchased large dental practice through a leveraged buy-out.
- Determined and successfully implemented long-term growth strategies.
- Supervised a staff consisting of two other dentists and six support personnel; providing comprehensive care for over 2000 patients.
- Doubled practice's growth through the implementation of a strategic marketing program.
- Led the office in steadily increasing production and revenues.
- Updated practice and computerized equipment.
- Presently facilitating transition of practice to new owner.

1991-1992   **Director/Dental Assistant**
                                                      Unit/Clinical Instructor
SEATTLE UNIVERSITY DENTAL SCHOOL   **Seattle, WA**
- Supervised clinic with rotating groups of seven dental students and eight support personnel.
- Evaluated student performance, analyzed financial viability of clinic and instituted plan to increase profitability.

1989-1991   **Dentist**
UNIFIED DENTAL CENTERS   **Moses Lake, WA**
- Provided comprehensive dental care and trained staff members.
- Allocated marketing budget.

1988   **Instructor of Clinical Periodontics**
UNIVERSITY OF WASHINGTON   **Seattle, WA**
- Supervised small groups of students during their first contact with patients.
- Developed lesson plans, demonstrated periodontal procedures, and evaluated student performance.

EDUCATION
1985-1989 **UNIVERSITY OF WASHINGTON, SCHOOL OF DENTAL MEDICINE**   **Seattle, WA**
Chairman of Ethical Board, Director of Veterinary School's Veterinary Dental Rotation, clinically rated top 5% of class, American Student Dental Association Student Representative.

1987-1989 **SEATTLE TECH**   **Seattle, WA**
Bachelor of Science Degree: Biology, 1987

■ Specific achievements and dynamic action verbs give resume impact.

■ Courses listed under education are related to candidate's field of interest.

DIETARY TECHNICIAN

CHRIS SMITH
178 Green Street
Topeka, KS 66621
(913) 555-5555

WORK EXPERIENCE:

HEARTLAND OSTEOPATHIC HOSPITAL, Topeka, KS
Dietary Technician   1992-Present
Supervise and coordinate activities for food
service employees. Assist with training new
employees. Plan menu selection for patients.
Manage the department when dietician/department
head is absent. Keep daily record of food,
refrigerator, and dish machine temperatures.

CRESCENT MOON HOSPITAL, Ottowa, KS
Nutrition Assistant   1990-1992
Trained and supervised diet aides in distribution
of patient trays. Consulted with patients on diet
therapy plans.

WHISPERING WOODS CHILDREN'S CENTER, Olathe, KS
Assistant Cook   1988-1990
Consulted with head cook on food preparation.
Planned menus in conjunction with the head cook.
Purchased food and supplies. Organized and
maintained stock inventory.

MCPHERSON GAS COMPANY, McPherson, KS
Customer Service Representative   1986-1988
Scheduled appointments for workmen. Visited sites
of rehabilitated properties to inform customers of
new appliances.

EDUCATION:

Washburn University of Topeka, Topeka, KS
Certificate in Food Service Preparation, 1989.
Topeka Junior College, Topeka, KS
Certificate in Food Service Supervision, 1988.

■ Reverse chronological format focuses employer's attention on candidate's most current position.

■ Relevant work experience is emphasized while other positions are de-emphasized.

DIETICIAN

CHRIS SMITH
178 Green Street
Atlanta, GA 30350
(404) 555-5555

WORK EXPERIENCE:
Dietician
Ellsworth Hospital, Atlanta, GA   **1992-Present**
- Confer with medical and multidisciplinary staffs.
- Prepare nutritional care plans.
- Interview patients.
- Maintain and document patients' medical records.
- Instruct patients and their families.
- Perform miscellaneous duties as a member of the hospital support team.

Dietary Aide
Bentley Nursing Home, Atlanta, GA   **1991-1992**
- Assisted in preparation of patient food trays.

Office Assistant
Morehouse College, Atlanta, GA   **1989-1991**
- Served as Receptionist for main office.

Library Assistant
Morehouse College Library   **Summer 1989**
- Worked in circulation and periodical sections.

EDUCATION:
Morehouse College, Atlanta, GA
B.S. Degree, 1992
Major: Consumer and Family Studies
Minor: Sociology

RELEVANT COURSES:
Human Nutrition; Family Financial Decision-Making; Professional Preparation;
Principles of Food I & II; The Four Food Groups; Interpersonal Communication;
Social Psychology; Human Relations.

INTERNSHIP:
Dowdell County Extension Service, Atlanta, GA (Fall 1991)
- Wrote weekly food/advice column, "Eat Up!"
- Developed chart and gave presentation on the major nutrients.

- Relevant course work adds depth to candidate's educational background.

- Job descriptions are straightforward and understandable.

EMERGENCY MEDICAL TECHNICIAN

Chris Smith
178 Green Street
Visalia, CA 93291
(209) 555-5555

QUALIFICATIONS

- Work well under pressure in crisis situations.
- Thorough knowledge of all Emergency Medical procedures.
- Certified, C.P.R. and Heimlich Methods of Resuscitation.
- Proven capabilities in adhering to standard methods of assisting in emergency childbirth and heart attacks.
- Demonstrated skills in applications of dressings, including burn dressings, tourniquets, oxygen, IVs.
- Familiar with procedures for critical burns, shock, gunshot wounds, physical manifestations of child abuse and wife battering.
- Provide emergency treatment for rape victims while staying within the guidelines of the law.
- Excellent knowledge of all main streets and secondary routes; strong sense of direction and map reading ability.

LICENSES/CERTIFICATIONS/TRAINING

Certified, E.M.T. License	**Visalia Hospital, 1990**
License #4490223	**State of California, 1990**
Recertification Credits	**California General Hospital, 1994**

E.M.T. EXPERIENCE

DOLAN AMBULANCE SERVICES   **Visalia, CA**
Head Emergency Medical Technician   **1993-Present**
Provide emergency response and care to primarily elderly patients with bone fractures, strokes, heart attacks, falls. Assist in standard hospital and legal procedures for fatalities and post-mortem crises management.

RUSSELL AMBULANCE SERVICES   **Los Angeles, CA**
Emergency Medical Technician   **1990-1993**
Assist in providing emergency response to 911 calls; emergency care to patients involved in traffic accidents, heart attacks, stroke, falls, industrial accidents.

■ Qualifications section accentuates candidate's acquired professional skills.

■ Candidate's necessary licenses/certification/training are bolded for impact.

FITNESS INSTRUCTOR

CHRIS SMITH
178 Green Street
Richmond, VA 23220
(804) 555-5555

PROFESSIONAL OBJECTIVE
A challenging position in fitness instruction in which tremendous energy, motivational skills and perseverance will have valuable application.

PROFESSIONAL EXPERIENCE

1990 to Present   THE BABY BOOM, Richmond, VA
Owner/Operator
- Provide comprehensive yet responsible exercise classes for the pregnant woman.
- Supervise staff of twelve. Hire/train employees, manage payroll, schedule work shifts, administer billing.
- Maintain steady contact with each client's physician so as to ensure absolute safety for her and the baby.

1988 to 1990   DEE DEE LEE'S FITNESS PHANTASMAGORIA, Richmond, VA
Aerobics/Calisthenics Instructor
- Taught intensive aerobics, calisthenics and stretching to co-educational classes of up to 25 adults in all physical conditions.
- Geared program toward intermediate and advanced levels.
- Used music as a motivational tool.

1986 to 1988   UP AND AT'EM STUDIO, Norfolk, VA
Manager/Exercise Instructor
- Handled all sales (telephone and direct), marketing and strategy development.
- Developed client referral network.
- Motivated clients to perform intensive calisthenics, yoga and stretching; taught techniques.
- Handled bookkeeping and all business activities.

EDUCATION
WILLAMETTE UNIVERSITY, Salem, OR
Bachelor of Arts in English, Minor in Physical Education, 1983
Studies in Physiology, Anatomy and Nutrition.
Captain of Women's Gymnastic Team.

PERSONAL INFORMATION
Associate member of Women in Fitness Association, Richmond Chapter; in excellent health; perform daily aerobics, Nautilus, and Universal workouts; enjoy hiking and run five to ten miles a day; willing to travel and/or relocate.

References are available upon request.

■ Personal information reinforces candidate's professional objective.

■ Courses listed under education are related to candidate's field of interest.

HEALTH SERVICES COORDINATOR

CHRIS SMITH
178 Green Street
Charleston, SC 29411
(803) 555-5555

PROFILE More than ten years of office experience in hospital settings. Accurate, detail-oriented, reliable. Excellent communication with strong customer service skills and ability to work effectively in high pressure environment. Skilled in grant writing. Excel in accounting, bookkeeping and mathematical calculations.

EXPERIENCE

Resource Coordinator, THE BAPTIST HOSPITAL, Charleston, SC   5/91-Present
Create and implement statistical reports for nursing home placement, utilizing spreadsheet software. Design a database file system to update nursing homes and rehabilitation facilities. Coordinate luncheons to introduce rehabilitation facilities and services to physicians. Work closely with physicians to identify patients who require referrals to long-term care facilities. Attend patient care rounds on all adult Med/Surg and conduct psycho-social assessments. Meet with social workers and family members to discuss nursing home placement. Organize and implement system to coordinate appropriate community beds and organize two health care teams. Coordinate discharges and maintain accurate records of referrals and transfers. Visit and identify all facilities.

Unit Coordinator, CHARLESTON CITY HOSPITAL, Charleston, SC   1989-1991
Supervised activities on hospital floor. Compiled and updated all medical records for patients, maintained all lab work and records. Received admissions and arranged discharges. Maintained inventory of supplies, and ordered when necessary.

Financial Coordinator, HALFWAY HOME INC., Charleston, SC   1987-1989
Prepared payroll for 60 clients. Created and implemented new budget utilizing Lotus 1-2-3. Designed file system for budget, and performed accounting duties. Trained and supervised mentally disabled employees. Maintained and created job folder files for vendors. Processed purchase orders.

EDUCATION FURMAN UNIVERSITY, Greenville, SC   1993-Present
B.S. in Human Services Management Candidate, 1995

CLEMSON UNIVERSITY, Clemson, SC   1989-1991
Business Administration Program, 2 years

COMPUTER SKILLS Lotus 1-2-3, WordPerfect, Microsoft Word

■ Profile sums up candidate's professional qualifications.

■ Valuable computer skills are highlighted in a separate section.

HOME HEALTH AIDE

CHRIS SMITH
178 Green Street
Decorah, IA 52101
(319) 555-5555

OBJECTIVE

To secure a challenging and responsible position that utilizes my supervisory skills and Home Health Care experience.

EXPERIENCE

HOMECARE INCORPORATED   Decorah, IA
1991-Present   Case Administrator
Manage the daily clinical operation of CPMS (Clozaril Patient Management System), monitor laboratory results and manage staff. Recruited to program at its infancy. Selected to develop, test and implement new home care system.
- Coordinate patient services, including blood draws and drug delivery.
- Establish and maintain service schedule for staff consisting of RN's, LPN's, phlebotomists and pharmacists.
- Assist in recruitment, selection and evaluation of RN's, LPN's and phlebotomists.
- Administer training and orientation for clinical staff.
- Generate monthly Quality Assurance reports and audit records and computer files.
- Monitor and report lab results to physicians for review and documentation.
- Identify and resolve service related incidents. Report and maintain record of incidents as described by quality assurance guidelines.
- Support marketing/sales teams of pharmaceutical companies.
- Assisted in selection and development of office/pharmacy.

1990   Nurse Clinician
Provided professional nursing support for home-bound patients in need of infusion therapy services.
- Worked closely with Nursing Supervisor, agency staff, and referring physicians.
- Attended to full range of patients, including those with AIDS.
- Provided patient, family/caregiver education.
- Educated members of nutrition support, oncology and IV teams in providing professional services.

1986-1990   **SIOUX CITY HOSPITAL**   Sioux City, IA
Staff nurse for the medical/surgical units.
- Responsible for assessment, planning, implementation and evaluation for primary care patients.
- Acted as resource nurse for staff of a 50-bed unit, with immediate responsibility for 12-15 patients.
- Supervised LPN's and ancillary staff.

EDUCATION

1986   SIOUX CITY HOSPITAL SCHOOL OF NURSING
Sioux City, IA

References Available Upon Request

- Job descriptions are brief and punchy, without being choppy.

- Education is listed towards bottom of resume because candidate's practical experience outweighs his/her degree.

HOSPITAL SUPERVISOR

CHRIS SMITH
178 Green Street
Northampton, MA 01060
(413) 555-5555

OBJECTIVE:

An opportunity to utilize technical and administrative experience in an institution or industrial plant.

EXPERIENCE:

Hospital Supervisor

Earnshaw Family Center, Northampton, MA   1990-Present

- Oversee the operation of the Laboratory, X-Ray Department, Inhalation Therapy Department, and Nursing Services.
- Public Relations - Set-up weekly public information lectures and discussions on alcoholism.
- Conduct tours of the hospital for the medical profession (students, doctors, nurses, etc.), industry executives and government officials.
- Hospital specializes in the treatment of alcoholics sent from major industries for treatment.
- Act in a consulting capacity with patients and families.

Laboratory Technician (Hematology)

Cooly Dickinson Hospital, Northampton, MA   1986-1990

- Supervised up to 12 technicians in the 500 bed teaching hospital which also operated a RN School and RT School for X-Ray Technicians.
- Monitored the quality and quantity of work performed.
- Requisitioned all laboratory supplies; participated in conferences with medical staff on patients with special laboratory needs.
- Trained new and/or inexperienced personnel in hospital techniques.

Supervisor (Laboratory and X-Ray Departments)

Trailwood Hospital, Chesterfield, MA   1984-1988

- Supervised four technicians; monitored the quality of all laboratory and X-Ray procedures.
- Requisitioned supplies for both departments.
- Sat in on conferences with medical staff since hospital lacked resident Pathologist.

EDUCATION:

Hampshire University, Hadley, MA
BS, Dual major in Biology and Management, 1979

■ Bullets make resume easy to read.   ■ Unrelated work experience is omitted.

LAB TECHNICIAN

CHRIS SMITH
178 Green Street
Hoxie, Kansas 67740
(913) 555-5555 (Work)
(913) 444-4444 (Home)

OBJECTIVE:
Seeking a position as a TECHNICIAN/COORDINATOR that utilizes my skills and experience.

EXPERIENCE:
1990-
Present

KANSAS GENERAL HOSPITAL, Topeka, KS
Medical Media Technical Coordinator, 1987-present
Coordinate, set-up and implement media services for hospital personnel and BU Medical School students and faculty. This includes supervising 3-8 Media Technicians. Complex medical and educational photography, processing, and slide reel set-up. Set-up and direction of medical videos and video equipment. Set-up, operation, and demonstration of medical equipment to medical students. Diagnostic troubleshooting, coordination, and problem solving. Departmental troubleshooting and problem solving. Conduct Hematological and Seratological medical testing. Work closely with undergraduate and graduate medical students, interns, faculty, physicians, and hospital staff.

Laboratory Supervisor
Coordinated laboratory operations, including media technology, analysis of test results, reporting and record keeping. Troubleshot and resolved departmental problems.

1989-1990 **Laboratory Technician**
DAMON CORPORATION, Shawnee Mission, KS
Conducted hematology and serology testing, as well as test sample photography. Recorded, analyzed, and communicated results to physicians, patients, and their families.

1984-1987 **Media Research Technician**
MAYFARB INSTITUTE, Wichita, KS
Produced synchronized audio and slide programs on medical and medical educational topics. Conducted cancer research. Served as a reference and research guide for institute staff and Harvard Medical School affiliates.

EDUCATION:
B.A., Media and Communications, 1984

References Available Upon Request

- Job descriptions detail candidate's responsibilities and accomplishments.

- Resume emphasizes contributions, achievements, and problems candidate has solved throughout his/her career.

MEDICAL RECORDS CLERK

Chris Smith
178 Green Street
Bismarck, ND 58501
(701) 555-5555

OBJECTIVE

An administrative position where experience and commitment will be utilized and advanced.

QUALIFICATIONS
- Computer Skills: IBM PC; WordPerfect; MS Word
- Outstanding interpersonal skills.
- Cooperative team player; equally effective and self-motivated working independently.
- Meet deadlines; work well under pressure.
- Detail-oriented, methodical, flexible, patient, organized, goal-directed.

EXPERIENCE

MICHAEL S. HUTCHENCE, M.D., P.C.   Bismarck, ND
Medical Records Librarian   1989-Present
Responsible for managing medical records department for large private practice of Glaucoma and Cataract specialists. Prepare medical records for appointments the following day. Facilitate scheduling between technicians and physician. Handle over 2,000 active patients, and 150,000 archival records. Reorganized charts and revamped original filing system into a universal filing system.

BISMARCK PAPER COMPANY   Bismarck, ND
Inventory Clerk   1987-1989
Assisted Inventory Manager in documentation and maintenance of paper supply. Performed clerical support as necessary.

EDUCATION

Jamestown College, Jamestown, ND
Courses in Business Administration, 1988.

INTERESTS

SINGING * PHOTOGRAPHY * CROSS-COUNTRY SKIING * SWIMMING

REFERENCES
Excellent references available upon request

■ Qualifications highlight candidate's acquired professional skills.

■ Personal interests can provide a great topic for conversation during a job interview.

MEDICAL TECHNOLOGIST

CHRIS SMITH
178 Green Street
Milwaukee, WI 53201
(414) 555-5555

SUMMARY

A Certified Medical Technologist seeking a challenging position in a private laboratory setting.

PROFESSIONAL BACKGROUND

1990 to MILWAUKEE HOSPITAL, Milwaukee, Wisconsin
Present *Senior Medical Technologist*
- Responsible for conducting laboratory tests and operating equipment at nights for all departments in hospital.
- Primary functions with Chemistry and Hematology Departments.
- Data entry via CRT to obtain test results.

1988 to 1990 BIOCARE, Ashland, WI
Medical Technologist
- Conducted laboratory test at Children's Hospital in Ladysmith, WI.
- Operated Nova for electrolytes, Coulters, and Fibrometer.

1985 to 1988 KIPLING HOSPITAL, Ripon, WI
Medical Technologist
- Conducted testing for several departments and operated Astra, Coagamate, and ELT.

1982 to 1984 DIALTEK, De Pere,WI
Medical Technologist
- Operated Coulters and utilized computer information in Hematology Department.
- Fielded calls for entire department.

1980 to 1982 AL KARTOUM M.D., La Crosse, WI
Private Hematologist Intern
- Operated hematology laboratory using haemacount machine, leitz photometer, and EKG Machine.

EDUCATIONAL BACKGROUND

UNIVERSITY OF WISCONSIN AT MADISON, Madison,WI
A.S. in Medical Technology, May 1981

PROFESSIONAL LICENSES

H.E.W. Certified Medical Technologist #3259050
Certified Laboratory Assistant #BID01359

■ Resume indicates increased responsibilities.

■ Including professional licensure and accreditations can be essential for certain fields of work.

MRI COORDINATOR

CHRIS SMITH
178 Green Street
Rigby, ID 83442
(208) 555-5555

OBJECTIVE:

To obtain a position in a medical environment where I can contribute skills in the field of Medical Office Management and Patient Relations.

WORK EXPERIENCE:

Rigby Community Hospital, Rigby, ID
MRI Coordinator   January 1990-Present
- Complete charge of setting up the new MRI Department including all front desk procedures.
- Implemented a new filing system, adapted new computer program to suit the department needs, developed a new booking system including design of protocol sheets, phone work, close interactions with in/out patients of 3 hospitals including: Jamison Parker Hospital, Children's Hospital, Durling Hospital.

Jamison Parker Hospital, Boise, ID
Clinical Practice Assistant - OB/GYN   1988-1990
- Monitored patient vital signs, assisting patients with ob/gyn problems, procedures, infertility, colposcopy, hysteros and endo-biopsy.

Children's Hospital, Rigby, ID
X-Ray Reading Room   1986-1988
- Worked closely with doctors. Monitored all inpatient x-rays, pulling conference films, presenting x-rays on alternators, assisted physicians with the presentation of conferences, entered data for all computer records.

Emergency Ambulance   1983-1986
- Worked midnight to 7:00 a.m. shift as an O.C. EMT

Radiology Reception Desk   1982-1983
- Required in-depth knowledge of all special exams, bookings, inpatient/outpatient computer programs, protocol, patient relations, all aspects of Radiology Department.

EDUCATION:

University of Rochester, Rochester, NY
Emergency Medical Technician, 1983

The Carleton Schools, Boise, ID
Medical Assistant/Office Management Diploma 1980-1983
- Specialized in front office procedures including insurance forms, patient and employee relations, phones, dictaphone, typing, various computer programs.

■ Resume illustrates continual career progression.

■ Job objective gives resume focus without limiting candidate's opportunities.

NURSE (Cardiac)

Chris Smith
178 Green Street
Kingsport, TN 37660
(615) 555-5555

PROFESSIONAL BACKGROUND
Danforth Women's Hospital, Knoxville, KY
Charge Nurse - C.T.I.C.U. AND C.T.P.C.U. (Cardio-Thoracic Intensive and Progressive Care Units), 1993-1994
Conducted development staff meetings.
- Supervised and evaluated all staff.
- Coordinated ICU (10 bed) and PCU (15 bed).
- Performed respective audits and monthly documentations.

Staff Nurse - Heart Transplant Unit, 1992-1993
- Participated in Clinical Practice and Staff Education Committees.
- Wrote standards for nursing practice, staged appropriately for various level of experience with emphasis on setting objectives for improvement; held monthly meetings to evaluate performance of department; targeted problem areas and set up resolutions.
- Conducted seminar on Patient Presentation and Utilization of the nursing Process and on Pacemaker Care.
- Invited to guest-lecture at Centre College. Gave presentation on "Care of the Patient with a Cardiac Valve Replacement."

Centre College, Danville, KY, 1990-1992
Clinical Instructor
- Supervised third year nursing students in medical/surgical/clinical setting.
- Taught clinical approach to cardiovascular physiological nursing one hour per week.

EDUCATION
Registration in Nursing, 1990
University of Colorado, Boulder
Bachelor of Science, Nursing, 1989
- Dean's List, 3.5/4.0 GPA.
- Participated in departmental meetings and briefings to insure effective interaction between UCB nursing students and City of Boulder personnel.
- Compiled and submitted proposals to the city government; stated objectives, targeted population, projected budget and benefits of program.
- Coordinated with American Heart and Lung Association, American Cancer Society and Boulder City Hospital to facilitate set-up of equipment and placement and staffing of stations for dissemination of Health Awareness materials.
- Post-project evaluation and statistical analysis.

■ Job descriptions highlight candidate's leadership skills and problem-solving abilities.

■ Impressive educational background strengthens resume.

NURSE (Home Health Care)

Chris Smith
178 Green Street
Yukon, MO 65589
(314) 555-5555

PROFESSIONAL EXPERIENCE

1989 to Present   **AIDS Clinical Coordinator/Home Infusion Nurse**
THE LAMONT CENTER   Yukon, MO
- Provide case management, teaching and follow up for AIDS patients receiving home infusion therapies.
- Identified need for study on the infection rate of venous access devices in AIDS patients; currently collecting pertinent data.
- Identify appropriate candidates for high tech home infusion therapies.
- Train patients and families to safely conduct these complex therapies within the home setting.
- Therapies include: total parenteral and enteral nutrition, IV antibiotic therapy, infusion chemotherapy, parenteral pain management and IV hydration.
- Member - The Lamont Center Home Care Committee

1983 to 1989   **Senior Staff Nurse (Level II)**
Oncology Division
- Functioned as Primary Nurse for the coordination of care for acute and chronic patients; emphasis on family centered care and patient education.
- Provided nursing care for chemotherapy and pain management patients.
- Facilitated discharge planning with home care agencies.
- Acted as Coordinator for Autologous Bone Marrow Transplant Program.
- Developed orientation program for new staff members.
- Conducted inservices for staff on procedural updates and progress of program.
- Served as hospital oncology resource for care of central venous catheters.
- Chairperson - Family Education Committee.

1978 to 1983   **Public Health Nurse**
SEDALIA HEALTH DEPARTMENT   Sedalia, MO
- Managed all operations for pediatric satellite clinic.
- Instructed families in maternal and well-child health practices.

PROFESSIONAL AFFILIATIONS
American Nurses Association
Intravenous Nurses Society

PROFESSIONAL LICENSES
Registered Nurse
State of Missouri #794791

EDUCATION
1990, Building Professional Skills to Work With Intravenous Drug Users
1987, AIDS Program for Clinical Nurses
RENDALL HOSPITAL SCHOOL OF NURSING
Saint Louis, MO
Diploma: Registered Nurse, 1978

■ Most recent job is listed in most detail while previous jobs are listed more briefly.

■ Job-related affiliations demonstrate candidate's active participation in his/her field.

NURSE (Intensive Care Unit)

CHRIS SMITH
178 Green Street
Cherry Fork, OH 45618
(513) 555-5555

SUMMARY OF QUALIFICATIONS:

Intensive Care Unit
- Working closely with recently graduated interns at major metropolitan trauma certified hospital.
- Accurate reporting and recording of lab values with follow up medical treatment.
- Recognizing life threatening arrhythmias and means of treatment for patients placed on cardiac monitors.

Post Anesthesia Care Unit
- Caring for arterial lines, monitoring BP and MAP, drawing arterial blood gases and other labs, interpreting and reporting abnormal values to physician for medical management.
- Providing specialized nursing and medical care in 17-bed unit for anesthetized patients following surgical procedures in the operating room.
- Calculating and recording cardiac output SVR and cardiac indexes.

EDUCATION:

UNIVERSITY OF CINCINNATI, Cincinnati, OH
Bachelor of Science in Nursing (1984)

MUSKINGUM COLLEGE HOSPITAL, New Concord, OH
Trauma Certificate (1991), Critical Care Course (1989)

EXPERIENCE:

OHIO STATE UNIVERSITY HOSPITAL, Columbus, OH
Staff Nurse, Post Anesthesia Care Unit and Trauma Unit
(10/90-Present)
Night Charge Nurse, making assignments and utilizing on-call nurses when necessary. Trauma certified for major trauma unit in the City of Columbus. PACU often turned into ICU for patients unable to get an ICU bed in high crime area location. Experience in treating patients, recovering from surgery for gunshot and stab wounds.

Staff Nurse, Medical Respiratory Intensive Care Unit

VIRTUE HOSPITAL, Dayton, OH
Nursing Internship, Medical-Surgical Unit (8/88-10/90)
Nurse's Aide (7/87-8/88)

REFERENCES:

Excellent references available upon request.

- Summary of qualifications details candidate's areas of expertise.

- Bullets call attention to candidate's key credentials.

NURSE (Medical/Surgical)

Chris Smith
178 Green Street
Boston, MA 02115
(617) 555-5555

PROFESSIONAL OBJECTIVE
A position as a professional Registered Nurse in Medical/Surgical, Intensive Care, Emergency Room, and/or Ambulatory arenas.

SUMMARY OF QUALIFICATIONS
- Specialize in ventilators, tracheotomy care, burn patients with extensive dressings, IV therapy.
- Expertise in coordinating discharge planning and home care with doctors, nutritionists, physical therapists, occupational therapists and social workers; strong on documentation and follow-through.
- Outstanding interpersonal and communication skills.
- Proven written and teaching/demonstration skills for extensive education regarding tracheotomies for in-home care.
- Co-produced educational videos for new staff with specialized information.

PROFESSIONAL EXPERIENCE
1992-Present **BOSTON HOSPITAL, Boston, MA**   **Staff Nurse, R.N.**
Thoracic Surgery
- Coordinate staffing issues, budget responsibilities, QA monitoring.
- Attend workshops, co-produce and act in educational videos; write working brochures for patients and families.
- Perform primary nursing care; communicate directly with doctors and other health care professionals.
- Participate in extensive post-op care with multiple problems.
- Deal directly with the families regarding hospital policies.

1989-1992 **ST. JOAN'S HOSPITAL, Medfield, MA**   **Professional Registered Nurse**
- As Charge Nurse, provided leadership on 40-bed Medical/Surgical unit with telemetry and provided IV therapy.
- As LPN, employed direct patient care with administration of medications.

EDUCATION
UNIVERSITY OF MASSACHUSETTS, Amherst, MA.
B.S. in Nursing. Graduated 1992 with Nursing GPA of 3.2/4.0.

DEAN JUNIOR COLLEGE, Franklin, MA.
A.S. in Nursing and Applied Science. Graduated 1989.

Major Course Work:
Nursing Research Seminar - Focusing on qualitative, quantitative and historic research methodology pertaining to nursing.
Community Health Nursing - A study on community and family environment.
Nursing Leadership and Management - An emphasis on nursing administration and budgetary responsibilities.

■ Resume is easy and quick to read; only relevant details are included.

■ Relevant course work adds depth to candidate's educational background.

NURSE (Psychiatric)

CHRIS SMITH
178 Green Street
Berry Creek, CA 95916
(213) 555-5555

OBJECTIVE

A daytime Nursing assignment in which to use training and broad-based experience as Staff or Charge Nurse in a Hospital environment.

SUMMARY

- Intensive experience working in diverse hospital and human services environments in a range from pediatric & medical/surgical clients to mixed adult/adolescent, manic depression, and borderline/acute personality disorders units (locked & unlocked units).
- Experience also includes crisis intervention, case management, working with conduct disorders, sexual & physical abuse, acute or chronic psychiatric distress, substance abuse, and work with the physically challenged.

PROFESSIONAL EXPERIENCE

1991-Present   **Dr. Felts Mental Health Clinic**
Nurse Manager   **Los Angeles, CA**

Manage third shift while supervising 3 nurses and associated staff, assigning patients for evaluation, working with social services representatives, patients' family and/or guardians, distributing medications, providing emergency medical assistance, and handling associated details of medical administration.

Note: Concurrently, 1991, was Case Manager, Jessamine Mutual. Approved hospital stays, therapies or treatments, worked with doctors, social workers and family or guardians, and handled related administration: Left to devote full time to Nurse Manager position.

1988-1991   **Renaissance Health Services**
Psychiatric Aide/Charge Nurse   **Los Angeles, CA**

Successfully completed assignments with 20 hospitals in the Greater Los Angeles Area. On-call status currently maintained by Renaissance.

EDUCATION

Associates Degree (3.7 G.P.A.), Mills College, Oakland, CA
- *Honors Award for Excellence in Nursing*
- Certified Psychiatric & Mental Health Nurse
- Gender & Stress counseling at Health Fairs
- Taught college level First Aid Course

REFERENCES

Available upon request.

- Limited education is balanced with medical certification, honors award, and high G.P.A.

- Summary grabs the reader's attention with powerful skills and qualifications.

NURSE (Psychogeriatric)

CHRIS SMITH
178 Green Street
Lodi, CA 95240
(209) 555-5555

SUMMARY

- **Psychogeriatric Nurse:** Progressively responsible and sophisticated clinical nursing experience; including responsibilities as Geriatric, Orthopedic, Plastic Surgery, Ophthalmology, Acute Medical, General Surgical and Medical-Surgical Nurse in Hospital, Clinical and Professional Health Care settings.
- **Bachelor of Science Degree, Nursing & Psychology,** with continuing education towards the Masters Degree.
- Expertise includes patient care involving both pharmacological & behavioral modification methods of treatment, as well as for drug & alcohol abuse, congestive heart failure, hospice care, pulmonary disease, and other severe medical or psychological conditions.

PROFESSIONAL NURSING EXPERIENCE

1989-Present   Midvale Counseling Services
PSYCHOGERIATRIC NURSE CLINICIAN   Lodi, CA
- Psychiatric & Psychological Counseling Center specializing in a full range of Mental Health Services. Service various area geriatric facilities in the provision of individual therapy to up to 40 geriatric residents, groups and family members/week for depression, lifestyle adjustment, grieving, and other physical and psychosocial needs.
- Perform medication assessments and consult with physicians about medication regimens. Provide nurse teaching and support services for staff regarding the identification and meeting of patient medical & psycho-social needs.

1984-1989   Unified Medical Center
RN/EVENING CHARGE   Fresno, CA
- Supervised up to 8, while responsible for 45-bed unit in this health care facility specializing in care for severe med-stress patients. Responsibilities encompassed admission assessment and care planning, including behavior modification and limit setting.
- Worked closely with Osteopathic Physicians & Psychiatric Staff in the care & assessment of Patients requiring treatment for drug and alcohol abuse, manic depression, and acute psychosis.

EDUCATION
Bellin College of Nursing, Green Bay, WI
Bachelor of Science Degree 1984

- Summary highlights candidate's acquired professional and educational training.

- Chrono-functional format is more flexible than a chronological resume, but stronger than a functional resume.

NURSING ADMINISTRATOR

Chris Smith
178 Green Street
Providence, RI 02903
(401) 555-5555

PROFESSIONAL EXPERIENCE
1992-Present VISITING NURSE ASSOCIATION OF PROVIDENCE, Providence, RI
Supervisor of Specialty Home Health Aides
Supervised 40 HHAs who care for pediatric patients with HIV.

1988-1992 **Reimbursement Specialist**, Northeast and Providence District Offices
Managed and evaluated all clinical documentation for Medicare and all third party related Medicare payers. Worked in cooperation with managers, clinicians, patients accounts and clerical staff to ensure quality documentation.

1985-1988 **Staff Nurse**
Provided skilled nursing assessment of primary patients and family needs. Utilized appropriate resource personnel and agencies in a collaborative effort to provide continuity of care to patient and family. Worked with liaison nurses to discharge patients to home with appropriate services and realistic expectation of third party reimbursement payers.

1984-1985 RHODE ISLAND PARAMEDICAL REGISTRY, Providence, RI
Visiting Nurse
Responsible for the home care of chronically ill children to give the primary caretakers physical and emotional respite.

1983-1984 THE CHILDREN'S HOSPITAL, Cranston, RI
Staff Nurse in cardiovascular/surgical intensive care unit. Provided surgical and medical management of critically ill children in collaborative effort with medical team. Supported parents and provided discharge teaching for comprehensive home care utilizing primary nursing.

1980-1982 KINGSTON HOSPITAL, Kingston, RI
Staff Nurse in pediatrics with charge responsibilities for a 20-bed ICU. Provided surgical and medical treatment for children, ages 3-17 years. Incorporated levels of development and psychosocial needs in teaching discharge goals. Counseled parents about disease process and child's needs.

EDUCATION
SALVE REGINA COLLEGE, Newport, RI. B.S. in Nursing;
Graduated 1979.
Summer Externship, Rollins Hospital, Orlando, FL, 1978.

■ Specifically citing number of employees supervised draws attention to candidate's leadership abilities.

■ Format is organized and visually appealing.

NURSING AIDE

CHRIS SMITH
178 Green Street
Ada, OK 74820
(405) 555-5555

OBJECTIVE: To obtain a position in a Health Care facility.

EDUCATION: EAST CENTRAL UNIVERSITY, Ada, OK
Diploma in Nursing, 1994.

CENTRAL STATE UNIVERSITY, Edmond, OK
Bachelor's Degree in Biology and Sociology, 1991.

EMPLOYMENT:

HOSPITAL EAST, Ada, OK   1993-Present
Nursing Aide
Responsible for tasks on the Medical/Surgical, Geriatric, Maternity and Cardiac units.
Assist in patient care; work on different floors as needed.

CENTRAL CITY HOSPITAL, Edmond, OK   1989-1993
Nursing Aide
Administered to patients' hygiene needs and everyday living functions. Counseled
patients and families on variety of health issues.

CENTRAL STATE UNIVERSITY, Edmond, OK   1990-1991
Teaching Assistant in Health Education
Taught Undergraduate Health Classes; supervised Health Education Library.

VOLUNTEER:

CENTRAL STATE UNIVERSITY, Edmond, OK   1989-1992
Health Worker/Heart Disease Prevention Program in High Schools
Focused on risk factors including smoking, cholesterol, exercise, blood pressure.

ELDERLY ASSISTANCE, Ada, OK   1991-Present
Elderly Advocate
Social work with geriatric population, working specifically with government benefits.

REFERENCES: Furnished upon request.

■ Unrelated work experience is omitted.

■ Volunteer work and community service lend strength to this resume.

NURSING HOME MANAGER

CHRIS SMITH, M.S.W., L.I.C.S.W.
178 Green Street
Sandy Springs, SC 29677
(803) 555-5555

PROFESSIONAL EXPERIENCE
Haversham Home, Sandy Springs, SC
Nursing Home Manager   1991-Present
- Coordinate provision of home care for elderly as part of state-funded program
- Train, supervise, develop, support and review staff of 7 to 8 case managers
- Review service plans for appropriateness, cost, and compliance with DEA regulations
- Determine client eligibility by need, age, and finances
- Act as liaison to service providers and community agencies
- Lead group meetings with case managers
- Plan and implement training programs; serve as member of Training Committee

Case Manager   1987-1991
- Developed comprehensive service plans for elderly clients; assessed needs, determined eligibility
- Coordinated in-home care, oversaw provision of all aspects of care
- Advocated for client in obtaining benefits and services; identified available services
- Administered case load of 80 to 90; prepared individual case records and reports

The Department of Youth Services, Suffolk, VA
Social Worker   1985-1987
- Performed casework, community service work, outreach, individual and family crisis counseling, and coordination with community agencies

EDUCATION
Licensed Independent Clinical Social Worker, October 1985

Master of Social Work, 1984
University of California, Davis, CA

Bachelor of Arts in Social Studies, 1982
University of Dubuque, Dubuque, IA

■ Impressive educational background strengthens resume.

■ Resume emphasizes achievements; doesn't simply list job responsibilities.

NURSING SUPERVISOR

CHRIS SMITH
178 Green Street
Giants Pass, OR 97526
(503) 555-5555

AREAS OF EXPERTISE

- Policy and Procedures Development
- Budget Preparation and Implementation
- Development of and instruction in formal education training programs
- Administration and supervision of patient care department
- Development of education/training of auxiliary staffs
- Personnel Recruitment/Administration (licensed/non-licensed)
- Direct Patient Care (medical/surgical)
- Geriatrics (long term/community care)

EXPERIENCE

Brixton Life Care Center   *1990-Present*
Director of Nursing Services

- Coordinate and direct all services related to direct patient care. Coordinate out-patient services rendering the life care residents in conjunction with director of Resident Care Services.
- Actively participate in all admission and discharge planning.
- Coordinate and oversee emergency services through the facility Digitizer, call service between the Life Care apartments and the medical building.
- Formed and actively participate in Restorative Service Committee for coordinating Rehabilitative Services.

Treehill Clinic
Director of Nursing Services   *1987-1990*

- Troubleshot and upgraded facility to a Level I - II (skilled care). Brought facility to successful relicensure.
- Hired a Staff Development Coordinator; reorganized and expanded staff to 130 licensed and non-licensed personnel including two new supervisors. Enforced on-going policies and procedures with regard to maintaining continuity with supplemental staff.

Day Supervisor   *1984-1987*

- Supervised delivery of patient care, including management and supervision of licensed and non-licensed personnel in this 200-bed, geriatric, long-term multi-level, skilled facility.

EDUCATION

Colby College School of Nursing, Waterville, ME
Bachelor of Science in Nursing, with honors, 1984

Georgia School of Nursing, Atlanta, GA
Graduated, 1980 - Registered Nurse

CERTIFICATION

ANA - Certification Nursing Administration, 1985

■ Candidate's areas of expertise are prominently listed.

■ Resume illustrates candidate's increased responsibility.

NUTRITIONIST

Chris Smith
178 Green Street
Winchester, MA 08190
(617) 555-5555

EDUCATION

Boston University, Boston, MA   **B.S., Public Health**
Graduated Cum Laude   1980
Laboure College, Dorchester, MA   **Food Service Supervision**
Certified   1970
American Dietetic Association (ADA)
Registered   1981

EXPERIENCE

Laboure College   Winchester, MA
Lecturer   1989-Present
- Instruct future dieticians and dietetic technicians in the science of foods and nutrition.
- Lecture on the role of dietetics in public and home health agencies, daycare centers, health/recreation clubs, and government funded food programs for the poor, elderly, malnourished, pregnant/nursing women, children, disabled and underprivileged citizens.
- Train dietetic technicians to perform nutrition screenings/ assessments, cholesterol reduction, portion control.

O'Donnell Medical Center   Winchester, MA
Nutritionist   1976-Present
- Train, supervise and coordinate all procedures for patients on strict food plans for cardiac, renal, diabetic, weight reduction and gain, post-surgical menus; plan menu selections.
- Provide analyses of patient dietary needs; ensure menu plan adheres to dietary needs in sports nutrition.
- Consult with facility cook concerning food preparation; assist in the budgeting and purchasing of foods.

Massachusetts General Hospital   Jamaica Plain, MA
Dietary Technician Supervisor   1970-1976
- Supervised and coordinated activities for food service employees.
- Trained new hires and diet aides in distribution of patient trays.
- Assisted in the planning of patients' menus.
- Took daily inventory of food. Monitored refrigerator and dish washer temperatures.

■ Candidate's professional certification is listed under education.

■ Work history is stated in reverse chronological order, with most recent employment listed first.

OCCUPATIONAL THERAPIST

CHRIS SMITH
178 Green Street
Topeka, KS 66621
(913) 555-5555

OBJECTIVE   To contribute excellent treatment planning skills to the position of **Staff Occupational Therapist.**

EXPERIENCE

1991 to Present
DIXON REHABILITATION CENTER   Hillsboro, KS
- Independently assessed clients with stroke and head trauma, ages 10 to 60.
- Initiated individual client treatment and implemented clinical therapy, utilizing standard disability interventions and physical management techniques.
- Monitored, identified and resolved client behavioral problems.
- Participated in rehab and clinical rounds and family conferences.
- Co-led a shopping and community re-entry group.
- Facilitated community field trips.
- Performed client treatment, notation, billing, statistical recording and assisted in training an O.T. Aide, on a daily basis.

1989 to 1991
WILD THORN CHILDREN'S CENTER   Sterling, KS
- Functioned as dyadic group leader for E.D. pre-adolescents with diagnoses of conduct, personality and affective disorders.
- Structured developmental group with parallel/project format utilizing cooking, games, leather and woodworking modalities.
- Observed, monitored and reported individual group interaction.
- Drafted weekly progress notes.

1986 to 1989
CURTIS SCHOOL FOR THE BLIND   Wichita, KS
- Evaluated, planned and established individual treatment interventions for clients with congenital disabilities and MR, Rubella, CP, Lebers and FTT diagnoses.
- Utilized Neurodevelopmental, Biomechanical, SI and Developmental methods.
- Coordinated program aids to implement treatment and documented quarterly progress notes.

EDUCATION

NEW YORK UNIVERSITY, College of Allied Health   New York, NY
Master of Science Degree: Occupational Therapy, 1986 G.P.A.: 3.8/4.0
Merit Scholarship, NYU College of Allied Health, 1986
Selected as Student Speaker for annual NYOT Conference, 1985

PROFESSIONAL AFFILIATIONS

Member - American Occupational Therapy Association
Member - Kansas Association for Occupational Therapists

■ Resume emphasizes candidate's strong work history.

■ Dynamic action verbs give resume impact.

OPTICIAN

Chris Smith
178 Green Street
Los Angeles, CA 90066
(213) 555-5555

CAREER OBJECTIVE
A challenging Senior Level/Management position as a **Ophthalmic Dispensing Optician**.

SUPPORTIVE QUALIFICATIONS
- Expertise in every optical environment; Private Practice, Optometric Practice, Large Retail Outlets, Ophthamalogical Groups, large eye-specialty Hospital.
- Broadbased knowledge of multidisciplined opticianary, low vision, binocular telescopes, microscopes, pediatric and geriatric opticianry, and specialty lens designs.
- Extensive knowledge of the latest technology in lens designs.
- Fellow, National Academy of Opticians; California State Optician Licensed.

HIGHLIGHTS OF PROFESSIONAL EXPERIENCE
1989-Present   Los Angeles Eye Infirmary, Los Angeles, CA
Director of Optical Services
- Ensured adherence to hospital, state and federal guidelines.
- Prepared financial reports; designed department budget.
- Responsible for purchasing of all lenses and frames.
- Supervised staff of 5.

Accomplishments
- Redesigned entire optical shop, laboratory and dispensary.
- Updated equipment to state-of-the-art machinery.
- Cut turnaround time by 75%.
- Consistently stayed within, or well under designated budget.
- Completely revamped line of inventory to more updated line of frames.
- Responsible for bringing outside clientele to hospital optical facility for the expressed use of our services.

1984-1989   THE PUPIL PLANET, Santa Ana, CA
Optician
- Quality control, dispensing eyeglasses, frame sales.
- Contact lens fittings.

1980-1984   DIPIETRO OPTICAL COMPANY, Los Angeles, CA
Optician
- Laboratory work.
- Eyeglass dispensing; stock control.

MILITARY
U.S. AIRFORCE - Three years Optical Lab Technician - Honorably Discharged

EDUCATION
BURBANK COMMUNITY COLLEGE, Burbank, CA. A.S., Ophthalmic Dispensing. Graduated 1980.

- Attention-getting resume focuses on accomplishments and uses dynamic language.

- Including a good military record can be advantageous if it relates to candidate's job objective.

ORTHODONTIST

DR. CHRIS SMITH
ORTHODONTIST

178 Green Street
Needham, MA 02192
(617) 555-5555

PROFESSIONAL EXPERIENCE
Private Practice, Weston, MA
Orthodontist, 1991 - Present
Treat up to 30 patients daily, ranging from teenagers to adults. Make adjustments to correct crooked teeth, treat accident victims, and fix problems related to TMJ. Practice Edgewise Orthodontics as well as Begg Orthodontics.

Greene and Associates, Brighton, MA
Orthodontist, 1987 - 1991
Treated a minimum of 40 patients daily with problems ranging from crooked teeth to TMJ complaints. Practiced Edgewise Orthodontics primarily on teenagers. Utilized porcelain braces as well as gold appliances.

EDUCATION
Tufts University, Medford, MA
Orthodontic Residency - 1987

D.M.D., 1984

Boston University, Boston, MA
B.S., Pre-Med Studies - 1978

LICENSES/CERTIFICATION
License to Practice Dentistry, 1985
Northeast Regional Board Certified, 1987

PROFESSIONAL AFFILIATIONS
American Dental Association
American Association of Orthodontists
Northeast Regional Association of Orthodontists
Massachusetts Association of Orthodontists

REFERENCES
Available upon request.

■ Resume format is neat and professional.

■ Job objective is unnecessary because resume illustrates a clear career path.

PEDIATRICIAN

CHRIS SMITH, M.D.
178 Green Street
Washington, D.C. 20020
(202) 555-5555

PROFESSIONAL OBJECTIVE
Admittance into the Internal Medicine Residency Program at a teaching hospital.

SUMMARY OF QUALIFICATIONS
- Fifteen years of professional experience in Pediatrics/Emergency Medicine.
- Six years as Emergency Room Physician including one year as Chief of the Department.
- Four years of experience as President of a free-standing emergency medical and surgical service.
- Completed American Board of Quality Assurance and Utilization Review examinations.
- Developed and directed a medical and support staff serving approximately 5,000 families.
- Currently Senior Resident - Washington D.C. Medical Center.
- Board Eligible in General Pediatrics, 1993.

EXPERIENCE
SENIOR RESIDENT   1993-Present
Washington D.C. Medical Center, Washington, D.C.
- Monitored intensive care, emergency room and inpatient services.
- Supervised staff of 15 including residents, interns and medical students.
- During day assignments, supervised three interns and 6 medical students (pediatric ward) with indirect responsibility for surgical patients. Extensive bedside teaching, rounds, conferences and lectures.
- Conducted research on intensive care on Validation of Admitting Leprosy Patients into Intensive Care. Developed a quality Assurance Plan for the Department of Pediatrics.
- Board Eligible in General Pediatrics, September 1993.

PEDIATRICIAN   1978-1993
R. MacDonald and Smith, Inc., Washington, D.C.
- Since 1978, established and developed a health care delivery practice for infants, children, and adolescents. Directed a staff of twenty nurses and administrative support personnel providing services for approximately 5,000 families.
- *Note:* Liquidated practice to accept Senior Residency Program.

PRESIDENT   1983-1987
Emergency Medical and Surgical Service of the Capitol, Washington, D.C.
- In conjunction with three other physicians, planned, organized and directed a free-standing emergency center. Center successfully grew to employ a support staff of 80, including associate physicians, nurses, technicians and administrative personnel.
- Selected site, equipped, staffed, and expanded the Center into a total self-contained operations including: laboratory; x-ray; fluoroscopy; occupational medicine; emergency room; and other health care services. Center was on 8:00 a.m. to 11:00 p.m., seven-day week operation which serviced from 200-300 patients per day.

(continued)

- Resume tracks candidate's long list of impressive accomplishments and promotions.

- Job descriptions are very specific.

- In addition to direct medical care, monitored financing, budgets, personnel and related business management activities.
- In 1987, resigned and liquidated holdings to concentrate on rapidly growing private practice.

CHIEF OF THE DEPARTMENT OF EMERGENCY MEDICINE/
EMERGENCY ROOM PHYSICIAN   **1978-1984**
Cook County Memorial Hospital, Washington, D.C.
- Function included all aspects of emergency patient care including physician and nurse coordination in both adult and pediatric care. Handled approximately 80,000 emergency visits per year.
- **As Chief of the Department of Emergency Medicine (1983-1984), and Emergency Room Physician,** was also responsible for quality assurance, utilization reviews, administrative functions and financial control.

EDUCATION
American University, Washington, D.C.
Master of Public Health 1977
Area of concentration: Maternal and Child Care

Children's Hospital, Washington, D.C.
Pediatric Internship/Residency 1971-1974
Palona Istak Award, Department of Pediatrics

Valparaiso University, Valparaiso, IN
Doctor of Medicine, 1971
BA, Chemistry, 1969

PROFESSIONAL ASSOCIATIONS AND ACTIVITIES
Member - American College of Utilizations Review Physicians
Member - American Medical Society
Member - Cook county Medical Society
Certified by National Board of Medical Examiners, 1977

PHARMACIST

CHRIS SMITH
178 Green Street
Lafayette, LA 70504
(318) 555-5555

PROFESSIONAL EXPERIENCE

1989 to Present   **Pharmacist**
ZERTEX ALLIED HEALTH SERVICES   Lafayette, LA
- Review and fill prescriptions and enter orders on computer.
- Coordinate total intravenous therapy program with nursing homes.
- Supervise staff and conduct purchasing procedures.
- Provide consultation for patients and nursing home staff on drug therapy and regulations.
- Simultaneously coordinate hospital and retail pharmacy services.

1987 to 1989   **Pharmacist**
BEAUCHAMPS HOSPITAL   New Orleans, LA
- Dispensed drugs to and counseled inpatients and outpatients.
- Advised professional staff re: drug information, interactions, etc.
- Trained new technicians in pharmacy computer operations.
- Assisted in decentralization of pharmacy services.
- Distributed unit doses, prepared intravenous and chemotherapy admixtures.
- Assisted in inventory control and performed various related duties.

1985 to 1987   **Clinical Pharmacy Clerkship**
VETERAN'S HOSPITAL   Baton Rouge, LA
- Worked with team of physicians and other health professionals on rotation through various hospital departments.

1984 to 1985   **Pharmacy Extern**
CUPID'S PHARMACY   Natchitoches, LA
- Assisted in the provision of pharmacy services, including: dispensation of medication, advising patients on usage of prescription and non-prescription drugs, monitoring patient profiles for interactions, medication compliance, inappropriate therapy, etc.
- Assisted in the processing and pricing of third-party prescription reimbursement claims.

EDUCATION

Bachelor of Science Degree: Pharmacy, 1985
TULANE UNIVERSITY   New Orleans, LA
Louisiana Registered Pharmacist #34217
Georgia Registered Pharmacist #36954

PROFESSIONAL DEVELOPMENT & AFFILIATIONS

Member - Louisiana Society of Hospital Pharmacy

■ Resume illustrates continual career progression.

■ Including professional licensure and accreditations can be essential for certain fields of work.

PHARMACY TECHNICIAN

Chris Smith
178 Green Street
Moss Point, MS 39563
(601) 555-5555

QUALIFICATIONS:
- Experience includes large metropolitan hospital, smaller community hospital, and retail experience.
- Skilled in all aspects of medication preparation and pharmacy operations.
- Excellent knowledge of medications/pharmaceuticals.
- Strong communications skills; computer experience.

EXPERIENCE:

1991-Present **Pharmacy Technician**
KENNSINGTON MEDICAL CENTER, Moss Point, MS
Perform pharmacy functions for satellite pharmacy serving the surgical and medical floors (100 beds). Pick-up and enter orders on computer. Fill and deliver orders. Check and replenish medical carts. Maintain narcotics controls, deliver IVs. Maintain computerized inventory controls and conduct monthly medication room audits. Communicate with physicians, nurses, and administrative personnel.

1986-1991 **Pharmacy Technician**
LAUREL GENERAL HOSPITAL, Laurel, MS
Full range of hospital (75 beds) and convalescent (100 beds) pharmacy responsibilities. Utilized computerized pharmacy system and administrative and documentation procedures. Prepared new medication and IV orders for hospital and convalescent facilities. Provided upkeep of daily orders for patient charts and MARS including allergies, special procedures, diet, treatments, lab procedures and diagnosis. Recorded strengths and dosages on "patient profile" forms. Priced and organized incoming stock. Prepared daily, physician's orders, MARS, month-end and Department of Welfare reports and forms. Communicated with pharmaceutical reps.

1983-1986 **Pharmacy Technician**
ST. MARTHA'S HOSPITAL, Jackson, MS
Filled medicine orders and recorded strengths and amounts on "patient profile" forms. Priced and organized incoming stock, prepared invoices for payment, and interacted with pharmaceutical reps. Prepared Department of Welfare forms and maintained accurate, long term patient files.

1981-1983 **Pharmacy Clerk**
THE MERIDIAN CENTER, Pascagoula, MS
Received in-person and telephone orders for prescriptions. Conferred with physicians regarding accuracy and clarifications on prescriptions. Maintained invoice and inventory information. Prepared Department of Welfare Forms. Updated "Physician's Desk Reference." Shared bookkeeping and general office responsibilities. Position required customer service and communications skills.

EDUCATION:
Mississippi State University at Starkville
B.S. in Pharmaceutical Procedure, 1980

■ Job objective is unnecessary because resume illustrates a clear career path.

■ Resume emphasizes candidate's strong work history.

PHYSICAL THERAPIST (General)

CHRIS SMITH
178 Green Street
Reading, PA 19602
(215) 555-5555

PROFESSIONAL OBJECTIVE
A physical therapy position in which planning, analytical ability, and communications skills will have useful application

EDUCATION
Albright College, Graduate School of Management, Reading, PA, 1993-Present
Candidate for MBA; enrolled part-time
Cumulative Average: 3.4/4.0

Baylor University, Waco, TX
Bachelor of Science in Physical Therapy, 1984
Waco Scholar; Dean's List three consecutive semesters
Course work in precalculus at Pennsylvania State in 1987

WORK EXPERIENCE
1992-Present DAVENPORT NURSES ASSOCIATION, Reading, PA
Senior Physical Therapist
- Assumed management responsibilities in absence of supervisor
- Served on staff/administration liaison committee
- Developed familiarity with third-party payments
- Served as clinical instructor and in-service instructor for community agencies

1990-1992 READING COMMUNITY HEALTH ASSOCIATION, Reading, PA
Rehabilitation Coordinator/Senior Physical Therapist
- Instructed and supervised Home Health Aides
- Oriented Rehabilitation staff
- Researched community resources for head injury patients

1988-1990 PYRENEES HOSPITAL, Pittston, PA
Staff Physical Therapist
- Served as clinical instructor for physical therapy students and Pulmonary Clinic
- Drafted physical therapy standards of care for selected surgical procedures

1984-1988 CRESTON REHABILITATION CENTER, Altoona, PA
Staff Physical Therapist
- Assisted management procedures in unique horizontal system; took part in cooperative hiring, firing, problem-solving, and formulation of personnel policies

■ Candidate's work experience reads like a series of accomplishments, not just a list of job duties.

■ Bulleted statements consistently begin with action verbs.

PHYSICAL THERAPIST (Orthopedic)

CHRIS SMITH
178 Green Street
Franklin, IN 46131
(317) 555-5555

PROFESSIONAL OBJECTIVE
A career opportunity in PHYSICAL THERAPY.

CLINICAL EXPERIENCE
MIDWEST MEMORIAL HOSPITAL, Indianapolis, IN
Orthopedic In- and Out-Patient Clinic   1993-1994
- Develop treatment plan for 10 patient caseload.
- Work extensively with chronic pain and cardiac patients.
- Present in-service on hip and knee prostheses.

DEARBORN COUNTY HOSPITAL, Richmond, IN
Cardiac Rehabilitation   1992-1993
- Acted as program coordinator for exercise regimen.
- Provided individualized treatments using modalities, such as ultrasound, electric stimulation, massage therapy, and stretching/strengthening exercises.
- Coordinated aquadynamics program for chronic pain patients.

CINNAMON MOUNTAIN, Mishawaka, IN
Pediatric Rehabilitation   1990-1992
- Coordinated the treatment of amputee children and children with congenital birth defects; created the "Alive with Pride" program that is now functional at thirty national hospitals.
- Encouraged regular exercise by developing child-oriented play program.
- Directed teacher workshops at local elementary schools.

EDUCATIONAL BACKGROUND
INDIANA UNIVERSITY, Bloomington, IN
<u>Bachelor of Science in Physical Therapy,</u> 1990
Awarded Indiana University Scholarship
Course work included Pediatric Therapy and research in the application placement of vibrator and effects of TVR.

GOSHEN COLLEGE, Goshen, IN
Biology Major; Chemistry, French, Calculus, 1987-88

SPECIAL PRACTICUM
INDIANA UNIVERSITY, Bloomington, IN
- Performed independent research evaluating back and shoulder strength of musicians who were suffering from tendinitis or bursitis.
- Presented findings to Physical Therapy Department; later published in the Indiana Journal of Medicine (Vol. X, pp. 20-24, August 1992).

■ Job descriptions detail candidate's responsibilities and accomplishments.

■ Independent research projects, like the special practicum listed here, illustrate candidate's initiative.

PHYSICIAN'S ASSISTANT

Chris Smith
178 Green Street
Topeka, KS 66614
(913) 555-5555

OBJECTIVE
A Physician's Assistant position within an organization offering opportunities for growth and advancement.

SUMMARY OF QUALIFICATIONS
- Clerical skills include typing, word processing, and computer literacy.
- Developed interpersonal skills, having dealt with a diversity of professionals, clients, and staff members.
- Administrative abilities in legal and business environments.
- Self-motivated; able to set effective priorities and implement decisions to achieve immediate and long term goals and meet operational deadlines.
- Function well in high-pressure atmosphere.

EDUCATION

MEDICAL EDUCATION CENTER, Topeka, KS
Medical Assisting Diploma, August, 1993
Specialized in Vital Signs EKG, Lab Procedures, Patient and Examining Room Preparation, Instrument Set-ups, CPR and First-aid.
Trained in front office procedures and typing. Completed 170 hours practical experience Externship.

LEDGER WORD PROCESSING CENTER, Topeka, KS
12-week training program in typing, word processing (MacIntosh and IBM), office procedures, accounting, and communications. Certified December 1986.

EXPERIENCE

BRYMAN ASSOCIATES, Topeka, KS   1992-1993
Receptionist
Typed legal documents, merchant agreements, and contracts. Handled filing, incoming/outgoing mail, general office equipment and PBX Telephone System.

MASTER PRESS, Topeka, KS   1987-1992
Receptionist
Dealt with incoming calls, mail and monthly reports. Typed correspondence and manuscripts. Managed varied aspects of final book production. Prepared shipping orders.

VANDELAY INDUSTRIES, Topeka, KS   1984-1987
Receptionist
Handled general office functions; arranged meetings; issued payroll.

- Since candidate has no experience in his/her field of interest, relevant education is listed before unrelated work history.

- Unrelated work experience is outlined only briefly.

PSYCHIATRIST

DR. CHRIS SMITH
178 Green Street
Taunton, MA 02718
(508) 555-5555

EDUCATION
Harvard University Medical School, Cambridge, MA
M.D., 1985

University of Massachusetts, Boston, MA
B.S., Pre-Med, 1981

CERTIFICATION / PROFESSIONAL AFFILIATIONS
Certified by the Commonwealth of Massachusetts

American Medical Association
Massachusetts Psychiatric Society
Greater Boston Psychiatric Society
Council of the American Psychiatric Association

PUBLICATIONS
American Journal of Medicine, August 12, 1993, Volume 9.
"Correlations of Neurological Biomechanics and Headaches."

New England Journal of Medicine, May 30 1991, Volume 19, Issue 5.
"Further Effects of Prozac on Depressed Patients."

PROFESSIONAL HISTORY
Borewood Hospital, Framingham, MA
On-Call Psychiatrist, 1990 - Present
- Assist permanent staff with severely ill psychiatric patients as needed.
- Sit in on individual and group therapy. Attend staff meetings. Dispense medication.
- Responsible for administrative reporting and preliminary diagnoses, as needed.

Greater Boston Psychiatrics Center, Boston, MA
Psychiatrist, 1985 - Present
- Provide outpatient psychiatric care to patients in low-income households and dispense medication as necessary.
- Provide treatment for grieving patients who have lost a spouse or child.
- Participate in group therapy sessions at Veterans Administration Hospital, Jamaica Plain assisting Vietnam and Desert Storm veterans with post-traumatic stress syndrome.
- Provide information for insurance companies, HMO's, and third party billing staff.

■ Publications are impressive and add weight to resume.

■ Resume format is neat and professional.

RESPIRATORY THERAPIST

CHRIS SMITH
178 Green Street
Wellesley, MA 02181
(617) 555-5555

PROFILE:
Demonstrated extensive professional achievement in not only respiratory therapy but also in the organization and coordination of the administrative end of the Respiratory Therapy Division of Massachusetts General Hospital.

Areas of Strength:

Highly Organized	Pleasant Bedside Manner	Strong Work Ethic
Creative Problem Solver	Crisis Management	Administration

EXPERIENCE:
Massachusetts General Hospital, Boston, MA
Respiratory Therapy Division Administrator   1989 - Present
- Responsible for smooth running and operations of Respiratory Division.
- Handle all incoming information from physicians, surgeons, other hospitals, and HMO's.
- Interview, hire, and train RT Division staff; evaluate and write personnel reports.
- Administer RT on the floor as necessary; assist anesthesiologist and physicians during surgery.

Respiratory Therapist   1977 - 1988
- Responsible for daily suctioning of vented patients, checking arterial blood gases.
- Administer inhalers and nebulizer treatments.
- Recommend therapies and Bi-pap vents.
- Set up and secure trach-masks.
- Work with doctors and specialists listening to breath sounds; ausculate breath sounds.

EDUCATION:
Simmons College   Boston, MA
B.S., Nursing   1974

Massachusetts General Hospital School of Continuing Medical Education   Boston, MA
Respiratory Therapy Training   **Certified R.T., 1976**

AFFILIATIONS:
New England Society for Respiratory Therapists

■ Attention-getting profile gives a snapshot of candidate's professional experience and strengths.

■ Job descriptions include technical jargon specific to candidate's field.

SPEECH PATHOLOGIST

Chris Smith
178 Green Street
Providence, RI 02918
(401) 555-5555

EDUCATION
Brown University, Providence, RI
Master of Education in Human Development and Reading, 1982
Cape Town University, Cape Town, South Africa
Bachelor of Arts with Honors in Speech Pathology and Audiology, 1979

PROFESSIONAL EXPERIENCE
1986 to   ST. CHRISTOPHER'S HOSPITAL, Providence, RI
Present   **Clinical Supervisor**, Bennet Hospital Satellite Speech and Language Program
- Started and direct Speech and Language Program under aegis of Bennet Hospital
- Market program: designed brochure, performed on radio talk shows, administer all advertising
- Provide in-service consultation to hospital staff, students, various agencies and organizations
- Hire, supervise, orient, instruct and discipline employees, graduate students, and clinical fellows
- Conduct quality assurance; appraise performance
- Evaluate, diagnose, and treat inpatients/outpatients, adults/children with variety of communication disorders
- Provide supportive and educational counseling
- Develop policies and procedures, perform various managerial and administrative tasks
- Perform Speech, Hearing, and Language screening
- Develop augmentative communication systems for non-verbal population
- Conduct aural rehabilitation for elderly

1983 to 1986   BENNET HOSPITAL, Providence, RI
Staff Speech-Language Pathologist, Speech, Hearing and Language Center
- Evaluated, diagnosed, and treated inpatients/outpatients, adults/children with variety of communication disorders including: apraxia, aphasia, dysarthria, head injury, fluency, voice, neurological impairments, language, mental retardation, phonology, laryngectomy, dialectal variances, hearing impairments, cleft palate, and cerebral palsy
- Ran preschool language group
- Participated on Stroke Team
- Provided in-service consultation to staff and agencies

1980 to 1983   PRIVATE PRACTICE, Cape Town, South Africa
Speech Pathologist
- Assessed, diagnosed, and treated adults and children exhibiting variety of communication disorders
- Conferred with physicians and schools
- Provided supportive/educational parent counseling

■ Reverse chronological format focuses employer's attention on candidate's most current position.

■ Job descriptions detail candidate's responsibilities and accomplishments.

SURGEON

Chris Smith, M.D.
178 Green Street
Providence, RI 02903
(401) 555-5555

EXPERIENCE

PROVIDENCE GENERAL HOSPITAL, Providence, RI
Staff Heart Surgeon
Appointed May 1988

RESEARCH EXPERIENCE

1989 INSTITUTE OF CHILD CARE, Harvard University, Cambridge, MA
Worked within Department of Developmental Anatomy. Conducted
research on cardiac anatomy and pathology. Research led to
awarding of Master of Science degree in Medicine.

1988 DEPARTMENT OF ANATOMY, University of Rhode Island, Kingston, RI
Conducted histochemical research on the urinary tract.

1987 MAXWELL HOSPITAL, Davis, CA
Conducted research on cardiac anatomy, within the Cardiac
Anatomy Laboratory.

1985 CHILDREN'S HOSPITAL, Davis, CA
Conducted part-time research in cardiac pathology.

192 to STANFORD UNIVERSITY, Stanford, CA
1984 Received general surgical training, at Burnt Oak Hospital,
General Hospital, and Abbey Road Hospital.

1975 to CHILDREN'S HOSPITAL, Pepperdine Medical School, Malibu, CA
1979 Performed research on congenital heart disease, as a medical
student, during elective periods.

EDUCATION

1987 UNIVERSITY OF CALIFORNIA, Davis, CA
1984 STANFORD UNIVERSITY, Stanford, CA
1981 PEPPERDINE UNIVERSITY, Malibu, CA
Doctor of Medicine Degree, M.D.

POST-GRADUATE TRAINING

1985-1987 Surgical Residency: City Hospital, Davis, CA
1982-1984 Surgical Internship: Good Fellow Hospital, Stanford, CA

LICENSURE

Rhode Island #MD-075261-E
Board Eligible: General Surgery/8

- Valuable research experience is highlighted in detail.
- Dates are clearly listed in left margin.

VETERINARIAN

Chris Smith, D.V.M.
178 Green Street
Mutt, NY 02135
(212) 555-5555

OBJECTIVE

A position in **Veterinary Medicine** where I can use my experience and education in an **Animal Hospital/Clinic** and/or in **Research** that will lead to further development within the field.

SUMMARY OF QUALIFICATIONS

- 13 years Veterinary Medicine research and assistance.
- Strong communication skills; team player; equally effective and motivated working independently.

EDUCATION

TUFTS UNIVERSITY, Medford, MA
D.V.M. - 1993

NORTHEASTERN UNIVERSITY, Boston, MA
B.S., Pre-Med/Biology - 1987

EXPERIENCE

DR. JAMES HERRIOTT, D.V.M.   Yorkshire, England
Animal Technician/Surgery   1988-1991
- Administered, assisted and maintained anesthesia operations during surgery.
- Performed duties with animal patients in ICU, under Doctor's orders including oral, IV, IM, SQ, fluid therapy, radiology, hematology, immunology, chemotherapy.

LUCKY DOG PET FOODS, INC.   Boston, PA
Animal Technician/Manager Assistant, Research Center   1978-1985
- Supervised and scheduled 20 center and union employees in conducting research.
- Conducted research on pet food products and analyzed studies on nutrition, zinc, urinalysis, fecal analysis, fluid therapy, medication, breeding and artificial insemination.
- Provided and submitted reports to government entities for FDA approval.
- Directed hygienic procedures on 300 animals including surgical and necropsies.
- Collaborated in testing new vaccine for feline leukemia.

- Professional title (D.V.M.) is listed directly after candidate's name.

- Summary of qualifications illustrates candidate's key credentials.

VETERINARY ASSISTANT

CHRIS SMITH
178 Green Street
Marylhurst, OR 97036
(503) 555-5555

OBJECTIVE
To obtain a position as an Animal Health Technician.

EXPERIENCE

PIAGETTI ANIMAL CARE CLINIC — Marylhurst, OR
Neonatal Intensive Care Nurse — 1992-Present
- Monitor patients and schedule work, personnel and supplies.
- Perform pre- and post-operative care and emergency care
- Collect and ship blood samples.
- Organize labs for veterinary students and for clinical instruction.
- Monitor ventilation and vital statistics of premature and critically ill animals.
- Collect blood, perform intravenous and arterial catheterization, intubation of endotracheal and nasogastric tubes.
- Member of Emergency Ventilation Team.

Surgery Staff Nurse — 1990-1992
Administered pre- and post-operative surgical care.
- Prepared animals for surgery.
- Administered antibiotics.

Rotating Staff Nurse — 1988-1990
- Assisted clinicians and students in treatment of patients.
- Room nursing; pre- and post-operative management of patients.

CERTIFICATIONS
Licensed Animal Health Technician, 1988
Veterinary Medicine, University of Portland, 1992
Applied Dentistry for Veterinary Technicians, 1992

EDUCATION
University of Oregon, Eugene, OR
B.A. Animal Health Technology 1992

University of Portland, Portland, OR
A.S. Animal Health Technology 1988

- Job objective is brief and to the point.

- Professional certifications and strong educational background add strength to resume.

14
Human Resources

Nature of Work

Human resource workers act as liaisons between top management and employees. Personnel managers recruit, interview, and hire employees according to their qualifications and suitability to the organization. Training and labor relations workers attempt to encourage a productive company culture by effectively utilizing employee skills and fostering job satisfaction. Benefits managers handle employee health and pension plans. Recruiting sometimes requires extensive travel and knowledge of government regulations regarding labor and employee benefit regulations.

Employment

Human resource workers are employed in virtually every organization. The majority of salaried jobs are found in the private sector—service industries, labor organizations, and manufacturing. Other jobs are located in government. Many human resource specialists are self-employed consultants serving both the public and private sectors.

Training

Human resource workers come from a variety of educational backgrounds. Although employers usually require at least a college degree, majors vary among human resource workers. A master's degree is helpful in seeking a labor relations or management position, while a law degree is beneficial in contract negotiations and employment benefits. Many employers encourage training seminars.

Job Outlook

The job market for human resources workers is expected to be better than average through the year 2005, although it is likely that the atmosphere will still be competitive due to the abundance of college students and experienced workers with suitable qualifications.

Most growth will occur in the private sector as employers, concerned about productivity and quality of work, devote greater resources to job-specific training programs in response to the increasing complexity of many jobs, the aging work force, and technological advances that can leave employees with obsolete skills.

Earnings

The median annual salary for human resources workers was approximately $30,000 in 1990. However, the range for yearly income is extremely wide, beginning at entry-level salaries of around $19,000, up to senior-level management positions with earnings over $65,000 per year.

ASSISTANT PERSONNEL OFFICER

CHRIS SMITH
178 Green Street
Vienna, VA 22180
(703) 555-5555

PROFESSIONAL OBJECTIVE

A position in the personnel field in which my experience and education will have valuable application.

PROFESSIONAL EXPERIENCE

VIRGINIA GENERAL HOSPITAL, Suffolk, VA
Assistant Personnel Officer, 1990-Present
- Recruited and trained administrative and clerical staffs, ancillary and works department staffs, professional and technical staffs.
- Supervised Personnel Assistant, Personnel Clerk and Secretary.
- Organized, revised, expanded and managed induction program.
- Evaluated personnel.
- Conducted disciplinary and grievance interviews.
- Signed employees to contracts.
- Advised staff on conditions of employment, entitlements, maternity leave, etc.

SOUTHERN CHARM STORES, Roanoke, VA
Assistant Staff Manager, 1986-1990
- Recruited and selected employees.
- Hired personnel and referred for termination.
- Administered wages, salary and workmen's compensation.
- Developed staff in various job descriptions.
- Performed inductions.
- Supervised personnel clerk.
- Served as interim Staff Manager at Raleigh.

EDUCATION

YALE UNIVERSITY, New Haven, CT
Bachelor of Science in Sociology, 1986.

COOK COLLEGE, Los Angeles, CA
Personnel Management Exams, 1985.

REFERENCES

Available upon request.

- Clean layout makes resume easy to read.

- Unrelated work experience is omitted.

ASSISTANT VICE-PRESIDENT OF HUMAN RESOURCES

CHRIS SMITH
178 Green Street
Longview, TX 75601
(903) 555-5555

PROFESSIONAL EXPERIENCE

RENFIELD CORPORATION, Longview, TX   **1991-Present**
Assistant Vice-President - Human Resources
Responsible for professional recruitment, human resources planning, benefits and compensation, employee relations, EEO/AA compliance and reporting, and service quality consultation.
- Spearheaded a project team for the development of a Home For Runaways.
- Evaluated the effectiveness of 30 incentive pay plans, recommending changes tied to service quality, and saving over $3 million in unproductive payouts.
- Reduced professional staffing costs by 10%, saving $400,000.

PHINEAS COMPANY, Killeen, TX   **1986-1991**
Director of Human Resources
Professionalized the human resources function by more cost-effective recruiting, designing a formal compensation program, implementing a performance management process, and inaugurating management and employee training.
- Analyzed pay practices and designed a more appropriate compensation system, including executive bonus plan, which was linked to performance goals, saving an estimated $300,000 in salary costs.

LANCOWSKI CORPORATION, U.S./Japan   **1982-1986**
Senior Consultant, Organization Effectiveness
Facilitated the implementation of Total Quality using employee involvement and supportive human resources systems; worked with executive and management teams in planning organization changes, and trained 40 facilitators and 200 employee teams in quality and problem-solving processes.

EDUCATION
M.S. Industrial Relations/HR Management
New York University, New York, NY, 1981

B.A. Economics/Psychology
Eugene Lang College, New York, NY, 1979

PROFESSIONAL AFFILIATIONS
Southwest Human Resource Planners Group
Association for Management Excellence

SPECIAL ACCOMPLISHMENTS
Vice-President and Co-Founder of the Longview Quality Club
Invited lecturer and adjunct faculty at two Longview universities
Authored 10 articles in leading professional journals and publications
Elected member of the Executive Leadership Committee, 1984-1985

■ Statistics and dollar figures quantify candidate's accomplishments.

■ Specific accomplishments highlight candidate's leadership abilities.

BENEFITS COORDINATOR

CHRIS SMITH
178 Green Street
Nordland, WA 98358
(509) 555-5555

WORK EXPERIENCE:
Jennings One Stop Stores, Inc., Seattle, WA
UNION BENEFITS COORDINATOR/ASSISTANT SUPERVISOR - PAYROLL   1992-Present
- Maintain and update all changes to the Union Benefits contract run for propriety, i.e., Pension/Health and Welfare reports, and mailed benefit checks to union offices.
- Handle weekly balancing of employee master file from all 450 stores and verify information before entering data into keypunch system.
- Research and resolve all errors and warning messages that appeared on the MSA edit.
- Edit the telxon field payroll transmissions.
- Reconcile all checks to the unclaimed wages account.
- Assist Department Supervisor in day-to-day operations; supervise staff of 30; handle special projects as assigned.

LEASE ADMINISTRATOR   1991-1992
- Analyzed and paid common area maintenance bills.
- Assisted in the preparation of monthly percentage rent accruals.
- Prepared quarterly gross sales reconciliation to the general ledger.
- Logged and filed lease agreements, amendments, etc., in the lease files.
- Reviewed and prepared lease summaries.
- Updated regular price files for stores with advance price reductions.
- Prepared gross sales figures.
- Updated and maintained automatic payment run for all theatre rents and payments as per lease agreements.

MARKETING RESEARCH ASSISTANT   1990-1991
- Primarily involved with gathering technical computer-related material for various Jennings publications.
- Duties included procurement of information, determination of accuracy, conscientious follow-through, continuous updating, as well as the ability to meet special deadlines.
- Chosen to train new employees in comprehensive aspects of computer trends throughout the United States.

EDUCATION:
University of Maine, Orono, ME
Bachelor of Arts Degree in Economics, 1988
G.P.A. 3.0
Concentration: Business/Finance/Communications

INTERESTS:
Jogging, fencing, cooking

Business and personal references are available upon request

■ Reverse chronological format focuses employer's attention on candidate's most current position.

■ Dynamic action verbs give resume impact.

COMPENSATION MANAGER

CHRIS SMITH
178 Green Street
Portales, NM 88130
(505) 555-5555

**CAREER
SUMMARY** A Human Resource Manager with extensive experience in maximizing corporate, team and individual performance through progressive human processes. Diversified generalist experience in strategic human resource planning, employee relations, employment, compensation, training, and organizational development.

**CAREER
HISTORY** **BANK OF NEW MEXICO,** Portales, NM
Compensation Manager (1994-Present)
Managed the Compensation and Payroll functions, which included the Job Analysis, Salary Administration, Employee Payroll and Personnel Records sections. Utilized the Hay job evaluation system and implemented a total HRIS conversion.

Compensation Representative (1992-1994)
Provided employee relations support and consultation to three departments. Specific activities included development, implementation and administration of compensation function. Responsible for all compensation activities, including position analysis and evaluation, benchmarking, salary surveys, and merit budget recommendations.

Employment Manager & Employee Relations Counselor (1990-1992)
Developed recruitment sources, college programs, internal staffing, outplacement, and provided employee counseling. Interpreted personnel policies for employee effectiveness.

M-N-M PLACEMENT AGENCY, Santa Fe, NM
Placement Counselor (1989-1990)
Recruited, screened, and placed candidates for permanent positions. Advertised, interviewed, and placed candidates for temporary assignments, as well as generated new business activity through cold sales calls.

EDUCATION **UNIVERSITY OF NEW MEXICO,** Albuquerque, NM
B.A. Political Science, 1989

PERSONAL Willing to relocate.

REFERENCES Available upon request.

■ Career summary grabs the reader's attention with powerful skills and qualifications.

■ Chronological format illustrates a clear career path.

DIRECTOR OF HUMAN RESOURCES

CHRIS SMITH
178 Green Street
Memphis, TN 38116
(901) 555-5555

OBJECTIVE

A career in Personnel Management/Administration.

PROFESSIONAL EXPERIENCE

TENNESSEE PAROLE BOARD, Memphis, TN
Director of Human Resources and Staff Development   1991-Present
Develop and implement policy. Provide leadership in the areas of personnel, payroll, labor relations, training, and affirmative action. Administer personnel/payroll system to meet management and employee needs. Consult with Chairman, Executive Director, managerial staff, and supervisors to ensure policy compliance with applicable statutes, rules, and regulations. Advance agency Affirmative Action Plan. Determine appropriate grievance procedures relief; resolve labor disputes. Act as liaison for regulatory agencies: EOHS, OER, DPA, State Office of A.A., and PERA. Maintain staff training program. Interface with Legal Staff in dealing with progressive discipline and grievances.

WILMONT INSURANCE CO., Nashville, TN
Director of Human Resources   1987-1991
Maintained smooth work-flow; supervised claim adjudication; performed claim payment internal audits; coordinated activity with reinsurance carriers. Hired/terminated, trained, oversaw, and delegated personnel. Determined technical decisions and payments. Responsible for computer maintenance (IBM Series I) and updating personnel files to ensure compliance with state/local regulations pertaining to holidays, vacations, etc.

Central Personnel Officer   1984-1987
Coordinated statewide reclassification study; organized questionnaires, individual interviews and desk audits. Evaluated/analyzed study data; rewrote job descriptions; prepared study package for legislative approval. Established related managerial files. Dealt with diverse personnel-related projects.

EDUCATION

Milligan College, Milligan College, TN
Course work in Personnel Management and Human Resources, 1990-Present

Tennessee Wesleyan College, Nashville, TN
B.A. Degree, Management, 1980

- Action verbs give job descriptions punch.

- Continuing education indicates candidate's ongoing commitment to his/her career.

EMPLOYER RELATIONS REPRESENTATIVE

CHRIS SMITH
178 Green Street
Provo, UT 84604
(801) 555-5555

CAREER HISTORY

1992 to DEPARTMENT OF EMPLOYMENT AND TRAINING   Provo, UT
Present *Supervisor*
- Assign and review applications, placement, initial claims and claims processing adjustments.
- Evaluate subordinate performance through both qualitative and quantitative analysis. Ensure compliance with established procedures.
- Recommend improvements in operations for enhanced public services.
- Supervise preparation and maintenance of statistical records. Ensure accurate reports.

1989 to DEPARTMENT OF UNEMPLOYMENT   Provo, UT
1992 *Claims Adjudicator*
- Interviewed employers; gathered information; determined status in claims cases.
- Analyzed/interpreted Utah Employment Security Law to ensure information completeness.
- Verified/supplemented case data via file searches and data base assessment.
- Trained new personnel.
- Maintained weekly case log and purge files, ensuring timely handling.

1987 to STEPHEN JOLIE JEWELS   Sandy, UT
1989 *Assistant Manager*
- Supervised/assisted with all facets of retail and wholesale operations.
- Hired, trained, scheduled and supervised personnel.
- Prepared daily balances; managed cash.
- Planned and implemented in-store displays/promotions.
- Coordinated advertising with media outlets.

EDUCATION

SMITH COLLEGE, Northampton, MA
Bachelor's Degree, Management 1987

AFFILIATIONS

- National Conference of Women - Secretary, 1989
- American Association of Business Managers, 1988-Present
- Smith College Alumni Association

■ Job descriptions highlight candidate's professional skills and responsibilities.

■ Job-related affiliations and elected positions within professional organizations accentuate candidate's dedication to his/her field.

EMPLOYMENT CONSULTANT (General)

CHRIS SMITH
178 Green Street
Orange, CA 92666
(714) 555-5555

PROFESSIONAL EXPERIENCE:

Chadd, Herman, Lombardi and Company   Los Angeles, CA
Employment Consultant (1984-Present)
- Coordinate complete employment services to a diverse client base throughout the area.
- Recruit applicants and provide career counseling, testing and quality matching to job.
- Established an employment service that promotes and integrates the Human Resource profession.

Emmanuel Cooperative Group   Los Angeles, CA
Employment Manager (1987-1989)
- Recruited candidates for non-exempt and exempt positions at stores, warehouses, and data ontry centers
- Developed low cost recruitment practices through supported work programs and career fairs.
- Administered and maintained performance and salary reviews.
- Advised managers on employee relation issues and counseled employees in the area of career/personal development.

Payroll Supervisor/Personnel Generalist (1986-1987)
- Performed weekly payroll functions, verified timecards and checked for non-work hours for over 650 employees.
- Solved weekly payroll problems.
- Maintained personnel records, attendance, and vacation schedules.
- Conducted systems and orientation training classes.
- Interviewed for non-exempt positions.
- Administration of benefit enrollment.

Department Manager (1986)
- Supervised daily floor operations and staff development.

EDUCATION:

Chapman College   Orange, CA
Master of Arts in Human Resource Management, May, 1993

University of Alabama   Birmingham, AL
Bachelor of Science, 1986
Major: Child Development and Family Relations

- Specific achievements and dynamic action verbs give resume impact.

- Job descriptions are brief and punchy, without being choppy.

EMPLOYMENT CONSULTANT (Specialized)

CHRIS SMITH
178 Green Street
Fort Worth, TX 76112
(817) 555-5555

SUMMARY OF QUALIFICATIONS:

- Supervisory/administrative experience with educational, recreational, vocational, and community programs.
- Actively involved in programs to motivate, counsel and tutor college freshmen.
- Superior communication skills and the ability to maintain cooperative spirit from individuals and groups at all age levels.

EXPERIENCE: *Consultant,* Murdock Corporation, Fort Worth, TX
1992-Present
Serve as a consultant on matters pertaining to effective methods for developing job openings and serving as a source of manpower supply to industry. Involved in planning, programming, and implementing training programs for the hard-core unemployed. Work as liaison between government agencies, industry, and the community.

Supervisor, The Metropolitan League, Dallas, TX
1988-1992
Served as a Member of the Personnel Committee, the function of which was to set up a policy for the operation of the League. Supervised the operation of the Metro League Office. Screened and tested prospective employees and matched skills and talents with several areas of employment. Worked with government agencies and industry to solicit jobs for unskilled, unemployed youths.

Recreational Supervisor, Dalton Neighborhood Action Program, Dallas, TX
1986-1988
Coordinated recreational activities in seven parks and supervised twenty employees.

Counselor, Berns House, Edna, TX
1984-1986
Coordinated sports programs for several teenage social clubs; counseled and tutored teenagers.

COMMUNITY ACTIVITIES: Elected to serve on the Board of Homeless Advocates, a non-profit organization formed to foster the socio-economic levels of individuals and small business aspirants in the Dallas and Fort Worth areas. Investigated business ideas and individuals, providing funds for those with entrepreneurial potential in the greater Fort Worth area.

EDUCATION: Bishop College, Dallas, TX
MA, Psychology, 1983

Boston University, Boston, MA
BA, Black History, 1981

■ Summary of qualifications illustrate candidate's key credentials.

■ Powerful adjectives (like "superior" and "hard-core") are chosen carefully and used sparingly to ensure maximum impact.

FACILITY MANAGER

Chris Smith
178 Green Street
Suquamish, WA 93982
(206) 555-5555

OBJECTIVE

Human Resources Management: Facility Manager.

EXPERIENCE

WOODLAND HALFWAY HOUSES, INC., Suquamish, WA
Facility House Manager   1992-Present
• Manage upkeep of the facility, assigning weekly maintenance and repair details.
• Supervise and assign office spaces and monthly collection of rents.
• Maintain inventory control of supplies, equipment, key control, first aid and hygiene kits.
• Provide front desk coverage, sign-in and sign-out logs by occupants, and verified incoming calls.
• Respond to programs involving informal counseling.

Volunteer Night Counselor   1991
• Responsible for nightly desk coverage.
• Maintained occupant sign-in/sign-out logs and worked with counselors in crises intervention programs.

CITY OF SEATTLE, Seattle, WA
Contract Administrator   1989-1992
• Monitored assigned programs by conducting quarterly on-site visitations and reviews.
• Reviewed monthly invoices and executed quarterly and final analysis of performance standards.
• Researched budget requirements and advised on budget revision requests.
• Participated in annual program planning and proposal review process.

Interviewer/Vocational Counselor   1987-1989
• Provided on-going vocational counseling to C.E.T.A. eligible clients and acted as liaison with program administrators.
• Clients represented ex-offenders and unemployed.
• Administered tests and referred applicants to various C.E.T.A. training programs.
• Responsible for documentaries, reports, and records on progress of programs.

EDUCATION

RANDLE HILL COMMUNITY COLLEGE, Randle, WA   1987
Studies: Human Resources/Criminal Justice/Accounting I/II

References available upon request

■ Work experience is emphasized, while limited education is de-emphasized.

■ Use of boldface and underlining provides a clean and crisp presentation.

JOB PLACEMENT OFFICER

CHRIS SMITH
178 Green Street
Kensington, MN 56343
(313) 555-5555

OBJECTIVE: A position in Industrial Relations and/or Human Resources.

EXPERIENCE: The Now Division, Kensington, MN
Job Placement Officer   1990-Present
Establish and maintain contact with various civic, cultural, and community organizations; actively participate in the development of programs designed to improve industrial and community relations through vocational training programs, OJT, and equal employment opportunities for the residents of Kensington and surrounding communities. Participate in programs, staff activities, community meetings, and conferences; prepare in-depth reports on proceedings. Establish contacts with prospective employers, union, public and private agencies, and associations to develop job opportunities for community residents. Recruit trainees from the community, and instruct them in good grooming and proper procedures for applying for a position.

Emmanuel Agency, Minneapolis, MN
Job Placement Officer   1987-1990
Conducted individual and group counseling of under-privileged youths for the purpose of developing positive attitudes and conduct for entry into the job market. Studied information on current labor trends and investigated areas of referrals. Maintained liaisons with available placement agencies throughout the city.

Borden's Boy's Club, Minneapolis, MN
Athletic Director   1985-1987
Developed and implemented recreational programs for approximately 700-800 boys, ages 7-15. Supervised staff of ten. Maintained all equipment and materials; established excellent relationships with participating children, parents, and other community agencies.

AFFILIATIONS: National Association of Human Resource Administrators
National Association of Job Placement Officers

EDUCATION: Clarke College, Dubuque, IA
Bachelor of Arts Degree, 1985
Major: Psychology

REFERENCES: Excellent references available upon request.

■ Job objective gives resume focus without limiting candidate's opportunities.

■ Professional affiliations show candidate's commitment to his/her field.

LABOR RELATIONS SPECIALIST

CHRIS SMITH
178 Green Street
New York, NY 10027
(212) 555-5555

OBJECTIVE
A challenging career continuation where labor relations experience will be utilized and advanced.

SUMMARY OF QUALIFICATIONS
- Over fifteen years of human resource and labor relations experience.
- Fluent in written and oral Spanish and English.
- Available to travel.
- Developed interpersonal and communication skills, having dealt with a diversity of professionals, clients, and staff members.
- Self-motivated; able to set effective priorities and implement decisions to achieve immediate and long-term goals and meet operational deadlines.
- Adept at anticipating and innovatively resolving potential problem areas.

PROFESSIONAL EXPERIENCE
THE CITY OF NEW YORK DEPARTMENT OF HEALTH   1984-Present
Labor/Management Relations Analyst
Represent over 4,000 employees. Investigate/mediate disciplinary actions taken by supervisors against employees; conduct grievance hearings. Collect, compile, and evaluate labor/economic data; write reports; present findings at City Hall hearings. Provide assistance in policy formation, implementation, planning, and dissemination. Aid/advise management staff with interpretation and application of collective bargaining agreements, supplemental agreements, personnel policies/practices, and grievance policy. Act as liaison with union representatives. Research and determine appropriate adherence to labor contract terms. Prepare documentation for evidence and mediate in diverse hearings. Interact with staff members, union representatives and management; develop recommendations; design agreements.

NEW YORK COMMISSION AGAINST DISCRIMINATION   1982-1983
Field Representative
Investigated alleged discrimination practices. Utilized paralegal training and analytical writing skills. Wrote recommendations and case dispositions.

NEW YORK HISPANIC LEGISLATIVE CAUCUS   1980-1982
Legislative Assistant
Served as liaison between Hispanic community, state legislators and business interests. Liaison responsibilities extended statewide to over 200 agencies. Organized/conducted legislative research projects. Interacted with senior staff researchers. Cooperated with Caucus in implementation of community outreach goals and general counseling needs.

EDUCATION
FORDHAM UNIVERSITY, Bronx, NY
B.S. Degree, 1979
Concentration: Government

- Resume accentuates candidate's experience dealing with cultural diversity issues.

- Foreign language skills are relevant to candidate's job objective.

PERSONNEL CONSULTANT

CHRIS SMITH
178 Green Street
Denver, CO 80208
(303) 555-5555

PROFESSIONAL EXPERIENCE

National Equipment Corporation   **Denver, CO**
Personnel Consultant, Software, Inc.   *1985-Present*
Provide consultation to and leadership for senior staff members and their management teams. Advise on organization and business issues, including needs assessment, diagnosis, transition planning, and problem solving. Develop positive and proactive employee relations, effective communications, employee advocate role, participative management, third party negotiation, interpreting company policies and procedures, employee development, compensation and benefits, and training design. Recommend organizational design and reorganization to maximize utilization of workforce. Design and/or facilitate group development activities, i.e., team-building programs. Communicate Affirmative Action/EEO policies and procedures to include: profile, climate, goal-setting, identification of problem areas and planning. Consult to effective management practices and behaviors, particularly in the areas of performance appraisal and reward system, and human resource planning.

Training Consultant, Sales Training Development, Barnes and Rogers   *1979-1984*
Consulted with product groups and other clients to determine training needs. Performed needs analysis and established program objectives. Recommended training solutions. Identified methods of introducing new information to increase job competence. Devised and documented training. Developed basic training materials and coordinated efforts of outside consultants and vendors. Assembled and organized all conceptual materials into course design. Determined effective instructional technique. Arranged for design and printing of material and preparation of audio-visual aids. Assisted in conducting pilot programs to train instructors. Evaluated and refined course materials in an effort to find optimum solution to training challenges.

State of Colorado   **Denver, CO**
Staff Assistant, Bureau of Employment   *1979*
Devised in-service staff development programs for state employees. Coordinated implementation with union and management. Planned career ladder education programs for upward mobility for state employees.

EDUCATION

M.Ed., 1978, University of Denver Graduate School of Education, Denver, CO
Administration, Planning and Social Policy Program

B.A., 1974, Colorado College, Colorado Springs, CO
Major: History

■ Job descriptions focus on candidate's ability to successfully complete projects and coordinate with various interest groups.

■ Diverse professional background includes positions held in both private and public sectors.

PERSONNEL MANAGER

CHRIS SMITH
178 Green Street
Franklin, IN 46131
(317) 555-5555

PROFESSIONAL BACKGROUND

PERSONNEL MANAGER
Cronin Construction, Franklin, IN
July 1994 to Present
- Adjust Human Resources policy to needs of expanding company.
- Develop Human Resources goals and objectives.
- Manage Human Resources budget.
- Handle employee relations.
- Direct employment and recruitment efforts.
- Manage company benefits and compensation.
- Compile statistics for employee benefits handbook.
- Assist in development of training programs.

PERSONNEL ADMINISTRATOR
Moschella Management Corporation, Franklin, IN
July 1992 to July 1994
- Initiated affirmative action program.
- Compiled policies and procedures manual for Human Resources Department.
- Coordinated recruitment program with agencies, and attended job fairs.
- Created advertising campaign for recruitment program.
- Developed and packaged new employee orientation.
- Implemented additional benefits, i.e., tuition reimbursement and employee referral program.

MANAGER OF PERSONNEL/PAYROLL
Purdue University School of Management, West Lafayette, IN
May 1990 to June 1992
- Supervised administrative and technical support staff.
- Interviewed, hired, and terminated personnel.
- Negotiated salaries, budgets, and business plan.
- Analyzed and resolved personnel grievances.

ASSISTANT MANAGER
Atwood Industries, Beloit, WI
September 1988 to May 1990
- Hired and terminated personnel; handled salary negotiations.
- Implemented billing and credit procedures (accounts payable and receivable).
- Served as liaison between client companies, East Coast office, and Home Office.

NOTABLE ACHIEVEMENTS
- Developed and managed Human Resources role as company grew from 140 to 275 employees.
- Completed course work in media presentations and computer applications (Lotus 1-2-3, WordPerfect, Pagemaker).

EDUCATION
Bachelor of Arts Degree in English, 1988
Beloit College, Beloit, WI

■ Bulleted statements are concise and begin with powerful action verbs.

■ Achievements demonstrate candidate's initiative.

RECRUITER (Agency)

CHRIS SMITH
178 Green Street
Willoughby, OH 44095
(216) 555-5555

SKILLS AND ACHIEVEMENTS PROFILE

- *Marketing Effectiveness: Perform market research and identify target populations to fill up to 83,000 vacancies; designed and created innovative programs. Increased recruitment market share from 14.9% to 34.4% with innovative marketing/advertising techniques.*
- *Staff Development: Select, train, supervise and counsel civilian and military recruiters and support personnel; market incisive individual performance evaluations. Record for inspiring team commitment to goals and quality standards.*
- *Public Relations: Articulate speaker; highly effective public presentations. Devised and implemented a comprehensive outreach program; significantly increased minority involvement with referrals from community organizations.*
- *Computer Proficiency: Utilize PARADOX, WINDOWS and other business-related software programs. Reduced inquiry response time with PARADOX for WINDOWS used for data management, scheduling and word processing functions.*

EXPERIENCE

RECRUITMENT COORDINATOR: Woodbine Job Corps Center   1992-1994
Coordinated efforts to attract, qualify and secure 500+ educational and vocational program vacancies for young adults annually while providing motivation and impetus for retention of program participants. Conceptualized, developed and implemented highly effective marketing campaigns. Trained, assigned and supervised support personnel in daily activities.
- *Increased the qualified candidate pool by 60%.*
- *Created innovative approaches to recruiting operations.*
- *Ordered daily work flow patterns and improved organization.*
- *Implemented tracking and monitoring systems.*
- *Created a computer database effectively managing applicant information.*
- *Inspired successful team effort to meet program recruitment and retention efforts.*
- *Initiated participative management style into the organizational and planning tasks.*

RECRUITMENT MANAGER   1988-1991
Directed regional recruitment activities for a $9 billion high tech organization with 83,000 job vacancies yearly. Designed, developed and implemented programs and campaigns to reach specialized target groups. Created and negotiated placement of a variety of advertising with the print and broadcast media. Developed and controlled annual operating budgets. Assigned, motivated and supervised a staff of 9 recruiters in goal setting and achievement.
- *Received numerous awards for meeting monthly quotas, motivating staff and professional expertise.*
- *Reduced applicant turnover rate by 15%.*
- *Increased goal reaching effectiveness by 25% with effective staff leadership.*

EDUCATION

University of Maine, Orono, ME
B.A. Management, 1987

- Skills and achievements profile summarizes candidate's areas of expertise.

- Job descriptions highlight candidate's on-the-job achievements.

RECRUITER (Human Resources Department)

178 Green Street
Boise, ID 83725
(208) 555-5555

OBJECTIVE A position in recruiting with a progressive, expanding firm offering growth potential within the organization's structure. Willing to relocate and/or travel.

ACCOMPLISHMENTS
- Established excellent relationships with employment agencies from California to Massachusetts; increased quantity and quality of resumes received by 200%.
- Developed monthly mailer directed to agencies.
- Implemented new administration procedures, increasing clerical productivity by 95% and reducing personnel department overhead by 30%.

EXPERIENCE Professional Recruiter - TAB/GTK Corporation, Boise, ID
August 1994-present
- Recruit sales and marketing support personnel.
- Plan and execute field recruiting trips to major cities, seminars, career centers, conferences, and universities.
- Design and implement college recruiting programs.
- Establish and maintain working relationship with select employment agencies.
- Prepare statistical reports relating to department expenditures and provide recommendations for eliminating excessive cost and overhead.
- Assist in the development of employee communication programs.

Personnel Manager - Bannen Boot Company, Syracuse, NY
May 1992-August 1994
- Established first complete personnel program including developing all procedures, records, programs, sources of hire and all administrative functions related to the recruiting and hiring of personnel.
- Established a child care service in-house.
- Worked on human relations problems arising with the introduction of newly established standards and work procedures.
- Developed new employee orientation programs including visual aids and prepared tests.
- Developed and maintained employee recreation program, music and PA system, bulletin boards, etc.

EDUCATION
Syracuse University, School of Communications, Syracuse, MA
BS Degree, Public Relations, 1989. Minor: Sociology.

■ Indicating a willingness to relocate and/or travel can be advantageous for a candidate in the field of recruiting.

■ Accomplishments section highlights candidate's most impressive achievements.

RECRUITER (Human Resources Department)

CHRIS SMITH
178 Green Street
New London, CT 06320
(203) 555-5555

OBJECTIVE

To contribute managerial skills to a challenging position as a Recruiter.

SUMMARY OF QUALIFICATIONS

- Extensive public relations work, dealing with all levels of employment.
- Self-motivated; able to organize, analyze and meet operational deadlines.
- Respond well in high-pressure atmosphere.
- Capable of handling a diversity of responsibilities simultaneously.

EXPERIENCE

NORMAN DEPARTMENT STORES, New London, CT
Manager of Executive Recruitment, 6/87-1/94
Oversaw college recruiting process, annual budget $75,000. Presented campus recruitment workshops; developed internship program. Hired/recruited support and merchandising staff. Organized Senior Executive involvement. Received award for overall achievement and outstanding performance in Human Resources, 3/92.

Department Manager, 9/85-6/87
Merchandised children's clothing and accessories. Analyzed/marketed $2 million inventory. Coordinated inventory control. Trained/developed staff of 15 sales associates in customer services skills and selling techniques. Achieved 20% sales increase over one year period. Chosen Manager of the Year for excellence in execution of responsibilities, 1986.

SEINFELD'S, Redding, CT
Selling Supervisor Trainee, 6/85-8/85
Coordinated merchandising and overall appearance of Men's Department. Evaluated sales data. Controlled inventory and placement of incoming merchandise. Executed price revisions.

EDUCATION

CONNECTICUT COLLEGE, New London, CT
B.A., Spanish Modified with Government Studies, May 1987

- Specific contributions display candidate's achievements and problem-solving abilities.

- Specific dates of employment (month and year) are ideal for candidates with no gaps in work history.

TRAINING COORDINATOR

CHRIS SMITH
178 Green Street
Orangeburg, SC 29115
(803) 555-5555

SKILLS

- ***Human Resource Development:*** Articulate and effective communicator and trainer. Inspire a team commitment to company goals, management objectives and high quality performance standards.
- ***Computer Systems:*** Skilled in use and development of data collection, and spreadsheet programs for accounting, statistical analysis and reporting functions. Assisted in computer systems installations and full training of employees.
- ***Troubleshooter:*** Analytical with an established track record for identifying complex problems; resourceful and inventive in developing and implementing creative solutions with enhanced sensitivity to cost, efficiency and deadlines.

EXPERIENCE

TRAINING COORDINATOR 1993-Present
Silver Guard Insurance Agency Orangeburg, SC
Develop training curriculum, aids and materials to instruct staff in division operations, corporate policy and procedure, and to maintain on-going personnel development in knowledge of current practices, increase job performance skills and maintain quality assurance for all office operations.
- Conduct highly effective classroom sessions and hands-on training encompassing billing, benefits, insurance industry regulations and relevant legal issues.
- Specialize in investigating and settling medical malpractice cases.

MANAGER 1991-1993
Orange Community Medical Center Orangeburg, SC
Managed and supervised daily credit and collections operations with responsibility for client billing and managing free care programs. Controlled operating budget and contributed to overall budget planning. Analyzed accounts status and implemented appropriate collections procedures; facilitated clear communications with service vendors; worked effectively with attorneys in cases involving legal proceedings.

ASSISTANT MANAGER 1987-1991
Contemporary Temps Hartsville, SC
Collected insurance statistical data; implemented cost avoidance programs and conducted training for temporary employees in billing procedures, government benefits programs, health care benefits issues, and insurance industry regulations.

EDUCATION
BACHELOR OF SCIENCE IN BUSINESS ADMINISTRATION, 1988
Coker College - Hartsville, SC

- Skills section draws attention to candidate's acquired professional qualifications.

- Chrono-functional resume has the strength of chronological format and the flexibility of functional format.

TRAINING SPECIALIST

CHRIS SMITH
178 Green Street
Winter Park, FL 32789
(305) 555-5555

CAREER OBJECTIVE A position in **Human Resources** in which professionally and educationally developed skills will be utilized and rewarded.

SUMMARY OF QUALIFICATIONS

- Over seven years generalist experience in Human Resources.
- Relevant education and training in the field.
- Excellent interpersonal and communication abilities.
- Strong employee relations.
- Proven recruiting, interviewing, evaluating and analyzing skills.

RELATED EXPERIENCE

ALLSAFE INSURANCE AGENCY, Orlando, FL

1988-Present **Training Specialist**

- Oversee employment process for assigned departments; conduct employment interviews, make hiring recommendations; network to maintain and expand base of contacts.
- Administer employee benefit programs, including Short/Long Term Disability and Medical/Dental Programs.
- Develop and conduct a variety of training programs with emphases on system instruction for all levels of employees.
- Develop/evaluate positions according to point system; assign salary grades; analyze and conduct periodic salary surveys.
- Recommend appropriate resolutions to employee relations problems; interpret company policies to management and staff.

1987 **Human Resources Assistant**

- Workmen's Compensation filings; temporary placements.

1986 **Human Resources Clerk**

- Human Resources office support

EDUCATION

ROLLINS COLLEGE, Winter Park, FL
Certificate in Human Resources Management; 1993.

ECKERD COLLEGE, St. Petersburg, FL
B.A. in Sociology; 1986.

■ Career objective gives resume focus without limiting candidate's opportunities.

■ Resume indicates a series of promotions.

VICE-PRESIDENT OF HUMAN RESOURCES

CHRIS SMITH
178 Green Street
Daytona, FL 32114
(904) 555-5555

OBJECTIVE

Executive-level position in Human Resources Management

PROFESSIONAL EXPERIENCE

Vice-President, Human Resources
Ann Davis Laboratories, Inc., Daytona, FL   1991-present
Direct a staff of 8 in the design and delivery of HR programs and services for this $175 mm
biotech/pharmaceutical business.
- Operate at Executive Staff Level in directing the business and resolving organizational issues.
- Changed existing Personnel Department into a streamlined HR department with bottom-line accountability.
- Recruit difficult to fill positions in an extremely competitive recruiting environment. Reduced turnover by 15%; managed cost per hire to below 30% for exempt hires.
- Introduced new performance compensation program — structure development, management guides and training, distribution curve, common reviews , and new survey participation. Formulated management incentive programs. Reconstructed field operations incentive program which greatly improved performance/morale.
- Formulate and administer new HR policies; employee suggestion system and opinion survey; various other employee motivational and communication programs.

Director, Human Resources
Olsen Laboratories, Inc., Sebring, FL   1987-1991
- Directed large staff (45-70) in providing all HR services and programs to the Corporate Headquarters organization.
- Introduced and directed a corporate centralized employment function operating as an in-house sourcing unit to reduce costs and streamline operations.

Corporate Compensation Manager
McCormick Inc., Tampa, FL   1983-1987
- Directed worldwide compensation programs including manufacturing facilities in the United Kingdom for the European sales force.

EDUCATION

M.A., Organizational Communications, Flagler College, St. Augustine, FL, 1982
B.A., Liberal Arts, University of Miami, Miami, FL, 1980

■ Percentages and dollar figures quantify candidate's achievements.

■ Job titles illustrate candidate's career progression.

15
Legal and Protective Services

Nature of Work

Laws define the society in which we live. It is the responsibility of lawyers and judges to interpret these laws, and police officers to enforce them. People such as paralegals, corrections officers, guards, and court officials act as support for our legal system. This includes people employed in correctional facilities, prisons, courts, and public or private businesses in security or claims departments.

Paralegals work directly under the supervision of an attorney. While the attorney assumes responsibility for the paralegal's work, a paralegal is allowed to perform all the functions of a lawyer other than accepting clients, giving legal advice, or presenting a case in court.

Guards, often called security officers, patrol and inspect property to protect against fire, theft, vandalism, and illegal entry. Their duties vary with the size, type, and location of their employer. Patrolling is usually done on foot, but some make rounds by car.

Correction officers are charged with the safety and security of persons who have been arrested, are awaiting trial, or who have been convicted of a crime and sentenced to serve time in a correctional institution. Correction officers may escort prisoners in transit between courtrooms, correctional institutions, and other points. They maintain order within the institution, enforce rules and regulations, and often supplement the counseling that inmates receive from psychologists, social workers, and other mental health professionals.

Employment

Law firms and courthouses employ a vast majority of the workers in legal and protective services. Lawyers, contracts managers, court officers, and paralegals work in one of these two locations. Paralegals can be found in almost every federal government agency, while the majority of guards are employed by industrial security firms and guard agencies.

Training

Educational requirements vary by profession. An attorney must be licensed, or admitted to its bar, under rules established by the jurisdiction's highest court. Nearly all require that applicants for admission to the bar pass a written bar examination. Civil service regulations govern the appointment of police and detectives in practically all States and large cities and in many small ones. Candidates must be U.S. citizens, usually at least 20 years of age, and must meet rigorous physical and personal qualifications. Eligibility for appointment depends on performance in competitive written examinations as well as on education and experience. Physical examinations often include tests of vision, strength, and agility.

There are several ways to enter the paralegal profession. Employers generally require formal paralegal training; however, some prefer to train paralegals on the job, promoting experienced legal secretaries or hiring persons with college education but no legal experience.

Job Outlook

Opportunities for people seeking positions as guards and corrections officers are expected to be plentiful through the year 2005, due to the rising inmate population. Employment of police officers is expected to increase about as fast as the average for all occupations. However, competition will be tough for those interested in positions as attorneys or judges.

Earnings

In 1990, security guards in 23 urban areas averaged about $6.28 per hour. Corrections officers at the State level had averaged yearly incomes of $22,900, with starting salaries being lower in the midwestern and southern states and higher on the East and West coasts.

Annual salaries of beginning lawyers in private industry were about $47,000 in 1990, but top graduates from the nation's best law schools started in some cases over $80,000 per year.

Police officers started at an average of $22,400 per year in 1990. Salaries for police chiefs ranged from about $22,000 in smaller jurisdictions to over $90,000 in larger jurisdictions.

ASSISTANT ATTORNEY GENERAL

CHRIS SMITH
178 Green Street
Madison, SD 57042
(605) 555-5555

EXPERIENCE:

OFFICE OF THE ATTORNEY GENERAL
FOR THE STATE OF SOUTH DAKOTA   Madison, SD
1991-Present   **Assistant Attorney General, Criminal Bureau**
• Prosecute false claims in Insurance Fraud Unit, including larceny, motor vehicle fraud and perjury.
• Argued before Supreme Judicial Court and Appeals Court on <u>Commissioner of the Department of Employment and Training v. Nicole J. Ross</u>, 145 (1994); and <u>D.E.T. v. Michael Meyers</u>, 66 (1993).

1989-1991   **Special Assistant District Attorney**
• Prosecuted criminal cases at district court in conjunction with Urban Violence Strike Force; prosecutions included rape and armed assault with intent to murder.

1986-1989   **SEAVER, MADDEN & BERMAN**   Aberdeen, SD
Attorney
• Prepared and presented civil and criminal motions before District and Superior Courts.
• Acted as co-counsel at trial; drafted memoranda, civil pleadings and appellate briefs.

1985-1986   **WADE COUNTY DISTRICT ATTORNEY'S OFFICE**   Rapid City, SD
Student Prosecutor
• Prosecuted criminal cases from arraignment to disposition.

Summer
1985   **Legal Intern**
• Researched, drafted memoranda for presentation in both criminal and civil actions.

EDUCATION:

1986   **HARVARD UNIVERSITY LAW SCHOOL**   Cambridge, MA
Juris Doctor
<u>Honors:</u>   Dean's List
Phi Delta Phi National Honors Fraternity
Top 10% of Class

1983   **PRINCETON UNIVERSITY**   Princeton, NJ
School of Business and Economics
B.S. in Business Administration
<u>Honors:</u>   Deans' List

■ Resume accentuates candidate's professional experience in both the public and private sector.

■ Strong educational credentials strengthen resume.

ATTORNEY (Civil Law)

CHRIS SMITH
178 Green Street
Atlanta, GA 30332
(404) 555-5555

PROFESSIONAL OBJECTIVE

A position in Civil Litigation within the business or environmental arenas.

PROFESSIONAL EXPERIENCE

1992-Present **Attorney**
EMERSON, LAKE & PALMER, P.C., Atlanta, GA
Trial attorney in medium-sized, general practice law firm with extensive corporate dealings. Areas of concentration have included environmental, public utility, general business and appellate litigation.

1984-1991 **Assistant District Attorney**
ATHENS DISTRICT ATTORNEY'S OFFICE, Athens, GA
Senior Trial Attorney responsible for prosecuting major felony cases in the Superior Court. Supervised criminal investigations and trained assistant district attorneys. Prosecuted over thirty major felony jury cases including murder, rape, and child abuse. Briefed and argued over forty cases before the Supreme Judicial Court and the Appeals Court.

1981-1983 **Law Clerk/Assistant Town Council**
TOWN OF MARIETTA, Marietta, GA
General municipal and appellate litigation.

EDUCATION

GEORGIA INSTITUTE OF TECHNOLOGY, Atlanta, GA
J.D., 1980, Cum Laude.

AGNES SCOTT COLLEGE, Decatur, GA
B.A., Political Science, 1975, Magna Cum Laude.

BAR MEMBERSHIPS

Georgia Bar Association, 1980
U.S. District Court for the District of Georgia, 1981

Professional and Legal References Available upon Request

■ Professional objective is clearly defined.

■ Resume is bolstered by candidate's strong educational credentials.

ATTORNEY (Commercial Law)

CHRIS SMITH, Esq.
178 Green Street
San Francisco, CA 94105
(415) 555-5555

EDUCATION

GOLDEN GATE UNIVERSITY, San Francisco, CA
Doctor of Law, 1994
- Semi-finalist, Golden Gate Moot Court Competition

NEW COLLEGE OF CALIFORNIA, San Francisco, CA
B.A., Communications, *Magna Cum Laude*, 1991
- Departmental Honors in Communication
- Dean's List
- Communications Department Teaching Assistant (faculty appointment)
- Captain of the Debate Team

LEGAL EXPERIENCE

KELLY, JACKSON & JAMES   San Francisco, CA
Associate   1994-Present
- Serve as Associate in the Commercial Law Department. Represent financial institutions, debtors and bankruptcy trustees in all phases of complex litigation and restructuring transactions. Possess substantial transactional and litigation experience in various facets of communication law; special emphasis on musical, artistic and literary property matters. Deal specifically with cases involving copyright registration and licensing, litigation and negotiation of trademark licensing; litigation of false advertising, unfair competition and defamation claims, and the negotiation and formulation of management agreements for entertainers.

FRANCIS, PARKER, MARKS & WILLIAMS   Los Angeles, CA
Summer Intern   1993

BOSLEY CHARLES & ANGEL   San Francisco, CA
Summer Intern   1992

VOLUNTEER WORK
- Serve on the Board of Directors of San Francisco General Hospital
- Offer Pro Bono legal services to non-profit organizations serving the arts.

References Available Upon Request

■ Internship experience and educational honors add depth to recent graduate's resume.

■ Volunteer work and community service lend strength to this resume.

ATTORNEY (Environmental Law)

CHRIS SMITH
178 Green Street
Bangor, ME 04401
(207) 555-5555

Admitted to Maine Bar, 1987
Admitted to Indiana Bar, 1986

EDUCATION
INDIANA UNIVERSITY, Bloomington, IN
Master of Studies in Environmental Law and Public Policy, magna cum laude, 1987
Juris Doctor, 1986
Environmental Action Group; National Lawyers Guild Indiana Chapter

ROCKFORD COLLEGE, Rockford, IL
Bachelor of Arts, 1983 Major: Sociology, cum laude
Editor, Environmental Newsletter

PROFESSIONAL EXPERIENCE
MAINE ENVIRONMENTAL RESEARCH GROUP, Waterville, ME   July 1988-Present
Environmental Program Director/Attorney
Coordinate environmental programs; develop policies; oversee campaign activities and staff. Draft legislation. Provide legal counseling. Develop media relations. Serve on state's acid rain and recycling program advisory committees. Initiated and successfully lobbied for state-wide moratorium on mandatory recycling. Strengthened state's acid rain regulations.

SOLO PRACTICE   August 1986-June 1988
Practiced before Water Resources Board. Negotiated small claims settlements; conducted title searches; advised clients on permitting processes.

LEGISLATIVE COUNCIL, 1985 Indiana General Assembly, Indianapolis, IN   Spring, 1985
Intern
Conducted legal research. Wrote memoranda. Presented testimony and drafted legislation primarily for House and Senate Health and Welfare and Government Operations committees. Worked with legislators, public and private interests. Addressed issues including toxics regulation, employment discrimination, and health care financing.

LAND USE CLINIC, Indiana University, Bloomington, IN   Fall, 1985
Investigated/analyzed Indiana design review ordinances. Searched records; attended administrative proceedings; interviewed planning officials; submitted report with recommendations for improving existing state enabling statute.

INDIANA ENVIRONMENTAL CONSERVATION BUREAU, Indianapolis, IN   Fall, 1984
Semester in Practice, Dept. of Hazardous Waste
Served on legislatively mandated advisory committee. Acted as liaison to Attorney General's office on uncontrolled hazardous waste cases. Addressed issues including pollution liability insurance, water protection, and non-hazardous waste disposal.

- Resume provides candidate's most essential qualification, bar accreditation, in the first two lines.

- Dynamic action verbs give resume impact.

ATTORNEY (Labor Relations)

CHRIS SMITH
178 Green Street
Alva, OK 73717
(405) 555-5555

PROFESSIONAL EXPERIENCE

1990-
Present   Alva School Department   Alva, OK
        Chief Negotiator for $375 million public agency, reporting directly to the Superintendent of Schools on collective bargaining issues with 15 unions of over 10,000 employees.

- Primary contract administration advisor for managers in 130 schools.
- Conduct or supervise all administrative hearings.
- Develop content and present training workshops for management staff.
- Oversee private sector labor relations with bus drivers union.
- Supervise and evaluate five member support staff.
- Design and implement modernization of office procedures.

1988-1990   Alan Pettybone, Esq.   Lawton, OK
        Principal

- Retained by the City of Lawton to provide management labor relations representation.
- Duties included: developing negotiation strategies, extensive hearing practice, and rendering legal opinions to personnel on labor relations issues.

1985-1988   Hollyhock, Stiller, and York   Langston, OK
        Associate

- Primary focus on labor law and litigation.
- Represented plaintiffs and defendants in general civil litigation cases in federal and state courts.

1982-1985   J.D. Simpson and Wrenwright   Alva, OK
        State Attorney

- Represented union members before government agencies, commissions and arbitrators.
- Drafted memorandums of law and wrote advisory opinions to legal staff.

EDUCATION

COLUMBIA UNIVERSITY LAW SCHOOL   New York, NY
J.D., June, 1981

COLUMBIA UNIVERSITY   New York, NY
B.S. HISTORY, Magna Cum Laude, 1978

- Job descriptions are straightforward and understandable.

- Use of boldface and underlining provides a clean and crisp presentation.

CONTRACTS MANAGER

CHRIS SMITH
178 Green Street
Cheyney, PA 19319
(717) 555-5555

OBJECTIVE: A managerial position in subcontract or materials management.

EXPERIENCE:

1992-Present   Thorndale Corporation   Cheyney, PA
Administrative Assistant
Placed all maintenance and repair contracts. Maintain various cost records
including capital projected costs; serve as liaison between the Chief
Engineer in all major departments. Contracts are for a ten story processing
plant; ten story filter house; machine shops; boiler house and engine room;
raw sugar warehouse; dock unloading facility; and plant with approximately
25,00 motors, etc. Place maintenance and repair contracts and after market
purchases of approximately $30 million, annually.

1989-1992   Redwood Corporation   Allentown, PA
Division Contracts Manager - responsible for service contracts with various
government agencies supporting Radar systems.
Asst. Purchasing Agent - responsible to purchasing agent for day-to-day
purchasing at the Chambersburg plant.

1986-1989   Berkowitz Inc.   Pittsburgh, PA
Contracts Manager - responsible for contractual support of special radar
program.

1984-1986   United States Air Force   Schenectady, NY
Lt. Colonel - member of procurement inspection teams performing management
inspections of the contractual, cost, production and quality aspects of
major procurement programs.

1981-1984   NBC Inc.   New York, NY
Asst. to President - special production problems, e.g. coordination of a
plant relocation and conveyorization of key production areas.

1976-1981   Spartan Manufacturing Corporation   Bismarck, ND
Asst. to Division Manager - responsible for the design, production and
marketing of a new tube fitting.

EDUCATION:

1976   North Dakota State University   Fargo, ND
B.S. Business Engineering Administration

■ Job objective is brief and to the
point.

■ Including a good military record
can be advantageous if it relates
to candidate's job objective.

CORRECTIONAL OFFICER

CHRIS SMITH
178 Green Street
Sabattus, ME 04280
(207) 555-5555

OBJECTIVE:
A challenging and responsible position in Law Enforcement, Criminal Justice, or related field where my education, experience, and capabilities can be fully realized.

EDUCATION:
BANGOR POLICE ACADEMY, Bangor, ME
Act 120 Certificate with 90% average (1987)

CERTIFICATIONS:
- NRA, shotgun and firearms; Monadnock PR 24; VASCAR plus
- CPR First Aid

EXPERIENCE:

1990-
Present **MAINE STATE PRISON**, Lewiston, ME
Correctional Officer
Responsible for control of 50 prisoners. Conduct population counts, cell checks and searches. Supervise dinner and yard duty. Monitor prisoner visitation. Issue money orders for prisoners. Assignments have included escorting special prisoners and serving as outside hospital guard. Prepare and file incident reports.

1989 **BIDDEFORD POLICE DEPARTMENT**, Biddeford, ME
Part-Time Police Officer

1988 **SOUTH PORTLAND POLICE DEPARTMENT**, South Portland, ME
Part-Time Police Officer
Responsible for routine patrol, issuing criminal arrest citations and testifying in court.

1985-1987 **FIRST FEDERAL SAVINGS BANK**, Cape Elizabeth, ME
Security Guard

VOLUNTEER:
Volunteer Fire Fighter, Cape Elizabeth Fire Co.

- "Certification" heading draws attention to candidate's specific professional qualifications.

- Volunteer work affirms candidate's commitment to community service.

CORRECTIONAL OFFICER/PEER COUNSELOR

CHRIS SMITH
178 Green Street
Lookout Mountain, TN 37350
(404) 555-5555

CAREER OBJECTIVE
To secure a position within the Department of Corrections.

SUMMARY OF QUALIFICATIONS
- Over 10 years experience in law enforcement.
- Proven ability in creating cooperation and good will within working environment.
- Demonstrated success in interfacing with marketing and public relations principles in substance abuse treatment centers.
- Excellent interpersonal skills with staff, inmate population and community.
- Crisis intervention with D.O.C. employees and families.
- Firearms qualified: 357, 9mm, M16, shotgun.

PROFESSIONAL EMPLOYMENT
1992 - Present   Department of Corrections Stress Program, Nashville, TN
Correctional Officer/Peer Counselor
- Worked with staff to identify troubled or "burnt out" employees by providing guidance, formulating treatment programs and informing them of community resources.

1989-1992   Knoxville SECC; Samuel Balderdash/TCI Nashville, TN
Correctional Officer
- Care, custody and control of inmate population assigned to my housing area.

1985-1989   Nashville Police Department, Nashville, TN
Patrolman
- Patrolled assigned areas, maintained peace, enforced Chapter 90 Motor Vehicle laws and City of Nashville By-laws; general patrol responsibilities.

ACCOMPLISHMENTS
- Was instrumental in preventing suicides; also dealt with families after suicide attempts.
- Arranged for scholarships/financial assistance, in amounts up to $10,000, for employees to receive treatment at inpatient facilities.
- Instructor, Stress Management for in-service employees as well as recruits.
- Commissioner's written Commendation for Perfect Attendance: 1990-92.

EDUCATION
- B.A., Criminal Justice 1984
  Hamline University, St. Paul, MN
- D.O.C. Training Academy, Nashville, TN 1985

■ Summary highlights candidate's acquired professional and educational training.

■ Professional accomplishments are highlighted in a separate section.

COURT OFFICER

CHRIS SMITH
178 Green Street
Trenton, NJ 08625
(609) 555-5555

SUMMARY OF QUALIFICATIONS

- Thorough knowledge in the provision of security and administrative support services within judicial and supreme court arenas, involving preparation of cases for trial proceedings, maintenance of official records, liaison functions between court and government agencies, custody/traffic direction processes.
- Adept with personnel management functions, requiring orientation, training, supervision, production of work schedules, delegation of tasks and evaluation.
- Superior communication, organizational, public relation and interpersonal skills; function well in high pressure arenas; regarded as a dedicated, trustworthy and loyal employee; able to prioritize assignments to meet operational deadlines.

PROFESSIONAL EXPERIENCE

STATE OF NEW JERSEY - Judicial Court, Trenton, NJ
Chief Court Officer, 1990-Present

- Coordinate general security procedures during court proceedings and in justice lobbies, accompany justices to outside engagements and manage public traffic.
- Serve as liaison for court and government agencies; transmit pertinent data.
- Produce work schedules, delegate responsibilities for staff, supervise in the execution of duties, train, coach and develop, as necessary.
- Prepare court room for trial proceedings, locate and supply precedent information for judges and counselors and record courtroom activity.

STATE OF NEW JERSEY - Judicial Court, New Brunswick, NJ
Court Officer, 1985-1990

- Attended court sessions and provided security for court room/judicial lobbies.
- Maintained court session and attorney appearance records and documents.
- Monitored activities of individuals held in custody and ensure public safety.
- Announce commencement and termination of court proceedings.
- Answered in-coming calls, obtained mail and distributed to justices.
- Received visitors; inspected guest credentials/directed to designated areas.
- Scheduled appointments for judges and provided courier services, as needed.

EDUCATION

CALDWELL COLLEGE, Caldwell, NJ
A.S., Criminal Law, 1985

- Education is listed towards bottom of resume because candidate's practical experience outweighs his/her degree.

- Bulleted phrases make for quick reading.

COURT REPORTER

CHRIS SMITH
178 Green Street
Buffalo, NY 14208
(716) 555-5555

PROFESSIONAL OBJECTIVE
A position as a court reporter.

EDUCATION
Mohawk Community College, Utica, NY
Certificate in Paralegal Studies, 1994

Canisius College, Buffalo, NY
Bachelor of Arts in Government, 1992
Continuing Education courses in writing, editing, and photography.

PROFESSIONAL EXPERIENCE
Courthouse Reporter
The Buffalo Times, Buffalo, NY (June 1994-Present)
Collect information from courthouses. Consult court transcripts for accuracy. Serve as liaison between paper and court officers.

Copy Editor
Metro Section, *The Central Standard Times*, Utica, NY (June 1993-May 1994)
Edited for style, content, and grammar; wrote headlines and photo captions; formatted copy.

Program Assistant
Canisius College, Buffalo, NY (January 1993-May 1993)
Responsible for registration for continuing education programs of up to 200 persons in the field of governmental communications. Served as a liaison between program directors and the general public.

Research Assistant
Political Research Group, Buffalo, NY (August 1992-December 1992)
Developed a plan for launching a communications vehicle, requiring an in-depth study of all aspects of newsletter publishing.

COMPUTER SKILLS
Lotus 1-2-3; IBM-PC; MacIntosh FileMaker, Pagemaker.

REFERENCES
Available upon request.

■ Specific dates of employment (month and year) are ideal for candidates with no gaps in work history.

■ Relevant course work adds depth to candidate's educational background.

FIRE FIGHTER

CHRIS SMITH
178 Green Street
Palos Heights, IL 60445
(312) 555-5555

SUMMARY OF QUALIFICATIONS:
- Emergency Medical Technician and volunteer Fire Fighter.
- Able to remain calm and take control in emergency situations.
- Have held numerous elective offices.

EDUCATION:

DEERFIELD COMMUNITY COLLEGE, Deerfield, IL
Emergency Medical Technician, 1988

Certified by the Illinois Department of Health
Illinois Association of Arson Investigators Certificate, Forensic Fire Photography
Chicago Electric Company Fire Academy
Gas and Electric Fire Fighting, 1974-5
Deerfield Fire Academy, Fire Fighting I, II, III, 1973-4

TRINITY VOCATIONAL-TECHNICAL SCHOOL, Deerfield, IL
Communications Technician, 1974-6
Photographic Technician, 1973-4

WORK EXPERIENCE:

1973 -
Present **PALOS HEIGHTS FIRE COMPANY** - Life Member
Fire Fighter, Emergency Medical Technician
- Ambulance Lieutenant, 1978, 1990 - conduct training drills.
- Ambulance Captain, 1979
- Ambulance Auxiliary Secretary, 1979
- Photographer, 1987 - Present

1989 -
Present **INTERNATIONAL FIRE PHOTOGRAPHERS ASSOCIATION**

1973 -
Present **DEERFIELD FIREMAN'S ASSOCIATION**

1979-1983 **MIDWEST AMBULANCE**, River Forest, IL
Assistant Manager/Crew
- Scheduled ten full time and eight part time Emergency Medical Technicians for emergency and hospital transportation of patients. Services Burn Center at River Forest Medical Center.

■ Relevant, job-specific training is listed under education.

■ Summary of qualifications illustrates candidate's key credentials.

GUARD

CHRIS SMITH
178 Green Street
Sundance, WY 82729
(307) 555-5555

OBJECTIVE

A position in security.

PROFESSIONAL EXPERIENCE

THE FIELDSTONE BANK   Sundance, WY
Bank Guard   1992-Present
- Responsible for ensuring safety and security of customers, bank employees, and bank assets.

WILLOW MEAD ART MUSEUM   Wolf, WY
Security Guard   1989-1992
- Responsible for patrol, surveillance, and control of facilities and areas.
- Maintained reports, records, and documents as required by administration.

CITY OF ROCK SPRINGS POLICE DEPARTMENT   Rock Springs, WY
Property Clerk   1987-1989
- Responsible for security, transfer, and storage of personnel effects/properties as evidence in trial and court cases.

CITY OF GILLETTE SCHOOL DEPARTMENT   Gillette, WY
Transitional Aid   1983-1987
- Responsible for ensuring safety of students and security of school property at Madison Park High School.

THUNDERBEAT CONSTRUCTION   Crowheart, WY
Weigher of Goods/Track Foreman   1982-1985
- Weighed materials and supervised track construction at University of Wyoming.

PINEDALE & SONS   Miami, FL
Mason   1980-1982
- Performed variety of duties including masonry, stucco, finishing work, and foundations for general contractor.

EDUCATION

UNITED STATES COAST GUARD, Miami, FL
Certificate, Interactive Query Language, 1980
Certificate, Advanced PMIS, 1979
Certificate, Coast Guard WP School, 1978
Winter Park High School, Winter Park, FL, 1978

■ Job objective is brief and to the point.

■ Military training strengthens otherwise limited education.

LAW CLERK (Corporate and Contract Law)

CHRIS SMITH
178 Green Street
Romeoville, IL 60441
(312) 555-5555 (work)
(312) 444-4444 (home)

EDUCATION   **DEPAUL UNIVERSITY SCHOOL OF LAW**, Chicago, IL
J.D. May, 1992
Specialized Course work: Environmental Law

ILLINOIS WESLEYAN UNIVERSITY, Bloomington, IL
B.A. in Political Science May, 1989
G.P.A.: 3.2/4.0

LEGAL
EXPERIENCE
June 1992-   **Law Clerk**, Hall & Gotes, Chicago, IL
Present   Research and write appellate briefs, draft motions, complaints and answers. Research and prepare
memoranda on corporate and contract law. Assist in attorney - client conferences by describing the
law as it pertains to the client's suit.

June 1989-   **Research Assistant**, Attorney Barbara Cady, Elgin, IL
May 1992   Researched and investigated important new issues in environmental law.

Summer 1988   **Law Clerk**, Justice Lori O'Connor
Supreme Court of Illinois, Chicago, IL
Researched and drafted decisions on motions, prepared and wrote memoranda on various issues.
Participated in pre-trial conferences.

Summer 1987   **Congressional Intern**, Rep. Wendy Millbauer (D-OH), Washington, DC
Conducted research for legislative bills, reviewed and reported on committee hearings,
corresponded with constituents.

OTHER
EXPERIENCE
Summer 1986   **Assistant Head Pro**
Lake Forest Country Club, Lake Forest, IL
Conducted clinics and gave tennis lessons to all ages, arranged and coordinated Midwest Junior
Tennis tournaments.

INTERESTS   History, Politics, Tennis.

References, writing samples, and transcript available upon request

■ Including a work telephone number is optional on a resume.

■ Work experience is effectively divided into subheadings: legal and other.

LAW CLERK (Criminal Law)

CHRIS SMITH
178 Green Street
Des Moines, IA 50311
(515) 555-5555

EDUCATION

DRAKE UNIVERSITY LAW SCHOOL, Des Moines, IA
Juris Doctor, June, 1994
Class Rank: 5 out of 300
Honors: Dean's List all semesters

CENTRAL UNIVERSITY OF IOWA, Pella, IA
B.A., American History, 1980
Internship, Washington, D.C., Office of Rep. William McCarthy,
September-December, 1980

EXPERIENCE

WARD, WESTON AND WOLCOTT, Des Moines, IA
1992-1994 **Law Clerk**
Researched and wrote motions and memoranda, prepared discovery, and trial assistance for three attorneys specializing in criminal law.

ADDISON AND HAYES, Des Moines, IA
1990-1991 **Law Clerk**
Responsibilities included: preparation of discovery and trial assistance.

FULTON ADJUSTMENT SERVICE, Des Moines, IA
1982-1989 **Road Adjuster** (two years)
Office Manager (one year), Portsmouth, NH
Suit Supervisor (nearly three years)
Responsibilities included: investigation, negotiation, trial preparation or settlement of first and third party insurance claims, particularly automobile and general liability. Some Workers' Compensation and property cases.

CAROLINA AND CO., Pella, IA
1979-1981 **Road Adjuster**
Handled third party liability and Workers' Compensation claims.

INTERESTS

Baseball, soccer, jazz.

■ Educational honors and internship strengthen candidate's short work history.

■ Personal interests can provide a great topic for conversation during a job interview.

LAW CLERK (Judicial)

CHRIS SMITH
178 Green Street
Irving, TX 75061
(817) 555-5555

BAR
STATUS

Texas Judicial Court, 1994
U.S. District Court for the District of Texas, 1994

EXPERIENCE

TRIAL COURT OF TEXAS, Irving, TX
Law Clerk to the Justices 1994-Present
Provided legal research and writing assistance with respect to substantive and procedural issues at various stages of civil and criminal proceedings to approximately twenty justices.

IRVING DISTRICT COURT, Irving, TX
Student Prosecutor 1993
Prosecuted misdemeanors under supervision of Suffolk County District Attorney's Office.

TEXAS JUVENILE COURT, Irving, TX
Law Clerk 1993
Drafted proposed findings of fact and conclusions of law in care and protection cases, conducted research, and assisted in a case management project.

UNIVERSITY OF DALLAS LAW SCHOOL, Irving, TX
Legal Research, Reference & Government Documents Assistant 1990-1994
Assisted in instruction of Legal Research course, assisted attorneys and students with legal research, helped maintain reserve materials, and updated collection.

KING'S PRESS, Kingsville, TX
Reporter, Feature Writer & Copy editor 1984-1990
Covered government, law enforcement, education, health issues, the environment, entertainment, and social trends.

EDUCATION

UNIVERSITY OF DALLAS, Irving, TX
Juris Doctor, *magna cum laude*, 1994, G.P.A. 3.5
Honors: Editor, New England Law Review
           Dean's List

TEXAS A & M UNIVERSITY, Kingsville, TX
B.S. Business, *cum laude*, 1989, G.P.A. 3.3
Honors: Dean's List

TEXAS CHRISTIAN UNIVERSITY, Fort Worth, TX
B.A. English & Journalism, 1984, G.P.A. 3.2
Honors: Dean's List

■ Candidate's key credential, bar status, is listed first and foremost.

■ Impressive educational background strengthens resume.

LAW STUDENT

CHRIS SMITH
178 Green Street
Ithaca, NY 14853
(607) 555-5555

EDUCATION

Cornell Law School, Ithaca, NY
Juris Doctor to be awarded May, 1997

City University of New York, NY
Bachelor of Arts in English, May 1994
Gold Key National Honor Society
Yearbook Editor

EXPERIENCE

Cornell Law Library, Ithaca, NY
Research Assistant   1994-Present
- Assist law students, lawyers and faculty with library research.
- Maintain and update newspaper clippings file of recent Supreme Court decisions.
- Train and supervise staff of five work-study students.

New York Attorney General's Office, New York, NY
Legal Intern   Summer 1994
- Acted as aide to Assistant Attorney General during court room proceedings, pre-trial conferences, interviewing of witnesses, and legal research.
- Prepared discovery motions, typed briefs, provided legal counsel in and prepared witnesses for grand jury testimony.

OTHER EXPERIENCE

CITY UNIVERSITY OF NEW YORK, ENGLISH OFFICE, New York, NY
Secretary/Receptionist   1990-1994

THE BAD SEED RESTAURANT, New York, NY
Bartender   Summers 1990-1993

REFERENCES AVAILABLE UPON REQUEST

■ Education in progress is listed before limited professional experience.

■ Internship experience is valuable for candidates with little job experience, particularly if it corresponds to the position sought.

LEGAL ASSISTANT

CHRIS SMITH
178 Green Street
Chicago, IL 60605
(312) 555-5555

EDUCATION

ROOSEVELT UNIVERSITY, Chicago, IL
Bachelor of Arts, *cum laude*, 1992
Major: Political Science; **Minor:** Economics

LEGAL EXPERIENCE

MUNICIPAL ASSOCIATION, Chicago, IL
Legal Assistant   July 1993-Present
Research impact of reduced State revenue sharing on municipal public safety staffing. Involved in needs assessment, strategy planning, community outreach, interviewing, data collection, analysis and reporting.

CHICAGO DISTRICT ATTORNEY'S OFFICE, Domestic Violence Unit, Chicago, IL
Victim Witness Advocate   May 1992-July 1993
Interviewed victims and witnesses, prepared documents and organized information for court appearances. Assisted attorneys during trials.

ILLINOIS PUBLIC DEFENDERS, Chicago, IL
Legal Intern   September 1990-May 1992
Researched and drafted motions on various criminal law and procedural issues. Interviewed clients at Illinois correctional institutions. Argued bail motions in several state district courts. Negotiated plea and bail agreements for defendants accused of misdemeanor crimes. Attended criminal trials and deposition hearings.

PRO BONO LEGAL ADVISORS COMMITTEE, Chicago, IL
Legal Intern   Summer 1990
Advised mentally handicapped clients on aspects of mental health law, including guardianship, commitment, discharge, and civil rights. Drafted motions, complaints, and discharge petitions for clients. Devoted part of time to advising clients at the Central Square Homeless Shelter.

ATTORNEY DANIEL BANNEN, Oak Park, IL
Legal Secretary   Summer 1989
Greeted clients. Prepared documents for legal proceedings involving real estate transactions. Entered all client information into new computer system.

COMPUTER SKILLS

IBM: WordPerfect, Word for Windows; MacIntosh: Microsoft Word, FileMaker.

■ Specific dates of employment (month and year) are ideal for candidates with no gaps in work history.

■ Valuable computer skills are highlighted in a separate section.

LEGAL SECRETARY (Civil Law)

CHRIS SMITH
178 Green Street
Danville, KY 40422
(606) 555-5555

OBJECTIVE

To acquire a **Legal Secretarial** position, preferably but not limited to Civil Litigation or Criminal Law, where my experience and commitment to excellence will be fully applied.

SUMMARY OF QUALIFICATIONS

- 15 years experience as a legal assistant/secretary in civil litigation.
- 10 years part time experience in general practice.
- Computer literate: IBM - WordPerfect 5.1 and Multimate.
- Notary Public.
- Supervisory skills, delegate and distribute workload evenly among secretarial staff.

HIGHLIGHTS OF LEGAL EXPERIENCE

1989-Present LAW OFFICES OF LANGSTON & GREY, Lexington, KY   **Legal Secretary**
Responsibilities include organizing pre-deposition conferences with doctors, attorneys, involved parties; handling, canceling, re-scheduling; setting up motions for court hearings; trial papers and schedules; researching files for necessary documentation, proofreading; notarizing legal documents.

1979-1987 THEODORE F. LOGAN, Danville, KY   **Legal Secretary**
Part-time evening duties involved court and client scheduling, typing legal documents, drafting wills, letters, complaints in general practice law office.

1975-1978 CUMBERLAND INSURANCE, Lexington, KY   **Secretary**
General secretarial tasks; typing correspondence and reports, filing, phones.

EDUCATION

CENTRE COLLEGE, Danville, KY Paralegal Studies, 1988-1989
Also participated in Communications Skills Workshop for Paralegals.

DANVILLE COMMUNITY COLLEGE, Danville, KY.
Relevant training and course work in legal issues and computers.

PERSONAL

Baseball, cooking, travel.

■ Unrelated work experience is omitted.

■ Courses listed under education are related to candidate's field of interest.

LEGAL SECRETARY (General Law)

CHRIS SMITH
178 Green Street
Shreveport, LA 40292
(502) 555-5555

OBJECTIVE

To contribute acquired clerical skills to a challenging position within an organization offering opportunities for growth and advancement.

SUMMARY OF QUALIFICATIONS

- More than eight years of progressive professional secretarial experience.
- Computer skills include: Epson, Multimate, and WANG word processor.
- Developed interpersonal skills, having dealt with a diversity of professionals, clients, and staff members.
- Self-motivated; able to set effective priorities to achieve immediate and long-term goals and meet operational deadlines.
- Adept at working independently and as team member.
- Adapt easily to new concepts and responsibilities.
- Function well in fast-paced , high-pressure atmosphere.
- Notary Public and CPR Certified.

PROFESSIONAL EXPERIENCE

1987-1993   THOMAS J. CUNNINGHAM, P.C., LAW OFFICES, Shreveport, LA
Secretary/Legal Assistant
Generated, typed, formatted and edited letters, documents, motions, briefs, and client forms. Handled incoming calls, scheduled appointments and immigration case conferences. Maintained case files.

1985-1986   BORDEN INSURANCE COMPANY, Shreveport, LA
File Clerk
General clerical responsibilities included typing correspondence, screening and referring calls, filing, and mail distribution.

EDUCATION

Shreveport Community College, Shreveport, LA
Courses in Legal and Business Studies.

REFERENCES

Furnished upon request.

- Summary grabs the reader's attention with powerful skills and qualifications.

- Chrono-functional format is more flexible than a chronological resume, but stronger than a functional resume.

LOSS PREVENTION MANAGER

Chris Smith
178 Green Street
Stillwater, OK 74078
(405) 555-5555

OBJECTIVE
A position in loss prevention management.

PROFESSIONAL EXPERIENCE

Vedder Toxic Waste — Norman, OK
Loss Prevention Manager — 1991-Present
Ensure proper operation of physical building security, alarms, and camera surveillance system. Prescreen/train loss prevention staff; enforce policies and procedures; devise incentive programs. Implement inventory control audits and investigations. Apply energy maintenance program to reduce equipment costs, repair, and efficiency.

Oklahoma State University Store — Stillwater, OK
Loss Prevention Manager — 1989-1991
Developed loss prevention department, manager and staff training; conducted comprehensive needs assessment, recommended improvements; created error notice system; implemented $3M anti-theft system; decreased cash register shortages 93% over six month period. Executed Merchant Alert Program with local merchants and police.

Oklahoma City University Store — Oklahoma City, OK
Loss Prevention Manager — 1987-1989
Redesigned departmental goals and direction. Development training and professional standards; created store wide, loss prevention awareness and in-house training; implemented cash register error notice program. Produced monthly employee newsletter.

Spruce Creek, INC. — Stillwater, OK
Operations Manager — 1986-1987
Maintained for $.5 M service maintained operations; directly managed 40-50 member supervisory/support staff. Hire/terminate, train, schedule, and oversee personnel; delegate responsibilities. Respond to client needs and queries; act as liaison with vendors. Provide cost analysis, budgeting, specifications/proposals, and service maintenance contracts for commercial accounts.

EDUCATION

Albright College — Reading, PA
Masters Degree, Private Law — 1985
Allegheny College — Meadville, PA
Bachelors Degree, Liberal Arts — 1983

■ Supporting statistics and dollar figures illustrate candidate's ability to cut costs, an essential attribute in a loss prevention manager.

■ Education is de-emphasized because candidate's work history is strong.

OMBUDSMAN

CHRIS SMITH
178 Green Street
Waukesha, WI 53188
(414) 555-5555

SUMMARY OF QUALIFICATIONS

- Over ten years of progressive, professional human services experience.
- Proven abilities in training, program development, and analysis of policies.
- Extensive knowledge of long-term care issues.
- Developed interpersonal skills, having dealt with a diversity of professionals, clients, and staff members on all levels.
- Tested communication skills, both oral and written.

PROFESSIONAL EXPERIENCE

WISCONSIN ELDER CARE INC., Waukesha, WI
Long-Term Care Ombudsman Program Director, 1988 to Present

- Developed local Ombudsman Program in 46 nursing and rest homes in fourteen cities and towns; required close cooperation with administrators and facility staff members.
- Investigated and resolved problems of long-terms care residents.
- Recruited, trained, and supervised staff of 30 volunteers; developed on-going training program for Ombudsman staff.
- Presented workshops and lectures.
- Refined data collecting and recording system.
- Actuated and implemented inquiry recording system.
- Developed comprehensive information/resources packet.
- Cooperated in team effort to develop and implement several special projects.
- Established productive and effective relationships with state and local agencies: Executive Office of Elder Affairs, Department of Public Health, Department of Mental Health, Home Care Corporation and Councils on Aging.

Case Manager, 1984 to 1988

- Assessed physical, environmental and emotional status of applicants; evaluated existing support systems; determined financial eligibility.
- Advocated for clients; handled crisis intervention.
- Developed/implemented client service plans.

EDUCATION

UNION COLLEGE, Schenectady, NY
Master of Science in Human Services/Gerontology, 1984

SALVE REGINA-THE NEWPORT COLLEGE, Newport, RI
Bachelor of Science in Health Services, 1982

■ Reverse chronological format focuses employer's attention on candidate's most current position.

■ Bullets make resume easy to read.

PARALEGAL (Civil Law)

CHRIS SMITH
178 Green Street
Santa Fe, NM 87501
(505) 555-5555

PROFESSIONAL OBJECTIVE
To contribute paralegal, managerial, and organizational abilities within the civil litigation process.

QUALIFICATIONS AND ACCOMPLISHMENTS
- Outstanding case research and writing skills; compiled Training Manual.
- Computer-oriented: IBM PC; WordPerfect; WordStar; DECMate; Rainbow 100; VT100; Wang.
- Programmed over 1,000 files onto WordStar with productivity increasing 70%.
- Revamped Accounting, and Debit and Credit systems.
- Received Digital Equipment's Achievement Award for having researched and retrieved lost accounts.

PROFESSIONAL EXPERIENCE
LAW OFFICES OF BRENDAN ELLIS   Santa Fe, NM
Civil Litigation Specialist/Office Manager   1988-Present
- Manage entire office and staff of three secretaries. Ensure smooth operation of small law firm. Control and maintain law office accounts.
- Interview clients; prepare all files/discovery.
- Negotiate and settle cases with defense attorney and insurance companies.
- Request and review all medical documentation; ascertain all evidence information and process all with the appropriate parties.
- Prepare clients for depositions/trials.
- Attend mediations and conciliations.

BROWNINGTON, INC.   Albuquerque, NM
Administrative Assistant   1983-1988
- Confirm all manpower hours and prepare monthly logs to bill various sites.
- Responsible for clerical support to 24 software engineers.
- Recognized for "Excellence in Customer Satisfaction—Southwest Region."

WILD RAIN EXOTIC GIFTS   Silver City, NM
Owner/Operator   1980-1983
- Responsible for eight sales personnel and incoming and outgoing orders.
- Accepted art and memorabilia on consignment.

EDUCATION/RELEVANT TRAINING
SAINT JOHN'S COLLEGE   Santa Fe, NM
B.S., Resource Management   1980
Numerous seminars on *Insurance Reform/Personal Injury Law*

■ Job objective is clearly defined.

■ Professional qualifications and accomplishments are listed prominently.

PARALEGAL (Corporate Law)

CHRIS SMITH
178 Green Street
St. Paul, MN 55104
(612) 555-5555

EXPERIENCE

1989 to BRODERICK & HOLMES, St. Paul, MN
present **Corporate Paralegal**, 1984-present
- Solely responsible for ensuring corporate compliance with Minnesota General Laws, meeting and filing requirements for 750 clients.
- Determine interstate corporate business status and handle registration process.
- Extensive contract with State Department of Revenue Compliance Bureau to verify corporate tax standing.
- Draft corporate votes, liquidation and dissolution plans, various agreements and supporting documents.
- Familiar with UCC financing statements; research liens in connection with corporate acquisitions and financing.
- Supervise, train and develop administrative staff.
- Determine and collect corporate data for implementation of computerized information system.
- Responsible for organization of new corporations including preparation of articles of organization, drafting of by-laws and issuance of stock.
- Guide legal interns in department procedure and scheduling.
- Trained on LEXIS and NEXIS legal research systems.

Legal Recruiting Coordinating, 1985-1989
- Aided in recruiting effort in all areas of practice.
- Scheduled interoffice interviews.
- Reviewed attorney and summer associate candidates.
- Coordinated recruiting effort in law schools; contacted placement agencies and established positive working relationships.
- Prepared all materials for hiring committee meetings.

EDUCATION MACALESTER COLLEGE, St. Paul, MN
Bachelor's Degree in Marketing, 1983
(GPA 3.85)

CARLELTON JUNIOR COLLEGE, Duluth, MN
Associate Degree in Secretarial Sciences, 1978
(GPA 3.75)

Ongoing professional development includes: managing complex financial transactions, organizational structure seminar, and national association for legal placement's annual recruitment conference.

REFERENCES Furnished upon request.

- Candidate's most recent position is outlined in detail.

- Continuing education indicates candidate's ongoing commitment to his/her career.

PARALEGAL (Real Estate Law)

CHRIS SMITH
178 Green Street
Jackson, MS 39217
(601) 555-5555

<u>**PROFESSIONAL EXPERIENCE**</u>

1987-present   OLIVER, FIELDING & OLIVER, Jackson, MS
Legal Assistant
- Provide paralegal services to attorneys in residential real estate sales within Mississippi and surrounding states
- Monitor transactions from start to final settlement statement; order and review titles, obtain plot plans and municipal lien certificates, research background, work successfully against deadlines
- Prepare loan documents
- Determine outstanding utility and tax bills
- Ensure completion of mortgage payments by previous owners
- Serve as liaison for clients, banks, and attorneys; schedule meetings, identify documents necessary for all parties
- Coordinate all post-closing functions, complete title insurance forms, send final payments to banks and municipalities, disburse funds
- Maintain constant communication with all parties involved throughout entire process

1981-87   HALPERN INSURANCE AGENCY, Jackson, MS
Subrogation Clerk, 1986-1987
- Negotiated payments with attorneys on Third Party Liability cases; reviewed medical records

Operator, Third Party Liability Dept., 1985
- Provided subscriber information to customers, assisted in completion of questionnaires

Senior Clerk, Hospital Claims Dept., 1981-1984
- Reviewed claims, made payments for patients with nerve and mental disorders

<u>**EDUCATIONAL BACKGROUND**</u>

BELHAVEN COLLEGE, Jackson, MS
Certificate in Paralegal Studies
- Introduction to Paralegal, American Legal System, Criminal Law, Litigation, Utilization of Legal Materials, Real Estate Law

HALPERN INSURANCE Courses:
- Legal Terminology, Contractual Terminology, Mathematical Skills

<u>**SKILLS**</u>   AT&T and Compaq PC's with Samna program; data entry, CRT, typing (55 wpm)

- Relevant company-sponsored course work strengthens candidate's educational background.

- Valuable computer and typing skills are highlighted in a separate section.

PARALEGAL (State Department)

CHRIS SMITH
178 Green Street
Rindge, NH 03461
(601) 555-5555

PROFESSIONAL OBJECTIVE
To obtain a position in the **Paralegal** field.

PROFESSIONAL EXPERIENCE
1993 to   SECRETARY OF STATE, AWARDS DIVISION, Rindge, NH
Present   **UCC Corporations Clerk**
Locate Uniform Commercial Code and obtain corporate documents for lawyers. Work with Limited Partnerships and trust. File Annual Reports and Articles of Organizations.

1991 to 1993   MILAND, GARLAND, AND TEEK, Manchester, NH
Local Searcher
Obtained documents for clients across the country. Documents: Uniform Commercial Code, Mortages, Plaintiff and Civil Probate Court, Land Court UCCs. Obtained Federal and State Tax Liens, Bankruptcy, Registry of Motor Vehicles, Marriage Certificates.

1986 to 1990   BLUE NOTES, Madrid, Spain
Salesman
Responsible for inventory control, customer service, billing and management liaison.

1982 to 1986   UNITED STATES AIR FORCE, Madrid, Spain
Administrative Personnel Management Clerk
Resolved all Personnel Problems or Requests: re enlistment, extension of tour of Europe, relocation within the USA and Europe, return of dependents to the United States or Europe, ensured receipt of awards, tracking of personnel, all records of accidents and injuries. Routed incoming Top Secret Messages. Typed correspondence for Commanding Officer. Honorably Discharged.

EDUCATION AND TRAINING
1990   FRANKLIN PIERCE COLLEGE, Rindge, NH
Certificate in Paralegal Studies

1984   Thirteen weeks training at Fort Bragg, N.C., assisting 109th Signal Battalion. Trained in Computer Science, using Microsoft Word, Lotus 1-2-3, and Excel.

■ Education is listed towards bottom of resume because candidate's practical experience outweighs his/her degree.

■ Including a good military record can be advantageous if it relates to candidate's job objective.

PATENT AGENT

CHRIS SMITH, Esq.
178 Green Street
Detroit, MI 48219
(313) 555-5555

EDUCATION

MICHIGAN STATE UNIVERSITY   East Lansing, MI
Doctor of Law   1992
Honors and Awards
- 3.0 GPA
- Semi-finalist, Cornell Winter Moot Court Competition

BATES COLLEGE   Lewiston, ME
B.A., Magna Cum Laude   1989
Honors and Awards
- College High Honors Scholar
- Department Honors in English
- Dean's List
- English Department Teaching Assistant
- Varsity Soccer

DAVID LEVINE PREP SCHOOL   Lewiston, ME
- National Merit Scholar - Letter of Commendation   1987

LEGAL EXPERIENCE

ANDERSON, BRUFORD, WAKEMAN & HOWE   Detroit, MI
Associate, Patent Division   1992-Present
Substantial transactional and litigation experience in various facets of intellectual property law, with special emphasis on musical, artistic and literary property matters, including copyright registration and licensing, litigation of false advertising, unfair competition and defamation claims, litigation and negotiation of trademark licensing issues in the context of bankruptcy proceedings, and the negotiation and formulation of management agreements for entertainers. Served as member of Anderson, Bruford's Hiring Committee.

KANE, GOLDSTEIN, & EDISON   Lansing, MI
Summer Associate   1991

MADISON, HARRIS, & LEE   PORTLAND, ME
Summer Associate   1989

- Educational honors and awards indicate candidate's ability to excel.

- Stating that "references are available upon request" is not essential; most employers will assume that references are available.

POLICE OFFICER (Campus)

CHRIS SMITH
178 Green Street
Baltimore, MD 21210
(410) 555-5555

PROFESSIONAL EXPERIENCE

1985 to present JOHNS HOPKINS UNIVERSITY POLICE DEPARTMENT, Baltimore, MD
Patrolman
- Protect life and property on and about the campus of Johns Hopkins University.
- Uphold laws and codes of the State of Maryland and Johns Hopkins University.
- Patrol on foot and via automobile; utilize strong observational skills.
- Cooperate with other law enforcement agencies; act as Deputy Sheriff, Essex County.
- Maintain community relations; give seminars on drunk driving.

1983 to 1984 BUCKMAN ASSOCIATES, Bethesda, MD
Head of Security
- Managed all aspects of security for hotels and adjoining properties.
- Hired, terminated, scheduled, supervised, and evaluated personnel.
- Provided all policing functions with emphasis on defusing potentially violent situations.
- Cooperated extensively with Baltimore and Bethesda Police Departments.
- Promoted from starting position as Patrol Officer.
- Received standing offer of return for emergency or full-time employment.

1978 to 1982 TOWN OF ROCKVILLE POLICE DEPARTMENT, Rockville, MD
Patrolman
- Performed all aforementioned policing functions.
- Oversaw proper use of Chapter 90 sheets and citations.
- Interacted and communicated with town officials.
- Kept records; maintained data.

EDUCATION AND TRAINING

Graduate, Baltimore Police Academy, 1985
Graduate, Rockville Police Academy, 1978

CERTIFICATION AND LICENSURE

- License to carry firearms
- Emergency Medical Technician, National Certification
- Certification in radar usage, Breathalyzer, and Identi-Kit systems

REFERENCES

Available Upon Request

■ Strong action verbs bring resume to life.

■ Valuable certification and licensure are highlighted in a separate section.

POLICE OFFICER (Municipal)

CHRIS SMITH
178 Green Street
Chicago, IL 60680
(312) 555-5555

LICENSES AND CERTIFICATES
- Illinois License to Carry a Firearm
- Certificate in Weaponry Training, October 1993
- Certified in Security Supervision
- Certified as Security Officer, K-9 Handler, and Park Ranger
- Certified in C.P.R.

EXPERIENCE

1990-Present   CHICAGO MUNICIPAL POLICE (P.F.D.)   **Special Police Officer**
Duties include protection of all properties owned or controlled by the City of Chicago. Educate staff and city employees on safety/self-protection. Discourage theft, arson and vandalism by patrolling various crime zones throughout the city.
- Respond to burglar alarms and citizen complaints on city property.
- Arrest/detain persons violating the law; assist Chicago Police and Fire Departments in security and safety related to municipal buildings security.

1987-1989   NEWBURY MEMORIAL HOSPITAL, Chicago   **K-9 Patrol Officer**
Patrolled high crime areas around hospital for employee safety and to deter crime.
- Conduct foot patrols with guard dog through hospital garage at night; investigate reports of suspicious persons; respond to alarms.

1988-1989   LAKEFRONT MEDICAL AREA PATROL, Chicago   **Special Police Officer**
Patrolled colleges and hospitals within Lakefront Medical area for safety and crime prevention.
- Inspected property to deter vandalism and theft; responded to burglar alarms.
- Utilized powers of arrest as Special Police Officer and assisted local police with criminal or emergency situations.

1987-1988   UNIVERSITY OF CHICAGO   **Institutional Patrol Officer**
Dispatcher and Desk Officer for Public Assistance at Campus Police Station.
- Inspected campus buildings for security, safety and fire prevention.

1985-1988   SAINT XAVIER COLLEGE SECURITY, Chicago   **Sergeant/Shift Supervisor**

1985-1987   EVANSTON POLICE DEPARTMENT, Evanston   **Auxiliary Police Officer**

EDUCATION AND TRAINING
CHICAGO POLICE ACADEMY-1989.
ILLINOIS POLICE DOG SERVICES-K-9 Handler (80 hours), 1985.
UNIVERSITY OF ILLINOIS, Chicago, IL
Bachelor of Science in Criminal Justice, 1984.

■ Resume format is neat and professional.

■ Work history is stated in reverse chronological order, with most recent employment listed first.

POLICE SERGEANT

Chris Smith
178 Green Street
Houston, TX 77030
(713) 555-5555

PROFESSIONAL OBJECTIVE
A position as a police sergeant in which professional background, management skills, and commitment to excellence will be effectively utilized.

PROFESSIONAL LICENSE
Certified Protection Professional

PROFESSIONAL BACKGROUND
HOUSTON CITY POLICE DEPARTMENT, Houston, TX
Sergeant/Chief Polygraphist **1986-present**
...Develop objectives, establish procedures, set policies, and maintain standards for two units.
...Supervise, train, schedule, and evaluate 25 employees.
...Forecast, prepare, and monitor budgets for both units.
...Order supplies and equipment.
...Design and execute workshops on fingerprints and polygraph techniques to maintain efficiency.
...Restructured record filing and material handling systems.
...Utilized computer to evaluate fingerprints.

Commander **1982-86**
...Maintained resident and building security in 50 building, 5000 resident Southwest Housing Project in Houston.
...Inspected premises to maximize crime prevention.
...Established goals with residents and adjacent commercial establishments.
...Reduced thefts, assaults, and property destruction by 55%.

Sergeant/Patrol Supervisor **1980-82**
...Directed 150 police officers in all aspects of their duties.

EDUCATIONAL BACKGROUND
Austin College, Sherman, TX
Bachelor of Science, Law Enforcement, 1978.

■ Education is listed towards bottom of resume because candidate's practical experience outweighs his/her degree.

■ Specifically citing number of employees supervised draws attention to candidate's leadership abilities.

SECURITY MANAGER

CHRIS SMITH
178 Green Street
St. Louis, MO 63103
(314) 555-5555

OBJECTIVE   A corporate management position in Security.

EXPERIENCE

FREEDMAN DEPARTMENT STORES   St. Louis, MO
Regional Manager, Loss Prevention/Safety   1991-Present
Responsible for Southeast Regional area. Implement Loss Prevention/Safety Program
within major department store chain.

HERRICK CORPORATION   St. Louis, MO
Loss Prevention Consultant   1988-1990
Assigned to Retail Corporation. Responsible for all required investigations.

LANDON, INC.   St. Louis, MO
Director of Loss Prevention, Security and Safety 1984-1987
Responsible for all loss prevention policies, procedures, contracts and personnel.
Implemented all training, investigations, loss prevention, safety and shrink programs.

M.L. FLEMING   St. Louis, MO
Loss Prevention Manager   1982-1984
Administered $2 million budget, 50 person department. Implemented all loss prevention
security programs for M.L. Fleming Distribution Center. Managed all loss prevention
systems with Parry Corporate facilities.

MAXIMUM LOCK & SECURITY CORPORATION   St. Louis, MO
Consultant   1980-1983
Advised major companies in Security Systems Development. Developed systems/
programs to reduce losses and prevent shortages.

MANNING COMPANIES, INC.   St. Louis, MO
Security Agent   1971-1979
Supervised all manufacturing and distribution centers security programs. Controlled all
guard forces. Conducted all investigations of losses. Coordinated inventory control
systems with management team.

Stores Security Agent   1970-1971
Supervised designated geographical areas containing stores of all types, including:
supermarkets, department stores, drug stores and tobacco stores. Supervised/evaluated
store detectives. Investigated all major losses.

EDUCATION

PARKER COMMUNITY COLLEGE, St. Louis, MO
Associates Degree in Criminal Justice, 1970.

- Job objective gives resume focus without limiting candidate's opportunities.

- Resume emphasizes candidate's strong work history.

16
Marketing and Sales

Nature of Work

The marketing and sales field encompasses a wide variety of professions, from cashiers and retail clerks to real estate brokers and merchandising managers. Real estate agents and brokers act as a medium for price negotiations between home buyers and sellers, while appraisers evaluate the construction of a home in order to estimate its market value. Telemarketers contact individuals by phone, mail or in person to interview and assist them in completing various forms. They then verify the information they obtain and perform various processing tasks.

Travel agents give advice on destinations, make arrangements for transportation, hotel accommodations, car rentals, tours, and recreation, or plan the right vacation package or business/pleasure combination. Manufacturers' and wholesale sales representatives market their company's products to manufacturers, wholesales and retail establishments, government agencies, and other institutions.

Employment

Those who work in marketing and sales can be found in a variety of areas. Travel agencies are located in rural areas as well as big cities. Manufacturing and wholesale sales representatives work mainly in wholesale trade, mostly for distributors of machinery and equipment, groceries, and motor vehicles and parts. Due to the diversity of products and services sold, employment opportunities for sales representatives are available in every part of the country. Real estate workers are usually employed in relatively small firms, concentrated mainly in large urban areas.

Training

The background for sales and marketing jobs varies by profession. For instance, manufacturing representatives with former sales experience yet no college degree might be hired, while real estate workers must be licensed in every state and in the District of Columbia. This requires passing a comprehensive written examination. Travel agents must also have some formal training, either in the form of a college degree in travel/tourism in vocational school programs or travel correspondence courses offered by certified travel agent societies.

Job Outlook

The employment of most professionals in sales and marketing is expected to grow as fast as the average for all occupations through the year 2005. Most openings will result from the fact that many experienced sales workers will transfer to other occupations, retire, or stop working for other reasons.

Earnings

Salary ranges vary dramatically for those in sales and marketing positions. Travel agents start at $12,000 annually, making up to $25,700 after ten years. Real estate brokers have a median gross personal income of $50,000 per year. Depending on their level of success, agents and brokers can earn considerably more.

Median annual earnings of full-time manufacturers and wholesale sales representatives were about $31,000 in 1990, while the top 10% earned more than $59,000 per year.

ACCOUNT EXECUTIVE

CHRIS SMITH
178 Green Street
Wise, VA 24293
(703) 555-5555

PROFESSIONAL EXPERIENCE

1988 to present   WCVT-TV (NLC-Channel 3), Wise, VA

Account Executive/Sales Department   1990-present
- Established and maintained new and existing corporate accounts representing more than $1.5 million in new clients.
- Initiated and developed marketing strategies and target grids for the second ranked TV station in fifth largest market for effective sales programs/promotions.
- Aided with potential clients in developing effective marketing strategies and programs.

Associate Director/Stage Manager   1989-1990
- Production Department Stage Manager for Noon, Five O'Clock, and News at Ten news casts, all public affairs programs, editorials, and news cut-ins.
- Assembled sets and operated chyron machine.

Production Intern   1988
- Wrote hard news, feature stories, scheduled/interviewed guests.
- Researched materials and packaged tapes for production.
- Operated teleprompter.

1986 to 1988   **UNIVERSITY OF VIRGINIA**, Charlottesville, VA

Producer, Television and Radio Station WNUV-Channel 62   1987-1988
- Responsible for researching materials for mini-documentary.
- Scheduled and interviewed guests for round-table discussions.
- Wrote and edited scripts and edited master tape.

Production Assistant   1986-1987
- Performed as camera technician, stage manager, and chyron operator.
- Assembled lighting and audio equipment.

EDUCATION

RANDOLPH-MACON WOMAN'S COLLEGE, Lynchburg, VA
B.A. Degree, Communications/Mass Media   1989
Magna Cum Laude. Concentration: Economics and Afro-American Studies

HONORS/AFFILIATIONS

Recipient, Virginia Chapter, National Association of TV Arts and Science Award. National Achievement Award. National Association of Women Journalists. National Association of Media Workers.

■ Resume emphasizes candidate's strong work history.

■ Impressive honors and affiliations further enhance candidate's credentials.

ACCOUNT MANAGER

CHRIS SMITH
178 Green Street
Winchester, VA 22001
(703) 555-5555

Experience:

Starbuck Computer, Inc.   Richmond, VA

10/93 to **National Account Manager**
present Responsibilities include developing and implementing national sales strategy for several Richmond based Fortune 500 corporations including Ackler Industrial, The Carnulton Group, Hanlon and Associates and Polamin Company. Position requires the identification and analysis of potential business applications within target accounts and the cultivation of key business relationships with senior management to facilitate sales.
- Average performance over five year period was 125%
- Grew Starbuck revenue 200% to $5M amidst decreasing unit pricing and increasing sales goals
- Completed all five years in the top 12% of the National Account Channel and received Golden Star Award every year
- Created new revenue streams resulting in an estimated $300M in Starbuck sales and $400M in new services for the company

10/85 to **Dealer Account Executive**
10/93 Responsible for the sale of Starbuck products into dealer locations. Initiated cooperative sales strategy with reseller business owners, designed marketing promotions and directed reseller's sales efforts into business and education accounts.
- Average performance over six year period was 110%
- Grew sales by 400% to $11M
- Received Golden Star Club Award every year

7/80 to **Corporate Chain Account Sales Representative**
10/85 Provided administrative and technical sales support to Richmond corporate chain account locations including Power Electronics, Computer Corral and Circonne Computer. Developed marketing promotions and trained store personnel.

10/77 to **Customer Support Representative**
7/80 Created and implemented customer service procedures for Richmond distribution facility. Resolved customer service issues including invoicing discrepancies, shipping errors and upgrades for hardware.

Education:
5/77 Randolph-Macon Woman's College, Lynchburg, VA
B.A., Communications and Political Science

■ Bullets draw attention to candidate's on-the-job achievements.

■ Education is de-emphasized because candidate's work history is strong.

ACCOUNT REPRESENTATIVE

CHRIS SMITH
178 Green Street
Clarksville, TN 37042
(615) 555-5555

CAREER OBJECTIVE

A position as an account representative calling on a background in marketing, management, and computer graphics/design.

QUALIFICATIONS

Computer graphic design using the Macintosh QuarkXpress program (3 years), Adobe Illustrator, and TypeStyler. Scanning techniques using the Ofoto and Microtek Scanners, and Adobe Streamline. Complete knowledge in traditional paste-up, stat camera work and print production including 4-color process.

EMPLOYMENT

MAPLE SKY ADVERTISING - Clarksville, TN   6/92-Present
Account Representative

Account Representative and troubleshooter for several different advertising accounts, including the creation, development, and management of each account. Projects include newspaper inserts, production, billboard and advertising, along with radio and other forms of media advertising. Assist in the creation and design of special advertising.

BLACKTHORN GARDEN CENTER - Clarksville, TN   2/88-6/92
Assistant Manager

Managing up to 20 employees while meeting the wants and needs of our customers. Advertising of current seasonal merchandise, through many different media, and purchasing inventory through representatives of many different distributors.

EDUCATION
- Graduated Cum Laude, Centenary College, Hackettstown, NJ
- BS in Business Administration, December, 1987
- Major Field: Marketing
- Minor Fields: Management, Psychology
- Cumulative G.P.A.: 3.5/4.0
- Honors: Who's Who in American College Students
- Financed 90% education through part-time employment, scholarships, and loans.

REFERENCES

Available upon request.

■ Candidate's technical qualifications are highlighted.

■ Specific dates of employment (month and year) are ideal for candidates with no gaps in work history.

AD COPYWRITER (Direct Mail)

CHRIS SMITH
178 Green Street
South Paris, ME 04281
(207) 555-5555

PROFILE A professional writer with demonstrated expertise in promotional concept, design, and copy. Proven ability to market product/company to best advantage.

EXPERIENCE A. MARTIN ART CATALOGUES, Bangor, ME
Direct Mail Copywriter, 1992-Present
Implement direct mail and all other in-print marketing/advertising campaigns for leading modern art catalogue service. Establish direct mail schedules for all products and coordinate activities with field sales and telemarketing. Write and track all brochures, catalogues, letters, and ads. Oversee outside freelance design and printing.

SEDOTE DESIGN, Newark, NJ
Senior Writer, 1990-1992
Wrote and edited direct mail brochures, letters, catalogues, and ads for a leading textbook publisher. Interacted with marketing and product development staff to produce effective promotional material. Planned and executed writing and production schedules, supervised staff of copywriters, and managed activities of designers, photographers, and printers. Promoted from position of Advertising Copywriter.

G. EDMUND SUKKIENIK PUBLISHING, South Paris, ME
Marketing Writer, 1988-1990
Wrote copy for direct mail catalogues and promotions. Worked closely with marketing and creative staff on press releases, space ads, posters, card decks, and dealer promotions.

NORTHERN LIGHTS ASSOCIATION, Northfield, MN
Public Relations Assistant, 1987-1988
Coordinated media relations, arranged promotional events, wrote press releases, press kits, and newsletters.

EDUCATION CARLETON COLLEGE, Northfield, MN
B.A. Communications, 1988
Concentration: **English**
- GPA: 3.75/4.0
- Summa cum laude
- Ranked 10th among 1000 students
- Minor: Journalism

REFERENCES Available upon request..

- Candidate's work experience reads like a series of accomplishments, not just a list of job duties.

- Reverse chronological format focuses employer's attention on candidate's most current position.

ADVERTISING ASSISTANT

CHRIS SMITH
178 Green Street
Buckeye, WV 24924
(304) 555-5555

OBJECTIVE
An entry-level position in the Advertising Department of an established corporation offering advancement potential based on performance excellence.

CAPABILITIES BRIEF
- Mass Communications
- Advertising and Promotion
- Marketing and Sales Support
- Customer Relations
- Sales and Sales Management
- Film/Video Production

SUMMARY
- **Bachelor of Arts Degree in Advertising**; Basic knowledge of Mass Marketing and Communications; Consumer Oriented; Computer Literate.
- Three years of full- and part-time employment experience in positions of supervisory responsibility.
- Excellent verbal and written communications skills; experienced in personnel relations, brochure and documentary film production; high aptitude for the acquisition of new business technologies.

EDUCATION
Bachelor of Arts Degree, University of Massachusetts, Amherst, MA, 1992
- Advertising major.
- Core GPA 3.48/4.0; Dean's List of Distinguished Students.
- Relevant courses include Organizational Communication - Interpersonal communication - Advanced Mass Media - Advanced Video - Consumer Motivation - Advertising - Writing for Film, Radio and T.V. - Graphic Design.
- Assisted in the production of an independent documentary film "Now I Lay Me Down to Sleep" about homelessness. Acted as script advisor, camera person, and sound assistant.
- Extracurricular activities include: Captain, Lacrosse Team (1981-92); Varsity Tennis (1990); Contributing Editor for *Little Green* school newspaper.

EMPLOYMENT EXPERIENCE
Fanfare, Inc.   **1991-94**
Assistant Manager   **Northampton, MA**
- Provided support services for the Operations Manager, including Determination of Costs and Analysis of old and current account.
- Oversaw distribution of warehouse inventory to branch offices.
- Scheduled and dispatched truck fleet.
- Documented billing and posting of union labor.
- Devised daily cut sheets.
- Operated Texas Instrument Computer System.

■ Capabilities brief and summary highlight candidate's professional qualifications and marketable skills.

■ Education is emphasized because candidate's employment history is limited.

ADVERTISING COORDINATOR

CHRIS SMITH
178 Green Street
Hammond, VA 70402
(504) 555-5555

OBJECTIVE

A challenging career in the advertising industry.

SUMMARY OF QUALIFICATIONS

- Eight years of progressive professional administrative, advertising, and client service experience.
- Self-motivated; able to set effective priorities and implement decisions to achieve immediate and long-term goals and meet operational deadlines.
- Adapt easily to new concepts and responsibilities.

PROFESSIONAL EXPERIENCE

BRADFORD'S DEPARTMENT STORE, Hammond, VA
Advertising Coordinator   1991-Present
Coordinate weekly, monthly, and seasonal advertising and sales campaigns. Actuate/update weekly advertising planning calendars. Input into computer system. Generate confidential reports and monthly communication packages; interact with Production Department and store managers. Update ad changes. Maintain/update media contracts and ratebook. Recreated daily calendar history for 92/93 season; verified information accuracy; entered into word processor.

Print Media Coordinator - Remote Stores   1990-1991
Planned, updated, and managed monthly remote market information; issued forecasts. Acted as liaison with Media Representatives, Store Executives, and Production Department in planning and problem solving. Developed strategies and budget recommendations. Required extensive knowledge of remote markets, media availability and coverage, and rate structures.

Advertising Administrator   1988-1990
Coordinated confidential reports and communication packages for seasonal planbook. Maintained media files. Gathered/entered historical data into weekly and monthly planbook. Dealt with storewide and direct mail information requiring strict adherence to deadlines. Coordinated/oversaw development of newspaper ad system.

XRAY VISION, Winchester, VA   1986-1988
Sales Representative/Telemarketer
Supervised/scheduled personnel. Headed payroll administration 100-member staff.

EDUCATION

UNIVERSITY OF VIRGINIA, Charlottesville, VA
B.A., Communications   1986

- Summary is concise and adds punch to resume.

- Resume illustrates continual career progression.

ADVERTISING MANAGER

CHRIS SMITH
178 Green Street
Nashville, TN 31210
(615) 555-5555

OBJECTIVE
A challenging career in Advertising.

PROFESSIONAL EXPERIENCE
1992 to   USA OLYMPIC PUBLICATIONS, Nashville, TN
Present   Advertising Manager
- Sell advertising space for a publication distributed at Olympic Conventions. Sell rental contracts for booths at trade shows, etc.
- Design flyers and brochures as part of promotions for conventions and trade shows. Handle other promotional work as assigned.
- Initiate, organize and promote trade show for Tennessee merchants and for others interested in area trade and commerce. Contact merchants to rent booths, send promotional materials to buyers and contract for media advertising.
- Coordinate and secure facilities and services for trade show project of approximately $150,000.

1989 to   GOOD MORNING NASHVILLE NEWS, Nashville, TN
1992   Executive Secretary to the Advertising Manager
- Prepared statistical analyses of advertising lineage for use in assessing competitive ranking.
- Typed, answered the Call Director and performed general secretarial duties for sales personnel as assigned.
- Provided resource contact and encouragement to Sales Staff.

1986 to   DEPARTMENT OF SOCIAL SERVICES, Memphis, TN
1989   Legal Secretary
- Handled correspondence, telephones and general secretarial/light research work.

1984 to   RYE BROOK COMPANY, Madison, TN
1986   Typist
- Mag card typist of specifications usually 40 to 50 pages long; compiled and typed statistical information for analyses.

INTERESTS   Rock climbing, gardening, 70s trivia.

REFERENCES   Furnished upon request.

■ Education is omitted due to candidate's extensive work experience.

■ Personal interests give a candid snapshot of candidate as a person.

ASSISTANT ACCOUNT EXECUTIVE

CHRIS SMITH
178 Green Street
Kutztown, PA 16233
(717) 555-5555

SYNOPSIS Area of expertise is in Advertising Production with a proclivity to TV and Magazine Production. Self-starter and excellent communicator with ability to project and elicit interest, enthusiasm, and drive using a common sense approach. Adept at sizing up situations, analyzing facts, and developing alternative courses of action to increase productivity and exceed desired results.

SUPPORTIVE QUALIFICATIONS

- 7 years advertising experience; handle accounts up to $3 million.
- Strong client service, professional, diplomatic, supportive; excellent interpersonal skills with clients, management, staff, public and media.
- Always meet deadlines with accuracy and quality; able to deal with extended pressure; strong on follow-through.
- Proven supervisory skills; organize, prioritize, and delegate tasks; effectively train staff in new concepts and procedures.

EXPERIENCE

THE MERCER GROUP, Meadville, PA
Assistant Account Executive   1992 to Present
Direct all phases of client services for national account, primarily based in the Mid-Atlantic Region. Plan media and placement. Direct creative services, copy and design.

Account Supervisor - Account Coordinator   1990 to 1992
Oversaw Coordinating Department; trained, guided and directed staff of five while monitoring ad placement system. Assisted in creation of advertising campaigns and acted as liaison between client, agency and media vendors, including selection, budget and advertisement placement.

THE ARIEL AGENCY, Newark, NJ and *MERTON, KASS & HOWE*, Pittsburgh, PA
Advertising Internship   1989
Responsibilities included: compiling market research, writing press releases, producing traffic reports, working media events, and assisting in advertising production.

EDUCATION

Rutgers University at Camden, B.A. in Mass Communication; minor in English.

PROFESSIONAL AFFILIATION

The Advertising Club of Pennsylvania, 1993 to Present

COMPUTER SKILLS

Microsoft Word, WordPerfect, Macintosh, Quark

■ Synopsis provides employer with summary of candidate's professional skills and working philosophy.

■ Professional affiliations illustrate candidate's dedication to a long-term career.

CALLBACK REPRESENTATIVE

CHRIS SMITH
178 Green Street
Poughkeepsie,NY 12601
(914) 555-5555

OBJECTIVE:

To contribute acquired skills to a sales position promoting the mutual funds of an industry leader.

EMPLOYMENT EXPERIENCE:

MANIFEST FATE, INC., Poughkeepsie, NY
Senior Callback Representative, 9/91-Present
- Troubleshoot problems on shareholder and broker accounts which require research.
- Analyze all relevant facts pertaining to each problem; implement a timely solution and inform the caller of the resolution.
- Interact with other departments to determine source of internal errors and prevent their re-occurrence.
- Approve all maintenance items submitted by phone representatives.
- Maintain smooth work flow and department standards in supervisor's absence.
- Train new telephone representatives in department procedures, telephone techniques, legal requirements, and portfolio objectives.

Telephone Representative, 1/89-9/91
- Informed shareholders and brokers about the Manifest family of funds, the mutual fund industry as a whole, activity in each portfolio, and Manifest policy.
- Interacted with portfolio managers concerning portfolio objectives, market trends, individual brokerage concerns, and changes in SEC regulations and tax laws.
- Educated shareholders and brokers about laws and SEC regulations as they pertained to their particular state.
- Researched difficulties with dealer commissions, registration data, taxable events, wire trades, and government allotments.

EDUCATION:

DAEMAN COLLEGE, Amherst, NY
Bachelor of Arts - Economics, 12/88

LICENSES:

Series 6, NASD Registrations

AWARDS:

Manifest Fate Employee of the Month - October 1993
2 Silver Service Awards
Attendance Award - last 5 consecutive quarters

■ Resume emphasizes contributions, achievements, and problems candidate has solved throughout his/her career.

■ Impressive awards indicate candidate's potential to excel.

DIRECTOR OF SUBSIDIARY RIGHTS

Chris Smith
178 Green Street
Kansas City, MO 64110
(816) 555-5555

EXPERIENCE

Chesapeake Company, Kansas City, MO

1992-Present *DIRECTOR OF SUBSIDIARY RIGHTS*
Negotiated subsidiary rights licenses for Trade and Reference publications in hard cover and paperback reprint, book club, large print, motion picture, merchandising, mechanical and audio recording. Oversaw the administration of departmental contracts and accounting noting systems. Prepared monthly forecast and quarterly budget reports. Supervised a secretary and two interns.

1991-1992 *MANAGER OF SUBSIDIARY RIGHTS*
Negotiated subsidiary rights licenses for Trade and Reference publications in hardcover and paperback reprint, book club and large print. Supervised administration of departmental contracts and accounting noting systems. Prepared monthly forecast and quarterly budget reports.

1988-1991 *SUBSIDIARY RIGHTS COORDINATOR*
Negotiated specialty book club and large print licenses. Administered the internal monitoring and processing of all subsidiary rights contracts and monies. Coordinated and fulfilled all manufacturing requests from licensees, including foreign and domestic co-productions. Generated all contractual reversions. Supervised an assistant.

1985-1988 *SUBSIDIARY RIGHTS ASSISTANT*
Assisted the subsidiary rights coordinator with submissions, preparation of various reports and fulfillment of manufacturing materials to licensees. Provided general secretarial support.

1982-1985 *ADMINISTRATIVE ASSISTANT*
Provided general secretarial support within the subsidiary rights department. Researched rights histories and availability of rights.

EDUCATION

Bernadette Tibbs Business School
Kansas City, MO 1980-1982

REFERENCES

Available upon request.

■ Work history is stated in reverse chronological order, with most recent postion listed first.

■ Job descriptions highlight candidate's leadership skills and problem-solving abilities.

INSURANCE AGENT

CHRIS SMITH
178 Green Street
Erie, PA 16505
(814) 555-5555

OBJECTIVE

To join the management team of an organization in need of comprehensive expertise in establishing, implementing and managing insurance programs in a non-carrier environment.

EXPERIENCE

SENIOR SUPERVISOR CLAIMS   **1989-Present**
Bimscala Risk Management   **Pittsburgh, PA**
- As Senior Supervisor, Claims, was accountable for all claims service provided by the Workers' Compensation and Liability units. Oversaw the delivery of a quality product which developed client confidence in the claims handling ability of Bimscala.
- Responsibilities encompassed direct claims handling, reporting and negotiating high exposure claims, conducting periodic claims reviews and loss report reviews.
- Established all opening reserves on cases and advised adjusters as to what specifics were needed. Instituted authority levels. Reported claims to excess carrier.

DIRECTOR OF RISK MANAGEMENT   **1988-1989**
Aspenwood and Co.   **Scranton, PA**
- Analyzed risk of potential loss to clients' assets and revenues.
- Consulted on property and casualty insurance for clients of various industries.
- Interacted directly with corporate financial and general management officers to establish insurance policies and procedures.

CLAIMS MANAGER   **1987-1988**
Jared Barkly, Inc.   **Reading, PA**
- Administered Workers' Compensation claims for Regional District; processed claims, hired independent adjusters, physicians and attorney.

EDUCATION

Grove City College, Grove City, PA
Master of Arts in Speech and Business Communications, 1987
Mansfield University, Mansfield, PA
Bachelor of Science in Visual and Verbal Communications, 1985

LICENSE

Licensed Insurance Agent, The State of Pennsylvania - #1068

- Work history is stated in reverse chronological order, with most recent employment listed first.

- Required license information is provided.

MANUFACTURER'S REPRESENTATIVE

Chris Smith
178 Green Street
Douglasville, GA 30134
(404) 555-5555

KEY QUALIFICATIONS

- More than ten years of successful experience in professional sales and marketing to manufacturers throughout New England. Experience includes prospecting, telemarketing, key account sales, customer follow-up and relations, product management and sales, as well as related aspects of sales administration and contract negotiation.
- Excellent verbal, written and interpersonal skills. Relate easily at all levels of the decision making process. Work well as individual producer or team member in the successful achievement of sale objectives. Very high aptitude for acquisition of new product sales and marketing technologies.
- Experience includes production and operational areas of management, such as scheduling, distribution, purchasing, inventory management, personnel supervision and relations, labor management relations and negotiations, and related aspects of business operations.

PROFESSIONAL EXPERIENCE

1990-Present   Blackwell Manufacturing Corp.
AREA MANUFACTURING REPRESENTATIVE   Atlanta, GA
- Hired to explore and develop unmarketed territory for expanding clothing manufacturer.
- Developed territory in declining market area from $0.00 to annual volume of over $500,000.
- Handled all aspects of professional sales, from cold calling, market research and follow-up on referrals/customer inquiries, to networking customer base and assisting with styling/complete design of product to customer specifications.

1984-1989   Birmingham Corp.
AREA MANUFACTURING REPRESENTATIVE   Decatur, GA
- Opened/developed Southeastern territory from $0.00 to annual sales of $600,000.
- Sold belts and children's clothing to accounts throughout the Southeast. Established and maintained good working relationship with all major manufacturers in the Southeast.

EDUCATION

Oglethorpe University, Atlanta, GA
Bachelor of Science Degree, Business Administration, 1983
Minor: Economics

REFERENCES

Furnished upon request.

■ Candidate's key qualifications are listed prominently.

■ Bullets make resume easy to read.

MARKET RESEARCH ANALYST

CHRIS SMITH
178 Green Street
Ossipee, NH 03864
(603) 555-5555

OBJECTIVE To apply marketing and problem-solving skills in a marketing research/analysis position for career growth.

EXPERIENCE

1991 to Present BRIODY ASSOCIATES, Derry, NH
Market Research Analyst
Build consumer behavior models for corporate clients using multivariate techniques, including regression and discriminant analysis, and cluster analysis. Analyze data from national probability survey to identify purchase intents and patterns for business to consumer direct marketers. Organize and present marketing information to executive staff for in-house promotions and press releases.

1986 to 1991 THOMSON AND COMPANY, Manchester, NH
Market Researcher
Member of Survey Research Group addressing all marketing research needs, i.e. marketing segmentation, concept testing, and product usage and awareness. Interviewed and gathered data from managers in a wide variety of industries including consumer goods, high technology, banking, retailing, and health care. Pre-tested, edited, and coded in-depth questionnaires.

1984 to 1986 STEVEN ICE, INC., Derry, NH
Market Researcher
Identified target markets, constructed complex questionnaires, conducted telephone interviews, compiled and analyzed the data, organized and conducted a focus group within market segment, analyzed and dovetailed the results from 2 data-gathering approaches, tested original assumptions, and wrote and presented a report to management including recommendations for future action.

EDUCATION

BABSON COLLEGE, Wellesley, MA
Master of Business Administration, Honors, 1984
PRINCETON UNIVERSITY, Princeton, NJ
Bachelor of Arts, Psychology, Honors, 1982

AWARDS

- Awarded U.S. Medal for Management Excellence, 1990
- Business Board Member of Princeton Yearbook Publication Inc., 1982

SKILLS IBM and Macintosh. Lotus 1-2-3 and Microsoft Word.

■ Resume includes additional information including candidate's awards, memberships, and extracurricular activities.

■ Valuable computer skills are highlighted in a separate section.

MARKETING AND SALES DIRECTOR

Chris Smith
278 Green Street
Greenwood, SC 29646
(803) 555-5555

OBJECTIVE

A career within sales and marketing.

PROFESSIONAL EXPERIENCE

JOLENE'S, Columbia, SC

Marketing Director/Amber Rain, 1989-Present

- Maximize sales in 19 stores; consistently achieve monthly sales plan.
- Recruit/interview/hire, train and develop counter managers and beauty advisors; stress improved customer service and follow through.
- Act as liaison between Jolene's and Amber Rain account executives; communicate/execute corporate plans.
- Merchandise cases/counters; oversee/organize stock areas; review stock control and productivity books.
- Actuate/implement promotional events to generate additional business. Hire/train freelance models to promote business. Conduct product sales and seminars for promotional agencies.
- Review and analyze goals and retail sales; interact with general managers and cosmetic buyers.
- Organize/supervise 25 clinics and special promotional events.

Marketing Director/Emerald Haze, 1984-1989

- Responsible for 25 stores and $3 million account. Improved staffing, increased business 30% in Spring '89, 60% Christmas '88, and 42% Fall '87.
- Restructured special events to generate business. Actuated "Days of Haze" program, stressing customer service/follow through; established goals to increase average unit sales, makeovers, and consultations.
- Brought account to #2 in the country; exceeded sales goals.
- Received numerous Jolene Marketing Awards.

EDUCATION

Columbia Institute of Aesthetics, Columbia, SC
Courses in Advanced Makeup Artistry, 1988

University of Florida, Gainesville, FL
B.A., Marketing, 1982

PERSONAL

Willing to relocate

- Percentages and dollar amounts quantify candidate's accomplishments.

- Courses listed under education are related to candidate's field of interest.

MARKETING ASSISTANT

Chris Smith
178 Green Street
Terre Haute, IN 47804
(812) 555-5555

OBJECTIVE

A position that will further develop my superior marketing skills.

EXPERIENCE

Marketing Assistant, The Art Lover's Institute
Indianapolis, IN   2/91-Present
- Temporary position assisting the Manager of Public Information on the exhibit "Proud Triangles; Gay Life in America."
- Executed the distribution of exhibit posters and organized the development of displays merchandising products to promote the exhibit at local retailers.
- Coordinated press clippings and releases about the exhibit.

Assistant Box Office Manager, Terre Haute Performing Arts Center
Terre Haute, IN   6/90-1/91
- Managed daily operations for a staff of 20 operators responsible for customer service and the sale of all tickets in a theater seating 5,000.
- Compiled all financial statements on a daily and monthly basis for each performance in the theater averaging 10 performances per month, including daily deposits and revenue from outlet sales on secondary ticketing systems.

Gallery Assistant/Window Exhibit Coordinator, Jim Cannon's Art Implosion
Bourbon, IN   5/89-6/90
- Developed marketing plan for fine art prints and coordinating notecards.
- Developed client base and serviced accounts.
- Coordinated special events relating to current exhibits, opening receptions, and artist signings. Handled press releases.

EDUCATION

Valparaiso University, Valparaiso, IN
Bachelor of Arts, 1991.
Arts Administration with a concentration in marketing/communications.

SKILLS

Macintosh: Pagemaker, Word.
IBM: WordPerfect, Excel and rBase.

- Job descriptions are straightforward and understandable.

- Specific dates of employment (month and year) are ideal for candidates with no gaps in work history.

MARKETING CONSULTANT

CHRIS SMITH
178 Green Street
Hawthorne, FL 32640
(904) 555-5555

EXPERIENCE

1994   **Hawthorne Management,** Hawthorne, FL
Consultant - *Market and Strategic Management Research*
Conducted large-scale quantitative research projects based in customer satisfaction measurement and total quality implementation, including design, coordination, statistical analysis and report generation. Specialized in business-to-business services and health care.

1992-93   **Scott, Wilder, Johanson and Rolfe,** Archer, FL
Research Associate - *Public Relations and Market Research*
Managed behaviorally-based research projects including proposal writing; methodology, instrument and sample development; field coordination; data coding, analysis and interpretation; report writing. Projects included customer and employee studies, communication audits, market analysis, name/logo testing, constituency relations research, positioning and purchaser/user studies.

1991   **International Research Group,** Gainesville, FL
Management Consultant - *Public Relations*
Provided counsel in areas of Marketing, Behavior and Research. Participated in internal and external strategic planning for Fortune 500 companies, government agencies, non-profit organizations and health care providers.

1990   **Webber and Sons, Inc.,** Ocala, FL
Research Assistant - *Market Research*
Conducted on-site survey groups, interviews, intercepts and telephone interviews. Recruited focus groups and pre-screened samples. Involved in project execution, coding and analysis.

EDUCATION

Stetson University, De Land, FL - 1990
Advanced Graduate Certificate *Marketing Management.* GPA 3.8

Georgetown University, Washington, DC - 1988
M.A. *Applied Psychology.* Concentration in Health Care research. GPA 3.6

Central Connecticut State University, New Britain, CT - 1985
B.A. *Psychology, minor Business Administration.* Field work in Puerto Rico.

- Use of boldface and underlining provides a clean and crisp presentation.

- Impressive educational background strengthens resume.

MARKETING DIRECTOR

CHRIS SMITH
178 Green Street
Covaillis, OR 97330
(503) 555-5555

PROFILE WITH SELECTED HIGHLIGHTS

- MANAGEMENT accountabilities include P&L responsibility for $500 million covering 100+ film products and 80+ cameras. Developed and implemented 5 operating plans covering 150 products. **Delivered and executed 5 national marketing plans.**
- SALES ACHIEVER: Created 4 new imaging categories and **negotiated $40 million in first year sales** with a projected 20% increase in high tech market sales in newly established distribution.
- KEY CUSTOMER RELATIONS: Fully profiled 30 multi-location customers and won them back to Cressidine, **securing $20 million in sales.** Handle Fortune 500 firms.
- GLOBAL MARKET PROSPECTIVE: As Product Manager of the International Division, traveled for 5 years between **5 South American countries and 10 European subsidiaries** building product launch plans and developing relationships and knowledge of foreign customs and business protocols.
- TEAMWORK STYLE MANAGER: Provide leadership for **national sales force of 500+.** Mentored and promoted numerous managers into key positions.

PROFESSIONAL EXPERIENCE
CRESSIDINE CORPORATION, Corvallis, OR

DIRECTOR OF MARKETING OPERATIONS: TECHNICAL IMAGING   1992-Present
Spearhead implementation of corporate objectives within the Technical Imaging Division. Conceive and energize all marketing strategies and provide feedback on program performance and recommendations to corporate senior managers. Direct and supervise a staff of 10 in responsibilities for generating $250 million in sales with a $150 million margin for core products. Prepare and effectively control a $7 million marketing expense and a $4 million advertising budget.

- *Created the first end user direct mail strategy generating a 30% response rate and selling 400,000 units within the first year.*
- *Mounted trade show exhibitions including designing booths, collateral materials and advertisements.*
- *Secured $200,000 in pre-booked sales within a month of trade show presentations for 4 new products.*

GROUP MARKETING MANAGER: TECHNICAL IMAGING   1987-1992
Responsible for developing relationships with major imaging companies and securing long term contracts for core products within a vertical market framework. Directed and monitored new product launch programs; developed pricing and selling strategies. Fostered and maintained key account relations.

EDUCATION
BACHELOR OF SCIENCE IN BUSINESS ADMINISTRATION, 1987
University of Oregon, Eugene, OR

- Profile sums up candidate's professional qualifications and highlights achievements.

- Statistics and dollar figures quantify candidate's accomplishments.

MARKETING INTERN

CHRIS SMITH
178 Green Street
Washington, D.C. 20020
(202) 555-5555

SUMMARY OF QUALIFICATIONS
- Successfully completed finance/marketing internship in Maastricht, the Netherlands.
- Performed market research for new Pinchot Fat Free Cakes.
- Computer Skills: MacIntosh; IBM PC and compatible systems.
- Excellent interpersonal and communication skills with verbal, written, presentation, and foreign language translations.
- Multi-lingual: Fluent in Dutch; Conversant in German, French, and Italian.
- Familiar and comfortable with multi-ethnic populations; well traveled and have resided and studied in Amsterdam, Munich, and Rome.
- Demonstrated marketing/public relations, events planning, and fund raising capabilities.

EXPERIENCE

LION BANK   Maastricht, the Netherlands
Finance/Marketing Intern   Spring 1994
Dealt with portfolios, stocks and bonds. Provided translations. Assisted with research on the Maastricht Treaty and the potential financial ramifications of a unified Europe. Selected as part of the Johns Hopkins-Maastricht Exchange Program as one of only seven students chosen to participate.

BANKS' HEALTH FOODS   Richmond, VA
Market Research Intern   Summer 1993
Assisted with new product research for Pinchot Fat Free Cakes; worked extensively on IBM system.

SWEET BRIAR PRODUCTS, INC.   Annapolis, MD
Research and Development Intern   Summer 1992
Worked for new product development research team.

JOHNS HOPKINS ALUMNI ASSOCIATION   Rockville, MD
Fundraiser   Summer 1991
Coordinated the procedures and implementation of securing funds for tutoring facility, career and alumni center.

EDUCATION

JOHNS HOPKINS UNIVERSITY   Baltimore, MD
B.S., Political Science; Minor, International Relations Anticipated   Spring 1995

JOHNS HOPKINS-MAASTRICHT   Maastricht, the Netherlands
Student Exchange/Internship   Spring 1994

■ Internship experience is valuable for candidates with little job experience, particularly if it corresponds to the position sought.

■ Foreign language skills and international exposure, via exchange programs and/or internships, are a valuable asset in today's global market.

MARKETING MANAGER

CHRIS SMITH
178 Green Street
El Paso, TX 79925
(915) 555-5555

OBJECTIVE

A position in **Sales/Marketing Management.**

EXPERIENCE

DENNISON PRESS, El Paso, TX
Trade Division
Marketing Coordinator   1993-Present
- Develop and supervise implementation of all Dennison marketing plans with the sales and marketing departments.
- Prepare and manage the annual marketing budget of $2 million.
- Supervise marketing assistant.
- Manage scheduling and production of all sales and marketing materials.
- Provide marketing information at biannual sales conferences and coordinate book presentations.

Professional Division
Children's Books Department
Editorial Administrator   1991-1993
- Managed revisions from manuscript preparation to bound book. Resolved author questions and problems. Ensured manuscript conformity to budgetary and scheduling constraints.
- Directed supplement program of over seventy books from budget management to project completion with specific emphasis in electronic manuscript preparation.
- Supervised and trained editorial assistant.
- Provided information to marketing department for direct mail promotions and reviewed copy for accuracy and content.

Children's Books Department
Editorial Coordinator   1988-1991
- Supervised the supplement program.
- Conducted editorial market research and assessed results with senior editors.

Children's Books Department
Editorial Assistant   1987-1988
- Provided general support for senior editors.
- Fulfilled various author requests.

EDUCATION   Baylor College, Waco, TX
B.A., English major, Economics minor, 1986

SKILLS   Proficient in Microsoft Word, WordPerfect, Lotus 1-2-3, and Quark.
Working knowledge of the French language.

■ Resume illustrates continual career progression.

■ Valuable software and foreign language skills are highlighted in a separate section.

MERCHANDISING MANAGER

CHRIS SMITH
178 Green Street
Bay City, MI 48708
(517) 555-5555

SUMMARY OF QUALIFICATIONS

Broad-based knowledge of product merchandising/display techniques, fashion coordinating, and retail management.
- Utilizing innovative techniques and creativity to maximize sales of fashion and other products.
- Training, scheduling, evaluating, and supervising personnel.
- Forecasting and monitoring operational budgets.
- Refinement and implementation of management systems, administrative policies and operational procedures.

PROFESSIONAL BACKGROUND

1990 to Present   THE PLASTER MASTER, Bay City, MI
Visual Merchandising Manager
- Supervise the creation of window and interior displays for eight stores in Michigan.
- Train, schedule, and supervise display staff.
- Teach merchandising concepts to sales personnel.
- Monitor budget and purchase merchandising materials.

1987 to 1990   LORD JASPER'S RETAIL RUMPUS, Saginaw, MI
Director of Visual Merchandising
- Responsible for creating and implementing design concepts for six department stores, division of Lady Lucy, Inc.
- Presented workshops on new fashion trends to store personnel.

1985 to 1987   ERNEST AND BERTRAM'S HIDEAWAY, Adrian, MI
Visual Merchandiser - Freelance
- Monitored merchandising of haute couture, European lines in boutique.
- Participated on buying trips to Europe.

1983 to 1985   MISS BESS' CLOSET MESSES, Minneapolis, MN
Department Manger
- Supervised operation of women's clothing, sportswear, and furnishings departments.

EDUCATIONAL BACKGROUND

DETROIT CONTEMPORARY SCHOOL OF BEAUTY CULTURE, Detroit, MI, 1985

MINNEAPOLIS COLLEGE OF ART AND DESIGN, Minneapolis, MN
Bachelor of Arts, Art History, 1983

- Summary of qualifications highlights candidate's acquired professional skills.

- Job descriptions are straightforward and understandable.

PRODUCT DEVELOPER

CHRIS SMITH
178 Green Street
Hattiesburg, MS 39401
(601) 555-5555

OBJECTIVE A progressive career in **Product Development and Sales.**

MAJOR QUALIFICATIONS
- 9 years managerial, 7 years sales, 6 years buying experience.
- Perform point of sale forecasting.
- Proven training record with ability to make complex concepts and items approachable and user friendly to customers and staff.
- Innovative in merchandising and display.
- Success and expertise in parallel exporting.

PROFESSIONAL EXPERIENCE
1991-Present **THE TWO WHEEL EXCHANGE,** Starkville, MS　　　**Product Developer**
Supervise up to 25 employees.
- Direct all Product Development Operations, including the fabrication and testing of prototype cycles.
- Conceive, develop and build bicycles for the physically handicapped.
- Fabricate, develop and supervise construction of a wheelchair bike for Bill Milton in his annual New York Marathon bid.
- Teach evening classes on bicycle repair/maintenance.
- Manage and equip a cycling team sponsored by The Two Wheel Exchange.
- Open/close store, scheduled and trained staff, ordered bikes.

1988-1991 **GIGI'S INC.,** Hattiesburg, MS　　　**Management/Sales**
Ensured the smooth operation of a prestigious, 150 year old store.
- Ordered and distributed several lines of merchandise.
- Coordinated product training and development.
- Opened and closed store; ensured safety of cash drawer, inventory and displays.
- Maintained strong customer relations.
- Ordered supplies, maintained inventory, developed creative window displays.

1986-1988 **HARVEY DAWSON MOTORCYCLES,** Boston, MA　　　**General Manager**
Responsible for the special ordering and purchasing of Harvey Dawson motorcycles in the U.S.

EDUCATION
NORTHEAST MISSOURI STATE, Kirksville, MO.
Bachelor of Arts, Marketing, 1985.

- Job objective gives resume focus without limiting candidate's opportunities.

- Chrono-functional resume has the strength of chronological format and the flexibility of functional format.

PURCHASING AGENT

CHRIS SMITH
178 Green Street
Bountiful, UT 84040
(801) 555-5555

EMPLOYMENT

PURCHASING AGENT   1990-Present
Data Basix, Westwood, MA
- Purchase Montgomery, Sprint and Miyako products, PCs, Laptops and peripherals.
- Maintain open-order status reports for Montgomery, Sprint, and Miyako products and expedited orders, as necessary, pertaining to inventory control.
- Return defective and obsolete inventory products.

PURCHASING AGENT   1989-1990
Radlett, Inc., Lark, UT
- Purchased Wellsville 1068, Moore Laptop PCs and peripherals. Interacted with sales and marketing departments, with total responsibility for overseeing all order processing, scheduling, and inventory control functions. Handled general supplies purchasing for the entire company.

REGIONAL DISTRIBUTION SUPERVISOR   1988-1989
Rybell Corporation, Teasdale, UT
- Purchased Apple IIe, Grinfeld, KRT, Willard, Moore Laptop micro computers, as well as software and peripherals to be sold to individuals and companies up through Fortune 500. Handled all purchasing for 10 retail outlets in Utah and Nevada. Successfully worked with vendors to maintain best and most current pricing. Supervised and trained a staff of eight in buying, order processing and billing; and five in warehouse administration and maintenance for the Western Region.
- Started as a Buyer, while with Microsource, responsible for annual purchases of $17 million in microcomputer equipment/peripherals, monitoring inventory, and preparing forecasts for a perpetual inventory system. Company sold to LCO; retained and promoted to Regional Distribution Supervisor by new management.

BUYER   1985-1988
O'Donnell Corporation, Oasis, UT
- Purchased electronic components, for a collision avoidance radar system used by both commercial and military shipping, from manufacturers and local distributors. Functioned as Assistant to the Mechanical Buyer. Purchased all office and miscellaneous supplies.
- Started as a Purchasing Secretary responsible for administrative support to Purchasing Agent and liaison to outside vendors. In 1986, based on performance, was promoted to position of Buyer.

EDUCATION

University of Colorado at Boulder
B.A. Business Administration 1985

■ Job descriptions detail candidate's responsibilities and accomplishments.

■ Education is listed towards bottom of resume because candidate's practical experience outweighs his/her degree.

REAL ESTATE APPRAISER

CHRIS SMITH
178 Green Street
Winona, MN 55987
(507) 555-5555

SUMMARY OF QUALIFICATIONS
Professional experience includes the following areas:
- Assessing property and real estate value for insurance claims, adjustments and repair.
- Successfully marketing services to Fortune 500 companies.
- Project and office management, supervising estimators, superintendent and construction crew.
- Demonstrating estimating software in Northern regions and following up with problem solving assistance.

EXPERIENCE
5/92-Present WINONA CONSTRUCT Winona, MN
Vice-President/Appraiser
Manage two estimators, a superintendent and 20-member construction crew, assessing damages, preparing estimates and proposals for insurance companies, and supervising reconstruction activities.
- Call homeowners, real estate companies, insurance company representatives and adjusters, promoting company's services.
- Achieved average annual sales of $950,000 with new clients.
- Provide demonstrations and training to groups of 10 to 30 persons in computer estimating software package, traveling to Maine, Florida, Georgia and Massachusetts. Followed up with problem solving services.
- Travelled to Los Angeles area to write estimates for apartment complexes damaged by 1994 Earthquake as special assignment.

1988-1992 NORTHERN STAR RESTORATION COMPANY Minneapolis, MN
General Manager
Worked closely with management companies and apartment complexes, managing restoration work for new company, hiring and supervising sub-contractors and supervising jobs from start to finish.

1984-1988 ST. PAUL LIFE & CASUALTY St. Paul, MN
Property Claims Representative (1985-1988)
Appraised all types of residential properties and investigated all types of damages to home, including water, fire, vandalism and "natural disasters." Determined value of claim and prepared report. Exceeded monthly claims quota by 40%.

Inside Auto Adjustor (1984-1985)
Investigated cause and perpetrators of accidents, dealing with attorneys, police officials, auto adjusters and clients.

EDUCATION
1984 BROWN UNIVERSITY Providence, RI
Bachelor of Arts in Education

■ Summary highlights candidate's experience and expertise in his/her field.

■ Resume indicates a series of promotions.

REAL ESTATE BROKER

CHRIS SMITH
178 Green Street
Fargo, ND 58102
(701) 555-5555

SKILLS:

- Real Estate Brokers License, North Dakota, 1983
- Closing High-End Sales
- Generating and Developing Prospective Clients
- Developing Sales and Support Networks
- Cold Calling, Telemarketing, Advertising Expertise
- Outstanding Interpersonal and Communications Skills

EXPERIENCE:

SMOOTH MOVES, INC.   **Fargo, ND**
Real Estate Broker   1991 to Present
Sell single, multi-family, and investment residential properties. Develop and utilize sales networks, cold calling, telemarketing, and advertising to generate buyers, sellers, and financiers. Specialist in no-money-down and foreclosure sales. Maintain active troubleshooting and negotiating involvement through closing.
- Originated Client Concerns Division of the company.
- Assisted in increasing market share from 10% to 30%.
- Sold over $2 million in downturned market.

GET OUT OF TOWN, INC.   **Minot, ND**
Real Estate Broker   1988 to 1991
Sales and Rentals of single and multi-family, high end homes and condominiums. Proficient in obtaining difficult to receive financing. Specialist in executive relocations. Adept at handling difficult and out-of-town clients.
- #1 Rental Broker in company history.
- Averaged $1.5 million in sales per year.

CATCH THIS PRODUCTIONS   **Bismarck, ND**
Owner/Operator   1985 to 1987
Founded and operated a musical booking agency, booking nightclubs, talent and tours on a local and nationwide basis. Developed and maintained profitable relationships with nightclubs and talent, as well as a nationwide network of other agents. Negotiated percentages, dates, and details.

BURNS & CLAP   **Bismarck, ND**
Sales Manager   1983 to 1985
Promoted from Rental Broker after 6 months, with added responsibility to motivate Brokers and coordinate marketing and advertising campaigns.

EDUCATION:

COLLEGE OF WOOSTER, Wooster, OH
B.A., Business Management, 1982

■ Candidate's skills are highlighted in a separate section.

■ Bulleted statements highlight candidate's on-the-job achievements.

REAL ESTATE MANAGER

CHRIS SMITH
178 Green Street
Lawton, OK 73703
(405) 555-5555

EXPERIENCE

DIRECTOR OF REAL ESTATE DEVELOPMENT
Wildoak, Inc., Lawton, OK   1989-Present
Responsibilities and Accomplishments:
- Started a real estate development division which grew to a professional and support staff of 30, and generated contracts in excess of $12 million.
- Manage development projects from inception to final use. Assign and manage direct company and contract professionals including controller, architects, estimators, designers, engineering and sale staff.
- Implement large scale development of single family detached home neighborhoods which range in price and market segment from first time buyers, upwardly mobile buyers, to luxury communities. Play a key role in directing all areas of projects.
- Plan and manage projects through the most efficient methods functioning as a General Contractor or working through a General Contractor.
- Interact with individual and corporate clients, local and state officials and inspectors, attorneys, contractors, utilities, financial institutions and real estate brokers for the planning, development, financing, and marketing of large scale investment.

VICE-PRESIDENT - PLANNING AND FINANCE
Village Realty, Inc., Muskogee, OK   1981-1989
General Information:
Started with this firm in real estate sales, 1981, and was involved in all phases of marketing and sales of residential and commercial properties. Based on performance was promoted to Manager of Sales and Marketing, and subsequently Vice-President of Finance and Planning, 1984.

As Vice-President of Finance and Planning:
- Assumed full responsibility for the planning, finance, sales, lease or rentals of all company development and construction projects. Supervised a staff of 18 in accounting, sales, construction and building management.
- Conferred and negotiated with financial institutions and private investors to obtain financing. Created and coordinated financial packages for new developments or expansions.
- Attended planning and zoning board hearings and meetings, and successfully obtained zoning approval to proceed with what resulted in a successful condominium complex.

EDUCATION
Oklahoma State University, Stillwater, OK
Bachelor of Arts Degree in Management/Economics, 1985
Honors: Dean's List
Cumulative Average: 3.5/4.0

■ Resume emphasizes achievements; doesn't simply list job responsibilities.

■ Format is neat and professional.

REGIONAL ACCOUNT MANAGER

CHRIS SMITH
178 Green Street
Fairfax, VA 22033
(703) 555-5555

OBJECTIVE A challenging Regional Sales/Management position.

EXPERIENCE

1990-Present **REGIONAL ACCOUNT MANAGER**
Global Trust, Fairfax, VA
Market trust and custody products and financial support services to qualified clients within a 12-state territory. Manage product sales with cycles from two months to one year in length and generating recurring revenue agreements to $2 million.
- *Develop leads and maintain a viable network of business contacts and prospective clients to consistently meet assigned sales quotas.*
- *Ascertain client needs and cost parameters; formulate appropriate product packages; make effective sales presentations.*
- *Negotiate and secure sales, developing existing accounts and acquiring new account business.*
- *Process and track fulfillment of customer orders, troubleshoot customer problems and ensure total client satisfaction.*
- *Monitor account performance; ensure collection of account balances.*
- *Review and analyze policy and procedures with a view toward enhancing sales productivity, efficiency and quality performance.*

1985-1990 **VICE PRESIDENT/PRINCIPAL**
Shrika Group, Falls Church, VA
Planned, directed, coordinated and executed marketing support operations for a firm specializing in benefits administration software for mid-size companies.
- *Researched market opportunities; prepared and drove the group's initial business plan.*
- *Developed contract options, sales techniques, efficient operations, staff training and administrative procedures.*
- *Trained, motivated, assigned and supervised performance of support staff.*

1982-1985 **ACCOUNT EXECUTIVE**
Raneri Company, Newark, NJ
Implemented marketing strategies for New Jersey state insurance products. Provided personal account information, counseling and advice as part of high quality customer service.

EDUCATION

1982 **DARTMOUTH COLLEGE,** Hanover, NH
BACHELOR OF SCIENCE IN BUSINESS ADMINISTRATION, 1982

- Dynamic action verbs give resume impact.

- Use of boldface and italics provides a clean and crisp presentation.

REGIONAL SALES MANAGER

CHRIS SMITH
178 Green Street
Toppenish, WA 98948
(509) 555-5555

PROFESSIONAL OBJECTIVE

A position in **Regional Retail Management** in which my strong interpersonal and organizational skills will have valuable application.

PROFESSIONAL EXPERIENCE

THE GIVING TREE, Seattle, WA   1989 to Present
Northwest Regional Manager
- Supervise all operations of 10 stores
- Regional warehouse accountability; supervise all inventories
- Hire/fire, train, supervise and develop managers
- Handle sales planning, administer loss prevention program
- Coordinate extensive marketing and merchandising functions

DEVONSHIRES, Lacey, WA
District Manager   1986 to 1989
- Oversee operations of 10 stores in metropolitan area
- Train district managers, hire/fire, train, supervise and develop managers
- Coordinate sales planning, loss prevention programs, extensive marketing and merchandising functions

District Manager, Portland, OR   1984 to 1986
- Oversee operations of 8 stores in metropolitan area
- Promoted from Manager in under 6 months

Manager, Forest Grove, OR   1983 to 1984

Assistant Manager, Salem, OR   1981 to 1983

TINY TOTS, Beloit, WI   1979 to 1981
Assistant Manager

EDUCATION

Beloit College, Beloit, WI
Bachelor of Arts in Philosophy, 1981
Magna Cum Laude

REFERENCES

Available upon request

- Indicating a promotion, in this case from Manager to District Manager, is excellent on a resume.

- Bolded job titles point to candidate's continuous career advancement.

RETAIL BUYER

CHRIS SMITH
178 Green Street
Baltimore, MD 21227
(301) 555-5555

OBJECTIVE

To contribute acquired skills and education to a challenging retail buying position. Willing to travel/relocate.

CAREER HISTORY

1987-Present **CALVIN CLOTHES COMPANY**, Baltimore & Bethesda MD, Washington D.C.

1991-Present **Buyer - Junior Apparel Departments** (Baltimore)
- Developed sales volume from 5.5 M to 7.5 M, 1991 to 1993. Consistently achieved net operating profit of 5% - highest in company.
- Implemented promotional strategies and developed key classifications which were directly responsible for volume increase.
- Developed a wide range of communication networks which not only supplied product knowledge to sales staff but also affected strategic planning of vendor programs.
- Chosen as Merchant of the Month, October 1992.

1989-1991 **Divisional Sales Manager** (Bethesda)
- Handled furniture, electronics, lamps and basement store. 1989 total volume reached 5.6 M.
- During mall expansion, instrumental in holding store sales volume within plan by achieving 12% increase. Priorities included constant evaluation of stock levels and content, goal setting, development of key personnel and achieving a high motivational level.

1985-1989 **Assistant Buyer** (Washington, D.C.)
- Handled men's coordinates, coats, swimwear/activewear.
- Interpreted, analyzed and responded to all reports, including: OTB, selling reports and seasonal plans.
- Acted as liaison with vendors and warehouse to assure timely merchandise delivery.

1979-1985 **Store Manager** (Washington, D.C.)
- Promoted from trainee to manager within eighteen months.
- Conceptualized and implemented employee training and effectiveness program.

EDUCATION

UNIVERSITY OF DELAWARE, Newark, DE
B.S., Marketing, 1986

- Indicating a willingness to relocate on a resume can be advantageous.

- Job descriptions emphasize candidate's ability to meet and exceed sales goals, an essential attribute in retail.

SALES ADMINISTRATOR

CHRIS SMITH
178 Green Street
Shreveport,LA 70460
(318) 555-5555

OBJECTIVE

A position in Sales Administration where I can contribute proven administrative and marketing skills.

WORK HISTORY

SOUTHERN TRAVEL, Shreveport, LA   1991-Present
Sales Administrator to Regional Vice-President
Assist sales personnel with outside sales and telemarketing to National/Group Associations. Create/proof camera ready ads and color brochures. Act as liaison for sales staff and passengers. Process travel orders and correspondence. Direct incoming invoices, outgoing commission checks, and passenger payments. Maintain records. Availability Coordinator for travel programs. Provide customer service. Utilize Trans-National Reservation System.

BEAUREGARD'S BRIGADE, Baton Rouge, LA   1989-91
Sales Manager
Managed/controlled all facets of $1.1 million annual volume men's clothing business. Hired, trained, and motivated 18 member staff. Achieved 19% increases in sales over 1 year period.

Manager   1987-89
Managed daily operations for national video store including the selection, training, and evaluation of ten sales associates. Successfully introduced profitable line of creative slogan T-shirts. Coordinated all advertising and displays.

ORSON'S PRIDE, New York, NY   1984-87
Manager
Managed Accessories Department of this $2.2 million international women's clothing store.

EDUCATION

FORDHAM UNIVERSITY, College at Lincoln Center
New York, NY
B.A. in Marketing, 1987

- Job objective focuses on the needs of the employer, not the job candidate.

- Reverse chronological format focuses employer's attention on candidate's most current position.

SALES ASSISTANT (Equity)

CHRIS SMITH
178 Green Street
Cortaro, AZ 85652
(602) 555-5555

EDUCATION: UNIVERSITY OF ARIZONA, Tuscon, AZ
B.S. in Business Administration, May 1992
Concentration: Marketing

EMPLOYMENT PROFILE:

SALINGER COMPANY, Tuscon, AZ   January 1993-Present
Equity Division - Research Sales Department
Sales Assistant
- Recorded salesman's trades and commissions
- Corrected various trade problems
- Gathered industry research
- Performed general office duties
- Interacted with clients

TEASDALE COMPANY, Tuscon, AZ   June-December 1992
Finance - Reporting Operations Department
Intern
- Performed general accounting functions
- Generated various accounting reports
- Designed Symphony work-sheet program

BARNEY COMPANY, Tuscon, AZ   January-May 1992
Mutual Funds Administration Department
Intern
- Generated daily reports for proprietary mutual funds
- Updated files on nonproprietary mutual funds
- Pursued stockbrokers who failed to take appropriate action on letters of intent
- Compiled directory of nonproprietary mutual fund firms
- Corresponded with clients

CAMP ARAPAHO, St. George, UT   Summers 1990, 1991
Counselor
- Supervised fifteen girls, ages nine and ten
- Planned and organized group activities

SPECIAL SKILLS: Use of IBM PC and Wang Word Processing. Familiarity with Lotus 1-2-3 and Symphony software packages. Educated in BASIC computer language

INTERESTS: Travel, Tennis, Swimming, Drawing

REFERENCES: Available upon request

■ Candidate's educational degree corresponds to his/her area of interest.

■ Internships strengthen candidate's short work history.

SALES ASSISTANT (General)

Chris Smith
178 Green Street
Fort Worth, TX 76112
(817) 555-5555

EXPERIENCE:

1990- REGENCY CORPORATION, Dallas, TX
Present **Sales Assistant:** Act as liaison between customer and sales representative. Provide customer service via telephone. Ascertain order accuracy. Track and expedite orders. Cooperate in team endeavors.

1987-1990 THE MUSIC MAKER, Inc., Houston, TX
Sales Assistant: Coordinated sales efforts of a staff of six for a large musical instruments dealership. Developed and maintained working relationships with manufacturers and customers. Supported top account executives. Maintained open files to ensure greatest customer satisfaction.

1985-1987 CITY OF DALLAS, TREASURERS DEPARTMENT, Dallas, TX
Research Assistant: Assisted in the collection of delinquent real estate, personal property and motor vehicle excise taxes. Matched instrument of taking against daily tax title receipts. Processed petitions of foreclosure for the legal section and title searches.

1984-1985 TRAFFIC AND PARKING DEPARTMENT, Dallas, TX
Senior Claims Investigator: Investigated and expedited claim settlements relating to ticket disputes and information request.

1983-1984 SHERMAN BANK FOR SAVINGS, Sherman, TX
Bank Teller: Interacted with customers, processed all money and check transactions, balanced all transactions at the end of each shift. Operated a Wang Word Processor, CRT and TRW terminal, and developed a working knowledge of money market funds and IRA accounts.

EDUCATION:

Austin College, Sherman, TX
A.S. Business Management, 1983

Texas Institute of Banking
Completed courses in Bank Organization and Business English, 1981

- Education is listed towards bottom of resume because candidate's practical experience outweighs his/her degree.

- Reverse chronological format focuses employer's attention on candidate's most current position.

SALES ASSISTANT (Investment)

Chris Smith
178 Green Street
Nashua, NH 03060
(603) 555-5555

EXPERIENCE

1993-Present   DIXON WALSTON RESEARCH, Nashua, NH
Sales Assistant: Support brokers and clients. Handle research, word processing and incoming calls. Input portfolios into Multimate C System.

1991-1993   CHAUNCY CO., INC., Derry, NH
Personnel Department Assistant: Verified employment, assisted employees to solve everyday problems, setting up personnel files, typing, phones, data entry, issuing check cashing cards to employees and registered representatives.

1989-1991   RUMNEY HEALTH, INC., Westmoreland, NH
Counselor/Office Clerk: Verified eligibility of members, entered data on intake forms, setting up appointments, heavy telephone work, various office forms, release of medical claims.

1988-1989   STEVE ANGELINO FITNET, Manchester, NH
Receptionist: Monitored switchboard, opened medical charts for patients, entered data in computer and updated information as necessary, met and greeted members.

1986-1988   CRYSTAL LAKE LAW, Crystal Lake, NH
Receptionist/Office Assistant: Heavy phones, typed various legal documents, filed office forms, translated legal documents from German into English.

EDUCATION

1989   **Bertha Tibbs Secretarial School,** Plymouth, NH
Options Program

1984   **The Austrian Institute,** Vienna, Austria
Degree in translation
German/English English/German

SKILLS

Typing (60 wpm), Shorthand (60-70 wpm), WANG Word Processing, knowledge of other word processing systems. Fluency in German, good verbal and written communications skills.

REFERENCES

Furnished upon request.

■ Resume emphasizes candidate's strong work history.

■ Candidate's special skills are highlighted in a separate section.

SALES EXECUTIVE

CHRIS SMITH
178 Green Street
Las Cruces, NM 88003
(505) 555-5555

Objective: A senior position in Sales/Marketing Management.

Qualifications:

Extensive experience in the high performance computing industry with a proven ability to increase sales. Able to obtain excellent sales results through direct calls on users and management of third-party distribution channels.

Employment:

Seldane Research, Santa Fe, NM   11/93 to Present

Vice-President of Sales and Marketing - Monitor end-user software and service sales, management of international distributors, OEM distribution, product planning and promotion.

Develop marketing and sales strategies designed to promote product awareness within the parallel computing community. Develop effective sales collateral and presentation materials. Aggressive new account development resulted in a 60% increase in installed accounts and a tripling of the identified qualified prospects.

Sell products to Government research laboratories, academic institutions and commercial scientific centers through direct sales, international distributors and OEM manufacturers. Strengthened Seldane's presence in Europe by identifying and negotiating agreements with distributors in France and The Netherlands and in the last year have negotiated distribution agreements with five OEM manufacturers in the parallel processing field. Personally responsible for generating individual sales leads, product presentations and contract negotiations. Year-to-date sales have increased 85% over the same period in 1993.

Nedline Research, Truth or Consequences, NM   1/87 to 11/93

National Program Manager, Government Marketing   6/90 to 11/93
Led marketing effort in developing and selling a new product for the real-time processing market. Developed product requirements and a comprehensive business plan resulting in approximately $3 million being allocated for the project. Responsible for overall market strategy, prospect identification and qualification with primary emphasis on US Government accounts.

Region Sales Analyst   1/87 to 6/90
Provided technical sales support to Nedline Research account managers including technical presentations and proposal preparation. Acted as lead analyst on three successful efforts within this period resulting in approximately $35 million in sales.

Education:

B.A. Math/Computer Science, University of Charleston, WV (1986)

■ Most recent position is described in great detail, including candidate's specific contributions.

■ Specific dates of employment (month and year) are ideal for candidates with no gaps in work history.

SALES MANAGER (Engineering)

CHRIS SMITH
178 Green Street
Providence, RI 02912
(401) 555-5555 (Days)
(401) 444-4444 (Evenings)

CAREER SUMMARY

Sales professional who, for seven years, has solved problems and met customer needs to consistently generate top sales. Acknowledged for pursuit of personal and professional growth through study and application of proven ability to create Win-Win opportunities for all parties involved.

RELEVANT EXPERIENCE

1990-Present **EAGLE TECH, INC.** Providence, RI

Sales Manager
- Marketed and sold engineering solutions and graphic equipment including workstations, terminals, printers, software, and other related peripherals.
- Generated a $350,000 order for color printers from Dublin Aircraft which was a result of business relationships cultivated with key corporate contacts.
- Convinced a major account on value of new terminal even though the required driver was not yet available. Persuaded the account to pressure their software vendor to write the driver for the terminal. Result: Closed a $400,000 sale of 40 terminals.
- Trained and supervised a new service technician to provide sales support. He was subsequently promoted for outstanding performance.
- Recognized as top sales performer in Eastern half of the United States and inducted into "Leaders." Achieved $4.1 million in sales and exceeded quota of $3.6 million.
- Orchestrated sales efforts with the U.S. Navy and a government contractor to implement a war gaming system. Commitment to service with rapid follow-up resulted in sales of $600,000. Anticipate additional sales of at least $1.4 million.

1988-1990 **LEONARD FINN CORPORATION** Newport, RI

Territory Manager
- Managed a remote territory while supervising sales and equipment installation in a wide range of companies throughout nine counties.
- Sold conversion from Macintosh system to The National Bank of Rhode Island, producing a sale of $75,000.

1987-1988 **PEARSON PROBLEM SOLVERS, INC.** Bristol, RI

Direct Marketer/Manager
- Created and implemented sales plan to promote inventory control system for retailers.

EDUCATION **COLBY COLLEGE,** Waterville, ME
B.S., Marketing, 1986

■ Career summary accentuates candidate's acquired professional skills and impressive track record.

■ Unrelated work experience is omitted.

SALES MANAGER (Industrial)

CHRIS SMITH
178 Green Street
Alexander, AR 72002
(501) 555-5555

PROFESSIONAL OBJECTIVE
A career continuation in Senior Level Industrial **Sales Management.**

QUALIFICATIONS/MAJOR ACCOMPLISHMENTS
- Awarded Outstanding Performance Award, a presidential award given to a select number of senior managers, chosen by company CEO.
- Developed solid team of 10 salesmen to accomplish goals; very low turnover rate.
- Expanded our Midwest territory from $15 million to $25 million gross sales in 5 years.
- In 1987, single-handedly developed and implemented a company distribution center in Springdale, AR, from finding location to hiring staff.

PROFESSIONAL EXPERIENCE
THE TORTEN GROUP, Little Rock, AR
Sales Manager   1991-Present
- Manage staff of 10 with volume of over $25 million.
- Negotiate large contracts; represent company; corporate field contact for service and maintenance.
- Set forecasts; coach sales staff and critique their abilities.
- Oversee and write all performance evaluations, salary reviews and expense accounts.

District Manager of Arkansas - Genevia, AR   1985-1990
- Managed and product-trained 5 salesmen, 3 application engineers, and 5 independent distributors in Midwest, resulting in new unit and after-market volume of over $10 million.

Branch Manger - Sherwood, AR   1981-1984
- Managed Arkansas office including independent distributors with total sales equaling $3 million.

Salesman - Cammack Village, AR   1977-1980

Application Engineer - Sweet Home, AR   1973-1976

EDUCATION/RELEVANT TRAINING
HARDING UNIVERSITY, Searcy, AR, **B.S. Mechanical Engineering,** 1970.

SOUTHERN ARKANSAS UNIVERSITY, Magnolia, AR, **Diploma, Financial and Entrepreneurial Studies,** 1973.

■ Candidate's qualifications/major accomplishments are highlighted.

■ Candidate's highest educational achievement is shown before other, less significant degrees.

SALES REPRESENTATIVE (Computers)

CHRIS SMITH
178 Green Street
Salt Lake City, UT 84102
(801) 555-5555

OBJECTIVE

To contribute exceptional sales ability, account management, and communications skills to a challenging Sales Representative position.

SUMMARY OF QUALIFICATIONS

- Thorough knowledge in the provision of sales services, account acquisition, and management; consistent enhancement of product and industry knowledge, reactivation of dormant accounts, and the development of successful sales techniques.
- Consistently meet and exceed sales quotas.
- Accumulated over six years experience within a major hardware/software company.

EXPERIENCE

2/92 to Present   **Sales Representative**
GRASSVILLE SYSTEMS   Salt Lake City, UT

- Sell computer hardware and peripherals to corporate accounts and dealer channels.
- Acquisition new accounts; maintain and reactivate existing accounts. Coordinate cold calling; process orders and sell service accounts.
- Devise solutions for customer microcomputer needs and after-sales support.
- Sell Panasonic, Hewlett Packard, IBM, and compatible desktops and laptops.

7/89 to 1/92   **National Sales Representative**
NIMBUS COMPUTERS   Provo, UT

- Acquisitioned new accounts, maintained and reactivated existing accounts.
- Instituted solutions for customer micro computer needs and after-sale support.
- Sold IBM, MacIntosh, Hewlett Packard, Compaq, and compatible desktop and laptop systems.

12/86 to 6/89   **Sales Associate**
SUEDE BOGGS COMPANY   Salt Lake City, UT

- Facilitated promotional activities, dealt with customers.

EDUCATION

NEW HAMPSHIRE COLLEGE, Manchester, NH
Bachelor of Arts: Communications, May 1987.

COMPUTERS

IBM, Compaq, Hewlett Packard, MacIntosh

- Summary of qualifications illustrates candidate's key credentials.

- Boldface type emphasizes key information, such as job titles and dates of employment.

SALES REPRESENTATIVE (Pharmaceuticals)

CHRIS SMITH
178 Green Street
Millington, TN 38053
(901) 555-5555

OBJECTIVE

A challenging position requiring strong sales, managerial and organizational skills with a firm where advancement and compensation are based on personal performance.

CAPABILITIES

Territory/Account Management
Sales/Merchandising
Promotional/Incentive Programs
New/Existing Account Development

EXPERIENCE

SALES REPRESENTATIVE   **September 1990-present**
Appleby Industries, Millington, TN

- Responsible for distribution, dollar volume and promotions of pharmaceutical products.
- Sell to major drug store chains, major wholesalers, deep discount stores, and mass merchandisers throughout Tennessee, including 2 national accounts.
- Prepare and present business reviews for key accounts.
- Develop and manage new and existing accounts.
- Analyze and propose alternatives to customers.
- Set up sales and new distribution contests for major wholesalers.
- Created a customer selling booklet for wholesalers' sales representatives to improve efficiency and sales.
- Won <u>Sales Representative of the Year Award</u>, 1993.

SALES REPRESENTATIVE   **June 1986-August 1990**
Clayton and Wallace, Inc., Bartlett, TN

- Promoted five divisions of Health and Beauty Aids and over-the-counter products, in drug, food and mass merchandiser accounts by selling display, shelf improvements and distribution programs. Involved implementation of creative ideas, brand initiative and headquarter activity.
- Became Account Coordinator for three major drug store chains.

EDUCATION

Memphis State University, Memphis, TN
Bachelor of Science, Health Care Administration, 1986
Courses: Business Management and Sales, Business Writing

References available upon request.

- Job descriptions are action-oriented.

- Courses listed under education are related to candidate's field of interest.

SALES REPRESENTATIVE (Technical)

CHRIS SMITH
178 Green Street
Savannah, GA 31404
(912) 555-5555

OBJECTIVE

The opportunity to join a rapid-growth organization that has the need for a technical sales executive with an established track record in handling state of the art electronic equipment.

EXPERIENCE

REGIONAL MANAGER   **1991-Present**
Dunsinane Corp., Savannah, GA
- Distribution management for Southern region of factory authorized dealers. Distribution maximization, appointment and quota assignment.
- Manage distributor sales hour and program commitment. Interview sales candidates.
- Consultant to professional engineers and architects. Formulated school and health care project specification and systems design, conduct product line presentations for consulting firms.
- Employed distributor computer project specifications and quoting system. Visit problem installations, trouble-shoot, and report failures.

SALES ENGINEER   **1988-91**
Patridge and Killarney, Atlanta, GA
- Monitored the marketing and sale of Dunsinane microprocessor communication systems.
- Researched, evaluated and selected subcontractors and negotiated contracts for the installation of systems. Handled customer relations and provided technical support during and post installation.
- Achieved 120% of quota.

LEAD SENIOR ELECTRONIC TECHNICIAN   **1985-88**
Hepburn Communications, Americus, GA
- Trained junior technicians on custom built test fixtures as well as company procedures and products; set up and repaired test fixtures. Tested, debugged and repaired hospital communications modules utilizing analog, digital and microprocessor-based electronics.

ELECTRONIC TECHNICIAN   **1983-85**
Patterson Research, Statesboro, GA
- Worked with production control, production, and service departments on the test and repair of equalizers and noise reduction units for consumer high-fidelity applications. Used oscilloscopes, spectrum analyzers, distortion analyzers, signal generators and custom designed test equipment.

EDUCATION

Savannah State College, Savannah, GA
B.A. Electronics Technology 1983

Kennesaw College, Marietta, GA
A.A. Business Management/Marketing 1980-81
- Worked part-time installing and repairing audio/video equipment.

- Resume emphasizes candidate's most recent position while only briefly touching on previous jobs.

- Candidate's work experience reads like a series of accomplishments, not just a list of job duties.

SALESPERSON

Chris Smith
178 Green Street
Lancaster, PA 17064
(717) 555-5555

OBJECTIVE:
An challenging position in sales.

EDUCATION:
LESLEY COLLEGE, Cambridge, MA
B.A., Politics and History, 1994
Minor: English

SALES EXPERIENCE:
PETIE'S PET LAND, Pittsburgh, PA   1992-1994
Salesperson
Sold merchandise. Developed ongoing customer relationships, enhancing future sales. Developed special seasonal sales. Handles cash transactions and kennel care.

THE TIRE BARON, INC., Beaver Falls, PA   Summer 1992
Upper Bay/Lower Bay Technician
Sold merchandise. Provided customers with technical advice. Trained new employees.

THE SUBVERSIVE PAGES BOOKSTORE, Erie, PA   Summer 1991
Salesperson
Sold merchandise. Provided customer service. Purchased materials and monitored books.

UNRELATED EXPERIENCE:
UNITED PACKAGERS, Boston, MA   Summer 1993
Material Handler

LESLEY COLLEGE, Cambridge, MA   Summer 1992
Maintenance Technician, Buildings and Grounds

ACCOMPLISHMENTS:
Fluent in French
Student Government Representative, 1992-93
Founder, Debate Team, 1993

■ Relevant work experience is emphasized while other positions are de-emphasized.

■ Candidate's most impressive accomplishments are highlighted in a separate section.

SENIOR ACCOUNT MANAGER

CHRIS SMITH
178 Green Street
Orem, UT 84057
(891) 555-5555

OBJECTIVE

Seek a position as a **Senior Account Manager** for a well-established, progressive organization or agency.

EXPERIENCE

Borton, Marsel, Pierbo, and Kane, Orem, UT   1991-Present
Senior Account Manager
Provide strategic planning and day-to-day management of northeast regional financial account and several non-profit accounts for leading advertising agency. Specific duties include supervision of junior staff, daily interface with clients; preparation of quarterly forecasts, budgets and management reports, research and analysis of marketing data, and coordination with creative teams. Accounts and special projects include:

- *Shay Bank* (New York State, Montana, Nevada, and Utah markets).
  Managed bank-wide advertising and promotions for consumer products and developed and implemented strategies for local promotions that maintained the integrity of the corporate position.
- *United Way of Utah* (Fundraising Campaign).
  Developed and implemented advertising positioning and strategy for the '92 campaign.
- *Beth's Place* (Advocacy and Counseling Center for Battered Women).

Monster Donut, Salt Lake City, UT   1989-1991
Project Consultant for Marketing
Provided strategic planning and implementation of the creative concept for the 1990 Monster Donut Calendar. As an annual promotional tool distributed among 1,800 franchises, it served to highlight unusual and humorous events incorporating the Monster Donut product. Creative and administrative responsibilities included:

- Selected calendar photos based on ability to incorporate product, visual appeal, strangeness and/or humor.
- Coordinated with events' organizers and local franchises to increase product recognition and promote positive company image.
- Developed publicity opportunities for Monster Donuts with local and regional press.

Danlon, Inc., Salt Lake City, UT   1987-1989
Marketing Supervisor

- Coordinated the development of market research and divisional business plan for manufacturer of popular men's and women's bathing suits.
- Supervised advertising agency and graphic design firm.

EDUCATION

College of The Holy Cross, Worcester, MA
B.A. Art History, 1987

■ Reverse chronological format focuses employer's attention on candidate's most current position.

■ Citing specific accounts and special projects adds weight to resume.

TELE-INTERVIEWER

CHRIS SMITH
178 Green Street
Jonestown, MS 38639
(601) 555-5555

OBJECTIVE

A diversified position where there is a need for an organized, communicative individual skilled in interacting with, selling to and/or training company/customer personnel.

SUMMARY OF QUALIFICATIONS

- Over five years of experience in telemarketing, tele-interviewing and customer service for projects involving industrial, commercial and consumer products, communications, and license regulatory issues.
- Well organized, good time manager and persistent in achieving or exceeding set objectives.
- Excellent communication skills and the ability to interact with people in sales, training, fundraising and other programs for profit and/or non-profit corporations.

EXPERIENCE

TELE-INTERVIEWER
The Telemasters, Inc., Yazoo City, MS   **1989-present**

- For this data collection/research company, call companies throughout the United States, establish correct contact, update records, and conduct telephone interviews for a variety of surveys dependent upon client needs.
- Train new tele-interviewers on effective interviewing techniques for completion of questionnaires.
- Responsible for calling prospective customers to explain type of service or merchandise offered.
- Utilize telemarketing techniques to persuade customers to purchase or follow-up on products or services available.
- Record names, addresses, purchases and/or reactions of prospects solicited; used city and telephone directories to develop lists of prospects.
- All positions require ability to interact with people in a wide variety of work or community environments to obtain accurate data upon which research and/or sales projections are based.

EDUCATION

University of Southern Mississippi, Hattiesburg, MS
Bachelor of Science in Elementary Education (With Honors), 1989
Cumulative average: 3.5/4.0

References available upon request.

- Summary of qualifications accentuates candidate's acquired telemarketing/communication skills and hardworking nature.

- Only most current and relevant position is listed.

TELEMARKETER

Chris Smith
178 Green Street
Saint Petersburg, FL 33713
(813) 555-5555

OBJECTIVE

A position in inside sales preferably in the telecommunications industry.

QUALIFICATIONS

- Outstanding selling and closing capabilities with proven track record.
- Excellent listener; patient and sensitive to clients' needs.
- Calm under pressure; meet deadlines; meet all sales quotas.
- Proven problem-solving skills.

EXPERIENCE

1992- ESP Telecommunications, Saint Petersburg, FL
Present **Telemarketing Professional**
Cold called residential consumers, discovered their domestic/international calling needs, recommended programs. Consistently achieved at least 125% of sales goals.

1991-1992 Kaybee Education Group, Miami, FL
Marketing Assistant
Cold called high school and college students selling diagnostic college and graduate school entrance exams.

1990-1991 Bill Wonka Quality Car Wash, Cambridge, MA
Bookkeeper
Performed bank reconciliations, trial balances, and general ledger.

AWARDS AND ACCOMPLISHMENTS

- Inducted into national club of Top Ten Percent, 1993.
- Awarded Golden Ring Award for meeting sales goals throughout 1991.

EDUCATION

Quincy College, Quincy, MA
B.S., Finance, 1991

COMPUTERS

Lotus 1-2-3, Windows, Pascal, Microsoft Word, Pagemaker

- Candidate's qualifications are listed prominently.

- Impressive awards and accomplishments point to candidate's ability to consistently meet sales goals.

TELEMARKETING DIRECTOR

CHRIS SMITH
178 Green Street
Mentele, PA 15761
(412) 555-5555

PROFESSIONAL OBJECTIVE:
Seeking a challenging management level position in Marketing/Telemarketing.

CAREER HISTORY:
1989-Present   DURITZ, INC., Mentele, PA
Director of Telemarketing
Solely responsible for 6 cold call sales generation centers, with a staff of 60 persons. 1989 estimated cold call generated revenues: $2.8 million. Manage media department to coordinate overall sales efforts.
- Recruit, interview, hire and train management staff; develop performance incentives; review staff production periodically through meetings with office managers.
- Expanded the Telemarketing division from one office with staff of 8 to present size and scope within 3 years.
- Develop all telemarketing scripts and assist in development of all print and radio marketing; monitor reply performance and develop improvements based on industry trends.
- Initiated and established a Quality Control department to verify sales appointments; reduced the number of unproductive sales calls.
- Organized and established division responsible for $2.5 million in sales annually.
- Coordinate telemarketing efforts with the Media Manager, Director of Sales and company president; provide input on all company marketing strategies.
- Designed new tally sheets for centralized reporting system.
- Improved performance of Telemarketing division for $60,000 net in 1988 to present $2.8 million; reduced average Cost-of Lead from 55% to 40%.

1985-1989   LYNWOOD MARKETING, INC., Glenn Willard, PA
Sales Manager
- Oversaw and directed 40 sales staff and 8 clerical assistants.
- Developed sales promotions and staff incentives; conducted all shift meetings.
- Wrote classified advertising and recorded ad response.
- Controlled sponsor relations, lead control, payroll preparation

EDUCATION: ALLEGHENY COLLEGE, Allegheny, PA
Bachelor of Science in Marketing, 1985

REFERENCES: Available Upon Request.

■ Specifically citing number of employees supervised draws attention to candidate's leadership abilities.

■ Percentages and dollar amounts quantify candidate's accomplishments.

TRAVEL AGENT (A)

CHRIS SMITH
178 Green Street
Joliet, IL 60435
(815) 555-5555

OBJECTIVE

A challenging career continuation where computer and travel experience will be utilized and advanced.

SUMMARY OF QUALIFICATIONS

- More than seven years of progressive, professional Computer Operator / Travel consultant experience; proven verbal sales skills.
- Detail-oriented, self-motivated; able to set effective priorities and implement decisions to achieve immediate and long term goals and meet operational deadlines.
- Developed interpersonal skills, having dealt with a diversity of professionals, clients, and staff members.
- Comfortable in fast-paced, high-pressure atmosphere.

PROFESSIONAL EXPERIENCE

SURGE AND SIEGE TRAVEL, INC., Joliet, IL   1989 to present
Air Coordinator
Coordinator air/ticketing requests and tour departures utilizing Apollo and Sabre computer systems. Resolve client problems and special requests. Verify international and domestic fares; input pricing data. Issue tickets and final itineraries. Maintain/file all pertinent materials. Assist with special projects; prepare reports.

GOTTA FLY TOURS, Wheaton, IL   1987-1989
Computer Operator/Supervisor
Responsible for all Sabre Computer operations. Administered ARC ticket stock and accountable documents. Managed office accounting. Supervised personnel. Group leader for Caribbean familiarization trips. Actuated/implemented system which eliminated Sabre computer costs.

QUICK TRIP TRAVEL, Evanston, IL   1986-1987
Travel Consultant
Arranged individual and group travel. Generated invoices.

EDUCATION

MIDWEST TRAVEL SCHOOL, Chicago, IL
Graduated third in class, 1986.

DEPAUL UNIVERSITY, Chicago, IL
Bachelor of Arts, History, 1985.

WINDY CITY COMMUNITY COLLEGE, Chicago, IL
Associate of Arts, Geography, 1983.

■ Including a telephone number is essential on a resume.

■ For upward-bound professionals with a strong track record, the chrono-functional resume is the strongest tool available.

TRAVEL AGENT (B)

CHRIS SMITH
178 Green Street
Plymouth, MA
(505) 555-5555

OBJECTIVE A challenging position within the Travel Industry.

SUMMARY OF QUALIFICATIONS
- Ten years of experience acquired during employment and educational training within the travel industry.
- Thorough knowledge of various reservation transactions, including: booking, bursting, ticketing, interfacing with contracted vendors to ensure realization of customer reservation specifications, sales and customer service.
- Competent familiarity with Sabre computer system.
- Proficient in the provision of general office duties.

EXPERIENCE
1990 to Present   **Support Agent**
AS THE CROW FLIES TRAVEL   Plymouth, MA
- Burst tickets and ensure correct formatting of ticket transaction data.
- Book hotel reservations and direct customer package specifications.
- Process ticket transactions via the Sabre computer system.
- Provide sales services and develop sales strategies.
- Respond to customer inquiries for general and package information.

1987 to 1990   **Sales Representative/Accountant**
BUZZWORD TRAVEL   Hyannis, MA
- Extensive accounting tasks in basic bookkeeping.
- Monitored the selling of corporate and leisure accounts.
- Researched and processed credit checks.
- Verified international and domestic fares.

1985 to 1987   **Tour Guide**
SILVER SENTINEL TRAVEL   Provincetown, MA
- Organized tour schedules for international students. Booked local cruises.
- Acted as assistant to company accountant. Performed general bookkeeping duties.

EDUCATION TRAVEL SCHOOL OF NEW ENGLAND, Springfield, MA, 1985

QUINCY COLLEGE, Quincy, MA, 1984
Completed travel and marketing courses, 1985

- Summary of qualifications clearly spells out candidate's area of expertise.

- Only relevant educational training is included.

VICE-PRESIDENT OF MARKETING

CHRIS SMITH
178 Green Street
Conyers, GA 30208
(404) 555-5555

EXPERIENCE:

Shockley Associates, Inc., Conyers, GA
Publisher of *Anarchists in Love Comedy Magazine*
Vice-President of Marketing   1991-Present
Manage all corporate day-to-day operations, including production, distribution, sales, marketing and administration.
- Increased annual sales by 10% while achieving net profit margins in excess of 35%.
- Strengthened company management structure by recruiting key personnel for production, distribution and accounting operations.
- Saved $70,000 annually and improved production schedule by switching printers.
- Reduced accounts receivables to average of 13 days.
- Improved effectiveness of distribution operation through daily contact with distributors and stores.
- Capped growth in production staff through aggressive work flow management.

Barton, Quivers, and Spunk, Athens, GA
Testing and Consulting Firm
Vice-President   1987-1991
Responsible for the strategic, sales, and business management of the company's publications operations.
- Doubled annual division sales to $2 million in 1987; increased sales by 400% in 5 years.
- Created $400,000+ in annual ad placements for parent company at no cost.
- Increased total advertising pages 30% over 2 years, versus 30-40% decreases for competitive publications.
- Built technical seminar business from scratch to $275,000 in annual revenues; developed seminars on EC 1991 and ISO-9000.

Edgewild Laboratories
Pharmaceutical Manufacturer
Marketing Representative   1985-1987
Sold proprietary pharmaceuticals and OTC medications in hospital and pharmacies.
- Doubled annual sales in 2 years, from $200,000 to $400,000.
- Achieved 110% of budget in 1st year.

EDUCATION:

New York University, New York, NY
M.S., Marketing, 1985

PERSONAL:

Willing to relocate

■ Bulleted statements highlight candidate's on-the-job achievements.

■ Facts and figures emphasize candidate's ability to increase profits and work within budget constraints.

VICE-PRESIDENT OF SALES (Furniture)

CHRIS SMITH
178 Green Street
Hartford, CT 06106
(203) 555-5555

PROFESSIONAL EXPERIENCE
WILLIAMS COMPANY

VICE-PRESIDENT OF SALES
HARTFORD, CONNECTICUT   1987-Present

Drive sales /marketing and all aspects of operations for a furniture dealership generating $50,000,000 in annual revenues. Formulate corporate policy, engage in long and short range business planning; devise and implement effective marketing strategies and sales campaigns. Responsible for branch profits and loss performances while maintaining $7,000,000 in yearly sales activity focused on the corporate market and the design community. Manage human resource issues, budget controls, purchasing, and sales/marketing.

- Increased sales from billings of $2,500,000 in 1987 to $4,000,000. Initiated the practice of visiting all customers in the interest of fostering and maintaining excellent client relations.
- Single most profitable division in the Williams organization in numerous years with a record for steady volume growth.
- Select, train, and motivate a staff of 15 branch personnel in all assigned duties.
- Develop and conduct in-depth sales trainings encompassing policy and protocols, product knowledge, sales and customer service techniques.
- Cultivate and maintain profitable relationships with 100+ furniture manufacturers,
- Effectively apply detailed knowledge of the relationships of manufacturing and distribution.

ACCOUNT MANAGER
HACKENSACK, NEW JERSEY   1980-87

Developed new and existing business within corporate and small business accounts. Directed a staff of junior sales representatives and support personnel in marketing furniture products. Provided personal consultation to clients and prospects.

EDUCATION
University of Pennsylvania, Philadelphia, PA
B.A. Management

COMPUTERS
DOS, Microsoft Word, IBM Compatible, Lotus 1-2-3

- Resume emphasizes achievements; doesn't simply list job responsibilities.

- Resume format is neat and professional.

VICE-PRESIDENT OF SALES (Pharmaceuticals)

CHRIS SMITH
178 Green Street
Pueblo, CO 81007
(719) 555-5555

SUMMARY

- **Vice-President, Sales,** with more than 30 years of successful experience encompassing Direct Sales and Sales Support, Project Management and Engineering, Research and Development, Engineering, and General Sales and Financial Administration.
- **Knowledge includes** customer buying policies and direct liaison with manufacturers, scientists and engineers in diverse specializations in the sales of products.
- **Highly organized,** good knowledge of contemporary electronics products and applications. Documented record of sales production in the millions of dollars in assigned territories.

PROFESSIONAL EXPERIENCE

1979-Present   **Pharmatech, Inc.**
Vice-President, Sales   **Pueblo, CO**

Began as Sales Engineer and assumed administrative and marketing responsibilities. Advanced on the basis of performance to the position of Vice-President, with responsibilities encompassing:

- Marketing and sale of pharmaceutical products. Handled related duties of sales administration and financial consulting.
- On-site presentations, telemarketing and promotion of product lines, including utilization of technical knowledge for analysis of customer needs, potential applications, definition of specifications and performance. Client base of hundreds of large and small companies.
- Responsibilities also included recommendation of new products/applications, marketing and sales aids, competitive pricing, detailed sales forecasts, attendance at trade shows, staff development, customer training and relations, and associated troubleshooting and problem solving.

1974-1978   **Paratronics, Inc.**
Systems & Liaison Engineer   **Canon City, CO**

- Started as Engineering Administrative Assistant, Research and Development — advanced to Project Manager, Manufacturing Division.
- Positions held included Senior Bid Specialist, Systems and Liaison Engineer, and Engineering Administrator, Research and Development. Responsibilities included Program Management, technical and cost proposals, field surveys, and liaison between customers, company and outside vendors.

EDUCATION

Adams State College   Alamosa, CO
Bachelor of Science Degree in Marketing, 1970

■ Summary grabs the reader's attention with powerful skills and qualifications.

■ Impressive promotions are indicated under "Professional Experience."

WHOLESALE BUYER

CHRIS SMITH
178 Green Street
Salt Rock, WV 25959
(304) 555-5555

SUMMARY OF QUALIFICATIONS:

- Ten years of experience, advancing from Follow-up Coordinator to Senior Buyer.
- Proven communication and organizational skills interacting effectively with suppliers, as well as engineering and production control personnel in support of engineering functions within Genova Industrial Corp.
- Extensive computer capability on many varieties of software and systems.
- Effectively negotiate procurements for major commercial and industrial firms, resulting in significant cost savings and in support of overall minority objectives.

PROFESSIONAL EXPERIENCE:

GENOVA INDUSTRIAL CORP   Huntington, WV
Senior Buyer - 1992-Present
Manage quotations, negotiations, proposals, documentation and order placement for various components for both commercial and industrial applications.

- Actively participate in multimillion dollar negotiations for company purchase agreements to set price, terms, and conditions.
- Write detailed basis of awards for price and source selections.
- Actively pursue new minority and small disadvantaged businesses.
- Comply with all government regulations.
- Assist in negotiations with suppliers for initializing supplier ship to stock programs.

Buyer - 1988-1991
Procured electrical and mechanical components to both government specifications and commercial levels.

- Purchased components via supplier stocking computer system with various distributors.
- Established computer tracking systems utilized by other personnel via Symphony for management reports.

Follow-Up Coordinator - 1984-1987
Expedited deliveries on critical items for both Research and Development

- Attended management critical status reviews in manufacturing facility.
- Established a system for solving invoice and packing slip problems.
- Created new system for easier expediting.

EDUCATION:
Shepherd College, Shepherdstown, WV
Bachelor of Arts in Philosophy, 1984

COMPUTER EXPERIENCE:
Systems: Lexitron, PTS 100, IBM Personal Computer
Software: WordStar, Accounting Plus, Symphony, Lotus 1-2-3, WordPerfect, DOS, Microsoft Word

---

- Impressive professional experience precedes education.

- Use of boldface and underlining provides a clean and crisp presentation.

17
Science

Nature of Work

The work done by scientists plays an important role in the quality of human life. Some scientists conduct basic research to increase knowledge of of the world we live in. Others use this knowledge and research to develop new medicines, increase crop yields, and improve the environment. Agricultural scientists study farm crops and animals and develop ways of improving their quantity and quality. Biologists study living organisms and their relationship to their environment, usually specializing in some area of biology such as ornithology (the study of birds) or microbiology (the study of microscopic organisms). Chemists search for and put to practical use new knowledge about chemicals, while geologists and geophysicists study the physical aspects and history of the Earth. Meteorologists study the atmosphere's physical characteristics, motions, and processes.

Employment

About one third of salaried scientists work for the Federal Government, in places such as the Departments of Agriculture, Interior, and Defense, and in the National Institute of Health. The rest work in state and local governments at colleges or research stations. Some work for commercial research and development laboratories, seed companies, pharmaceutical companies, wholesale distributors, and food products companies.

Training

Training for scientists depends upon the specialty and the type of work performed. A bachelor's degree in the particular science is sufficient for some jobs in assisting basic research, while a master's or doctoral degree is required for most other positions. A Ph.D. is usually needed for college teaching and for advancement to administrative research positions.

Job Outlook

Job opportunities in the science fields are expected to be good through the year 2005 because enrollments in science curriculums have dropped considerably over the past few years and because employment is expected to grow faster than average for all occupations. Efforts to clean up and preserve the environment will continue to add to this growth, as more scientists will be needed to determine the environmental impact of industry and government actions. Chemists will be in demand due to the expanded research and development in pharmaceutical and biotechnology firms.

Earnings

Median annual earnings for biological and life scientists were about $31,300 in 1990; the middle 50% earned between $20,700 and $42,500. Ph.D.s usually make higher wages, averaging $55,000 to $70,000 per year. Education is definitely the key to a high salary in science professions.

AGRICULTURAL SCIENTIST

CHRIS SMITH
178 Green Street
Cambridge, MA 02139
(617) 555-5555

SUMMARY:
- Fluent in Spanish language, written and spoken.
- Extensive background in Agriculture, specializing in plants/animals.
- Proven abilities as team member.
- Developed communication skills, both oral and written.

EXPERIENCE:

1991-1994 PEACE CORPS, Ghana, West Africa
Livestock Extension Agent
- Organized groups.
- Conducted classroom-style lectures.
- Promoted improved animal health practices.
- Coordinated vaccination schedules.
- Solicited funds.
- Began and supervised continuation of small businesses.

1989-1991 UNIVERSITY OF MASSACHUSETTS CATTLE UNIT, Amherst, MA
Student Assistant Herdswoman
- Assisted animals with difficult deliveries.
- Diagnosed/treated common illnesses.
- Controlled inventory and supply orders.
- Assisted in record keeping.
- Operated several types of farm equipment.
- Trained new employees in animal care and feeding.

1989-1990 UNIVERSITY OF MASSACHUSETTS MEAT SCIENCE LAB, Amherst, MA
Student Assistant
- Operated equipment commonly used in meat processing industry.
- Implemented sanitation procedures as per USDA regulations.
- Trained personnel in clean-up procedures.
- Answered customer questions; took meat orders.

EDUCATION:
UNIVERSITY OF MASSACHUSETTS, Amherst, MA
B.S., International Agriculture, 1991
Concentration: Agricultural Development, emphasizing both Animal and Plant Sciences

AWARDS:
- Woman of Distinction, 1988, University of Massachusetts
- Rookie of the Year, Cymbidium Society
- Service Award, Animal Science Department, University of Massachusetts

■ Awards heading draws attention to candidate's significant accomplishments.

■ Peace Corps experience can be advantageous for certain positions.

ASTRONOMER

Chris Smith, Ph.D.
178 Green Street
Jupiter, FL 33477
(407) 555-5555

OBJECTIVE: A senior level position as **LEAD ASTRONOMER**, preferably in a university setting utilizing research, computer-assisted and telescopic lens equipment.

PROFILE: Versatile Physicist and Astronomer who through 12 years in education and privately funded organizations has demonstrated proven effectiveness in the calculations and measurements of stars' magnitudes. Strong ability to write and transform technical data into interesting and informative reading.

EDUCATION:

Massachusetts Institute of Technology, Cambridge, MA
Ph.D., Contemporary and Ancient Astronomy   1990
- Doctoral Thesis: "The Effect of Gamma Gamma Rays on Man in the Moon Marigolds," 1988. Published by Bob Adams, Inc., 1989.

Oxford University
M.S., Astral Physics   1985
- Doctoral Thesis: "The Hubble vs. Jodrell Bank: A Question of Perspective."

Renselear Polytechnic Institute
B.S., Astronomy   1982

EXPERIENCE:

NASA, Cape Canaveral, FL   1989-Present
Head Researcher
- Monitor progress of Hubble telescope as it relates to super novae, the moon, and the planets.
- Investigate binary stars and their movements.

Harvard University Cambridge, MA   1986-1989
Research Assistant
- Conducted experiments and provided findings in 200-plus page reports on the magnitude of old stars; monitored their demise.
- Ensured smooth running of the lab and orderly maintenance of telescopes; ordered equipment and supplies.

PUBLICATIONS:
- "Pulsars and Black Holes: Relatives or Diametric Opposites?" *New England Science Journal,* May 1991.
- "Moon Rock or Hard Rock: Our moon in Music." *Rolling Stone Magazine,* February 1988.

■ Profile highlights candidate's educational achievements and professional skills.

■ Publications attest to candidate's expertise in astronomy.

CHEMIST (Analytical)

CHRIS SMITH
178 Green Street
Norfolk, MA 02056
(508) 555-5555

PROFESSIONAL OBJECTIVE
A responsible and challenging position in the field of chemistry.

PROFESSIONAL BACKGROUND
1983 to   BOSTON HOSPITAL, Boston, MA
Present   **Chemist**
- Responsible for conducting more than 500 manual and computerized assays of steroids, carcinogenic analyses, vitamins, fibrinogens, and other chemicals in hospital laboratory.
- Position involves rotation of duties and includes usage of the following instrumentation: HPLC, GSC, Nephelometer, Boehringer-Mannheim Multichannel Analyzer, Beckman Astra, Centrifichem, Spectrofluoromter, Electrophoresis, Spectrophotometer, and Flame Photometry.
- Knowledge of quality control systems and techniques.
- Perform maintenance and ensure proper calibration of instrumentation.
- Interface with physicians regarding test results and methodology.
- Train new employees.

1980 to 1981   TUFTS UNIVERSITY CHEMISTRY DEPARTMENT, Medford, MA
Teaching Assistant
- Instructed General Chemistry classes and laboratories.

1979   MASSACHUSETTS INSTITUTE OF TECHNOLOGY, Cambridge, MA
Guest Speaker
- Planned and conducted 3-day seminar on analysis of metals in soil for national chemistry convention.

EDUCATIONAL BACKGROUND
FLORIDA INSTITUTE OF TECHNOLOGY, Melbourne, FL
Master's Degree Program in Chemistry (1980-1985)

FLORIDA INTERNATIONAL UNIVERSITY
Bachelor of Science Degree with Honors in Chemistry (1979)
- Thesis: Analysis of Metals in Soil

CERTIFICATION
Certified in Chemistry by ASCP

- Bullets make resume easy to read.
- Professional certification adds weight to candidate's credentials.

CHEMIST (Instrumentation and Computer Science)

CHRIS SMITH, Ph.D.
178 Green Street
Wellborn, TX 77881
(409) 555-5555

OBJECTIVE

A position as a Chemist utilizing my education and experience with microcomputer systems in a laboratory setting.

PROFESSIONAL EXPERIENCE

Menden Corporation, Bryan, TX
Chemist I - Instrumentation and Computer Science (1991-Present)
Developed laboratory microcomputer systems for instrument automation and custom and specialized instrumentation/test equipment. Programmed technical applications on various microprocessors, minicomputers and mainframe systems.
- Engineered a patented design and coordinated construction of ten particle size instruments for Quality Control and Research saving $150,000 over commercial alternatives while providing improved performance and reliability. Received Award for Technical Excellence.
- Designed and built a continuous viscometer detector for gel permeation chromatography to provide absolute molecular weight and branching data. Design was later commercialized by Cook Associates.

EDUCATION

Texas A & M University, College Station, TX
Ph.D., Chemistry, Anticipated, 1997

Baylor University, Waco, TX
M.S., Chemistry 1991

Austin College, Sherman, TX
B.S., Chemistry 1989

- Job objective is clearly defined.

- Job descriptions focus on achievements, instead of simply listing job responsibilities.

CHEMISTRY RESEARCH ASSISTANT

CHRIS SMITH
178 Green Street
West Hartford, CT 06117
(203) 555-5555

OBJECTIVE:
To use extensive experience in recombinant DNA technology to help solve molecular biological problems.

EXPERIENCE:
1985-1993　RESEARCH ASSISTANT
New England Cancer Institute, Hartford, Connecticut
Performed DNA sequence analysis, S1 Mapping, plasmid and miniprep DNA purifications; made plasmid constructions.

1977-1984　CHEMIST
Drew Chemical Co., Hartford, Connecticut
Developed chemical synthetic procedures and isolation schemes for various nucleotides, nucleosides, and their derivatives.

1973-1976　GRADUATE STUDENT
Department of Physiological Chemistry, University of Connecticut, Storrs, Connecticut
Developed biochemical procedures for study of ribosome structure with respect to the RNA component.

1969-1972　RESEARCH ASSISTANT/TECHNICIAN
Department of Chemistry, Western Connecticut University, Danbury, Connecticut
Researched fungal cell metabolism; isolated plant alkaloids and their bacteria; performed various organic syntheses.

EDUCATION:
Master of Science - Physiological Chemistry, 1976
University of Connecticut, Storrs, CT

Bachelor of Science - Chemistry, 1969
Fairfield University, Fairfield, CT
Emphasis in the field of biochemistry.

■ Strong educational credentials strengthen resume.

■ Appropriate use of specialized terminology displays candidate's familiarity with advanced scientific procedures.

CONSERVATION SCIENTIST

CHRIS SMITH
178 Green Street
Oberlin, OH 44074
(216) 555-5555

Objective: A challenging position in the environmental science field.

Education: OBERLIN COLLEGE, Oberlin, OH
Environmental Science, Bachelor of Science Degree
May, 1994
Physics, Associate of Science Degree
May, 1990
Senior Thesis: "After the Rain: The Decline of Brazil's Forests"

Experience:

Sept. 1992-   Environmental Research Associates, Oberlin, OH
Present   *Laboratory Assistant*
Organic extractions laboratory assistant processing soil and water samples for trace organic analysis of pesticides, and herbicides. Performing set funnel extractions, creating surrogate solutions, maintaining laboratory inventory of glassware and chemicals, waste disposal, and clean up.

Summer   Brazil Forestry Station for Research, Brasilia, Brazil
1992   *Volunteer*
Volunteer laboratory assistant testing soil samples and cuttings for traces of pesticides and pcb's. Performed organic analysis of vegetation. Maintained records of daily temperature and precipitation level.

Sept. 1991-   Oberlin College-Science Laboratory, Oberlin, Ohio
May 1992   *Customer Service Representative*
Performed computer record maintenance and customer service.

Summer   Town of Pepper Pike, Pepper Pike, Ohio
1990   *Surveyor's Assistant*
Assisted civil engineer in surveying, also researched municipal records.

Sept. 1988-   Oberlin College-Physics Department, Oberlin, Ohio
May 1990   *Research Assistant*
Research assistant for Advanced Electronic Measurements course, involved general electronic repair.

Skills: FORTRAN and basic computer programming.
Certified in Laboratory Standards and Safety Course, 1992.

- Relevant volunteer work and/or summer employment strengthens recently graduated candidate's resume.

- Valuable skills are highlighted in a separate section.

FARM MANAGER

Chris Smith
178 Green Street
Ayer, MA 01432
(508) 555-5555

OBJECTIVE

To acquire a career continuation in **farm management** including animal husbandry.

AREAS OF EXPERTISE
- ✓ Animal Husbandry/Livestock
- ✓ Lambing/Foaling
- ✓ Accounting
- ✓ Crop/Produce
- ✓ Dairy Production

PROFESSIONAL EXPERIENCE

1988-
Present
La Grange Farms   Ayer, MA
FARM MANAGER
Responsible for the operation of a livestock and produce farm, its marketing and accounting tasks, selling beef, lamb, and produce to supermarkets, restaurants, and roadside vegetable stands.

1975-1988
Corny-Copia Farms   Lexington, MA
ASSISTANT FARM MANAGER
Handled all livestock, dairy cows and goats, assisted in lambing season checking for newborn foal diseases and malformations. Raised lambs and hens; baled and sold hay.

1960-1975
Pleasure Acres Farm   Brigham, KY
FARM HAND
Grew up on family owned and operated dairy and livestock farm; baled hay, collected eggs from hens, milked cows; assisted in the birth of cows and horses, assisted father and uncle in marketing meat and dairy produce to restaurants, supermarkets and local dairies.

EDUCATION

Bunker Hill Community College, Charlestown, MA
Business Management Certificate   1987

Lexington Community College, Lexington, MA
A.S., Animal Husbandry   1979

- Candidate's areas of expertise are prominently listed.

- Hands-on experience, essential in farm management, is listed before candidate's classroom experience.

FOREST SCIENTIST

CHRIS SMITH
178 Green Street
Olympia, Washington 98502
(206) 555-5555

-EXPERIENCE-

WASHINGTON STATE PARK, Olympia, WA   7/92-Present
Director of Buildings & Grounds
- Handle administrative duties for 850-acre state park.
- Oversee an annual operating budget in excess of $500,000.
- Supervise field surveys and database development.
- Prepare bid documents for contractual services.
- Consult and coordinate scientists, engineers and other professionals for special projects.
- Develop maintenance schedules for pruning, pest and weed control, fertilization and pH adjustments. Maintain park records, inventories and maps.
- Propagate desirable trees and/or plants from seed or cuttings to increase or replace plants in the park collection.
- Provide information to horticulturists, arborists, students, teachers and the public regarding plants and trees in the park.

WINSTON-SALEM PARK COMMISSION, Winston-Salem, NC   7/88-6/92
Forest Scientist
- Designed and supervised the layout and implementation of horticultural plantings for several state-owned parks and land reservations.
- Supervised total maintenance program.
- Researched and sought sources for tree and plant acquisitions.
- Planned pest control program.
- Handled overall curation of the collections.

PRINCESS GARDENS, Winston-Salem, NC   6/85-8/88
Worked summers and weekends during college, gaining experience in all phases of planning and planting public display gardens.

-EDUCATION-

WAKE FOREST UNIVERSITY, Winston-Salem, NC
Bachelor of Science in Environmental Science
                                                            1988

-COMMUNITY ACTIVITIES-

Save America's Plants (SAP), Washington Chapter - Vice-president
Forest Conservation Society-Board Member, Chief Spokesperson for the Northwest Region

---

■ Specific dates of employment (month and year) are ideal for candidates with no gaps in work history.

■ Community activities display candidate's dedication to the environment.

FORESTER/PARK RANGER

CHRIS SMITH
178 Green Street
Felda, FL 33930
(407) 555-5555

OBJECTIVE

A challenging career as a Forest Ranger where environmental and horticultural experience, education, skill, combined with motivation and a commitment to our forests will be utilized and advanced.

EXPERIENCE

FOUNTAIN OF YOUTH NATIONAL PARK — Felda, FL
Manager, Agrarian Development — 1984-Present
- Monitor and evaluate areas of agriculture, timber/forestry, and agrarian-based industries.
- Provide consultations to U.S. Wildlife Department with regard to national and regional objectives and priorities.
- Examine all aspects of forestry/timber credit, marketing, labor and productivity, with strict adherence to territorial logging and replacement of new pine and oak shoots.
- Generate field support for project budgetary controls on lumber projects; negotiate pricing and products with mill contractors.
- Extensive involvement in environmental protection of forests, land, fisheries and wildlife activities.
- Document existing state of forest destruction and increase public awareness through public relations; conducted start-up group of concerned citizens and school children through field trips, lectures, films and videos.

MYLES STANDISH STATE FOREST — Plymouth, MA
Manager, Planning and Development — 1977-1984
- Performed case studies on marketing forest and public recreation areas, including inefficiencies concerning fisheries, wildlife, fire prevention/fire fighting techniques, and cost of educating both public and private sectors.
- Appraised financial and economic projects for expanding public recreation areas with feasibility studies; monitored water supply, drainage and irrigation, flood protection, and ground water.

U.S. PEACE CORPS - SALIM ABBAS RESERVATION — Malaysia
Case Worker - Forester — 1974-1976
- Evaluated areas of lumber, fisheries and wildlife; examined and planned turf management.

EDUCATION

University of Massachusetts — Amherst, MA
M.S., Forest/Plant Science and Management — 1983
B.S., International Agriculture — 1974

■ Job descriptions detail candidate's responsibilities and accomplishments.

■ Education is listed towards bottom of resume because candidate's practical experience outweighs his/her degree.

GEOLOGIST

CHRIS SMITH
178 Green Street
Brookfield, WI 53305
(414) 555-5555

OBJECTIVE: A supervisory/management position with a progressive firm offering the opportunity to utilize geological background.

EXPERIENCE: **Geologist** - Daystar Co., Brookfield, WI (1988-Present)
Carry out research and development work on ceramics. Worked with group on the geological aspects of client projects. The types of work performed covered research on production problems and product work for a lime manufacturer. Directly responsible to the client's research director.
Handled research problems on the preparation of raw materials for production handling, i.e. preparing feed prior to heat treatment. (Pelletizing and briquetting).
   Set up and supervised a brief training program for a manufacturer to train non-technical personnel in the methods of firing and testing light weight aggregates for the purpose of evaluating quality.
   Handled petrographic and mineralogical work on processed and raw materials to evaluate mineral content and structure as well as other characteristics which can be determined only by the use of petrographic techniques.

Engineering Aide - Harmony Inc., Milwaukee, WI (1984)
Worked with a field crew performing various types of soil testing, to assure contractors adherence to government contract specifications.

Research Assistant - Pennsylvania Geological Survey, University of Pennsylvania (1983)
Worked on heavy and light mineral separation and analysis for the purpose of correlating various Pennsylvania glacial deposits.

EDUCATION: Boston University, Boston, MA
Chatham College, Pittsburgh, PA
B.A. degree in Geology, 1982

University of Pennsylvania, Philadelphia, PA
One year of graduate study in Geology, 1983.
(Research Assistant, Pennsylvania Geological Survey).

MILITARY SERVICE: U.S. Army (1985-1988). Served in the Infantry and Engineers. Tour of duty in Iceland for one year. Worked with Engineering Corps on demolition and other field problems.

■ Field experience, essential in scientific work, is listed before education.

■ Including a good military record can be advantageous if it relates to candidate's job objective.

GEOPHYSICIST

CHRIS SMITH
178 Green Street
Canyon, TX 79015
(806) 555-5555

SUMMARY OF QUALIFICATIONS

- Planning, coordinating and directing geophysical exploration programs and acreage evaluation, worldwide.
- Serving as a company representative in negotiation and problem resolution to contractors, industry committees, foreign governments, consortiums, and other individual companies.
- Experience in areas involving strategic planning, profitability analysis, organizational design and preliminary acquisition studies.

EXPERIENCE

SENIOR EXPLORATION GEOPHYSICIST
The International Petroleum Company
Amarillo, TX (1989-Present)

- Full responsibility for geophysical exploration and evaluation of the Plateau of Tibet.
- Instrumental in the selection of lease blocks for application by International Petroleum.
- Responsible for projects ranging in value from $75,000 to 2 million and equipment valued in excess of $1.5 million, while supervising up to 50 people under extreme working conditions at locations both domestic and foreign.
- Originated a well logging cost saving operation which saved as much as $100,000 per well on wells in the Persian Gulf.
- Served as company representative in exploration committees of oil company consortiums and to various service companies in contract negotiation and supervision.
- Instrumental in development of amphibious surveying operation which saved the company over $100,000 per month on eight month project.
- Helped set up and manage the first company production digital recording geophysical crew.

SENIOR COMPUTER
Oil Works, Inc., San Antonio, TX (1985-1988)

- Worked in nearly all field and office positions on company geophysical crew.
- Worked on staff of geophysical crew, using digital equipment and processing on a production basis.
- Completed assignments at numerous locations in Texas, New Mexico, and Mexico.

EDUCATION

FLORIDA INTERNATIONAL UNIVERSITY, Miami, FL
Bachelor of Science degree in Geological Sciences, 1981

BRIGHAM YOUNG UNIVERSITY, Provo, UT
Master's degree in Geology-Geophysics, 1984

■ Summary highlights candidate's experience and expertise in his/her field.

■ Statistics and dollar figures quantify candidate's accomplishments.

LABORATORY ASSISTANT

CHRIS SMITH
178 Green Street
Manchester, NH 03102
(603) 555-5555

PROFESSIONAL OBJECTIVE
A challenging and rewarding position as a Laboratory Assistant in the field of Molecular Biology.

EDUCATION
NOTRE DAME COLLEGE, Manchester, New Hampshire
Master of Science degree in Microbiology, 1993

ST. ANSELM COLLEGE, Manchester, New Hampshire
Bachelor of Science degree in Biology, 1991
- Dean's List
- Natural Sciences Department Award
- Senior Class President
- Named to Who's Who in American Colleges and Universities

EXPERIENCE
ST. ANSELM COLLEGE, Manchester, New Hampshire
Laboratory Assistant to Microbiology Department Head, 1993-Present
- Prepare all media and cultures for microbiology classes.
- Order supplies for department, monitor inventory.
- Act as informal tutor, help other students.

DURHAM MEDICAL ASSOCIATES, Durham, NH
Laboratory Technician for four doctors, 1991-1993
- Initiated running of laboratory; organized equipment and materials.
- Ran tests for patients, reported on same-day basis.
- Ordered supplies; maintained inventory.

REFERENCES
Available on request.

■ Impressive educational background helps to compensate for limited work experience.

■ Unrelated work experience is omitted.

LABORATORY TECHNICIAN

CHRIS SMITH
178 Green Street
Dayton, Ohio 45469
(513) 555-5555

CAREER OBJECTIVE
To secure a challenging position in Biological Research.

SUMMARY OF QUALIFICATIONS

Laboratory
Expertise
- Proven ability in analysis, scientific theories and procedures.
- Collect and study data from various biological and ecological sources.
- Produce and process blood components.
- Perform tissue experiments using electron microscopy.
- Learn and perform complicated tasks quickly and accurately.
- Member, American Association of Clinical Pathologists.

Technical
Writing
- Organize, write and edit detailed reports and research papers.

Interpersonal
Skills
- Speak and write French, Spanish, Italian, and English fluently.
- Work well independently and as a team player.
- Able to work long hours under deadline pressure.

Training
- Train biochemists in routine blood banking procedures.

EMPLOYMENT

1988-Present **American Red Cross**, Cleveland, OH
Laboratory Technician involved in production and processing of blood components, labeling and release, for transfusion and manufacture. Viral immunology testing of blood products. Irradiation of blood products.

1993-Present **College of Wooster**, Wooster, OH
(Part-time) **Clinical Research Technician.** Perform hormonal assays using RIA, ELISA and nucleic acid hybridization in clinical research of fertility patients.

1985-1987 **Roma Color**, Cincinnati, OH
Research and development in organic pigment.

EDUCATION
Nebraska Wesleyan University, Lincoln, NE
Bachelor of Science, Biology/Chemistry; 3.5 GPA. Graduated 1987.

- Chrono-functional format focuses attention on candidate's relevant skills while de-emphasizing limited work experience.

- Relevant part-time work accentuates candidate's dedication and hardworking nature.

MARINE BIOLOGIST

CHRIS SMITH
178 Green Street
Tacoma, WA 98416
(206) 555-5555

Professional Experience

1992-
Present
Staff Environmental Scientist. Puget Sound Project/U.S. E.P.A.
National Estuary Program, Tacoma, WA
Made written, editorial, and research contributions to ten briefing papers and a comprehensive management plan for Puget Sound. Oversaw publication of research reports funded by the Project: provided grant tracking support to authors, coordinated reviews and revision, formatted the reports, and facilitated printing and distribution.

1991-1992 **Aquatic Toxicologist/Culturist.** Flint River Project, Flint, MI
Performed toxicity tests on industrial wastes, effluents, drilling fluids, and dredge materials. Conducted wet chemistry, Microtox, and dilutor system analyses. Coordinated acquisition and culture of all fish, invertebrate, and algal organisms used in tests and for the operation and regulation of the culture facility.

1989-1991 **Inland Fisheries Extensionist.** Peace Corps/Mexico City, Mexico.
Technical advisor and regional outreach coordinator for koa and tilapia aquaculture projects in ten rural communities. Provided support and assistance in construction and repair of fish ponds and instruction in management techniques.

1987-1989 **Marine Science Technician.** Cavendish Laboratory, Mashpee, MA
Processed benthic samples and identified infaunal organisms collected on Atlantic and Gulf Coast petroleum monitoring programs. Member of scientific crew on Atlantic Ocean monitoring survey.

Publications

Smith, C.A., P.N. Toolman, G.B. Zeserson. 1992. *The Lonely Death of Puget Sound.* Puget Sound Project.

Graber, S.T., P.T. Hale, K.B. Rooks, C.A. Smith. 1993. *The Toxic Distillery Called Flint River.* Flint River Project.

Education

B.S. in Biology, minor in Chemistry. Montana State University, Bozeman, MT 1987.

Computer Skills

WordPerfect, MacIntosh Microsoft Word, Microsoft Excel, FileMaker.

■ Education is de-emphasized because candidate's work history is strong.

■ Relevant publications illustrate candidate's expertise in the field of marine biology.

METEOROLOGIST

CHRIS SMITH
178 Green Street
Bar Harbor, ME 04609
(207) 555-5555

OBJECTIVE To secure a position as a Meteorologist at an International Airport or for Local Television.

EXPERIENCE MAINE OCEANOGRAPHIC INSTITUTE, Bar Harbor, ME
Meteorologist   **1987-Present**
- Analyze and interpret data gathered by surface and upper-air stations, satellites, and radar, and those effects on the surface and subsurface of the ocean and coastline; prepare reports and forecasts.
- Prepare special forecasts and briefings for air and sea transportation, fire prevention, and air pollution.
- Observe and record weather conditions, including upper-air data on temperature, humidity, and winds using weather balloon and radiosonic equipment.

WAYN-TV, Bar Harbor, ME
TV Meteorologist/Announcer   **1992-Present**
- Weekend TV weather forecaster and announcer for local cable TV.
- Broad based knowledge of TV broadcasting and forecasting weather for seasonal climate conditions affecting Bar Harbor tourism and/or natural disasters that affect the harbor's special ecosystem.

PORTLAND AIRPORT, Portland, ME
Meteorologist   **1987-1989**
- Part-time and on-call emergency situation staff member at small airport.
- Observe and record weather conditions utilizing weather balloon and radiosonic equipment.
- Prepare specific, timely forecasts for air transportation.
- Assist in forecasting for hurricanes, northeasters, and natural disasters.
- Conduct pilot briefings.

EDUCATION CORNELL UNIVERSITY, Ithaca, NY
B.S. and M.S. Degrees in Meteorology   **1985, 1987**

Excellent References Available On Request

- Education is listed towards bottom of resume because candidate's practical experience outweighs his/her degree.

- Part-time positions are treated on resume like full-time positions.

PHYSICIST

CHRIS SMITH
178 Green Street
Albuquerque, NM 87131
(505) 555-5555

PROFESSIONAL OBJECTIVE
A challenging position in **Research and Development**.

PROFESSIONAL EXPERIENCE
1991 to
Present

RADIATION MONITORING DEVICES, INCORPORATED, Santa Fe, NM
Staff Scientist
- Conduct materials research in semiconductors for semiconductor neutron detector.
- Design cadmium telluride gamma ray detector for dental x-ray calibration.

1987 to 1991 UNIVERSITY OF NEW MEXICO, Albuquerque, NM
Research Assistant
- Conducted experimental research in nonlinear optics, stimulated Brillouin scattering in organic liquid crystals for Professor Rao on government research grant.
- Operated Q Switched Ruby Laser, Helium Neon Laser and Fabry-Perot Interferometer.
- Taught physics labs.

1986 to 1987 UNIVERSITY OF NEW MEXICO, Albuquerque, NM
Research Assistant
- Conducted experimental research in positron annihilation spectroscopy for Professor Shah on National Science Foundation research grant.
- Recorded and analyzed data on computer.

1984 to 1986 UNIVERSITY OF NEW MEXICO, Albuquerque, NM
Research Assistant
- Conducted experimental research in organic synthesis for Professor Becker on government research grant.

EDUCATIONAL BACKGROUND
UNIVERSITY OF NEW MEXICO, Albuquerque, NM
Master of Science Degree in Applied Physics, 1990
Concentration in Nonlinear Optics and Stimulated Sound Scattering.
- GPA 3.8/4.0
- Thesis: Stimulated Sound Scattering in a Vacuum

Bachelor of Science Degree in Chemistry and Physics, 1987
- Society of Physics Students, Member
- Sigma Pi Sigma - Physics Honor Society, Member
- Physics Club, Vice-president

■ Dynamic action verbs give resume impact.

■ Educational honors, including honor society memberships, high GPA, and/or honors thesis written, attest to candidate's strong work ethic and ability to excel.

RESEARCH ASSOCIATE

CHRIS SMITH, Ph.D.
178 Green Street
Los Angeles, CA 90041
(213) 555-5555

PROFESSIONAL EXPERIENCE

1989 to present SUN LABORATORIES, Los Angeles, CA
Manufacturing Research Associate II
- Developed expertise in research through production via process experimentation and operation of pilot plant equipment
- Performed large-scale fermentation, protein purification, and other processes under GMP regulations
- Developed system for preparing media
- Performed related protein assays

1974 to 1984 GRAYSON RESEARCH CORPORATION, Los Angeles, CA
Research Technician, Cell Propagation Department
- Optimized growth parameters of fibroblast and epithelial cellines
- Scaled up culture from 25-cc T-flasks up through to 40-L fermentor microcarrier cultures; worked independently
- Established media unit for exclusive use of department
- Set up perfusion system

Technician-2, Media Department
- Filtered and sterilized various media under GMP regulations

Assistant Supervisor, Glassware Department
- Supervised department of 15 employees
- Prepared, sterilized, and distributed tissue culture glassware to different departments

EDUCATION

Ph.D. Program in Biology, 1989
California Institute of Technology, Pasadena, CA
Course: Biochemistry, Molecular Biology, Protein Chemistry

Master of Liberal Arts in Biology, 1986
Occidental College, Los Angeles, CA
Concentration: Immunology

Bachelor of Science in Agricultural Engineering, 1974
Huntingdon College, Montgomery, AL

■ Job descriptions include technical jargon specific to candidate's field.

■ Impressive educational background strengthens resume.

SCIENCE WRITER

CHRIS SMITH
178 Green Street
Newport, RI 02840
(401) 555-5555

OBJECTIVE: A research, science or technical writing position.

WRITING EXPERIENCE: Science Writer (Freelance) - Blake Astoria Publishing Company, (1990-Present)
Responsibilities:
- Wrote text "Physics Principles and Problems", by Murphy and Sloat.
- Wrote eighth grade science textbook.

Science Writer - Braeridge Publishing Company, Trenton, NJ (1988-1990)
Responsibilities:
- Wrote Earth Science Series (science texts on elementary level).
- Wrote a series of slides to supplement the text.
- Wrote a set of correlated workbooks.
On a free-lance basis, edited teacher's editions of textbooks (grades 1-6; and a mathematics text, grade 8).

TEACHING EXPERIENCE: Physics/Physical Science Teacher - Purchase High School, Purchase, NY (September 1985-June 1988)
Responsibilities:
- Taught the following courses: Honors Physics (Text: Physics for High School by Jacob Tern). Science Survey which included the following disciplines: Astronomy, Geology, Ecology, Chemistry and Physics.

Lecturer - Rollins College - University College, Winter Park, FL (1981-1985)
- Taught a survey course including the following disciplines: Astronomy, Meteorology, Geology, Physics, Chemistry, and Biology.

EDUCATION: Graduate Study:
Dickinson College, Carlisle, PA
Master of Science degree, Geophysics (1980)
Geophysics courses: Physics of the Earth, Seismology, Elastic Wave Theory, Meteorology, Geomagnetism.

Columbia University, New York, NY (1979)
Courses: Mineralogy, Sedimentology, Petrology, Chemistry, Thermodynamics, Electricity and Magnetism, Potential Theory.

Trenton State College, Trenton, NJ
B.A.degree, Mathematics (1978)
Related subjects: Physics, Geology, Geophysics.

■ Experience is divided into functional categories, writing and teaching, but also includes dates of employment.

■ Courses listed under education are related to candidate's field of interest.

ZOOLOGIST

Chris Smith
178 Green Street
Lexington, KY 21345
(606) 555-5555

OBJECTIVE

A challenging position as a zoologist in the natural habitat of studied subjects or in the laboratory.

EDUCATION

Boston University, Boston MA
M.S., Zoology, September 1988.

Northeastern University, Boston, MA
B.S., Zoology with a concentration in Genetics, June 1985.

Internships: Center for DNA Research, Cambridge, MA; Spring, 1985.
Truman Thoroughbred Stables, Hamilton, MA; Spring 1984.
Stoneham Zoo, Stoneham, MA; Spring/Fall 1984.
Center for Genetic Research, New York, NY; Summer 1983.
Chacombe Kennel, Cohasset, MA; Spring/Fall 1982.

EMPLOYMENT

1991-
Present
Uphill Thoroughbred Stables & Stud, Lexington, KY
Genetics/Breeding Specialist
- Work directly with doctors of veterinary medicine and racehorse trainers in the breeding and grooming of top quality thoroughbreds for racing and dressage.
- Investigate genetic factors, forecast cross breeding and artificial insemination considerations of specific mares and studs.
- Provide vets, trainers, owners, and investigators with pertinent information regarding the designated forecasts, mating seasons/procedures, and expected inherited traits.

1985-1991
Center for DNA Research, Cambridge, MA
Researcher
- Studied the effects of altering proteins in compositions of DNA.
- Closely monitored mutations and aberrations in basic cellular structure.
- Reported findings to doctors and researchers in public and private sectors; interfaced with the media.
- Coordinated teams for various experiments and procedures.

REFERENCES

Furnished upon request.

- Valuable internship experience is included under education.

- Resume format is neat and professional.

18
Service

Nature of Work
The role of people working in service organizations is as the name says: to provide quality service to its customers. The performance of service employees is often what makes (or breaks) a business.

Some examples of service occupations are food preparation workers, make-up and hairstylists, hotel employees, and flight attendants. All of these jobs involve direct responsibility for customer satisfaction.

Employment
Most food service employees work in restaurants and other retail eating and drinking establishments. Others are employed in institutions such as schools, hospitals, and nursing homes.

Barbers, hairstylists, and cosmetologists traditionally work in beauty salons, barber shops, and department stores. Some are employed by hospitals, hotels, and prisons. About 75% of all workers in this section of the service industry are self-employed.

Flight attendants held over 100,000 jobs in 1990. Most of these positions were stationed in major cities at the airlines' home bases.

Training
Some positions within the service industry require little or no experience, and in some cases the employer is willing to train new and inexperienced people. Jobs such as cooks, hotel clerks, and wait staff do not require a college degree, and allow much room for promotion. People in these positions start out at entry-level, and work their way up from there.

Chefs and hair and make-up professionals must go to special schools for training specifically geared for their occupation.

Flight attendants must be at least 19 to 21 years old, and have excellent health, good vision, and the ability to speak clearly. Fluency in the appropriate foreign language is required for people desiring to work on international flights.

Job Outlook
Jobs for food service workers, including cooks and wait persons, are expected to be plentiful through the year 2005, due to the large number of people who leave the industry each year.

Overall employment of barbers and cosmetologists is expected to grow about as fast as the average for all occupations. Population growth, a greater number of women in the labor force, and rising incomes will stimulate demand for these workers.

Employment of flight attendants is expected to increase at the average rate for all occupations from now until 2005. Growth in both population and income are contributing factors toward this trend.

Earnings

Earnings for kitchen workers vary, depending on what part of the country they are in. Similarly, annual salaries for other food service workers, barbers, and cosmetologists are difficult to pinpoint, as their income is a combination of hourly wages and customer tips. In 1990, median hourly earnings (including tips) of full-time waiters and waitresses were $4.80, whereas the top 10 percent earned at least $9.00 an hour. According to limited information, most barbers and cosmetologists earned between $7.00 and $14.00 an hour in 1990.

Flight attendants had median earnings of about $13,000 per year in 1990. Those with six years of flying experience had average annual earnings of about $20,000, while some senior attendants earned as much as $35,000 per year. Flight attendants receive extra compensation for overtime and for night and international flights. In addition, flight attendants and their immediate families are entitled to reduced fares on their own and most other airlines.

CASHIER

CHRIS SMITH
178 Green Street
Dillon, MT 59725
(406) 555-5555

OBJECTIVE

To contribute acquired skills to a retail position.

SUMMARY OF QUALIFICATIONS

- Developed interpersonal skills, having dealt with a diversity of professionals, clients, and staff members.
- Adept at cashiering and reconciling cash.
- Proven communication abilities, both oral and written.
- Function well, independently and as team member.
- Self-motivated; able to set effective priorities to achieve immediate and long-term goals and meet operational deadlines.

EDUCATION

BURDAN JR. COLLEGE, Missoula, MT
Major: Criminal Justice   BA Candidate, 1996

WORK HISTORY

YOUR STORE, Dillon, MT   1994-Present
Cashier
Provided customer and personnel assistance. Handled cash intake, inventory control, and light maintenance. Trained and scheduled new employees. Instituted store recycling program benefiting the Dillon Homeless Shelter.

RONDELL IMAGE, Helena, MT   1993-94
Data/File Clerk
Assisted sales staff. General office responsibilities included data entry, typing, and filing invoices.

TARPY PERSONNEL SERVICES, Bozeman, MT   1991-93
General Clerk
Duties included shipping/receiving and filing invoices.

TELESTAR MARKETING, Great Falls, MT   1989-91
Telephone Interviewer
Conducted telephone surveys dealing with general public and pre-selected client groups in selected demographic areas. Required strong communication skills.

REFERENCES

Furnished upon request.

■ Typewritten resume is acceptable for most entry-level retail positions.

■ Job objective is brief and to the point.

CATERER

CHRIS SMITH
178 Green Street
Las Vegas, NV
(505) 555-5555 (Work)
(505) 444-4444 (Home)

ACCOMPLISHMENTS
- Named "Best & Brightest New Business Owner" by The Entrepreneurial Expo, 1993.
- Coordinated and implemented CCC Employee Training Program, voted "Most Effective" by the Restaurant Association of New Mexico.
- Catered The Governor's Dinner, 1994.

PROFESSIONAL EXPERIENCE
6/93- **CHRISTINE'S CATERING COMPANY,** Las Vegas, NV
Present **Owner/Manager**
- Manage operations and service, handling $30,000/week sales.
- Organize weekly work schedules for staff of 35.
- Troubleshoot staff and client problems.
- Create innovative incentive programs to motivate staff and improve customer service.

9/89-5/93 **CAMPUS CATERERS,** Hobbs, NV
Banquet Supervisor
- Coordinated banquets for up to 450 guests.
- Organized dining area.
- Trained new employees
- Supervised staff of 15.

6/88-8/89 **THE OASIS COUNTRY CLUB,** Las Vegas, NV
Server
- Handled cash and credit card transactions.
- Resolved customer complaints.
- Trained new bus and wait staff.

EDUCATION
COLLEGE OF THE SOUTHWEST, Hobbs, NV
Bachelor of Science in Management, 1993

ASSOCIATIONS
Southwest Restaurant Association, member since 1993
The National Caterer's Guild, member since 1990

- Candidate's most impressive accomplishments are featured first.

- Professional memberships show candidate's commitment to his/her field.

CHEF (Assistant)

CHRIS SMITH
178 Green Street
Boston, MA 02116
(617) 555-5555

PROFESSIONAL OBJECTIVE
To obtain a position as a Pastry Chef in a restaurant environment.

PROFESSIONAL EXPERIENCE

1991 to THE WILLARD HOTEL   Boston, MA
Present **Assistant Pastry Chef**
- Work directly with the executive pastry chef. Monitor the baking, mixing and finishing of cakes, pastries, and a full range of bakery products on an as-needed basis.
- Includes work to Special Order, for banquets, special functions, and the Hotel Restaurant. Schedule and management of personnel. Supervise a four member staff.

1990 CATERING BY C. SMITH   Everett, MA
Pastry Cook
- Worked concurrently with above position, helping out during the busy season on a half-time basis, with the baking and finishing of breads and pastries.

1989 to 1990 THE BANNEN INN   Bangor, ME
Rounds Cook
- Cooked dishes to order as needed. Streamlined work flow, acted as management liaison, scheduled shifts, provided inventory control, and the troubleshooting of related problems on an as-needed basis.

1988 to 1989 LE HOTEL DE VIVRE   Bangor, ME
Pastry Cook
- Assisted the manager with all phases of shop management; the production of baked goods, the servicing of accounts, etc. Performed the baking, mixing, and decoration of cakes. Provided inventory control.

1986 to 1988 KIKI COUNTRY CLUB   Boston, MA
Saute and Broiler Cook
- Performed all associated Prep Work, with the handling of stations and the cooking of food items.

EDUCATION

1987 AMERICAN PASTRY ARTS CENTER   Medford, MA
Course in Chocolates and Candy
- Understudy of Sid Cherney

1986 GOURMET INSTITUTE OF AMERICA   Boston, MA
A.O.S. Degree
- Earned Certificates in Food and Management Sanitation.

■ Chronological format illustrates a clear career path.

■ Job objective is supported by the facts and accomplishments stated in resume.

CHEF (Executive)

CHRIS SMITH
178 Green Street
Hytop, AL 35768
(205) 555-5555

EXPERIENCE

1992 to Present **TORPEDO CLUB**, Montego Bay, Jamaica
Executive Chef - Sand Dollar Restaurant
165 seat restaurant - two seatings for dinner, all inclusive concept. Supervise head chef, sous chef, pastry chef, butcher, and 53 additional staff. Trained all staff with exception of pastry and head chefs. Run complete party system with 15 sections, including breakfast, lunch, garde manager, vegetables, roasts and sauces, soups, pastry staff, butchering, kitchen clerks, buffet runners. and sanitation section. Plan menu.

1990 to 1992 **THE SIN SHACK**, South Negril Pt., Jamaica
First Sous Chef
Responsible for overall running of two kitchens. Oversee kitchen and 38 additional staff. Seating 165 on a la carte menu.

1988 to 1989 **THE BARNYARD**, Mandaville, Jamaica
Head Chef
Hired and trained all staff to provide 30 entrees and 175 a la carte dinners per night. Reported directly to executive chef. Primary responsibility to serve highest quality dishes at lowest possible cost.

1986 to 1988 **CLUB CURPCO - HOTEL BRIGADOON**, Lucea, Jamaica
Sous Chef
Directly responsible to head chef. Complete charge of 52-member brigade. Assisted with menu planning. Responsible for cost and quality control, production, and food cost.

1985 **THE OCHO RIOS SUNRAY INN**, Ocho Rios, Jamaica
Broiler Chef
Responsible for all grilled foods, quality, presentation, waste control.

1983 to 1985 **SQUIRE CRUISE SHIPS**
Breakfast Cook
Prepared up to 600 meals per day; promoted to Breakfast Chef.

EDUCATION

Jamaica Community College, Mandaville, Jamaica
1989 - Food and Beverage Management

Jamaica Hospitality Center, Lucea, Jamaica
1986 - Dessert Finesse

Jamaica Hotel School, Ocho Rios, Jamaica
1985 - Basic Cookery

■ Figures, such as restaurant capacity and number of meals prepared, indicates candidate's ability to work in a high-pressure environment.

■ Courses listed under education are related to candidate's field of interest.

CHEF (Pastry)

CHRIS SMITH
178 Green Street
Eugene, OR 97401
(503) 555-5555

OBJECTIVE
To contribute extensive experience, educational background and culinary skills to the position of Pastry Chef within a restaurant environment.

SUMMARY OF QUALIFICATIONS
- Thorough knowledge in the preparation of an extensive assortment of baked goods, including: pastries, cookies, puddings, muffins, breads and specialties.
- Consistently utilizing creative talents to develop attractive presentations and proficient in the production of original creations.
- Competent in organizing production to maximize use of available space.
- Able to direct work flow in an accurate, timely and efficient manner.
- Recipient of numerous Culinary Awards for superior creations.

EXPERIENCE

1/92 to Present *Pastry Chef*
THE BEVENSHIRE HOTEL Eugene, OR
- Plan and prepare three desserts on a daily basis for Faculty Club.
- Produce truffles and special tea pastries for Deans House.
- Prepare desserts for in-house groups, serving 100-200 people.

10/90 to 1/92 *Pastry Chef*
DELTA PINES BAKERY & CAFE Corvallis, OR
- Prepared an extensive assortment of desserts, rotating on a weekly basis, including cakes, cookies, cobblers, puddings, tarts, special order desserts and wedding cakes.
- Mixed puff pastry, croissant and Danish doughs.
- Created breakfast pastries and breads for lunch specials.

3/87 to 10/90 *Pastry Chef*
THE PLUMROSE RESTAURANT Corvallis, OR
- Planned and executed monthly menu which included six desserts, two sorbets, two ice cream dishes and two fresh breads daily for lunch and dinner.
- Ordered all bakery and dairy supplies and created Brunch breads.
- Prepared desserts for retail store and special orders.

EDUCATION

6/81
ESTERBROOK INN New York, NY
American Culinary Federation: Certified Cook

10/84 to 7/87
- Butcher Assistant, Rodeo Ranch, 6 months
- Soup and Sauce preparation, 6 months
- Carde Manager, ice and tallow sculpture, 6 months
- Pastry Assistant, 1 year

■ Summary of qualifications accentuates candidate's areas of expertise and related achievements.

■ Relevant apprenticeships augment impressive list of professional experience.

COSMETOLOGIST

CHRIS SMITH
178 Green Street
Marion, IN 46952
(317) 555-5555

PROFESSIONAL EXPERIENCE
1990-Present **LATITIA GREEN ACADEMY,** Marion, IN
<u>Instructor</u>
- Provide instruction to all levels in cosmetology theory and practical applications.
- Develop lesson plans in all subjects; Administer tests; Give demonstrations.
- Motivate and counsel 20-student classes; Evaluate tests and performances.

1987-Present **LE SALON DESIREE,** Lafayette, IN
<u>Owner/Operator</u>
- Hairdresser/Cosmetologist, performing all relevant functions.
- Arranged for promotion of business and maintained good customer relations.

1983-1987 **DYE HEALTHY SALON,** Muncie, IN
<u>Hairdresser</u>
- Performed hairdressing, manicuring, skin care, hair coloring and hair styling.

1982-1983 **BORELLI MORTALIO SALON,** Lisbon, Portugal
<u>Hairdresser</u>
- Provided hairdressing, skin care, facials, permanents and hair coloring.

1980-1982 **ZACHARY DRAKE'S SHOP,** Lisbon, Portugal
<u>Hairdresser</u>
- Service customers with hairdressing, manicuring, skin care, facials.

EDUCATION
WINNIFRED ACADEMY, Muncie, IN; Completed Cosmetology course work.
Received License #1 (#1372), 1984
BONNY LASS BEAUTY ACADEMY, Lisbon, Portugal; Completed one-year course in Cosmetology, 1980.

PERSONAL
Bilingual in English and Portuguese; Managed a grocery store in Lisbon, Portugal, for 3 years.

REFERENCES
Furnished upon request.

- Experience as an instructor indicates candidate's expertise in the field of cosmetology.

- Resume illustrates continual career progression.

CUSTOMER SERVICE MANAGER

CHRIS SMITH
178 Green Street
San Francisco, CA 94111
(415) 555-5555

CAREER OBJECTIVE
A management position in customer service or field support.

BACKGROUND SUMMARY
Dedicated, resourceful, and decisive individual. Successfully maintained multiple accounts. Demonstrated skill in working independently or with a group. Order and data entry experience. Proven ability to work under changing fast-paced priorities. Handle multiple tasks concurrently. Organized. Experience in problem resolutions.

CAREER HISTORY

BURBA AND QUATTRUCCI DATA, San Francisco, CA   1991-Present
Customer Service Manager of Parts Department National Accounts
- Supervise and maintain 250 clients working with debits, credits and shipping errors.
- Investigate and resolve customer complaints both international and domestic.
- Coordinate clients' problem resolution with co-workers and supervisors.
- Demonstrated ability to make quick and accurate decisions.
- Received letters of commendation for work performed under stressful conditions.

BIRKENSTOCK AUTO, San Gabrielle, CA   1988-1991
Personal Secretary
- Coordinated transportation of vehicles to and from locations for clients both international and domestic.
- Organized and implemented a filing system for each client and vehicle.
- Maintained and balanced the company's finances.

MORRISEY ART GALLERIES, Santa Ana, CA   1986-1988
Sales Representative
- Generated and organized showings and sales of artwork.
- Motivated clients to have showings and to purchase.
- Assisted in sourcing network.

EDUCATION
San Rafael High School, diploma 1986

COMPUTERS
Thorough knowledge of Microsoft Word and Lotus 1-2-3.

PERSONAL
Willing to relocate.

- Background summary gives a snapshot of candidate's work personality.

- Work experience is emphasized, while limited education is de-emphasized.

CUSTOMER SERVICE REPRESENTATIVE (Credit)

CHRIS SMITH
178 Green Street
Volga, SD 57071
(605) 555-5555

CAREER DEVELOPMENT

Credit Office Representative, **The Gillis Corporation, Volga, SD**   **(October 1991-present)**
- Work with customers to resolve problems concerning billing.
- Assist sales staff with questions on transactions and billings.
- Responsible for cash reconciliations from all registers in store.

Customer Service Representative/Medical Underwriter   **(June 1987-September 1991)**
Desmond Insurance Company, Sinai, SD
- Responsible for underwriting/enrollment of insurance applications and requisitions for change.
- Dealt directly with applicants advising them of enrollment options, plan design features, billing processes and resolution of problems.
- Handled enrollment/underwriting reports; provided marketing/installation support.

Employment Interviewer, **State of South Dakota**   **(June 1986-May 1987)**
Department of Labor, Brookings, SD
- Interviewed job applicants in unemployment office.
- Reviewed applications for job placements; fielded job openings from local employers and assisted employers in filling job orders.
- Received job orders over phone and entered them in IBM computer to facilitate selection and referral process.
- Attended classes on Public Speaking and Interviewing Techniques.

OTHER EXPERIENCE

Shoe Sales Representative - Tilden Department Store, Aurora, SD   **(Summers 1982-1985)**
- In conjunction with the above, worked for this Department Store assisting customers in selecting footwear; cashiering, totaled department daily sales amounts, trained new associates.

Arlington Day Camp, Arlington, SD   **(September 1985-May 1986)**
- Supervised and coordinated activities for children. Prepared schedule and payroll for all employees.

President and Founder - Brookings Baby-sitting Service   **(September 1982-May 1984)**
Brookings, SD
- Established baby-sitting service for local residents in Brookings area. Acted as referral service for associates. Created business protocol and guidelines

EDUCATION

South Dakota State University, Brookings, SD
Bachelor of Arts degree in Health Care, 1986

■ Career-related positions are detailed, other positions are briefly listed under "Other Experience."

■ Resume format is neat and professional.

CUSTOMER SERVICE REPRESENTATIVE (Sales)

CHRIS SMITH
178 Green Street
Broken Arrow, OK 74011
(918) 555-5555

SUMMARY OF QUALIFICATIONS

- Demonstrated ability in the provision of sales support services. Includes establishment of the client base, extensive customer servicing, telemarketing, cold calling and sales territory development.
- Consistently met/exceeded sales goals and instituted sales programs; sales increased from $8 to $25 million.
- Thorough knowledge of management production; assure timely and accurate presentation of goods; adept at coordinating delivery processes, organization of delivery schedules and monitoring delivery personnel.
- Extensive experience in facilitating operational procedures. Respond to customer complaints; resolve problem elements, interact with credit department to ascertain customer account status. Handle sourcing of vendors, contract negotiation, purchasing, correspondence, account adjustments and inventory control.
- Exceptional communication/interpersonal and organizational skills.

EXPERIENCE

OXBRIDGE, INC.   Broken Arrow, OK
Sales/Customer Service Representative   **1989-Present**
- Interface with merchandising personnel, at all levels, and provide technical information on company products and services.
- Interact with customers, providing advice in the selection of products. Monitor production to ensure realization of customer specifications.
- Collaborate with contracting merchandisers for contract negotiation on supplies. Conduct extensive materials costing processes.
- Coordinate delivery schedules and monitor delivery personnel.
- Organize promotional demonstration activities for home and New York marketing office.
- Respond to and resolve customer complaints.
- Manage office operations and produce correspondence.
- Control stock and conduct purchasing procedures.
- Assist sales department in establishing client base/sales territories.

EDUCATION

PROPHET JUNIOR COLLEGE   Broken Arrow, OK
Associate Degree Program   1993 to Present
Computer Operations Program: Lotus 1-2-3, Database III, Typing, Word-processing (Multimate), Business Math, Speech Communication, Introduction to Computers and English Composition.

- Background summary accentuates candidate's acquired professional skills and impressive track record.

- Listing relevant courses adds weight to candidate's educational credentials.

FAST FOOD WORKER

Chris Smith
178 Green Street
Carson City, NV 89703
(702) 555-5555

PROFESSIONAL OBJECTIVE

A challenging, growth-oriented position in the fast food industry in which academic training, work experience, and a commitment to excellence will have valuable application.

EMPLOYMENT

1993-Present   THE PIZZA PALACE, Carson City, NV
Server
- Participate in opening of new store outlets.
- Assist with public relations, food service and register control.
- Resolve conflicts in high pressure environment.

1992-1993   NEVADA TELEPHONE, Las Vegas, NV
Data input/Repetitive Debts Collection/Commercial
- Responsible for commercial account installation and verification of records/old accounts for new service.
- Maintained Wang Computer for bill revisions through referrals.
- Executed customer services, fielded inquiries, and consumer services.

Summers   BLACKTHORN DAY CAMP, Plaston, NH
1989-1992   **Recreation Director**
- Planned, programmed, and supervised camp activities for summer outdoor education/camping services for juvenile coeds.
- Supervised cabin group, counseled, and instructed in aquatics, sports, special events, and parent visitations.

1987-1988   SISYPHUS GROCERY, Manchester, NH
Cashier/Produce Section
- Maintained produce inventory, cash control, public relations, and in-house advertising for special sales and events.
- Strong communications and interpersonal skills required.

EDUCATIONAL BACKGROUND

MANCHESTER HIGH SCHOOL, Manchester, NH
Diploma, College Preparatory, 1989
Varsity Sports (4 years), Blue Key Club.

- Education is listed towards bottom of resume because candidate's practical experience outweighs his/her degree.

- Use of boldface and underlining provides a clean and crisp presentation.

FLIGHT ATTENDANT (Lead)

CHRIS SMITH
178 Green Street
Troy, MI 48098
(313) 555-5555

OBJECTIVE
To secure a position as a Flight Attendant.

SUMMARY OF QUALIFICATIONS
- Broad knowledge of airline safety and service procedures.
- Positive attitude and patient with challenging and difficult passengers.
- Excellent rapport with children, elderly and handicapped passengers.
- Enjoy working with the public.
- Conversant in Spanish.
- Knowledgeable about fine foods and domestic wines.

PROFESSIONAL EXPERIENCE

1994-
Present
TRANS AIR BUSINESS CONNECTION, Detroit, MI
Lead Attendant
Oversee up to ten attendants. Greet and assist passengers boarding and leaving plane. Instruct passengers in the use of emergency equipment. Care for small children, elderly, and handicapped. Administer first aid. Assist and instruct passengers during emergency situations.

1987-1994
Flight Attendant
Expertise and accuracy with pre-flight procedures; the safety and comfort of all passengers; serving food and beverages, stowing carry-on luggage; CPR/First Aid if necessary.

1985-1987
KALEIDOSCOPE CAFE, Utica, MI
Head Waitress and Manager of Banquet Wait Staff
Served as hostess, banqueting and catering assistant for elegant, upscale restaurant. Seated and served patrons gourmet meals, mixed cocktails; cash and credit card transactions. Trained minimum of five wait staff and performed scheduling calendar.

CERTIFICATIONS
Trans Air Business Flight Attendant * CPR

EDUCATION
THE PERRY SCHOOL, Ann Arbor, MI. Travel Industry Program
Graduated 1987 * G.P.A. 3.8

CONCORDIA COLLEGE, Ann Arbor, MI
A.S. in Communications, 1985

■ Previous restaurant experience, though different from candidate's job objective, illustrates relevant skills in customer service and hospitality.

■ "Certifications" heading draws attention to candidate's specific professional qualifications.

FLIGHT ATTENDANT (Reserve)

CHRIS SMITH
178 Green Street
Peoria, IL 61603
(309) 555-5555

PROFILE
Certified flight attendant with over four years experience working overseas/domestic flights. Specialized training in CPR and emergency evacuation/crisis procedures. Fluent in Slavic and English; knowledgeable in German language.

SKILLS
Communication
- Bachelor of Arts degree in Communications.
- Developed interpersonal skills, having dealt with a diversity of professionals, clients, and associates.
- Fluent in Slavic and English; knowledgeable in German language.

Customer Service
- Over five years experience in retail/sales, dealing with a wide variety of clients.
- Adept at handling customer complaints and problem-solving.

Specialized Training
- Certified flight attendant.
- CPR-certified.
- Participated in three-day intensive training seminar: "Reacting in an Emergency."

PROFESSIONAL EXPERIENCE
9/92-Present WANDER IN WONDER WORLD AIRWAYS, O'Hare Airport, Chicago, IL
Flight Attendant, overseas/domestic flights
- Assist in customer boarding.
- Supervise equipment/supply loading.
- Ensure passenger safety and comfort.
- Maintain passenger manifest and seating allocations.
- Handle bilingual safety instructions and travel problems (emergency landings, etc.).

OTHER EXPERIENCE
1992   THE CRAFTY BOUTIQUE, Orlando, FL, **Salesperson/Manager's Assistant**

1990-1992 BEST BET BUSINESS TEMPS, Chicago, IL, **Account Representative**

1989-1990 THE TAX TASKMASTER, Normal, IL, **Sales Assistant**

1987-1989 THE CHASIN BANK, Joliet, IL, **Teller/Customer Service Representative**

EDUCATION
FANTASTIC FLIGHTS TRAINING CENTER, Orlando, FL
Received Flight Attendant Certificate, 1992
ILLINOIS COLLEGE, Jackson, IL
BA in Communications, August, 1989

PERSONAL
Extensive travel including Europe, Asia, and the Untied States. Willing to relocate.

■ Attention-getting profile gives a snapshot of candidate's professional experience and strengths.

■ Chrono-functional format is more flexible than a chronological resume, but stronger than a functional resume.

FOOD INSPECTOR

CHRIS SMITH
178 Green Street
Rome, GA 30160
(706) 555-5555

SUMMARY/OBJECTIVE

To utilize a strong academic background and experience in the food areas of the public health care field. Experience encompasses the development and implementation of systems and direction of services within the food inspections standards and industry.

EXPERIENCE

THE CITY OF ROME — 1986-Present
Director, Food Inspector and Public Health — Rome, GA
Establish all executive guidelines and centralized management systems for Rome restaurants (sit down/take out), hospitals/health care facilities, schools/campus dining halls, airlines, public and private cafeterias.
Interface directly with Public Health, Public Safety and food service distributors throughout the city.
Provide documentation and distribute warnings to establishments and distributors that fail food inspections.

GREATER ATLANTA HEALTH DEPARTMENT — 1979-1986
Chief Food Inspector — Atlanta, GA
Participated in exams and regulatory inspections of food distributors/warehouses/ refrigerated facilities, restaurants, supermarkets/convenience stores, and commercial buildings' food service areas.
Ensured all inspections were within regulations of the Georgia General Laws, State Sanitary Codes and Local Ordinances.

PLYMOUTH COUNTY HEALTH DEPARTMENT — 1978-1979
Internship - Food Inspectors' Offices — Hingham, MA
Accompanied and assisted food inspectors on their rounds of food distribution warehouses, supermarkets, restaurants, hospital kitchens.

EDUCATION

UNIVERSITY OF SOUTHERN CALIFORNIA
B.S. Environmental Health, 1978

CERTIFICATION

Registered Sanitation Inspector, 1979

- Resume format is neat and professional.

- "Certification" heading draws attention to candidate's specific professional qualifications.

HAIRSTYLIST

CHRIS SMITH
178 Green Street
Menoken, ND 58558
(701) 555-5555

OBJECTIVE:
A position with a reputable hair salon.

SUMMARY OF QUALIFICATIONS:
- Certified hairstylist.
- Ability to work efficiently, thus reducing customer waiting time.
- Coordinated promotional events with local radio stations, including The First Annual Much Ado About Hair-Do's and Don'ts.
- Named "Most Promising Hairstylist" by the *Bismarck Gazette*.

PROFESSIONAL EXPERIENCE:

1988-Present **The Hair Studio, Mandan, ND**
Hairstylist
- Skilled in various hair cutting techniques such as texturizing.
- Working knowledge of permanents, body waves, and spiral perms.
- Use prepared dyes; also create colors as desired by clients.
- Perform waxing services.
- Style hair for local fashion shows: French braids, twists, floral weaves.
- Doubled base clientele within first two months.
- Answer phones and schedule appointments.

1984-1987 **Hair America, McKenzie, ND**
Hairstylist
- Performed duties as above.
- Independently sold hair care products.
- Manicured nails.

EDUCATION:

National Hair Academy, Bismarck, ND
Hair Styling Certification, 1984

INTERESTS:

Skiing, Scuba Diving, Mystery Novels.

REFERENCES:

Available Upon Request.

■ Summary of qualifications highlight candidate's skills and qualifications.

■ Interests give candidate's resume a personal touch.

HEALTH CLUB MANAGER

CHRIS SMITH
178 Green Street
Anchorage, AK 99502
(907) 555-5555

OBJECTIVE
To contribute developed skills to a Management/Supervisory position.

SUMMARY OF QUALIFICATIONS
- Strong interpersonal skills.
- Hardworking and goal-oriented.
- Self-motivated.

PROFESSIONAL DEVELOPMENT

MUSCLE MANIA, Anchorage, AK
Manager   1993-Present
- Initiate and execute sales/marketing and promotional efforts for corporate membership packages.
- Plan budget for facility operations, supplies, and equipment.
- Schedule and train personnel in sales and service.
- Actuate and implement programs and operations.

Program Director   1991-1993
- Designed comprehensive Health/Fitness Evaluation, incorporating components of strength, flexibility, cardiovascular/muscular endurance, and cardiac risk factors.
- Organized/instructed fitness classes for special interest groups (i.e. pre-post natal exercise, aerobics for learning-disabled children and exercise for the elderly).
- Developed and administered monthly seminars, workshops, and special interest groups to enhance public relations.

ACCOMPLISHMENTS
- National Wrestling Champion, 1990.
- Consultant for the U.S. Olympic Wrestling Team, 1992.
- Certified in CPR/First Aid.

EDUCATION

UNIVERSITY OF MAINE AT ORONO
B.S. in Physical Education, 1991
Major—Exercise Physiology.
Minor—Recreational Sports Management.
Activities: Wrestling (Team Captain), Weightlifting Trainer.

■ Unrelated work experience is omitted.

■ Highlighted accomplishments are related to candidate's field of interest.

HOTEL CLERK

CHRIS SMITH
178 Green Street
Halstead, KS 67056
(316) 555-5555

OBJECTIVE

To contribute developed customer relations and administrative skills to a challenging position in a hotel.

SUMMARY OF QUALIFICATIONS

- Developed interpersonal skills, having dealt with a diversity of clients, professionals, and staff members.
- Detail- and goal-oriented.
- Function well in high-stress atmosphere.
- Knowledgeable on both EECO and APTEC computers systems.

CAREER HISTORY

THE OLIVER HOTEL, Whitewater, KS   1992-Present
Hotel Clerk
Resolved guests' needs. Controlled reservation input utilizing EECO computer system. Handled incoming calls. Maintained daily reports involving return guests, corporate accounts, and suite rentals. Inspected rooms.

WALDEN HOTEL, Walton, KS   1988-1991
Hotel Clerk
Trained personnel. Handled telephone, international fax and telex bookings. Maintained daily and monthly reports tracking demands and guaranteed no-show billing. Utilized APTEC computer for inputting group bookings and lists.

READ ALL ABOUT IT, Newton, KS   1986-1987
Sales Associate
Assisted customers. Maintained stock. Opened/closed shop. Tracked best selling novels, and made recommendations to customers.

BETHEL COLLEGE, North Newton, KS   1983-1985
Secretary
Responsible for general clerical duties. Resolved inquiries. Assisted in locating guest speakers.

EDUCATION

BETHANY COLLEGE, Lindsborg, KS
Bachelor of Science: Sociology, 1983

REFERENCES

Furnished upon request.

- Candidate's customer relations and administrative skills, essential in the hotel/hospitality field, are emphasized throughout the resume.

- Education is de-emphasized because candidate's work history is strong.

HOTEL CONCIERGE

Chris Smith
178 Green Street
Milwaukee, WI 53233
(414) 555-5555

PROFESSIONAL EXPERIENCE
1990 to   JAMESON HOTEL, Milwaukee, WI
present   **Concierge**, 1992-present
- Promoted to establish Concierge Department in 350-room luxury hotel.
- Responsible for setting tone and image of hotel through providing guest services, including tourist information, tour arrangements, and hotel and airline reservations.
- Procure theater and symphony tickets.
- Arrange car rentals and limousine hires.
- Handle and route guest mail and faxes.
- Make restaurant recommendations and dinner reservations based on comprehensive knowledge and contact with area restaurants and management.
- Supervise/manage 40-person hotel staff including Concierge Department Assistants, Mail and Information Clerks, Bell Staff, Doormen, Valet Parking and Hotel Garage Staff, and Telephone Operators.
- Flexible schedule includes weekends and evenings.
- Extensive knowledge of all areas of hotel operation.
- Interact with other hotel departments to ensure full guest service.
- Diplomatically and effectively resolve guest grievances/problems; compose responses and make follow-up phone contact.
- During hotel's promotion, handled all guests from check-in to check-out; coordinated 2,500 museum tickets, consulting with guests on preferred times.
- Assist in hotel promotions and marketing strategies; coordinate all Bridal Package arrangements.
- Administer emergency life saving procedures as necessary; work well under pressure and in difficult situations.
- Ability to function in a variety of capacities within the hotel structure.

Bell Captain, 1991-1992
- Supervised all Bellman and Doormen.
- Acted in role of Concierge prior to establishment of Concierge Department.

Doorman/Bellman, 1990
- Greeted guests; fostered positive impression of establishment.

EDUCATION

Sorbonne University, Paris, France: Summer 1985
Marquette University, Milwaukee, WI: 1984-1986

ADDITIONAL

Working knowledge of French
Certified in CPR & First Aid

- Current position is detailed while previous positions are listed briefly.

- Additional qualifications supplement candidate's acquired professional experience.

HOTEL MANAGER (Front Desk)

CHRIS SMITH
178 Green Street
Phoenix, AZ 85021
(602) 555-5555

OBJECTIVE

A position in hotel management.

PROFESSIONAL EXPERIENCE

4/94-present **DESERT SANDS HOTEL,** Phoenix, AZ
Front Desk Manager
- Manage front desk operations for this 500 room Three Star Hotel.
- Interview, hire, and supervise a staff of 15.
- Book and coordinate local and national business conventions/seminars.
- Designed and implemented a guest survey to gauge satisfaction with the hotel, its staff, and services.

5/92-4/94 **LA MIRAGE HOTEL,** Phoenix, AZ
Front Desk Clerk
- Handled reservations, guest check in/out.
- Dealt with cash/credit card transactions for 250 rooms.
- Resolved guest complaints.

9/89-5/92 **GOTTA FLY TRAVEL,** Tucson, AZ
Travel Agent
- Assessed client needs.
- Handled plane reservations and hotel bookings.

COMPUTER SKILLS
- IBM (Logistics II and Series 1)
- SABRE Computer System

EDUCATION

UNIVERSITY OF ARIZONA, Tucson, AZ
Bachelor of Science in Business Administration, 1992

REFERENCES

Available on request.

- Job objective gives resume focus without limiting candidate's opportunities.

- Specific dates of employment (month and year) are ideal for candidates with no gaps in work history.

HOTEL MANAGER (Housekeeping)

Chris Smith
178 Green Street
Charleston, WV 25314
(304) 555-5555

OBJECTIVE
To contribute developed customer relations, managerial and accounting skills to a challenging position in hotel management.

SUMMARY
- Capable manager and motivator of staff.
- Function well in high-stress atmosphere.
- Detail- and goal-oriented.
- Highly developed interpersonal skills.
- Developed innovative and efficient system of reconciliation.
- Skilled in utilization of various computer systems.

EXPERIENCE
1990-Present   DONNELLY HOTEL, Charleston, WV
Assistant Manager, Housekeeping
- Manage 100 employees.
- Ensure standards of guest rooms.
- Prepare biweekly/monthly housekeeping inventory.
- Develop budget worksheets utilizing FileMaker.
- Assist in weekly labor forecasting and scheduling.
- Certified in Interaction Management.

1988-1990   NEWPORT HEIGHTS HOTEL, Montgomery, WV
Chief Night Auditor/Manager On Duty
- Managed technically proficient and hospitality-oriented staff.
- Supervised reconciliation of all Front Desk and Food and Beverage transactions.
- Maintained hotel computer system. Required weekly reorganizations and various other functions.
- Compiled and distributed Daily Business Summary, using Lotus 1-2-3.
- Administered overnight operations of Front Desk, Security, and Food and Beverage outlets.
- Nominated Manager of the Year, 1989.

1985-1987   **Night Auditor**
- Coordinated check-in/check-out of guests.
- Assisted in reconciliation of all transactions.
- Cooperated in implementation of Food and Beverage cashiering system.
- Developed and implemented efficient system to reconcile Food and Beverage transactions.
- Dealt with preparation of Daily Business Summary.

EDUCATION   WEST VIRGINIA STATE COLLEGE, Institute, WV
Course: Principles of Accounting I & II, 1985.

■ Summary grabs the reader's attention with powerful skills and qualifications.

■ Bulleted job descriptions are concise and begin with action verbs.

RESTAURANT MANAGER (Fast Food)

Chris Smith
178 Green Street
Colchester, VT 05446
(802) 555-5555

PROFESSIONAL OBJECTIVE
To obtain a challenging position in the field of Restaurant or Food Service Management.

PROFESSIONAL EXPERIENCE
1991 to Present BURGER CHEF, Colchester, VT
Manager
- Responsible for Shift Scheduling, Personnel Management, Inventory Control, maintenance of Physical Plant and Lockbox.
- Supervise up to twenty employees per shift.
- Responsible for all cash received per shift.
- Completed Management Training Program.

1988 to 1991 BLACK DIAMOND ICE CREAM CORPORATION, Mount Snow, VT
Shift Supervisor
- Controlled Shift Management, Personnel, Cash Deposits, Opening and Closing, Inventory Control and Management Reports.
- Promoted to manager from cook.

1986 to 1988 GRIMSHAW LOUNGE, South Burlington, VT
Manager
- Supervised staff of thirty employees per shift.
- Monitored food costs, filed reports.
- Planned weekly menu, made changes where necessary.

1985 to 1986 THE YEE HAH RESTAURANT, Brattleboro, VT
Manager
- Responsible for Night Shift Management, Special Function Catering, and Kitchen Personnel.
- Hired/trained staff, monitored payroll, supervised banquets.

EDUCATION
1983 to 1985 CHURCHILL CULINARY ARTS SCHOOL
- Completed two year course of study successfully.

1980 to 1983 UNITED STATES AIR FORCE
- Completed Class A & C Cooking School successfully.
- Honorably Discharged.

COMMUNITY ORGANIZATIONS
- Volunteer time and cooking skills at Snacks on Tracks and the Boys Club of Colchester.

- Resume emphasizes appropriate aspects of candidate's military training.

- Volunteer work and community service lend strength to this resume.

RESTAURANT MANAGER (Fine Dining)

Chris Smith
178 Green Street
Waterville, ME 04901
(207) 555-5555

PROFESSIONAL OBJECTIVE
A responsible and challenging position in Restaurant Management.

SUMMARY OF QUALIFICATIONS
- Design and implementation of management systems, administrative policies, and operational procedures.
- Qualified Butcher, Saucier, Baker, and Chef.
- Menu planning and experience with Italian, French, Oriental, Mexican, and Nouvelle American cuisine.
- Hiring/termination, supervising, scheduling, training, evaluating, and motivating professional and support staffs.
- Troubleshooting actual and potential problem areas, and implementing viable solutions that are both profitable and efficient.
- Purchasing food and supplies, and monitoring inventory.
- Knowledge of financial systems and procedures.
- Exceptional interpersonal, customer service, liaison, and follow-through skills.
- Presentation of a positive and professional image.

PROFESSIONAL BACKGROUND
1982-Present   THE TEMPEST, Waterville, ME
Manager/Chef
- Assisted in the start-up of 200 seat restaurant featuring 120 item menu containing Italian, French, Oriental, Mexican and Nouvelle American cuisine prepared from scratch.
- Standardized recipes, procedures, and systems including written test that all employees must pass.

1981-1982   NO FRILL COUNTRY COOKING, Orono, ME
Manager Trainee
- Learned all aspects of restaurant management for 250 seat establishment with $125,000 weekly volume.
- Stations included Saute, Fry, Salad, Baking, Hot/Cold Sauces, Portioning, Inventory, Ordering, Scheduling, and Supervision.

EDUCATION
Johnson and Wales, Providence, RI
B.A. Hotel and Restaurant Management, 1980

- Summary of qualifications highlight candidate's leadership and problem-solving skills.

- Figures, like seating capacity, weekly volume, and number of menu items, give a snapshot of candidate's working environment.

SANITATION INSPECTOR

Chris Smith
178 Green St.
Rockford. IL 61110
(815) 555-5555

OBJECTIVE: Seeking a challenging position in the Sanitation Field where experience and proven sanitation skills will have valuable application.

PROFILE: Registered sanitation inspector with over 20 years of experience. Proven effective in strict adherence to issues of public health and safety.

EXPERIENCE:

Colorado Board of Health, Denver, CO   1980-Present
Chief Sanitation Inspector
- Ensure all department regulations are adhered to in an orderly, strict and timely fashion; supervise staff of twelve.
- Conduct inspections in restaurants, retail food stores, bath/massage establishments, funeral parlors.
- Provide documentation to Board of Health; distribute warning and/or terminate existence of establishment fail inspections.

Chicago Health Department, Chicago, IL   1970-1980
Sanitation Inspector
- Participated in exams and regulatory inspections of restaurants, supermarkets, funeral parlors, commercial buildings and housing facilities in the greater Chicago area.
- Ensured all inspections were within regulations of the Illinois General Laws, State Sanitary Codes and Local Ordinances.

Chicago Health Department, Chicago, IL   Fall 1969
Internship-Inspectors' Offices
- Accompanied and assisted inspectors in their rounds of restaurants and fast food facilities, hospital kitchens, and bath houses.

EDUCATION:

University of Chicago 1970
B.S. Environmental Health and Sciences
Certification: Registered Sanitation Inspector, 1970

REFERENCES:

Available upon request.

■ Profile sums up candidate's professional qualifications.

■ Resume illustrates continual career progression.

WAIT PERSON

CHRIS SMITH
178 Green Street
Kaneohe, HI 96744
(808) 555-5555

EXPERIENCE

THE PALMS, Kaneohe, HI   5/94-Present
Head Waiter
- Managed, opened/closed high volume restaurant. Hired, terminated, trained, scheduled, and supervised wait staff.
- Reconciled cash intake.

PALUA SAILS RESTAURANT, Kaneohe, HI   5/92-5/94
Head Waiter
- Provided efficient service to full bar and serving area.
- Chosen Employee of the Month.

CANDLE IN THE WIND, Honolulu, HI   10/91-5/92
Barback
- Handled customer service and cash intake.
- Assisted with liquor inventory.

BLUE HAWAII RESTAURANT, Honolulu, HI   7/90-10/91
Busboy
- Organized large dining room.
- Trained new bus people.

ADDITIONAL TRAINING
- Certified in the SIPS Program for responsibly serving alcohol.
- Attended Restaurant Association training session: "Customer Satisfaction in the 90s."

EDUCATION

HAWAII LOA COLLEGE, Kaneohe, HI
Major: Liberal Arts
Degree Expected: 1996

INTERESTS

Photography, parasailing, surfing.

■ Additional training adds weight to resume.

■ Personal interests can provide a great topic for conversation during a job interview.

19
Social and Human Services

Nature of Work
Those professionals who work in social and human services attempt to improve the emotional well-being of individuals in need. Psychologists study human behavior and mental processes to understand, explain, and change people's behavior.

Urban and regional planners, often called community or city planners, develop programs to provide for growth and revitalization of urban, suburban, and rural communities and their regions. They help local officials make decisions on social, economic, and environmental problems.

"Human services workers" is a generic term for people with job titles such as social service technician, case management aide, community outreach worker, residential counselor, alcohol or drug abuse counselor, and gerontology aide. They work in group homes and halfway houses, correctional, mental retardation, and community mental health centers. They generally perform under the direction of social workers or in some cases psychologists, helping clients obtain benefits or services.

Employment
Most social and human services workers are employed by state and local governments, primarily in hospitals and outpatient mental health centers, facilities for the mentally retarded and developmentally disabled, and public welfare agencies. They also hold jobs in clinics, community mental health centers, and private psychiatric hospitals.

Training
Educational requirements for social and human service professionals vary within fields. For urban planners, a Ph.D. or equivalent degree is a minimum requirement for most positions in colleges and universities and is important for advancement to many top-level non-academic research and administrative posts.

A doctoral degree is generally required for employment as a psychologist, those with doctorates qualify for a wide range of responsible research, clinical and counseling positions in universities, private industry, school settings, and government.

Job Outlook
Employment of social and human service workers is expected to grow much faster than the average for all occupations through the year 2005, largely because there will be more

demand for programs to combat the increase in alcohol abuse, drug dependency, marital strife, and family violence.

Earnings

Earnings vary among social and human service professionals. The median annual salary of psychologists with a doctoral degree is about $55,000. The middle 50% of urban planners earn between $22,000 and $52,000 annually. Social workers employed by the Federal Government averaged $38,200 in 1991. According to limited data, social workers in all types of settings generally earned between $23,000 and $36,000 in 1990.

CASE MANAGER

Chris Smith
178 Green Street
Golden, CO 80401
(303) 555-5555

PROFESSIONAL EXPERIENCE

1988-Present DYLAN HIGH SCHOOL, Golden, CO
<u>Case Manager</u>
- Work closely with at-risk students
- Coordinate outreach and referral services
- Maintain records/statistics
- Supervise staff
- Assist community-based agencies and educational institutions in all activities involved with students

1985-1987 LIVINGSTON SCHOOL, Golden, CO
<u>School/Family Counselor</u>
- Conducted intake and admissions
- Coordinated parent-teacher conferences
- Advocated community outreach with outside agencies
- Participated in staff training and development
- Maintained records, documentation, and monthly reports

1984-1985 DEPARTMENT OF PUBLIC WORKS, Denver, CO
<u>Placement Specialist</u>
- Coordinated placement services for discharge planners, community and families
- Maintained up-to-date list of services available for difficult-to-place clients
- Conducted in-service training
- Counseled families in crisis
- Compiled and updated all records and weekly statistics reports

1979-1984 FAMILY SERVICES OF DENVER, Denver, CO
<u>Social Worker</u>
- Worked directly with Housing Authority
- Coordinated services for clients/families at risk
- Conducted family life education groups
- Supervised agency volunteers and students
- Worked collaboratively with various community agencies

EDUCATION

1983 **Colorado State University**, Fort Collins, CO
Major: Social Work
Licensed Social Worker

1989 **Colorado Community College**, Denver, CO
Major: Sociology

■ Resume stresses broad range of experience.

■ Clean layout makes resume easy to read.

CASE WORKER/LEGAL ADVOCATE

Chris Smith
178 Green Street
East Troy, WI
(414) 555-5555

PROFESSIONAL EXPERIENCE

1993-
Present **Case Worker/Legal Advocate, The Women's Safe Place** East Troy, WI
Night manager at shelter for abused women and their children. Monitor 24-hour hot line and authorize admitting residents on an emergency basis. Organize, prepare, and present seminars to high school students on domestic violence and lead discussions to raise awareness. Assist Associate Director in planning public relations and fundraising events. Assist women in completing Temporary Restraining Orders. Provide support and access to legal resources to women in crisis situations. Advocate for women before judges in family court proceedings. Act as Coalition observer during domestic violence legal cases and report outcomes to staff.

1991-1993 **Associate Editor/Program Coordinator**
Baby's Breath Press Madison, WI
Developed, wrote and edited articles for monthly business management newsletter. Writing involved combining multiple sources of information and organizing pertinent facts for a business-oriented audience. Developed and wrote articles with outside authors involving case studies on management development within their organizations. Assisted editorial department in planning content of newsletter by selecting topics for publication. All work performed in a strict deadline-oriented environment. Worked with the 50 people who presented at the annual conference by assisting them with their presentations.

1990-1993 **Writer, *The Republic*** Madison, WI
Researched a variety of sources incorporating various philosophies and wrote articles on women's issues for a Quarterly Literary Magazine in Madison.

EDUCATION

1991 Beloit College Beloit, WI
Bachelor of Arts in Sociology. Concentration in Economic Stratification and Social Hierarchies. Courses include Poverty and Crisis, Gerontology, and Women in Society. Independent study topic: "The Feminization of Poverty in the United States." Member of The Phi Beta Kappa honor society. Member of student-run Volunteers for a Better World program. Co-directed campus food drive. Contributing writer for *The Vanguard Press*.

■ Including detailed information about education can be advantageous for candidates with less than five years professional experience.

■ Use of boldface calls attention to key information.

COUNSELOR (Career Changer)

Chris Smith
178 Green Street
Washington, DC 20008
(202) 555-5555

OBJECTIVE

A challenging and progressively responsible position in COUNSELING.

ECUATION

American University, Washington, DC
Bachelor of Science in Psychology and Sociology, 1980

Course work included the following:
Drugs and Society
Sociology of Medicine
Speech Pathology

Death and Mourning
Psychology of Women
Experimental Psychology

STRENGTHS

Fluent German; mature, sound decision-making skills; ability to establish trusting relationships with individuals; accurately keep records; positively relate with people from diverse backgrounds; strong communication skills; enthusiastic and positive; genuine desire to be of service to people.

EMPLOYMENT HIGHLIGHTS

American University, Washington, DC
Recorder Coordinator Create, maintain and update academic records. Assess student charges. Instruct and assist students in registration procedures. Act as liaison with academic and administrative offices. Supervise activities of part time personnel.
(1981- Present)

Natak & Company, Washington, DC
Assistant Controller/Full Charge Bookkeeper Directed activities of all bookkeeping personnel, including training and orienting. Prepared quarterly reports and financial statements.
(1971-1979)

REFERENCES

Furnished upon request.

- List of course work demonstrates candidate's specialized knowledge in his/her field of interest.

- Candidate's abilities are highlighted under "strengths" heading.

COUNSELOR (Mental Health)

Chris Smith
178 Green Street
Atlanta, GA 30314
(404) 555-5555

OBJECTIVE

To contribute relevant experience and educational background to a challenging Counseling position, offering ample skill utilization and growth opportunities.

SUMMARY OF QUALIFICATIONS

- Experienced in the development of treatment plans for various populations within social service arenas, to constitute initial evaluation and assessment of clientele; coordination of special service networks; collaboration with health service professionals for the establishment of procedural guidelines; placement of individuals and advocacy in trial proceedings.
- Completed training with the Department of Social Services.
- Proficient in recruitment of prospective parents for adoption purposes, execution of home studies, assignment of children and application of follow-up processes.
- Knowledgeable in formulation and composition of various legislative documents and provision of programming and curriculum recommendations; complemented by exceptional administrative, communication and organizational skills.

EXPERIENCE

1990 to Present   **Residential Counselor**
MENTAL HEALTH SERVICES OF ATLANTA   Atlanta, GA

- Collaborate with health service professionals for development of treatment plans for emotionally disturbed adolescents.
- Assist clients in formulating survival skills to aid in transition from residential to independent living situations.
- Coordinate service networks for academic, psychological and social assistance.

1989 to 1990   **Agency Recruitment Specialist**
TYLER ADOPTION AGENCY   Atlanta, GA

- Travelled to various community sites and executed presentations for the recruitment of prospective parents for minority children.
- Conducted home studies of prospective parents to determine eligibility for program.
- Placed children with families and followed up for situation evaluation.

1988 to 1989   **Social Worker**
DEPARTMENT OF SOCIAL SERVICES   Atlanta, GA

- Assessed client need, developed treatment plans and managed cases.
- Communicated with court officials for the handling of cases.
- Served as child advocate for court proceedings and provided inclusive testimonies.
- Placed children in foster homes and coordinated specialized services.

(continued)

- Broad work experience shows candidate's adaptability to various environments.

- Summary of qualifications high-lights candidate's achievements.

<u>**EXPERIENCE**</u> (continued)

Summer 1988   **Legislative Assistant**
ATLANTA CITY HALL - INTERNSHIP   Atlanta, GA
- Assisted in the generation and composition of protective custody bills and policies.
- Conducted legislative research and resolved constituent concerns.
- Executed survey, incorporating budget and non-budget public response data.

1987 to 1988   **Director/Head Teacher**
DEPARTMENT OF HUMAN SERVICES   Atlanta, GA
- Supervised first and second grade classes/staff, developed and implemented sound curriculum.
- Led staff meetings and provided curriculum recommendations for teaching staff.
- Coordinated administrative operations for after-school program and served as liaison between department and teaching staff.

1986 to 1987   **Tutor**
TUTORING PLUS   Athens, GA
- Provided individualized academic instruction for school-aged children.
- Devised and instituted activities for youth program and generated participants.

<u>**EDUCATION**</u>

EMORY UNIVERSITY, 1989   Atlanta, GA
Master's Degree, Social Work

UNIVERSITY OF GEORGIA/ATHENS, 1987   Athens, GA
Bachelor of Arts Degree: Sociology - Minor: Criminal Justice
Graduated Cum Laude
Member - Sociology Honor Society, 1987
Member - Criminal Justice Honor Society, 1987

<u>**PERSONAL**</u>

Willing to relocate.

COUNSELOR (School)

Chris Smith
178 Green Street
Fort Lauderdale, FL 38314
(305) 555-1212

PROFESSIONAL OBJECTIVE

A counseling position in which my education and bicultural experience will have valuable application.

PROFESSIONAL EXPERIENCE

1984 to
Present
AMERICAN SCHOOL OF RECIFE, Recife, Brazil
Counselor, International Primary School
- Administer psychological and educational testing for students ranging from pre-kindergarten to fifth grade
- Counsel students, families, and teachers
- Design remedial and therapeutic plans
- Lead group activities for self-image enhancement and behavior modification
- Work with teachers in preventive strategies for social and disciplinary problems

1983 to
1985
INSTITUTE OF AMERICA, Sao Paulo, Brazil
Guidance Counselor
- Counsel individuals and families for students ranging from pre-kindergarten to twelfth grade
- Designed complete record-keeping system for all students
- Performed value clarification exercises with students
- Implemented behavior modification programs
- Administered achievement, vocational, and college-prep tests
- Made policy on admissions and discipline
- Worked with teachers on individual educational programs

1983 to
Present
PRIVATE COUNSELING PRACTICES, Miami, Recife, and Sao Paulo
Counselor
- Bilingual English and Spanish counseling

EDUCATION

Master of Arts in Counseling Psychology, Nova University
Fort Lauderdale, Florida, 1983
Concentration: Community Clinical; GPA: 3.7
Bachelor of Arts in Developmental Psychology, Barry University
Miami Shores, Florida, 1981
Associate of Arts in Human Development, Barry University
Miami Shores, Florida, 1980
Cum Laude Graduate

References available upon request

- Resume highlights bicultural and bilingual experience.

- Strong educational credentials strengthen resume.

ECONOMIC DEVELOPMENT COORDINATOR

CHRIS SMITH
178 Green Street
Cambridge, MA 02139
(617) 555-5555

PROFESSIONAL OBJECTIVE

To secure a challenging position overseas in **Economic Development** for a non-governmental organization.

SUMMARY OF QUALIFICATIONS

- Several years experience working overseas in developing countries.
- Fluent in Spanish; Foreign Service Level 4.
- Proficient in Japanese; Foreign Service Level 2.
- Empirical Analysis: Hypothesis Testing, Regression Analysis, Accounting and Budgeting.
- Micro and Macro Economic Analysis.

OVERSEAS EXPERIENCE

WORLD FRIENDS, U.S.A./Ethiopia   1992-Present
Economic Development Coordinator
Implemented a rural, small scale enterprise and credit program. Planned and ran workshops for village councils and entrepreneurs in credit management and accounting. Assisted entrepreneurs with feasibility analysis and loan applications. Did research for senior thesis on rural, small scale enterprise and credit, which was subsequently sent to S.C.F. in Ethiopia.

INDEPENDENT TEACHER, Bombay, India   1989-92
English Teacher
Taught English conversation and grammar to students, ages seven through adult, both privately and in classroom.

WORLD FRIENDS, U.S.A./Japan   1985-89
Proposal Writer
Researched and wrote a position case study on landlessness in one district of Japan. Contributed to the development of a new small scale enterprise project.

HELPING HANDS, Ashau Valley, Vietnam   1982-85
Health Projects Coordinator
Worked on health-related issues including community mobilization for latrine construction and education for strategies to combat water-borne diseases.

EDUCATION

School of Government, Harvard University, Cambridge, MA
Masters Degree in Public Policy; concentration in International Development, 1982.

College of Arts and Sciences, Harvard University, Cambridge, MA
Bachelor of Arts in International Development.
Graduated Summa Cum Laude, with distinction, 1979.

- Job objective is clearly defined.

- Resume emphasizes candidate's international experience and impressive foreign language skills.

HUMAN SERVICES WORKER (General)

CHRIS SMITH
178 Green Street
Columbus, IN 47201
(812) 555-5555

WORK EXPERIENCE

1987 to **Human Service Relief Worker: Temporary Resources, Columbus, IN**
Present Work as a temporary substitute in a variety of human service programs including specializing clients in hospital, direct care of developmentally delayed clients, counseling and supervising adolescents in group homes and substitute teaching at institutions such as the Stafford School for the Deaf.

1984 to **Residential Manager: Allied Group Homes, Columbus, IN**
1986 Worked in several residential programs for all levels of developmentally delayed clients. Taught skills in daily living, cooking, hygiene, and community awareness. Provided emotional support to clients. Interacted with clients' families. Implemented behavioral programs.

1982 to **Residential Counselor: Harrison House, Mooresville, IN**
1983 Staffed community residence for five developmentally delayed clients. Implemented behavioral programs. Taught activities of daily living skills directed toward independent living and community integration.

1981 to **Nurse's Aide: Center Street Nursing Home, Franklin, IN**
1982

1980 **Mental Health Assistant: Bethany School, Bethany, IN**

1979 **Employment Counselor: Jobs Plus, Franklin, IN**
Interviewed and counseled clients for the purpose of placement in jobs or training programs. Made referrals for employment or training programs.

1978 **Social Worker: State of Indiana—Division of Child Welfare**

1972 to **Social Worker: State of Indiana**
1977

EDUCATION

1975 to Franklin College
Present Graduate-level courses in psychology, education, and counseling

1971 Bachelor of Arts in Social Sciences

- Job descriptions are clear and to the point.

- Use of bold type calls attention to key information.

HUMAN SERVICES WORKER (Juvenile and Family)

Chris Smith
178 Green Street
Elmhurst, IL 60126
(312) 555-5555

OBJECTIVE

To contribute comprehensive experience and educational background to a challenging position as a Human Services Worker.

SUMMARY OF QUALIFICATIONS

- Thorough knowledge management of cases for juveniles and families, which required assessment, development of clinical treatment plans, facilitation of crisis intervention procedures and informal family therapy.
- Developed exceptional counseling skills, motivating several individuals to enter programs for substance abuse treatment.
- Extensive experience and familiarity with child abuse/neglect cases.
- Excellent rapport with children; superior communication abilities.

EXPERIENCE

1988 to Present   **Investigator/Ongoing Case Manager**
SOCIETY FOR THE PREVENTION OF CRUELTY TO CHILDREN   Chicago, IL
- Conduct assessments and develop treatment plans for family caseload.
- Maintain ongoing written documentation of contracts.
- Provide crisis intervention and informal family therapy.
- Serve as advocate for clients in court and with community agencies.

1986 to 1987   **Intern**
FARMINGTON JUVENILE COURT   Farmington, IL
- Established monitor contacts and composed monitor reports.
- Tracked abuse/neglect cases to ensure that status reports and petitions were filed accurately and on time.
- Observed court hearings and trials and established court expectations.

1985 to 1986   **Intern**
PEORIA JUVENILE COURT   Peoria, IL
- Provided individual and group counseling for juvenile offenders in detention.
- Reviewed case files and incident reports.

1984   **Intern**
DEPARTMENT OF MENTAL HEALTH   Gardena, IL
- Assisted retarded adults in the enhancement of motor skills and encouraged the development of self esteem and self sufficiency.

EDUCATION

BRADLEY UNIVERSITY   Peoria, IL
Bachelor of Science Degree: Human Services, 1987

REFERENCES FURNISHED UPON REQUEST

- Bullets make resume easy to read.
- Summary of qualifications highlight candidate's skills.

PROGRAM COORDINATOR

Chris Smith
178 Green Street
Alexandria, VA 22311
(703) 555-5555

OBJECTIVE
The coordination of production for advertising and promotion, mass communication, or related areas.

SUMMARY OF QUALIFICATIONS
- Bachelor of Arts Degree in Political Science
- Coordination of all production activities associated with fund raising through mass mailing programs
- Grant proposal preparation
- Fund raising and staff training
- Computerized list maintenance

PROGRAM COORDINATOR **1990-Present**
Watercrest Developers, Alexandria, VA
Responsibilities with this fundraising arm of Watercrest Developers includes:
- Provide direct assistance to the Director of Fundraising Programs; emphasis on direct mail aspect of the Annual Giving Program.
- Coordinate planning, copywriting, production and analysis of program results as well as procedural detail and in-house consultant reports.
- Streamlined procedures for mailings of 80,000 pieces and saved 40% in printing costs through vendor survey and negotiation.
- Conduct market research, copy editing and consulting supervision of telemarketing activities and other functions required in the smooth enactment of 16 annual mailings totaling approximately 300,000 pieces while managing a $600,000 budget. Overall results, 1993, $3.1 million.

FUND RAISER/SUPERVISOR **1988-90**
Nathan Hawke Associates, Manassas, VA
- Director of fund raising team responsible for initiating and developing contacts with political contributors for conservative parties and organizations.
- Interviewed, trained and supervised staff of 20, while managing coordination of work flow.
- Assisted with preparation of promotional letters for campaign fund solicitations.

DEVELOPMENT/ADMINISTRATIVE ASSISTANT **1987-88**
Appleton Art Abode, Appleton, WI
- Assisted in preparation of grant proposals; prepared and reviewed proposals for events at Art Center, while organizing and providing production support for publication of the Appleton News.

EDUCATION
Lawrence University, Appleton, WI
Bachelor of Arts Degree, 1986
Major: Political Science

■ Statistics and dollar figures quantify candidate's accomplishments.

■ Candidate's most relevant work experience is prioritized throughout resume.

PROGRAM DIRECTOR

Chris Smith
178 Green Street
Treynor, IA 51575
(912) 555-5555

OBJECTIVE
A position as Director of a Social Services organization.

PROFESSIONAL EXPERIENCE

1983 to Present — ROUMAN MEMORIAL HOSPITAL, Council Bluffs, IA
Program Director, Psychotherapy Ward, 1988 to present
- Manage all aspects of residential treatment facility for mentally ill adolescents
- Prepare and manage $500,000 annual budget
- Supervise clinical and clerical staff of twenty; hire/fire, schedule, motivate, and guide professional development
- Oversee physical plant; ensure compliance with licensing standards, contact and direct vendors, order supplies, etc.
- Reorganized administrative structure; develop policies and procedures; wrote new policy manual
- Act as liaison to Department of Mental Health, juvenile and adult courts, and all outside service providers
- Coordinate outside consulting work
- Supervise and approve intakes/referrals
- Coordinate monthly treatment team meetings

Assistant Program Director, 1985 to 1987
- Performed various administrative duties as above under direction of Program Director

Clinical Supervisor, 1983 to 1984
- Supervised clinical staff
- Planned and directed activities
- Served as milieu therapist

1980 to 1982 — KING HILL REHABILITATION CENTER, Sioux City, IA
Staff Supervisor/Rehabilitation Counselor
- Supervised counseling staff of fifteen
- Coordinated programming and supervised clinical practices
- Coordinated and led group therapy sessions
- Served on administrative teams to develop long-term treatment plans, agency cooperation, personnel and program policies

EDUCATION

Morningside College, Sioux City, IA
Bachelor of Arts in Sociology, December, 1979
Cum Laude

- Resume indicates promotions within one organization.

- Objective is clearly defined.

PSYCHIATRIC COUNSELOR

Chris Smith
178 Green Street
Otter Creek, FL 32683
(904) 555-5555

EXPERIENCE

1990 to Present   **CAUFIELD PSYCHIATRIC HOSPITAL, Usher, FL**
Psychiatric Counselor
Responsible for crisis intervention for both adult and adolescent clients, psychiatric assessments and evaluations, patient admission to specific unit. Observe suicidal patients on a one-to-one basis and use physical restraint when necessary. Manage and stabilize unit teams in resolving problems. Submit reports.

1987 to 1989   **CROSS CITY HOSPITAL, Psychiatric Unit, Cross City, FL**
Psychiatric Counselor
Handled psychiatric assessments, evaluations and attendant reports. Conducted adult and geriatric counseling as well as group community meetings. Taught daily living skills. Prepared treatment plans. Monitored vital signs. Dealt with crisis intervention and assessment of suicidality. Acted as in-service educator.

1984 to 1986   **PRIMECARE, Jasper, FL**
Counselor
Responsible for unit management, primary care, cooking, feeding residents, nursing care and crisis intervention. Taught daily living skills to facilitate independence.

1982 to 1983   **VERNON HOUSE, Monticello, FL**
Psychiatric Counselor
Taught patient independence at halfway house. Provided crisis intervention, house management, case management and case presentation in addition to cooking, feeding and assisting with cleaning.

1980 to 1981   **FLORIDA STATE HOSPITAL, Ponce de Leon, FL**
Counselor
Supervised activities and recreation for twelve boys. Submitted reports. Acted as liaison between center and District Court.

1975 to 1979   **PANAMA CITY HOSPITAL, Panama City, FL**
Psychiatric Counselor
Handled psychiatric admissions and case presentations. conducted community meetings. Provided in-service education for counselors and nurses.

1973 to 1974   **WEST FLORIDA REHABILITATION CENTER, Pensacola, FL**
Psychiatric Counselor
Provided individual, group and family counseling, case management and presentations. Conducted film presentations and discussion groups.

EDUCATION

UNIVERSITY OF WEST FLORIDA, Pensacola, FL
Bachelor of Science in Developmental Psychology, 1973

■ Resume illustrates continual career progression.

■ Emphasis is placed on most recent positions.

PSYCHOLOGIST

Chris Smith
178 Green Street
Ames, IA 50011
(515) 555-5555

PROFESSIONAL BACKGROUND
1987-1993   INSTITUTE OF HUMAN RESOURCES, Des Moines, IA
Psychologist
- Coordinated admissions, procuring and assessing information from referral requests to determine appropriateness of psychiatric admissions
- Interviewed patients for admission, which included history, social and familial associations, medical condition, evaluation of mental status, and familiarizing patient with hospital structure
- Consulted with staff on therapeutic intervention
- Performed routine monitoring of patients on unit
- Assessed crisis situations and collaborated on suitable staff intervention
- Initiated one-on-one meetings with suicidal and violent patients
- Documented patient care and progress

1984-1987   DES MOINES COUNSELING SERVICES, Des Moines, IA
Psychotherapist
- Conducted individual psychotherapy sessions with clients, who included community residents and out-patients
- Consulted with co-therapists in private group practice

1980-1984   KNOXVILLE PSYCHIATRIC HOSPITAL, Knoxville, IA
Mental Health Worker
- Supervised floor of 15 patients, aged 13 and up; performed intake, counseling, limit setting, general observation, progress charting; and assisted with physical needs
- Rendered support and guidance to patients undergoing drug and alcohol detoxification
- Provided crisis intervention and maintenance services for patients on unit
- Acquired knowledge of medications and ability to read medical charts
- Served as liaison between nursing staff and patients

EDUCATIONAL BACKGROUND
IOWA STATE UNIVERSITY, Ames, IA
Master of Arts Degree in Counseling Psychology, 1984

CENTRAL UNIVERSITY OF IOWA, Delta, IA
Bachelor of Science Degree in Psychology, 1980
Graduated Cum Laude

MOUNT VERNON COMMUNITY COLLEGE, Mount Vernon, IA
Associate of Arts Degree in Medical Laboratory Technology, 1975

■ Extensive educational background further strengthens resume.

■ Resume demonstrates continual increase in job responsibilities.

SOCIAL WORKER (Juvenile)

Chris Smith
178 Green Street
Chalmette, LA 70043
(504) 555-5555

EDUCATION

TULANE UNIVERSITY — New Orleans, LA
Master's in Social Work — May, 1987

LOYOLA UNIVERSITY — New Orleans, LA
Bachelor of Arts, Psychology — May, 1985
Research assistant to Dr. Sophie Dillon. Project involved studying intrinsic and extrinsic motivation in children.
Dean's List.

PROFESSIONAL EXPERIENCE

CHALMETTE CHILDREN'S HOSPITAL,
Early Intervention Program — Chalmette, LA
Social Worker/Case Manager — August 1987-Present
Member of interdisciplinary team servicing children who are at environmental and/or biological risk. Responsibilities include: clinical, concrete and supportive services, education for families, and developmental stimulation for children. Services provided via home visits and participation in classroom team for children.

NEW ORLEANS TEEN CLINIC — New Orleans, LA
Intern — September 1987-May 1987
Provided individual social work to children and adolescents, including pregnant teens and foster parents. Cooperated with Department of Social Services regarding treatment and placement of children in foster care.

VETERAN'S ADMINISTRATION HOSPITAL OF NEW ORLEANS — New Orleans, LA
Intern — September 1985-May 1986
Medical and psychiatric social work involving direct patient care with both individuals and groups at outpatient clinic. Cooperative experience with nationally recognized pain team at New Orleans Outpatient Clinic.

PROFESSIONAL INTERESTS

Adolescent Behavior, Gifted Children, Neuropsychology

REFERENCES

Available upon request.

- Layout is clean and well-organized.

- Dynamic action verbs give resume impact.

SOCIAL WORKER (School)

Chris Smith
178 Green Street
Baltimore, MD 21218
(301) 555-5555

PROFESSIONAL EXPERIENCE
1985 to 1994   DEPARTMENT OF DEPENDENT SCHOOLS
Vienna, Austria
Clinical Social Worker, Vienna Center for Education
Provided direct social work services to elementary and high school students and their families. Member of on-call child psychiatry emergency team. Conducted parent education groups. Supervised interns and trained school personnel.

1980 to 1984   **Clinical Social Worker,** American School of Vienna
Provided outreach clinical services to American elementary schools in addition to responsibilities similar to those described above.

FIELD TRAINING
1980 to 1981   ANDREW T. FERRIS CHILDREN'S CLINIC, Baltimore, MD
Second Year Field Placement
Primary duties included diagnostic evaluation and treatment of children, adolescents, adults and families, and investigation of Care and Protection Petitions within multidisciplinary team.

Summer   BALTIMORE COMMUNITY CENTER, Baltimore, MD
1980   **Intern**
Responsibilities included: intake, evaluation and treatment of individuals, couples and families in a medical and social service setting.

1979 to 1980   BALTIMORE JUVENILE COURT CLINIC, Baltimore, MD
First Year Field Placement
Responsibilities included: diagnostic evaluation and treatment of children, adolescents, adults and families. Participated in multidisciplinary evaluations.

EDUCATION
JOHNS HOPKINS UNIVERSITY, Baltimore, MD
Master of Social Work, 1979

COLBY COLLEGE, Waterville, ME
Bachelor of Psychology/Sociology, Cum Laude, 1975

AFFILIATIONS
• Academy of Certified Social Worker
• International Association of Social Workers

References available upon request

■ Job-related affiliations demonstrate candidate's active participation in field.

■ Candidate's international work experience adds to qualifications.

THERAPIST

Chris Smith
178 Green Street
Houma, LA 70363
(504) 555-5555

EXPERIENCE

THERAPIST 1991-Present
Private Practice Houma, LA
Render quality counseling services to private clientele with varied psychological disorders. Develop rapport and relationships of trust; facilitate clear communication. Assess symptoms and personal information to diagnose problems and devise effective treatment strategies.
- Assess client progress and effectiveness of treatment plans
- Involve guardians and family members in supporting therapeutic activities.
- Make referrals to specialists or social service organizations as appropriate.
- Maintain knowledge of new developments in the field and applications to personal practice.

COORDINATOR OF PROGRAM SERVICES
COUNSELOR/ADVOCATE 1988-1991
Domestic Violence Services, Inc. Orono, ME
Provided leadership and management expertise for efficient daily operations of this non-profit organization specializing in counseling and services for victims of domestic violence. Assessed needs and coordinated delivery of information, referrals, advocacy, and counseling.
- Responded appropriately to hot line calls and emergency situations.
- Provided one-on-one counseling to battered women and children.
- Conducted play groups for children living in the shelter as volunteer in 1988.
- Served as Intern Advocate for victims before the Orono Superior court.

EDUCATION

MASTER OF ARTS IN PSYCHOLOGY, 1991
Teacher's college, University of Maine, Orono, ME
Masters Thesis: Impact of Classroom Learning on Students' Behavior

BACHELOR OF ARTS IN PSYCHOLOGY, 1988
Colby College, Waterville, ME

Additional courses, workshops, and seminars:
Identification and Treatment of Trauma and Abuse ● Rational Emotive Therapy
CareerPro Leadership Seminar ● Group Facilitation ● Cultural Diversity
AIDS ● Drugs and Alcohol Abuse ● Supervision and Management Training
Family Therapy ● Battered Woman Syndrome ● Women Portrayed in Media

---

■ Bullets call attention to candidate's most significant qualifications.

■ Strong educational background is emphasized.

URBAN PLANNER

Chris Smith
178 Green Street
Lansing, MI 48906
(517) 555-5555

PROFESSIONAL EXPERIENCE

DIRECTOR, OFFICE OF ECONOMIC DEVELOPMENT

1984-Present Community Development Group. Manage $5 million budget. Supervise staff of ten. Develop policy and direction for grant programs. Evaluate activities of non-profit organizations statewide. Initiate new programs in response to identified constituency's needs, and oversee proposal review, grant monitoring and training and technical assistance. Serve as liaison with public and private agencies supporting non-profit community-based organizations.

SPECIAL ASSISTANT TO THE DIRECTOR

1982-83 Community Development Group. Oversaw foundation fundraising, public relations and information referral. Assisted in project development, implementation and administration. Organized training programs for Board and staff.

TECHNICAL ASSISTANCE COORDINATOR

1980-81 Community Development Group. Provided all training and technical assistance as required by agency's contract with Office of Neighborhood Development. Planned and presented seminars for local organizations. Coordinated technical assistance for various community agencies outside Michigan including project areas such as housing development, housing management, commercial development and industrial retention and expansion.

1980 **GOVERNOR'S TASK FORCE ON ECONOMIC DEVELOPMENT OF WOMEN**
Member of Task Force to make recommendations to Governor concerning assistance to female small-business owners.

EDUCATION

MASTERS IN CITY AND REGIONAL PLANNING
Michigan State University, East Lansing, MI, 1980

BACHELOR OF ARTS
Albion College, Albion, MI, 1976
Major: Geography
Honors: Cum Laude

- Chronological format emphasizes clear career path.

- Job descriptions stress candidate's accomplishments, instead of simply listing job responsibilities.

20
Students

Whether you're graduating from high school or college, those of you with little or no work history face the same dilemma: it's tough to get a job without experience and it seems to be impossible to gain experience without getting hired. But, as you will see, there are ways to get around this by emphasizing your strengths and educational achievements.

Which Type of Resume Is Right For You?

The type of resume you should use really depends on your job experience. If you don't have any work history, you should use a functional resume format, emphasizing your strong points, such as:

- Education. This should be your primary focus.
- Special achievements. This could be almost anything from having an article published to graduating with honors.
- Awards and competitive scholarships.
- Classes, internships, theses, or special projects that relate to your job objective.
- Computer knowledge. Are you familiar with a Mac or PC? What software programs do you know?
- Language skills. Are you fluent in a foreign language? Be sure to indicate both written and verbal skills.
- Volunteer work.
- Committees and organizations.
- Extracurricular activities.

If you have some work experience, such as a part-time job as the editor of your school paper or waiting tables, you should use the chrono-functional resume format. Recruiters like to see some kind of work history, even if it doesn't relate to your job objective, because it demonstrates that you have a good work ethic. However, it's also important to emphasize any special skills or qualifications you have, including the above information.

Resume Tips and Pointers

Your resume should fit onto one page and everything should be easy to find. Use bullets to highlight your most important skills, qualifications, and achievements. You should try to avoid paragraphs longer than six lines; if necessary, rewrite the material into two or more paragraphs.

It's a good idea to use a brief, general job objective. This will give your resume focus while keeping all your opportunities open. A good job objective would be "A career in public relations" or "An entry-level position within an operations management environment."

Unless you have more than two years of full-time work experience, you should emphasize your education most. You can accomplish this by listing your education at the top of your resume and by elaborating on special classes you took, achievements you made, and awards you received. If you have already graduated, you should begin "Awarded the degree of. . ." If you are still working on your degree, you should begin with the phrase "Candidate for the degree of . . ." If you did not graduate and are not currently pursuing your degree, you should simply list the dates you attended and the courses studied. For example, "Studied mathematics, physics, chemistry, and statistics."

Never include a grade point average (GPA) under 3.0 on your resume. If your GPA in your major field of study is higher than your overall GPA, include it either in addition to or instead of your overall GPA.

Including high school information is optional for college grads. If you have made exceptional achievements in college and in your summer or part-time jobs, you should omit your high school information. If you decide to include your high school achievements, describe them more briefly than your college achievements.

When describing your work history, you should avoid simply listing your job duties. Focus on accomplishments and achievements, even if they are small. Consider the difference:

> *Weak:* "Lifeguard at busy public beach. Responsible for safety of bathers and cleanliness of the beach and parking areas."

> *Strong:* "Lifeguard at busy public beach. Established recycling program for bottles and cans."

If you have held many different jobs, you may choose to emphasize only two or three and list the rest under the heading "Other Experience" without individual job descriptions. For example:

Other Experience:

Floor and stockroom clerk at university bookstore, server, lifeguard, and courier.

Bear in mind that your resume is an advertisement for yourself, not an affidavit. Do not feel compelled to list every job you've ever had. Instead, focus on the positions you've had that relate to your current objective or that speak most positively of your experience.

Although you will want to present yourself in the best possible light, always be truthful on your resume. More and more companies are checking resumes these days and false information is often considered grounds for dismissal, even years after you are hired.

And don't forget to proofread for spelling errors and accuracy!

COLLEGE STUDENT APPLYING FOR AN INTERNSHIP

Chris Smith

School Address:
178 Green Street
Skidell, LA 70458
(504) 555-5555

Permanent Address:
23 Blue Street
New Orleans, LA 70128
(504) 555-5555

OBJECTIVE
A summer internship in the book publishing industry.

SYNOPSIS
Self-starter and fast learner with positive attitude regarding goal direction.
Excellent communicator with the ability to project and elicit interest and enthusiasm using a common sense approach. Adept at analyzing and sizing up situations; diligent, hard worker and strong on follow-up. Enjoy developing and implementing new ideas, techniques, and the creative process as a whole.

SUMMARY OF QUALIFICATIONS
- Well-traveled.
- Public speaking.
- Copyediting/proofreading.
- Intermediate-level French.
- American Sign Language.
- Prolific writer; voracious reader.
- Computer skills: Microsoft Word.

EDUCATION
TULANE UNIVERSITY, New Orleans, LA. **Bachelor of Arts in English and American Literature** with a concentration in film. Degree to be awarded May 1996.
Dean's List; GPA in major: B+.

UNIVERSITY OF MANITOBA, Winnipeg, Manitoba, Canada. Semester Abroad, Fall 1993. Studied photography, literature, Canadian drama/theater.

EMPLOYMENT HIGHLIGHTS
2/94 to THE NEW ORLEANS PEOPLE FIRST PROGRAM, Skidell, LA
Present **Adult Literacy Tutor**
Travel to various prisons, nursing homes, boarding houses, and learning centers. Tutor residents in the basic elements of spelling, grammar, and parts of speech. Issue progress reports, bestow awards, etc.

10/93 to TULANE UNIVERSITY, New Orleans, LA
Present **Manager, Film Series**

Summer PETIE'S DEPT. STORE, Skidell, LA. Direct sales, cosmetics.
1992

Spring 1992 TULANE MAILROOM, New Orleans, LA. Mail sorter.

■ Job objective gives focus to student's resume, without limiting his/her opportunities.

■ Synopsis and summary of qualifications highlight student's skills.

RECENT GRAD SCHOOL GRAD (Communications)

Chris Smith
178 Green Street
Mossyrock, WA 98564
(509) 555-5555

PROFESSIONAL OBJECTIVE
A career opportunity in Technical Editing/Writing.

EDUCATIONAL BACKGROUND
WHITWORTH COLLEGE, Spokane, WA
Master of Science Degree in Mass Communications, 1994

WALLA WALLA COLLEGE, College Place, WA
Bachelor of Arts in Communication and Theater, 1992

PROFESSIONAL BACKGROUND
1992 to LOCKWOOD ENGINEERING, Ravensdale, WA
Present Editor/Writer - Worldwide Business Development Division
- Responsible for editing, writing, format design, and production coordination of bid proposals for government, industrial, and utility engineering and construction contracts.
- Act as liaison between Proposal/Marketing Engineer and graphic arts, word processing, and production departments; monitor and oversee production schedule
- Organize and maintain up-to-date dummy book throughout several revision cycles
- Interpret client RFP requirements; determine applicability of proposal response to RFP

1990 to 1992 GLACIER PEAK, INC., Nahcotta, WA
Assistant to the Director - Publications Department
- Researched, wrote, and supervised production of employee orientation brochures.
- Edited and proofread most intra-company published materials.
- Special projects included establishment of corporate slide library and preparation of quarterly budget forecasts/analyses.

1988 to 1990 RUSTLEAF PAGING SERVICES, INC., Deerpark, WA
Assistant to the Manager - Computer Resources Department
- Developed computerized report program to track personnel productivity and department project/task management.
- Monitored customer accounting including answering inquiries and preparing service reports.

TECHNICAL EXPERIENCE
BASICS, SPSS, UNIX Operating System, UNIX INFORMIX Relational Data Base, Apple LISA Software, IBM PC 1-2-3, SuperComp, and EZ Calc Spreadsheets, SSI and PEN Word Processing Programs

■ Listing education before work experience draws attention to student's impressive academic credentials.

■ Valuable computer skills are highlighted in a separate section.

RECENT GRAD SCHOOL GRAD (Criminal Justice)

Chris Smith
178 Green Street
Seattle, WA 98102
(206) 555-5555

EDUCATION

EVERGREEN STATE COLLEGE
M.S., Criminal Justice; G.P.A., 3.5, 1994
WHITMAN COLLEGE
B.A., Psychology; G.P.A., 3.3/4.0, 1993

Olympia, WA

Walla Walla, WA

Honors:
Psi Chi National Honor Society in Psychology
Dean's List six consecutive semesters
Who's Who in American College Students

EXPERIENCE

OFFICE OF THE COMMISSIONER OF PROBATION, Seattle, WA   1994
INTERNSHIP
- Assisted with the integration of probation violators into the Seattle Boot Camp; researched and prepared results for the Commissioner on recidivism rate; attended meetings with judges.

CORBAIN HOUSE HOTEL, Seattle, WA   1993
INTERNSHIP - SECURITY DEPARTMENT
- Worked directly with Director of Security in developing a fire safety and security manual for evacuations with floor plans and procedures to facilitate emergency situations.

UNIVERSITY OF WASHINGTON, Seattle, WA   1992
RESEARCH ASSISTANT-DEPARTMENT OF PSYCHOLOGY
- Assisted Dr. Rocky Clapper, Professor of Research Methods and Psychology in coding and data entry for experiments on drug use in juvenile delinquents.
- Trained in research methods and interpretation of collected data.

EMPLOYMENT

BINNACLE FASHIONS, Seattle, WA   1991-Present
COUNTER ASSOCIATE-JUNIOR MANAGEMENT
- Responsible for customer returns/service; nightly financial transactions.
- Oversee employees; vigilant regarding shrinkage problems and loss prevention.

COMPUTERS

WordPerfect and MacIntosh

- Educational honors, such as Dean's List standing and national honor society membership, indicate candidate's potential to excel.

- Internships bolster student's otherwise limited professional experience.

RECENT GRAD SCHOOL GRAD (Finance)

Chris Smith
178 Green Street
Whitewater, WI 53190
(414) 555-5555

OBJECTIVE
A Mortgage Banking position in Loan Origination or Processing.

EDUCATION
Beloit College, Beloit, WI Bachelor and Master of Science Degree in Finance and Management. Graduated June 1989 and June 1994, respectively.

SUMMARY OF QUALIFICATIONS
- Current knowledge of all relevant FNMA, FHLMC, FHA , VA Guidelines.
- 3 years experience in loan processing and servicing.
- Excellent capacity to establish informative rapport with correspondent lender, broker and borrower.
- Above average communication skills, both oral and written.

RELEVANT EXPERIENCE
Loan Processing
- Analyzed incoming loan package documentation to determine necessary requirements for underwriting of loans.
- Ordered and reviewed credit and appraisal reports to establish subject property suitability and to determine credit eligibility.
- Verified all assets and employment to show stable savings and career history.
- Examined initial Loan Analysis Worksheets to determine borrower's qualification according to applicable guidelines.
- Reviewed all matters pertaining to the borrowers in order to explain any inconsistencies found.

Loan Origination
- Aided potential borrowers by providing product information interest rate figures.
- Determined borrower's maximum loan amount, closing costs and monthly payments using pre-qualification guidelines.

EMPLOYMENT HISTORY
1993-Present LOAN PROCESSOR
Urban Finance, Whitewater, WI

4/93-7/93 LOAN SERVICING/Temp
Milwaukee City Bank

2/93-3/93 LOAN ORIGINATION/Temp
Milwaukee City Bank

■ Functional portion of resume focuses attention on student's practical and professional skills.

■ Chronological portion of resume lists employment history, including job titles and dates of employment.

RECENT GRAD SCHOOL GRAD (Journalism)

Chris Smith
178 Green Street
Minneapolis, MN 55455
(612) 555-5555

EDUCATION University of Minnesota, Twin Cities, Minneapolis, MN
M.A. Journalism (Print)
June 1994
University of Minnesota, Maris, MN
B.S. Media Communications, June 1992
Journalism minor/Photography concentration

RELEVANT **The St. Paul Times, St. Paul, MN**
EXPERIENCE *Freelance Writer*   *7/92-10/93*
• Wrote human interest sports features.

Minneapolis Magazine, Minneapolis, MN
Editorial Intern   *Summer 1993*
• Conducted research for staff writer, senior editor, and Literary News editor.
• Other responsibilities included organizing and writing for Fashion editor.
• Gained knowledge of XyWrite, and IBM word processing package.

The FAN Newspapers, Duluth, MN
Editorial Intern   *Summer 1990*
• Responsible for writing short features for managing editor.
• Responsible for event listings and short features used in the City Time section of the St. Paul edition.

Editor - Life Saves   *1/90-Present*
• Duties include assigning and editing stories for in-house employee newsletter, in addition to coordinating bimonthly production schedule and distribution.

Staff Writer - The Translator   *11/88-4/89*
• Wrote feature stories for in-house employee newsletter, published quarterly.

ADDITIONAL **People Count, Inc., Minneapolis, MN**
EXPERIENCE *Central Monitor*   *10/92-Present*
• Receive customer help calls promptly and follow through to completion, including dispatching police and medical personnel and notifying family members and friends of emergency situations. Troubleshoot unit malfunctions and provide customer service.

Program Manager   *4/89-1/90*
• Responsible for the day-to-day operation of nine satellite hospital programs located in Southwestern and Pacific Northwest United States.

Leasing Associate   *2/88-11/88*
• Performed month-end cash and equipment reconciliations, handled consumer billing inquiries, and provided customer service.

■ Relevant internships demonstrate student's initiative and desire to enter his/her field of interest.

■ Job descriptions are short, concise, and effective. This resume will likely be examined more carefully than a long-winded one.

RECENT GRAD SCHOOL GRAD (Marketing)

Chris Smith
178 Green Street
Plymouth, New Hampshire 03264
(603) 555-5555

EDUCATION

Plymouth State University, Plymouth, NH
M.A. in Marketing, Dec. 1994
Courses include International Marketing, Marketing Research, Business Communications, and Statistics.
Member, National Honor Society.
Pratt University, Brooklyn, NY
B.A. in Accounting, 1992

EMPLOYMENT

THE PLYMOUTH PLAYER, Plymouth, NH
6/94 - New Hampshire's largest daily newspaper (circ. 30,000)
Present *Marketing Assistant* (part-time)
- Design and manage market research to determine the satisfaction of former subscribers with editorial content. Supplement data with focus group research.
- Develop strategic marketing plans. Propose new marketing management strategies and systems; studied on-line news distribution, and creation of new print publications.
- Initiate telemarketing campaign to sell ads for a special section. Targeted advertisers outside usual geographic territory. Although 1/10 of salesforce, sold 1/3 of total ads (sold 6.0k of total sales of 20k).
- Selling display advertising space. Meet with advertisers, negotiate prices and design ads.

PILGRIM TRAVEL, Plymouth, NH
1/94 - 6/94 Discount travel company specializing in trans-Atlantic cruises
Marketing Intern
- Managed nation wide client base. Monitored sales, marketing, research, analysis, reports and presentations.
- Developed and executed marketing plan. Coordinated marketing communications, published monthly client newsletter, created, marketed and conducted seminars, and managed direct mail campaigns.
- Analyzed finances of client organizations.. Performed analysis of multivariate revenue, insurance revenue, and accounts receivable.

COMPUTERS

IBM: WordPerfect, Lotus 1-2-3, Macintosh, Microsoft Word.

REFERENCES

Available upon request.

■ Part-time work experience during school indicates a strong work ethic.

■ Stating that "references are available upon request" is not essential; most employers will assume that references are available.

RECENT GRAD SCHOOL GRAD (Sociology)

Chris Smith
178 Green Street
Alamogordo, NM 88310
(505) 555-5555

PROFESSIONAL OBJECTIVE

To secure a position in Government.

EDUCATION

New Mexico State University, Las Cruces, NM
Master of Science Degree, Sociology, 1994
Courses: Politicians and Society, International Relations, The Global Marketplace.
Thesis: *Personalities and Politics: A Study of The North American Free Trade Agreement.*
Bachelor of Science, Sociology, 1986

MILITARY TRAINING

U.S. ARMY, 1988-1992, Athens, GA
Sergeant, U.S. Army
Prepared briefings concerning material management. Composed graphics as a precedent to the preparation of transparencies via the IBM P.C. computer. Supervised and trained staff members to utilize various software packages, and to achieve proficiency in material management specializations. Assigned to Istanbul in the capacity of U.S. Army translator and liaison between military personnel and Turkish officials. Trained and supervised local population and unit members in settlement construction.

OTHER EXPERIENCE

SINGLETON AIR FREIGHT CO., Raleigh, NC 1986-1988
International Cargo Agent
Prepared international documentation, as required, for the transportation of goods by air and sea. Responded to client inquiries regarding available services. Implemented collection procedures, and recorded invoice statements.

NEW MEXICO STATE UNIVERSITY, Las Cruces, NM 1984-1986
Research Assistant, Sociology, Department
Conducted research in the area of Gerontology, and interpreted data for the presentation of a report to the Midwest Sociological Society's annual convention.

Teaching Assistant (Office of Minority Affairs) 1982-1984
Tutored minority students in various subjects, including sociology, mathematics, and methods of statistical research for the humanities.

■ Courses listed are pertinent to student's professional objective.

■ Military training section indicates student's leadership abilities and technical skills.

RECENT HIGH SCHOOL GRAD (Administration)

Chris Smith
178 Green Street
Seattle, WA 98104
(206) 555-5555

OBJECTIVE:
An entry-level position in administration.

SUMMARY:
- Precise and accurate worker with background demonstrating pride in performance and successful work accomplishment.
- Strong problem solving, organizational and communicative skills, paying professional attention to detail.
- Welcome new challenges, quickly learning new skills and procedures with excellent memory retention.

EDUCATION:
RYDELL HIGH SCHOOL, Seattle, WA
Activities: Editor-in-Chief, School Newspaper; Literary Editor, Yearbook; Captain, Drill Team, 1994.

EXPERIENCE:
LANCELOT NATIONAL BANK, Seattle, WA
Customer Service Representative (6/94-Present)
Open new accounts, take applications and process loans, handle customer transactions, cross-sell bank products, purchase supplies, and resolve customer problems and complaints. Other duties include collection of overdrawn accounts, answer telephones, utilize CRT, and clerical duties (light typing, filing).
Winner of Premier Performance Award.

MY SPECIAL PLACE, Seattle, WA
Sales Associate - Children's Department (9/93-6/94)
Provide sales and customer service, resolve customer problems, receive merchandise, arrange displays, set up sales and operational paperwork, i.e., price mark downs, transfers.
- Department Selling Star, among Top Five Salespeople in the store, Fall 1993.
- Award for opening most store credit cards, December 1993.

DAMON AND BLAINE, Seattle, WA (11/92-6/93)
Sales Associate - Linens

WINDSOR SPORTING GOODS, Seattle, WA (1/92-9/92)
Sales Associate - Promoted to Lead Sales Associate.

■ Job descriptions indicate how student contributed to his/her previous employers.

■ Extracurricular and work-related awards add weight to student's resume.

RECENT HIGH SCHOOL GRAD (Child Care)

Chris Smith
178 Green Street
Jamaica, NY 11451
(718) 555-5555

OBJECTIVE
A responsible position as a Governess.

WORK HISTORY
1995 to MR. AND MRS. KURT URBANE
Present 15 Goldstone Road, Jamaica, NY
Governess
- Provide full-time care for a 6-year old girl.
- Duties include dressing, tutoring, chauffeuring, running errands, housework, cooking and seeing to the child's needs and well-being.
- Live-in position.

1994 MR. AND MRS. PAUL MCMAHN
145 Nicole Lane, Kutztown, PA
Governess
- Responsible for care of 3 children: an infant, 3-year old girl, and 5-year old boy.
- Live-in position.

1990-1994 MR. AND MRS. STEVE MCGUYVER
333 Sunshine Court, Loveland, CO
Babysitter
- Provided care for an infant girl and toddler twin brothers.

EDUCATION
Boulder High, Bolder, CO
Concentration in Psychology, 1994

PERSONAL INFORMATION
- Interests include: Skiing, Reading, Horseback Riding, Traveling, Swimming.
- Valid Driver's License; Perfect driving record.
- CPR/First Aid Certified.

REFERENCES
Excellent references available upon request.

- Including a telephone number is essential on a resume.

- Personal information is pertinent to student's job objective.

RECENT HIGH SCHOOL GRAD (Public Relations)

Chris Smith
178 Green Street
Gaffney, SC 29341
(803) 555-5555

OBJECTIVE

An entry-level position in the public relations and/or media field.

EDUCATION

GAFFNEY PUBLIC HIGH SCHOOL
Graduated with academic degree, 1994

SKILLS

Typing, data entry, IBM computer system, word perfect format, editing, fax machine, filing and calculator. Has worked with Video, Video Production and Editing. Have a pleasant and professional phone manner. Work well with little supervision; energetic, responsible, well organized and work well under stress. Capable of light bookkeeping, customer service and inventory. Enjoy working in a busy environment.

EXPERIENCE

LAUREL PARK CINEMAS, Gaffney, SC
10/93 - Ticket Agent/Concessions Manager
Present Greet moviegoers, provide tickets, drop nightly deposit at bank, provide food service. Assume responsibilities of manager in event of his absence; open and close facility, call in nightly sales to national entertainment center, schedule employee shifts, etc.

STATE OF SOUTH CAROLINA: DEPARTMENT OF PUBLIC WELFARE
6/93-9/93 Summer Intern
Wrote and edited articles for the newsletter, edited forms, data entry, greeted people, confirmed appointments, answered phones and filed manuscripts.

BROADWAY VIDEO, Gaffney, SC
1/92-5/93 Sales Assistant
Took inventory of merchandise, greeted/served customers, placed and took orders, answered phones, and performed general office work.

THE BURGER VASSAL, Gaffney, SC
1/91-1/92 Cashier
Provided customer service, performed monetary transactions, took weekly inventory of food/paper supplies.

■ Skills section highlights student's professional skills and work habits.

■ Part-time work experience during school indicates a strong work ethic.

RECENT HIGH SCHOOL GRAD (Service)

Chris Smith
178 Green Street
Emory, VA 24327
(703) 555-5555

OBJECTIVE
Seeking a long-term position as a Field Service Representative.

SUPPORTIVE QUALIFICATIONS
- Two years experience in the field.
- Expertise with copier and fax models made by Toshiba, Mita, Gestener, Adler-Royal, Monroe, Ricoh, Xerox.
- Dependable, flexible, patient.
- Perfect driving record. Excellent sense of direction.
- Bilingual: Fluent in speech, reading, writing English and Spanish.

EXPERIENCE

1994 - KRIS ELLIOT DUPLICATING SYSTEMS, Emory, VA.   **Field Service Rep**
Present Hired to service Boston Metro area working as troubleshooter.
Received five to six daily client appointments; serviced both facsimile and copiers;
Weekly administrative follow-up tasks for contract maintenance calls.

1993 - 1994 BIJOV OFFICE SYSTEMS, Richmond, VA.   **Field Service Rep**
Serviced copiers for the largest Mita dealer in Virginia. Repaired, adjusted and performed maintenance on all machines; completed six to eight customer calls daily in both Virginia and California regions. Received "Employee of the Month" award three times for recognition of service and no call-backs.

TRAINING AND CERTIFICATIONS
BURDETT TRAINING SCHOOL, Atlanta, GA. Certified III-555, 1993.
SALAMANCA TECHNICAL SCHOOL, Salamanca, Spain. 1993 Graduate.
RICHMOND HIGH SCHOOL, Richmond, VA. 1993 Graduate.

ACTIVITIES
Richmond High Debate Team (Captain, 1992)
Class Secretary (1991)
Basketball (Captain, 1991, 1992, State All-Star, 1992)

■ Supportive qualifications accentuate student's acquired skills.

■ Elected positions of authority, like team captain, indicate student's leadership abilities.

RECENT MBA (A)

Chris Smith
178 Green Street
Goodwell, OK 73939
(405) 555-5555

PROFESSIONAL OBJECTIVE
To secure a position in the field of Accounting/Billing.

EDUCATION
UNIVERSITY OF MIAMI, Coral Gables, FL. M.B.A. with concentration in Finance, 1994.
COLLEGE OF THE HOLY CROSS, Worcester, MA. Bachelor of Science
Degree in Economics/Finance, 1991.

EMPLOYMENT
1994 to
Present   NAOT, INC., Goodwell, OK   **Accountant**
Responsible for preparation of monthly financial statements and general ledger
reconciliations, project management, billing and maintenance of Timberline Software
System for all company projects, cost proposals on government and commercial accounts.
Payroll, general ledger, daily cash, accounts payable and receivable.

1990 to 1992   O'CONNOR, RAISTY, & ROSS, Oklahoma City, OK   **Contract Billing Administrator**
Worked for BBN Systems & Technologies; interpreted billing provisions of government and
commercial contracts, maintained interactive billing systems, prepared accounts
receivable and sales adjustments. Maintained MIS database, and reconciled mailing list to
invoice register.

THE MUTUAL CORP., Shawnee, OK   **Coordinator, ABI-Boston**
Designed procedures for implementation of new Automated Brokerage Interface.
Supervised transformation from manual to computerized operation and trained personnel
accordingly. Maintained system software and daily records. Researched and reconciled
complex international transactions.

ACTIVITIES
Broadcaster, SportsNet Football for local cable company.
Coached Okie Acorns Soccer Team, B.A.Y.S. League.

COMPUTERS
Excel   DOS
Lotus 1.2.3   Timberline
dBase II   WordPerfect

■ Work experience emphasizes
most positive or relevant aspects
of each position, rather than summarizing each position like a job
description.

■ Personal interests and activities
add depth to resume.

RECENT MBA (B)

Chris Smith
178 Green Street
Phoenix, AZ 85044
(602) 555-5555

PROFESSIONAL OBJECTIVE
A position in the ACCOUNTING department of a growing corporation.

SUMMARY OF QUALIFICATIONS
- Academic training is represented with an MBA Degree, an MS Degree in Taxation, and a BSBA Degree in Accounting.
- Strong venue in interpreting complex tax matters with concern for savings plans, investment avenues, and credits.
- Skill in establishing profit and loss projections, cash flow projections, and financial controls.
- Ability to draft, write, and edit technical publications with clarity and conciseness.

EDUCATION

GRAND CANYON COLLEGE, Phoenix, AZ
M.B.A. Degree, 1994
Magna Cum Laude
Who's Who in American Graduate Students

HENDRIX COLLEGE, Conway, AR
B.S.B.A. Degree with honors, Accounting, 1986

PROFESSIONAL EXPERIENCE
1991 - Present DEVONSHIRE TECHNICAL SUPPORT, INC., Phoenix, AZ
Assistant Controller
- Establish corporate accounting systems and procedures with the design of a computerized system for current accounting practices.
- Provide audit preparation and write-up; post journal entries to general ledger; compile working papers and monthly financial statements for auditors.
- Responsible for profit and loss projections, cash flow projections, and cash disbursements.
- Prepare all Federal/State tax returns consistent with statutory requirements.

1988 - 1991 THE SHONDELL CRIMSON CORPORATION, Chandler, AR
Assistant Controller
- Designed and implemented a new accounting system with two-member support staff.
- Maintained accounts payable verification, check writing, and weekly cash flow forecasts.
- Prepared journal entries to general ledger.
- Responsible for Federal/State corporate income tax returns.

1986 - 1988 IVANHOE EQUIPMENT CORPORATION, Flagstaff, AZ
Accounting Conversion Staff
- Contracted assignment through the Technical Aid Corporation.
- Performed accounting duties and functions during conversion of manual accounts payable procedure to computerized system.

■ Summary of qualifications highlights student's academic credentials and professional skills.

■ Resume is tailored to student's job objective; unrelated jobs and other irrelevant information is de-emphasized or omitted.

RECENT MBA (C)

Chris Smith
178 Green Street
Ogden, UT 84404
(801) 555-5555

PROFESSIONAL OBJECTIVE
Seeking a position in the Human Resource/Management field.

EDUCATION

BRIGHAM YOUNG UNIVERSITY, Provo, UT
Master of Business Administration, 1994
GPA: 3.74
Honors: Salutatorian of Graduating Class, Academic Scholarship, Social Service Award for work with disadvantaged teenagers.

UNIVERSITY OF UTAH, Salt Lake City, UT
Master of Public Administration Degree, 1991
Concentration: Financial Management
GPA: 3.50

PROFESSIONAL EXPERIENCE

SUNRIDGE LABORATORIES, Ogden, UT
Supervisor   1993-Present
- Provide personnel with secretarial, transcription, computer equipment operations and general clerical services
- Interview, select and manage support services staff; developed training and facilitating programs for various levels; and created a secretarial floater pool.

Technical Employment Representative/Affirmative Action Counselor   1992-1993
- Acted as initial contact for prospective employees; evaluated resumes, conducted preliminary interviews, calculated salaries, etc.
- Participated in job/career fairs.
- Served as Loden Valley Summer Program Administrator.
- Active member of the Loden Valley Affirmative Action Committee
- Community Relations duties included representing company on various boards ranging from Chambers of Commerce to Social Service agencies.

OFFICE OF MANAGEMENT SERVICES/DEPARTMENT OF PUBLIC WORKS
Salt Lake City, UT
Intern   1991
- Coordinated complete automation of the Office of Management Services by establishing an "Engagement Plan" outlining the time frame to complete all phases of the system; generated a final report, incorporating the system's effects on user personnel and corresponding recommendations, evaluation of supporting software and related matters.

■ Internships supplement student's classroom learning with valuable, hands-on experience.

■ Job descriptions indicate how student contributed to his/her previous employers.

RECENT MBA (D)

Chris Smith
178 Green Street
Lexington, KY 40508
(606) 555-5555

CAREER OBJECTIVE
To secure a challenging position within the fields of **Finance, Mutual Funds** and/or **Investments.**

EDUCATION

TRANSYLVANIA UNIVERSITY, Lexington, KY.
Master of Business Administration.
Graduated, Magna Cum Laude, May 1994.

BEREA COLLEGE, Berea, KY.
Bachelor of Business Administration.
Graduated, Cum Laude, May 1992.

MARKETING COURSE WORK
STATISTICS * CORPORATION FINANCE * BUYER BEHAVIOR/MARKETING RESEARCH
SALES MANAGEMENT * INTERNATIONAL MARKETING * BUSINESS POLICY/STRATEGY
PROMOTIONAL STRATEGY * ACCOUNTING I AND II * CALCULUS II
PRINCIPLES OF MARKETING * WRITING FOR BUSINESS

SUMMARY OF QUALIFICATIONS
- M.B.A. and Bachelor of Business Administration.
- Internship, course work and relevant training in marketing.
- Strong interpersonal abilities; professional, organized, cooperative, diplomatic and trustworthy team player.
- Computer Literate: Basic; Lotus 1 2 3; d-Base III; WordPerfect.
- Goal-directed; meet deadlines, good under pressure and strong on follow-up.

EMPLOYMENT HIGHLIGHTS

Give 'em the Boot   Lexington, KY.
Assistant Manager   1991-Present
Supervise staff of 5, manage customer service, bookkeeping, displays, ordering, transfers.
Tops in sales. Average $5,000 weekly.

SID'S Country Market   Scuddy, KY.
Assistant Buyer   1988-1990
Planned marketing strategies; developed new customer service program; displays; payroll.

ADDITIONAL EXPERIENCE
KENTUCKY OUTLET; LE JOLIE CAFE; TRAN O MARKETING and BUSINESS CLUBS.

■ Summary grabs the reader's attention with powerful skills and qualifications.

■ Resume includes course work that corresponds to the position desired.

RECENT MBA (E)

Chris Smith
178 Green Street
Sanford, FL 32771
(415) 555-5555

OBJECTIVE

Management, marketing, or sales position in an organization valuing logical but imaginative thinking.

QUALIFICATIONS

Experience in organizing, accepting responsibility, and making decisions. Ability to supervise and deal successfully with others. Valuable experience in gathering, recording, and interpreting marketing research data. Strong academic background in marketing, sales, management, and economics.

EDUCATION

STANFORD UNIVERSITY, Stanford, CA
GRADUATE SCHOOL OF BUSINESS ADMINISTRATION
Master's Degree in Business Administration, May 1994.
Major fields of study: marketing, sales, and management.

EMPLOYMENT

CAMAROON SALES, INC.   New York, NY
Research Assistant   1993-94
Employed part-time during academic year doing industrial marketing research. Worked on nation-wide studies with WATS lines. Learned to be proficient at telephone surveying, editing, and analyzing results. Recommended for position by Chairman of Marketing Department, Stanford University. Delivered report on Industrial Marketing Research to graduate students, New York University.

DEER SPRING BREWING COMPANY   Daytona, FL
Warehouse Assistant   1992-93
Assisted in Production, Packaging, and Shipping.

BENNY'S   Boca Raton, FL
Associate   1991 Summer
Salesman of men's clothing and specialty goods.

COMPUTERS

Lotus 1-2-3, dBase III+, SPSSX, Excel.

REFERENCES

Available upon request.

■ After education, job experience is listed in reverse chronological order, with student's most recent job appearing first.

■ Powerful skills and abilities are listed under "Qualifications."

RECENT MBA (F)

Chris Smith
178 Green Street
Greenville, SC 29649
(803) 555-5555

OBJECTIVE

A position in medical sales/marketing with a firm that offers the opportunity to utilize technical training and experience.

EDUCATION

Furman University, Greenville, SC
Master of Business Administration, 1994
National Honor Society
Spanish Club
Awarded Partial Scholarship

Clemson University, Clemson, SC
Bachelor of Science Degree, Biology, 1989

QUALIFICATIONS

- Nationally registered as MT (ASCP) and CLS (NCA).
- Two years experience as a Blood Bank Medical Technologist and In-service Educational Coordinator.
- Sound knowledge of biomedical instruments and scientific reagents.
- Hands-on technical experience and effective training and communications skills.
- Additional experience in sales and business procedures.
- A self-motivated achiever who is efficient, well organized and capable of dealing with people in a sales, service or support function.

STAFF MEDICAL TECHNOLOGIST
Greenville Union Hospital Blood Bank
Greenville, SC   1989-Present
- Perform all blood bank procedures using a wide variety of biomedical instruments (IBM 2997) and scientific reagents.
- Serve as Technical Advisor on weekends and week nights to laboratory staff.
- Serve as In-house Educational Coordinator, planning and organizing in-service seminars and workshops on current technology for blood banking.
- Provide didactic and technical instruction to blood bank internists.
- Maintain monthly inventory of blood bank reagents and daily inventories of blood bank donor bloods.
- Monitor quality control of reagents and blood bank instruments.
- Represent the hospital at medical conventions to learn about new equipment and procedures, and subsequently present and instruct hospital personnel in application of the latest equipment and procedures.
- Position requires the ability to carry a heavy workload, work extra shifts, and deal with people in pressured situations in a precise manner.

■ Listing special academic awards, honors, competitive scholarships, and/or thesis topics gives student a competitive edge.

■ Working experience relates to student's job objective and is featured prominently.

RECENT MBA (G)

Chris Smith
178 Green Street
Pittsburgh, PA 15218
(912) 555-5555

EDUCATION

Duquesne University, Pittsburgh, PA
Master of Business Administration, December 1994
Concentration in Marketing and Strategic Planning
Worked full-time while taking courses at night.

Swarthmore College, Swarthmore, PA
Bachelor of Science in Engineering, May 1984

EXPERIENCE

1991- **Bomarc, Blue, and Spruce**, Pittsburgh, PA
Present *Sales and Marketing Manager*
Examined new services and changing markets and developed a
detailed marketing strategy resulting in the addition of two new
business units for the company. Designed and implemented a
company sales and marketing campaign targeting emerging markets
with new promotional and communication materials. Identified
specific action oriented tasks required to sustain growth;
resulted in significant improvement in company's overall
financial and operating condition. Designed a three pronged
incentive sales program for telecommunications client wanting to
protect installed base and increase market share. Developed
push pull marketing program for software company wanting to
expand its channels of distribution. Positioned client's products
with innovative promotional campaigns. Designed team-building and
gain-sharing programs for clients with a focus on quality, cost
reduction and safety.

1986-1991 **Dunkeith Woods, Inc.**, Pittsburgh, PA
Regional Sales Manager
Established and managed Regional Sales Office for this leading
compiler and marketer of business and consumer information
database used by direct marketing companies. Worked closely with
clients to prepare and implement marketing plans for a variety of
products and services. Integrated proprietary Database America
information with information brokered from other sources to
ensure coverage of established markets and test new potential
markets. Recommended and provided necessary data processing
services, data file maintenance and customized enhancement
programs. Additional responsibilities included prospecting for
new business, attendance at trade shows and conferences and
report preparation.

■ Resume focuses on valuable full-time experience gained while attending school at night.

■ Student's work experience reads like a series of accomplishments, not just a list of job duties.

SOME COLLEGE BUT NO DEGREE (Accounting)

Chris Smith
178 Green Street
Dahlonega, CA 31597
(404) 555-5555

PROFESSIONAL OBJECTIVE
A challenging career continuation as an Accounting Assistant.

SUPPORTIVE QUALIFICATIONS
- Eight years experience and broad-based knowledge of the accounting field.
- Proficient with Lotus 1-2-3 Spreadsheets; general ledger, accounts receivable and payable, auditing and cash flow functions.
- Strong numerical and administrative abilities.
- Experience training incoming personnel.

HIGHLIGHTS OF PROFESSIONAL EXPERIENCE
1990-Present SAVANNA COMPTROLLER'S OFFICE, Dahlonega, CA
Accounting Assistant
- Monitor funding and financial reporting associated with various federal sponsors.
- Perform internal cost audits of terminated research contracts and grants.
- Coordinate audit and cash flow functions between CAO and other university departments.
- Audit and create financial reports, monthly/quarterly reports, government requirements and correspondence.

1987-1990 NOSTRADAMUS CORPORATION, Dahlonega, CA
Accounting Assistant
- Held complete responsibility for all receivables and payables.
- Implemented CRT operations; computerized financial reports and auditing.
- Strong telephone and personal contact in customer service and problem solving with purchasing department.
- Maintained computer master files and related input data.

EDUCATION
CREIGHTON UNIVERSITY, Omaha, NE
Course work in accounting, statistics, corporate finance, business law, and computers, 1985-1987.

PERSONAL INTERESTS
Photography * Tennis * Marathon Running

- Although student did not earn a degree, he/she lists courses taken.

- Supportive qualifications illustrate candidate's key credentials.

SOME COLLEGE BUT NO DEGREE (Administration)

CHRIS SMITH
178 Green Street
Mitchell, SD 57301
(605) 555-5555

OBJECTIVE
To secure an administrative position where supervisory and training experience will be fully utilized.

QUALIFICATIONS
- 7 years administrative experience.
- 5 years experience in the Health Care field.
- Supervised and trained up to 10 on staff in Medical Records.
- Organized and revamped medical records filing system as well as Navy personnel filing system.
- Computer Skills: MS DOS Windows Microsoft Works.
- Extensive telephone/communications experience with work on the 46-line SB 4303 Switchboard.

STRENGTHS

• Accurate	• Enthusiastic
• Dependable	• Calm under pressure
• Organized	• Strong written communication skills

EXPERIENCE

1991 -   MILITARY/HEALTH CARE
Present   U.S. NAVY / E-4 Specialist   **Switching Systems Operator**
- Performed extensive administrative tasks, including the maintenance of records of Navy personnel. Composed and typed correspondence.
- Set up equipment, antennae, security codes, and ensured communications were established.
- Honorably Discharged.

1987 - 1989   HUMAN NUTRITION RESEARCH CENTER, Rapid City, SD   **Nurse's Aide**
- Took patients' vital signs, specimens; stock supplies.

1983 - 1987   S. DAKOTA GENERAL HOSPITAL, Shadehill, SD   **Medical Records Controller**
- Trained and supervised staff.
- Provided record maintenance in File Room.

EDUCATION

NATIONAL COLLEGE, Rapid City, SD 1987-88
HURON COLLEGE, Huron, SD 1988-1989
Courses in Marketing, Business Administration, Statistics, Computer Science, and Liberal Arts, Volunteer for Student Legal Aid.

- Chrono-functional format is more flexible than a chronological resume, but stronger than a functional resume.

- Professional experience and special qualifications are accentuated while limited education is listed at bottom of resume.

SOME COLLEGE BUT NO DEGREE (Management)

Chris Smith
178 Green Street
Walcott, IA 52773
(319) 555-5555

OBJECTIVE
To secure a full-time management position.

EXPERIENCE

10/89 - KLINE AND COMPANY, Moline, IA
Present **Supervisor, Mailroom Services**
Coordinate incoming mail; disperse inter-building correspondence. Manage courier services and shipping/receiving. Administer employee evaluations/appraisals; schedule hours. Research and account for certified, registered, and express mail. Responsible for office supply procurement. Obtain/maintain lease agreements for electronic machinery and equipment.

3/89-9/89 EXPRESSMAIL, Blue Grass, IA
Courier
Delivered time sensitive packages throughout area. Sorted incoming/outgoing express packages.

1/86-2/88 GASTON, ROSE & BROOKS, Milan, IA
Supervisor, Mailroom Services
Supervise shipment of weekly overseas pouches and biweekly payroll to 30 domestic offices. Sorted/distributed in-house payroll for 500 employees. Coordinated in-house and U.S. office stock distribution. Acted as building management contact and Chief Fire Warden for 75,000 square feet of office space. Assisted in office relocations throughout U.S.

12/82-12/85 P. GEDELLO FINANCIAL GROUP, Bettendorf, IA
Supervisor, Incoming Mail/Messengers and Stock Distribution
Manage of computer facility forms and negotiable forms stored in-house vault.

EDUCATION

9/80-11/82 SAINT AMBROSE COLLEGE, Davenport, IA
Course work concentrated in Personnel and Human Resources Management. Participant in SAFE Escort Program for Students.

9/79-5/80 LOVAS COLLEGE, Dubuque, IA
Two courses in Communications.

REFERENCES
Furnished upon request.

■ Courses listed under education are related to candidate's field of interest.

■ Stating that "references are available upon request" is not essential; most employers will assume that references are available.

TRANSFER STUDENT

Chris Smith
178 Green Street
Rochester, NY 14623
(716) 555-5555

EDUCATION:

Conell University, Ithaca, NY
Bachelor of Science, Earth Science, 1994
Greenpeace Student Representative
Cornell International Club Member

Massachusetts Institute of Technology, Cambridge, MA 1992
Course work in biology, chemistry, and environmental science

WORK EXPERIENCE:

Biobased Materials Center, Forest Products Dept., Cornell, Ithaca, NY
Intern 1993-1994
Developed an understanding of the materials science aspects of polysaccharide (cellulose, hemicellulose, chitin) regeneration in the form of hydrogen beads. This research has been focusing on the examination of relationships between the nature of the polysaccharide (chemistry, molecular weight, viscosity, etc.) and important hydrogen parameters, such as gel structure, morphology, bead pore size, flow characteristics, mechanical strength, and reactivity.

Wood Chemistry Laboratory, Forest Products Department, Cornell, Ithaca, NY
Assistant 1992
Assisted professor on chemical modification of lignin with propylene oxide for the synthesis of urethanes and thermoplastic elastomers.
Developed methods for the synthesis of telechelic oligomers from lignin with controlled number and length of arms.
Performed the synthesis and full characterization (chemical, thermal, mechanical and morphological) of multiphase block copolymers containing lignin and either polycaprolactone, cellulose propionate or polystyrene, as the hard segments.
Produced blends of thermoplastic formulations of multiphase block copolymers containing lignin as compatibilizers in polymer blends with commercial polymers such as PVC, polystyrene, and cellulose propionate.

American Center of Technology (ACT), Boston, MA
Assistant 1991
Developed projects on alternative energy from biomass residues, mainly sugar cane bagasse. Worked on projects for ethanol production either from acidic or enzymatic hydrolysis of wood, sugar cane bagasse, and manioc.

PERSONAL:

Fluent in English and German, proficient in Spanish, working knowledge in Dutch. Interests include reading, billiards, and running. Willing to relocate.

AFFILIATION:

American Chemical Society - member since 1992
International Club, Cornell - member since 1993
Greenpeace - member since 1993

■ College from which student graduated is listed before and in greater detail than the school which he/she transferred from.

■ Professional affiliations indicate student's active participation in his/her field.

ACCOUNTING MAJOR

Chris Smith
178 Green Street
Auburn, WA 28764
(206) 555-5555

EDUCATION

BS in Accounting, May 1994
University of Washington, Seattle, WA
Course work included Finance, Bookkeeping, Business Law, and Computer Science.
Founder of Student Credit Union, a credit union run solely by and for students. Treasurer
of Senior Class Council. Member of Women's Rugby Team.

EXPERIENCE

SUNNYBRAE STREET BANK   **AUBURN, WA**
Portfolio Accountant   June 1994-Present
Determined cash available for daily security investment on $4.0 billion portfolio. Ensured
timely settlement on all fixed income and equity trades. Calculated and posted
amortization of all long-term fixed income holdings. Computed net asset value of funds
on a monthly basis. Calculated interest accruals on fixed income securities.

GENTLE WARRIOR MARKETING   **VANCOUVER, WA**
Marketing Intern   Summer 1993
Created project timelines, drafted budget estimates; created copy, edited, proofread,
supervised time production.

RAINY DAY BUSINESS MACHINES   **BELLVUE, WA**
Marketing Support Assistant   Summer 1992
Assisted marketing reps in making sales calls. Participated on sales team supporting
account executives.
Maintained a P.C. hot line for customer questions.

UNIVERSITY OF WASHINGTON COFFEEHOUSE, INC.   **SEATTLE, WA**
Bar Director   1991-1994
Managed student run concession for college community. Supervised daily operation with
a staff of 30+ employees. Operated with a budget of $175,000 a year. Directed numerous
capital improvement projects.

SKILLS

Microsoft Word, Lotus 1-2-3, WordPerfect, Pagemaker.

PERSONAL

Willing to relocate.

■ Specific numeric and dollar figures quantify candidate's achievements.

■ Extracurricular activities relate to student's field of interest.

AFRICAN-AMERICAN STUDIES MAJOR

Chris Smith
178 Green Street
Sunapee, NH 03782
(603) 555-5555

Education: **Kalamazoo College**, Kalamazoo, MI
B.A. African American Studies, May 1994
Minor: Political Science
Awarded the Lieberman Scholarship.
Member, Volunteers in Action (VIA).

Experience: **Computer Consultant** *11/93-5/94*
Personal Computer Classroom Operations
- Maintained classroom equipment.
- Assisted users with MS Word, Pagemaker, Hypercard and Superpaint for the MacIntosh computer.
- Developed knowledge of WordPerfect on IBM compatible.

Resident Assistant *9/93-5/94*
University Housing Services
- Coordinated activities for 50 international students in residence halls.
- Enforced policies.
- Counseled students.
- Performed administrative duties.

President *9/92-5/93*
Student House Council
- Volunteer, elected position.
- Facilitated meetings.
- Organized events.
- Worked with other officers.
- Acted as liaison between resident director and house council.
- Acted as representative to area government.

Vice-President *2/92-5/92*
Dormitory Council
- Volunteer, elected position.
- Assisted in organizing social events.
- Arranged fund-raisers.
- Coordinated activities with other officers.
- Acted as representative to area government.

Skills: Typing (approx. 60wpm), MS Word on MacIntosh.

- Part-time college jobs are listed in detail under "Experience."
- Resume is easy and quick to read; only relevant details are included.

ANTHROPOLOGY MAJOR

Chris Smith
178 Green Street
Neopit, WI 54150
(715) 555-5555

EDUCATION

Ripon College, Ripon, WI
B.A. cum laude with distinction in Anthropological Studies, 1994
Art history courses completed on Greek and Roman Art
Milwaukee Center for Adult Education, Milwaukee, WI
Classes in Calligraphy and Graphic Design, Summer 1993

EXPERIENCE

Ripon Journal of Anthropology
Assistant Editor   Ripon, WI
Responsible for production of journal and office management.   Feb. 1993-Present
Monitor and maintain production schedule with typesetters and printers.
Design layout, create mock-ups for journal, and complete paste-up.
Proofread all articles and book reviews, some reference checking.
Complete occasional artwork as needed.
Office management responsibilities include:
*   Order all supplies, approving bills for payment, answering mail and phones.
*   Create and maintain databases for exchange agreements and fundraising activities.
*   Type all correspondence with authors and service providers.
*   Manage occasional temporary workers.

Wider View Program
Student Anthropologist   Queensland, AUS
Developed a thesis paper at program's conclusion.   Summer 1993
Studied gender roles in four Aboriginal tribes within a six mile area in one outback.

Camp Meteetsee
Counselor   Fort Kent, ME
Responsible for daily activities of campers aged 5 to 16.   Summers 1988, 1989
Coordinated Arts and Crafts Program, organized and ran Music Library.

VOLUNTEER POSITIONS
Capella Alamire
Treasurer   Ripon, WI
In charge of bookkeeping for orchestral society.   Sept. 1992-present
Coordinate grant applications.

Ripon Gilbert and Sullivan Society
Coordinator   Ripon College, Ripon
Produced H.M.S. Pinafore and Ruddigore.   1992-1993
Organized Society functions.

SKILLS

Knowledge of Microsoft Word, FileMaker; Basic knowledge of Pagemaker, Quark XPress
Working knowledge of German and Latin.

■ Volunteer experience supplements student's classroom learning with valuable hands-on experience.

■ Valuable computer and language skills are highlighted in a separate section.

ART HISTORY MAJOR

Chris Smith

School Address: Permanent Address:
178 Green Street   23 Blue Street
Providence, RI 90666   Los Angeles, CA 90666
(401) 555-5555   (813) 444-4444

EDUCATION

PROVIDENCE COLLEGE, Providence, RI
Bachelor of Arts Degree in Art History to be awarded May, 1995.
Concentration in the History of African and African-American
Art. Courses include: New Trends in Modern Art, Introductory
Museum Science, and Modern Sculpture.

THE INTERNATIONAL SCHOOL, Nairobi, Kenya
High School Diploma, May, 1990.

EXPERIENCE

9/91 to **COPLEY SOCIETY OF LOS ANGELES—ART GALLERY**, Los Angeles, CA
present Internship
Assisted customers, sales, setting up displays and mailings for
exhibitions. Some clerical work.

7/91 **RAISON CENTER Cultural Center,** Paris, France
Internship
Learned all facets of the Center, including Publicity,
Technical, Planning, House Management, and Art Gallery
Departments. Some duties included layouts for concert and play
programs, contact promoters, distribution of leaflets on
oncoming events, behind stage lighting, sound, equipment, etc.
Hung displays and exhibitions. Solicited subsidiary funding.

7/91 **LAPIS GALLERY**, Lisbon, Portugal
Assistant to the Head of Lapis Tate International Council
Worked on the opening of a Klimt Exhibition entitled "Golden
Rebellion". Organized a dinner for 1000 Art-Sponsors and
Artists.

Summer **EUROPEAN TEEN ORCHESTRA** , Conductor: Leonard Bernstein
1987 General Secretary
Orchestra toured to Hamburg, Athens, Hiroshima, Osaka, Hong
Kong, and Vienna. Assisted in administrative Duties.

LANGUAGES

Fluency in English and French, working knowledge of Spanish.

- Internship experience is valuable for students with limited paid experience, particularly if it corresponds to his/her field of interest.

- Foreign language skills further strengthen candidate's qualifications.

BIOLOGY MAJOR

Chris Smith

School Address:
178 Green Street
Oneonta, NY 13820
(607) 555-5555

Home Address:
23 Blue Street
Houston, TX 77024
(713) 444-4444

Career Objective A permanent position that would allow me to utilize my skills in scientific writing and editing.

Education Hartwick College, Oneonta, NY
B.S. in Biological Sciences, Anticipated May 1995

Writing Experience

Student Affairs, Hartwick College
Writer
Revise the text and design of Science Section of *The Word*, a 120-page student handbook, and work to incorporate student input into the undergraduate course catalog. May 1993-present.

The Bunsen Science Newsletter
Copy Manager
Duties included organizing a staff of eight to ten proofreaders, scheduling their hours, and doing some proofreading and copy editing. Act as the authority on style and layout and also participated in editorial decisions. January 1992-January 1994.

Science News Editor
Assigned and wrote science oriented stories, edited, designed the layout, and put together a five to seven page section of a monthly science newspaper. October- December 1991.

Production Manager
Supervised an eight member staff, designed and typeset advertisements, designed the newspaper pages, and oversaw the final production of the weekly color, broadsheet newspaper. February-October 1991.

Activities

Head Orientation Counselor, Hartwick College
Worked with five others to organize and oversee a week-long Orientation program for incoming students. Organized and kept a budget of approximately $100,000. September 1992-September 1993.

Jones Lab, Hartwick College
Laboratory Assistant
Prepared and set up equipment for researchers in the laboratory. May 1992-October 1993.

Computer Skills

Microsoft Word, MacWrite, Pagemaker, Aldus Freehand, FileMaker Pro, and Excel. Basic Knowledge of Photoshop, Word Perfect, and QuarkXpress.

■ Resume indicates writing experience relating to student's major.

■ Computer skills, highlighted in a separate section, are particularly valuable for careers in writing.

BUSINESS ADMINISTRATION MAJOR

Chris Smith
178 Green Street
Elsah, IL 62028
(708) 555-5555

EDUCATION

NORTHWESTERN UNIVERSITY SCHOOL OF PUBLIC HEALTH, Evanston, IL:
Part-time studies toward Master Of Public Health. Degree to be awarded May, 1997.

NORTHWESTERN UNIVERSITY, Evanston, IL 1994
B.S., Business Administration/Marketing. Member, Alpha Beta Gamma;
National Business Honor Society. Certificate of Award for Outstanding Business
Administration Graduates. Varsity Soccer.

LARSON COLLEGE, Malibu, CA 1987
A.A., Merchandising/*Certificate in Professional Modeling*. Emphasis on Communication
and Public Presentation.

EXPERIENCE

1992 -   *RED SAVIOR INSURANCE*, Elsah, IL   **Information Consultant**
Present   Trained on all contracts and systems. Assist Department Supervisor as required with
responsibility for work assignments, quality control, and troubleshooting.
- Educate public on applicable BC/BS policies, guidelines and procedures.
- Resolve Complaints and disputes in billing or contract specifications.
- Research and write customer requests for appeal and present findings.
- Identified existing problems and provided research data to Ombudsman which
contributed to revision of applicable underwriting policy.
- Selected to assist the Consumer Relations Department with inquiries from the media
and third party inquiries from the Division of Insurance.
- P.A.C.E. 5 Awards (Public Acknowledgment for Conscientious Effort).

1990 - 1992   **Senior Information Representative**
- Assisted in training and orientation of new information representatives.
- Interacted directly with Research on legal cases for Law Department.
- Selected to attend training program on new EDS computer system with subsequent
responsibility to train co-workers.
- Responded to inquiries, identified and researched subscriber problems.
- Drafted series of form letters to accompany payments to participating medical
providers.

1988 - 1990   *THE CLOTHES CRITERION*, Chicago, IL   **Sales Associate**
Responsible for customer sales and service. Assisted with new employee training.
- Ranked among Top 15 Salespeople in the country.

- ■ Job descriptions detail candidate's responsibilities and accomplishments.

- ■ Student indicates that he/she has not yet graduated by stating "Degree to be awarded..."

BUSINESS MANAGEMENT MAJOR

Chris Smith
178 Green Street
Raleigh , NC 27611
(919) 555-5555

CAREER OBJECTIVE

To secure a responsible, entry-level position as a Sales Representative within a progressive company.

SUMMARY OF QUALIFICATIONS

- Goal-oriented, hard worker with supporting background and education capabilities.
- Energetic self-starter with highly effective problem solving skills.
- Demonstrated organizational effectiveness; strong on follow-up.
- Proven interpersonal and negotiating skills. Excellent in dealing with staff and management. Good listener, cooperative.
- Responsible, trustworthy and versatile team player.

EDUCATION

Muskingum College, New Concord, OH; **Bachelor of Science Degree**
Business Management; Minor in Political Science. Graduated 1994.

RELEVANT COURSE WORK AND ACTIVITIES

- Organizational Theory/Behavior, Principles of Management, Advertising/Promotion, Business Policy, Computer Programming, Communications.
- Vice-President, Student Government.
- Model United Nations Representative (three years).
- College Management Club.
- Executive Board Member, Lambda Chi Fraternity.
- College Orientation Staff Leader.

WORK EXPE'RIENCE

Summers: 1990- Present
Carpenter Apprentice
Craven Construction Co., Raleigh, NC
Performed jack hammering, drilling, sawing, clean-up and stocking of materials on construction sites.

Summers: 1988 - 1990
Landscaper
B. Baggins Landscaping, Mars Hill, NC
Landscaping tasks: Mulched, planted, dug holes, laid sod, created drainage, laid bricks.

PERSONAL

Willing to travel and/or relocate.

■ Relevant course work and activities strengthen student's resume.

■ Summer employment indicates student's initiative and sense of responsibility.

CHEMISTRY MAJOR

Chris Smith
178 Green Street
Snylna, GA 30082
(404) 555-5555

OBJECTIVE
To work as a research assistant and/or lab technician in an organic, inorganic or analytical environment.

EDUCATION

EMORY UNIVERSITY, Atlanta, GA
Bachelor of Science degree in Chemistry awarded in December 1994. Minor in Biology with a concentration in Biochemistry. Courses include Anatomy and Physiology, Environmental Science, and Modern Laboratory Technology. Member of Students for Environmental Protection. Organized Green Earth Clean-Up Program for campus/city.

EXPERIENCE

DAVENPORT COMPANY, Atlanta, GA
Chemical Division, Part-time Assistant   1992-Present
Provided technical assistance and support to management. Ran trials on the bleaching process using different chemicals in order to improve the process and reduce the outflow of dioxins. Calculated flow rates and meter pump settings for the chemical polymer feed system in the filter plant. Assisted outside engineering firm in designing a new bulk storage tank system and piping for the main polymers used for filtration.

EMORY UNIVERSITY, Atlanta, GA
Research Lab/Intern/Rheumatology/Immunology   1990-present
Ran and maintained high-pressure liquid chromatograph system for proteins (leukotrienes). Prepared standards and titration of antibodies used by the whole department for RIAs. Culture and bovine endothelial cells. Radioligand binding studies with leukotrienes. Knowledge of spectrophonometer to obtain concentrations; purifying of polymorphonuclear leukocytes and monocytes.

MOONSTONE AND WICCA COMPANY, INC., Atlanta, GA
Engineering Department, Internship   1990-1992
Assisted a DuPont Test Specialist in the operation of a two-column distillation pilot plant. Responsible for starting the pilot plant, monitoring the control panel, making process adjustments as needed to maintain steady state operation and shutting the pilot plant down when needed. Compiled pilot plant data and performed associated calculations on an IBM PC.

■ Listing courses taken and extra-curricular activities is especially important for students with low GPAs.

■ Student's experience and accomplishments correspond with the position desired.

CLASSICAL CIVILIZATION MAJOR

Chris Smith
178 Green Street
Louisville, KY 40292
(502) 555-5555

OBJECTIVE: To obtain an entry-level position in Administration.

SKILLS: Excellent written and verbal communication skills.
Ability to work well with a variety of people.
Several years of experience as a temporary worker for over 50 employers.

EDUCATION: University of Louisville, Louisville, KY
Bachelor of Arts, May, 1994 - Major in Classical Civilization.
GPA: 3.6 in major. Dean's List.

EXPERIENCE:

1992-
Present
Cartel, Manpower, Berman, TAC Temps and Brooks Temporary Services
Involved in a wide variety of temporary employment including warehouse work, carpenter's assistant, plumber's assistant, furniture moving, construction work, plaster and drywall work, security guard, retail clerk, satellite dish installation, office filing and Goodwill trailer attendant.

1992-
Present
"Louisville Music Magazine" Louisville, KY
Album Reviewer. Occasionally published as an album reviewer in independently produced music publication.

1991-1992
Jon's, Calvert City, KY
Cashier and Stock Clerk in retail department store.

1990-1992
Appleby Communications, Lexington, KY
Performed various tasks at independent publisher of Financial Services Times and Kentucky Insurance Times, including paste-up, making copies and media kits, phone reception, small repairs, mail preparation, etc.

ACTIVITIES:

House Program Council, contributor to Louisville Collegian, intramural sports.

REFERENCES:

Available upon request.

■ Computer and typing skills are valuable assets, particularly for entry-level administrative positions.

■ Only a few, carefully chosen extra-curricular activities are listed, indicating depth of interest and commitment.

CLASSICS MAJOR

Chris Smith
178 Green Street
Albany, NY 12203
(518) 555-5555

OBJECTIVE

An entry-level position in magazine publishing.

EDUCATION

Millsaps College, Jackson, MS
B.A. Classics, June 1994
Full tuition scholarship on the basis of academic merit.

EXPERIENCE

WRITING CLINIC TUTOR, Millsaps College. Answered questions about individual work. Critiqued rough drafts. Made suggestions for structural and stylistic improvement. September 1993 - May, 1994.

CLASSICS TEACHING ASSISTANT, Millsaps College. Ran a weekly discussion meeting focused on course readings for Classics 101. Explicated difficult passages. Answered students' questions. Critiqued rough drafts. Semester I, 1993-94.

TEMPORARY OFFICE POSITIONS, including Receptionist, Mail Room Assistant, and Data Entry, for New York Temps, Inc., Albany, NY. Worked with Microsoft Word. Filed. Verified auto insurance coverage. Directed calls. Entered client data into computerized archive system. Summers 1992, 1993.

SKILLS

Proficient with Microsoft Word, Word 4.0. Type 50 wpm. Trained in Basic Programming. Excellent writing and editing skills. Working knowledge of French. Some experience with computerized paste-up, spreadsheets.

ACTIVITIES

STAFF WRITER, *Millsaps College News.* Wrote biweekly feature articles on various campus events. Aided in the decision of which issues to cover. Assisted in paste-up.

LITERARY EDITOR, *Hetaera,* a literary magazine produced by Millsaps and Belhaven Colleges. Reviewed and rated contributions. Determined what to include in collaboration with other staff members.

EDITOR-IN-CHIEF, *Another COG,* Albany High School, Albany, NY.
Assigned and edited articles. Managed staff of fifteen. Composed editorials, features, and news articles. Created advertisements. Supervised paste-up and lay-out.

FOUNDER AND EDITOR-IN-CHIEF, *Juggernaut Cover Girl,* an independent satire magazine, Albany, NY. Founded magazine with the help of six other high school students. Edited and assigned satirical articles on high school life. Solicited advertising and created advertisements. Supervised paste-up and lay-out.

■ Resume is tailored to student's job objective; unrelated jobs and other irrelevant information is de-emphasized or omitted.

■ Job descriptions are short, concise, and effective. This resume will likely be examined more carefully than a long-winded one.

COMMUNICATIONS MAJOR

Chris Smith
178 Green Street
Magnolia, DE 19962
(302) 555-5555

OBJECTIVE
To contribute education and experience in an entry-level position in Communications.

SUMMARY OF QUALIFICATIONS
- Heavy course work in all areas of communications, marketing, PR, writing, public speaking, presentations, and advertising.
- A one-year internship at a radio station.
- Bilingual: Fluent in speaking, reading and writing German.
- Member of Communications Club and Yearbook staff at UCONN.
- Dedicated, cooperative, flexible team player.

EDUCATION

D'YOUVILLE COLLEGE, Buffalo, NY
Bachelor of Arts, Communication Sciences   May, 1994
Specialized course work included Public Relations Writing, Advertising, Promotions and Publicity, Marketing, Consumer Behavior, Interpersonal Communication, Persuasion, Mass Media, Quantitative Analysis.

EUROCENTERS, Hamburg, Germany
German Certificate (120 hours intensive, four-week course.)   July, 1993

EXPERIENCE

DELAWARE MEDICAL CENTER   1993-Present
Secretary: Psychiatric Day Hospital responsible to 15 doctors. Type vouchers, office logs, letter files, and perform other general secretarial duties. Assisted in Ophthalmology, maintaining over 3,000 charts as well as typing and faxing documents.

104.25 WSTV-FM, Buffalo, NY   1993
Internship: Assisted the Promotion Department by participating in their on-location promotional events and programming activities. Aided on-air personalities during their shows.

THE HARTFORD GOLD CLUB, Buffalo, NY   1991-1993
Receptionist: Received members/guests, made reservations, and performed general clerical tasks.

COMPUTER SKILLS:
WordPerfect 5.0; Lotus 1-2-3; MacIntosh; Paradox; DOS 4.0

PERSONAL
Travel, photography, dance

■ The chrono-functional resume format is ideal for college students with some work experience.

■ Foreign language skills, useful for positions in communication, further strengthen student's credentials.

COMPUTER SCIENCE MAJOR

Chris Smith
178 Green Street
Goshen, IN 46526
(219) 555-5555

OBJECTIVE

A career in computer programming.

EDUCATION

United States Naval Academy, Annapolis, MD
B.S. Computer Science, May 1994.
Curriculum had emphasis on the analytical and technical skills for identifying, studying and solving informational problems in business organizations.

SKILLS

- DEC PDP 11/70, VAX 11/780, and the IBM-compatible AT&T PC.
- Programming in COBOL, BASIC, Ada, RBase 5000, and dBase II.
- Hardware-oriented courses: Microprocessors.
- Software-oriented courses: Programming in BASIC, Operating Systems, File Structures, DATA Structures, COBOL, Data Base Techniques, Ada, and Software Engineering.
- Analysis and Design courses: Systems Analysis, Systems Design, and Programming Languages.

EXPERIENCE
Summers
1992-1994   The Let It Rise Restaurant, Goshen, IN
- Waited tables, acted as host; developed good personal relation skills.
- Took in deliveries and supplies and distributed them throughout the restaurant.
- Managed Inventory.

COLLEGIATE

United States Naval Academy is the nation's oldest private military college, which places demands upon its students beyond academic curriculum. The Academy develops leadership and organizational skills through a disciplined environment.

Charter Member of the Association for Computing Machinery (ACM).
Member of the USNA Division 1 Crew Team.

Selected by the Harvard University crew coach to play for a rugby all-star team in the Netherlands.

Intramurals: softball, volleyball.

Anderson College Hockey Team Manager.

Other interests: football, wrestling, beach combing.

■ Extensive computer skills, a must for jobs in programming, are listed in detail near top of resume.

■ Including some job experience on a resume is important, even if it doesn't relate to student's job objective.

CRIMINAL JUSTICE MAJOR

Chris Smith
178 Green Street
Edgerton, KS 66021
(913) 555-5555

OBJECTIVE:
A position in a corrections facility.

EDUCATIONAL BACKGROUND
BAKER UNIVERSITY, Baldwin City, KS
Bachelor of Arts degree in Criminal Justice, May 1994
Minor: Sociology
Dean's List. 3.2 grade point average. Courses include U.S. Government, Business Law, Ethics in Public Life, The Politics of Economics, Sociology of Poverty, and Public Speaking.

Financed 100% of education through various full- and part-time jobs

INTERNSHIP
Sept. 1993 - GARDNER MUNICIPAL COURT, Probation Department, Gardner, KS
Dec. 1993 **Intern Probation Officer**
- Supervised, counseled, and advised adult probationers on community service
- Conducted initial interviews of all criminals to obtain personal history for court records
- Located positions for community service
- Monitored progress through regular meetings with probationers and their supervisors
- Provided referrals to counseling groups for drug and alcohol treatment
- Maintained list of employment agencies for job referrals

STUDENT WORK EXPERIENCE
Summer THE SQUEAKY CLEANERS, Wellsville, KS
1993 **Night Manager**
- Responsible for in-coming cash
- Oversaw pick-up and drop-off of customers' clothing

1988-1993 OVERBROOK FOOD, Overbrook, KS
Assistant Manager, Grocery Department
- Trained and supervised clerks on shift
- Hired as clerk; awarded increased responsibility through excellent performance

REFERENCES
Available upon request

- Impressive grade point average is listed under education; a GPA under 3.0 should not be included on a resume.

- Job descriptions are short, concise, and effective. This resume will likely be examined more carefully than a long-winded one.

CULINARY ARTS MAJOR

Chris Smith
178 Green Street
Cavendish, VT 05142
(802) 555-5555

OBJECTIVE
To contribute acquired culinary skills to a restaurant position.

SUMMARY OF QUALIFICATIONS
- More than four years of progressively responsible food-related experience.
- Bachelor's degree in Culinary Arts.
- Dependable, detail-oriented team worker; capable of following directions precisely.

EDUCATION:

CULINARY INSTITUTE OF AMERICA, New Haven, CT
Bachelor's degree in Culinary Arts
Culinary Arts Diploma (1994)

UNIVERSITY OF WASHINGTON, Department of Correspondence Study
Nutrition Course - 3 semester hours credit (1993)

EXPERIENCE

AUTUMN OAKS INN, Cavendish, VT   1994-Present
Cook
Assist chefs in meal preparation. Responsibilities include cutting meat, making sauces, rotating food, cooking and serving special faculty functions and on-line service of more than 300 patrons.

SHADE HILL INN, Branford, CT   1993-1994
Cook
Prepare breakfast for over 200 patrons daily.

REDWING FOOD SUPPLY, Hartford, CT   1992-1993
Stock Person
Dated and rotated products. Supplied food to homeless shelter cafeterias.

THE WOLFSONG TAVERN, Butte, MT   Summer 1992
Prep Cook
General responsibilities as above.

Assistant Prep Cook   Summer 1991
Busperson   Summer 1990

- Summary calls attention to student's strongest qualifications.

- Resume illustrates continual career progression.

EARTH SCIENCE MAJOR

CHRIS SMITH

<u>School Address:</u>
178 Green Street
Corvallis, Oregon 97335
Phone: (503) 555-5555

<u>Permanent Address:</u>
23 Blue Street
Portland, Oregon 98651
Phone: (503) 444-4444

Education
1991- **OREGON STATE UNIVERSITY**   <u>CORVALLIS, OR</u>
Present

Bachelor of Arts degree to be awarded in June 1995, majoring in Earth Science and minoring in Forestry. Courses of study include Forest Economics, Range Management, Ecology, Soil Science, Hydrology, Wildlife, and Agronomy. Independent Research topic: The Effect of Hydrolechicin Treatment on Blue Alpine Firs Infected with Pulloma Disease. 3.7 grade point average.

Member of the Oregon State Ecological Society. Awarded the Tepper Badge for outstanding achievement in the natural sciences.

Internship
summer **OREGON STATE SOIL CONSERVATION SERVICE**   <u>PORTLAND, OR</u>
1994

Provided technical assistance to farmers, ranchers, and others concerned with the conservation of soil, water, and related natural resources. Aided in the development of programs designed to maximize land productivity without harm or damage. Developed programs to combat soil erosion.

Experience
summer **OREGON STATE UNIVERSITY FIELD CAMP**   <u>KLAMATH FALLS, OR</u>
1993

Planted and maintained trees and rare natural vegetation, recorded and charted growth. Tracked wildlife species and worked to preserve natural habitats for endangered species. Tested soil and water samples.

part-time Unrelated work positions include Bus Person, Cashier, and Service Station
1991-1993 Attendant.

Interests

Playing acoustic guitar, hiking, camping, and competition swimming.

References

Available upon request.

■ Listing a permanent address in addition to a school address is a good idea for students who have not yet graduated.

■ Internships supplement student's classroom learning with valuable, hands-on experience.

ECONOMICS MAJOR

Chris Smith
178 Green Street
La Houna, HI 96761
(808) 555-5555

OBJECTIVE

An entry-level position with a financial services firm.

EDUCATION

BOSTON COLLEGE, Chestnut Hill, MA
Bachelor of Arts in Economics, May 1994
Minor areas of concentration: Business Administration,
Mathematics Communications

ACTIVITIES

Member, Debate Team
Member, Finance Society
Member, College Republicans

PROFESSIONAL EXPERIENCE

TROPICAL WORLD BANK AND TRUST COMPANY, Lattaina, HI
summers 1989-91
Conducted daily processing of option pledges and releases into
the depository trust and options clearing computers.

MICHAELS, DOUGLAS AND ROWE, Honolulu, HI
summer 1992
Performed investment research of prospective companies' various
stock options and economic events, cold calling and stock trading
for a broker.

UNRELATED EXPERIENCE

THE FENCE PRINCE, Boston, MA 1993-94
Independent installation of boundary, swimming pool and tennis
court fencing.

DAVIERWEILLER, INC., Dorchester, MA 1992-93
Fork lift operator for the third largest supermarket
warehousing firm in the nation.
Additional Work Landscaping and Maintenance.

INTERESTS

Stock market, skiing, and water sports.

■ Extracurricular activities add weight to student's resume.

■ Experience is effectively divided into two categories: professional and unrelated.

EDUCATION MAJOR

Chris Smith

School Address
178 Green Street
Dayton, OH 45469
(513) 555-5555

Permanent Address
23 Blue Street
Oakwood, OH 45873
(419) 444-4444

EDUCATION

University of Dayton   **Dayton, OH**
Bachelor of Arts Degree, Summa Cum Laude, May 1994
G.P.A.: 3.6/4.0 Dean's List, First Honors
Majors: Secondary Education, English

HONORS

Selected to speak at Commencement ceremonies
National Education Award, 1992
National Dean's List, 1990-1991, 1991-1992, 1993-1994
Who's Who Among Students, 1991,1992

ACTIVITIES

Student Admissions Program
Peer Advisement Program
Freshmen Assistance Program
School of Education Senate
Student Representative to Educational Policy Committee

EXPERIENCE

Spring **Substitute Teaching**   **Oakwood High School, Oakwood, OH**
1994 Work as substitute teacher in various disciplines for students in grades 7-12.

Fall 1993 **Student Teaching Full-Time Practicum**   **Kerrigan High, Kerrigan, OH**
Travel to site daily and assume full teaching responsibility for two junior accelerated American Literature classes and one freshman fundamental English class. Prepare, lecture, discuss, and evaluate units in literature and writing. Design and present lessons on Puritan writers, focusing on Nathaniel Hawthorne's *Scarlet Letter*. Provide writing instruction for paragraphs and essays.

Fall 1992 **Student Teaching Field Pre-Practicum**   **Central High School, Dayton, OH**

Spring **Kerrigan High School**   **Kerrigan, OH**
1992 Visit site weekly to observe classes and gain practical teaching experience.

REFERENCES

Available upon request.

■ Teaching practicums are an essential aspect of an education major's resume.

■ Special honors indicate student's potential to excel.

ELECTRICAL ENGINEERING MAJOR

CHRIS SMITH

CURRENT ADDRESS:	**PERMANENT ADDRESS**
178 Green Street	23 Blue Street
Santa Clara, CA 95050	Beaverton, OR 97007
(408) 555-5555	(503) 444-4444

OBJECTIVE
A challenging entry-level electrical engineering position.

EDUCATION
BACHELOR OF SCIENCE IN ELECTRICAL ENGINEERING, 1994
San Jose State University, San Jose, CA
Laboratory work included: Microelectronics Fabrication, Communications, Microprocessors,
Electronics, Circuit Analysis, Digital Logic Design
Electronics Labor - San Diego Technical Community College, 1993

COMPUTER PROFICIENCY
SPICE/WORKVIEWCAD/AUTOCAD/BASIC/PASCAL/FORTRAN

WORK EXPERIENCE

Castello Corporation   Santa Clara, CA
Engineering Assistant   1993-Present
Planned, organized and prioritized production operations and rendered technical support for the U.S. Government
Secure System, PCs, mid-range computer systems, work stations and printers. Dealt with assembly, test and
configuration issues; implemented and monitored the effectiveness of manufacturing procedures. Worked with R&D
in readying product upgrades and newly designed products for production.
- Achieved optimum efficiency in productivity, manufacturing process and design.
- Boosted product quality with effective controls.

Baldwin Inc.   Malibu, CA
Group Leader   1992-1993
Responsible for equipment maintenance/operation and supervision of 4 trimming department employees. Oversaw
machine set up; served as technical consultant to new employees and offered instruction on various machinery
operations. Operated several cutting machines and ensured smooth departmental assembly-line flow and compliance
with quality assurance standards.

Melvin Inventory   Beaverton, OR
Inventory Clerk   Summer 1992
Performed inventory control for several area retail stores. Duties included taking inventory; entering SKU numbers,
prices and quantities into hand-held computer; ensured accuracy.

VOLUNTEER WORK
Member - Santa Clara Volunteer Firefighter's Association

INTERESTS & ACTIVITIES
Skiing/Weight Training/Football

■ Job objective gives focus to student's resume, without limiting his/her opportunities.

■ The chrono-functional resume format is ideal for college students with some work experience.

ENGLISH LITERATURE MAJOR

Chris Smith
178 Green Street
Forsyth, GA 31029
(912) 555-5555

SKILLS:
- **Writing:** Over three years experience writing articles for various newspapers on topics ranging from politics to theater.
- **Deadlines:** Extremely reliable under pressure, consistently meet deadlines.
- **Computers:** Knowledgeable in many types of computer software packages, such as Microsoft Word, WordPerfect, and Pagemaker.

EDUCATION:

Tift College, Forsyth, GA
Bachelor of Arts in English Literature, May 1994
Minor: Journalism
Magna Cum Laude

EXPERIENCE:

Editor, *The Spectrum*   Sept. 1992-May 1994
Forsyth, GA
Held weekly meetings with up to 25 students to select poetry, short fiction, prose, and art work for school literary magazine, published once per semester. Worked closely with printer on page layout and cover design. Made final decisions on submissions. Carefully proofread final product. Distributed magazine to area locations.

Feature Writer, *The Sentinel*   Sept. 1990-May 1993
Forsyth, GA
Wrote weekly articles for Arts and Entertainment Section of campus newspaper reviewing movies, plays, novels, and new music releases. Was also a guest columnist for viewpoint, sports, and News Sections.

Intern, *The Forsyth Gazette*   Sept. 1993-Dec. 1993
Forsyth, GA
Contributed weekly articles on current events to local newspaper. Interviewed local businessmen and townspeople for experimental section on area residents.

AFFILIATIONS:

English Society
Society for Academic Excellence
Young Journalists of America

REFERENCES:

Available upon request.

■ Internships and jobs at college newspapers supplement student's classroom learning with valuable, hands-on experience.

■ Professional affiliations illustrate student's commitment to his/her field.

ENGLISH MAJOR

Chris Smith
178 Green Street
Columbia, MO 65201
(314) 555-5555

OBJECTIVE
To contribute developed skills to a challenging position in the publishing field.

SUMMARY OF QUALIFICATIONS
- Four years publishing experience.
- Completely bilingual in English and Spanish; some knowledge of French.
- Extensive computer experience (formerly a Computer Science major): IBM, MACINTOSH, Compu-graphics, VAX.
- Proven writing skills; authored hundreds of pages of fiction in the past three years.
- Excellent communication abilities; lectured to a wide variety of audiences in a museum setting.

EDUCATION
DOWLING COLLEGE, Oakdale, NY
B.A., English, magna cum laude, May, 1994

COLLEGE ACTIVITIES
Plume, Literary Magazine   Fall 1990-Spring 1994
Editor (from Spring 1992), **Production and Business Coordinator**
Responsible for composing magazine budget and arranging specifications with printers.

Free-Lance Writer   Spring 1991-Spring 1994
Published book and movie reviews, essays and short stories on different campus publications.

Dowling College Pictures   Spring 1992
Founding Member/Screenwriter
Wrote short movie production.

WORK EXPERIENCE
The Damien House Museum, Oakdale, NY   Spring 1994
Museum Assistant
Interpreted exhibits for visitors. Prepared/delivered short talks on historical subjects. Participated in organization of creative educational programs.

Bindings Bookstore, Oakdale, NY   Fall 1992
Sales Clerk/Floor Person
Maintained stock; helped customers make selections; registered sales.

Collectible Canvas Store, Creve Coeur, MO   Summer 1992
Framer
Handled frame/glass cutting and mounting of prints and artwork.

- Summary of qualifications highlights student's acquired skills.

- College activities are related to student's field of study and career objective.

FINANCE MAJOR

Chris Smith
178 Green Street
Georgetown, TX 78676
(517) 555-5555

CAREER OBJECTIVE
To secure a responsible, entry-level position in Finance.

SUMMARY OF QUALIFICATIONS
- College major, relevant course work and tutoring experience in finance, economics and accounting.
- Strong analytical and numerical abilities.
- Proven interpersonal skills: cooperative team player, yet equally effective, motivated and hard working independently.
- Excellent sales and closing skills.
- Calm under pressure; meet deadlines; strong on follow-up.
- Bilingual: Fluent in French.

STRENGTHS

GOAL -DIRECTED * ENTHUSIASTIC * HIGH ENERGY * DEPENDABLE

EDUCATION

SOUTHWESTERN UNIVERSITY, Georgetown, NY
Bachelor of Science in Finance; Major GPA 3.55/4.0. May 1994

ALLAPOLOOSA ACADEMY, Hadley, MA 1990

L'ECOLE DE TROIS FILLES, Paris, France 1988

EMPLOYMENT

THE TURKEY TROUGH, Alpine, TX   1993-Present
Assistant to Manager/Server and Bartender
Responsibilities included customer service; balancing of nightly receipts.

SOUTHWESTERN UNIVERSITY, Georgetown, TX   1991-1993
Teaching Assistant/Tutor in Finance, Economics, Accounting
Tutored students and assisted professor in Corporate Finance course.

BENNOIT ASSOCIATES, Austin, TX   1989-1991
Payroll and Daily Journal Bookkeeper

COMPUTERS

DOS, Lotus 1-2-3, WordPerfect

PERSONAL

Water and snow skiing * tennis * snorkeling

■ Summary of qualifications highlights student's professional and educational training.

■ Personal interests can provide a great topic for conversation during a job interview.

FOOD SCIENCE MAJOR

CHRIS SMITH

School Address	**Permanent Address**
178 Green Street	23 Blue Street
Newport, RI 02840	Hull, MA 02045
(401) 555-5555	(617) 444-4444

OBJECTIVE
A challenging CHEF/MANAGERIAL position in the FOOD SERVICE INDUSTRY.

EDUCATION
JOHNSON & WALES COLLEGE, Providence, RI
A.S. Degree - Food Science/Degree to be awarded: 1995
Dean's List student

PROFESSIONAL EXPERIENCE
PHEASANT LANE RESTAURANT, Newport, RI   1994-Present
Sous Chef
Main duties involve capably assisting the owner and Executive Chef in overall operations of this nouvelle cuisine specialty restaurant.
- *Ensure and arrange for selective and adequate ordering of all meat, fish and produce for the cafe.*
- *Interview, hire, train and supervise all new kitchen employees.*
- *Skilled in the preparation and production of quality cuisine, and in the planning, development and execution of innovative recipes.*
- *Conceptualize and design creative and original menus.*

OCEANVIEW INN, Providence, RI   1992-1994
Banquet Manager/Food & Beverage Director
- *Organized functions, including scheduling employees, ordering food and beverages, and overseeing functions.*
- *Organized dining areas.*

RHODE SIDE INNS, Providence, RI   1991-1992
Server
- *Trained new bus and wait staff.*
- *Resolved customer complaints.*

Busperson
- *Set up and dismantle dining area..*
- *Promoted to server within six months.*

- Student indicates that he/she has not yet graduated by stating "Degree to be awarded..."

- Resume indicates student's ongoing interest in a particular industry.

GEOGRAPHY MAJOR

Chris Smith
178 Green Street
Maize, KY 41160
(316) 555-5555

OBJECTIVE
Seeking a challenging entry-level position in convention/function planning where related education and experience will be utilized.

EDUCATION
TULANE UNIVERSITY, New Orleans, LA
B.S. Degree in Geography, 1994. Concentration: **Travel and Tourism**. Dean's list seven semesters.
Course work included: Comprehensive Travel, Travel Management and Planning, Tourism Development, Retail Travel, Tourism Development, Domestic and International Geography.

SUMMARY
- Completed special tourism development project (The New Orleans Facility Report); produced a guide to area function facilities and developed facility marketing strategies.
- Hands-on travel marketing and development experience.
- Experienced in itinerary preparation, proper usage of Official Airline Guide, Hotel Indexes and Thomas Cook Timetables, and international and domestic manual ticketing.
- Ability in map reading, accounting, reservations and administration.
- Experience in the food and beverage industry.

EXPERIENCE

THE NEW ORLEANS VISITORS CENTER   **Intern**   Fall 93
- Researched and compiled information for directories which included Calendar of Events, Catalog of Historic Sites, and Music Festival Directory.
- Represented Massachusetts Division of Tourism at the World Trade Center Travel Show; answered questions and provided tourist information on New Orleans cultural events, places of interest and sightseeing.
- Assisted in marketing effort to promote New Orleans; contacted tour planners nationwide.
- Provided tourist information at the New Orleans Visitors Center.
- Completed special project involving compilation and analysis of data on all Mardi Gras visitors; Analyzed market potential for industry expansion and provided detailed reports regarding benefits to affected industries.

PALMETTO AUTO, New Orleans, LA   **Receptionist**   1992-93
- Performed a variety of administration support functions.
- Interacted with customers; extensive telephone communication.

CANDLEBERRY COURT, New Orleans, LA   **Server**   1991-92

THE TEAKWOOD INN, New Orleans, LA   **Server**   1990-91

■ Resume includes course work that corresponds to the position desired.

■ Format is organized and visually appealing.

GERONTOLOGY MAJOR

Chris Smith
178 Green Street
San Francisco, CA 94133
(715) 555-5555

EDUCATION:

SAN FRANCISCO STATE UNIVERSITY, San Francisco, CA
Bachelor of Arts in Gerontology, 1994. G.P.A.: Overall 3.1, Gerontology, 3.6. Worked to finance nearly 50% of college tuition.

EMPLOYMENT:

VETERAN'S CLINIC, SAN FRANCISCO, CA   1994-Present
Ward Medical Clerk
- Serve as an administrative aid to the medical personnel on the wards.
- Carry out doctor's orders such as ordering lab work, scheduling tests, and maintaining accurate patient records.
- Duties require a high level of interaction with staff, patients, and family members.

BARBOSA LIBRARY, SFSU, San Francisco, CA   1990-1993
Interlibrary Loan Assistant
- Assisted librarians in interlibrary loan office of main college library.
- Processed incoming mail, notified students of receipt of requests, and updated transactions on the computer.

VETERAN'S CLINIC, San Gabriel, CA   Summer 1992
File Clerk, Record Retirement Project
- Worked as part of eight-person team on special record retirement project.
- Located, consolidated and packaged inactive medical records for shipment to storage.
- Chosen to accurately roster and enter data into word processing system.

COMMUNITY SERVICE:

STUDENT PROGRAM FOR CHILDREN'S WELFARE   1990-1992
Big Friend/Little Friend Program
Participated in program to aid disadvantaged San Francisco youth from the Staron Village housing project.
VELSOR MIDDLE SCHOOL, San Francisco, CA   Fall 1993
TUTOR
Tutored 7th grade boy in need of academic assistance.

OTHER SKILLS:

- Familiar with Microsoft Word and WordPerfect
- Working knowledge of written and spoken German

■ Education is listed at the top of resume because it is student's strongest qualification.

■ Community service indicates student's altruistic nature, a positive attribute in a health/social services-related field.

HISTORY MAJOR

Chris Smith

Current Address	Permanent Address
178 Green Street	23 Blue Street
Baltimore, MD 21218	Aurora, ME 04408
(301) 555-5555	(207) 444-4444

OBJECTIVE
To contribute acquired skills and recent educational background to an entry-level administrative position within an organization offering opportunities for growth and advancement.

SUMMARY OF QUALIFICATIONS
- Adapt easily to new concepts and responsibilities.
- Diverse background in both business and outdoor skills.
- Self-motivated; detail-oriented; function well both independently and as team member.
- Proven communication skills, both oral and written.

EDUCATION

UNIVERSITY OF MARYLAND, College Park, MD
Bachelor of Arts Degree, History, expected May 1995.

WORK HISTORY

THE SPORTS SPOT, Baltimore, MD   1993 - Present
Sales Associate
Consistently meet/exceed monthly sales quotas in all market areas.

BLUE BAYOU ENTERPRISES, College Park, MD   1991-1992
Owner/President
Conceived, developed, marketed, and sold various products to 30,000 student and faculty population.

BERMAN FOUNDATION, Aurora, ME   Summer 1991
Work Camp Supervisor
Responsible for twelve European University students through Volunteer for Peace Program.

Wilderness Trip Co-Leader   Summers 1988-1990
Co-led a seven-week canoeing and backpacking expedition for ten teenage participants in Northern Maine, 1988, 1989. Co-led a family canoeing trip on the Alaska Wilderness Waterway, ages 12 to 65, 1990.

UNIVERSITY OF MAINE, Orono, ME   Winter 1988-1992
Registrar's Office
Administrator
Processed transcripts; researched records on data base, microfilm, and hard copy; responded to student inquiries/complaints. Required familiarity with PC and Main frame data entry.

- Objective accentuates student's educational background as well as professional skills.

- After education, job experience is listed in reverse chronological order, with student's most recent job appearing first.

INTERNATIONAL RELATIONS MAJOR

Chris Smith

School Address
178 Green Street
Ripon, WI 54971
(414) 555-5555

Permanent Address
23 Blue Street
Charlotte, NC 28277
(704) 444-4444

EDUCATION

RIPON COLLEGE
B.S. International Relations: G.P.A. 3.20, Major 3.33
Minor: Marketing
Courses: Marketing Research, Sales and Distribution, Management, Promotional Management, Consumer Behavior, Global Communications, Social Change in Developing Nations.

OXFORD UNIVERSITY   Oxford, England
Spring 1993
Related Courses: International Marketing and Advertising, International Economics and World Trade.

*Financed 50% of college tuition as well as all personal expenses through part-time college and full-time summer employment.

WORK EXPERIENCE

JACKSON ELECTRIC COMPANY   Ladysmith, WI
Customer Service Representative   Summer 1994
Worked in the Marketing Department for the Power Integrated Circuits Division of Jackson answering both domestic and international customer inquiries regarding product and pricing. Processed product sample requests, packaged and shipped samples. Developed reports on sample requests and manufacturing orders received for District Managers worldwide. Assisted other marketing personnel in various tasks as required.

THE INTERNATIONAL CONNECTION   Ripon, WI
Evaluation Intern   Spring 1994
Composed, edited, and dispersed to Management summaries of project reports for IESC, a non-profit organization which sends retired corporate executives into third world countries to advise and assist them in efficient production methods.

THE WOODTIP CORPORATION   Ripon, WI
Student Manager   1991-1994
Organized blueprint files, order entering, and materials inventory; handled accounts payable and account receivable; worked with materials purchasing; and replaced receptionist for plant which manufactures aircraft engine parts.

ADDITIONAL EXPERIENCE

Ripon College Marketing Club (1992-1994), College Marketing Association (1992-1994), International Relations Club (1992-1993), Circle K Club (1990-1991).

Studied in London, England (1993) and traveled through Western Europe and the United Kingdom. Working knowledge of French.

■ Valuable foreign travel and study abroad experience is related to student's major.

■ Student's financial contribution to education indicates maturity and strong sense of responsibility.

JOURNALISM MAJOR

Chris Smith
178 Green Street
Willamette, OR 97301
(503) 555-5555

EDUCATION:
University of Oregon, Eugene, OR
Bachelor of Arts in Journalism, May 1994
The Writer's Block, 1992-1994
Vice-President of a student-run journalism/writing group producing a biweekly newsletter and providing a forum for creative expression by students.

EXPERIENCE:

Kids Abroad 4/93 to Present
Administrative Director, Western Region USA; Supervise, from inception to completion, all incoming foreign exchange student programs. Assign program location and coordinator. Annually monitor 800 high school foreign exchange students. Act as liaison between foreign clients and American personnel. Evaluate, edit, and choose texts used to teach English to the exchange students.

Kids Abroad 4/90 to Present
Contributing columnist for public relations newspaper.

Kids Abroad Western Regional Office 9/90 to Present
Manage 800 person field staff across United States. Place, counsel, and monitor high school foreign exchange students and host families throughout United States. Tutor English As A Second Language. Annually direct French student orientation in Portland. Write public relations and promotional materials. Manage office.

Journalism Department University of Oregon 9/92 to 6/93
Peer academic advisor; professor's assistant; office support staff.

INTERNSHIP:

Jade Ryder Enterprises 7/92 to 9/92
Researched and organized celebrity biographies for promotional flyers; writing and computer graphics; administrative duties.

VOLUNTEER:

Tutoring Program 1/91 to 6/92
Participated in an independent tutoring program in which college students tutored junior and high school students in academic subjects and motivational skills.

SKILLS:

WordPerfect 5.1, Microsoft Word for Windows, Editing.

■ Extracurricular activities add weight to student's resume.

■ Valuable computer skills are highlighted in a separate section.

LINGUISTICS MAJOR

Chris Smith

School Address	**Permanent Address**
178 Green Street	23 Blue Street
Sterling, VA 20165	Westhampton, MA 01027
(703) 555-5555	(413) 444-4444

PROFESSIONAL OBJECTIVE
An entry-level position in linguistic analysis.

EDUCATION

Bachelor of Science in Linguistics, 1994
Roanoke College, Salem, VA
Graduated third in College of Arts & Sciences
Cumulative Average: 3.8/4.0
Howard Payne University, Brownwood, TX

SPECIAL COURSES & SKILLS
Linguistics courses included Semantics, Syntax, Phonetics, and
Psycholinguistics
Experience in COBOL, BASIC, FORTRAN, and PASCAL programming
languages
Speak French at conversational level
Have taken various mathematics and science courses

ACTIVITIES
Member, Phi Kappa Phi National Honor Society
Member, The Academy Honor Society, Roanoke College
Staff Writer, Student Newspaper, Howard Payne University
Calculus Tutor, Howard Payne University
Member, Orientation Staff, Howard Payne University
Member, Education Club, Howard Payne University
Tour Guide, Admissions Office, Howard Payne University

PRACTICA

ROANOKE COLLEGE, Salem, VA Winter/Spring 1993
• Studied and evaluated performance of DEC talking computer
• Assisted development of classroom applications for phonetics
class; assessed needs in six-month practicum

NEUMANN SCHOOL, Westhampton, MA, Summer 1993
• Evaluated disadvantaged students to determine effects of
socioeconomic background on linguistic skills and scholastic
performance

■ Education is elaborated upon by including special courses and skills.

■ Extracurricular activities demonstrate that student is sociable and gets along well with a diversity of people.

MANAGEMENT INFORMATION SYSTEMS (MIS) MAJOR

Chris Smith
178 Green Street
Chicago, IL 60611
(312) 555-5555

OBJECTIVE
An entry-level position in Management Information Systems.

PROFESSIONAL PROFILE
- Experienced in client relations.
- Organized, dedicated with a positive attitude.
- Fluent in French, born and raised in France.
- Excellent written and spoken English.
- Excellent in Mathematics.
- Developed computer programs in COBOL and Pascal.

EDUCATION
Loyola University of Chicago, Chicago, IL, May 1994.
Bachelor's Degree in Management Information Systems.
Dean's List status, Honors student. Helped to organize the first Annual Loyola State Computer Symposium.

PROFESSIONAL EXPERIENCE
Tierney Temps, Inc., Chicago, IL, 1992-Present
Reception, data entry, word processing.

Loyola University of Chicago, Chicago, IL, 1991-1993
Computer Lab Assistant. Helped students to get started on computers, assisted during classes. Peer tutored in different fields.

D. McGill & Associates, Chicago, IL, 1990-1991
Data Entry Clerk for busy accounting firm. Also maintained correspondence with key accounts. Found major billing error that saved company over $3,000.

COMPUTER SKILLS
Programming Languages - COBOL, BASIC, PASCAL.
Software - MS DOS, dBase III+, Quattro Pro, Word Processors.
Hardware/Mainframe - Bitnet, Internet, DOSVS, VSE.
Hardware Micros - IBM PSII, IBM 386, AT&T PC, Macintosh.

- College students should never submit a resume more than one page long. If necessary, a smaller typeface or narrower page margins can be used.

- Student's educational background corresponds with his/her job objective.

MARKETING MAJOR

Chris Smith
178 Green Street
Berrien, MI 49104
(616) 555-5555

EDUCATION:

University of Michigan at Ann Arbor
Bachelor of Science in Marketing, May 1994
Concentration: Communication Studies
Minor: Sociology
G.P.A.: 3.4/4.0
University of Michigan at Flint
Studies in Liberal Arts/Theater, 1990-92

AWARDS AND ACTIVITIES:

Dean's List   Stage Troupe
Golden Key National Honor Society Member   Somerville Community Chorus
Student Government Representative   International Leadership Award Recipient
University Chorus   Student Government Advertising Committee

EXPERIENCE:

Rodriguez Inc., *Ann Arbor, MI*   January-April 1994
Public Relations Intern
• Interned in a large Portuguese jewelry manufacturer.
• Researched information on Portuguese and American precious metal trade.
• Compiled status reports and press releases for the company.

University of Michigan Ad Center, *Ann Arbor, MI*   September 1991-October 1993
Account Leader
• Attended weekly client and team meetings.
• Created copy for and produced brochures for Ann Arbor Youth Guidance Center.
• Produced informational slide show and video for Champions organization.
• Compiled weekly status reports for clients and team.

Sacajawea Marketing, *Detroit, MI*   Summer 1993
Salesperson
• Arranged meetings with prospective buyers of knives from reputable company.
• Managed monetary transactions between the company and the client.
• Attended valuable seminars on self presentation and salesmanship.

University of Michigan International Scholars Office *Ann Arbor, MI*   Summer 1992
International Orientation Leader
• Participated in a program to welcome international students to Boston University.
• Implemented many techniques of intercultural communication during the session.
• Planned and directed a talent night for the students.

SKILLS:

Speech writing and public speaking.
Proficient in MacIntosh software including Microsoft Word and Aldus Pagemaker.

■ Listing impressive awards and activities gives student's resume a competitive edge.

■ Relevant internships demonstrate student's initiative and desire to enter his/her field of interest.

MATHEMATICS MAJOR

Chris Smith

Current Address
178 Green Street
Sioux Falls, SD 57103
(605) 555-5555

Permanent Address
23 Blue Street
Wounded Knee, SD 57794
(605) 444-4444

Education: Back Hills State College, Spearfish, SD
Bachelor of Science, May 1994
Concentrations: **Mathematics and Economics**
Independent Study: Comparison of Six Women Mathematicians

Dakota Wesleyan College, Mitchell, SD
September 1990 to May 1992
Concentrations: **Mathematics and Economics**

Memberships:
Debate Club
Economics Faculty/Student Liaison Committee
Mathematics Faculty/Student Liaison Committee

Special Skills: Basic Programming, Fortran Programming, COBOL Programming, Accounting, Word Processing

Experience:

1/94 - Present **Research Analyst**, South Dakota Urban Reinvestment Advisory Group, Sioux Falls, SD. Senior internship. Research and analyze the lending policies of banks.

1/94 - Present **Computer Consultant**, Micro-Computer Laboratory, Estelline, SD Assist students, faculty, and alumni with software and hardware problems.

9/93-12/93 **FORTRAN Tutor**, Black Hills State College, Spearfish, SD

5/93-8/93 **Customer Service Representative**, Oacoma Savings Bank, Oacoma, SD. Handled up to 350 transactions per eight hour day. Processed all address changes for main bank and four branches. Used computers to enter all data.

9/92-5/93 **Mathematics Tutor**, Ecumenical Social Action Committee, Spearfish, SD

Activities:

9/90-5/92 **Big Brother/Big Sister Program**, Mitchell, SD
Participated in a one-to-one relationship with a disadvantaged child.

9/90-5/91 **Political Campaign Worker**, Worked on political campaigns of various candidates for state and national offices.

■ Listing a permanent address in addition to a school address is a good idea for students who have not yet graduated.

■ Activities section highlights student's involvement in community service and politics.

MECHANICAL ENGINEERING MAJOR

Chris Smith
178 Green Street
Dobbs Ferry, NY 13026
(914) 555-5555

OBJECTIVE
To obtain an entry-level position in Mechanical Engineering.

SUMMARY OF QUALIFICATIONS
- Excellent grounding in all areas of Engineering with ability and desire to continue learning.
- Outstanding abilities with figures, technical and manual operations.
- Highly developed interpersonal skills.
- Experienced in VAX and UNIX operating systems, WANG and IBM PCs.
- Knowledge of FORTRAN Programming.
- Working knowledge of Japanese.

EDUCATION

STATE UNIVERSITY OF NEW YORK, Ireland
Bachelor's Degree in Mechanical Engineering, Honors, 1994
Specialized in Design Engineering.

WORK HISTORY

UNITED PARCEL SERVICE, Dobbs Ferry, NY   6/94-Present
General Office Clerk
Responsibilities include: customer service, billing and credit control.

STONEY BROOK BUILDERS, Stoney Brook, NY   1/91-1/92
Engineering Intern
Involved in all departments of this Electronics Company including Workshop, Wiring, Soldering, Testing, and Design Departments.

REFERENCES

Available upon request.

■ Chrono-functional format is more flexible than a chronological resume, but stronger than a functional resume.

■ Standard, inexpensive white office paper (20# bond) is acceptable for resumes for most entry-level positions.

MUSIC MAJOR

Chris Smith

School Address
178 Green Street
New York, NY 10012
(212) 555-5555

Home Address
23 Blue Street
New Rochelle, NY 10801
(914) 444-4444

OBJECTIVE

To participate in various musical settings as a drummer/vocalist and to perform and record my own original material.

EDUCATION

THE JUILLIARD SCHOOL, New York, NY
Dual Major: **Performance and Songwriting**, B.A. May 1994. Dean's List.
Played piano for school band. Performed in annual Christmas concert to benefit the homeless.

Resident Assistant for Freshman Dormitory for two consecutive years. Organized student activities and field trips. Managed $500/semester budget.

ACCOMPLISHMENTS

- Broad based knowledge and comprehensive academic training in music for 13 years in jazz, rock, pop, Latin and classical music.
- Principle instrument: Drums with expertise on piano, guitar, voice; songwriting: words and music.
- Strong grounding in harmony and theory.
- Experience in performance and recording both in the U.S. and Puerto Rico.
- Own copyright on 25 original pieces of Rock Memorabilia.
- Bilingual: Spanish and English, verbal, written, reading, musical.
- Sat on jury for Spin Digest's International Songwriting Contest, July 1992.
- Appeared and played drums in rock video for famous Puerto Rican group, Los Hombres Guapos, Christmas 1992.

EMPLOYMENT EXPERIENCE

The "Record" Record, New York, NY   1993-Present
Served as **Assistant Editor** at this up-and-coming monthly chronicle of rock music's early years. Selected feature artists for impending Issues, conducted interviews, researched backgrounds, and assisted in editing final product.

The Salmon Run, New York, NY   1991-Present
Weekly performer with band.
Acquired weekly performance slot at this star-studded night club. Played one hour set, opening for such bands as **The Dead Onions**, **Pain Cave**, and **Burnt Retina**.

REFERENCES

Available upon request.

■ Elected positions of authority indicate student's leadership abilities.

■ Student's accomplishments are highlighted in a separate section.

NURSING MAJOR

Chris Smith
178 Green Street
Bennington, VT 05201
(802) 555-5555

CAREER OBJECTIVE
To acquire a Nursing position in a hospital or health care facility.

SUMMARY OF QUALIFICATIONS
- Nine years experience in a medical/health care setting.
- R.N. completion in December 1995; B.S.N. anticipated 1996.
- Certified Phlebotomist.
- Demonstrated composure under pressure.
- Flexible, decisive, patient.
- Intuitive; enjoy patients and work well with them.
- Prepared, organized and ready for daily tasks.
- Excellent interpersonal skills; cooperative with co-workers.
- Hard worker; dependable; prompt.
- Computer skills: IBM, WordPerfect, Lotus 1.2.3, Apple, Hospital-related PCs.

EDUCATION
VERMONT SCHOOL OF NURSING, Montpelier, VT
R.N. Diploma expected December, 1994.
Awarded Bailey Howe Award for Outstanding Students in Nursing, 1993.

EMPLOYMENT
October **TRINITY HOSPITAL**, Burlington, VT Per Diem/16-24 hours
1993 - **Intensive Care Aide/Surgical Floor Aide - Floater**
Present Assist with burn dressings and trauma patients. Post-surgical care assistance with vital signs, ADLs, insertion of Foley catheters, dressing changes, monitor IV fluids, blood sugar monitoring, and collect specimens.

1991-1993 **VERMONT GENERAL HOSPITAL**, Bennington, VT
Undergraduate Nursing Assistant - Phlebotomist
Monitored all aspects of patient care; Vital signs, ADLs, input/output records, collected specimens; monitored IVs.

1990-1991 **NEW AGE PUBLISHERS**, Killington, VT
Graphic Designer
Designed newspaper and high quality magazine ad work.

PERSONAL INTERESTS
KARATE * TROPICAL FISH * HORSEBACK RIDING

■ Relevant academic awards and practical experience illustrate student's dedication to the field of nursing.

■ Personal interests can provide a great topic for conversation during a job interview.

NUTRITION MAJOR

Chris Smith

Current Address
178 Green Street
Bloomington, IN 47405
(812) 555-5555

Permanent Address
23 Blue Street
Evansville, IN 47712
(812) 444-4444

OBJECTIVE
To utilize acquired skills in biotechnology research toward project responsibility in nutrition/health industry.

EDUCATION

Bachelor of Science in Nutrition
INDIANA UNIVERSITY
Degree Anticipated: 1995
Courses include Organic Chemistry, Anatomy and Physiology, and Food Service Administration.
Thesis topic: "Advances in Refrigeration Techniques and Their Application to the Fresh Meats Industry.

EXPERIENCE

1994 to Present   **Intern**
Nutrition Evaluation Laboratory, Human Nutrition Research
CENTER ON AGING AT INDIANA UNIVERSITY
- Assist seven researchers in routine and esoteric biochemical analysis. Implement 10 different non-clinical assays of vitamins, amino acids and other biomolecules in support of human and animal tissue culture studies. Develop and implement new types of assays and improve existing analytical techniques.
- Interact with investigators and assist in organization and implementation of analysis. Provide literature search and publication of developed methodologies in scientific journals.
- Provide maintenance for a wide variety of laboratory and analytical equipment.
- Train on microprocessor and personal computer driven analytical instruments and robots: Waters hardware and software, analytical, chromatography software.
- Initiated independent research project concerning detection of non-enzymatically glycated amino acid residues in proteins.

1993 to 1994   **Teaching Assistant**
Department of Biochemistry and Biophysics
INDIANA UNIVERSITY
Bloomington, IN
- Led group of seven students in weekly laboratory experiments.
- Administered quizzes and evaluated lab results.

PERSONAL

Willing to travel.

■ Student indicated he/she has not yet graduated by stating "Degree Anticipated ..."

■ Internship experience is valuable for students with little job experience, particularly if it corresponds to the position sought.

OCCUPATIONAL THERAPY MAJOR

Chris Smith
178 Green Street
Ypsilanti, MI 48198
(313) 555-5555

Education Eastern Michigan University, Ypsilanti, MI
Bachelor of Science, Occupational Therapy, 1994
Dean's list four consecutive semesters.

Clinical LEARNING PREP SCHOOL, Ypsilanti, MI   1993-Present
Affiliations *Assistant Occupational Therapist*
Work with students having Developmental Delays, Mental Retardation and Related
Learning Disabilities.
* Interventions include Gross and Fine Motor Therapy, Visual-Perceptual-Motor
Therapy, Vocational Training and Neurodevelopmental Technique in individual
therapy.
* Supervised Community Outings, Supervised Visual-Perceptual-Motor Group,
Pre-vocational and Vocational Work Centers.

SPAULDING REHABILITATION HOSPITAL   Summer 1992
Assistant Occupational Therapist
Caseload included patients with Cardiac and Pulmonary Disorders, Lower Limb
Amputations, Stroke, Brain Injury and Reflex Sympathetic Dystrophy.
* Interventions included Neurodevelopmental Technique, joint mobilization, Deep
Friction Massage, Computer Assisted Cognitive Therapy, Community Mobility,
Home Program Planning, Home Evaluations and Evaluations in all related areas.

MORING PSYCHIATRIC HOSPITAL   Summer 1991
Occupational Therapy Internship
Work with adolescent, adult and geriatric patients with Affective, Chronic Thought
Process, Social and Personality Disorders, as well as Substance Abuse Disorders.
* Supervised General Activities Period.
* Administered initial evaluations, vocational readiness evaluations, and leisure
planning evaluations.
* Student Project—Occupational Therapy in Psychiatry.

Professional Michigan Occupational Therapy Association, American Occupational Therapy
Associations Association.

Related SUGAR CREEK CHILDREN'S UNIT, Michigan State Psychiatric Hospital
Work *Mental Health Assistant*   Fall 1992
Experience Worked with adolescents ages 12-16 on a 30 patient unit. Responsibilities included
Milieu Therapy, counseling, behavioral management, restraint of aggressive or
self-abusive patients, and custodial care.

■ Clinical experience is an essential aspect of a resume for students entering medicine.

■ Professional affiliations indicate student's dedication to the field of occupational therapy.

PHILOSOPHY MAJOR

Chris Smith

School Address
178 Green Street
Charlotte, NC 28277
(704) 555-5555

Home Address
23 Blue Street
Banner Elk, NC 28604
(704) 444-4444

EDUCATION:

University of North Carolina at Charlotte
Bachelor of Arts, Projected May, 1995
Major: Philosophy
GPA 3.8/4.0
Dean's list seven consecutive semesters.
One of five candidates chosen to assist in teaching Freshman
Seminar orientation class.
Self-financed 50% of education.

EXPERIENCE:

9/93-   **Cake Decorator**
Present HARPER LEE SUPERMARKETS, Charlotte, NC
Fill custom cake orders and maintain cake shelf on sales floor.
Associate of the Month award in August, 1993. Received
corporate-wide recognition for cake production idea which increased
company cake sales 10%. Represented Bakery in Associate Task Force.
Time commitment of 30 hours per week.

9/92-   **Learning Center Tutor**
Present UNIVERSITY OF NORTH CAROLINA AT CHARLOTTE
Tutor students on an individual basis in all aspects of writing
and literature and the concepts of molecular, genetic and
evolutionary biology. Average of three hours per week.

Summers **Store Manager**
1991-92 JERRY K. PANTS, INC., Charlotte, NC
Full profit and loss responsibility for high volume package store
employing 25 people. Managed purchasing, inventory control, cash
handling, financial reporting, merchandising, advertising, special
promotions, and personnel hiring, training and supervision.
- Implemented purchase control system, thus reducing inventory
  levels by $75,000.
- Achieved average annual sales growth of 20%.

1988-90 **Assistant Store Manager**
ANCIENT OAK FOOD MARKET, Wilmington, NC
Scheduled and supervised 15-20 staff members and managed daily
operations and inventory. Involved in extensive customer service
and cash handling during full- and part-time employment. High
volume store with up to $300,000/weekly.

■ Education is listed at the top of resume because it is student's strongest qualification.

■ Typewritten resume is acceptable for most entry-level positions.

PHYSICAL THERAPY MAJOR

Chris Smith

School:
178 Green Street
East Lansing, MI 48824
(517) 555-5555

Home:
23 Blue Street
Rockland, MA 02370
(617) 444-4444

PROFESSIONAL OBJECTIVE
To secure a teaching position in Physical Therapy with potential for professional growth and advancement.

EDUCATION

MICHIGAN STATE UNIVERSITY, East Lansing, MI
Bachelor of Science Degree in Physical Therapy
To be awarded: May, 1995.
President of the local chapter of the Disabled Students Union. Led crusade resulting in increased accessibility of the campus to physically challenged students, including more wheelchair ramps, designated parking, and special class scheduling.

ACCOMPLISHMENTS / AWARDS
- Dean's List Standing.
- Student-Athlete of the Year, 1994.
- Michigan State University Varsity Hockey, 1991-Present; Captain, 1993-Present.

EXPERIENCE

1992-Present   MICHIGAN STATE UNIVERSITY, East Lansing, MI
Athletics Instructor
- Organize coed intramural sports for the entire campus.
- Lead numerous outdoor, physical activities.
- Assist and teach undergraduates.

RELATED EXPERIENCE

Summers   EAST LANSING DAY CAMPS, East Lansing, MI
1991-1993   **Activities Coordinator**
- Organized and guided inner city youth in recreational activities, new games, arts and crafts.

Summer   ROCKLAND PARKS COMMISSION, Rockland, MA
1990   **Activities Supervisor**
- Involved in weekend field days, organized sports and recreational activities.

1988-1990   ROCKLAND SKATING RINK, Rockland, MA
Skate Guard/Instructor.

■ Major accomplishments and awards are related to student's major field of interest.

■ Resume indicated student's ongoing interest in athletics.

PHYSICS MAJOR

Chris Smith

Current Address:
178 Green Street
Pasadena, CA 91125
(818) 555-5555

Permanent Address:
23 Blue Street
Milton, MA 02186
(617) 444-4444

EDUCATION

California Institute of Technology. Pasadena, CA
Bachelor of Arts in Physics, to be awarded: May 1995
Additional areas of study include Chemical Engineering, Mathematics, and Systems Applications. 3.42 grade point average.
Golden key honor society. Cycling Team. Varsity Wrestling.

Milton Academy, Milton, MA
High School Diploma, May 1992

SKILLS

Programming experience in:

C	FORTRAN
PASCAL	MACRO-11 ASSEMBLY LANGUAGE
PL/1	MACHINE LANGUAGE
BASIC	FORTH

Experience with several different machines and operating systems including VAX and UNIX.

ACHIEVEMENTS

- Chosen by Caflo Limited to develop new currency options trading strategies using advanced mathematical and statistical modeling.
- Developed and wrote an original bond pricing program for Caflo Limited in the 'C' programming language.
- Served as president of The Physics Club.
- Wrote for *The Pasadena Sun Times*, College Section.
- Entered college at the age of 17.
- Accepted by and participated in the Physics Project at the University of Chicago; received a grade of 'A'.

WORK EXPERIENCE

5/93-11/94 Caflo, Limited, Pasadena, CA

Intern Software Systems Analyst
Helped develop and write a software package in 'C' to manage the company's accounts.

- High school information is optional and should be listed more briefly than college achievements.

- Academic and professional achievements are highlighted in a separate section.

PSYCHOLOGY MAJOR

Chris Smith

School Address
178 Green Street
Canton, OH 44709
(216) 555-5555

Permanent Address
23 Green Street
Quincy, MA 02169
(617) 444-4444

SUMMARY OF QUALIFICATIONS
Background combines academic achievement, competitive success in pageants, and a record of success in roles requiring diverse public relations skills. An energetic individual with a commitment to personal and professional excellence.

EDUCATION
MARIETTA COLLEGE - Marietta, OH
B.A., Psychology - May 1994 - Departmental Honors
Minor: English
G.P.A.: 3.42/4.00 Overall; 3.61/4.00 Major

HONORS
Dean's List 6 Terms
Nominated for two Senior Class Awards
2nd Runner-Up Miss Ohio - Winner Talent Award - 1994
Periclean Honor Society - 1993-1994
Psi Chi - National Honor Society for Psychology - 1994
Named, Outstanding College Students of America - 1992

EXPERIENCE
9/92 to 6/94 MARIETTA COLLEGE AREA-AID - Marietta, OH
Co-Founder/Director
Developed a comprehensive community service program. Activities included holding fundraisers and organizing student volunteers for a wide variety of causes.

6/93 to 8/93 DEFENSE DEPARTMENT - Marietta, OH
Business Manager - Liberty Misses Program
Performed organizational, press and public relations functions for an international tour of military bases. Made travel and show arrangements, acted as press liaison, and handled accounting and travel expenses.

9/91 to 5/93 MARIETTA COLLEGE - Marietta, OH
Peer Advisor Leader
Oriented incoming freshmen to college life. Gave academic and personal counsel. Trained eleven other advisors.

ACTIVITIES
Senator: College Government Association - 1993-1994
Liberty Misses Troupe Performer - 1993 - 1994
Speaker: Alumni Officers Panel on Student Life Today - 1993
Student Teacher - New Family Project - 1993
Miss Ohio USO Troupe Performer - 1992-1993
Miss Ohio Scholarship Pageant 4th Runner-Up - 1992

- Impressive grade point average is listed under education; a GPA under 3.0 should not be included on a resume.

- Academic honors and a variety of extracurricular activities and achievements indicate a well-rounded student.

SOCIOLOGY MAJOR

Chris Smith
178 Green Street
Belle Chasse, LA 70037
(504) 555-5555

OBJECTIVE
To contribute acquired skills and recent educational background to an organization offering opportunities for growth and advancement.

SUMMARY OF QUALIFICATIONS
- Adept at dealing with ethnic relations, handicapped individuals, and emergency situations.
- Proven supervisory skills; able to work in groups.
- Self-motivated; able to set effective priorities and implement decisions to achieve immediate and long-term goals and meet operational deadlines.
- Fluent in verbal and written Spanish.

EDUCATION
DILLARD UNIVERSITY, New Orleans, LA, 1994
B.A., Sociology, G.P.A. 3.0
Minor: Spanish
Independent Study: "The Feminization of Poverty in the United States."
Member of the Phi Beta Kappa honor society.
Contributing writer for The Vanguard Press.

PROFESSIONAL EXPERIENCE
1992-94 GRETNA CITY, Gretna, LA
Weekend/Evening Telecommunications Shift Supervisor
- Supervised staff of five handling incoming calls; ensured smooth work-flow and prompt attention to emergency situations.
- Notified key personnel of incoming emergencies; coordinated security efforts to ensure hospital safety; initiated appropriate measures during fire alarms.
- Reported shift inadequacies; recommended resolutions.

1991-92 HARVEY MEDICAL CENTER, Harvey, LA
Assistant Translator
- Translated Spanish medical documents; edited previously translated documents.

REFERENCES
Furnished upon request.

- Scholarly research, such as an independent study and/or theses, indicates student's ability to successfully complete an in-depth project.

- Part-time employment during college indicates student's ability to handle multiple responsibilities.

SPEECH MAJOR

Chris Smith
178 Green Street
Bar Harbor, ME
(207) 555-5555

EDUCATION

HUSSON COLLEGE, Bangor, ME
Bachelor of Arts in Speech, May, 1994
Course work in: Radio Announcing, Advanced Public Speaking, T.V. Production, Interpersonal Communications.

WKPL-FM HUSSON COLLEGE, 1990-1994
Sports Director, two consecutive semesters
Assigned daily sportscasts to all 22 department members. Assisted Program Director and Station Manager in scheduling Husson College athletic events to be broadcast. Set up remote broadcast equipment for athletic events. Assigned department members to broadcast events and biweekly, hour long, phone-in sports talk show.
Won: MOTORMOUTH PRESS AWARD, best sports coverage for a college radio station.

Board Operator, 1990-1994
Formatted/hosted local music show. Featured live interviews with local bands. Coordinated ticket giveaways with Promotion Department.
Involved with various other formats.

Class Orator, Husson College Commencement Exercises, May, 1994.

WORK EXPERIENCE

CITY OF BANGOR, Public Facilities Department, Bangor, ME   2/92-5/94
Office Clerk
Witnessed/assisted bid openings for city contracting jobs. Delivered/received documents to and from Bangor offices. Reorganized filing system. Handled blue print orders and general office functions - filing, typing and mail delivery.

HUSSON COLLEGE, Bangor, ME   10/90-1/92
Social Science Office Assistant
Delivered/received exams and important documents to Campus Copy Room. Made deliveries on campus. Coordinated student evaluations of faculty members.

SUMMER EXPERIENCE

RORSHERCH CLUB, Bar Harbor, ME
Bus Boy
DURLET RECREATION CENTER, Bangor, ME
Laborer

■ Extracurricular activities relate to student's field of interest.

■ College students should never submit a resume more than one page long. If necessary, a smaller typeface or narrower page margins can be used.

STATISTICS MAJOR

Chris Smith
178 Green Street
Oklahoma City, OK 73132
(405) 555-5555

OBJECTIVE:

To secure an entry-level marketing position.

EDUCATION:

OKLAHOMA CITY UNIVERSITY
Oklahoma City, OK
Bachelor of Science degree in Statistics, September 1994.
Member of the Math Club. Recipient of The Connor Foundation Scholarship in 1991.
Varsity Basketball.

EXPERIENCE:

Melvin Corporation   Oklahoma City, OK
Product Specification Specialist   10/93 - Present
- Coordinate the input and editing of market research data to produce a weekly report providing advertised pricing from 10 markets for Home Entertainment categories.
- Assist in the input, graphing and editing of a monthly in-store survey report furnishing retail shelf pricing, placement data and trend analysis.
- Assisted Database Manager and Sales Representative with customized information for various client requests.

Genoa Publishing Inc.   Tulsa, OK
Marketing Intern   Summer 1993
- Conducted competitive analysis in the consumer health and personal financial investment markets.
- Researched possible entry into the facsimile fulfillment market.
- Assisted in developing new products, including positioning of products, writing direct mail advertisements, conducting competitive market research, and developing a fulfillment plan.
- Developed written and telephone surveys covering marketing management issues. Analyzed surveys and wrote summary reports of survey results.
- Organized focus group on mutual fund investors: hired and supervised independent moderator; developed working outline; and wrote summary report of focus group findings.

International College News   Oklahoma City, OK
Assistant Managing Editor   9/92-5/93
- Supervised project progress of contributing writers, artists, and in-house staff.
- Developed readership surveys to evaluate paper's readership in campus community.
- Used survey input to redesign paper content and appearance, increasing response rate.
- Edited manuscripts for accuracy, readability, and grammar.

SKILLS:

Lotus 1-2-3, Microsoft Word, DOS, Quark Express.

■ Impressive competitive scholarships add weight to student's educational background.

■ Student has valuable work experience pertaining to his/her major.

STUDIO ART MAJOR

Chris Smith
178 Green Street
Ewing, NJ 08625
(609) 555-5555

FORMAL EDUCATION
HAMPSHIRE COLLEGE, Amherst, MA. **B.A. in Studio Art/Sculpture**. 1994.
Also extensive studies in Chinese, Environmental Issues, Politics, and Women's Studies.

THE RAINBOW HERMITAGE; Nova Scotia; A humanistic, alternative high school. 1990.

INFORMAL EDUCATION
Lived and traveled extensively in
GREECE * VIETNAM * THE PEOPLE'S REPUBLIC OF CHINA
CANADA * INDIA * UNITED STATES * HONG KONG

LANGUAGES
English * Spoken Mandarin Chinese * French

WORK EXPERIENCE
HEALWELL, Ewing, NB   1991-Present
Co-Leader, Art Therapy Groups
For children, ages 4-10, of battered women.
Child Care Supervision
For children, ages infant-12 years, whose mothers are in counseling.

REESE PARK EXPRESS, Durango, CO   Summer 1990
Counselor
Co-Leader for coed, teenage group which explored cultures and wilderness areas of the
southwestern U.S.; planned and led backpacking trips.

BUSINESS TIMES, Boston, MA   Summer 1989
Proofreader and Unofficial Copyeditor
Proofread and edited copy for internationally distributed magazine.

HAMPSHIRE COLLEGE, Amherst, MA   Winter 1988
Workshop Leader
Led Sexual Assault Education Program workshops.
Organized Women's Self Defense workshop.

THE SILENT BLOOM, Hanoi, Vietnam   Fall 1987
English Teacher
Developed and implemented lesson plans for four levels of English, from six year old
beginners to adult intermediates.

■ Extensive travel and foreign language skills are valuable com-
modities in today's global market.

■ High school information is optional
and should be listed more briefly
than college achievements.

THEATER MAJOR

Chris Smith

School Address:
178 Green Street
Raleigh, NC 27610
(919) 555-5555

Home Address:
23 Blue Street
Asheville, NC 28804
(704) 444-4444

Hair: Dk. Brown   Eyes: Green   Height: 6'2"
Weight: 180   Age: 21   Age Range: 15 - 30   Voice: Bass

PERFORMANCE EXPERIENCE

Play	Role	Produced By	Year
Love Letters	Andy	Meredith College	1993
Machinal	The Husband	Meredith College	1993
Carousel	Mr. Bascomb	Ferndale River Playhouse	1993
Black Coffee	Cptn. Hastings	Ferndale River Playhouse	1993
Brigadoon	Mr. Lundie	Ferndale River Playhouse	1993
The Wake of Jamie Foster	Leon Darnell	Ferndale River Playhouse	1993
A Bright Called Day	Baz	Meredith College	1993
Oklahoma!	Slim	Meredith College	1993
The Mikado	Chorus	Ferndale River Playhouse	1992
Chamber Music	The Man in White	Meredith College	1992
The Time of Your Life	Dudley	Meredith College	1991
Twelfth Night	Sir Andrew	Meredith College	1991
Becoming Memories	Stephen/Jerry	Meredith College	1990
Guys and Dolls	Arvide Abernathy	The Meadowlark Playhouse	1990
Mirrors	Chip	Ridgehollow Country Players	1989

OTHER EXPERIENCE

Two seasons of cabaret with the Ferndale River Playhouse - singing, dancing, improvisation, comedy sketches; 1992 & 1993
Two seasons of Ship-Ahoy! children's theater in Ferndale River, NC - improvisational story theater; 1992 & 1993
Creative Arts at Park summer camp, Rocky Mount, NC - CIT (two years) and counselor (two years) teaching improvisation, play writing and creative dramatics to children ages eight to fifteen; 1989 - 1992

TRAINING/SPECIAL SKILLS

Bachelor of Arts degree in the Dramatic Arts. Merideth College. To be awarded May 1995.
Acting, Directing - Jasmine Elwood
Improvisation - Maury Firethorn
Theatrical Design - Lark Hartshorne
Stage Combat (epee, hand-to-hand) - Alexander Kennybunk
Play Writing - written/directed *The Sapphire Runway*, *Relieving Atlas* at Meredith College
The Sapphire Runway, produced at Theater Americana in Altadena, CA
Comedy sketches performed at Cabaret in Ferndale River, NC

■ Descriptive information (height, weight, etc.) is appropriate to include on resume for students in certain areas of the performing arts.

■ Valuable performance experience, essential to theater majors, is the focal point of resume.

THEOLOGY MAJOR

Chris Smith

School Address
178 Green Street
Immaculata, PA 19345
(215) 555-5555

Home Address
23 Blue Street
Clifton Forge, VA 24422
(703) 444-4444

EDUCATION:

Immaculata College, Immaculata, PA
Candidate for Bachelor of Arts degree in Theological Studies, May 1996.
Courses: Religion in Society, Eastern Religions, Church vs. State.
Honors/Activities: Dean's List all semesters, Sailing Club Co-Captain, Editor-in-Chief of campus magazine, Immaculata Concepts, Community Task Force Member.

EXPERIENCE:

Teaching Assistant, Immaculata College. Fall 1994.
Selected by Chair of Theology Department to assist in instruction of Introductory to Eastern Religion course. Conducted regular review sessions, helped students with papers, facilitated classroom discussions.

Teaching Intern, Immaculata School System. Spring 1993.
Taught special needs class math, science, and writing in cooperation with full-time staff member. Prepared lessons, graded daily assignments, organized afternoon activities and field trips. Participated in parent-teacher conferences.

Tutor, Immaculata Tutoring Program. 1992-1993.
Tutored elementary school children in history and reading for 8-10 hours a week.

SUMMER WORK:

File Clerk, Clifton Medical Center, Clifton Forge, VA. Summers 1991-1994.
Maintained active patient files and assisted office manager with computerized billing of patients and insurance companies.

TRAINING:

Computers: IBM - Word for Windows, WordPerfect
Languages: Proficient in French; Rudimentary knowledge of Latin.

INTERESTS:

Travel, antiques, sailing.

■ Extracurricular activities demonstrate that student is sociable and gets along well with a diversity of people.

■ Job titles are simple and straightforward, not exaggerated.

WESTERN CIVILIZATION MAJOR

Chris Smith
178 Green Street
Presque Isle, ME 04769
(207) 555-5555

EDUCATION

UNIVERSITY OF MAINE AT PRESQUE ISLE — Presque Isle, ME
Bachelor of Arts Degree: Western Civilization — 1994
Concentration: European Studies
Secretary of Alpha Chi Epsilon sorority.
Member of the Ski Team. Regular competitor in downhill ski races, including three annual state-wide competitions.

INSTITUTE OF WESTERN STUDIES — Paris, France
Student Exchange Program — Spring 1993
Major: French Cultural and Economic Studies

EXPERIENCE

Intern — Bangor, ME
STEADMAN TRADE — Spring 1994
- Marketed imported French products.
- Prospected territories and acquisitioned clientele.
- Performed cold calling and seed sales.
- Developed sales strategies.
- Conducted research to ascertain target market.

Sales Representative/Administrative Assistant — Boston, MA
BENSONHURST AND DYNELL — Summer 1993
- Provided customer and sales assistance.
- Performed various general office duties, including: filing, light typing, greeting guests, responding to customer inquiries, delivering messages and controlling inventory.

Customer Service Representative — Paris, France
LA BANC DE FRANCE — Spring 1993
- Sold bank products, opened and closed customer accounts.
- Calculated and deposited currency.
- Provided customer service and supervised staff members.

SPECIAL SKILLS

Fluent in French Language.
Exceptional translation and interpretation capability.

VOLUNTEER EXPERIENCE

BOSTON UNIVERSITY MEDICAL CENTER — Boston, MA
Assist handicapped patients with daily living skills. — 1992-Present

INTERESTS

Foreign languages, sports, travel.

■ Internship experience is listed with past jobs whereas volunteer work is listed separately.

■ Extracurricular activities indicate sociability, motivation, and initiative.

WOMEN'S STUDIES MAJOR

Chris Smith
178 Green Street
Newark, NJ 07102
(201) 555-5555

Education:

Rutgers University, Newark, NJ
Bachelor of Arts in Women's Studies, 1994. Thesis topic: *The Political Economy of Our Domestic Health Care System.* 3.63 Grade Point Average.
Member of Varsity Crew Team. Designed and painted university-sponsored mural with the theme of cultural diversity.

Work Experience:

12/93-6/94 Summer Orientation Leader
Rutgers University, Newark, NJ
- Aided over 400 students in registration process.
- Led groups through rigid itinerary in strict time schedule.
- Provided initial contact to services and advisors for freshmen and transfer students.
- Facilitated dialogue on issues following group diversity exercise.
- Presented campus-wide tours to incoming students and their families for University Open House.

9/90-8/93 Editor-in-Chief, Layout and Design Editor, Activities Editor
The Amber Store, Rutgers University
- Successfully worked within a $30,000 budget to create a 400-page publication from scratch.
- Served as accountable leader of student-run organization.
- Interviewed and selected personnel.
- Acted as teacher, advisor and supervisor to team of eight.
- Established deadlines fro book completion and staff contracts based upon academic calendar and publisher expectations.

Summer/Winter Breaks
1990-1994 Teller
Alpine Savings Bank, New Brunswick, NJ
- Achieved excellent balancing record with daily cash flows.
- Processed large and numerous transactions responsibly.
- Promoted bank services and benefits.
- Mastered the Unysis computer terminal.

1988-1989 Snack Bar Staff
Clover Fields, Camden, NJ
- Organized inventory, storage and daily tasks for new snack bar.
- Assisted in managing front line customer transactions and behind the scenes operations while training new applicants.

Interests:

Enjoy photography, yoga, and collecting 19th Century Russian novels.

- Attention-getting resume focuses on accomplishments and uses dynamic language.

- Personal interests give a candid snapshot of candidate as a person.

21
Technical

Nature of Work

Technical professionals, whether working at a desk, in the field, on-line, or at 30,000 feet in the air, apply their specialized knowledge to making our lives run more safely and efficiently. Aircraft pilots transport passengers, cargo, and mail, while others dust crops, spread seed for reforestation, test aircraft, and take aerial photographs. Aircraft mechanics inspect, maintain, and repair the engines, landing gear, instruments, and other parts of aircraft to keep them in top operating condition.

Architects design buildings that are functional, safe, economical, and suit the needs of the people who use them. Landscape architects design residential areas, public parks, college campuses and shopping centers, making them not only functional and beautiful but compatible with the natural environment.

Surveyors measure and map the earth's surface to establish official land, air space, and water boundaries. Electricians install and maintain electrical systems for a variety of purposes, including climate control, security, and communications. They may also install and maintain the electronic controls for machines in business and industry.

Employment

Approximately three-fifths of all civilian pilots work for airlines. Others work as flight instructors, fly for air taxi companies, dust crops or inspect pipelines for private businesses, work for the government, or are self-employed. Similarly, most airline mechanics work for airlines; the rest work for aircraft assembly firms, the federal government, or for independent repair shops.

Architects generally work in small architecture firms or are self-employed, whereas most landscape architects work for companies that provide landscaping services or in architecture firms. Most surveyors work within engineering, architectural, and surveying firms. The majority of electricians are employed in the construction industry, while others work as maintenance electricians and are employed in virtually every industry.

Training

Training for those in technical professions is varied. Many start as helpers or apprentices to gain a thorough knowledge of all aspects of their trade. In addition to on-the-job training, most technical professionals are also required to provide tangible proof of their expertise. Pilots undergo vigorous training and must pass written, practical, and physical examinations before they are able to fly craft on their own. In order to be certified, aircraft mechanics are required to take oral and written tests in addition to practical training.

Architects and landscape architects must also have practical experience and pass an exam before they can provide services to clients. Most persons prepare to be a licensed surveyor by combining post-secondary school courses in surveying with extensive on-the-job training, although some universities and vocational schools offer programs in both surveying and surveying technology. Most electricians are trained by completing a four- or five-year apprenticeship program.

Job Outlook

The employment outlook for professionals in technical occupations varies greatly. The job outlook for pilots should be favorable in the long run, due to an expected shortage of pilots. Employment growth coupled with an expected wave of retirements will provide many of these job openings. The number of aircraft mechanics is expected to increase at an average rate over the next decade.

Opportunities for architects will also increase at an average rate, while the job outlook for landscape architects is expected to be highly favorable. Employment of surveyors is expected to grow at an average pace through the year 2005, with openings arising from increased demand for surveyors and from replacement needs.

Employment of electricians is expected to increase faster than average for all occupations through the year 2005, due to a growing population and economy, and new technological advances. However, people wishing to become construction electricians should be prepared to experience periods of unemployment, resulting from the limited duration of construction projects and the cyclical nature of the construction industry.

Earnings

Airline pilots averaged $80,000 per year in 1990, whereas pilots working outside the airlines earned anywhere from $43,000 to $74,000 per year in late 1989. Aircraft mechanics earned approximately $30,000 per year. The median annual earnings for salaried architects who worked full-time was about $36,000 in 1990, whereas the top 10 percent earned more than $66,300.

According to the limited data available, the median annual earnings for surveyors were about $25,600 in 1990. Median weekly earnings for full-time electricians who were not self-employed were $524.

AIRCRAFT MECHANIC

CHRIS SMITH
178 Green Street
Northfield, MN 55057
(507) 555-5555

OBJECTIVE

A challenging position in AIRCRAFT MAINTENANCE which allows for broadening professional experience and room for growth toward management.

EDUCATION

NORTHFIELD COMMUNITY COLLEGE, Northfield, Minnesota
Currently attending <u>Applied Science Degree Program in Aeronautics</u>

UNITED STATES AIR FORCE AIRCRAFT MAINTENANCE SCHOOL
Grisham Air Force Base, Indiana
Graduated 170 hour program - KC/RC/EC-135, Periodic
December 1992
Graduated 110 hour program - KC/RC/EC-135, Able Chief
May 1992

UNITED STATES AIR FORCE AIRCRAFT MAINTENANCE SCHOOL
Sheppard Air Force Base, Texas
Graduated 150 hour program in Tactical/Airlift Bombardment
December 1991

AIRCRAFT MAINTENANCE COURSE
Lubouk Air Force Base, Texas
Graduated 120 hour program
September 1990

PRACTICAL EXPERIENCE

Trained in maintenance, servicing, and troubleshooting on all areas of KC/RC/EC-135 aircraft from wing tips to landing gear, nose to tail, interior and exterior, including removals and replacements of component parts, repairs, lubrications, refueling, and flight-line launching and recoveries.

Perform inspections of J57-59 Turbo Jet Engines, plus troubleshooting of component parts. Certified in aircraft towing, aircraft power and battery connections and disconnections, engine cowl removal and installation.

RELATED INFORMATION

Received honorable discharge.

Available immediately . . . Willing to relocate . . . References on request.

■ Strong educational credentials are stressed while limited work experience is de-emphasized.

■ Resume format is neat and professional.

AIRCRAFT PILOT

CHRIS SMITH
178 Green Street
Glendale, AZ 85306
(602) 555-5555

OBJECTIVE Flight Officer

FLIGHT Total Time   6500   Jet Engine   900
TIME   Pilot in Command   3800   Turbine   5200
            Second in Command 2600   Instrument   350

QUALIFICATIONS

AIRLINE TRANSPORT PILOT
- Airplane Multi-Engine Land
- BAE 3100 Type
- FAA Class I Medical
- Flight Engineer-Basic-Turbojet written
- SF-340 Type

EDUCATION EMORY-RIDDLE AERONAUTICAL UNIVERSITY   Daytona Beach, FL
Professional Pilot   January 1980 to April 1981

MISSISSIPPI STATE UNIVERSITY   Starkville, MS
Business Administration   January 1972 to May 1974

SAINT LOUIS UNIVERSITY   St. Louis, MO
Business Administration/Physical Education   August 1969 to December 1970

EMPLOYMENT

SOUTHWEST AIRLINES   Phoenix, AZ
First Officer   January 1990 to June 1993
DC-9

NORTHEAST AIRLINES   Portland, ME
Captain   August 1986 to December 1989
Saab-Fairchild 340

VANTAGE ENTERPRISES, INC.   Wayne, NE
Line Pilot   March 1984 to July 1986

IPHAGENA INDUSTRIES   Wayne, NE
Line Pilot   May 1983 to February 1984

REFERENCES

Furnished upon request

■ Nontraditional format emphasizes candidate's qualifications and flight-time while listing employment only briefly.

■ Clean layout makes resume easy to read.

ARCHITECT

CHRIS SMITH
178 Green Street
East Brunswick, NJ 08816
(908) 555-5555

SUMMARY

Over seven years in Architecture and Facility Management (FM) related industries with emphasis in Computer Design Base (CDB), Education, and Communication.

PROFESSIONAL EXPERIENCE

CDB INC., East Brunswick, NJ   1992-Present
Architect
Provide industry consultation and implementation expertise in architecture and FM, Computer-Aided Design and Database Management software packages. Experience with IBM Mainframe, Workstation, and PC based products.
- Provide demonstration, presentations and technical support for pre- and post-sales activity
- Act as subject matter expert for future software enhancements and requirements
- Lead role in various joint studies teaming with IBM and other major corporations in the evaluation CDB software for architecture

CITY OF PITTSBURGH, Pittsburgh, PA   1988-1992
Building Inspector
Worked within both the Public and Private Sector. Required knowledge of local government agency procedures (e.g. obtaining permits, variances, interfacing with the Building, Planning, and Engineering Departments). Projects included:
- Commercial and industrial interior spaces
- Small commercial and low-rise buildings
- Large customer and multi-family residential housing
- Architectural renderings, presentation graphics

PROFESSIONAL REGISTRATIONS

LICENSED ARCHITECT - State of New Jersey   C100468

EDUCATION

MASTER OF ARCHITECTURE   1988
University of Pennsylvania
Philadelphia, PA

BACHELOR OF SCIENCE, ARCHITECTURE   1986
Massachusetts Institute of Technology
Cambridge, MA

COMPUTER SKILLS
DOSS, IBM, Microsoft Word, Pascal, Lotus 1-2-3

- Summary highlights candidate's experience and expertise in his/her field.

- Including professional licensure and accreditations can be essential for certain fields of work.

BROADCAST TECHNICIAN

CHRIS SMITH
178 Green Street
Burlington, VT 05405
(802) 555-5555

OBJECTIVE:
To pursue a technical career in television or video with opportunities for training and merited advancement.

EDUCATION:

Trinity College, Burlington, VT
Associate Degree in Radio-Television-Film Technology, Dec. 1994
Cumulative GPA: 3.4, GPA in major: 3.7
Selected Radio-Television-Film Courses: Newswriting and Production, Film Production, Television Production, Community Video and Industrial Production, Writing for Radio-Television-Film, Station Organization and Operation (FCC Laws).

Film Direction Workshop. Sponsored by the American Film Institute. Covered the essential narrative, visual and organizational elements of the director's craft. Examined all phases of film production from the special point of view of the director.

Scriptwriting: An informal discussion. Sponsored by the Burlington Film Festival. Workshop explained how a studio system works, how scripts are submitted and evaluated.

EXPERIENCE:

December
1994-Present
Master Control Room Technician, **KSTG** Channel 68, TTP Affiliate
Responsible for "on-air" switching of various program sources, commercials, promos and public service announcements. Recorded satellite feeds. Dubbed commercials and movies. Maintained proper transmitter, program and operational discrepancy logs. Required the ability to perform with accuracy during periods of high stress.

Fall 1994
Internship. **KARR-TV** Channel 3, NLS Affiliate
Worked as a community production intern in the Community Service Department. Assisted in producing and writing public service announcements and special news packages. Participated in editing process, using a Sony BVE-3000A editing system.

Spring 1993
Internship, **KLAG-TV** Channel 7, MPT Affiliate
Operated Ampex BCC-10 studio camera and Telescripter, Inc., television prompter. Lighted commercials and public service announcements using Kliegal Brothers fresnel 2K, 1K, lights and scoop lights, Century Strand 1000 750 lights and Mole-Richardson type 2561 molequartz super-softlite 2000 watt. Operated Kliegal Brothers dimmer board.

Spring 1993
Film Production Class
Wrote, produced and directed for short films. Acted as camera person for two short films.

Fall 1992
Community Video and Industrial Production Class
Operated a JVC-KY 1900 portable camera. Directed two exercise videos.

- Relevant course work adds depth to candidate's educational background.

- Internships strengthen candidate's short work history.

BUILDING INSPECTOR

CHRIS SMITH
178 Green Street
Prichard, AZ 36610
(205) 555-5555

SUMMARY OF QUALIFICATIONS

- More than 15 years of experience ranging from Carpenter Apprentice to general contractor/project superintendent in military, custom, and general construction.
- Most recent eight years of experience as Permanent Building Inspector, with three years as Acting Building Commissioner during absence of incumbent Commissioner.
- Sound knowledge of state building codes and the inspection of all construction projects.
- Expertise in inspecting new and existing buildings and structures to ensure conformity to building, grading, and zoning laws and approved plans as well as specifications and standards.
- Experience working with engineers and architects on design, coordination and building of construction projects.
- Capable of enforcing full range of building codes and working with all construction and mechanical trades on codes including electrical and plumbing regulations.

EXPERIENCE

PERMANENT LOCAL BUILDING INSPECTOR, City of Prichard, AL (1988-present)
As Local Inspector:

- Assigned to inspect Mobile District. Position requires application of sound knowledge of state building codes in inspecting residential, commercial, industrial and other buildings during and after construction to insure that components such as footings, floor framing, completed framing, chimneys and stairways meet provisions of building, grading, zoning and safety laws.
- Interact with all construction and mechanical trades as well as architects and engineers to assure adherence to improved plans, specifications and standards.
- Prepare reports concerning violations which have not been corrected, interpret legal requirements and recommend compliance procedures to contractors, craft workers, and owners.
- Maintain inspection records and prepare reports for use by administrative or judicial authorities.

As Acting Building Commission:

- During the absence of the Building Commissioner, assume full responsibility for administering and enforcing state building codes as well as all state rules and regulations involving construction in Mobile.

GENERAL CONTRACTOR

Prichard Construction (1978-1987)

- Formed company in 1978 and applied education, training and experience in building custom style homes for clients insisting on high degree of skill, quality workmanship, and ability to complete projects to schedule and budget.
- Negotiated all subcontracts. Supervised up to 25 carpenters and laborers.

EDUCATION

Mobile Junior College, 1976, Mobile, Alabama.
Associate Degree in Industrial Arts.
Completed Apprenticeship with John Skrensky.
Journeyman Carpenter, 1978, Mobile, AL.

- Summary grabs the reader's attention with powerful skills and qualifications.

- Job descriptions detail candidate's responsibilities and accomplishments.

DRAFTER

CHRIS SMITH
178 Green Street
Richmond, VA 23201
(804) 555-5555

SUMMARY OF QUALIFICATIONS
- 15 years experience in various aspects of electronics.
- Broad knowledge of product development; mechanical/electronic detailing and drawing; regulatory compliances, codes and standards; and managerial skills.

PROFESSIONAL EXPERIENCE
1990-Present **Supervisor, Drafting Department** - SHAMROCK INDUSTRIES, Richmond, VA
- Monitor all drafting responsibilities, products and drawings in Optical Division.
- Manage hybrid microcircuit design and drawing for production.
- Assist with documentation of federal licensing/certification for government projects.
- Coordinate all aspects of detailing with schematic capture, wiring, harnessing, cable drawings, and sand casting.

1988-1990 **Drafting Technician and Designer**-GRAPHIQUE CORPORATION, Dallas, TX
- Performed schematical, electrical, P.C.B. designs and CADD development.
- Responsible for drawings development and detailing from conceptualization stage through final release.
- Prepared and coordinated ECNs, along with necessary concurrence mark-ups.

1986-1988 **Mechanical Detailer**-ECO-LAST CORPORATION, Hoya, TX
- Analyzed client specifications and aided in initial design development.
- Calculated extrusions and flat patterns for sheet-metal fabrication.
- Utilized basic dimensioning system and datum structure for machine drawings.

1985-1986 **Detailer**-MUNSON MECHANICAL CO., Hemingway, TX
- Prepared sheet metal drawings, component drawings.
- Created artistic illustrations for advertising and marketing purposes.

EDUCATION
VIRGINIA COLLEGE OF ART, Richmond; Drafting and Design - Transferring to WORTH INSTITUTE, Richmond - B.S. in Drafting and Design. Graduation anticipated 1996.

EL GRECO COMMUNITY COLLEGE, Austin, TX; Course work in Drafting Technology and Architectural Development.

COMPUTERS
CV/4X, CADD, Xerox Expert Schematic capture systems, Loading Digital Software from hard drive onto mag maps.

- Valuable computer skills are high-lighted in a separate section.

- Job descriptions include technical jargon specific to candidate's field.

ELECTRICIAN

CHRIS SMITH
178 Green Street
Manchester, NH 03103
(603) 555-5555

OBJECTIVE
A challenging career utilizing more than fifteen years of progressive, professional electrical, general repair, and small plumbing/heating experience.

QUALIFICATIONS
- Self-motivated; able to work independently and as team member to meet operational deadlines.
- Function well in high-pressure atmosphere.
- Adapt easily to new concepts and responsibilities.
- Developed interpersonal skills, having dealt with a diversity of professionals and clients.

PROFESSIONAL EXPERIENCE
1987-Present MANCHESTER COMPANY, Manchester, NH
Owner/Electrical Contractor/Electrician
Write proposals/estimates for residential and commercial wiring, then perform work as requested. Handle advertising, bookkeeping, electrical and general repairs (including washers, boilers, burners, and lock repair). Hire/oversee assistants as required.

1981-1984 FREELANCE
General Assistant
Dealt with residential electrical, heating, and plumbing needs.

1984-1987 LAMPWORKS, INC., Bedford, NH
Electrical Assistant
Demonstrated knowledge of electricity via wiring lamps; ensured proper connections and working order.

RELEVANT TRAINING/LICENSURE
MANCHESTER TECHNICAL COMMUNITY COLLEGE, Manchester, NH
Associate of Science Degree in Electrical Technology, 1976
Journeyman Electrician State License, 1976

AFFILIATIONS
Associate Member, N.F.P.A.
Associate Member, I.A.E.I.

REFERENCES
Furnished upon request.

■ Job objective is supported by the facts and accomplishments stated in resume.

■ Professional affiliations illustrate candidate's dedication to a long-term career.

ELECTRONIC EQUIPMENT REPAIRER

```
                        CHRIS SMITH
                      178 Green Street
                       Warwick, RI
                      (401) 555-5555
```

SUMMARY OF QUALIFICATIONS
13 years of experience as a customer service hardware specialist and field service engineer. Extensive electronics and mechanical background.

EXPERIENCE

1992 TO   VI-TAL COMPUTERS   CONCORD, MA
Present   Customer Service Repair/Refurb Technician.
             Rebuild and repair the GS1000, GS2000, vistra800 Titan graphic workstation product lines, using Unix sys5, STARDENT Stellix and MS-DOS. Perform system test and configuration of both hardware and software to meet the customers needs. Track vender repaired items including HP tape drives, X-terminals, Sony 8mm tape drives and Optical drives. Maintain refurb inventory for all product lines. Assist less experienced technicians with software and operating systems. Reduced testing and configuration time for HP drive by 60% by developing more streamlined procedures.

1987 to   THE BREWMAN CORPORATION   SLOCUM, RI
1992   Customer Service Repair Technician/Group Leader.
             Repaired Raster Technologies Model One graphics controller product line, using Unix, VMS, MS-DOS and Prime OS. Repaired and tested all cpu cards, floating point processors, image and bulk memory cards, genlock video sync boards and a variety of customer products including video adjuster boards, video latch boards used for overlay applications and driving two or more monitors. Utilized as a consultant in customer support.

1985 to   DAMMON LEE INC.   WATCH HILL, RI
1987   Electronic Test/Repair Technician.
             Repaired and upgraded field service and system test boards. Provided test, repair and calibration of a variety of high-speed logic boards, primarily dealing with ECL logic, but also including TTL and analog.

EDUCATION

1983 to   THE GORTEK INSTITUTE
1985   Graduate of an 700 hour computer technology curriculum. Basic electronics, digital concepts, hardware, software, and microprocessor principles.

TRAINING

             VI-TAL COMPUTER INC.
             Unix System Administration AT&T sys5 rev5.

             BREWMAN COMPUTER SYSTEMS INC.
             Introduction to Unix.

             DAMMON LEE, INC.
             Managing Multiple Priorities

■ Summary of qualifications is con-   ■ Relevant education and training
cise and adds punch to resume.   strengthen resume.

ENGINEERING TECHNICIAN

CHRIS SMITH
178 Green Street
Salem, OR 97301
(503) 555-5555

OBJECTIVE
A position as an ENGINEERING TECHNICIAN.

QUALIFICATIONS
- Strong desire to work and learn in a technical environment.
- Ability to work efficiently and compatibly on a team.
- Ability to read and produce working drawings.
- Adept in the construction and modification of prototype systems and devices using a wide variety of power and hand tools.
- Substantial experience in the organization, execution, and documentation of testing programs.

EXPERIENCE

1991 to Present — NUTECH MACHINE COMPANY, Salem, OR
Technical Engineering Aide to Vice President of Operations
- Create and interpret testing programs to evaluate and modify product performance and reliability for manufacturer of commercial kitchen equipment.
- Present written and oral reports on test results, proposing changes to design, manufacturing, or marketing problems in the product.
- Conduct meetings with component manufacturer representatives, evaluate components and present findings for inclusion in final product design.
- Assist in the implementation of new office procedures including a parts numbering system and a project scheduling priority system.
- Collect and organize information for both production cost analysis and marketing surveys.

1988 to 1991 — BRYTECH R/D COMPANY, Portland, OR
Engineering Aide in Fluid Mechanics Department
- Assist engineers in producing flow models to evaluate and improve fluid system designs.
- Design scale models from field drawings.
- Supervise model construction and assembly.
- Produce drawings, charts, and illustrations for presentations and final reports.

EDUCATION
WILLAMETTE UNIVERSITY, Salem, OR
A.S., Mechanical Engineering 1987

■ Job objective clarifies candidate's career goal.

■ Chrono-functional resume has the strength of chronological format and the flexibility of functional format.

LANDSCAPE ARCHITECT

CHRIS SMITH
178 Green Street
Prescott, AZ 86301
(602) 555-5555

OBJECTIVE: A challenging and responsible entry-level **Architectural Landscaping** position where my experience, capabilities and career interest can be utilized.

EDUCATION:

UNIVERSITY OF NEW MEXICO, Albuquerque, NM
Bachelor of Science in Environmental Science Studies to be awarded May, 1995.

UNIVERSITY OF ALBUQUERQUE, Albuquerque, NM
Architectural Landscape Design Program (1980-1983)

ACME GASOLINE CORPORATION, Prescott, AZ
Management, interviewing and hiring and EEO training (1986-1987)

SKILLS: Strong mechanical aptitude. Experienced with power mower, small tractor and other small equipment. Knowledgeable in planting and care of trees, shrubs, bulbs, annual and perennial flowers and vegetables.

EXPERIENCE:

1987-Present   **ACME GASOLINE CORPORATION**, Prescott, AZ
Station Manager, Prescott, AZ (1987-Present)
Responsible for all phases of operations for full service gas station including maintaining appearance standards and landscaping, customer service, hiring and supervising personnel, fuel product and merchandise ordering.

Shift Manager, Walker, AZ (1985-1987)
Responsible for full service convenience store including store appearance, customer service, ordering merchandise, cost control, and personnel functions.

Cashier, Alameda, NM (1983-1985)
Maintained station appearance and provided customer service.

1970-1983   **FORD WORKS INCORPORATED**, Alameda, NM
Assistant Manager
Supervised twelve employees. Act as liaison between upper management and associates.

PERSONAL:

Enjoy working outdoors. Own pick-up truck.

REFERENCES AVAILABLE UPON REQUEST

- Job objective is supported by the facts and accomplishments stated in resume.

- Personal information is relevant to candidate's job objective.

MILLWRIGHT

CHRIS SMITH
178 Green Street
Gary, IN 46408
(219) 555-5555

OBJECTIVE   To secure a position as a Millwright.

SUMMARY OF QUALIFICATIONS

- Eight years experience as a millwright.
- Strong mechanical and analytical attributes.
- Highly effective supervisory skills.
- Constructed Turbo Z-58 and VCC turbines; overhaul and repair turbines; turbine assembly and alignment.
- Member, Local Millwright Union.

EXPERIENCE

1989-Present   HARRISON INC., Fort Wayne, IN   **Millwright**
Supervise staff of 4 to 30 millwrights. Start-up support for Turbo and VCC. Assemble/disassemble turbines on Resnik Ltd., Gary, IN job site.

1986-1989   STEEL THE SKY, INC., Kokomo, IN   **Millwright and Foreman**
Oversee plant construction; set/align turbines and pumps; construct air-cooled condenser.

1980-1986   PERFORMANCE AUTOMOTIVE, Notre Dame, IN   **Owner**
Manage sales, service of foreign cars; import autos from Japan; possess emissions certificates and comply with DOT regulations. Fabricate race cars and engines.

EDUCATION

OAKLAND CITY COLLEGE, Oakland City, IN.
Automotive Technology; certified and graduated 1980.
INDIANA UNIVERSITY, Bloomington, IN. A.S. Accounting 1978.

COMPUTER SKILLS
IBM-PC, Quicken, Q&A, WordPerfect, Lotus 1-2-3.

REFERENCES
Furnished upon request.

- Summary grabs the reader's attention with powerful skills and qualifications.

- Listing former business ownership accentuates candidate's initiative and entrepreneurial spirit.

PRECISION INSPECTOR

CHRIS SMITH
178 Green Street
Raymore, MO 64083
(816) 555-5555

PROFILE:
More than ten years experience in:
- First piece, in-process and other phases of precision inspection.
- Background in wide variety of production manufacturing departments shops and associated inspection areas.
- Inspection procedures and methods pertaining to machined and fabricated complex parts from in-plant and vendors.
- Worked to industrial and government specifications, and interpreted drawings.
- Capable of making complicated set-ups and using tools and techniques to inspect with a maximum amount of efficiency and minimum supervision.

EXPERIENCE:

1991-present Precision Inspector - Dyers Corp., Grandview, MO
- First piece, in-process and other phases of precision inspection on all types of manufactured products.
- Involved in sheet metal layout inspection; machine and sheet metal parts inspection; incoming material and in-process inspection as well as final inspection.
- Inspect machine and fabricated complex parts from in-plant and vendors.
- Create intricate set-ups and use tools and inspection techniques to inspect with maximum efficiency and minimum supervision.
- Design functional templates for multi-shaped parts.
- Perform complicated calculations and apply formulas; interpret more difficult drawings along with working to specifications and applying control charts.
- Operate from routing sheets and drawings to ensure correct fabrication or machining of products.

1989-1991 Precision Inspector - Carothers Company, Independence, MO
- Assigned to various production manufacturing departments and inspection areas to plan and carry out complex sample, model, first piece in-process and other types of product parts.

1985-1988 Steel Inspector - Dorsey Steel Corporation, Kansas City, MO
- Inspection of steel using all types of inspection methods and equipment applications for this type of inspection.

EDUCATION:

DeVry Institute of Technology, Kansas City, MO 1984

- Attention-getting profile gives a snapshot of candidate's professional experience and strengths.
- Most recent position is highlighted while previous positions are de-emphasized.

QA TEST TECHNICIAN

Chris Smith
178 Green Street
Las Vegas, NV 89154
(702) 555-5555

OBJECTIVE:
A position in computer repair with opportunities for advancement.

EXPERIENCE:

1989-
Present
Lakinakis Corporation, Wendover, NV
Customer Service Receiver
Quality Assurance Test Technician
Handled receiving of computer work station units that failed in the field; tested and repaired all computer work stations; ran diagnostic tests and handled troubleshooting on the sub-assembly level.

1988-1989
Ostow Stores, Search Light, NV
Area Specialist/Department Manager
Performed managerial duties for retail camera and electronics department.

1986-1988
Woodruff Electronics, Las Vegas, NV
Field Service Technician
Repaired IBM stations and POS terminals on site. Performed preventative maintenance and customer service.

EDUCATION:

1986-1990
New York University, New York, NY
Bachelor's Degree in Computer Science
Maintaining G.P.A. of 3.9.

1984-1986
Colgate University, Hamilton, NY
Physics Major
Successfully completed four semesters toward a B.A. Achieved a 3.8 G.P.A. before transferring to New York University for completion of studies.

1983-1984
Spinack Data Institute, Brooklyn, NY
Electronics Technology
Received a Certificate in Electronics Technology. Achieved Honors for maintaining a 95+ average.

REFERENCES:
Available upon request.

■ Job descriptions are straightforward and understandable.

■ Strong educational credentials strengthen resume.

QUALITY CONTROL INSPECTOR

Chris Smith
178 Green Street
Crittenden, KY 41030
(505) 555-5555

OBJECTIVE

To secure a position where I can contribute Quality Assurance and Project Management experience.

EXPERIENCE

NEWPORT NAVAL SHIP YARD   Newport, RI
Boiler Systems Inspector, Quality Assurance Office   11/90-6/94

Accountable for all phases for inspection of surface ship propulsion systems and main boiler plants. Position requires full knowledge and experience of Boilermaker duties combined with additional certifications and training.

- Conducted working audits on final systems operational test performed by all shops.
- Certify acceptance of systems whose testing was audited.
- Submit reports and recommendation on all work on systems.
- Maintain files, charts and reports on work in progress and inspections.
- Investigate and report on problem areas and special projects.
- Perform inspections on handholes, manholes, pressure parts, piping, condensers, pressure fuel oil tanks and support machinery.
- Submit all reports to Design and Planning and Estimating to initiate all work.

Boilermaker/Boilermaker Foreman   2/89-11/90

Manufactured and overhauled surface ship propulsion systems and main boiler plants to within very close tolerances and adhering to strict quality control.

- Performed shipfitter and structural steel work to assemble cylinders, pipes, tank heads, condenser heads and shells.
- Produced pipefitting for boiler hookups, tanks and pressure chambers.
- Utilized mason/insulator skills to install fire brick, insulating brick, calcium silicate block, burner tiles, and baffle tiles.

EDUCATION AND SPECIALIZED TRAINING

Steam Generating Plant Inspector   San Francisco, CA
U.S. Navy Main Propulsion Steam Generating Plant Certificate   6/90-10/90

American Society for Quality Control   New York, NY
Inspection Gaging Workshop   6/89

Newport Naval Ship Yard Apprentice School   Newport, RI
Boilermaker Apprentice   9/85-5/89

■ Format is organized and visually appealing.

■ Candidate lists only most relevant education and specialized training.

RESEARCH AND DEVELOPMENT TECHNICIAN

CHRIS SMITH
178 Green Street
Ames, IA 50011
(515) 555-5555

CAREER SUMMARY

An accomplished Research and Development Technician with solid Quality Control experience. Knowledgeable in testing, product specifications, inspection methods, documenting, and electrical/mechanical components. Well developed problem solving skills. Contributions which improved quality and effectiveness.

BUSINESS EXPERIENCE

SYSTEMS SCIENCE, INC.   1990 to Present
Des Moines, IA
A manufacturing company specializing in desktop and portable computers for the home, business, and educational markets.

Test Specialist
Provide research and development for compliance, testing, verification, and submittals. Data testing standards for VDE-0871-B, EN55022, CISPR 22, NEMCO, and FCC Class B.
- Identified test equipment and procedure, reducing test time from 2 days to 1 day.
- Co-developed basic programs for compliance testing of new equipment.
- Maintained test equipment and components to eliminate measurement error thereby reducing product failure.

TOWNSEND COMPANY   1983 to 1989
Des Moines, IA
Technician
Provided testing for compliance of computers to meet safety standards and requirements. Conducted component evaluation to assure attainment of print specifications. Coordinated in-coming Quality Assurance inspection of electrical and mechanical components.
- Developed various test programs for equipment, assuring attainment of product.
- Reduced overall testing time by creating and documenting program to calculate test results.

PREVIOUS EXPERIENCE

Served as Computer Operator for Security in the United State Navy.

EDUCATION

Electronics, Luther College, Decatur, IA, 1980 to 1982

COMPUTER EXPERIENCE

8088, 80286, 80386, 80486, Pentium, Window, Word for Windows, Excel

■ Summary highlights candidate's experience and expertise in his/her field.

■ Bulleted statements highlight candidate's on-the-job achievements.

SURVEYOR

CHRIS SMITH
178 Green Street
Billings, MT 59102
(406) 555-5555

OBJECTIVE: A position in construction, project, or related areas of management. Willing to relocate.

EXPERIENCE: Public Works Department, Billings, MT
Chief Surveyor (1994-Present)
Perform highway, water shed, and topographical surveys. Supervise preparation of plans and specifications for all county highways, bridges, park buildings, and related structures. Maintain a private practice as a surveyor handling site surveys, real estate development layout, and topographical surveys.

Office Engineer (1992-1994)
Developed standard designs for retaining walls and reinforced concrete bridge abutments the designs of which are still currently being used.

Job Works Program, Billings, MT
Seminar Teacher (1994-Present)
Instructed construction foreman in construction methods and leadership.

LICENSES: Professional Engineer, Montana
Surveyor, Montana
Builder, Montana

EDUCATION: Montana State University, Bozeman, MT
B.S. degree in Civil Engineering (with honors), 1992.
Additional course work in concrete design, FORTRAN programming, and computer-aided design. Maintain state-of-the-art skills through extensive reading on construction and business topics.

HOBBIES: Golf, running, racquetball, music.

REFERENCES: Furnished upon request.

■ Continuing education indicates candidate's ongoing commitment to his/her career.

■ Personal interests give a candid snapshot of candidate as a person.

TECHNICAL ILLUSTRATOR

CHRIS SMITH
178 Green Street
Montevallo, AL 35115
(205) 555-5555

CAREER OBJECTIVE
To secure a position as a Technical Illustrator.

BACKGROUND SUMMARY
Extensive experience in creating technical drawings.
Expertise in generating different types of line artwork for
charts, graphs, exploded view and assembly drawings.

QUALIFICATIONS
- Used both computer software and pen and ink materials to produce line artwork for service manual publication.
- Utilized knowledge of variety of software tools such as Auto CAD-12, Fast Links, Norton Utilities and CCMail.
- Drew objects as specified by technical writer.
- Consolidated and resized complex drawings and blueprints for publication use.
- Used verbal specification to develop electronic illustration for new and changed products.

CAREER HISTORY
Alexander Information Systems, Birmingham, AL
Computer Aided Illustrator I   1990-Present

Singleton Company, Birmingham, AL
Illustrator 3   1986-1990
Illustrator 2   1980-1982
Illustrator 1   1978-1980

EDUCATION
Associate's degree in Technical Illustration, 1978
Auburn University, Auburn AL

MILITARY
Veteran, U.S. Air Force - Honorable Discharge

REFERENCES
Available upon request.

■ Qualifications are emphasized while job descriptions are omitted.

■ Education is listed towards bottom of resume because candidate's practical experience outweighs his/her degree.

TECHNICAL INSTRUCTOR

CHRIS SMITH
178 Green Street
Alpha, NJ 08865
(609) 555-5555

CAREER OBJECTIVE:
Develop training programs in a corporate or academic environment and present the material in a clear and interesting manner.

BACKGROUND SUMMARY:
Fifteen years of experience in the microcomputer industry with skills ranging from system design to Project Management. Special expertise in creating and presenting training programs covering a wide variety of topics.

EMPLOYMENT
THE RACE BANNEN COMPANY, Rockaway, ME
Program Management Training Specialist/Network Administrator   1989-Present
Prepare and teach classes in program management techniques and the use of program management software. Manage and maintain the computer network for the department of Program Management. Reconfigure the computer network resulting in 60% increase in the efficiency of the Electronic Mail system. Developed the course material for seven different classes and presented them to over 300 employees.

Program Manager Computers   1987-1989
Coordinated all efforts going into the successful development of computer products from their inception through their discontinuance. The activities managed included electrical and mechanical engineering, publications, purchasing and regulatory. Successfully managed seven different computer models to market including the company's first 83962 based portable.

Marketing Support Engineer   1984-1987
Possessed working knowledge of all Zenith computer products. Represented the company at computer trade shows. Answered technical questions from dealers, distributors and prospective customers. Field tested computer products and performed other "continuing engineering" functions.

Software Documentation Writer   1981-1983
Authored documentation for Computer Products including a complete revision of the original CP/M operating system manual.

SINEAD KIERNEY CORPORATION   1979-1981
Technical Staff
Co-designed a disk interface for word processor to photo-typesetting equipment. Wrote all of the machine language firmware for the design.

EDUCATION:
Ramapo College of New Jersey, Mahwah, NJ
Master's degree in Physics   1979

COMPUTERS:
Programming: FORTRAN, Basic, Assembly
Applications: MS-DOS, Word, Pagemaker, Corel Draw, Management programs

---

- Resume indicates a series of promotions.

- Dynamic action verbs give resume impact.

TECHNICAL SUPPORT SPECIALIST

CHRIS SMITH
178 Green Street
Fairbanks, Alaska 99775
(907) 555-5555

1/91-Present *SASQUATCH HEALTH CARE*, Fairbanks, AK
TECHNICAL SUPPORT SPECIALIST
Structure the submission of test files for electronic billers, according to the required specification manual, which imposed significant changes in physicians' reimbursements. Developed and designed test data formats for telecommunications claim billers, relative to internal technical operations and equipment.
Monitored effective working relationships with external credentialing groups, linking users to meet shared objectives. Formulated and edited technical user specification manual. Submitted weekly patient accounting check writing jobs on the Tape Operating System controlled by Job Control Language and operated the Series 1 mainframe for electronic billers.

6/90-1/91 **INTERNAL SUPPORT SPECIALIST**
Communicated with physician and health providers desiring to submit patient billing claims on the professional line of business, Medicaid, including initiating the activities related to their acceptance and approval of all tape, diskette, and telecommunications billers.
Acted as corporate liaison, communicating and monitoring the providers fraud list for active, suspended, or deceased physicians, and reviewed contracts for credentials of providers anticipating the acquisition of technical billing authorization and a physician provider identification code. Updated and maintained all Alaskan Professional input providers and billers authorization file for all Medical reimbursement billing system.

3/88-6/90 **DATA CONTROL ANALYST**
Serviced local and regional billing agents who submitted weekly hardware on tapes and diskettes for printing and cutting a weekly check writing voucher file. Created and maintained a database on the facility line of business for all input files. Distributed hard copies of vouchers for health care services provided by hospital facilities, to aid as balance control documents.
Allocated missing data that controlled the mechanisms for billing tape submissions; analytically identified and resolved data processing problems and communicated the solution. Promoted from Statistical Analyst and Keypunch Operator.

EDUCATION

FAIRBANKS COMMUNITY COLLEGE, Fairbanks, AK
ASSOCIATE OF ARTS, Computer Science, May 1993, GPA 3.7

ALASKA INSTITUTE OF COMPUTERS, Fairbanks, AK
DIPLOMA, Computer Programming, May 1990, GPA 3.6

PERSONAL
Willing to relocate.

■ Chronological format illustrates a clear career path.

■ Indicating a willingness to relocate on a resume can be advantageous.

TECHNICAL WRITER

CHRIS SMITH
178 Green Street
Melrose, FL 32666
(904) 555-5555

PROFESSIONAL OBJECTIVE
A position as a **Technical Writer**.

PROFESSIONAL EXPERIENCE
1991 to   RIZZO ASSOCIATES, Melrose, FL
Present   **Technical Writer/Project Administration**
- Research data and accurately describe the installation, removal, erection, and maintenance of all military hardwares.
- Outline wiring diagrams and drew part breakdowns for illustrators.
- Serve as administration lead for specific projects in A-3, EA-3, and EP-3E programs.
- Work on IPB, MIM, and IFMM for all maintenance levels.
- Read from various source materials including engineering drawings, wiring diagrams, etc.

1986 to   CAPABIANCO PUBLISHING, Winter Park, FL
1991   **Technical Writer**
- Performed duties as above for military hardware.
- Performed duties of project lead, including editing, lay-out, and corrections.
- Started in Report Storage/Administrative Assistance. Promoted quickly to technical writer.

1984 to   DARK WILLOW ENGINEERING CORPORATION, Killarney, FL
1986   **Editor/Writer**
- Edited, wrote, designed format, and coordinated production of large proposals for government contracts.
- Organized and maintained up-to-date dummy book throughout several revision cycles.
- Interpreted client RFP requirements and determined applicability of proposal response to RFP.

EDUCATION
Curtis College, Winger Park, FL
B.S. in Civil Engineering, 1988.
Course work in English Composition, Drafting, and Computer Science.

REFERENCES
Available on request.

- Job objective is brief and to the point.

- Stating that "references are available upon request" is not essential; most employers will assume that references are available.

TELECOMMUNICATIONS CONSULTANT (Cable)

CHRIS SMITH
178 Green Street
Robbinsdale, MN 55422
(612) 555-5555

OBJECTIVE

A challenging position in telecommunications where my international perspective will be utilized.

EXPERIENCE

May 1993-January 1994 | **CANADIAN CABLE COUNSEL** **Vancouver, Quebec, and Minneapolis**
Consultant
- One of five consultants assigned to research/recommend a strategic alliance for Canadian Cable Corporation.
- Conducted on-site research at CCC's Vancouver offices and at its home office near Quebec.
- Presented final recommendations in video conference. Recommended alliance with Truglia Corp. to produce a multimedia product in anticipation of the merging of telecommunications and computer technology.

September 1992-May 1993 | **THE INTERNATIONAL JOURNAL OF TELECOMMUNICATIONS** **Minneapolis, MN**
Market Researcher
- Researched the effects of worldwide television deregulation on broadcast, cable and satellite television, international broadcasting, and advertising industry.
- Researched direct mail advertising as an international marketing tool. Examined political campaigns, image design, and information distribution.

May 1990-August 1992 | **AROUND THE WORLD CONSULTANTS** **Saint Paul, MN**
Market Research Project Support
- Built database of international publishing & printing firms. Researched list sources, acquired lists, created, merged and purged database.
- Conducted, coded and edited telephone market research surveys to identify and track trends in the electronic publishing and information networking industry.

EDUCATION

SAINT CLOUD STATE UNIVERSITY, St. Cloud, MN
B.S. in Engineering, Minor: French, 1990
- Spent junior year studying and traveling in France.

TRAINING

Seminar in "Global Relations and American Business."
Training session on the uses of the Internet.

- Resume emphasizes achievements; doesn't simply list job responsibilities.

- Relevant training strengthens resume.

TELECOMMUNICATIONS CONSULTANT (General)

CHRIS SMITH
178 Green Street
Binghamton, NY 13901
(607) 555-5555

PROFESSIONAL BACKGROUND
1983-present SUNLINE COMMUNICATIONS, Binghamton, NY
Senior Consultant
- Hired as Director of Marketing in 1983.
- Created department and was responsible for all functions, strategies, and sales tactics. Company doubled billings during this period.
- Promoted in 1985 to Senior Consultant.
- Performed analyses and reconfigurations for a variety of clients, ranging in size from single location companies and municipalities to international multi-location companies with annual network costs in excess of $2 million. Network design included use of computer programs for simulations and modeling.
- Responsible for projects dealing with formulation of specifications, review of vendor bids, and system recommendations.
- Wrote reports dealing with discounted cash and analysis and cost/benefit analyses.
- Responsible for inventory and facility justification of systems and networks.
- Dealt with several major universities and governmental agencies and included station reviews, department interviews for needs and analysis, vendor conferences, and site surveys.

1977-1982 COMMUNET, INC., Yorkville, NY
Account Executive
- Responsible for network facilities, services, sales, and territory management.
- Consistently over quota.
- Assisted in development of following programs: Telemarketing, Customer Service Representative, and Customer Training.

1975-1977 THE SELANEY COMPANY, Utica, NY
- Hired into Customer Relations; moved into Sales.

EDUCATIONAL BACKGROUND
FORDHAM UNIVERSITY, Bronx, NY
Bachelor of Fine Arts Degree in Theater, 1975
Concentration in Management and Technical Theater.

PROFESSIONAL ORGANIZATIONS
President, Professionals in Telecommunications.
Member, Society of Telecommunications Consultants.

- Resume format is neat and professional.

- Job-related affiliations demonstrate candidate's active participation in his/her field.

22
Visual and Performing Arts

Nature of Work
People in the visual and performing arts field create and entertain. Their creative energies inspire everything from criticism to admiration, tears to laughter.

Designers organize and design articles, products, and materials in such a way that they not only serve the purpose for which they were intended but are visually pleasing as well. Photographers accurately or artistically portray people, places, and events. Visual artists use an almost limitless variety of methods and materials to communicate ideas, thoughts, and feelings. Actors, directors, and producers make words come alive by creating a visual and oral presentation based on the written words of a script. Dancers express ideas, stories, rhythm, and sound with their bodies, either performing as a group or solo, while choreographers are those professionals who create dance interpretations.

Employment
A much higher proportion of people working in the field of visual and performing arts are self-employed than those working in other occupations. Performing artists usually work on a per project basis. Photographers, and other visual artists may work exclusively for an advertising agency, newspaper, or magazine, but most often hire out their services to a number of clients. Likewise, interior and fashion designers may work for a design firm or independently.

Training
Creativity is crucial in all visual and performing arts occupations, whether it lies in a strong sense of color and design, fluidity of movement, or an ear for music. A good portfolio, performance video or audio tape is often the deciding factor in landing a job. However, formal preparation is important in all fields.

Some design occupations require a bachelor's degree, while the only prerequisites for acting and musical careers are strong ability and drive.

Job Outlook
The employment of visual and performing arts professionals is expected to grow as fast as average for all occupations. Stimulating a demand for photographers will be the growing importance of visual images in education, communication, entertainment, mar-

keting, and research and development. Employment of actors, director, and producers will rise due to increased demand for American productions fueled by the growth of cable television, home movie rentals, and television syndication.

Earnings

The salaries among visual and performing arts professionals vary greatly. The minimum weekly salary for actors in Broadway productions was $850 in 1991, though most actors earn considerably less.

Earnings of most professional dancers are governed by union contracts. In 1991, the minimum weekly salary of dancers in ballet and modern dance productions was $555.

In regional orchestras, the minimum salaries of musicians were between $212 and $637 per week, and the seasons last eight to forty-two weeks.

Salaried photographers doing fairly routine work averaged $24,800 per year, while those doing difficult and complex work averaged $37,300 in 1991.

ACTOR/ACTRESS

CHRIS SMITH
178 Green Street
Seattle, WA 98105
(206) 555-5555

Hair:	Blonde	D.O.B.:	7/20/65
Eyes:	Hazel	Height:	5'8"
Sex:	Female	Weight:	135 lbs.

EXPERIENCE
1994   WHITEWATER COMMUNITY THEATER, Seattle, WA
Mrs. Babson, *Lights, Camera, Action*

SUMMER ARTS THEATER, Seattle, WA
Karen Arnold, *Life In The Slow Lane*

NIGHT OWL THEATER, Seattle, WA
Candice Lloyd, *World's End*

1993   ST. MARY'S CONGREGATION, Black Diamond, WA
Director, Assorted children's plays

REGGAE FEST, Jamaica
Actor/Director, Several "Festival" performances during this annual national celebration

CHARLES STREET THEATER, Black Diamond, WA
Therese Dupuis, *The Deal*

EDUCATION
1994 to   ACTING UP DRAMA WORKSHOP, Seattle, WA
Present   **Advanced Acting, Acting for Stage and Television, Ritual and Performance**

Related performances:
- **Carolyn Christian**, *Many Moons*
- **Sarah Downs**, *Two For Lunch*
- **Maryanne Walsh**, *Computer Geeks*
- **Lisa**, *Cranberry With a Twist*

1992   EMERSON COLLEGE, Boston, MA
Bachelor of Fine Arts, Acting

ADDITIONAL
Bilingual: Fluent in Italian and English

- Age, sex. and physical appearances are immediately relevant to some jobs in acting, modeling, and the electronic media. In all other cases, these characteristics are inappropriate on a resume.

- Nontraditional resume format works for this nontraditional job.

ART ADMINISTRATOR

Chris Smith
178 Green Street
San Bruno, CA 94066
(415) 555-5555

OBJECTIVE

To contribute teaching and artistic experience and education to an organization where a commitment to excellence will be utilized and advanced.

SUMMARY OF QUALIFICATIONS

- Extensive training in Traditional Art and Drawing.
- Knowledgeable in many different areas of art, including Airbrush, Pastels, Corporate Design, and Book Illustration.

PROFESSIONAL EXPERIENCE

Italian Art Administrator   1993-Present
Organize exhibits. Locate potential sites; actuate presentations; coordinate slide materials. Interact with clients. Generate advertising.

JONAS PUBLISHING CO., San Bruno, CA   1990-93
Graphic Artist
Produced lay-out, paste-up, and mechanicals of full color, bound printed material.

CALIFORNIA CHAPTER OF THE HARE KRISHNAS, San Francisco, CA   1986-89
Graphic Artist
Responsible for artwork, paste-up, and mechanicals for brochures, invitations, newsletters, and printed materials used for annual fundraising campaign. 1989 campaign effort raised $20 million.

EDUCATION

A. MONTERNO, Venice, Italy - Traditional Painting and Drawing, 1991-92
K.S. KUHN STUDIO, San Francisco Artists' Guild, San Francisco, CA - Traditional Painting and Drawing, 1990-91
ACADEMY OF ART COLLEGE, San Francisco, CA
Commercial Art Certificate, 1989
ART CENTER COLLEGE OF DESIGN, Pasadena, CA
Courses in corporate Design, 1986
CALIFORNIA INSTITUTE OF THE ARTS, Valencia, CA
Courses in Air Brush and Portraits in Pastel, 1985
SAN FRANCISCO ART INSTITUTE, San Francisco, CA
Courses in Children's Book Illustration, 1984

HONORS

Outstanding Achievement Award, *American Artist Magazine*, 1993

EXHIBITS

K.S. KUHN STUDIO, San Francisco, CA
Group Exhibition, January-February 1989
CREATIVE ARTS WORKSHOP, Sausalito, CA
Juried Exhibition, May 1987

Letters of recommendation and portfolio available upon request.

- For certain artistic positions, it is advantageous to cite that a portfolio is available.

- Impressive educational background and noteworthy award enhance candidate's qualifications.

ART DIRECTOR

Chris Smith
178 Green Street
Bristol, RI 02809
(401) 555-5555

OBJECTIVE:
Freelance or full-time agency employment as Art Director in an established advertising agency.

EMPLOYMENT:

CURTIS ASSOCIATES/CHERRY HILL, Boston, MA
Art Director, 1991-Present
Major responsibilities included:
- The design, art direction, illustration and concept development of black and white and full color promotional samples for black and white, color copying and ink jet printing divisions.
- Art direction on photography sessions for direct mail marketing pieces.
- Quality control management on press runs for promotional pieces printed in- and out-of-house.
- Design in-house company morale promotional pieces such as anti-drug abuse posters, company picnic and Christmas dinner/dance posters and tickets as well as completing most of the paste-up on all projects.

WOLFSONG, INC., Northampton, MA
Assistant Art Director, 1988-1991
Designed and/or rendered full page cooperative free standing insert ads for regional and national name brand pet food companies.
- Designed and/or rendered FSI's accompanying point-of-sales materials (header cards, tear-off pads, soft sheets and shelf talkers), trade promotions (ad reprints, dealer sell sheets and marketing lists), and bounce-back coupons.
- Utilized illustrative talents to complete black and white product illustrations for bounce-back coupons and ad slicks. Also performed some paste up and type specing.

EDUCATION:

RHODE ISLAND SCHOOL OF DESIGN, Providence, RI
Associate's Degree in Specialized Technology (1988)

MONTSERRAT COLLEGE OF ART, Beverly, MA
Completed three-year program in Commercial Art (1986)

SKILLS:

MacIntosh based Letra Studio, McDraw, Superpaint, Quark Express and Pagemaker software; Itek Stat machine, Iris 3024 and 3047 Inkjet printers, Cannon CLC500 color photo copiers, IBM based Network Pictures Systems' retouching and page layout software, and EICONIX full color flat bed scanner.

- Computer and other job-related skills are highlighted in a separate section.

- Boldfacing calls attention to candidate's strongest qualifications.

CHOREOGRAPHER

Chris Smith
178 Green Street
Pegram, TN 37143
(615) 555-5555

SUMMARY OF QUALIFICATIONS
- Ten years of successful experience as dance studio owner, manager, and instructor.
- Instruction - jazz, ballet, tap, modern and creative dance.
- Planning, coordination, and management of numerous show productions including lighting, staging and sound.
- Travel and function planning.

SKILLS
(Management/Production)
- Successfully plan, organize and manage studio specializing in on-stage dance (jazz, ballet, tap, modern and creative dance).
- Hire, schedule and supervise staff of instructors, receptionist and support personnel working with a student base of 75 to 150.
- Plan, direct, produce, and choreograph shows. Coordinate and manage all phases of publicity, press releases, advertising, artwork and mechanicals for program reproduction.
- Design stage sets, hire and manage stage hands; plan, coordinate, and direct lighting, staging and sound work administered by stage hands for these productions.
- Select, order and distribute costumes; arrange for ticketing and other needs to establish high visibility and audience appeal.

(Dance)
- Choreograph and assist director for show at The Presidential Hotel.
- Work professionally at the Brevard, Robinson, Main House, Rutherford, Bluegrass, Oglethorpe, and other internationally recognized resort hotels.
- For several years was lead dancer with the Mitchell Company.

(Theatre/Drama)
- With the Nashville Theatre, appeared in numerous theatre productions with professionals from New York Stage and Broadway during six to eight-week engagements.

PROFESSIONAL EXPERIENCE
Nashville On-Stage Dance Studio, Nashville, TN
The Presidential Hotel, Nashville, TN
The Nashville Theatre, Nashville, TN

EDUCATION
Memphis State University, Memphis, TN
Bachelor of Arts Degree in Psychology with Minor in Drama, 1981

REFERENCES
References and demo tape of performances available upon request.

- Functional format focuses attention on candidate's major skills and accomplishments.

- For certain jobs in the performing arts, it can be advantageous to indicate that a demo tape is available upon request.

COMEDIAN

CHRIS SMITH
178 Green Street
Miami, FL 33199
(305) 555-5555

PROFILE:
Charismatic, crazy, creative, daring, dastardly, hilarious, hyper, hysterical and of course zany!

PERSONAL:
D.O.B.: 9/5/68   Height: 6'1"
Hair: Brown   Weight: 165 lbs.
Eyes: Blue   Sex: Male

LAST SEEN:

MIAMI Comedians At Large   Beachside Comedy Review
Miami Moon   Laughter Unlimited
Carlisle's Lounge   Give It Up
Kevin's Connection   Pleasure Island

CHICAGO Wind It Down   The Funny Farm
Comedy Central

DETROIT Let It Slide   Can You Stand It?
Barry's Bar & Grill   The Haverill House

SAN Wild Child   The Funny Bone
FRANCISCO Check It Out   Tickle My Fancy

ORLANDO Church Street Station   The Mad Hatter
Mickey's

TELEVISION LOSIN' IT
• Co-producer of local cable program, showcasing a variety of
stand-up performers
COMEDIANS FOR HIRE
• Numerous stand-up appearances

KNOWN ASSOCIATES:
The American Comedians Association

CAUTION:
Mr. Smith is armed with a sharp tongue and a quick wit. He has
been known to strike without warning!

■ Resume lists candidate's most recent appearances.

■ Zany tone of resume corresponds to candidate's career.

COMMERCIAL ARTIST/INSTRUCTOR

Chris Smith
178 Green Street
Cordova, MD 21625
(301) 555-5555

CAREER OBJECTIVE
A position as ART INSTRUCTOR in a Museum/Academic environment.

RELATED EXPERIENCE
ARTIST/CARPENTER
Cordova, MD   Fall 1994
Coordinated creative planning sessions and budget discussions for two downtown promotional events. Developed prototype designs; constructed and painted various props and backgrounds. Designed and implemented lighting effects.

ARTIST
Bartlett's, Baltimore, MD   1992-Present
Awarded commission for creating Japanese motif sketch design for front window display in upscale retail store. Administered project budget for labor and materials; utilized large rolls of paper and ink to paint 16 panels of oriental designs.

ARTIST/CARPENTER
The Tyler Center, Riverdale, MD   1990-1992
Participated in advertising promotion of new men's fragrance. Created large superstructure using tension and fiberglass with a red cloth recreating the product bottle. Room walls were shaped with reliefs of the bottle image.

ARTIST
The Perry Hotel, Westminster, MD   1990
Worked in artist shop creating various props including tropical set for disc jockey. Created palm trees, built bamboo hut, integrated lighting effects into structure/scene.

EDUCATION & TRAINING
AMOS SCHOOL OF DESIGN - Boston, MA
MASTERS DEGREE IN FINE ARTS, 1989
Volunteer work at the Larson Museum
Studied abroad in Europe; travels included France, Germany and Italy

EXHIBITS
Zone "Tri-Town Siege" - Baltimore, MD
Bonfried Scott Gallery - Gaithersburg, MD
The Mystic Gallery - Manhattan, NY

■ Job objective is clearly defined.   ■ Unrelated work experience is omitted.

DANCER

CHRIS SMITH
178 Green Street
Las Vegas, NV 89154
(702) 555-5555 (Day)
(702) 444-4444 (Evening)

TALENTS:
- Ballet
- Jazz
- Modern Dance
- Tap
- Singing
- Acting
- Choreography
- Directing

EXPERIENCE:
DANCING
September 1992-Present: Soloist with Mormon Youth Ensemble. Presentations include:
- "Summer Winds" - Contemporary ballet
- "Peace at Heart" - Modern piece
- "Travels Afar" - Classical ballet
- "Italian Gondolas" - Contemporary ballet
- "Two Stars" - Jazz piece
- "Clouds Above" - Dream ballet, musical
- "The Gosling" - Classical ballet
- "A Little Bit Country" - Modern ballet, musical

CHOREOGRAPHY
- Special events and shows, 1991-Present
- Rocket Dance Club, Las Vegas, NV, 1992-Present
- Copa Cabana Club, Las Vegas, NV, 1991-1992

EDUCATION:
Sierra Nevada College, Incline Village, NV
BFA in Dance and Choreography, 1994

TRAINING:
- Ballet: NV Ballet, NV Academy of Ballet
- Jazz: Genevieve le Fleur, James Ivan
- Tap: Jackie Rose Studio

DEMO TAPE AVAILABLE UPON REQUEST

■ Candidate's special talents are emphasized in a separate section.

■ Indicating both a daytime and evening telephone number can be beneficial.

DESKTOP PUBLISHER

CHRIS SMITH
178 Green Street
Revere, MA 02151
(617)555-5555

PROFILE

Experienced design professional with background in desktop publishing, graphic design and technical art. Proficient in Ventura Publisher 4.0, PerForm Form Designer, Micrografx Designer, QuarkXpress and WordPerfect 5.1.

EXPERIENCE

LYERLA LIFE INSURANCE COMPANY, Revere, MA   1992-Present
DESKTOP PUBLISHER
- Produced brochures, personnel forms and policy pages using WordPerfect 5.1, PerForm, Ventura, Designer and quark in a Windows environment.
- Created layout & design of brochures detailing product lines for sales representatives and convention participants. Worked with sales representatives and printers regarding bid specifications and deadlines for three color brochures.
- Extensive experience in WordPerfect designing and formatting over 350 policy pages.

KANE INC., Welch, WV   1988-1992
TECHNICAL ILLUSTRATOR/GRAPHIC DESIGNER
- Created complex diagrams, schedules, charts and signs for use in proposals, reports and division communications. Designed and updated organization charts for division.
- Designed and formatted an eight page employee newsletter. Sized photos and used stat camera for art. Worked with outside vendors for photos and final printing of newsletter.
- Produced photo contest poster, Employee of the Year poster, booklets, brochures and invitations promoting company events.
- Within TQM environment assumed management responsibility, prioritized assignments, delegated tasks and planned schedules. Prepared material for presentation by TQM groups.
- Organized and led departmental meetings, successfully resolving problems with product quality. Established department standards for artwork and documents; published handbook of standards implemented department wide.

JUNIOR TECHNICAL ILLUSTRATOR/TECHNICAL TYPIST   1982-1988
- Responsible for technical drawings, newspaper paste-up, diagrams and illustrations for technical reports and proposals. Assisted photographer in photo lab.
- Typeset copy for proposals and viewgraph presentations using Wang word processor and IBM Composer. Typing speed 80+wpm.

EDUCATION

University of Tennessee, Knoxville, TN
Graphic Design Certificate, 1982

Benkart Junior College, Benkart, TN
WordPerfect 5.1 Applications, 1981

■ Profile grabs the reader's attention with powerful skills and qualifications.

■ Resume emphasizes achievements; doesn't simply list job responsibilities.

FASHION DESIGNER

CHRIS SMITH
178 Green Street
New York, NY 10019
(212) 555-5555

OBJECTIVE A position in apparel and accessory design where illustration, design and technical skills will be creatively utilized.

SUMMARY Diversified background offers expertise in:
- **Illustration:** Design sketching and fashion illustration.
- **Sewing:** Tailoring, mass production, fabrication, pattern making, construction.
- **Design:** Specializing in custom evening wear and women's special occasion and sportswear.

EXPERIENCE THE NEW COLLECTION, New York, NY
Tailor, 1992-Present
- Specialize in fashionable women's working apparel.
- Provide tailoring, wardrobe consultation, and custom design of suits and evening wear.
- Sketch original designs, create patterns and construct garments.

Freelance Fashion Designer, 1990-Present
- Create custom clothing for fashion shows.
- Provide wardrobe, fabric and color consultation.
- Have developed a solid, recurring client base.

COLOR CONTOURS, Albany, NY
Seamstress, 1988-1990
- Fabrication, woolen and knit ponchos and fur accessories.
- Production sewing, Merrow, single-needle and fur machines.

GALLUZO MANUFACTURERS, Saugerties, NY
Assistant Designer, 1986-1988
- Designed for High Street label and line.
- Selected fabric, color, and pattern.
- Achieved minimum production costs on first pattern estimates.

EDUCATION
FASHION INSTITUTE OF TECHNOLOGY, New York, NY
Associates in Applied Science: Fashion Design Major, 1993.

HONORS/EXHIBITS
- Prize-winning garments for design and construction
  Fashion Union Fashion Show, 1993
- Best Bikini Design
  New York Swimwear Associates, 1990

■ Summary clearly spells out candidate's areas of expertise.

■ Impressive honors and exhibits further enhance candidate's accomplishments.

FILM PRODUCTION ASSISTANT

CHRIS SMITH
178 Green Street
Los Angeles, CA 90049
(213) 555-5555

PROFESSIONAL OBJECTIVE
A film production position where I can contribute a broad range of relevant experience and education.

EXPERIENCE

1993-
Present **HOLLY CAN PRODUCTIONS**, Burbank, CA
Production Assistant
- Assisted in production of "Chuck's Gals."
- Shot and edited commercials for Indian Outfitters.
- Research and recommend prop and wardrobe choice.

1990-
Present **Freelancer**
- Videotaped improvisational workshop for the L.A. Entertainment Theatre, and comedy sketches for local talent.
- Wrote material for various Los Angeles comedians.
- Wrote jokes published in *Side-Splitters* Magazine.

1992-93 **Intern**
- Observed techniques in video editing and pre-production of feature films and slide shows for corporations and universities

WRITING
- Radio/TV commercial scripts
- 35-page comedy
- Several short narrative sketches
- Several short comedy films

EDUCATION

Bachelor of Arts in Film Production
Emerson College, L.A. Program, May 1993

PORTFOLIO

Portfolio of writing and productions available upon request.

■ Internships strengthen candidate's short work history.

■ Writing experience is outlined in a separate section.

GRAPHIC ARTIST/DESIGNER (A)

Chris Smith
178 Green Street
Honey Grove, TX 75446
(210) 555-5555

PROFILE
Business and art professional with broadbased knowledge and expertise in a variety of art forms. Excellent organizer and communicator with the ability to project and elicit interest, enthusiasm and energy, using a common sense approach. Over five years professional art experience. Strong conceptual skills; able to translate ideas into realities.

ART/DESIGN EXPERIENCE

MICHAEL JUDGE GALLERY, Dallas, TX   Spring 1994
Displayed and sold several art pieces. Illustrations used in advertisements and gallery logo.

CAROL OATES INC., Keechi, TX   1993-1994
Freelance work for national stationery and social invitation firm.
- Design invitations, personal stationery, business cards, and logos.
- Implemented italic method as well as numerous hand-designed, stylized lettering.

BYRON KATZ, Kress, TX   1991-1992
Freelance calligrapher for national stationery company.
- Design invitations and logos.

BARBARA B. DOLE, Kress, TX   1989-1991
Self-promoting/advertising, freelance calligrapher for local clients.
- Design wedding and party invitations.
- Provide artwork and calligraphy for accompanying accessories.

ACCOMPLISHMENTS
- Designer of logo for Connection Street Gallery, its storefront sign, T-shirts, jackets, business cards and stationery, advertising, and greeting cards.
- Designer of logo for *Brazen Attachment* Magazine; artwork for advertising appeared in *Her View*.
- Designer for calligraphic artwork for Texas History Museum.

EDUCATION
CONCORDIA COLLEGE, Bronxville, NY
Bachelor of Fine Arts, 1988

PUBLICATIONS
Missed Grits: How to Cook Southern Favorites No Matter Where You Live, Reni Watts. 1991. Cover Design.

References and Portfolio Available On Request

- Profile sums up candidate's professional qualifications.

- Impressive accomplishments and publications add depth to candidate's qualifications.

GRAPHIC ARTIST/DESIGNER (B)

Chris Smith
178 Green Street
Elk Rapids, MI 49629
(517) 555-5555

CAREER OBJECTIVE
A challenging position in the field of COMMERCIAL ART where I can contribute highly developed graphic design skills and technical aptitude.

RELATED EXPERIENCE

GRAPHIC ARTIST   1984-Present
Packard Army Reserves, Elk Rapids, MI
Serve as artistic support for Army Base; create flyers, charts, brochures, tickets, diagrams, maps and design logos. Document work order requests; plan and organize work to meet all deadline requirements. Purchase materials and supplies; document materials received and perform graphics department inventory. Maintain accurate and timely department records.

GRAPHIC ARTIST/ELECTRONIC DESIGN   1988-Present
Midland Products, Alden, MI
Produce camera ready art utilizing Apple computer system with laser printing equipment. Proficient in use of MacDraw, Pagemaker and Freehand programs. Process film, operate reproduction camera for stats, positive and negative images. Utilize Diffusion Transfer machine. Effectively organize time and work to consistently meet critical deadlines. Keep artwork and files up to date.

TECHNICAL LINE ARTIST   1984-1988
Marmoset Electric Company, Rapid City, MI
Performed drafting work; inked illustrations. Produced paste up and mechanical preparation for Detroit Transit Railcar Inspection Manuals.

ARTIST/PASTE UP   1982-1984
Sharona's Art Emporium, Ellsworth, MI
Created art for viewgraphs and slide presentations; designed ads for newspaper; provided computer art for Sharona's computer facility. Set up mechanicals for print orders including business cards and stationery. Ran blueprints, made negatives, and opaqued negatives.

EDUCATION
ASSOCIATE'S DEGREE in GRAPHIC DESIGN, 1980
Kendall School of Design, Grand Rapids, MI

PORTFOLIO AND REFERENCES AVAILABLE UPON REQUEST

- Job objective focuses on the needs of the employer, not the job candidate.

- Resume illustrates continual career progression.

INTERIOR DESIGNER

Chris Smith
178 Green Street
Murfreesboro, TN 37129
(615) 555-5555

PROFESSIONAL OBJECTIVE
A responsible and challenging position as a SENIOR INTERIOR DESIGNER.

SUMMARY OF QUALIFICATIONS
- Broad-based knowledge from over four years of professional experience in architectural and interior design including space planning, product knowledge, specification and drafting techniques.
- Training and coordination of administrative and operational support personnel, with the ability to work productively and effectively with all levels of management and a full range of personalities.
- Ability to meet deadlines and work well under pressure.
- Exceptional interpersonal, client service and liaison skills.
- Presentation of a positive and professional image.

EMPLOYMENT HISTORY
1988 to   MERRIMONT BUSINESS SETTINGS, INC., Jackson, TN
Present   Senior Interior Designer
- Responsible with team of six designers for producing space plans and interior finishes for corporate offices, schools, libraries, and banks.
- Developed expertise in field measuring, architectural planning, inventory, product specification, finish selection, renderings and presentation boards, and supervision of installation.
- Enjoy extensive client contact throughout design process including resolution of problems.
- Train and supervise junior designers.
- Plan budgets, make estimates, and negotiate final sales agreement with client.

1985 to   LAWRENCE LOWFERN ASSOCIATES, Nashville, TN
1988   Junior Interior Designer
- Conducted preliminary inventory work, site measurement, drafting of space plans, 1/4 scale details, elevations, choosing and paste-up of finishes on presentation boards, budgets, specification writing and follow up work.

EDUCATIONAL BACKGROUND
MEMPHIS COLLEGE OF ART, Memphis, TN
Bachelor of Fine Arts in Interior Design, 1984

Portfolio available upon request

■ Resume illustrates continual career progression.

■ Format is organized and visually appealing.

MODEL

Chris Smith
178 Green Street
Acworth, GA 31707
(912) 555-5555

Height: 5'9"	Bust: 36"
Weight: 120 lbs.	Waist: 28"
Hair Color: Auburn	Hips: 35"
Eye Color: Green	Dress Size: 5
Age Range: 18-30	Shoe Size: 7

TRAINING

Rick Bass Casting, Modeling and Acting
Joy DeVivre, Modeling and Acting

EXPERIENCE

Fashion BRYDIE'S BRIDAL SHOP, Atlanta, GA
Shows Fashion Show, May 1994

RAYANNE'S FASHIONS, Albany, GA
Runway Show, July 1993

Film EBONY'S FINE ARTS SCHOOL, Alphoretta, GA
Modeled for Photography class, Summer 1992

GOLD MORNING PRODUCTIONS
Extra for three scenes at Downtown Crossing, Boston, MA, October 1992

Competition EVAN HAWKE MODELING CONTEST, Atlanta, GA
First Runner-up, December, 1993

SPECIAL SKILLS

Sports: swimming, ice skating, snow and water skiing, bicycling, baseball, basketball, tennis, jogging, aerobics.
Dancing: jazz, tap, ballet.
Play classical piano.
Familiar and comfortable working with animals (dogs and cats, large and exotic species included).

EDUCATION

Georgia County Community College, Atlanta, GA
Chemical Engineering Studies.

■ For all but a few positions in acting, modeling, and electronic media, physical characteristics are inappropriate on a resume.

■ Unrelated work experience is omitted.

MUSICIAN

Chris Smith
178 Green Street
New York, NY 10019
(212) 555-5555

SUMMARY OF QUALIFICATIONS
- More than six years orchestral experience as violinist/violist.
- Ability to comprehend administrative needs from the perspective of a performer.
- Acquired skills as orchestra librarian/personnel manager
- Organizational abilities; detail-oriented.

RELEVANT EXPERIENCE

Orchestra - 2nd Violin
- La Musique, C'est Magnifique!
  Play, Paris, France
- White Willows in Glasgow
  Opera and Ballet, Scotland
- Sun Symphony Orchestra of L.A.
  Los Angeles, California
- The Minot Lighthouse Orchestra
  Bar Harbor, ME
- Bang a Ceramic Gong: The Tale of a Chinese Emperor
  Play, Boston, MA

MIDAS TOUCH CHAMBER ORCHESTRA, New York, NY   1990-92
Personnel Manager. Recruited players. Arranged for substitutes.
Assisted Conductor/Music Director. Scheduled recitals,
announcements and member contact regarding changes, problem
resolution, etc. Required ability to deal with personality
conflicts and musical problems as well as fielding suggestions
from members. Instituted rotating string sections. Handled
membership payment. Acted as liaison between musicians and union.

EDUCATION

O'BURN INSTITUTE, New York, NY   1992
Teacher Workshop Courses

THE JUILLIARD SCHOOL, New York, NY   1989
Bachelor of Arts, Music

References and Audio Tape Available on Request

■ Summary of qualifications illustrate candidate's key credentials.

■ Resume emphasizes contributions, achievements, and problems candidate has solved throughout his/her career.

PHOTOGRAPHER

CHRIS SMITH
178 Green Street
Burlington, VT 05405
(802) 555-5555

OBJECTIVE
A position in photography utilizing my outstanding production and creative skills to improve a company's services and profitability.

KNOWLEDGE/SKILLS
- Black and White film development and printing
- Color Film development and printing, negative and direct positive processes
- Large format view cameras 4x5; 8x10; Medium format cameras; 35mm equipment
- Studio and location lighting equipment setups
- Special effects, multiple imagery, conventional and electronic manipulation techniques
- DOS, MAC, Windows Software: Adobe Photoshop, Quark Xpress, Aldus Photostyler, Persuasion, Freehand, Pagemaker, Lotus Freelance, and Paintbrush

EXPERIENCE
Photographer/Assistant   1991-Present
Worked on a variety of location and studio assignments, developed curriculum, and instructed photography classes. Produced superior photo work in a number of venues:
- Articles in National Stamp Collector Magazine
- Photographs for portfolio reproductions and theatrical head shots at Goddard College
- Photo essay for Jake's Fisheries: "A Day Offshore"
- Interpreted layouts, designed and constructed sets for complete on-figure fashion shoots
- Highly skilled at laying out and shooting hard-line advertising

Photographic Assistant   1987-Present
- Frank Zanna, still life, Hubbel Pen, Dom Champagne, 1992-Present
- Jack Camp, still life, Merry Maids, 1991-Present
- Les Meyers, location editorial Goddard College 1987-1991

ACCOMPLISHMENTS
- Location photography of Men's Swim Team for U.S. Olympic Committee, 1992
- Hard line advertising/marketing brochures/corporate portraits, Kenerson Industries, Burlington, VT, 1991
- Promotional photography for ballet recital, University of Vermont, Burlington, VT, 1991

EDUCATION
Goddard College, Plainfield, VT
Bachelor of Fine Arts in Visual Arts, 1991
Concentration: Photography

■ Knowledge/Skills section calls attention to valuable technical knowledge.

■ Specific accomplishments add depth to candidate's experience.

PRODUCTION COORDINATOR

Chris Smith
178 Green Street
Bristol, RI 02809
(401)555-5555

EXPERIENCE
1993-present | **Production Coordinator.** Formington Corp.   Bristol, RI
Supervise all steps in the production and printing processes for new book titles; design and produce book covers and marketing materials as assigned by the Corporate & Professional Production Manager. Coordinate and maintain schedules and budgets for each project, hire and manage vendors as necessary. Utilize QuarkXpress, FileMaker Pro, Excel, and Microsoft Word on a daily basis; familiar with Canvas, Aldus Freehand, and Adobe Illustrator.

1991-1993 | **Production Assistant.** Formington Corp.   Bristol, RI
Assisted General Books Production Manager and Departmental Art Directors in mechanical paste-up corrections for reprint titles. Coordinated new covers for Special Markets Division, produced numerous production reports utilizing Macintosh software, maintained various departmental database networks and filing systems, and prepared interior text corrections for printing.

1989-1991 | **Quality Control Inspector**. Martinson Inc.   Providence, RI
Inspected software packages, interrupted assembly line errors, prepared weekly and monthly production reports on an IBM.

1986-1989 | **Jacket Art Department Intern.** Ricolla Co.   Boca Raton, FL
Responsibilities included photostat production, bookkeeping, operating fax machine, telex machine and photocopier, illustrator correspondence, photo research, routing mechanicals, and distributing printed jackets to department and company supervisors. Also assisted sketch comprehensives, type layout and mechanical paste-up.

EDUCATION | **Bachelor of Fine Arts.** Villanova University   Villanova, PA
1986 | Studio Art curriculum with an elected Design and Biology minor. Dean's List, Cum Laude.

ADDITIONAL | Completed a QuarkXpress training class at Tech Computer in Bristol, attended
EXPERIENCE | Book Builders seminars on desktop color and pre-press, completed Publication Design class at Abarstow School of Art and Design, and several graduate painting classes at Rhode Island College of Art.

REFERENCES | References and portfolio available upon request.

■ Resume includes course work and seminars related to candidate's field of interest.

■ Format is organized and visually appealing.

PRODUCTION (TOUR) MANAGER

Chris Smith
178 Green Street
Boston, MA 02115
(617) 555-5555

SUMMARY OF QUALIFICATIONS

- Five years of progressive, professional tour management/production experience requiring ability to coordinate tours, video, T.V., fashion/tradeshows, and conventions.
- Self-motivated; able to set effective priorities and implement decisions to achieve immediate and long term goals and meet operational deadlines.
- Capable of organizing projects from initiation through completion; adept at troubleshooting and resolving problems.
- Proven liaison and negotiating skills coordinating worldwide tours.
- Deal with daily expenses, cost projections, and show settlements.

PROFESSIONAL EXPERIENCE

STRANGE MAGIC MANAGEMENT COMPANY, Boston, MA — 1990-Present
Tour/Production Manager
Oversaw diverse aspects of on the road tours including Crypt Keeper and Adis Ababa. Managed finances/budget. Hired outside contractors/road crews. Coordinated travel arrangements, including four worldwide tours. Dealt with visas, freight, hotel accommodations, etc. Acted as liaison with local labor unions and security. Resolved problems as necessary.

MILQUETOAST, LIE TO YOUR MOTHER TOUR — 1990
Production Manager
Oversaw/directed six-month worldwide tour.

WENDELL THE PAPERBOY, WHY BOTHER? TOUR — 1990
Production Manager
Coordinated all aspects of six month tour.

NO ARTICULATION, HEART ON YOUR SLEEVE TOUR — 1989
Back-Line Technician
Served as Drum Technician. Assisted in stage management. Arranged equipment rental for worldwide tour including: Bangkok, Saigon, and Taiwan. Developed endorsements with instrument companies and backstage catering.

THINK TANK, KISS IN THE RAIN TOUR — 1989
Back-Line Technician/Stage Manager
Worked directly under Production Manager on this arena level tour. Served as Drum Technician.

BURNT RETINA, BREAD & WATER TOUR — 1988
Lighting Technician
Dealt with complicated lighting system, rigging, loading/unloading, and working with union crews.

EDUCATION
CURRY COLLEGE, Milton, MA
B.A. Public Relations, 1987

■ Summary of qualifications highlights candidate's acquired professional skills.

■ Education is listed towards bottom of resume because candidate's practical experience outweighs his/her degree.

TALENT AGENT

Chris Smith
178 Green Street
Winterthur, DE 19735
(302) 555-5555

OBJECTIVE

To become an artist and repertoire representative for a major label.

EXPERIENCE

Ricochet Management Inc., Wilmington, DE
Personal Manager (1990 to present)
- Selected six local bands and brought them to national recognition: Top of the Charts, Sights, New York Talk, and Spunk Awards 1992
- Advised artists on performance and repertoire, resulting in three major label signings
- Oversaw and coordinated the production, promotion and marketing of 4 major label projects
- Initiated and devised extraordinary pre-release promotions for a debut album, resulting in immediate college chart movement on release (Kieley and Briody)
- Tour managed three album tours, one regional and the others national, all 20-25% under budget

Moonchild Records, New York, NY
Label Manager (1988-1990)
- Achieved three regionally top 10 selling and charting records, and a top selling single in Europe.
- Devised and oversaw promotion and marketing on limited budgets of $10,000 to $15,000
- Oversaw production, mastering, manufacturing, artwork and distribution
- Coordinated career development with artists and their management

Aural Erosion Records, Los Angeles, CA
Product Manager (1987-1988)
- Effected the release of 3 independent records by 3 local bands: each record reaching top 10 regional sales and radio charts, with each subsequently signed to a major label

Mudsling Song, Inc., Los Angeles, CA
Operations Manager/Booking Agent (1985-1987)
- Created a showcase club for up-and-coming alternative acts: Crudeness, Drink the Foam, Your Mangy Mother, Corporate Mind Wipe, Clubbed Knee, and Four Evil Extraterrestrials and their Dad
- Conceived entirely new club concept: music format, design and marketing strategy. Increased revenues from an average $100,000 to over $2 million, and profit on live shows from 52% to 99%

EDUCATION

Stanford University, Stanford, CA
Major: Public Relations
Master's Degree, May 1985

■ Specific numeric and dollar figures quantify candidate's achievements.

■ Resume emphasizes qualifications pertaining to candidate's job objective.

THEATRICAL DIRECTOR

CHRIS SMITH
178 Green Street
Chicago, IL 60622
(312) 555-5555

OBJECTIVE

A career continuation as a Director of legitimate theatre on or off Broadway.

SKILLS AND QUALIFICATIONS

- Over 13 years experience stage directing with clear understanding of playwrights' texts and creative analysis.
- Provide theatrical direction to actors attuned to both the Stanislavsy and Method styles of acting.
- Focused on the physical requirements and restrictions of stages ranging from in-the-round, proscenium arch, mechanical stages, and special effects.
- Communicate well with actors in relation to lighting and sound technicians.
- Involved in all aspects of costuming and make-up to enhance actors' performances and facilitate their taking direction accurately and precisely while maintaining their own "voice" and force on stage.
- Able to deal with producers and financial backers in structural, aesthetic, and artistic feasibility of a play.
- Work closely with producers and board of directors on time, focus, budget, creative and practical expectations between director-actors-and-powers that be.

SELECTED DIRECTORIAL EFFORTS

- *THE IMPORTANCE OF BEING ERNEST*
- *SUNSET STRIP*
- *FENCES*
- *THE FANTASTICKS*
- *PEARLIE*
- *GREASE*
- *THE WIZ*
- *THE REAL INSPECTOR HOUND*
- *SHADOWLANDS*
- *AGATHA CHRISTIE'S THE MOUSETRAP*
- *EVITA*
- *OLIVER!*
- *BARNUM*
- *THE LITTLE FOXES*
- *WAITING FOR GODOT*

EDUCATION

EMERSON COLLEGE, Boston, MA	M.A., Directing	1980
EMERSON COLLEGE, Boston, MA	B.A., Theatre	1978

References and Portfolio Available On Request

- Nontraditional resume format is acceptable for certain nontraditional careers.

- Resume is tailored to candidate's job objective; unrelated experience is omitted.

VISUAL ARTIST

Chris Smith
178 Green Street
Pittsburgh, PA 15221
(412) 555-5555

OBJECTIVE   To apply educational background and acquired experience to a challenging position in Visual Presentation Management.

SUMMARY OF QUALIFICATIONS
Extensive experience in the implementation and revision of visual presentation standards for a chain of 40 stores, requiring creation and implementation of a visual checklist, visual criteria standardization, conduction of visual audits, imparting of display techniques, creating and writing operational manuals, development of promotional campaigns, costing, purchasing, inventory control, training, enhancement of personnel, and conduction of marketing surveys.

EXPERIENCE   **MARK'S GRAFFITI GARAGE**   **Visual Presentation Coordinator**
1992-Present   Pittsburgh, PA
- Revise and implement standards of presentation for a retail chain, consisting of 40 stores.
- Created and implemented a visual checklist, which standardized company wide visual criteria; through utilization by district managers during weekly visits to stores.
- Conduct frequent visual store audits, for the purpose of enforcing visual standards and imparting display techniques to field personnel.
- Design, execute and direct seasonal floor sets with corresponding window displays, requiring communication of updates to field personnel as the flow of merchandise changes.
- Establish and maintain consistency within stores with regard to what, where, when and how merchandise is presented.
- Periodically update and implement window display fixture to maintain consistency with company image.

1990-1992   **Pennsylvania Area Manager**
- Directed, developed and supported a team of 26 store managers and assistant managers for the Pennsylvania Region.
- Trained store management teams to provide customers with a firm conceptualization of company's image, through the development of visual presentation, operational procedures and service skills.
- Provided managerial support and direction for twelve stores, with a cumulative yearly volume of $8.4 million.

EYE OF THE STORM   **General Manager/Buyer**
1988-1990   Levittown, PA
- Created and wrote an operational manual for a twelve store chain in Pennsylvania and New York which standardized employment and sales policies for 155 employees.
- Revamped a retail computer network by installing inventory controls that produced a substantial increase in revenue.

EDUCATION   **GENEVA COLLEGE**   Beaver Falls, PA
Bachelor of Science Degree, Business Administration, 1987

- Specifically citing number of employees supervised draws attention to candidate's leadership abilities.

- Background summary accentuates candidate's acquired professional skills and impressive track record.

23
Resumes and Cover Letters in the Electronic Age

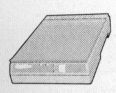

Welcome to the electronic age! As computers have impacted many other aspects of our lives, they have dramatically changed the way we go about job hunting, too. With companies slashing recruiting budgets and trimming hiring staffs, they rely increasingly on automated applicant tracking systems to process and sort employment applications. Other companies hire electronic employment database companies to fill specific openings. This means that your resume will be read by more computers and fewer people. Your resume, therefore, must be in a format that is easy for a computer to recognize and understand. Otherwise, your application will quickly begin collecting dust. For more examples visit our web site at: http://www.careercity.com/resumes/howto.htm

Basically, this is how it works: Your resume is fed through a scanner, which sends an image of the document to a computer. The computer then "reads" your resume, looking for key words, and then files your resume accordingly in its database. When an employer has an opening to fill, he or she will search the database for applications that have key words associated with the requirements of the position.

The good news about this technology is that it enables you to market your resume to hundreds of thousands of employers very easily. The bad news is that you must create an "electronic resume" in order to take advantage of the technology. But don't panic! An electronic resume is simply a modified version of your conventional resume. And though an electronic resume is very different from other types of resumes, it's easy to create. Here's how.

Content
Name. Your name should appear at the top of your resume, with your address following underneath.

Abbreviations. Most resume scanning systems will recognize a few common abbreviations like BS, MBA, and state names. Widely used acronyms for industry jargon, such as A/R and A/P on an accounting resume, are also generally accepted. But if there's any question of whether an abbreviation is a standard one, play it safe and spell it out.

Key Words. Using the right key words or key phrases in your resume is critical to its ultimate success—or lack thereof. Key words are usually nouns or short phrases that the computer searches for when scanning your resume. They usually refer to experience, training, skills, and abilities. For example, let's say an employer searches an employment database for a sales representative with the following key word criteria:

> sales representative
> BS/BA
> exceeded quota
> cold calls
> high energy
> willing to travel

Even if you have the right qualifications, if you don't use these key words on your resume, the computer will pass over your application.

To complicate matters further, different employers search for different key words. These are usually buzzwords common to your field or industry that describe your experience, education, skills, and abilities. Though there is no way to know for sure which key words employers are most likely to search for, you can make educated guesses. Check the classified ads for job openings in your field. What terms do employers commonly use to describe their requirements? Executive recruiters who specialize in your field are also a good source of this kind of information. Of course, you'll want to use as many key words in your resume as possible to maximize your chances.

Key-Word Summary. This is a compendium of your qualifications, usually written in a series of succinct key-word phrases, that immediately follows your name and address.

Experience and Achievements. Your professional experience should immediately follow the key-word summary, beginning with your most recent position. (If you are a recent college graduate, however, you should list your education before your experience.) Be sure that your job title, employer, location, and dates of employment are all clearly displayed. Highlight your accomplishments and key responsibilities with bullets.

Education. This section immediately follows the experience section. List your degrees, licenses, certifications, relevant course work, and academic awards or honors. Be sure to clearly display the name of the schools, locations, and years of graduation.

References. Don't waste valuable space with statements like "References available upon request." Though this section was standard fare for resumes of old, it won't win you any points on an electronic resume.

Format

Length of the Resume. Ideally your resume should be one to two pages in length. If you go over one page, make sure your name appears on the top of each subsequent page. Do not staple or fold your resume.

Paper. Don't bother with expensive papers or fancy colors. Use standard, twenty pound, 8$^1/_2$-by-11-inch paper. Because your resume needs to be as sharp and legible as possible, your best bet is black ink on white paper.

Font. Choose a non-decorative font with clear, distinct characters, such as Helvetica or Times.

Font Size. A font size of 12 points is ideal. Don't go below 10 or above 14 points, as type that is too small or too large is difficult for the scanner to read.

Font Style. Most scanners will accept boldface, but if an employer specifically tells you to avoid it, you can substitute boldface with all capital letters. Boldfacing and all capitalization are best used only for major section headings, such as "Experience" and "Education."

Graphics, Lines, and Shading. A resume scanner will try to "read" graphics, lines, and shading as text, resulting in computer chaos. You should also avoid using nontraditional layouts for your resume, such as two-column.

Printing. Whatever type of printing process you use, make sure the end result is letter quality. Ideally, you should have it printed at your local copy shop. Otherwise, a laser printer is perfectly acceptable. Avoid typewriters and dot matrix printers, since the quality of type they produce is inadequate for most scanners. Because your resume needs to be as sharp and legible as possible, you should always send originals, not photocopies. For the same reason, you should always mail, not fax, your resume.

Should You Include a Cover Letter with Your Electronic Resume?

Yes. Though cover letters are generally not scanned, some systems will take a "photograph" of it, and store it electronically with your resume. And while your cover letter will not help you in the initial selection process, it can help distinguish you from the competition in the final rounds of elimination. If you've taken the time to craft a letter that reiterates a couple of your strongest qualifications, you'll have the edge over other contenders who skipped this important step.

As with your resume, your cover letter should contain key words reflecting your strongest qualifications. If you're responding to a classified ad, be sure to echo as many of the key words mentioned in the ad as possible. And if you're sending your resume to a new networking contact, be sure to mention who referred you. Even in this anonymous electronic age, the old adage "It's all in who you know" still holds true.

ELECTRONIC COVER LETTER

47 Lake Shore Drive
Cambridge, MA 02138
(617) 555-5555

September 3, 1996

Ms. Pat Cummings
Controller
Any Corporation
1140 Main Street
Boston, MA 02215

Dear Ms. Cummings:
This letter is in response to your September 2 advertisement in the *Boston Globe* for the position of Assistant Controller. I am very interested in the position and believe I have the qualifications you are looking for. Please consider the following:

- Over twenty years experience in Accounting and Systems Management, Budgeting, Forecasting, Cost Containment, Financial Reporting, and International Accounting.
- Implemented "team-oriented" cross-training program within accounting group, resulting in timely month-end closings and increased productivity of key accounting staff.
- MBA in Management from Northeastern University.
- Results-oriented professional and proven team leader.
- These are only a few of my credentials that may be of interest to you. I look forward to discussing them with you further in a personal interview. Thank you for your consideration.

Sincerely,

Chris Smith

Enc. Resume

■ Letter echoes the key words used in the employment ad.

■ Candidate uses bullets to emphasize his/her key credentials.

ELECTRONIC RESUME

CHRIS SMITH
47 Lake Shore Drive
Cambridge, MA 02138
(617) 555-5555

KEY WORD SUMMARY

Senior financial manager with over twenty years experience in Accounting and Systems Management, Budgeting, Forecasting, Cost Containment, Financial Reporting, and International Accounting. MBA in Management. Proficient in Lotus, Excel, Solomon, Real World, Windows.

EXPERIENCE

COLWELL CORPORATION, Wellesley, MA
$100 Million Division of Bancroft Corporation

Director of Accounting and Budgets, 1988 to present
Directed staff of 20 in General Ledger, Accounts Payable, Accounts Receivable, and International Accounting. Facilitated month-end closing process with parent company and auditors.

- Implemented "team-oriented" cross-training program within accounting group, resulting in timely month-end closings and increased productivity of key accounting staff.
- Developed and implemented a strategy for Sales and Use Tax Compliance in all 50 states with 100% compliance for both parent company and subsidiaries.
- Prepared monthly financial statements and analyses for review by management executive board.

Accounting Manager, 1985-1988
Managed a staff of 6 in General Ledger and Accounts Payable. Responsible for the design and refinement of financial reporting package. Assisted in month-end close.

- Established guidelines for month-end closing procedures, thereby speeding up closing by 5 business days.
- Promoted to Director of Accounting and Budgets.

FRANKLIN AND DELANY COMPANY, Melrose, MA
Senior Accountant, 1979-1985
Managed A/P, G/L, transaction processing, and financial reporting. Supervised staff of two.

- Developed Management Reporting package, including variance reports and cash flow reporting.

Staff Accountant, 1975-1979
Managed A/P, including vouchering, cash disbursements, and bank reconciliation. Wrote and issued policies. Maintained supporting schedules used during year-end audits. Trained new employees.

■ Resume contains many key words such as Budgeting, Forecasting, and MBA

■ Format is "computer-friendly": non-decorative font, traditional layout, no italics or special graphics.

Junior Accountant, 1973-1975
Assisted in general ledger closing. Monitored cash collections and accounts receivable.

EDUCATION

MBA in Management, Northeastern University, Boston, MA, 1985
BS in Accounting, Boston College, Boston, MA, 1973

ASSOCIATIONS

National Association of Accountants

Index

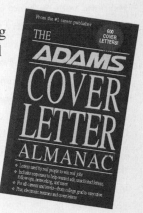